Explaining Criminals and Crime

Essays in Contemporary Criminological Theory

Raymond Paternoster
University of Maryland

Ronet Bachman
University of Delaware

Roxbury Publishing Company
Los Angeles, California

Library of Congress Cataloging-in-Publication Data

Explaining criminals and crime: essays in contemporary criminological theory
  Raymond Paternoster, Ronet Bachman [editors].
  p. cm.
Includes bibliographical references and index
ISBN 1-891487-32-9
1. Criminology. 2. Crime - Sociological aspects. I. Paternoster, Raymond.–
II. Bachman, Ronet.
  Explaining Criminals and Crime
HV6018.E94 2001
364—dc21   99-35826
                                                                                                  CIP

Publisher: Claude Teweles
Managing Editor: Dawn VanDercreek
Production Editor: Joshua H. R. Levine
Production Assistant: Kate Shaffar
Copy Editor: Ann West
Typography: Synergistic Data Systems
Cover Design: Marnie Kenney

Printed on acid-free paper in the United States of America. This book meets the standards for recycling of the Environmental Protection Agency.

ISBN 1-891487-32-9

ROXBURY PUBLISHING COMPANY
P.O. Box 491044
Los Angeles, California 90049-9044
Tel.: (310) 473-3312 • Fax: (310) 473-4490
E-mail: roxbury@roxbury.net
Website: www.roxbury.net

Dedicated with awe and wonder to John Phillip Bachman-Paternoster, the son around whom we both revolve.

Contents

Chapter 5

Social Disorganization and Crime

Chapter 6

Anomie/Strain Theories of Crime

Chapter 7

Differential Association and Social Learning Theories

Chapter 8

Labeling or Social Reaction Theories of Crime

Chapter 9

Radical and Feminist Theories of Crime

Chapter 10

Theoretical Development in Criminology: Falsification, Integration, and Competition

Preface

Our purpose in assembling this collection of readings on criminological theory was simple—we wanted to make an important part of our discipline more accessible to both undergraduate and graduate students. For the most part, undergraduate students learn about criminological theory secondhand. They read about theory as filtered through the lens of the author or authors of their undergraduate textbook in criminology and through the point of view of the professor teaching their course. Graduate students generally get a more firsthand account of criminological theory. They usually are instructed to read the one or more journal articles where a theorist has initially laid out their work, or, in other instances, read an entire book that the theorist has devoted to their theory. Unfortunately, journal articles and theoretical monographs are not written in a style that many graduate students would find cordial. For both undergraduate and graduate students, then, criminological theory remains only partially understood and appreciated.

What we wanted to do was to have some of the major theorists in criminology write an essay in which they provide a simple and clear description or explanation of what their theory is all about. When we approached contributors to this volume we emphatically requested that they employ what we called, for lack of a better term, "an easy exposition." Now that the volume has been assembled, we think all authors have more than achieved that objective. We think the essays in this book do two things: (1) they cover some of the most important criminological theories in our field today, and (2) they do so with a style that all students can almost effortlessly comprehend. We also asked each theorist to cover three areas in his or her essay: (1) what the theory says about crime and criminals, (2) some assessment of what the empirical literature says about the theory, (3) the policy implications of the theory. Again, we think these objectives were met in each case.

The specific theories covered in this volume are:

- Deterrence, Rational Choice, and Routine Activities Theories
- Biological Theories
- Control Theories
- Social Disorganization Theories
- Anomie/Strain Theories
- Differential Association and Social Learning Theories
- Labeling or Social Reaction Theories
- Radical and Feminist Theories
- Integrated Theories

As the reader can quickly surmise, the book covers a lot of theoretical ground. Moreover, the author of each essay is either the original author of the theory or has invested a substantial amount of his or her professional life writing about it. While we feel good about the wide sweep of theory the book covers, we nevertheless acknowledge that there are some important criminological theories that, for reasons of space, had to be omitted.

As we noted at the beginning of the Preface, our intention was to make criminological theory more accessible to undergraduate and graduate students of criminology. We hope that we and the authors of these essays have done that. We also hope that our colleagues will find these essays enlightening. We have benefited greatly from a careful reading of what each author had to say and have, in the process, learned a few new things about each of the theories in this book.

1

The Structure and Relevance of Theory in Criminology

Knowledge itself is power.

—Sir Francis Bacon,
Meditationes Sacrae

The criticism and transformation of society can be divorced only at our peril from the criticism and transformation of theories about society.

—Alvin W. Gouldner,
The Coming Crisis of Western Sociology

One of the most difficult classes to teach, and we readily admit one of the most difficult classes to take in a criminology, criminal justice, or sociology curriculum, is a class on criminological theory. This difficulty is certainly not because of a lack of subject matter. Criminologists have been exceptionally fertile, professionally speaking, and in a very short time they have generated more than their share of possible explanations about why crimes are committed and why offenders behave the way they do. We believe that, instead, criminological theory is problematic primarily because for too many students it is simply irrelevant, and irrelevant things are difficult to focus on. Students often believe that this theory has nothing to do with the "real world"—the places where they anticipate working and living.

Many students correctly observe that criminological theory is the product of professors who sit in university offices rather than in places where "the action is"—police stations, courtrooms, or correctional institutions. And that in a nutshell, they conclude, is the source of its fatal flaw. These theoretical writings may get published as journal articles and books, but they then simply sit on the stacked, dusty shelves of other professors (and their students). Perhaps this theory is of interest to those scholars who are forced to read it, but some students say it simply is not useful, interesting, or meaningful to them.

We happen to think that this perception is short-sighted and mistaken. Criminological theory is relevant for the world. It tells us what we need to examine in the world in order to understand crime and what we need to change, and leave unchanged, in order to reduce crime. By explicitly telling us what we need to look at (e.g., peer groups, the quality of neighborhoods, psychological states), theories of crime and criminality also implicitly tell us what we may ignore or what we do not really need to pay attention to. Thus public policy is informed and guided by theory, even if this connection is not always made explicit. In other words, criminological theory suggests some lines of action for policy makers to take and rules out others, and these lines of action certainly have ramifications for real human lives.

As an example, consider the implications of rational choice/deterrence theory, which asserts that criminal behavior is rational conduct that occurs when the benefits of committing crime are perceived by a would-be offender to be greater than both the costs of crime and the benefits of noncrime. That is, would-be offenders contemplate and are affected by the consequences of their actions. If the benefits of crime are high and the costs low, crime will occur. If, however, the benefits of crime are lower than the costs, crime will not occur. An implication of this theory, then, is that if the costs of crime are made to be high, would-be rational offenders will be restrained or deterred from committing it. Consider also that many state legislators have argued in favor of death penalty legislation by claiming that the threat of execution will keep someone contemplating murder from committing the crime. In other words, although the penalty of life imprisonment might not deter murder, increasing the penalty to death would. At least partly on the basis of their predicted deterrence benefits, such death penalty statutes are now legal in a majority of states.

A theory of crime does then have an influence on what is done in the real world. Furthermore, other theories of crime and punishment, for example retribution theory, would also support the execution of convicted murderers. In fact, much of what is done in criminal justice policy is at least implicitly guided by some theory of crime. Rational choice/deterrence theory is not unique in this. We believe that all theories of crime contain within them suggestions or implications for criminal justice policy. We also believe that those who make decisions about criminal justice policy use and are informed by theory. Hence, theory and policy are inextricably related.

To continue with our example: Any theory of crime which argues that offenders can be deterred from committing criminal acts by making the punishment more severe does two things. First, it emphasizes the importance of criminal sanctions in the causation of crime. As a result, rational conduct theory highlights the arsenal of penalties at the disposal of the state to discourage crime (e.g., more police for certain and swift apprehension, longer confinement for more severe punishment, and capital punishment rather than life imprisonment). This theory, therefore, focuses our attention on issues like the certainty, swiftness, and severity of criminal penalties.

The second, and perhaps less obvious, thing that this theory does, however, is that it implicitly suggests *what not to look at*. For instance, arguing that criminal conduct is rational and is responsive to the punishment policies of government implies that crime is not due to broken and dysfunctional families, or psychological traits such as a weak superego, or to any constellation of biological abnormalities that criminal offenders may have. These things are simply not relevant to rational choice/deterrence theory; and if it is not relevant, we do not need to pay attention to it or do anything about it. The point is that just as theory brings some

things to light, by its silence, it keeps other things in the dark.

Perhaps the most important lesson to draw from this discussion is that even if it is not made explicit (and it rarely is), public policy about crime is in fact generally driven by some criminological theory. That is, criminological theory does not simply lead an idle existence in books and obscure journal articles, but actually serves as a guide to criminal justice policy. As testimony to this, thousands of offenders are currently incarcerated across the United States under the implicit theoretical rationale behind "three-strike" laws, scores are executed each year, and still more are in job, education, and therapeutic programs. To understand policy, therefore, it is necessary to understand theory, and to critique policy is to critique theory.

This talk about the public policy implications of theory may sound quite odd to you. After all, you may have started this chapter thinking that criminological theory and criminal justice policy live in separate worlds. You may now very well be asking yourself, "So where can I find policy within theory?" It is to this important question that we now turn our attention.

Articulated Propositions

In his discussion of the content of social theory, Alvin Gouldner (1970) pointed to a complement of both articulated or explicit propositions, and what he calls an infrastructure of sentiments and the personal dimension of theory—the implicit part of any theory. We will divide these components of theory into articulated and unarticulated propositions.

Formal or Written Context

A theory's set of *articulated* propositions consists of its formal or written content. That is, in a theory, theoretical concepts are linked by relationship statements. For instance, conventional beliefs and crime are theoretical concepts found side by side in some control theories, and the statement "As conventional beliefs get stronger the likelihood of crime decreases" is a relationship statement. Theoretical concepts identify key terms of the theory and relationship statements link these concepts with one another into propositions or hypotheses. These articulated propositions are the formal structure and content of a theory because this is the part of theory that is made explicit by the theorist when words are put on paper. In other words, when we read a theory in a book or article and learn about what the theory says, we are learning its set of articulated propositions.

For example, when we read Robert Agnew's (1992) journal article that describes his general strain theory, he states (among other things) that:

- Persons feel strain when they have unpleasant experiences.

- One response to unpleasant experiences is to feel anger, and blame someone or something for those feelings.

- These outwardly-focused feelings of anger may be difficult to deal with, and it may be difficult to "calm down."

- Those who feel uncontrolled anger may have a set of rationalizations for criminal conduct and a collection of like-minded others willing to provide support and companionship.

- Persons who are both strained and angry, and who have both justifications for and assistance with crime, are more likely to commit criminal offenses than others.

Although a simplified rendition of Agnew's theory, these five statements form a set of articulated propositions about general strain theory. We arrived at these propositions because Agnew articulated or discussed them in writing. In fact, each of the criminological theories in this book has a set of articulated propositions about the process it thinks best accounts for variation in criminal behavior. Moreover, as a formal exposition of a theorist's point of view about the causes of crime, the articulated propositions of a theory are a professional product. They reflect the theorist's own scholarly training, reading, and understanding of the phenomenon of crime.

The Cognitive or Empirical Validity of Theory

One of the questions that any discipline asks about the formal or articulated propositions of a theory is whether or not they are true, or "fit the facts." After all, a theory at its most basic level is an explanation or description about how the world operates (in the case of the theories in this book, it is a description about what produces crime), and one of the features that we demand of a "good" theory is that it portrays the world accurately. What we would expect, therefore, is that the propositions alleged by the theory be true—that they accurately map with reality.

In language that is very helpful, Gouldner (1970, 13) refers to this truth element of a theory as its *cognitive validity*. A good theory with high cognitive validity is the product of an intellectual, cerebral, or cognitive (i.e., with the mind) exercise. Determining the cognitive validity of a social theory is generally done by conducting research—specifically, by collecting data (via questionnaires, interviews, or secondary sources) and by determining how well these data fit with what the theory has predicted. If, for instance, the theory says that persons who have unpleasant experiences, and who react to such experiences with anger, and who have peers to act delinquent with, will be more likely to commit crimes than others, then this is exactly what we should see when we collect information about persons' strain, anger, stock of peers, and criminal activity. If we do our empirical study, collect and analyze our data, and find that the expected relationships are not true, then the theory is empirically or cognitively suspect. The cognitive validity of a theory with weak empirical support is, therefore, low. If we see the things in our data that our theory predicts, then the theory enjoys some empirical support and we have strengthened its cognitive validity. Because the cognitive validity of a theory depends upon how closely it fits with empirical facts, it is also referred to as *empirical validity*.

In sum, we would argue that every formal criminological theory has a set of articulated or written propositions that link via relationship statements the theoretical concepts of the theory (e.g., strain, anger, supportive beliefs, offending). As an explanation about the expected process that generates crime, criminological propositions can be, and generally are, "put to the test" by empirical research. The purpose of this is to determine if what the theory says is true maps accurately with the world (i.e., do offenders behave the way the theory says they should behave?). To the extent that a theory's propositions about the causes of crime match or are consistent with research findings, the theory is said to contain some empirical "truth" or cognitive validity.

The cognitive validity of a theory is directly linked to its professional popularity, "career," or success. Generally, theories that have low cognitive validity, that enjoy little empirical support and therefore seem not to be accurate descriptions of reality, are not likely to be supported by the community of scholars. In the field of criminology, theories with little empirical support are not likely to appear long in journals, are not likely to be taught in undergraduate classes, are not likely to be part of the training of graduate students, and are, therefore, not likely to have long "careers." At least one reason for the decline of a theory's professional popularity, then, is that it lacks sufficient cognitive or empirical validity.

Unarticulated Propositions

The articulated propositions of a theory are a professional product, the result of the theorist's own scholarly training and thinking about crime. We now examine theory as a *personal product* (Gouldner 1970) containing propositions that reflect the theorist as a person, a human being with a history, with tastes, feelings, and preferences. These are referred to as *unarticulated* propositions expressly because a theorist usually does not make them apparent when describing the theory. Instead, they are implicit. That is, when you read a scholar's theory, you are unlikely to find a formal written treatment of these unarticulated propositions. Unlike articulated propositions that are written, knowledge about a theory's unarticulated propositions often must be inferred or dis-

covered by implication and careful reading and re-reading. Another difference between articulated and unarticulated propositions is that although the former are subject to empirical examination and falsification, the cognitive validity of unarticulated propositions is rarely empirically tested. As you will see, however, readers of theory do evaluate these unarticulated propositions and they do influence the career and popularity of a theory.

Types of Unarticulated Propositions

There are different types of unarticulated propositions in criminological theory. One type concerns the assumption that all criminological theorists must inevitably make about human beings. This assumption is implicit and unexamined, but forms an important context or background for their work. In fact, this assumption is influential in the kind of theory that is actually constructed. An example may help.

As you will soon discover, a rather broad class of theory in criminology is referred to as *control theory* (Toby 1957; Nye 1958; Reckless 1967; Hirschi 1969). Specific control theorists emphasize different things in their explanations, but they all share a common assumption about human beings—that humans are generally self-interested, asocial beings who would naturally (i.e., without much additional motivation) commit criminal or deviant acts if they thought it would be to their benefit. To control theorists, rule-breaking is not problematic, and because it frequently satisfies human desires and wants as well as or better than conformity, no special explanation need be made for it. If persons are assumed to be asocial, self-interested beings, the real question for control theorists is not "Why do some people commit crime?" but "Why do some people not commit crime, and why do those who do commit crime not do it more often?" Because of their assumption of human nature, therefore, control theorists do not have to account for antisocial conduct. Instead, they must account for conformity or obedience. As a result, control theorists talk about restraints or controls on rule-breaking and criminal impulses.

A different class of criminological theories are called *strain theories* (Merton 1938, 1968; Cohen 1955; Cloward and Ohlin 1960; Agnew 1992). There are some subtle differences among these, but they all share a common assumption about the nature of human beings. Strain theories essentially assume that human beings are social creatures who have internalized the existing belief or normative system (system of rules) within which they exist. That is, strain theorists assume that people are naturally inclined to conform because they believe in the "rules of the game." Thus, strain theories take conformity for granted. Unlike control theorists, they do not have to explain why people conform to rules. If, however, you assume that people are basically social beings, what you do have to account for is rule-breaking. In other words, if you take conformity for granted, then deviance and crime are problematic and you must in your theoretical work be able to explain and account for it. For this reason strain theorists must build an incentive or motivation to do crime and deviance into their theories. This is why it is useful to think of strain theories as motivational theories. The general explanation for these theories is that persons are under strain or pressure to break rules.

As you can perhaps surmise, assumptions about human nature are an important component in any criminological theory. If you adopt the assumption that humans are basically asocial, you assume rule-breaking and develop a theory of restraint and control. If, however, you assume that humans are essentially social creatures, you assume conformity and must develop a theory that includes deviant or criminal motivation. In spite of their centrality, however, assumptions about the nature of human beings are rarely made explicit by theorists. You do not, for example, read about the essential nature of human beings when you read Albert Cohen's (1955) strain theory found in his book, *Delinquent Boys*, nor is there such a discussion in Jackson Toby's (1957) control theory essay about the failure of delinquents to have a stake in conformity. Instead, these assumptions are an unarticulated or implicit component that forms the background and context of the theorist's work.

Another type of unarticulated assumption embedded in criminological theories concerns the public policy implications of the theory. We have alluded to the fact that criminological theory does indeed have consequences for the real world. Every criminological theory accepts some part of the world and challenges others. In his discussion of general social theory, Gouldner (1970) noted that, by its implicit suggestions for public policy, theory advocates some lines of political activity at the expense of others, and that "every social theory is thus a *tacit theory of politics*"(40). Thus, the written work of social theorists encourages people to do things in the world (and by implication, discourages other things):

> Rooted in a limited personal reality, resonating some sentiments but not others, and embedded in certain domain assumptions, *every social theory facilitates the pursuit of some but not of all courses of action, and thus encourages us to change or accept the world as it is, to say yea or nay to it. In a way, every theory is a discreet obituary or celebration for some social system.* (Gouldner 1970, 47, emphasis added)

This emphasizes our point that inevitably every criminological theory both sheds light on some things and hides or masks others.

Tacit Implications for Public Policy

You may be used to thinking of criminological theory as a purely intellectual product that is scientifically "neutral" without any political or policy component, so a few examples to the contrary might be helpful. Our first example comes from August Aichhorn's (1935) psychoanalytic theory of delinquency. This theory proposed that diverse forms of rule-breaking are due to a time-stable individual trait that Aichhorn referred to as "a predisposition to delinquency," possibly rooted in the child's early emotional experiences:

> When I ask parents how they account for the dissocial behavior of their children, I usually receive the answer that it is a result of bad company and running around

on the streets. To a certain extent this is true, but thousands of other children grow up under the same unfavourable circumstances and still are not delinquent. There must be *something in the child himself* which the environment brings out in the form of delinquency. If for the moment we call this unknown something a predisposition to delinquency, we have the factor without which an unfavourable environment can have no power over the child. . . .We like to think that this predisposition is inherited. Psychoanalysis has shown us that heredity cannot explain everything, that *the first experiences of childhood are important in determining later development.* (39–40, emphasis added)

The explanation of crime, this theory tells us, is anchored in one's "first experiences of childhood." Accordingly, we need look no further than events that occur very early in life, most importantly, those interactions that take place between parents and very young children. What crime is *not* due to, therefore, are events and experiences that occur in adolescence and adulthood—like unemployment, the stigma received from processing by a criminal court, divorce, drug addiction, or the strains and pains of adolescence. Aichhorn's theory clearly places the light of scientific scrutiny solely on early life experiences and internal emotional states.

There is an implicit or tacit theory of public policy here, too. According to Aichhorn's thesis, "doing something about" crime means focusing attention on early life experiences. Even though we may be a little powerless in manipulating the kinds of experiences people have, this theory implies that we can do something about how those events and experiences have subsequently been interpreted. This is particularly true for those unpleasant events and experiences Aichhorn (1935, 46) refers to as "psychic traumas." The insights provided to individuals by psychoanalysis and psychotherapy, for example, are needed to help people discover and overcome their psychic traumas. Aichhorn's theory, therefore, would be compatible with any number of psychological and psychiatric treatments (i.e., individual and perhaps group therapy). Structural changes, such as

a redistribution of wealth, higher wages for the working class, athletic programs for the idle, work programs for the young urban poor, and a decriminalization of status offenses, would not be appropriate according to his theory. By linking deviance and crime to a pathology of the individual rather than the criminogenic nature of the social system, Aichhorn's body of criminological theory constitutes a celebration of the existing social order.

A second, and entirely different, example comes from Richard Quinney's (1974) conflict/Marxist theory of crime. In his book, *Critique of Legal Order: Crime Control in Capitalist Society,* he writes the following:

> . . . the legal system is an apparatus created to secure the interests of the dominant class. Contrary to conventional belief, law is a tool of the ruling class. The legal system provides the mechanism for the forceful and violent control of the rest of the population. In the course of battle, the agents of the law (police, prosecutors, judges, and so on) serve as the military force for the protection of domestic order. Legal order benefits the ruling class in the course of dominating the classes that are ruled. (52)

Clearly, Quinney's theory of crime is much different from Aichhorn's. Instead of one's early life experiences as the cause, for Quinney the social system itself breeds crime. Thus, capitalist society uses the legal system to maintain existing economic inequalities. The criminals are not biologically or psychically inferior; they simply do not have control over the means of economic production. The theoretical light of the conflict perspective is, therefore, cast away from the individual and turned on social, economic, political, and cultural institutions.

In his discussion of the state and the legal system, Quinney has some clear policy implications as well. In order to reduce crime, we would not need to provide psychoanalytic understanding for individuals who have experienced "psychic trauma." Rather, we should work on creating a more equitable economic order. Quinney's charge would be that, in their current form, criminal laws favor the economically powerful, who translate economic power into political power by having the behaviors of the lower/working classes (e.g., robbery, theft) deemed "crimes," while comparable acts committed by the powerful are treated as either "shrewd" business practices or minor, sometimes noncriminal offenses. Thus, the explanation and prevention of crimes require us to focus on the relationship between economic and political power. By implication, what we need not examine are things like the biology and psychology of offenders or their set of peer relationships. Whereas Aichhorn's theory can be seen as a celebration of the existing social system (criminal propensity resides in the personal psychological backgrounds of offenders), Quinney's is clearly an obituary for American society (more friendly to social-economic change than individual change).

We readily admit that these are dramatic examples to forcefully illustrate our point: every criminological theory discussed in this book implicitly contains some prescriptions for public policy. That is, in line with Gouldner's "tacit theory of politics," each theorist suggests what we should do in the world in order to reduce crime. Naturally, in telling us what to do, a criminological theory also implicitly tells us what we can ignore. Because most theorists do not usually make the policy implications of their theory explicit, we take special care in this book to have all the writers do so.

The Sentiment Relevance of Theory

In our discussion of a theory's articulated propositions, we alluded to the fact that the popularity and career of a criminological theory are in part determined by its cognitive or empirical validity. A great many scholars interested in the study of crime spend their professional careers collecting data and objectively testing whether theories are true to the known facts about crime. In his discussion of social theory in general, Gouldner (1970) argued that although evaluating the scientific merit of theory is crucial, scientific considerations alone *do not* and *should not* completely determine the validity or acceptability of a theory:

That the ideological impli[…] cial consequences of an i[…] tem do not determine its v[…] in the least denied here. Ce[…] *nitive* validity of an intell[…] cannot and should not be[…] ideological implications or […] sequences. But it does not follow from this that an intellectual system should be (or, for that matter, ever is) judged only in terms of its cognitive validity, its truth or falsity. In short, it is never simply a question of whether an intellectual system, or a statement that it implies, is true or false. (13)

The point that Gouldner makes is an important one. He argues that a theory should be judged in part by how well it fits the facts—its cognitive validity. Every theory must, therefore, be evaluated in terms of the collection of empirical findings about it. But this is not the only basis upon which to evaluate theory. There is another, much more subjective, basis upon which we can evaluate theory. This is not an objective intellectual approach driven by concern for the empirical facts; rather, as Gouldner (1970) eloquently notes, "some theories are simply experienced as *intuitively* convincing" (30). Notice the language here. A theory is *experienced* as intuitively convincing when the sentiments it contains reflect the sentiments of the reader. Now, how do sentiments enter a theory?

You will recall that in addition to the articulated propositions of a theory that are subject to empirical falsification and verification, a theory contains a cache of unarticulated propositions, such as assumptions about human nature and prescriptions for what to do in the world. Gouldner argues that these unarticulated propositions become the foci for sentiments, and that people subjectively sense or feel, based on their own personal history and experience, that the theory is valuable. In other words, some theories are *felt* to be true because the sentiments captured in the theory resonate with the sentiments of the reader. Other theories, independent of the scientific evidence, are thought to "ring hollow" for the same reasons. The "reasons" are, however, affective rather than cognitive and intellectual. In this

theory as a personal product of the
er either reflects or is antagonistic to the
ersonal history of the reader and consumer
of theory.

For example, for reasons that have nothing to do with its scientific validity, many students and scholars reject a Marxist explanation of crime such as that previously described by Richard Quinney. To its critics, such a theory, with its implication of economic class conflict in American society, simply does not feel intuitive or comfortable. Marxist criminology suffers because the sentiments it contains are not reflected in the personal histories of some readers. Others may reject control theory because they do not find intuitively satisfying its assumption that human beings are basically self-interested and asocial, and that their appetites must be restrained for social order to be possible. Others feel hostile to a biological theory of crime because, to them, it seems to have connotations of racial inferiority or suggests that criminal behavior is somehow predetermined. Empirical research findings have virtually no impact on these intuitive and emotional perceptions. Readers may reject a theory simply because it does not reflect their own assumptions about human nature or the foundation of social order.

This means that the popularity or career of a theory, in addition to its truth value or cognitive validity, is also determined by extra-scientific or nonintellectual criteria. There is an affective evaluation of theory that sticks to its collection of unarticulated propositions. Some theories simply feel right to us and we accept them. Just as the construction of a theory is both an intellectual and personal product for the theorist, it is also an intellectual and personal product for the reader. Moreover, the truly important point is not whether we should evaluate criminological theory by its sentiment relevance, we just need to acknowledge that we often do. A theory may be accepted and rejected, enjoy professional popularity and suffer professional anonymity, in part because we may not like what it implies about things like the essence of human nature or what it suggests we do in the world to reduce crime.

The rise and demise of social reaction or labeling theory is a perfect illustration of this point (see also Chapter 8). One of the features of the labeling school of criminology and deviance is that it implies a deep distrust of government and formal means of social control. Formal institutions like courts, prisons, and law enforcement are portrayed as *contributing* to the crime problem by the processes of stigmatization, role engulfment, and deviance amplification (Schur 1971). The basic suspicion of the state can be seen in the labeling theory proposition that intervention by formal agencies of control usually will make things worse for someone caught up in them. As a theory of crime, labeling theory probably reached the height of its popularity during the late 1960s and early 1970s. This surge in its popularity could not be attributed to the fact that empirical evidence suddenly emerged to support its articulated propositions. In fact, for the most part, the jury was still out regarding the cognitive validity of this theory. Instead, the appeal of labeling theory probably had to do more with the fact that its theme of heavy-handed and malignant authorities resonated with the anti-government sentiments of the time. That is, an unpopular war in Vietnam and internal turmoil brought about by the civil rights movement had bred a distrust of formal institutions. When the intellectual climate changed over time and became more conservative, the popularity of labeling theory waned to the point that many scholars considered it "dead" (Tittle 1980). This is one of numerous instances where the career of a criminological theory was influenced by nonscientific criteria.

Conclusion

We encourage you to put your sentiment-based, affective evaluations of the theories in this book out into the open. When reading, be clearly mindful both about what each theory says and what it is silent about, its fit with the facts, and its views on human nature and social action. With this goal in mind, you may use the major points of our introduction that follows as a useful guide to organizing as you read.

- Criminological theory contains a set of articulated propositions.
- These articulated propositions are an intellectual product and consist of relationship statements that link theoretical constructs.
- The articulated propositions of a theory are what we usually find when we select a book or journal article and read about a theory.
- The articulated propositions of any criminological theory are evaluated in accordance with their cognitive or empirical validity. The cognitive validity of a theory is the extent to which a theory "fits the facts." Generally, scholars do this by gathering data and testing empirical hypotheses derived from the theory.
- The cognitive validity of a theory, the amount of empirical support it has, influences its professional popularity and career.
- Criminological theory also contains a set of unarticulated propositions.
- These unarticulated propositions do not generally comprise the formal, written part of the theory. They are generally implicit.
- The unarticulated propositions of a theory are an intensely personal product and pertain to issues such as the nature of human beings assumed by the theorist.
- Part of these unarticulated propositions also include a "tacit theory of politics"—prescriptions for what one should do in the world in order to deal with the "crime problem." Implicitly, implications about what one should do to in order to deal with crime also carry ramifications for what one need not look at or need not do.
- A criminological theory's set of unarticulated propositions become the foci for sentiments or feelings.
- Sometimes the sentiments embedded in a theory are reflected in the sentiments of a reader. When this occurs, a theory is felt to be intuitively correct. When the reader's sentiments are not resonated by the theory, it may be viewed with suspicion.
- In addition to their cognitive validity, therefore, theories are also evaluated with respect to their sentiment relevance.
- Because they contain suggestions for what to do (and what not to do) in the world, theories have real consequences for real people. Although the connection is not always made clear, criminal justice policies are virtually always based on some theory about the causes of crime. To understand policy, therefore, one must understand theory.

The essays in this book were written by the major criminological theorists of our time. In the course of each essay, you will find a discussion of the essential propositions of the theory (i.e., each theorist's account of what explains crime). You will also find a review of the empirical work to date on the theory, and some understanding of the extent of empirical support the theory enjoys, and where additional research needs to be conducted. Finally, each theorist has explicitly spelled out some of the policy implications of his or her work.

References

Aichhorn, August. (1935). *Wayward Youth.* New York: Viking.

Agnew, Robert. (1992). "Foundation for a general strain theory of crime and delinquency." *Criminology,* 30:47–88.

Cloward, Richard and Lloyd Ohlin. (1960). *Delinquency and Opportunity.* Glencoe, IL: Free.

Cohen, Albert K. (1955). *Delinquent Boys.* Glencoe, IL: Free.

Gouldner, Alvin W. (1970). *The Coming Crisis of Western Sociology.* New York: Basic.

Hirschi, Travis. (1969). *Causes of Delinquency.* Berkeley: University of California Press.

Merton, Robert K. (1938). "Social structure and anomie." *American Sociological Review,* 3:672–682.

——. (1968). *Social Theory and Social Structure.* Glencoe, IL: Free.

Nye, F. Ivan. (1958). *Family Relationships and Delinquent Behavior.* New York: Wiley.

Quinney, Richard. (1974). *Critique of Legal Order: Crime Control in Capitalist Society*. Boston: Little, Brown.

Reckless, Walter . (1967). *The Crime Problem, Fifth Edition*. New York: Appleton-Century-Crofts.

Schur, Edwin. (1971). *Labeling Deviant Behavior*. Englewood Cliffs, NJ: Prentice Hall.

Tittle, Charles R. (1980). "Labeling and crime: An empirical evaluation." Pp. 241–269 in W.R. Gove (ed.), *The Labelling of Deviance*, Second Edition. Beverly Hills, CA: Sage.

Toby, Jackson. (1957). "Social disorganization and stake in conformity: Complementary factors in the predatory behavior of hoodlums." *Journal of Criminal Law, Criminology, and Police Science*, 48:12–17.

2

Classical and Neuve Classical Schools of Criminology

Deterrence, Rational Choice, and Situational Theories of Crime

Introduction

Theories of crime are typically classified as falling into one of two larger and more general schools of thought—the classical school or the positive school of criminology. The older classical school dates back approximately to the middle of the eighteenth century. In 1764, the Italian scholar Cesare Beccaria wrote his *Essay On Crimes and Punishments,* a document of slightly more than 100 pages providing many of the fundamental themes of the classical school. A little later, near the end of that century, the English philosopher Jeremy Bentham (1789) published *An Introduction to the Principles of Morals and Legislation,* another compilation of the key ideas of classical criminology.

Both of these men were utilitarian philosophers, which means, among other things, they believed that government programs (like judicial and penal policies) ought to be evaluated on the extent to which they maximize social benefits (i.e., maximize utility). This implies that in evaluating whether or not a given social policy is a "good" one, "good" is determined by a cost and benefit analysis. For example, if a state sanction such as capital punishment (generally a bad thing because punishment produces pain, it

may set a bad example, and there is a risk of executing innocent persons) deters would-be murderers from committing a crime (a good thing), one has to balance the bad and good consequences. A "good" policy is one that has more net good consequences than bad. In this sense, the good policy possesses "utility." Notice that the policy would not be evaluated on the basis of whether or not it was the "morally right" thing to do, just on the basis of whether or not it produced a net benefit or utility to society.

The classical school of criminology was the product of a more general intellectual and cultural tradition in Europe known as the Enlightenment and influenced by the moral philosophers and political theorists Rousseau, Voltaire, Montesquieu, Bentham, Locke, and Hobbes, among others. One key theme of the classical school is that crime is in large measure the product of the free will and rational deliberation of individuals. Persons rationally contemplate committing crimes; they are not compelled by forces beyond their control to do so. In this contemplation, would-be offenders consider the benefits to be gained by the crime and the costs or penalties they could incur. They also consider the costs and benefits of noncriminal conduct. Crime is either selected when it is estimated to be beneficial or rejected when thought to be too personally costly. Criminals choose to commit their deeds, therefore, because they calculate that they will profit by them. In order to minimize crime, would-be offenders must be convinced that the likely punishment for crime would be swift, sure, and severe enough to counter any anticipated gain.

The principal themes of the classical school of criminology, then, incorporate the belief that human beings are rational, calculating, and hedonistic (self-interested) beings. Hence, their goal is to maximize their own pleasure and minimize their own costs or pain. Given their innate self-interest, crime is a natural act because it is often an easy way to secure things that are wanted. However, just as easily as one may commit crime, one may become the victim of a crime. In a state of nature each individual is fearful of being a victim. In the words of

Thomas Hobbes, without some restraint over their conduct, human beings are in danger of falling into a war "of every man against every man," where there is "continual fear and danger of violent death; and the life of many, solitary, poor, nasty, brutish, and short" ([1651] 1962, 100). In a state of nature, therefore, liberty or freedom is rendered practically useless because if I have complete freedom to do anything I want, including harm and steal from you, you have the same freedom to act in an identical manner toward me.

In order to prevent this war of all against all, rational human beings join together and surrender some of their freedom to a governing body or state (what Hobbes referred to as *Leviathan* and Rousseau ([1762] 1967) as the *social contract*). By agreeing not to do some things that might be individually profitable (like robbing and violently injuring others for one's own personal gain), rational beings enjoy the protection that the state offers. Although they lose some liberty, there is still a net gain in joining the social contract because one is relatively free from wanton harm (i.e., a "nasty, brutish, and short" life). The function of the state, therefore, is to use as little force as possible (because the use of force against one's citizens is painful, and the purpose of any action is to maximize pleasure while minimizing pain) in order to ensure compliance with the terms of the social contract.

You get a sense from this brief discussion that the classical theorists were not much interested in what we might call "criminal motivation," or to why criminals commit crimes. Actually, they did develop a theory of criminal motivation. Essentially, they believed that because all persons possess rationality, all persons also possess the capacity to commit crimes for their own benefit. That is, everyone runs the risk of committing a crime if the right circumstances exist—if, for example, the expected benefits are very high, the risk of detection is very low, the expected penalty if caught is minor, and if they can satisfy their need through no other means. The theorists of the classical school were really interested in what can be done in order to maximize the expected costs of crime,

without, of course, being too harsh and thus threatening the social contract that beings freely entered into and could freely dismiss themselves from. When classical theorists looked at what could be done to maximize costs, they looked at how the state could reduce crime by making the costs high or at least appear to be high through its punishment policies. As a result, classical criminology is often referred to as "penal criminology," "bureaucratic criminology," or "administrative and legal criminology." In other words, rather than explain what made people commit crimes, classical criminologists proposed a body of principles for legislators to follow when creating and enforcing criminal justice policies. This is no more clearly seen than in Beccaria's own work, *Essay on Crimes and Punishments* ([1764] 1985).

Beccaria's Contribution to the Classical School

Cesare Bonesana, Marchese de Beccaria, was born in Milan, Italy, in 1738 to an aristocratic family. After years of formal education and an undistinguished career as a professor and petty state official, Beccaria joined with a group of intellectual dissidents who met regularly to discuss the latest Enlightenment philosophies. This group, known among themselves as the "academy of fists," published a journal within which they advanced various political and social reforms. As part of this effort, Beccaria was asked to write an essay on penal reform. The result was his now famous *Essay on Crimes and Punishments*. Beccaria first published his work anonymously because he feared he would be prosecuted or even put to death for espousing such radical and potentially revolutionary ideas. His treatise harshly criticized the penal policies used by the existing governments of Europe, such as torture, forced confessions, arbitrary decisions, brutal punishments, and other abuses. Although Enlightenment philosophers like Beccaria espoused freedom of expression, that notion was not generally shared by the somewhat tyrannical rulers in power. Moreover, Beccaria's concern was not unwarranted. When first published, the *Essay* was soundly condemned by the Catholic Church and placed on its list of forbidden books, the *Index Librorum Prohibitorum*.

Beccaria's *Essay* specifically condemned such common state practices as obscure laws, unlimited judicial power that enabled judges to dismiss cases or impose sentences according to their personal whim, secret accusations, confessions obtained by torture, and use of punishments that far exceeded the harm caused by the crime itself. The first important component of the work, therefore, was a harsh rebuke of the irrationality, cruelty, and capriciousness of existing laws and the judicial and penal system.

The second thing Beccaria did in his essay was to propose a series of reforms for the existing legal system which would make it more enlightened, that is, more humane, rational, efficient, and fair. Beccaria forcefully argued for laws to be clearly written and publicized, leaving authorities with little room for discretion and disparate handling; the use of sworn and freely given testimony; the elimination of the death penalty except for a few crimes; the treating of all citizens as equals before the law; and the creation of a system of punishment that was swift and certain, but only severe enough to deter someone contemplating a crime from committing it.

Beccaria was no expert on either legal matters or matters that pertained to punishment and penal practices. Nevertheless, his small book was to have an immediate and profound impact in both intellectual and political circles. In addition to its original Italian publication and six subsequent editions, the *Essay* was quickly translated into both French and English (Beccaria 1985, x). It found a home among leading French Enlightenment thinkers such as d'Alembert, Helvetius, and the Abbe Morellet. Voltaire himself referred to the book as the "code of humanity," and Bentham heaped high praise upon it (Beccaria 1985, x). In addition to acclaim from intellectuals, the book also influenced a practical response. The Empress Maria Teresa of Austria and the Grand Duke Leopold of Tuscany in Italy proclaimed their intention to enact some of the *Essay*'s proposed legal reforms. Beccaria was also in-

vited to the court of Catherine the Great of Russia to personally preside over her intended judicial reforms (Beccaria 1985, x). Finally, Beccaria's ideas were enacted in part in the French Legal Code of 1791, immediately after the revolution (Vold and Bernard 1986, 25).

In spite of the appeal and modest influence of Beccaria's work, after about one hundred years of intellectual dominance, the field of criminology would soon experience a sudden shift of its axis. Ironically, one of the consequences of the Enlightenment was the ascendance of the belief in the scientific study of the world, free from both superstition and religious restraint. In the early 1800s, Europe witnessed an explosion of scientific work and discoveries in diverse fields, including criminology. Out of this intellectual mix developed the positive school, which was responsible for shifting the study of crime from a concern with legal systems and reform toward the empirical examination of human behavior, including criminal behavior. This positive school of criminology eclipsed the classical school by the middle of the nineteenth century and has dominated criminological thinking ever since.

Beginning in the 1960s, however, the classical school was to witness a rebirth with respect to some of the very issues that it championed two centuries earlier. We will refer to this rebirth as the *neuve* or *new classical school*. It first took the form of an interest in the process or theory of criminal deterrence, which we will briefly discuss next. Sparked by renewed interest in what was referred to as the *deterrence doctrine*, scholars began to expand its boundaries to a more general rational choice theory of crime. In addition, out of this concern with offenders' decision making came a body of work known as routine activities theory. The two essays in this chapter deal with these two new versions of the classical school. First, however, we turn our attention to the notion of deterrence.

Deterrence Theory

If there was one clear principle of the classical school of criminology it was that criminal punishment should be certain, swift, and proportionately severe. Beccaria (1985) spoke directly about each of these three characteristics of punishment:

> One of the greatest curbs on crimes is not the cruelty of punishments, but their infallibility. . . . The certainty of punishment, even if it be moderate, will always make a stronger impression than the fear of another which is more terrible but combined with the hope of impunity. (58)

> The more promptly and the more closely punishment follows upon the commission of a crime, the more just and useful will it be. . . . I have said that the promptness of punishments is more useful because when the length of time that passes between the punishment and the misdeed is less, so much the stronger and more lasting in the human mind is the association of these two ideas, *crime and punishment;* they then come insensibly to be considered, one as the cause, the other as the necessary inevitable effect. (55–57)

> For a punishment to attain its end, the evil which it inflicts has only to exceed the advantage derivable from the crime. . . . [A]ll beyond this is superfluous and for that reason tyrannical. (43)

The certainty of punishment refers to how likely it is to be caught and punished if one has committed a criminal offense, the swiftness or celerity of punishment refers to how quickly punishment follows the commission of the offense, and the severity of punishment refers to the magnitude or intensity of punishment. The reason that punishments should be certain, swift, and only severe enough as the harm generated by the offense is that these characteristics will have the greatest impressions on reasoning beings, and forcefully make the connection between the crime and the possible punishment.

An association between crime and punishment is necessary so that when would-be offenders contemplate committing a crime, they will bring vividly to mind all possible legal consequences. In other words, the connection between crime and punishment forges the link in the mind of the offender between the commission of a criminal act and the experience of some cost or pain. If the expected cost outweighs the anticipated gain,

the would-be offender will not, it is predicted, commit the offense. When would-be offenders refrain from committing a crime because of the anticipated legal punishment that follows, they are said to be *deterred*. Deterrence, then, is a process of inhibition— someone does not commit a crime because they think a punishment will certainly follow their deed, that it will swiftly follow, and that it will be of sufficient strength to offset any expected benefit or pleasure derived from the crime.

What makes deterrence work is the fact that human beings are both rational and self-interested beings. Persons make rational assessments of the expected costs and benefits of making numerous decisions— buying a house or car, changing jobs, committing a crime—and choose the line of behavior that is most beneficial (profitable) and least costly. The idea of deterrence is that if criminal behavior is consistently met with swift and strong enough punishment, it will tilt the balance of that calculation away from criminal to noncriminal behavior. Persons contemplating theft, for example, will consider that they might be arrested within the week for the crime, and will almost certainly be convicted of the crime, and once convicted will have to serve a year or two in the penitentiary. When these potential costs are considered, deterrence theory would predict that a dull job with a mediocre salary will be preferred to crime because the costs of crime are just too high. In other words, deterrence counts on the truth that "crime does not pay."

Conceptualizing Deterrence

The simple notion of deterrence, then, is that it occurs when someone refrains from committing a crime because he or she fears the certainty, swiftness (celerity), and severity of formal legal punishment. Beyond this simple definition, however, lurk some complexities. For example, different kinds of deterrence work for different kinds of people. There is, for instance, the difference between general and specific deterrence. *General* deterrence occurs when someone who is contemplating but has not yet committed an offense is inhibited from doing so because of the fear of legal punishment. *Specific* deterrence occurs when the one being punished refrains from committing another crime because of the fear of additional punishment. When the state punishes those who have committed criminal offenses, then, it is trying to specifically deter them from committing other crimes, and, by making them an example, trying to generally deter others who might be thinking about committing the offense.

Scholars have made other distinctions as well concerning deterrence. *Absolute* deterrence occurs when I refrain from committing any offense because of the fear of legal punishment. If knowing that my spouse has been caught and fined for speeding (or being caught and fined myself) causes me to stop speeding completely, I have been absolutely deterred. *Restrictive* deterrence occurs if I commit fewer offenses or less serious offenses because of the fear of punishment. If knowing that my spouse has been caught and fined for speeding causes me to speed only when I am in the car that has the radar detector or only on open rural roads, but not in my other car or on interstate highways, I have also been restrictively deterred. If knowing that my spouse has been caught and fined for speeding causes me to reduce my speeding to only 10 miles over the posted limit and not 20, I have also been restrictively deterred (see Zimring and Hawkins 1973; Gibbs 1975).

In an important modification to deterrence theory, Stafford and Warr (1993) argued that the previous understanding of general and specific deterrence as applying to different kinds of people (the unpunished and punished, respectively) is seriously flawed. They asserted that both kinds of deterrence can operate on the same person. This can occur, according to Stafford and Warr, because general and specific deterrence should refer to different kinds of punishment and nonpunishment experiences. General deterrence concerns one's indirect or vicarious experiences with punishment, while specific deterrence concerns one's own personal experience. Moreover, because nonpunishment or getting away with a crime also carries a message—that crime

perhaps does pay—it, too, is relevant for deterrence. We will try to explain what Stafford and Warr mean and their new conceptualization of deterrence.

If I know that someone has committed a crime and has been caught and punished for it, my fear of the law will likely increase and will restrain me from committing a crime. Thus, knowledge of someone else being punished (indirect or vicarious experience, because I was not the one actually punished) increases my fear of sanctions and strengthens my conformity. This is general deterrence via indirect experience. If, however, I know that someone has committed a crime and has gotten away with it, this too is knowledge about the law and its efficiency; but it is likely to lead me to doubt the credibility of legal sanctions and may incline me to break the law. Thus, knowledge of someone not being punished for a crime (the vicarious experience of nonpunishment or punishment avoidance) both reduces my fear of the law and weakens my conformity. This is a breakdown in general deterrence via indirect or vicarious experience.

Similarly, if I have been punished for a crime, the act of being caught and sanctioned is a direct or personal experience that the law "means business." This direct experience with punishment is likely to lead me to fear the law more, and may lead me to avoid criminal acts in the future. This is specific deterrence due to personal experience with punishment. If I have committed a crime and have escaped punishment, this direct or personal experience with punishment avoidance will weaken my fear of the law and may embolden me to commit new criminal acts. This is a breakdown of specific deterrence due to personal experience with punishment avoidance. In reconceptualizing deterrence, then, Stafford and Warr have suggested that it consists of four broad types of experience: (1) personal experience with punishment, (2) personal experience with punishment avoidance, (3) vicarious experience with punishment, and (4) vicarious experience with punishment avoidance.

In Stafford and Warr's view, the process of deterrence consists of a complex interplay of direct and vicarious experiences with punishment and punishment avoidance. Moreover, it is now easy to see how absolute and specific deterrence can operate on the same person. For example, suppose a "deadbeat dad" refuses to pay child support. He may be apprehended by the police and taken into custody pending trial. This is direct or personal experience with punishment. While in jail awaiting trial, he may mingle with other jailed child support violators who share their own stories of getting caught and punished for failing to pay child support. This is vicarious experience with punishment. Both of these experiences, personal and vicarious, are jointly communicating the vitality of the law's threats. If I "get the message" and start paying child support both because I have been punished and because others I have come into contact with have been punished, I have been both specifically and generally deterred by my personal (direct) and vicarious (indirect) experiences with punishment.

On the other hand, it is not difficult to see that the deterrence message may get mixed because often our personal and vicarious experiences may be at odds. For example, I may cheat on my taxes without discovery (personal experience with punishment avoidance) but know of others who have been audited and fined (vicarious experience with punishment). In this case, the deterrence messages are mixed and the effect on my behavior is likely to be different than if they were in harmony.

Empirical Research on Deterrence

Even though a prominent part of the classical school of Beccaria and Bentham, the theory of deterrence was buried by the end of the nineteenth century with the theoretical and empirical work of scholars from the positive school. Belief in free will, self-interest, and rational human behavior was replaced by the positive criminologists' search for the biological, psychological, and environmental causes of crime. A concern with legal punishment and the workings of the legal and judicial system was replaced by a focus on theories of criminal motivation. When interest in the deterrence process was later revived by economists and sociologists in the mid-1960s, it generally took the form of a hy-

pothesized relationship between the "objective properties of punishment" and crime rates.

Objective properties of punishment referred to the actual certainty and severity of punishment that existed in a given political jurisdiction. That is, it was predicted that political jurisdictions having higher levels of the certainty and severity of punishment would have lower levels of crime. For example, State "A," which had convicted a higher proportion of those arrested for armed robbery than State "B" (greater certainty), and which had sentenced them for longer periods of confinement (greater severity), would be expected, under deterrence theory, to have lower levels of armed robbery. The swiftness or celerity of punishment was given only very limited attention by deterrence researchers. Gibbs (1975) has suggested that it is difficult to predict what effect swift punishment would have on would-be offenders. The original theory would predict that a punishment that swiftly follows a crime is more likely to deter because it makes an immediate connection between the act and the punishment. Gibbs counterargued that a delayed punishment may be more painful because offenders have to endure the psychological stress of thinking about the punishment that awaits them.

On the basis of this, numerous empirical studies tested the prediction that crime rates are lower when the objective properties of punishment are higher, and much of this research provided some support for deterrence theory (Gibbs, 1975; Nagin, 1978). Although some exceptions did exist, and some methodological questions were raised about these studies, most data seemed to show some deterrent effect for certain punishment. The evidence with respect to the severity of punishment was much less supportive of deterrence theory. The evidence did indicate, however, that the observed deterrent effect for certain legal sanctions was fairly modest.

Various explanations have been offered to account for this generally weak deterrent effect, such as that there is a "tipping effect"— at low levels, certainty and severity of punishment fail to deter because the law does not have a credible threat (Tittle and Rowe 1974). Sanctions deter, it is argued, only when they cross a certain threshold of credibility and become meaningful to those who contemplate offending. Another explanation put forth for the generally weak deterrent effects reported in the literature was that deterrence theory is really a social psychological theory of threat communication (Geerken and Gove 1975). That is, people may be inhibited from committing crime not by what the legal punishment actually is, because most of us are unaware of the real certainty, severity, and celerity of punishment, but *what we think* it is. In this view, the critical variables are not the actual or objective properties of punishment, but persons' subjective assessment of those properties—the *perceptual* properties of punishment.

For example, suppose I live in a state where, compared to other states, very few armed robbers actually get caught, and those who are caught are not likely to be convicted or punished by a long prison sentence. According to the old way of thinking, I am unlikely to be deterred because the actual risk of being punished is low, as is the severity. However, suppose that, for whatever reason, I perceive law enforcement in my state as very effective in apprehending armed robbers, and I further perceive that prosecutors, judges, and juries in my state convict a high proportion of those charged with armed robbery and sentence them to long periods of confinement. Suppose that I think this is true because my brother-in-law committed an armed robbery for the first time and was caught, convicted, and punished for it. According to the perceptual version of deterrence theory, I am likely to be deterred from committing armed robbery because my behavior is affected by what I think to be the case with respect to legal sanctions, not by what they actually are. In other words, deterrence operates on the perception of certain, severe, and swift legal punishment.

Sparked by this new understanding of deterrence as a perceptual theory, numerous research studies were conducted to see if those who perceive certain and severe punishment are less likely to commit crimes than those who perceive that there is little

risk and little cost. Early attempts to demonstrate a link between the perceived certainty and severity of punishment and self-reported involvement in delinquency and crime were not particularly successful (Paternoster 1987). More recent studies, however, have asked subjects to report their intentions to offend in response to hypothetical situations ("would you do crime x in this circumstance?"); these have found a modest correlation between perceived certainty of punishment but a much weaker correlation for perceived severity (Klepper and Nagin 1989; Bachman, Paternoster, and Ward 1992).

In addition to the information provided by these recent studies, other evidence shows that the risk of legal penalties does deter crime. For example, ample evidence indicates that increasing the certainty of punishment by enhanced police enforcement carries with it a deterrent effect. Studies of police strikes have found that during these unusual times of low certainty (most police are not out on the street making arrests), crime does substantially increase (Zimring and Hawkins 1973; Sherman 1995). Moreover, the studies of Levitt (1997) and Marvell and Moody (1996) have shown that the crime rate is lower in cities that have more police officers (more officers translates into greater certainty of punishment).

Research has also demonstrated that increased police presence in localized high crime areas known as *hot spots* has a crime reduction effect (Koper 1995; Sherman 1995; Sherman and Rogan 1995; Sherman and Weisburd 1995; Weisburd and Green 1995). Experimental studies have suggested that, under certain conditions, arresting males suspected of misdemeanor domestic violence reduces the incidence of new violence (Sherman 1992). Research on police crackdowns on drinking and driving and other criminal acts suggests that such interventions have at least an initial deterrent effect, but one that likely decays over time (Ross 1982; Sherman 1990). Finally, there is evidence that when police crack down on minor kinds of crimes, the increased police presence may "spill over" and reduce the amount of other, more violent crimes

(Sampson and Cohen 1988). This is the law enforcement strategy of New York City Mayor Rudolph Giuliani and former Police Commissioner William Bratton, who have argued that vigorous policing of "civil disorders" (panhandling, public urination, etc.) will have a more general deterrent effect on serious crime in the city (see Wilson and Kelling 1982).

Some evidence also suggests that increasing the severity of punishment may generate a crime reduction effect. Research by Levitt (1996), Marvell and Moody (1994), and Spelman (1994) has suggested that recent increases in the prison population have resulted in less crime (for counter evidence, however, see Zimring and Hawkins 1995). In fact, Levitt (1996) has estimated that each additional prisoner in custody deters 15 crimes. Recent work on the effect of the elimination of parole via determinate sentencing laws, however, has not been successful in identifying any deterrent effect.

In sum, there is a vast amount of evidence on the deterrent effect of the law enforcement, judicial, and corrections system. While not all of the findings are supportive of a deterrent effect, the collective landscape of findings does seem to suggest that offenders are sensitive to the risks and costs of doing crime. While perhaps somewhat overstated, Daniel Nagin's (1998) recent conclusion is one we would agree with after reviewing this voluminous literature:

> . . . my review leads me to conclude that the evidence for a substantial deterrent effect is much firmer than it was fifteen years ago. I now concur with [the] more emphatic conclusion that the collective actions of the criminal justice system exert a very substantial deterrent effect. (3)

Extensions of Deterrence Theory

There is some controversy in the field about the inclusiveness or scope of deterrence theory. Some have argued that the deterrence process must be limited to the restraining effect of the threat or use of legal sanctions alone (Gibbs 1975). In this very narrow view, deterrence theory "refers only to the threat of legal punishment" (Akers 1997, 23). If persons refrain from crime be-

cause they fear other kinds of costs or negative consequences—the loss of a valued relationship or job—they may be inhibited from committing crime but cannot be said to have been deterred.

Other deterrence scholars, however, take a broader, more expansive view of the deterrence process and include the inhibition produced by informal as well as formal sanctions (Anderson et al. 1977; Grasmick and Green 1980; Paternoster et al. 1983; Williams and Hawkins 1986; Nagin and Paternoster 1991). In this sense of the word, *informal* means "a nonlegal kind of punishment," and includes such sanctions as social censure and expressed disapproval from parents, spouses, lovers, friends, co-workers— virtually anyone whose good opinion matters to us and who, therefore, influences our conduct. It also includes any anticipated moral costs or self-inflicted punishment via feelings of remorse and shame (Grasmick and Bursik 1990; Bachman, Paternoster, and Ward 1992). This expanded conceptualization asserts that deterrence occurs whenever persons refrain from committing a criminal act because they fear possible negative consequences.

When the more broadly conceived version of deterrence theory has been empirically tested, it has generally been found that so-called informal sanctions inhibit crime better than the threat of legal sanctions. This should not surprise us. Most of the time, what keeps us from violating the law is not the fear of legal punishment, but the loss of valued social relationships, the fear of jeopardizing commitments we have made and time we have spent in building up our conventional lives, and the possible loss of opportunities for success in the future. We will return to this issue when we discuss control theories of crime in Chapter 4.

The introduction of informal sanctions into the deterrence equation has inevitably led scholars to question the relationship between these kinds of sanctions and formal legal punishment. It has been argued that what makes formal penalties effective as a deterrent is that they trigger informal punishments. That is, in part what makes getting arrested a punishment to be avoided is that being arrested creates the constellation of informal penalties like possibly losing one's job, one's spouse, and the esteem of one's neighbors, as well as creating other nonlegal costs.

The Neuve Classical School

With the rebirth of interest in the themes of the classical school (e.g., the assumption of rational and self-interested beings), empirical work proliferated in the area of criminal deterrence, as we have shown. Now we turn to the theoretical developments that built upon yet moved beyond deterrence theory: the rational choice theory of crime and routine activities theory. We have categorized these as belonging to the neuve or "new" classical school, because they make the same basic assumptions about the rationality of human conduct as deterrence theory and the classical school theories of the eighteenth century. A prominent part of thinking about crime since the mid-1980s, both the rational choice and routine activities concepts have played an important role in crime prevention efforts.

Rational Choice Theory

Rational choice theory in the study of crime was really imported from economic studies. In 1968, the economist Gary Becker published a paper, titled "Crime and Punishment: An Economic Approach," in which he made the simple observation that a useful theory of crime would ". . . simply extend the economist's usual analysis of choice"(170). Thus, Becker started to lay the foundation for a theory of crime that viewed the decision to commit crime as involving the same essential mechanisms as making the choice to purchase an automobile, or attend college, or buy a particular television set. In this *expected utility model,* as it was later called, individuals make decisions even under uncertain conditions because they most likely do not have all the necessary information at their disposal and cannot anticipate all responses and consequences. In spite of their uncertainty, persons still use the information that they possess at the moment to determine which of the many possible decisions they could make in a given situation will produce the most favorable outcome. In other words, they choose behaviors that they expect will be most satisfying or beneficial for them (hence, the idea of expected utility). More specifically, because the outcome is expected to be beneficial in the eyes of the one making the decision (i.e., the determination of what is or is not "beneficial" is a subjective and not an objective determination), this model of decision making has also been termed a *subjective expected utility model (SEU).*

Subjective expected utility model models do not need to assume that human beings are like computers, which are fully rational and completely competent in gathering, storing, and analyzing information. Nor do such models need to assume that people try to achieve the best possible (or optimal) outcomes. What SEU theories do assume is that human beings are at least minimally rational in the sense that they do collect information about a decision (however imperfectly), that they do store this information in memory (however imperfectly), that they do analyze or process this information when it comes time to make a decision (however imperfectly), and that when they do make a decision they do so in consideration of the anticipated costs and benefits of the action and make an attempt to minimize their costs and maximize their gains. That is, persons do not possess perfect rationality; rather, they have limited or "bounded rationality" (Simon 1957).

Bounded rationality simply means that humans have bounds or restrictions on their capacity to plan and reason, bounds that include the fact that they gather, store, access, and process information imperfectly, that they make errors of judgment and take shortcuts in the decision-making process. What this implies is that persons create impressions of the world out of their capacity to reason and then act on the basis of these impressions, but that these are imperfect creations and that action that springs from them will not be perfectly rational or optimal. The economist and decision theorist Herbert Simon (1957) probably described human rationality and decision making best when he observed that what people try to do is to "satisfice" rather than optimize. That is, humans choose the line of action that seems to satisfy their needs at the moment rather than that which provides the maximum possible benefits.

Subjective expected utility theory was developed in the study of crime principally through the work of Ronald Clarke and Derek Cornish in the mid-1980s (Clarke and Cornish 1985; Cornish and Clarke 1986: Clarke and Felson 1993). The position advanced by Clarke and Cornish was that offenders are modestly rational in that most criminal acts involve some element of planning (even if for only a moment) and foresight. As rational beings, would-be criminals contemplate the costs and benefits of committing a crime, and the costs and benefits of alternative lines of action, and any possible social or moral costs involved. Because it is possible for researchers, often with the direct cooperation of criminals themselves, to reconstruct the decision-making process that offenders go through, it would be but a short step to devise policies to make crime more costly.

For example, if would-be robbers of convenience stores consider how much of the store windows are covered by advertisements when deciding which stores to rob, convenience store workers can reduce the risk of being robbed by keeping their windows clean so passers-by can see what is going on. There is, then, direct policy relevance for crime prevention in rational choice theory, and scholars who work within this tradition have been very concerned with the kind of situational crime prevention discussed above (Newman, Clarke, and Shoham 1997). In the first essay of this section, Professors Clarke and Cornish outline in considerable detail exactly what a rational choice theory of crime is, to what extent the empirical evidence supports it, and how it may be used to reduce crime.

Routine Activities Theory

Another criminological theory that has its roots squarely in the traditions of the classical school is routine activities theory. Routine activities theory is not really a theory of criminal offending, but more like a theory of victimization risk. It attempts to explain why crime occurs in certain places under certain conditions and more or less presumes a steady supply of motivated offenders. Rather than focusing on offender characteristics, this theory examines the effect of situational obstacles and attractions on the target selection decision of offenders. In a nutshell, a routine activities theorist would presume that persons are more likely to be victims of a crime if they are attractive targets for an offender (high benefit) and if the crime would involve little risk to complete (low cost). As you can see, while routine activities theory does not focus on the offender's motivations, it presumes that offenders do make decisions to commit crimes based on their subjective assessment of target attractiveness (i.e., benefits) and obstacles (i.e., risks and costs).

According to the most prominent version of the theory, a crime is likely to occur when three elements converge in time and space: (1) a motivated offender, (2) a suitable target, and (3) the absence of guardians capable of defending the target. In the theory, offenders are generally assumed to be motivated to do crime because of their self-interest. A suitable target is one which provides immediate benefits, for example, goods that are lightweight and easy to carry when stolen or a bank that is situated near a freeway, allowing easy escape. *Guardians* refer to people or objects that provide some coverage and protection for possible targets. By increasing the possible costs of crime, guardians make targets less suitable. A guardian may consist of an adult or a dog, or both, who stay at home during the day, protecting it from a break-in; a "Club," "Lo-Jack," or other theft-protection device is an automobile's guardian.

The term *routine activities* refers to the fact that during the daily and mundane (i.e., routine) activities of life, people put themselves in situations which increase or decrease their risk of being criminally victimized. For example, the routine activity of going to work lowers the risk of many street crimes for those who take private transportation (their car), but it increases the risk among those who take public transportation (a bus). This is because by using private transportation, one is less likely to be exposed to motivated offenders on the street or at a bus stop. Routine activities theory was developed by Lawrence Cohen and Marcus Felson (1979; Clarke and Felson 1993), and in the second essay of this section, Professor Felson provides an overview of the theory.

References

Akers, Ronald L. (1997). *Criminological Theories: Introduction and Evaluation*. Los Angeles: Roxbury.

Anderson, Linda S., Theodore G. Chiricos, and Gordon P. Waldo. (1977). "Formal and informal sanctions: A comparison of deterrent effects." *Social Problems*, 25:103–114.

Bachman, Ronet, Raymond Paternoster, and Sally Ward. (1992). "The rationality of sexual offending: Testing a deterrence/rational choice conception of sexual assault." *Law and Society Review*, 26:434–372.

Beccaria, Cesare. [1764] (1985). *Essay on Crimes and Punishments*. Translated by H. Paolucci. New York: Macmillan.

Becker, Gary S. (1968). "Crime and punishment: An economic approach." *Journal of Political Economy*, 76:169–217.

Bentham, Jeremy. [1789] (1962). "An introduction to the principles of morals and legislation." In *The Works of Jeremy Bentham*. J. Bowring (ed.). New York: Russell and Russell.

Clarke, Ronald V. and Derek B. Cornish. (1985). "Modeling offenders' decisions: A framework for research and policy." Pp. 147–185 in M. Tonry and N. Morris (eds.), *Crime and Justice: An Annual Review of Research*, Vol. 6. Chicago: University of Chicago Press.

Clarke, Ronald V. and Marcus Felson. (1993). *Routine Activity and Rational Choice: Advances in Criminological Theory*, Vol. 5. New Brunswick, NJ: Transaction.

Cohen, Lawrence E. and Marcus Felson. (1979). "Social change and crime rate trends: A routine activities approach." *American Sociological Review*, 44:588–608.

Cornish, Derek B. and Ronald V. Clarke. (1986). *The Reasoning Criminal: Rational Choice Perspectives on Offending*. New York: Springer-Verlag.

Geerken, Michael R. and Walter R. Gove. (1975). "Deterrence: Some theoretical considerations." *Law and Society Review*, 9:498–513.

Gibbs, Jack P. (1975). *Crime, Punishment, and Deterrence*. New York: Elsevier.

Grasmick, Harold G. and Robert J. Bursik, Jr. (1990). "Conscience, significant others and rational choice: Extending the deterrence model." *Law and Society Review*, 24:837–862.

Grasmick, Harold G. and Donald E. Green. (1980). "Legal punishment, social disapproval, and internalization as inhibitors of illegal behavior." *Journal of Criminal Law and Criminology*, 71:325–335.

Hobbes, Thomas. [1651] (1962). *Leviathan*. New York: Macmillan.

Klepper, Steven and Daniel S. Nagin. (1989). "The deterrent effect of the perceived certainty and severity of punishment revisited." *Criminology*, 27:721–746.

Koper, Christopher S. (1995). "Just enough police presence: Reducing crime and disorderly behavior by optimizing patrol time in crime hot spots." *Justice Quarterly*, 12:649–671.

Levitt, Steven. (1996). "The effect of prison population size on crime rates: Evidence from prison overcrowding litigation." *Quarterly Journal of Economics*, 111:319–352.

———. (1997). "Using electoral cycles in police hiring to estimate the effect of police on crime." *American Economic Review*, 87:270–290.

Marvell, Thomas and Carlisle Moody. (1994). "Prison population growth and crime reduction." *Journal of Quantitative Criminology*, 10:109–140.

———. (1996). "Specification problems, police levels and crime rates." *Criminology*, 34:609–646.

Nagin, Daniel S. (1978). "General deterrence: A review of the empirical evidence." Pp. 95–139 in A. Blumstein, J. Cohen, and D. Nagin (eds.), in *Deterrence and Incapacitation: Estimating the Effects of Criminal Sanction on Crime Rates*. Washington, DC: National Academy Press.

———. (1998). "Criminal deterrence research at the outset of the twenty-first century." Pp. 1–42 in M. Tonry (ed.) *Crime and Justice: A Review of Research*, Vol. 23. Chicago: University of Chicago Press.

Nagin, Daniel S. and Raymond Paternoster. (1991). "Preventive effects of the perceived risk of arrest: Testing an expanded conception of deterrence." *Criminology*, 29:561–585.

Newman, Graeme, Ronald V. Clarke, and S. Giora Shoham. (1997). *Rational Choice and Situational Crime Prevention*. Brookfield, VT: Ashgate.

Paternoster, Raymond. (1987). "The deterrent effect of the perceived certainty and severity of punishment: A review of the evidence and issues." *Justice Quarterly*, 4:173–217.

Paternoster, Raymond, Linda E. Saltzman, Gordon P. Waldo and Theodore G. Chiricos. (1983). "Perceived risk and social control: Do sanctions really deter?" *Law and Society Review,* 17:457–480.

Ross, H. Lawrence. (1982). *Deterring the Drinking Driver: Legal Policy and Social Control.* Lexington, MA: DC Heath.

Rousseau, Jean-Jacques. [1762] (1967). *The Social Contract and Discourse on the Origin of Inequality.* Edited by L.G. Crocker. New York: Washington Square Books.

Sampson, Robert J. and Jacqueline Cohen. (1988). "Deterrent effects of police on crime: A replication and theoretical extension." *Law and Society Review,* 22:163–189.

Sherman, Lawrence W. (1990). "Police crackdowns: Initial and residual deterrence." Pp. 1–48 in M. Tonry and N. Morris (eds.), *Crime and Justice: A Review of Research,* Vol. 12. Chicago: University of Chicago Press.

——. (1992). *Policing Domestic Violence: Experiments and Dilemmas.* New York: Free.

——. (1995). "The police." Pp. 327–348 in J.Q. Wilson and J. Petersilia (eds.) *Crime.* San Francisco: ICS.

Sherman, Lawrence W. and Dennis P. Rogan. (1995). "Effects of gun seizures on gun violence: 'Hot spots' patrol in Kansas City." *Justice Quarterly,* 12:673–693.

Sherman, Lawrence W. and David Weisburd. (1995). "General deterrent effects of police patrol in crime 'hot spots': A randomized, controlled trial." *Justice Quarterly,* 12:625–648.

Simon, Herbert A. (1957). *Models of Man: Social and Rational.* New York: Wiley.

Spelman, William. (1994). *Criminal Incapacitation.* New York: Plenum.

Stafford, Mark and Mark Warr. (1993). "A reconceptualization of general and specific deterrence." *Journal of Research in Crime and Delinquency,* 30:123–135.

Tittle, Charles R. and Allan R. Rowe. (1974). "Certainty of arrest and crime rates: A further test of the deterrence hypothesis." *Social Forces,* 52:455–462.

Vold, George B. and Thomas J. Bernard. (1986). *Theoretical Criminology,* Third Edition. New York: Oxford University Press.

Weisburd, David and Lorraine Green. (1995). "Policing drug hot spots: The Jersey City drug market analysis experiment." *Justice Quarterly,* 12:711–735.

Williams, Kirk R. and Richard Hawkins. (1986). "Perceptual research on general deterrence: A critical overview." *Law and Society Review,* 20:545–572.

Wilson, James Q. and George Kelling. (1982). "Broken windows: The police and neighborhood safety." *Atlantic Monthly,* March, pp. 29–38.

Zimring, Franklin E. and Gordon J. Hawkins. (1973). *Deterrence: The Legal Threat in Crime Control.* Chicago: University of Chicago Press.

——. (1995). *Incapacitation: Penal Confinement and Restraint of Crime.* New York: Oxford University Press.

Rational Choice

Ronald V. Clarke
Rutgers University

Derek B. Cornish
London School of Economics

Consider the words of some active armed robbers from St. Louis discussing their crimes (Wright and Decker 1997):

You are sitting there alone and you feeling light in your pocket, your rent is due, light and gas bill, you got these bill collectors sending you letters all the time, and you say, "I wish I had some money. I need some money." Those are the haints. [You haint got this and you haint got that.] Your mind starts tripping cause you ain't got no money and the wolves are at the door. . . . [After my last stickup] I gave my landlord some money and sent a little money off to the electric company, a little bit off to the gas company. I still had like twenty or thirty dollars in my pocket. I got me some beer, some cigarettes, and [spent] some on a stone [of crack cocaine]; enjoy myself for a minute. I let the people know I'm trying to pay you and they ain't gonna be knocking on my door. Now I can do me legitimate hustles until the crunch comes again. (43–44)

Robbery is the quickest money. Robbery is the most money you gonna get fast. . . . Burglary, you gonna have to sell the merchandise and get the money. Drugs, you gonna have to deal with too many people, [a] bunch of people. You gonna sell a fifty-dollar or hundred dollar bag to him, a fifty-dollar or hundred-dollar bag to him, it takes too long. But if you find where the cash money is and just go take it, you get it all in one wad. No problem. I've tried burglary, I've tried drug selling. . . the money is too slow. (51–52) See, I know the places to go [to locate good robbery targets]. Usually I go to all the places where dope men hang out. . . but I [also have] done some people coming out of those instant tellers. (78)

That's all I done robbed is drug dealers. . . they not gonna call the police. What they gonna tell the police? He robbed me for my dope? They is the easiest bait to me. I don't want to harm no innocent people, I just deal basically with drug dealers. (64)

Well, if [the victim] hesitates like that, undecided, you get a little aggressive and you push them. . . . I might take [the] pistol and crack their head with it. "Come on with that money and quit bullcrapping or else you gonna get into some real trouble!" Normally when they see you mean that kind of business they. . . come on out with it. (109)

These quotations vividly depict the immediate circumstances of offenders' lives that give rise to decisions to offend and the ways in which offenders go about translating these decisions into criminal action. A pressing need for cash and a lack of other practical alternatives, criminal or noncriminal, can make armed robbery an attractive option. Furthermore, knowledge of settings where cash-rich victims can be found, as well as of strategies for overcoming any opposition, may make the likely rewards well worth the risk and effort. For criminals, doing their best to "get by" in their everyday lives, choices and decisions like these, however rudimentary, play a significant role in determining the nature and frequency of their offending. The theoretical importance and practical benefits of investigating such decision making are two of the main contributions of the rational choice approach that we describe in this chapter.

This theoretical approach begins with the observation that crime is chosen because of the benefits it brings to the offender. This holds in all cases of crime, with the possible exception of some crimes committed as a result of serious mental illness. This starting point leads to a theory that differs in many ways from others in this volume. It explains the conditions needed for specific crimes to occur, not just why people become involved in crime. It makes little distinction between offenders and nonoffenders and emphasizes the role of crime opportunities in causation. And it is as much designed to serve policy making as criminological understanding.

Rational choice theory is the mainstay of economics and has been applied widely in sociology (Hechter and Kanazawa 1997). Although it is comparatively new to criminology, its focus on offenders as rational decision makers calculating where their self-interest lies, and pursuing it, puts it squarely in the classical tradition as developed by Beccaria in the eighteenth century. Several criminological versions of rational choice theory exist, but what we (Clarke and Cornish 1985; Cornish and Clarke 1986) have developed has probably attracted the most research attention. It is called the *rational choice perspective* and is the focus of this chapter.

The next few pages describe the principal features of the rational choice perspective, focusing on six basic propositions. We go on to explain the main points of difference between the rational choice perspective and other theories. Some applications of the theory are then described that illustrate its value in explaining crime and guiding prevention efforts. In the final section, the main criticisms of the theory are discussed.

Fundamentals of the Theory

A theory or model is a simplified representation of some aspect of the real world, such as crime. It is designed to assist in explaining, predicting, or controlling the phenomena falling within its general subject matter. While serving these purposes, the theory must also be internally consistent. This means that its various assumptions and propositions must fit together to form a logical and satisfying whole. In addition, if it is to be widely used, the theory must be simply stated. With this need in mind, we begin by identifying six basic assumptions or propositions forming the core of the rational choice perspective. Having stated these, we then go on to give greater detail.

Six Basic Propositions

1. Crimes are purposive and deliberate acts, committed with the intention of benefiting the offender.

2. In seeking to benefit themselves, offenders do not always succeed in making the best decisions because of the risks and uncertainty involved.

3. Offender decision making varies considerably with the nature of the crime.

4. Decisions about becoming involved in particular kinds of crime (involvement decisions) are quite different from those relating to the commission of a specific criminal act (event decisions).

5. Involvement decisions can be divided into three stages—becoming involved for the first time (initiation), continued involvement (habituation), and ceasing to offend (desistance)—that must be separately studied because they are influenced by quite different sets of variables.

6. Event decisions include a sequence of choices made at each stage of the criminal act (e.g., preparation, target selection, commission of the act, escape, and aftermath).

The Purposive Nature of Crime

As will be clear from the contents of this book, there are many different ways to explain crime. This is not just because criminology borrows theories from other disciplines, such as psychology and sociology, but also because so little agreement exists within these disciplines about the best ways of explaining human behavior. Thus, in psychology, there are fundamental differences of approach between (a) behaviorists, who view criminal behavior as being shaped, as all behavior is, by external rewards and punishments, and (b) psychoanalysts, who see offending as the outcome of internal mental conflicts. And, even within schools, many differences of opinion occur that at first might seem insignificant, but which can have important implications for explaining or controlling crime.

Particularly important is a theory's starting point. For the rational choice perspective it is that criminal acts are never senseless. To the contrary, they are purposive acts intended to bring some benefit to the offender. These benefits are most obvious when they come in the form of money or material goods, but they can also include excitement, fun, prestige, sexual gratification, and defiance or domination of others. A "wanton" act of smashing a window might actually be committed because of the fun of breaking something or the excitement of running away afterwards. A man might brutally beat his wife, not simply because he is a violent thug, but because this is the easiest way of getting her to do what he wants. "Senseless" acts of football hooliganism or gang violence might confer considerable prestige on the perpetrators among their peers. The term *joyriding* accurately conveys the main reason why cars are stolen—juveniles enjoy driving around in powerful machines. And it may not be the height of folly to provoke a police chase, as joyriders occasionally do. On the contrary, the added excitement, as well as the stories that can be told later, may more than compensate for the usually light punishments if caught.

These examples of crimes making sense when the motives and rewards are clarified could be multiplied over and again. Indeed, the cardinal rule of the rational choice perspective is never to dismiss as senseless or irrational any criminal act without first trying to understand its purposes from the perspective of the offender.

Limited or Bounded Rationality

We mentioned earlier that several varieties of rational choice theories exist in criminology (Hechter and Kanazawa 1997). Even though all assume that crime is the outcome of choice, they differ in their concept of what constitutes a "rational" choice. Opp (1997) has argued that most of these differences can be subsumed under the concept of *wide* and *narrow* formulations of rational choice. Wide formulations, which include the rational choice perspective, assume that an individual's behavior is characterized by "limited" or "bounded" rationality. This is to say that criminal decision making is inevitably less than perfect, because it reflects imperfect conditions under which it naturally occurs. Because offending involves risk and uncertainty, offenders are rarely in possession of all the necessary facts about costs and benefits (the risks, efforts, and rewards of crime). Although they try to act as effectively as they can, choices may have to be made quickly and revised hastily. And, because

there are constraints on human information-processing abilities, criminals, like the rest of us, may use rules of thumb to guide their actions. Instead of planning their crimes down to the last detail, they may rely on a general approach that has worked before, improvising when they meet with unforeseen circumstances. Once the decision to offend has been made, they may focus on the rewards of crime rather than its risks; and when considering these risks, they focus on the immediate possibilities of getting caught, rather than on the punishments they might receive.

To use the technical terms, their decision making is *satisficing* rather than *optimizing*—it gives reasonable outcomes ("it seems to get me mostly what I want") rather than the best that could be achieved ("all I can get with the least effort"). Like the rest of us, of course, offenders often act rashly and fail to consider the long-term consequences of their actions. They may be encouraged to take risks by their peers, and their decisions may sometimes be made in a fog of alcohol or drugs. As a result, offenders can make foolish choices that result in capture and severe punishment. Their mistakes and failures contribute further to the view that such behavior is irrational. To offenders, however, and to those taking a rational choice perspective on their crimes, they are generally doing the best they can within the limits of time, resources, and information available to them. This is why we characterize their decision making as rational, albeit it in a limited way.

The Importance of Crime Specificity

Specific offenses bring particular benefits to offenders and are committed with specific motives in mind. Cash is the motive for bank robbery, whereas for rape it is usually a desire for domination/power or sexual gratification. Similarly, the factors weighed by offenders, and the variables influencing their decision making, will differ greatly with the nature of the offense. This is especially true of event decisions because these are more heavily influenced by immediate situational factors. For example, the circumstances surrounding the commission of a mugging and the setting in which it occurs are quite different from those of a computer fraud.

For these reasons, criminal choice cannot properly be studied in the abstract. Instead, descriptions of criminal choice in the form of simplified models, such as flowcharts depicting involvement or event decision processes, have to be developed for specific categories of crime. Broad legal categories such as auto theft or burglary are far too general to model because they include many differently motivated offenses, committed by a wide range of offenders, employing a variety of methods and skills. For example, theft of a car for joyriding is a very different kind of offense from theft for temporary transport. Both are different from theft for "stripping" of the radio or theft for "chopping" of the body into its major parts. All these are different again from theft of cars for selling to local customers or for selling overseas.

There comes a point when increasingly finer distinctions between offenses result in tedious and unproductive study. For instance, separate choice models for joyriding thefts committed (a) in commuter parking lots and (b) in shopping malls may be of little value. So, what is the rule for deciding how crime specific to become? This question cannot be detached from the purpose of detailed modeling of criminal choices, which in most cases is to assist thinking about prevention. The question then becomes one of practicality and can be phrased as follows: Would drawing finer distinctions among a specific category of offenses result in large enough collections of offenses to justify separate interventions? If so, the distinctions should be made. If not, solutions should be sought that will address the variety of crimes subsumed under the broader category.

The emphasis on specificity does not mean that the rational choice perspective ignores the large body of evidence that many offenders, particularly juvenile delinquents and street criminals, are generalists, not specialists. Even when offenders commit a wide range of crimes, however, their motives and methods can vary greatly. Consider robbery and rape. These are sometimes committed by the same offenders, but against quite different victims. In the case of robbery, victims tend to be men with money, and in rape, younger women. The crimes also tend to be committed in different settings and, even though both may involve violence, the weapons used and injuries inflicted may be quite different. All these facts may result in different ways to prevent these crimes, which is reason enough for a crime-specific focus.

It is also the case that many offenders are not generalists. This is true of people who succumb to specific temptations to commit crime in the course of their work or everyday lives. People of this kind, who are generally law-abiding but who sometimes fall to temptation, commit a large proportion of all crime (Gabor 1996).

The Distinction Between Involvement and Events

Criminal choices can be divided into two broad groups, *involvement* and *event* decisions. Event decisions relate to the commission of a particular offense. They concern such matters as the choice of a particular target and ways to reduce the risks of apprehension. Involvement decisions are more complex and are made at three separate stages in a delinquent or criminal "career." Offenders must decide whether (1) they are ready to begin committing crime to get what they want, and (2) having started, whether they should continue with crime, and (3) at some point, whether they ought to stop. The technical terms used by criminologists for these three stages of involvement are *initiation*, *habituation*, and *desistance*.

It is easy to see why event decisions need to be understood and modeled separately for different kinds of crime. For example, the task of escaping apprehension is very different for bank robbers than for someone vandalizing a parked car. But crime specificity is just as important at the various stages of involvement. Thus, the issues faced by people deciding whether to become involved in particular crimes, and the background of relevant experience brought to bear, can vary greatly. The point can be illustrated with perhaps the two extreme examples of juveniles from the ghetto thinking about joining the neighborhood drug dealers and bank employees planning to defraud customers. The factors relevant to the decisions being made by these two groups are so different that they must be separately studied. These factors include the backgrounds and current circumstances of the two groups, the legitimate opportunities available to them for meeting the needs of their everyday lives, and the costs of being arrested and punished.

Where the same offenders are involved, more overlap is found in the background factors influencing their decisions about becoming involved in different crimes, such as drug dealing and shoplifting. Involvement in either of these crimes might also increase the probability of involvement in the other. But the opportunities for each, the skills and contacts needed, and the risks and rewards are likely to be so different that involvement will still need to be separately modeled.

It is also a mistake to assume that offenders involved in one kind of crime could just as easily be involved in another. Little research exists on this topic, but it is most unlikely that even for hardened offenders, all crimes carry the same moral costs. For instance, some muggers say they would never attack an old lady. This may help to rationalize their behavior and to present themselves in a better light, but it is not difficult to imagine that offenders make genuine moral distinctions between crimes. For instance, a deprived juvenile might have few inhibitions about shoplifting, particularly where the victim is a large, anonymous corporation. But he or she might be resolutely opposed to drug dealing because a brother or friend has died of a drug overdose. Scruples of this kind may turn out to be rare or relatively unimportant, but for the present they should be included in models of criminal decision making.

The Separate Stages of Involvement

Not only must involvement decisions be separately modeled for specific kinds of crime, but so must each stage of criminal involvement—initiation, habituation, and desistance—because decisions at each stage are influenced by different sets of variables. These variables fall into three groups:

(1) *background factors*, including personality and upbringing,

(2) *current life circumstances*, routines and lifestyles, and

(3) *situational variables* that include current needs and motives, together with immediate opportunities and inducements.

These are of differing importance at the various stages of involvement. At initiation, background factors have their greatest influence, because they shape both the nature of the individual's accumulated learning and experience as well as his or her current life circumstances. At habituation, current life circumstances, which now increasingly reflect the ongoing rewards of crime, may be of principal importance. Current life circumstances, together with accumulating experience of the costs of crime, also weigh heavily in decisions to desist. During all stages, however, it is the immediate influence of situational variables, such as needs and motives, and opportunities and inducements, that trigger the actual decision on whether or not to commit a particular crime.

Further details of the kinds of variables relevant at each stage are given in the accompanying decision diagrams. In keeping with the need for crime specificity, these diagrams relate to one particular kind of crime—burglary in a suburb. This might seem to be taking specificity too far, but Poyner and Webb (1991) have shown in their study undertaken in England that burglaries committed in suburbs are quite different from those committed in the city center. The latter tends to be committed by offenders on foot who are looking for cash and jewelry. Because access is restricted to the side and rear of older town houses in England, entry is often gained through the front door or a front window. Burglars operating in the suburbs, on the other hand, use cars and target electronic goods. They are as likely to enter from the back or side of the house as the front.

Figure 1 illustrates the factors influencing the initial decision to become involved in suburban burglary. Box 1 encompasses the various background factors that are thought by most theorists to determine the values, attitudes, and personality traits that dispose people to commit crime. In a rational choice context, however, these factors are reinter-

Figure 1
Initiation Model for Suburban Burglary

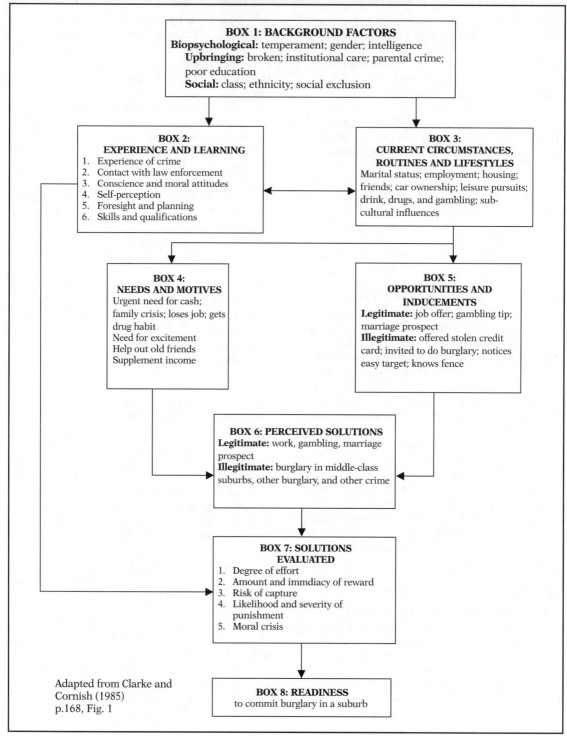

BOX 1: BACKGROUND FACTORS
Biopsychological: temperament; gender; intelligence
Upbringing: broken; institutional care; parental crime; poor education
Social: class; ethnicity; social exclusion

**BOX 2:
EXPERIENCE AND LEARNING**
1. Experience of crime
2. Contact with law enforcement
3. Conscience and moral attitudes
4. Self-perception
5. Foresight and planning
6. Skills and qualifications

**BOX 3:
CURRENT CIRCUMSTANCES,
ROUTINES AND LIFESTYLES**
Marital status; employment; housing; friends; car ownership; leisure pursuits; drink, drugs, and gambling; sub-cultural influences

**BOX 4:
NEEDS AND MOTIVES**
Urgent need for cash; family crisis; loses job; gets drug habit
Need for excitement
Help out old friends
Supplement income

**BOX 5:
OPPORTUNITIES AND
INDUCEMENTS**
Legitimate: job offer; gambling tip; marriage prospect
Illegitimate: offered stolen credit card; invited to do burglary; notices easy target; knows fence

BOX 6: PERCEIVED SOLUTIONS
Legitimate: work, gambling, marriage prospect
Illegitimate: burglary in middle-class suburbs, other burglary, and other crime

**BOX 7: SOLUTIONS
EVALUATED**
1. Degree of effort
2. Amount and immdiacy of reward
3. Risk of capture
4. Likelihood and severity of punishment
5. Moral crisis

BOX 8: READINESS
to commit burglary in a suburb

Adapted from Clarke and Cornish (1985) p.168, Fig. 1

Figure 2
Habituation Model for Suburban Burglary

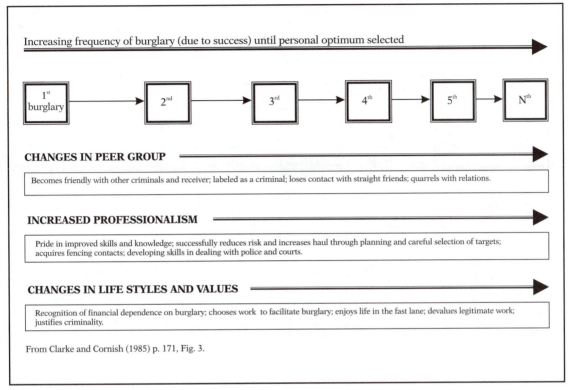

From Clarke and Cornish (1985) p. 171, Fig. 3.

preted as influencing the judgments and perceptions leading the individual to make a criminal choice. Box 3 deals with the offender's current life circumstances—employment, housing, marital status, aspects of lifestyle, and so forth. These help to determine the shape of an individual's needs and motives (Box 4), as well as the opportunities for meeting these needs and the inducements that may trigger or increase them (Box 5). The other boxes show how these needs are translated by the offender, based on his or her accumulated experience and learning (Box 2), through a process of evaluating alternative courses of action (Boxes 6 and 7), into a readiness to become involved in this form of crime (Box 8).

During habituation (Figure 2), background factors play a reduced role in decisions. Instead, the dominant roles are exercised by the rewards of crime and by changes in the offender's circumstances (new friends, increased professionalism, changes in life-

style, and associated values). At the stage of desistance (Figure 3), background factors have ceased to play any significant part in decision making. Rather, it is lack of success (including brushes with the law) and increasing reluctance to take risks, together with further changes in life circumstances (such as marriage and increasing family responsibilities), that play the important roles in the decision to desist.

The Sequence of Event Decisions

As mentioned, the rational choice perspective is comparatively new and is still being developed. This can be seen in the treatment of the criminal event, which initially focused on just one of the steps involved—the choice of targets (see Figure 4 depicting the suburban burglar's choice of house). But events often unfold in such a way that offenders are presented with a sequence of decisions. Sometimes these have to be made rapidly, one after the other, al-

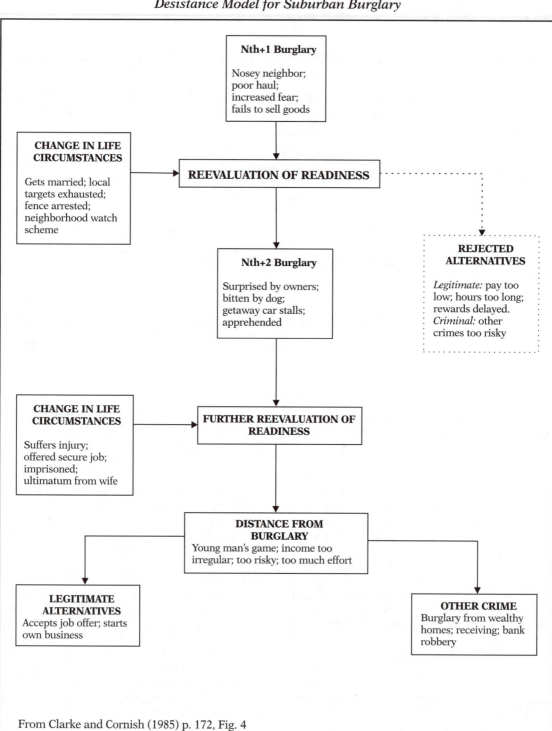

Figure 3
Desistance Model for Suburban Burglary

From Clarke and Cornish (1985) p. 172, Fig. 4

though in other cases they can be made at greater leisure.

In the case of a suburban burglary, the event may be sparked by some random occurrence, such as two burglars meeting up, both of whom need money. (Cusson, 1993, calls this stage "the precriminal situation.") Plans begin to be made and a car or van may be stolen for transport. The next step involves traveling to the neighborhood selected and identifying a house to enter. Ideally, this holds the promise of good pickings without the chance of being disturbed by the owners. A point of entry that is not too difficult or risky must then be found. Getting into the house and rapidly choosing the goods to steal follows this stage. The goods must then be carried to the car without being seen by neighbors or passers-by. Afterwards, they may have to be stashed safely while a purchaser is found. Finally, they must be conveyed to the buyer and exchanged for cash.

This account shows that the choice of a target is just one stage in the complex process of completing a criminal act. To assist analysis of this process, Cornish (1994) has proposed the concept of *crime scripts*, step-by-step accounts of the procedures used by offenders to commit crime. Crime scripts help to identify the decisions that the offender must make at each step and the situational variables that must be taken into account if the rewards of crime are to compensate for the risks and effort involved.

What Makes the Theory Different?

In this section we describe the main differences between the rational choice per-

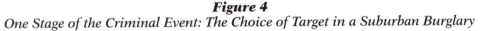

Figure 4
One Stage of the Criminal Event: The Choice of Target in a Suburban Burglary

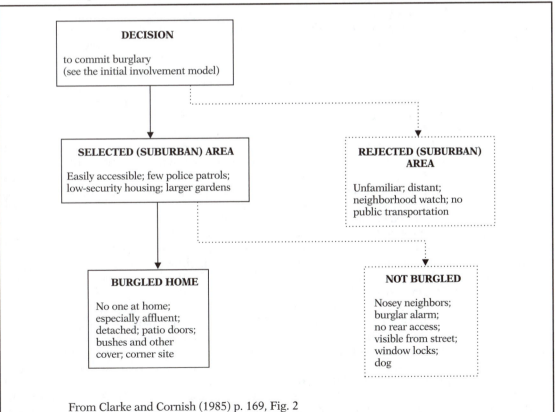

From Clarke and Cornish (1985) p. 169, Fig. 2

spective and other theories in this book. We do this to assist learning, not to suggest that there is little common ground with other theories. Rational choice perspective shares many assumptions, as indeed every theory borrows from others. What matters is the way in which the elements are packaged together. More important than anything else is the starting point of the rational choice perspective that crime is chosen for its benefits.

The Focus on Choice

Many other theories of crime, apart from rational choice, assume some choice on the part of the offender. Gibbons has pointed out, for example, that ". . . Sutherland's (1994) arguments about criminality resulting from an excess of definitions favorable to lawbreaking over definitions unfavorable to law violation are not entirely unlike rational choice contentions" (Gibbons 1994, 123). In other cases, choice assumptions are more explicit. For instance, the authors of an influential theory of deviancy state: "A social theory must have reference to men's teleology—their purposes, their beliefs, and the contexts in which they act out these purposes and beliefs" (Taylor, Walton, and Young 1973, 61). They give the example of bank robbers who, as they rightly observe, are not propelled through the door of the bank by their genes. Instead, ". . . men rob banks because they believe they may enrich themselves" (Taylor, Walton, and Young 1973, 61).

For these theorists, however, the purposive nature of crime is subsidiary to the wider social and political contexts that mold beliefs and structure choice. Consequently, they have taken little interest in the details of criminal decision making. For the rational choice perspective, however, it is these details that need to be understood. Bank robbers must actually make a decision to rob a particular bank and have to make at least some rudimentary preparations to accomplish the act. Even when offenders appear to behave impulsively and seize an opportunity that is suddenly presented, they must still make a choice to act, and this choice is facilitated by their general readiness to take advantage of such opportunities. Understand-

ing the background to such choices, the manner in which they are made, and how offenders set about their tasks is the business of the rational choice perspective.

A Theory of Both Crime and Criminality

Most criminological theories are geared to answering just one question: What makes certain people or groups of people more likely to become involved in crime and delinquency? In current criminological language, this makes them theories of criminality. When it focuses on involvement, the rational choice perspective is also a theory of criminality, albeit one that gives a fuller role to current life circumstances, needs, and opportunities. But when it focuses on the event, and seeks to understand why offenders choose to commit particular offenses, or how they undertake them, it becomes a theory of crime.

The Dynamic Nature of Crime

Preoccupied with explaining offending in terms of longstanding and relatively unchanging motives, criminological theories have often failed to capture the ever-changing, open-ended, contingent reality of offending. The rational choice perspective offers just such a fluid, dynamic picture—one that views offending as much more present-oriented and situationally influenced. Not only do offenders continually make decisions about whether or not to commit particular crimes, but they also constantly reassess their involvement in criminal activity. This assessment is deeply affected by their experience of committing particular acts and what they learn from the consequences. Cohen (1966) describes this as "a tentative, groping, feeling-out process, never fully determined by the past alone but always capable of changing its course in response to changes in the current scene" (45). It can result in desistance from offending or concentrating on some new form of crime. In addition, as Felson (1998) has explained, the commission of a particular crime can bring in its wake the need or the opportunity to commit other crimes. Thus, a burglar might decide to rape a woman he finds sleeping in the house, or a prostitute might decide to rob a drunken client. The notion of the crime script was specially developed to explore extended sequences of criminal decision making and links between crimes.

The Importance of Situation and Opportunity

With a few important exceptions, such as routine activity theory (Cohen and Felson 1979; Felson 1998), most criminological theories ignore or downplay the importance of situational factors in crime causation. However, the rational choice perspective pays as much attention to the causal role of immediate situational variables as to more remote variables such as family background and upbringing. It pays particular attention to opportunities for crime, which are perceived, evaluated, and acted upon by offenders. In some cases, opportunities are sought and created. But they also play a more active role. They may tempt an otherwise law-abiding person into occasional transgressions. And, the existence of easy opportunities in society might attract some people into a life of crime. These facts have important implications for prevention, as we shall see below.

The Distinction Between Motivation and Motive

Most theories are preoccupied with the factors giving rise to criminal motivations—deep-rooted inclinations or dispositions to commit crime. The rational choice perspective, on the other hand, takes more interest in criminal motives—more fleeting needs or wishes that might be met by crime. Table 1 lists some of the many motives that can drive the decision to commit crime.

The Normality of Crime

Unlike many other theories, the rational choice perspective makes no hard-and-fast distinction between offenders and the law-abiding. It recognizes, of course, that for some people crime is more consistently chosen in a variety of circumstances than for other people. However, this is as much the result of their present material circumstances as of their backgrounds. Given a change in their circumstances, they might easily begin to choose legal means for meeting their needs and desires. Likewise, people

Table 1
Common Motives for Crime

- to obtain money or goods
- to gain access to services
- to gain pleasure from intoxication
- to obtain sexual gratification
- to obtain excitement, fun, or thrills and to relieve boredom
- to achieve peer approval, admiration, status, or popularity
- to prove toughness and bravery
- to show off or gain attention to reduce tension due to anger or anxiety
- to escape or avoid aversive situations
- to see someone suffer or become frightened
- to gain compliance with orders or wishes
- to assert dominance or control
- to hurt an enemy
- to avenge an insult

who have generally avoided criminal choices might cease to do so in the face of overwhelming need or temptation. Many a respectable bank clerk has resorted to fraud in the face of pressing financial need. On occasion, all of us will commit an offense when we think we can get away with it. Even the most respectable among us, with steady, well-paid jobs, will cheat on expense claims and pilfer our employers' property.

A General Theory

Unlike many theories, which focus on particular kinds of delinquency and crime (usually committed by the lower classes), rational choice theory provides a general framework for understanding every kind of crime. It is as much concerned with crime in the suites as in the streets, as much with incivilities and disorder as with organized crime, with property crime as with violent crime, with crime committed by women as with crime committed by men. In short, there is no kind of crime for which choice and purpose play an unimportant part.

Policy Relevance

Both authors of the rational choice perspective spent their early careers in the British government's criminological research department (Clarke and Cornish 1983). This made them acutely aware of the need for criminology to be useful in solving policy and practical problems, and it helps to explain why the rational choice perspective was explicitly developed to assist policy thinking. It is by this standard that they would like the theory to be judged rather than by its ability to predict crime or crime trends. This policy purpose is served principally through detailed modeling of criminal decision making, as a result of which many potential points of intervention can be identified.

Theorists making use of the rational choice perspective reject the view of most criminologists that a policy-oriented stance limits the theoretician's objectivity and skews understanding of causes. Rather, they take the position that speculation unrestrained by practical demands often leads the theorist unduly to elevate the importance of motives or variables that may play very minor roles in crime causation. This has contributed to a criminology comprised mainly of theories that can never lead to practical action (Wilson 1975) and which is widely perceived among ordinary people as self-indulgent and politically motivated.

Compatibility With Criminal Justice

Worse still, most theories of crime put criminologists at odds with the criminal justice system, particularly with the concepts of punishment and deterrence lying at its heart. If crime is due to social or psychological deprivation, which is the position of most theories, it seems irrelevant or unfair to respond with punishment. This explains why many criminologists are hostile to criminal justice and reluctant to become involved in policy studies. Law enforcement and criminal justice professionals often detect this hostility and, in turn, disparage criminology.

This is unfortunate for both sides—and for society.

The rational choice perspective provides an escape from this situation. It recognizes that many offenders from deprived backgrounds have more limited opportunities for meeting everyday needs than more privileged members of society. To this extent, their crime choices are more readily understandable. However, in only very rare cases are people forced to commit crime by virtue of their background or current circumstances. Nor do all disadvantaged or deprived people turn to a life of crime. On the contrary, every act of crime involves some choice by the offender. He or she can be held responsible for that choice and can legitimately be punished. Rather than seek to excuse crime and oppose punishment, criminologists should therefore pursue a different agenda—one that seeks to make criminal choices less attractive. This does not mean that the rational choice perspective supports deterrent policies. In fact, research suggests that these play little part in most decisions to offend. In any case, punishment is expensive and often out of proportion to the harms caused by crime.

Application of the Rational Choice Perspective

Once stated, the basic propositions of the rational choice perspective seem intuitively obvious, if not commonsensical, and there seems little point in attempting to test their validity. Instead, we believe that the rational choice perspective should be evaluated by its usefulness in explaining crime and in suggesting novel forms of prevention. Judged by these standards, it has been quite successful in its short history. The examples given below have been chosen to illustrate the theory's power and versatility.

Explaining Repeat Victimization

Fattah (1993) has argued that the rational choice perspective shares many assumptions with recent theorizing about how people become victims. In both cases, these approaches are predicated on ideas that criminal behavior depends as much on situational opportunities as on upbringing and predisposition, that it cannot be understood without studying motives and purposes, and that it is essentially normal, not pathological. Fattah concludes,

> All this shows that the rational choice perspective and the victimological perspective do have much in common and could easily be linked together via some common and potentially unifying concepts such as "rationality/rationalization," "choice," "risk," "opportunity," "association/exposure," "target selection," and so forth. (239)

The explanation for "repeat victimization" given by Farrell, Phillips, and Pease (1995) illustrates these points. They argue that criminals repeatedly offend against the same targets for essentially rational reasons. For example, interviews with burglars show that they sometimes return to the same houses because they are familiar with the layout and can predict the likely haul. Occasionally, they return soon after the first burglary to collect items that they have left behind. Sometimes they return later when there has been time for owners to replace items stolen such as TVs and VCRs. In other cases, the burglars are local youths looking for small amounts of cash, who know when the occupants are away. All these are essentially rational explanations for an initially puzzling phenomenon.

Explaining the Preferences of Thieves

In their seminal paper on routine activity theory, Cohen and Felson (1979) identified four salient characteristics of suitable targets for predatory crime summarized by the acronym VIVA. This refers to a target's *visibility, inertia, value,* and *accessibility.* Criminologists showed little interest in VIVA until quite recently when they began to study "hot products," or the objects favored by thieves (Clarke 1999). They wanted to find ways of protecting these goods or of disrupting the illegal markets for them (Sutton 1998). While VIVA proved to be a useful starting point, its emphasis on the tangible, physical attributes of targets has resulted in neglect of their more subjective qualities. It also underplays attributes important at the stage of disposing of stolen goods.

With its emphasis on offender perceptions and on the sequential, extended nature of criminal events, the rational choice perspective provides the conceptual framework for a more complete model of target choice. Working within this framework, Clarke (1999) proposed the CRAVED model that refers to six important attributes of hot products: they must be *concealable, removable, available, valuable, enjoyable,* and *disposable.* Again, these attributes are mostly obvious. The one exception is enjoyable, but many studies have found that thieves tend to steal things that people enjoy owning or using (e.g., name-brand sneakers, VCRs, tobacco and liquor) rather than useful objects such as microwave ovens or undershirts.

Not all the attributes of CRAVED are of equal importance for all forms of theft. For example, all cars have wheels and motors, and the security measures built into most of them offer little resistance to theft. Thus, they are all readily removable. Even so, they still vary considerably in their risks of theft. In fact, these differences can only be explained when distinctions are made among the different kinds of theft. Clarke and Harris (1992) found in the United States that cars stolen for resale tended to be expensive models such as Lincolns and Mercedes. Those stripped of components tended to be widely available foreign imports, such as VWs with good radios that could be fitted to a variety of models. Those taken by joyriders tended to be domestic models, such as the Chevrolet Camaro, with powerful engines that were fun to drive. Viewed from the rational choice perspective, these results make good sense. They also provide examples of the theoretical importance of being crime specific and of paying closer attention to those properties of crimes, victims, and targets (*choice-structuring properties,* as they have been termed) that make them especially salient to criminal decision making.

Tracking Serial Killers

Most studies of target choice, such as those reviewed above, have been undertaken to find better ways of protecting targets from criminal attack. Studies of the victims of serial killers and rapists, and of the settings (e.g., murder scenes, body or property dumping sites) in which such crimes occurred, have been undertaken with a quite different objective—identifying and arresting the offender. Rossmo's (1995) *geographic profiling* is the best example of this approach. It is based on findings from environmental criminology (Brantingham and Brantingham, 1991) that most crime is committed within the *activity spaces* of offenders, those places routinely visited during their daily patterns of work and leisure. There are many reasons why this should be so. For example, offenders notice possible targets in the course of their routine activities. They become familiar with police activity in the area. And it is easier for them to commit crime during their daily routine than to make a special journey to do so.

Within every activity space is an *anchor point* or base, which for most people is their residence. By plotting where victims of the same offender are picked up and released (or their bodies found), Rossmo (1995) has had considerable success in identifying the approximate location of the offender's residence. His predictions are improved when he takes account of geographic features such as highways, parks, or shopping malls, all of which affect travel patterns. He has also found that offenders create a *buffer zone* around their homes where they avoid selecting victims—for the very good reason that they might be seen and recognized.

Knowing the likely anchor point has helped investigators to focus their efforts in a more confined area or on a narrower range of suspects, with the result that some very dangerous criminals have been arrested. Without the assumption of rationality, which to many people is contrary to the image of the serial killer, criminologists would not have contributed to this success.

Explaining a Dramatic Fall in Suicide

During the 1960s and 1970s, the national suicide rate in Britain dropped by about 40 percent. This was puzzling, as suicide rates had increased during the same period in most other European countries. Moreover, the economy in Britain was depressed during the period and morale in the country was low. This would normally lead to increased suicide, not the reverse. When found, the explanation for the drop proved quite simple: people in Britain were no longer able to kill themselves by using the domestic gas piped into their homes for cooking and heating. This was the result of two changes in the gas supply. In the 1960s, gas became less poisonous because it began to be made from oil, not coal. In the 1970s, the discovery of gas fields in the North Sea led to the replacement of manufactured gas by natural gas. This contains no poison and is difficult to use for suicide. Prior to these changes in the gas supply, about 50 percent of people committing suicide in Britain used domestic gas. After the changes, which were made for commercial reasons, this proportion dropped to less than 1 percent.

Wouldn't persons bent on suicide use another method? To explain why this did not occur, Cornish and Clarke (1987) analyzed the choice structuring properties of gas that led to it being preferred as a method of suicide. These include the facts that gas was available in nearly every home, it was simple to use, and it was highly lethal. It was also painless, left no marks or blood, and required relatively little courage. No other alternative possessed all these advantages and would therefore have been readily chosen as an alternative by someone thinking about committing suicide. For example, jumping from a high place or in front of a train requires more courage. Overdoses are rarely lethal and guns are not widely available in Britain. Cutting with a knife or razor is painful and can result in carpets or furniture being stained by blood. Consequently, when gas was made harmless, there was relatively little displacement to other methods. Given that suicide is usually seen as a deeply motivated act, this fact has important implications for preventing crime, as discussed below.

A Framework for Situational Crime Prevention

Although the rational choice perspective has been used in studying deterrence (Paternoster and Piquero 1995), perhaps its most important policy application to date has been in the field of situational crime prevention—a broad set of techniques designed to reduce opportunities for crime (Clarke 1997). These are classified under the four rational choice objectives: (1) increasing the perceived effort required by crime, (2) increasing the perceived risks, (3) reducing the anticipated rewards, and (4) removing excuses for crime.

Many notable crime prevention successes have been achieved by using these techniques. Clarke (1997) has republished 23 evaluated successes and there are dozens more. Some spectacular examples include the following:

- The virtual elimination of airline hijackings in the 1970s by baggage screening;

- The elimination of robberies of bus drivers in U.S. cities in the 1970s by the introduction of exact fare systems;

- The 40 percent reduction in credit card fraud achieved in the United Kingdom through a variety of situational controls introduced after 1992;

- The virtual elimination in the 1990s of graffiti on New York City subway cars by systematic and prompt graffiti removal; and

- The creation of a safe Metro system for the crime-ridden city of Washington, DC, by using crime prevention through environmental design (or CPTED) principles initially developed by Jeffery (1971).

In these and other cases, situational prevention is vulnerable to the criticism that reducing opportunities merely results in crime being displaced, for example to some other target or location. The rational choice perspective has helped to show why displacement does not necessarily occur. Much crime is the result of easy opportunities, and offenders may be unwilling to incur the additional risks and effort involved following the implementation of situational measures. In any case, other crimes may not provide the same rewards as those they previously committed.

Just as people are not compelled to commit suicide, offenders do not have to commit crime. Faced with reduced opportunities for crime, they can make do with less money and drugs or they can try to obtain these in noncriminal ways. In fact, a recent review found no evidence of any displacement in 22 out of 55 crime prevention projects studied (Hesseling 1994). Some displacement was reported in the remaining 33 projects, but in every case there was still a net gain in preventive benefits. Displacement is therefore not as much of a threat to situational prevention as was once thought. Evidence has also been accumulating that, far from simply displacing crime with little real benefit, situational measures often reduce crime more widely than expected. This is because offenders often believe that situational measures are more far-reaching than they really are (Clarke 1997).

Criticisms

The rational choice perspective has attracted much criticism, partly because it is new, partly because it is so different from other theories, and partly because it most resembles economic models that are specially disliked by sociologists. It has also fallen foul of political correctness among criminologists who, from a laudable desire to improve society, have often sought to portray deprivation and disadvantage as the sole, or at least the most important, causes of crime.

Some criticisms, however, result from legitimate differences of opinion about what is important in theory. For instance, it is true that the rational choice perspective pays relatively little attention to the motivational variables of traditional theories, except as background to understanding decisions about becoming involved in certain forms of offending. There are so many of these variables and their relationship to crime is so unclear that they become unrewarding to study. This is particularly true when the goal is to develop practical prevention policies. In addition, the rational choice perspective pays little attention to the broad social and political contexts that help to determine which acts are criminalized. It is not that these contexts are unimportant; rather, they play little direct part in most offender decision making.

We do not have space here to review all the criticisms made of the rational choice perspective. Instead, we concentrate on three of the most important: (1) that the defining characteristic of offenders is not rationality, but irrationality, (2) that some crimes might be rational but many are not, and (3) that the rational choice perspective offers little that is new to criminology.

Criminals Are Far from Rational

Much support for the rational choice perspective is found in ethnographic research in which offenders have been interviewed about their lifestyles, their criminal choices, and their motives and methods. This is conceded even by critics of the rational choice perspective, such as Gibbons, who states that recent studies of predatory offenders ". . . provide considerable support for a 'limited rationality' view of offender decision making by lawbreakers" (Gibbons 1994, 124). These studies include ones of burglars, shoplifters, car thieves, muggers, and robbers of banks and other commercial targets. However, some of the authors (e.g., Cromwell, Olson, Avery 1991; Shover 1996; and Wright and Decker 1994) have concluded that these instrumental offenders show less rationality than might have been expected. In particular, they do little planning of even serious crimes such as burglary and robbery. They often seem to rely on a set formula for committing crime and sometimes seize opportunities with little forethought. They frequently seem content to improvise solutions as the events unfold, without thinking much about alternative courses of action. Finally, they seem to think little about the consequences of being caught.

Whether these facts are evidence of irrationality is a matter of judgment. Given an initial willingness to commit crime, there might in fact be little point in spending much time and effort in planning offenses that have low returns and for which the risks are minimal. Dwelling too long on unlikely con-

sequences could paralyze action and too much planning could hinder improvisation when events take an unexpected turn. In any case, it is better to be optimistic and assume that tactics that have worked before are likely to work again. It could be argued therefore that the offenders are more "rational" than the researchers give them credit for. Altogether, this debate seems to be another example of assessing whether the glass is half full or half empty.

Other supposed evidence of irrationality in these interview studies is found in the value placed by offenders on a hedonistic, pleasure-loving lifestyle. Indeed, their criminal activity supports this lifestyle. Once again, pleasure seeking is not evidence of irrationality. It may indeed be an eminently reasonable goal for individuals whose opportunities are limited for the pursuit of longer-term career or financial objectives.

Finally, the element of excitement or fun in crime, which forms the basis of Katz's (1988) views about the seductions of crime, is sometimes seen as being antithetical to rational choice. But fun and excitement are legitimate goals, and therefore Katz's theory is one (important) variant of a rational choice position.

Only Some Crimes Are Rational

Some critics concede that organized and white-collar crime is largely rational, and that this may also be true of predatory crime such as burglary and robbery. However, they believe that many other crimes cannot be seen as rational. The examples most frequently cited include crimes with bizarre sexual components and, more generally, personal crimes of violence.

It is tempting to exclude crimes that are driven by clinical delusions or pathological compulsions from rational choice analysis. But even in these cases, rationality is not completely absent. For instance, serial killers of prostitutes who hear voices telling them to kill may still take pains to avoid arrest—and may succeed in doing so for a long time. In any case, pathological crimes are a tiny proportion of all criminal acts and their exclusion from rational choice theory hardly weakens its claims to generality.

As for violence, reluctance to accept its rationality comes from a failure to recognize (or admit) that it brings rewards. To understand these, one must see the crime from the offender's perspective. Apparently senseless fights between rival gangs or groups of football supporters can generate tremendous excitement among participants and great camaraderie among the youths on both sides. Getting into a brawl at the pub might be worth it—even when injuries result—so long as a reputation for toughness is not tarnished. Threatening or using violence is the quickest way for a robber to get the money. Hurting somebody that one hates can be pleasurable. For some men, beating their wives may be the only way to win an argument.

Recognition of these rewards has led Tedeschi and Felson (1994) to argue that all violence is instrumental and is used or threatened because of the benefits it brings. Their rational choice approach has been supported by detailed analyses of interactions that take place between victims and aggressors. These show that situational factors and incremental choices made by both parties interact to result in violence occurring or being averted. In a sense, violence is negotiated between both parties. Kennedy and Forde (1998) neatly capture this idea in the title of their recent book on violence, *When Push Comes to Shove*.

The foregoing arguments suggest that criticism of criminals or crimes as "irrational" often stems from the current lack of detailed information about the contexts, motivations, options, and decision-making processes that lead to offending. They may also arise from a reluctance to admit that wrongdoing could ever be considered rational, in case this might encourage (or be seen to encourage) more people to offend. But the notion that criminal behavior may be more rational than we sometimes like to think fits in well with evolutionary accounts that emphasize both the opportunistic nature of humans and other animals and the adaptiveness of antisocial behavioral strategies under a range of circumstances (Cohen and Machalek 1995).

The Rational Choice Perspective is Nothing New

The rational choice perspective is sometimes regarded as a version of neoclassical criminology and, as we have mentioned, it shares some assumptions with other modern theories. Consequently, some critics have claimed that it offers little not already provided by other theories. Those most often mentioned in this context are economic theory, social learning theory, routine activity theory, and Gottfedson and Hirschi's (1990) general theory of crime.

Economic theory. The rational choice perspective is sometimes said to be just another version of economic theory, even though most economists would reject this description. In particular, they would say the perspective does not attempt to express relationships between basic concepts in mathematical terms and cannot be used to predict levels of crime under varying conditions of costs and benefits. Nevertheless, other differences make it, in our view, more flexible and useful than economic models (Clarke and Felson 1993; Opp 1997). For example, it does not ignore rewards that cannot readily be expressed in monetary terms. It does not treat all crimes as functionally equivalent. It does not treat crime predominantly in terms of an occupational choice when most delinquents are too young for the labor force. It does not put faith in punishments that are difficult and costly to deliver in a modern society. It makes no use of the confusing economic concept of *demand* for crime when most victims have no wish to be victimized. Finally, the rational choice perspective is designed to assist understanding of why people commit specific forms of crime and of how they might be prevented from doing so. Consequently, it pays much closer attention to the details of crime and its commission than does the rational choice theory of economists.

Social learning theory. Perhaps the most explicit charge that the rational choice perspective is redundant has been made by Akers (1990), who sees it as little different from the social learning theory he has done so much to develop in criminology. This criticism has been rebutted by Cornish (1993), an author of this essay. In general, we would agree that there are many similarities between the two theories. Both are focused on the criminal actor and are thus micro theories; both assume rationality; both give importance to immediate situational rewards and punishments; and both give an important role to learning. Indeed, before developing the rational choice perspective, we regarded ourselves as learning theorists (see Cornish and Clarke 1975). We still believe social learning theory has much to offer criminology, but we found it of limited value in our own work. We came to believe that crime cannot be understood without attempting to discover how offenders think about their behavior and how they make their choices. We also thought that social learning theory paid insufficient attention to the vast differences in situational cues and influences for specific forms of crime. And it seemed not to pay enough attention to the need for separate modeling of the different stages of criminal involvement.

These differences might be interpreted as merely ones of emphasis, but in our view they carry important implications for understanding and explaining crime. For us, however, the crucial test of a theory is its value in helping to develop policy. The rational choice perspective underpins situational crime prevention—a successful approach to crime control based upon reducing crime opportunities. This is completely ignored by Akers, who seems to believe that the policy implications of the rational choice perspective are limited to deterrence. This may reveal how different is his approach from ours.

Routine activity theory. The rational choice perspective is also very different from routine activity theory, even though both are described as opportunity theories and are commonly discussed together. Clarke and Felson (1993) have enumerated the differences between the two approaches, but we believe that the most important is that routine activity theory is a macro theory dealing with changes at a societal level that expand or limit crime opportunities. The rational choice perspective, on the other hand, is a micro theory dealing with the ways in which these opportunities are perceived, evalu-

ated, and acted upon by individual offenders. Both have important, complementary roles in modern criminology. Routine activity theory is unsurpassed as a tool for understanding the relationship between crime and everyday life, while the rational choice perspective has proved invaluable for thinking about practical ways to block opportunities for crime.

The general theory of crime. The rational choice perspective shares with Gottfredson and Hirschi's (1990) general theory of crime a stress on the importance of the role of opportunity in offending. However, unlike Gottfredson and Hirschi, we take no particular view on whether offending is, in addition, the outcome of low self-control. Different offenses require varying degrees of planning, and offenders of different ages, experience, and skills may well exhibit varying degrees of understanding and concern about the consequences of their actions.

But before assuming that offenders as a whole lack self-control or, indeed, that such a lack is a defect (and therefore leads to less than "rational" behavior), we need to be sure that alternative explanations have been ruled out. For example, to the casual onlooker some offenses may well look more impulsive and ill-judged than they are. And, without a better knowledge of the typical life chances of those in similar socio-economic circumstances to those of offenders, it is hard to judge to what extent offending—even persistent offending—represents an imprudent choice. Where careers are nonexistent and the long-term is bleak, a life of autonomy, "partying" without concern for the future, may have more to offer at fewer costs than the middle-class criminologist thinks.

Conclusion

In general terms, defense of rational choice theory is hardly necessary: its heuristic value is incontrovertible. As Herrnstein (1990) points out, ". . . it comes close to serving as the fundamental principle of the behavioral sciences. No other well-articulated theory of behavior commands so large a following in so wide a range of disciplines" (356). As far as its application to criminology is concerned, we have yet to set out in detail all the components of this powerful perspective or to fully explore its potential. But to be of practical utility, the rational choice perspective needs only to be "good enough" for the explanatory or policy purpose in hand. At the same time, it must be flexible enough to accommodate new needs. In fact, it is continually being refined and its description in this chapter contains several elements not included before. If we were called upon to make a fresh statement of the theory some years from now, we believe this too would incorporate new or more fully developed concepts. Otherwise, we will have failed in our objective of providing a useful tool, capable of being honed and improved, to assist criminologists in thinking about the practical business of controlling crime.

Acknowledgments

We thank Mangai Natarajan and Martha Smith for their helpful comments on the draft of this essay, and we also thank the former for help with the diagrams.

References

Akers, R.L. (1990). "Rational choice, deterrence and social learning theory in criminology: The path not taken." *Journal of Criminal Law and Criminology* Vol. 81, pp. 653–676.

Brantingham, P.J. and Brantingham, P.L. (eds.). (1991). *Environmental Criminology* Second Edition. Prospect Heights, IL: Waveland.

Clarke, R.V. (ed.). (1997). *Situational Crime Prevention: Successful Case Studies,* Second Edition. Albany, NY: Harrow and Heston.

Clarke, R.V. (1999). "Hot products: Understanding, anticipating and reducing demand for stolen goods." *Police Research Series,* Paper 112. London: Home Office.

Clarke, R.V. and D.B. Cornish (eds.). (1983). *Crime Control in Britain.* Albany: State University of New York Press.

Clarke, R.V. and D.B. Cornish. (1985). "Modeling offenders' decisions: A framework for research and policy." In M. Tonry and N. Morris, (eds.), *Crime and Justice,* Vol. 6, pp. 147–185. Chicago: University of Chicago Press.

Clarke, R.V. and M. Felson (eds.). (1993). "Routine activity and rational choice." *Advances in Criminological Theory,* Vol. 5. New Brunswick, NJ: Transaction.

Clarke, R.V. and P.M. Harris. (1992). "A rational choice perspective on the targets of autotheft." *Criminal Behaviour and Mental Health,* Vol. 2, pp. 25–42.

Cohen, Albert. (1966). *Deviance and Control.* Englewood Cliffs, NJ: Prentice Hall.

Cohen, L.E. and M. Felson. (1979). "Social change and crime rate trends: A routine activity approach." *American Sociological Review,* Vol. 44, pp. 588–608.

Cohen, L.E. and R.S. Machalek. (1995). "Behavioral strategy: A neglected element in criminological theory and crime policy." Pp. 157–178 in H.D. Barlow (ed.), *Crime and Public Policy: Putting Theory to Work.* Boulder, CO: Westview.

Cornish, D.B. (1993). "Theories of action in criminology: Learning theory and rational choice approaches." Pp. 351–382 in R.V. Clarke and M. Felson (eds.), "Routine Activity and Rational Choice." *Advances in Criminological Theory,* Vol. 5. New Brunswick, NJ: Transaction.

Cornish, D. (1994). "The procedural analysis of offending and its relevance for situational prevention." In R.V. Clarke (ed.), *Crime Prevention Studies,* Vol. 3. Monsey, NY: Criminal Justice Press.

Cornish, D. and R.V. Clarke. (1975). "Residential treatment and its effects on delinquency." *Home Office Research Study,* No. 178. London: Her Majesty's Stationery Office.

Cornish, D. and R.V. Clarke (eds.). (1986). *The Reasoning Criminal.* New York: Springer-Verlag.

Cornish, D. and R.V. Clarke. (1987). "Understanding crime displacement: An application of rational choice theory." *Criminology,* Vol. 25, pp. 933–947.

Cromwell, P., J. Olson, and D. Wester Avery. (1991). *Breaking and Entering: An Ethnographic Analysis of Burglary.* Beverly Hills, CA: Sage.

Cusson, M. (1993). "A strategic analysis of crime: criminal tactics as responses to precriminal situations." Pp. 295–304 in R.V. Clarke and M. Felson (eds.), "Routine Activity and Rational Choice." *Advances in Criminological Theory,* Vol. 5. New Brunswick, NJ: Transaction.

Farrell, G., C. Phillips, and K. Pease. (1995). "Like taking candy: Why does repeat victimization occur?" *British Journal of Criminology,* Vol. 35, pp. 384–399.

Fattah, Ezzat. (1993). "The rational choice/opportunity perspectives as a vehicle for integrating criminological and victimological theories." Pp. 225–258 in R.V. Clarke and M. Felson (eds.), Routine Activity and Rational

Choice. *Advances in Criminological Theory*, Vol. 5. New Brunswick, NJ: Transaction.

Felson, M. (1998). *Crime and Everyday Life*, Second Edition. Thousand Oaks, CA: Pine Forge.

Gabor, T. (1996). *Everybody Does It! Crime by the Public*. New York: Macmillan.

Gibbons, D. (1994). *Talking About Crime and Criminals: Problems and Issues in Theory Development in Criminology*. Englewood Cliffs, NJ: Prentice Hall.

Gottfredson, M.R. and T. Hirschi. (1990). *A General Theory of Crime*. Stanford, CA: Stanford University Press.

Hechter, M. and S. Kanazawa. (1997). "Sociological rational choice theory." *Annual Review of Sociology*, Vol. 23, pp. 191–214.

Herrnstein, Richard J. (1990). "Rational choice theory: Necessary but not sufficient." *American Psychologist*, Vol. 45, pp. 356–367.

Hesseling, R.B.P. (1994). "Displacement: A review of the empirical literature." Pp. 197–230 in R.V. Clarke (ed.), *Crime Prevention Studies*, Vol. 3. Monsey, NY: Criminal Justice Press.

Jeffery, C.R. (1971). *Crime Prevention Through Environmental Design*. Beverly Hills, CA: Sage.

Katz, J. (1988). *Seductions of Crime: Moral and Sensual Attractions of Doing Evil*. New York: Basic.

Kennedy, L.W. and D.R. Forde. (1998). *When Push Comes to Shove*. Albany: State University of New York Press.

Opp, K.D. (1997). "Limited rationality and crime." Pp. 47–63 in G. Newman, R.V. Clarke and S.G. Shoham (eds.), *Rational Choice and Situational Crime Prevention: Theoretical Foundations*. Dartmouth UK: Ashgate.

Paternoster, R. and A. Piquero. (1995). "Reconceptualizing deterrence: An empirical test of personal and vicarious experiences." *Journal of Research in Crime and Delinquency*, Vol. 32, pp. 251–286.

Poyner, B. and B. Webb. (1991). *Crime Free Housing*. Oxford, UK: Butterworth Architect.

Rossmo, D.K. (1995). "Place, space and police investigations: Hunting serial violent criminals." In J. Eck and D. Weisburd (eds.) Crime and Place. *Crime Prevention Studies*, Vol. 4, Pp. 217–235. Monsey, NY: Criminal Justice Press.

Shover, N. (1996). *Great Pretenders: Pursuits and Careers of Persistent Thieves*. Boulder, CO: Westview.

Sutton, M. (1998). "Handling stolen goods and theft: A market reduction approach." *Home Office Research Study*, No. 178. London: Home Office.

Taylor, I., P. Walton, and J. Young. (1973). *The New Criminology*. London: Routledge and Kegan Paul.

Tedeschi, J.T. and R.B. Felson. (1994). *Violence, Aggression and Coercive Actions*. Washington, DC: American Psychological Association.

Wilson, J.Q. (1975). *Thinking About Crime*. New York: Basic.

Wright, R.T. and S.H. Decker. (1994). *Burglars on the Job*. Boston, MA: Northeastern University Press.

Wright, R.T. and S.H. Decker. (1997). *Armed Robbers in Action: Stickups and Street Culture*. Boston, MA: Northeastern University Press.

The Routine Activity Approach

A Very Versatile Theory of Crime

Marcus Felson
Rutgers University

The routine activity approach was first named in a paper published in 1979. It was subsequently applied to direct-contact predatory crimes. Since then, it has proven to be versatile for different types of crime and levels of analysis, at different ages, for individual and group crime, for comparisons across nations, states, regions and cities, and for trends and cycles over time. It even applies to electronic and other remote crimes and to domestic violence. This versatility strengthens its potential as a general theory.

The routine activity approach began as a relatively simple theory of limited application (Cohen and Felson 1979). It first applied only to direct-contact predatory offenses, when at least one person directly took or damaged the person or property of another. This had to occur in the same place at the same time, involving three minimal elements: a likely offender, a suitable crime target, and the absence of a capable guardian against crime.

The hallmark of the theory is its de-emphasis upon the offender and shift of attention towards the target and guardian (for a review, see Garland 1999). The guardian is usually a friend or relative whose proximity assists your safety; or you yourself are guardian for your own person and property. The target can be any person or property that any offender would like to take or control, whether it is a woman he wants to rape or a piece of candy he would like to shoplift. Using the impersonal word *target* rather than *victim* emphasizes the physical nature of each criminal act.

Indeed, a predatory offender has to find a target with a guardian absent or indisposed. For example, she might find your home empty and the neighbors gone, then break in to take your jewels. Or he might find you walking down a dark street without a friend or anybody else to discourage an attack. The most likely guardians are other people, not usually police or security guards. These assumptions of routine activity theory are quite consistent with rational choice theory (see Clarke and Felson 1993): in picking good targets with guardians absent, offenders make calculations about how to succeed in illegal acts. Their focus is not the eventual punishment of a slow criminal justice system but rather the immediate rewards and punishments of a crime situation.

From the outset, the routine activity approach worked at both the very local and very large-scale level of analysis. It considered not only the presence of the three minimal elements in each situation but also the population of situations producing such presences. The latter helped explain how crime rates change over years in the entire society. Thus, the national crime rate could go up for at least four reasons: more offenders, more targets, fewer guardians, or fewer convergences of offenders and targets with guardians absent. This also meant that crime rates could rise without having any increase whatever in the number of offenders or any moral breakdown. The routine activity approach shifted attention away from illegal intentions and towards the ability to carry out those intended acts.

The theory also shifted the focus away from the criminal justice system and towards changes in larger society that might provide crime opportunity. Although related developments in Europe used the term *opportunity theory,* the word *opportunity* in the United States normally refers to economic opportunity. In addition, that word is vague and imprecise in meaning. Routine activities refer more precisely to everyday behaviors giving rise to specific chances to put an illegal act into motion at the moment an offender finds a target with all guardians indisposed. For example, someone who gets drunk most nights and staggers home is likely to be mugged. Going to taverns or bars dominated by young males and staying late also generates risks. Letting crowds of people enter any door of your shop and exit any other door leads to more shoplifting. Leaving your home empty most days makes it more subject to the risk of burglary. Any large-scale social change that allows offenders to find targets with guardians absent will generate more crime. Any social change that reduces these convergences will tend to reduce crime. For example, in the 1990s the shift towards electronic money offered the best explanation of lower crime rates.

Initially, the routine activity approach emphasized two driving features of crime rates in the larger population: more light-weight goods that are easier to steal and the dispersion of activities away from family and household settings. The latter applied to both property and violent offenses. As people left family and household, they would be most likely to fall victim to crime as well as to perpetrate it. People and property were less supervised. Homes and cars were also subject to more risk in nonfamily, nonhousehold settings. Note that the family and household features were combined. Thus, if you left the household accompanied by parents, although your home might be burglarized, you would not very likely get drunk and into trouble as a victim or offender. If you stayed within the household, however, you might still get into difficulties while your parents were away. The *combination* of family and household provided the most powerful discouragement against victimization or offending.

This point gave rise to a critique of the routine activity approach as inapplicable to domestic violence, which occurs mostly (although not entirely) at home. Indeed, the common exaggeration that most violence is at home seems to threaten routine activity thinking or at least lead to the assertion that its applicability is limited. Nevertheless, further thought leads elsewhere. That is, the routine activity approach takes into account

the time that people spend in various settings. The initial work calculated risks per hours spent in each type of setting. These calculations showed clearly (Cohen and Felson 1979) that an hour on the street is far more risky than an hour at home. Even if one multiplies risks to take into account underreporting of domestic violence, it is still far safer at home than on the street. To be sure, workplaces are safe for most occupations. Yet, the routine activity approach assists in explaining why nighttime jobs, delivery work, and jobs in bars bring greater risk (see Block, Felson, and Block 1985; NIOHS 1996). Although women with a drunken and abusive husband could be safer at work than at home, this does not disprove the general point that most women are safer at home.

The emphasis in the initial routine activity approach upon activities away from home has given rise to a naïve interpretation of the theory. That interpretation treats activities away from home as definitive, when in fact these activities are merely the simplest examples of how the basic principles can apply. The fundamental point is that a predatory crime usually requires the convergence of a likely offender and a suitable target with a capable guardian absent. When such a convergence occurs inside or even among relatives, crime can still occur.

For example, domestic violence generally occurs indoors with isolation from those who might best stop it. This point is confirmed by Baumgartner (1993) and is explained further by Tedeschi and Felson (1994). Mannon's (1997) study of intimate violence considers access of stepparents to stepchildren, priests to choir boys, childcare workers to young children and lovers to each other. Such access depends also upon absences. Thus, a choir director attracted to young boys finds the right setting to make his move on a single youth with others absent. Or a man beats his girlfriend after friends or neighbors are out of sight or earshot. A father raping a stepdaughter depends upon the mother being away. A youth may be more likely to hit his girlfriend when his roommate is away. The old criticism that the routine activity approach does not apply to these offenses is clearly obsolete. But it is important to react creatively rather than defensively.

As we work out more thoughts and gather more information, we begin to see that the routine activity approach must not be defined narrowly as "a dispersion of activities away from family and household." That particular set of activity analyses is appropriate to many crimes, but other crimes depend upon other activity patterns. The type of housing and its remoteness influences a husband's ability to attack a wife and get away with it, or to beat the charge in court because nobody is around to help a judge sort out competing stories. For routine activities to help us study diverse offenses, we must focus our thinking and fact gathering.

In its earliest pronouncement, the routine activity approach virtually said there was nothing to do about crime; indeed, it stated that crime was built into the very structure of everyday life. It is now clear that the conclusion that crime could not be prevented was premature. If more crime opportunity makes more crime, then less crime opportunity has to make less crime. Over the past two decades, criminologists and others have discovered many ways in which to reduce crime opportunities. These methods are collected and explained by Clarke (1997), whose work on situational crime prevention is the mirror opposite of the routine activity approach. Indeed, Clarke and Felson (1993) brought the two approaches together and thus dispelled the misconception that the routine activity approach has nothing practical to offer. It is, in fact, part and parcel of crime prevention as both an intellectual and practical field. The routine activity approach has as its policy prescription a major program to reduce crime opportunities in local settings via diverse applications of situational crime prevention.

In short, the routine activity approach should no longer be defined narrowly. It includes or at least reaches out to situational prevention. It goes beyond the dispersion of activities away from family and household settings. It means much more today than it did in 1979. Indeed, it is closely linked to an entire cluster of theories and prevention approaches (Garland 1999).

The routine activity approach initially applied to violent offenses only so long as the latter were predatory. However, many violent offenses have no clear distinction between offender and victim. For example, two men get into a fight for which they are equally responsible. This cannot be called a predatory offense, yet it still depends upon routine activities. Alcohol in the blood, the structure of barrooms, the presence of peacemakers or provokers, the proximity of an audience for insults—all of these play a role in the development and escalation of disputes into violence (see Tedeschi and Felson 1994; Forde and Kennedy 1999).

Diverse offenses not formerly considered amenable to the routine activity analysis are now suitable for exactly that. First, drug sales have very strong routine elements that apply to their growth and prevention. Open-air drug markets, drug houses, and drug apartments—all of these have strong routine activity features (see Eck and Wartell 1998). Second, suicide—a crime in the United States—has strong routine activity features, such as a dependency on weapons or toxic gas, the absence of which can lead to dramatic declines in suicide rates (see Clarke and Lester 1989). In addition, telecommunications crimes have detailed modus operandi that can readily be analyzed in routine activity terms. These include illegal interceptions, electronic vandalism and terrorism, stealing telecommunications services, offensive content, electronic fraud, money laundering, and use of communications to further criminal conspiracies (see Grabosky and Smith 1998).

The routine activity approach is also increasingly suitable for making comparisons at various levels of analysis (see Felson 1998). For example, auto theft is greater in more densely populated cities with worse parking, while burglary rises in less dense metropolitan areas with larger backyards hiding burglars as they enter. School terms and weather produce crime cycles over the months of the year. Climatic variations are well explained by heavy beer drinking in warm months. The northern tier of the world, with its greater climatic variations, produces wider amplitudes in its monthly crime cycles than the zone of more even temperatures. Crime rates vary dramatically over hours of the day, probably the strongest pattern of all, itself reflective of dramatic differences in the daily cycle. Indeed, routine activity thinking generates hypotheses and simpler explanations for many more crime phenomena than previously found.

Even the classic but messy link between poverty and crime gains new clarity when put in routine activity terms. Some high-income areas are also high in crime and some low-income areas are low in crime. How can we reconcile this with the rule? Some low-income areas often offer excellent crime targets, such as warehouses and abandoned properties. Other low-income areas, however, are quite stable in population and have good sight lines to provide guardianship against crime. Some areas of relatively higher income offer excellent crime opportunities, such as larger backyards, shopping malls, and schools with plenty of trees to hide behind. Other areas with relatively higher income are abandoned in daytime, have high rates of geographic mobility, and few residents who know one another—these features feeding crime. The routine activity approach sharpens our thinking and thus helps replace the vague hypotheses about social disorganization and crime with something better.

References

Baumgartner, R. (1993). "Violent networks: The origins and management of domestic conflict." In R.B. Felson and J.T. Tedeschi (ed.), *Aggression and Violence: Social Interactionist perspectives*. Washington, DC: American Psychological Association Books.

Block, Richard, Marcus Felson, and Carolyn R. Block. (1985). "Crime victimization rates for incumbents of 246 occupations." *Sociology and Social Research*, 69:442–451.

Clarke, Ronald V. (1997). *Situational Crime Prevention: Successful Case Studies*, Second Edition. New York: Harrow and Heston.

Clarke, Ronald V. and D. Lester. (1989). *Suicide: Closing the Exits*. New York and Berlin: Springer-Verlag.

Clarke, Ronald V. and Marcus Felson. (1993). "Routine activity and rational choice." *Advances in Criminological Theory*, V. New Brunswick, NJ: Transaction.

Cohen, L.E. and M. Felson. (1979). "Social change and crime rate trends: A routine activity approach." *American Sociological Review*, 44:588–608.

Eck, J.E. and J. Wartell. (1998). "Improving the management of rental properties with drug problems: A randomized experiment." In L.G. Mazerolle and J. Roehl (ed.), *Civil Remedies and Crime Prevention. Crime Prevention Studies*, 9:161–187.

Felson, Marcus. (1998). *Crime and Everyday Life*, Second Edition. Thousand Oaks, CA: Pine Forge.

Forde, D. and L. Kennedy. (1999). *When Push Comes to Shove: A Routine Conflict Approach to Violence*. Albany: State University of New York Press.

Garland, D. (1999). "Review essay: The commonplace and the catastrophic." *Theoretical Criminology*, 3:3.

Grabosky, P.N. and R.G. Smith. (1998). *Crime in the Digital Age: Controlling Telecommunications and Cyberspace Illegalities*. New Brunswick, NJ: Transaction.

Mannon, J.M. (1997). "Domestic and intimate violence: An application of routine activities theory." *Aggression and Violent Behavior*, 2:9–24.

NIOHS (National Institute for Occupational Health and Safety). (1996). "Violence in the workplace: Risk factors and prevention strategies." Washington, DC: U.S. Department of Health and Human Services.

Tedeschi, J. and Richard Felson. (1994). *Violence, Aggression, and Coercive Action*. Washington, DC: American Psychological Association Books.

3
The Positive School of Criminology
Biological Theories of Crime

Introduction

In the previous chapter of this book, we noted that during the early part of the eighteenth century, thoughts about criminals and the criminal justice system were dominated by the broad intellectual tradition in Europe known as the Enlightenment. The moral philosophy of the Enlightenment emphasized, among other things, the rational capacities of human beings. An implication of this was the belief that humans possessed the ability, through the application of reason, first to understand and then change the world within which they lived. We know that a child of Enlightenment thought was the classical school of criminology, with its emphasis on human beings as rational, calculating, and self-interested creatures. We also learned that there was a strong public policy emphasis in the early classical school. Theorists like Beccaria [1764] (1963) and Bentham [1789] (1962) were more than just interested in developing theories of criminal justice. They wanted to devise policies to do something about it. A prominent component of the classical school, therefore, was the development of principles by which legislators could more efficiently and rationally rule.

The *classical school of criminology* was the dominant voice in criminological thinking for over a hundred years. By the beginning of the nineteenth century, however, there was a revolution in intellectual thought throughout Europe. This revolution was based upon the objective empirical examination of the natural world and was driven by important discoveries in chemistry, astronomy, and physics. This scientific revolution, and the use of the scientific method to acquire knowledge, had a profound impact on the world, the role and purpose of human beings in this world, and how the world was both viewed and could be understood. The scientific revolution also touched the biological sciences. Among the most important biological works of the time was Charles Darwin's *On the Origin of Species*, [1859] (1996). In that important book, Darwin advanced the thesis that, rather than representing a radical break with the animal world, human beings were simply more highly evolved forms of animal life. The works of Darwin and other scientific biologists were to influence an Italian physician, Cesare Lombroso, whose own work was instrumental in establishing a new criminological point of view—the *positive school of criminology*. If the classical school was influenced by the Enlightenment and its belief in a free will-based moral philosophy, the positive school of criminology was influenced by the newly developing natural sciences and the scientific method.

Cesare Lombroso and the Positive School

Lombroso (1835–1909) was an Italian professor of medicine at the University of Turin who conducted research in the Italian penal system. As part of his research, he collected detailed anatomical and physiological measurements (for example, the length of the arms, the size of the ears, the distance between the eyes, the amount of body hair) of Italian prisoners and noncriminal Italian citizens. His comparative work indicated to him that there were substantial differences between the physical characteristics of the prisoners and the noncriminal civilians.

To summarize his numerous findings, Lombroso noted that the prisoners bore certain physical characteristics or *stigmata* that indicated that they had not quite sufficiently evolved: they had long arms and fingers, they had abnormal amounts of body hair, they had developed sharp teeth and had extended lower jaws. In a nutshell, Lombroso thought that criminals were more apelike or Neanderthal than noncriminals. He referred to them as *atavists* or biological throwbacks to an earlier period of human evolution. Under Lombroso's classification scheme, five or more of these physical characteristics or stigmata identified the person as a "born criminal." The born criminal supposedly has the biological and mental capabilities of primitive humans, and as such, is unfit for modern society. Atavists or born criminals commit criminal acts simply because it is instinctive for them to do so. They can no more exercise free will than the tiger who pursues and kills the antelope. In fact, the idea of the atavistic criminal being a biological throwback to a more primitive period of evolution sprang directly from the work of Darwin ([1871] 1981, 137), who wrote, "[W]ith mankind some of the worst dispositions which occasionally without any assignable cause make their appearance in families, may perhaps be reversions to a savage state, from which we are not removed by many generations."

Let us stop for a moment and look at Lombroso's approach to the study of crime, because it captures most of the important themes that are to characterize the positive school of criminology. First, Lombroso was interested in the detailed measurement of things; in his case it was the physical characteristics of people. He wanted to precisely capture the characteristics of criminals, and he did this by painstaking measurements of bodily features, calibrating them down to very fine units. He was interested in *quantification*—the precise and accurate measurement of objects in the world (see Taylor, Walton, and Young 1973). Second, his measurements of the physical characteristics of criminals and noncriminals led him to the conclusion that criminal motivation was not, like rationality, a characteristic that all people equally possessed. In fact, Lombroso's notion of the atavist was based on the important premise that criminals are qualitatively as well as quantitatively different from noncriminals. Lombroso, therefore, believed in the notion of the *differentiation* between offenders and nonoffenders.

Finally, because criminals are the product, at least in his view, of biological forces, they lack free will and are not morally responsible agents. They are instead, the product of pathology and are in need of isolation or treatment rather than punishment.

Lombroso's findings with respect to the atavistic criminal were first published in his 1876 book, *The Criminal Man (L'uomo Delinquente)*. In this first edition of his book, the born criminal made up the bulk of the criminal population, and Lombroso's theory of crime was heavily biological. With subsequent editions, however, Lombroso acknowledged the existence of other types of criminals, some of whom were not influenced by their biological characteristics, but by environmental factors. In fact, by the time of his death in 1909, Lombroso's (1912) thought had moved to the point where the born criminal comprised a minority (approximately one-third) of the criminal population. In addition to the atavist, Lombroso identified two other criminal types: (1) the insane criminal who was characterized by mental defects and sub-intelligence and (2) criminaloids who comprised the largest category of criminals and possessed no obvious biological or mental abnormalities but were easily provoked to crime by environmental and situational factors.

The early scientific work of Lombroso, and the publication of the first edition of *The Criminal Man*, marked the beginning of the positive school of criminology. This approach differs in both content and method from the earlier classical school, which premised that human beings are rational and hedonistic and possess free will. That is, persons freely choose to commit crime because they have determined that it will net them some profit or benefit. The key to understanding and minimizing crime, therefore, is to ensure that the laws are clearly written and provide swift, certain, and severe punishment. The positive school generally rejects (more accurately, it greatly weakens) the notion of complete free will that is at the core of the classical school. According to the positive school, human beings behave in accordance with scientific laws. Depending upon one's disciplinary training, these laws might be biological, psychological, economic, or sociological, but human conduct is in large part governed by determinate laws.

This does not mean that human conduct is completely determined, however. While there are some biologically-based theories of crime that are very deterministic, and provide little room for the exercise of free will, most (especially more recent) biological theories could be described as "softly-deterministic." Such theories would argue that persons' biological traits place limits or boundaries on the exercise of free will. For example, persons with organic brain damage and of very limited intelligence would have some lines of action that were beyond their limits (astronaut, physician, etc.), but could utilize their limited rationality and make conscious (i.e., with free will) decisions within certain restrictions.

Because human conduct is strongly determined by the laws that govern behavior, the task for those in the positive school of criminology is to use the objective stance of the scientific method to discover what these laws are and apply them to behavior. Naturally enough, the positive criminologist believes that if she only applies the scientific method to criminal behavior (observation, experimentation, quantification, and statistical analysis), she will uncover the causes of crime. Once these causes are understood, policy makers can use this knowledge to design scientific programs of crime treatment and prevention. For example, if it is discovered that poor prenatal diets lead to a deficit in a given brain neurotransmitter, and that a deficit in this neurotransmitter is strongly correlated with violent childhood behavior, then programs that provide adequate diets for pregnant women could be implemented. Notice that the positive criminologist, unlike his classical counterpart, would not suggest that crime could or should be reduced by swift law enforcement and punitive sanctions. After all, children who behave violently toward their parents and other children because they lack sufficient levels of a particular neurotransmitter in their brain cannot really help themselves, nor are their actions under their conscious control, sensi-

tive to rational calculations of cost and benefit. There may be other reasons to punish, retributive ones for example, but the positive criminologist would argue that there is no scientific basis for swift, certain, and severe punishment of criminals. They would argue instead for the scientific study of crime, the determination of the causes of crime, and ultimately the use of that knowledge for crime prevention and treatment.

Early Biological Theories of Criminology

The positive school of criminology, then, marked a radical break with the classical school of thought, and Cesare Lombroso is often considered the "father of positive criminology." It was Lombroso who laid the foundation for the scientific study of the causes of crime, including the use of control groups of noncriminals and the strategy of statistical comparison. He was not by far, however, the last criminologist to be influenced by biological thinking. Lombroso's work sparked a great deal of interest not only in his notion of the born criminal, but in his general thesis that criminals differed in important biological ways from noncriminals.

One who took up Lombroso's research interest was Charles Goring (1913), a medical officer in the prison system of Britain. In his work, Goring and his colleagues collected detailed anatomical and physiological information from approximately 3,000 English convicts and a large group of noncriminal English males (university students, hospital patients, and soldiers). After amassing volumes of measurements on the two groups and conducting numerous statistical comparisons between them, Goring concluded that he could identify none of the physical differences (i.e., the stigmata) alluded to by Lombroso. His data lead him to the conclusion that Lombroso was wrong and that there was no such thing as a born criminal or even a distinctive criminal type. What Goring did find, however, was that the criminals were consistently smaller in height and lighter in weight than the noncriminals, and they seemed to be of diminished intelligence (though Goring did no formal IQ testing).

Perhaps indicative of a strong inclination to see criminals as not like the rest of "us," however, Goring made much of these differences. He concluded that although not a distinct type, criminals were physically inferior to noncriminals and were likely of defective intelligence. He believed the criminal's inferiority was inherited and came with an innate moral inferiority as well.

Goring's own theory and methods came under attack by the American anthropologist Earnest A. Hooten (1939). In his own description of criminals found in his book, *Crime and the Man*, based on detailed physical data collected from some 17,000 criminal and noncriminal subjects, Hooten reported that they were "organically inferior." In what we can now regard as "colorful" language, he referred to criminals as "low grade human organisms." The basis of this conclusion was Hooten's findings, more like Lombroso's than Goring's, that his criminal group differed from the "normal" group in a substantial number of bodily measurements. These physical differences implied to Hooten that the class of criminals was physically, mentally, and morally inferior, and that this inferiority was genetically transmitted rather than due to environmental influences.

Well, of course, Hooten's findings and conclusions were subject to reanalysis and criticism, as were those of Goring and Lombroso before him. There was a lot of common ground in the criticisms directed against all three scholars: they made much of observed small differences between the criminals and noncriminals, their statistical comparisons were technically faulty, they did not adequately take into account social class or other environmental factors that could account for any observed differences, and they made too little of the great disparity in the physical measurements within the criminal and noncriminal groups compared with that which existed across the groups (Akers 1994; Vold and Bernard 1986; Wilson and Herrnstein 1985). Although the theorizing and research of the early biological positivists did not long survive (with the exception of their claim that criminals have diminished intelligence), their guiding belief in innate and enduring biological differences between criminals and noncriminals did.

For example, in the 1940s the American psychologist William Sheldon (1949) and his colleagues developed a theory of crime that related it to differences in body types and a corresponding personality type. Taking his cue from the fact that the human embryo contains three different kinds of tissues: (1) the endoderm or fatty tissue, (2) the mesoderm or muscular tissue, and the (3) ectoderm or nervous tissue, Sheldon developed a scheme or typology of three body types or physiques: the *endomorphic* type, the *mesomorphic* type, and the *ectomorphic* type. There are combinations of all three types in each person, but one type usually dominates. The endomorphic body type has an abundance of fat, and the body is soft and round. The mesomorphic body type has an abundance of muscle; the body is rectangular and somewhat lean. The ectomorphic body type is fragile and bony with sharp features.

The respective personality types associated with each distinct body type were the viscerotonic temperament, an extroverted personality with a fondness for luxury and an aversion to physical activities; the somotonic temperament, an excited, aggressive, and assertive personality; and the cerebrotonic temperament, an introverted, shy, and withdrawn personality. Sheldon "scored" each body type on a 1–7 scale (see the reliance on quantification), so that persons with a body type of 1–7–1, for example, would be pure mesomorphs because their body type is predominantly composed of mesomorphic tissue. In his research, Sheldon collected photographs of the bodies of both known incarcerated offenders and nonoffenders and rated them on the level of each of the three body types. He found that criminal offenders were substantially more mesomorhpic (muscular) and less ectomorphic than the nonoffenders. The muscular body and its associated aggressive and assertive temperament were clear markers of a distinctive criminal type according to Sheldon.

The idea of body type differences that distinguish criminals from noncriminals was also a minor part of the work of Sheldon Glueck and Eleanor Glueck (1956) in their study of 500 delinquents and nondelinquents. As in William Sheldon's work, photographs of the two groups of boys were mixed together and each was rated or scored by an investigator on the presence of fatty, muscular, and skeletal tissue. The Gluecks, too, found that there was a pronounced proportion of the delinquents (60 percent) who possessed a mesomorphic body build when compared with the nondelinquents (31 percent). The Glueck study also included a substantial amount of information on the boys' personalities. They reported that the mesomorphs possessed personality traits that were consistent with aggression, a volatile temper, impulsivity, and self-centeredness. Although the Gluecks adopted a more multifactored approach to delinquency in their work (i.e., they believed that delinquency was due not to one or a few but many causal factors), they nonetheless believed that there was a link between the biology of body type and criminal and delinquent offending.

Sheldon's and the Gluecks' work on body type, personality, and criminal offending receded into the background of the discipline, however, as the sociological positivism of scholars like Sutherland, Cloward and Ohlin, and Cohen took center stage. By the 1960s, the dominant scholars of crime were more likely to be sociologists, and the focus on the causes of crime was fixed on environmental factors (neighborhoods, families, peer groups) rather than biological ones. At the same time, interest in the connection between biological factors and crime never really disappeared, and this perspective remained prominent in European criminology. Beginning in the 1980s, American scholars rekindled the interest in this relationship, interest that was reflected in numerous empirical studies of the biology crime link and in theories with a biological focus. As a vivid indication of the rebirth of older biological conceptions of crime, two prominent scholars, the political scientist James Q. Wilson and the psychologist Richard J. Herrnstein (1985), put forth a biologically-based theory of criminal offending in their

book, *Crime and Human Nature.* They resurrected the notion that constitutional factors like body build (body type is a largely inherited characteristic) are related to criminal behavior. This was followed by other important works on biology and crime, like those of Eysenck and Gudjonsson (1989) and Raine (1993).

A Brief Survey of Biological Approaches to Crime

There is no easy or noncontroversial way to organize or categorize the various biological approaches to the study of crime that have appeared in the past 15 to 20 years. What we will do is provide a brief overview of the research focus that some of these biological approaches have taken, because some of them cannot really be said to be biological "theories" of crime. In fact, our efforts are primarily directed at discussing some of the recent biological "independent variables" that purport to explain crime, whether or not they are organized into a coherent theory.

IQ and Crime

It cannot be said that interest in the relationship between intelligence and crime is new. In fact, ever since people began formally to think about the causes of crime, one of the most consistently identified causes has been a diminished intellectual capacity. The belief in a connection between things like low intelligence, feeblemindedness, and crime is, therefore, quite established (Goddard 1913). Literally hundreds of empirical studies have been directed at the relationship between intellectual deficits and crime. These studies consistently have shown that, compared with noncriminals, offenders have substantially lower-scored IQ values (Hirschi and Hindelang 1977; Rutter and Giller 1983; Wilson and Herrnstein 1985; Raine 1993). More specifically, it has been estimated that the IQs of criminals are generally 8–10 points lower than those of noncriminals. Although they do evidence general intellectual dysfunction, criminal offenders also have shown a specific deficit (of about 10–12 points) in verbal intelligence compared with performance or spatial IQ.

Even though a consensus in the field suggests that IQ and delinquency are related, there is little agreement as to why. Some have speculated that criminals have lower IQs than nonoffenders simply because, unlike their more intelligent counterparts, dim-witted offenders are more likely to get caught by the police, found guilty in court, and then sent to institutions where they become part of IQ-crime studies. This is an interesting speculation, and certainly intuitively plausible, but not likely to account for all or even a large part of the observed IQ-delinquency relationship. Research has shown that self-reported delinquency is related to delinquency at about the same magnitude as official delinquency (Hirschi and Hindelang 1977; Farrington 1989). Even delinquents who have successfully evaded detection, therefore, have lower IQ scores than nondelinquents.

Other scholars (Raine 1993) have offered a biological explanation that the IQ deficit in offenders, particularly a deficit in verbal intelligence, is due to some sort of brain dysfunction. It is argued that damage to the left hemisphere of the brain, caused by birth trauma or early head injury from child abuse or an accident, could lead to lower verbal IQ scores. Another suggested biological link between low IQ and delinquency is a genetic one, but even here there is disagreement as to the specifics. Gordon (1976), for example, has suggested that IQ measures abstract reasoning ability, which is genetically transmitted. However, the direct link to delinquency is social because he suggests that low-IQ parents have poor childrearing techniques, which eventually causes the delinquency of their children. Not surprisingly, more sociologically-minded scholars have suggested that the connection is due to educational and social factors. Hirschi and Hindelang (1977), for example, suggest that low IQ leads to a cascading constellation of effects, such as school failure, disenchantment with education, poor self-esteem, and ultimately delinquency and crime. Still other work suggests that low intelligence is related to delinquency because a deficit in intelligence is related to low "moral reasoning" (Kohlberg 1976). In this more psychological view, those with less intelligence are less competent in distinguishing right from wrong.

These are only a few of the numerous offerings that purport to account for the consistent IQ crime relationship. The simple but brute fact, however, is that there is very little solid research that can support these explanations. For the moment, our safest conclusion is that there is a relationship between diminished intelligence and delinquency, although the causal process through which this occurs is as yet not well known.

Genetic Links with Crime

A belief that delinquency and crime are inherited traits can be traced to the very beginnings of the positive school of criminology with the work of Lombroso. In the early 1900s the American criminologist Henry Goddard thought that the primary trait leading to criminality, feeblemindedness, was an inherited one. He traced the descendants of a illegitimate union between a normal man and a feeble-minded barmaid. A large proportion of these decendants had some mental or emotional defect. The descendants of the same man and his Quaker wife, Goddard reported, were completely normal, well adjusted, and successful. This convinced Goddard that crime and other dysfunctional behaviors had a genetic cause.

One thing to keep in mind when reading this section on genetics and crime is that virtually no scholar has argued that there is a specific "crime gene" that is inherited which directly leads to criminal behavior. Rather, even when the most biologically-oriented scholars of crime talk about a genetic link, they are referring to a predisposition or tendency to behave in a particular way that is inherited. What is inherited, then, is not a specific behavior or even set of behaviors but a proclivity to respond to environmental stimuli in a given consistent manner. Further complicating things is that it is unlikely that a single gene is implicated in criminal and delinquent behavior. The evidence is more compatible with the position that several genes are involved in combination to create a predisposition to criminal behavior (Raine 1993). Finally, even the most ardent biological criminologist would argue that even if genetics does play a substantial role in criminal behavior, a person's environment is also an important contributing factor. That is, the issue of a genetic contribution to crime is not an "all or nothing" issue; it is just that—a genetic *contribution* to crime.

In addition to intelligence, another inherited characteristic that in the past has been suggested to be connected to crime, particularly violent crime, is an extra *y* chromosome for males. The normal complement of sex chromosomes for men is one *x* and one *y*, while women receive two *x* chromosomes (the labels of *x* and *y* come from the shape of the chromosome). These sex chromosomes determine the sexual characteristics of the person. Sometimes there is a genetic disorder or mutation and a male is given an extra male or *y* chromosome. These *xyy* males have been thought to possibly possess "super male" characteristics—such as a predisposition to violence and aggression. Early research by Jacobs and her colleagues (1965), who conducted their work in a Scottish mental hospital for criminal defendants, showed a greater than expected number of *xyy* males among the violent inmates confined in the institution. In addition to having an extra male sex chromosome, these men were tall and bulky, and Jacobs (1965, 1351) described them as possessing "dangerous, violent, or criminal propensities."

Subsequent research, however, has failed to substantiate the link between an *xyy* chromosome complement and violent behavior. A definitive study by Witken and his colleagues (1977) found that those with the *xyy* syndrome are not more likely to be aggressive, but instead are more prone to property and nonviolent crimes. Though the findings by Witken do throw some cold water on the hypothesized link between the *xyy* chromosome complement and violent crime, they do not on their face disprove a possible role for inherited factors in crime. This is because (1) the findings did (as did others) show a strong relationship between the *xyy* factor and property crime, (2) the *xyy* syndrome is not really an inherited trait, but an abnormality that is due to a genetic mutation at conception, and (3) there are other possible inherited traits that may be related to crime (Raine 1993).

Some discussions of heredity and crime do not, however, focus on what is inherited, but on how one goes about demonstrating a genetic link to crime. Because identical twins have identical DNA and come from one fertilized egg (monozygotic), whereas fraternal twins have no more of a shared genetic background than regular siblings and they come from two separate eggs (dizygotic), it was thought that a genetic basis to crime might be demonstrated by conducting "twin studies." That is, twin studies could show the magnitude of the *concordance* between the traits of each pair of twins. Concordance occurs when both twins have the same characteristics. If, for example, one twin is delinquent and the other twin is also delinquent, then there is concordance with respect to delinquency. If, however, one twin is delinquent but the other identical twin is not, concordance has not been established. If there is an inherited criminal tendency or propensity, then we should see more concordance in delinquency and criminality among identical than among fraternal twins.

For example, suppose there are 25 pairs of identical twins. Further, suppose that there are eight cases where both twins are delinquent and five cases where one twin is delinquent but the other is not (and, of course, 12 twin pairs where neither is delinquent). Because there are eight out of 13 cases where if one twin was delinquent the other one was also, the concordance rate is approximately 62 percent. Now suppose there are 20 pairs of fraternal twins. In this group there are four cases where both twins are delinquent and 11 cases where one twin is delinquent but the other one is not. Because there are four out of 15 cases where the delinquency of the twins is the same, the concordance rate is 27 percent. Because the concordance rate is substantially higher among identical twins, who have identical genetic material, the position that there is a genetic component to crime cannot be rejected.

To date, there has been a great deal of twin research on crime. Although the results of these studies are controversial (see

Gottfredson and Hirschi 1990, 53–61; Raine 1993, 64–66), the most reasonable conclusion seems to be that the twin studies are consistent with some genetic link to crime. Raine (1993, 55–59) reports that, consistent with a genetic link, monozygotic twins are about twice as likely to show concordance with respect to delinquency as dizygotic twins. Critics of this research would point to two things. Although the results from twin studies are consistent with a genetic connection to crime, any possible genetic factor most likely has a very weak influence on crime. Second, twin studies are biased in favor of showing greater concordance with identical twins because identical twins share a more common environment than fraternal twins (parents frequently dress them alike, treat them alike, etc.).

The issue of the strength of any genetic link to crime is difficult to assess, and our conclusion is that the field is sharply divided about this in the face of limited evidence for either point of view. With respect to the issue of the confounding produced by shared environment, however, biological criminologists have attempted to addresses this issue by examining the concordance rates between identical twins reared together (shared heredity and shared environment) with identical twins reared separately (shared heredity with different environment). Because all they share is common heredity, a genetic link with crime would be supported if the concordance rates for the identical twins reared apart were approximately the same or greater than for those reared together. Understandably, there are few studies that meet these demanding criteria, but those that do generally find that, consistent with a genetic link, identical twins reared apart are at least as concordant with respect to crime as those reared together.

In addition to twin studies, studies of adopted children are relevant to the study of a genetic relationship to crime. In this design, the offspring of criminal parents who have been adopted are compared with the adopted offspring of noncriminal parents. If there is a genetic component to crime, the adopted children of criminal parents should show higher levels of delinquency and crime

than the adopted children of noncriminal parents. Although there has not been a great deal of research with this design, those studies that have been conducted are generally supportive of a relationship between the criminality of the parent and the subsequent criminality of the child (Raine 1993). Suggesting that the important relationship might involve both heredity and environment, a few studies have shown that the children of criminal parents are particularly likely to become involved in crime when they are in a poor or high-risk environment (for example, they live in a lower-class, high-crime area) (see Fishbein 1990). Interestingly, most of this evidence finds support for a genetic connection to property but not to violent crime.

Biochemistry and Crime

Another possible connection between biology and crime concerns the role of biochemical substances. For example, chemicals called *neurotransmitters* are secreted by the brain and have been consistently associated with other types of aberrant behaviors besides crime. Increased levels of the neurotransmitter dopamine, for instance, have been shown to be related to schizophrenia, while reduced levels of the neurotransmitter serotonin have been implicated in depression (Raine 1993). Neurotransmitters are instrumental in basic brain function, such as the retrieval and storage of information, communication, and emotional balance. As such, any neurotransmitter deficit or excess can have profound implications for one's behavior.

Research conducted to determine if violent or antisocial patients have neurotransmitter imbalances has produced interesting findings. In a detailed summary of this literature, Raine (1993) reported that antisocial and violent subjects tended to have lower levels of the neurotransmitter serotonin than nonaggressive subjects. If neurotransmitters are related to criminal or violent behavior, then behavior should change with planned attempts to lower or increase the amount of a given neurotransmitter. Attempts to alter behavior by deliberately manipulating the amount of a particular neurotransmitter has met with some, but limited, success. For example, Raine (1993; see also Fishbein 1990) showed that increasing the level of serotonin decreases aggressive behavior, while increasing the amounts of norepinephrine and dopamine tends to increase aggressive behavior. He cautioned, however, that the empirical base is thin because of few studies and a limited number of subjects studied so far. Nevertheless, the evidentiary base for the possible role of serotonin in aggressive and violent behavior is more substantial than that for norepinephrine and dopamine (Berman, Kavoussi, and Coccaro 1997).

Another biochemical substance that has been linked to crime, particularly violent crime, is the male hormone testosterone. It was believed that high levels of this steroid would lead to violence and other problematic or antisocial behaviors. Animal studies have linked high levels of testosterone to aggressive behavior, and moderate relationships have also been found in studies with human populations, although other studies have failed to find the expected effect (Raine 1993; Brain and Susman 1997).

Booth and Osgood (1993) have advanced a theory indirectly linking testosterone and adult criminality. They have hypothesized two mechanisms to show this conclusion: (1) high testosterone levels indicate high levels of a propensity to commit antisocial acts, which is manifested early in life and affects behavior throughout life, and (2) high testosterone levels make it difficult for persons to make and maintain conventional social relationships (i.e., their social bonds to a conventional life are weak). With a sample of Vietnam veterans, Booth and Osgood received some empirical confirmation of their theory. Critics (Akers 1994), however, caution that such support for the theory in this study was very modest.

Other Biological Correlates of Crime

In this review, we have scratched only the surface of a possible biological connection to delinquent and criminal behavior. The following essay by Professors Yaralian and Raine presents some of the other biological factors that appear to correlate with crime. In terms of whether or not the empirical research to date can prove a biological cause of criminal behavior, we urge modesty and caution in making any conclusion. Certainly, the empirical evidence suggests some connection between the biological characteristics of individuals and antisocial behavior. Those who are interested in the study of crime, therefore, ignore the study of biological factors at their peril. Exactly how strong a role such factors play and the processes connecting biological variables and crime are issues that have yet to be resolved. The answers may not be far off because biologists, biochemists, and neuropsychologists are making important new discoveries about human behavior every year. At the moment, however, we may conclude only that some biological factors have been related to criminal and other antisocial behaviors, and that these biological factors are not the sole cause of crime. Rather, biological causes work in concert with other, social factors. We think this is a conclusion with which most biologically and sociologically-oriented crime scholars would agree.

References

Akers, Ronald L. (1994). *Criminological Theories: Introduction and Evaluation*. Los Angeles: Roxbury.

Beccaria, Cesare. [1764] (1963). *On Crimes and Punishments*. Translated with an introduction by H. Paolucci. New York: Macmillan.

Bentham, Jeremy. [1789] (1962). "An introduction to the principles of morals and legislation." Reprinted in *The Works of Jeremy Bentham*. J. Browning (ed.). New York: Russell and Russell.

Berman, Mitchell, Richard J. Kavoussi, and Emil F. Coccaro. (1997). "Neurotransmitter correlates of human aggression." Pp. 305–313. In *Handbook of Antisocial Behavior*. D.M. Stoff, J. Breiling, and J.D. Maser (eds.). New York: Wiley.

Booth, Alan and D. Wayne Osgood. (1993). "The influence of testosterone on deviance in adulthood: Assessing and explaining the relationship." *Criminology*, 31:93–117.

Brain, Paul F. and Elizabeth Susman. (1997). "Hormonal aspects of aggression and violence." Pp. 314–323. In *Handbook of Antiso-*

cial Behavior. D.M. Stoff, J. Breiling, and J.D. Maser (eds.). New York: Wiley.

Darwin, Charles R. [1859] (1996). *On the Origin of Species.* G. Beer (ed.). New York: Oxford University Press. Reprint.

Darwin, Charles R. [1871] (1981). *The Descent of Man.* Introduction by J. Bonner and R.M. May. Princeton, NJ: Princeton University Press.

Eysenck, Hans J. and G.H. Gudjonsson. (1989). *The Causes and Cures of Criminality.* New York: Plenum.

Farrington, David P. (1989). "Early predictors of adolescent aggression and adult violence." *Violence and Victims,* 4:79–100.

Fishbein, Diana H. (1990). "Biological perspectives in criminology." *Criminology,* 28:27–72.

Glueck, Sheldon and Eleanor Glueck. (1956). *Physique and Delinquency.* New York: Harper and Row.

Goddard, Henry H. [1913] (1972). *Feeblemindedness: Its Causes and Consequences.* New York: Macmillan. Reprint. Freeport, NY: Books for Library Press.

Gordon, Robert. (1976). "Prevalence: The rare datum in delinquency measurement and its implications for the theory of delinquency." Pp. 201–284. In *The Juvenile Justice System.* M.W. Klein (ed.). Beverly Hills, CA: Sage.

Goring, Charles. [1913] (1972). *The English Convict: A Statistical Study.* London: His Majesty's Stationary Office. Patterson Smith Reprint. Montclair, NJ: Patterson Smith.

Gottfredson, Michael R. and Travis Hirschi. (1990). *A General Theory of Crime.* Stanford, CA: Stanford University Press.

Hooten, Earnest A. (1939). *Crime and the Man.* Cambridge, MA: Harvard University Press.

Hirschi, Travis and Michael J. Hindelang. (1977)."Intelligence and delinquency: A revisionist review." *American Sociological Review,* 42:571–587.

Jacobs, P.A., M. Brunton, M.M. Melville, R.P. Brittian, and W.F. McClemnot. (1965). "Ag-

gressive behavior, mental sub-normality, and the XYY male." *Nature,* 208:1351–1352.

Kohlberg, Lawrence. (1976). "Moral stages and moralization." Pp. 31–53. In *Moral Development and Behavior: Theory, Research and Social Issues.* T. Lickona (ed.). New York: Holt, Rinehart and Winston.

Lombroso, Cesare. (1876). *The Criminal Man (L'uomo Delinquente).* First Edition. Milan: Hoepli. Second Edition (1878) through Fifth Edition (1896). Turin: Bocca.

———. (1912). *Crime: Its Causes and Remedies.* Patterson Smith Reprint, 1968. Montclair, NJ: Patterson Smith.

Raine, Adrian. (1993). *The Psychopathology of Crime: Criminal Behavior as a Clinical Disorder.* San Diego, CA: Academic.

Rutter, Michael and H. Giller. (1983). *Juvenile Delinquency: Trends and Perspectives.* Harmondsworth, England: Penguin.

Sheldon, William H., E.M. Hartl, and E. McDermott. (1949). *Varieties of Delinquent Youth.* New York: Harper.

Taylor, Ian, Paul Walton, and Jock Young. (1973). *The New Criminology.* New York: Harper and Row.

Vold, George B. and Thomas J. Bernard. (1986). *Theoretical Criminology,* Third Edition. New York: Oxford University Press.

Wilson, James Q. and Richard J. Herrnstein. (1985). *Crime and Human Nature.* New York: Simon and Schuster.

Witken, H.A., S.A. Mednick, F. Schulsinger, E. Bakkestrom, K.O. Christiansen, D.R. Goodenough, K. Hirschhorn, C. Lundsteen, D.R. Owen, J. Phillip, D.B. Rubin, and M. Stocking. (1977). "Criminality, aggression and intelligence among *xyy* and *xxy* men." Pp. 165–188 in *Biosocial Bases of Criminal Behavior,* S.A. Mednick and K.O. Christiansen (eds.). New York: Gardner.

Biological Approaches to Crime

Psychophysiology and Brain Dysfunction

Pauline S. Yaralian
University of Southern California

Adrian Raine
University of Southern California

In the field of crime research, psychophysiological and neuropsychological paradigms have provided extensive information about the biological underpinnings of antisocial and violent behavior. The application of these paradigms to crime research has enabled scientists to uncover various biological anomalies that may interact with certain environmental conditions to predispose some individuals to engage in antisocial and violent behaviors. Although biological research in the area of crime will continue to elucidate the processes by which individuals become violent, we believe that it is the complex interplay among a variety of factors (including biological, environmental, and social influences) which ultimately brings about criminal behavior.

This chapter highlights some of the major biological approaches to crime. Following a brief introduction to psychophysiology, the literature relates psychophysiological abnormalities to antisocial behavior as well as theoretical interpretations of these deficits. Both cognitive and brain imaging studies are also discussed. Birth complications, a substantial source of brain damage, comprise a final set of biological factors to be reviewed. The chapter concludes with a discussion of how biological approaches to crime may advance crime prevention and reduction ef-forts. While the biological paradigms described here are commonly applied to crime research, please bear in mind that not all areas of biological functioning are covered in this chapter (see Raine 1993 for review).

Introduction to Psychophysiology

Psychophysiology is the science that deals with the interplay between psychological and physiologic processes. Skin conductance (SC) activity, heart rate activity (HR), electroencephalogram (EEG) activity, and event-related potentials (ERP) are among the most frequently recorded psychophysiological measures. Findings for SC and HR activity in relation to antisocial behavior are discussed below.

Skin Conductance Activity and Crime

Skin conductance activity is generally recorded by electrodes placed on the fingers or palm of the hand. Variations of the electrical activity of the skin lead to fluctuations in SC activity. For example, increased activity occurs following increased sweating. Using a polygraph, these changes can be recorded for subsequent measurement. Electrodermal arousal is inferred by measuring resting SC levels (SCLs) and frequency of occurrence of nonspecific fluctuations (NSFs; spontaneous SC responses, which are not elicited by external stimuli). Thus, individuals with high resting SC levels or a relatively large number of NSFs, or both, are said to be highly aroused, while those with lower resting SCLs and less frequent NSFs have relatively lower arousal levels. Responses that occur following the presentation of a neutral external stimulus (i.e., responses that do not occur during resting states) are termed *orienting responses* and are discussed below.

Skin Conductance Underarousal

The collective results of numerous studies assessing SC arousal in various antisocial populations (e.g., psychopathic criminals, nonpsychopathic criminals, and conduct disordered samples) indicate reduced SC activity during resting situations. Raine (1993)

57

has provided a review of studies of arousal conducted since 1978 and reported that four of ten studies found significant effects for resting arousal levels. Of these four studies, only one found significant effects for lower SCLs, while three found significantly fewer NSFs among the antisocials. In a more recent study, Kruesi et al. (1992) have shown that in a sample of behavior disordered children, low SCLs measured at age 11 predict institutionalization at age 13. Thus, although findings for the link between underarousal and antisocial behavior appear to be mixed, some evidence shows that general antisocial behavior is associated with fewer NSFs and lower SCLs (Raine 1997).

Skin Conductance Orienting

In response to the presentation of novel stimuli in one's environment, changes in the electrical activity of the skin occur, thus altering SC levels. For example, the presentation of a new tone generally causes an orienting response (or a "what is it?" response) that is accompanied by increased SCLs. These increased SCLs are comparable to orienting responses that occur at the behavioral level (e.g., when an individual turns and looks in the direction of a loud sound). The SC orienting response (SCOR) is a measure of information processing in that it indirectly reflects how a person attends to and processes novel environmental stimuli (Dawson and Nuechterlein 1984; Dawson, Filion, and Schell 1989).

According to Ohman's information processing perspective (1979, 1985), orienting responses occur when preattentive processes alone are insufficient for processing a novel stimulus and require augmentation by additional, controlled processing mechanisms. That is, certain types of stimuli, by virtue of being more salient or important, are processed more actively than others. Novel stimuli are initially stored in short-term memory where they form neural "templates." When subsequent stimuli are presented, they are compared to the template currently stored in short-term memory. If the two stimuli differ, preattentive or basic processing mechanisms will be unable to

recognize the newly presented stimulus and will require additional controlled processing of the new stimulus. In contrast, if the newly presented stimulus matches the template already stored in one's short-term memory, an orienting response does not occur because that stimulus is relatively less salient and, thus, "ignored." In such cases, active processing of the new stimulus is not needed. In addition to situations in which the "stored" stimulus (the "template") and the newly presented stimulus are mismatched, controlled processing is also necessitated when the novel stimulus is recognized as significant or something to be attended to, such as a sign of danger. Thus, the occurrence and size of the SCOR provides information about central nervous system functioning by indirectly assessing the allocation of attentional resources to the processing of external stimuli. Significant stimuli (e.g., signs of danger, aversive or novel stimuli) are generally expected to elicit large SCORs.

Evidence of orienting deficits in antisocial populations in the form of reduced frequency of SCORs has been found in numerous studies. Raine (1993) provides a summary of eight studies assessing SC orienting in criminals, including psychopathic criminals, a subset of criminals characterized by psychopathic traits (e.g., the lack of remorse and superficial charm). Of the eight studies reviewed, four found significantly reduced frequency of orienting responses to neutral stimuli among the antisocial groups.

Reduced orienting was found to be particularly characteristic of psychopathic, antisocial, and criminal subjects who also exhibit schizotypal or schizoid features, such as recurrent illusions and beliefs in the possession of magical powers or social isolation and emotional coldness (Blackburn 1979; Raine and Venables 1984a; Raine 1987). These results are consistent with findings of deficient SC orienting in both schizotypal personality disorder, a lifelong disorder involving oddities of thinking and behavior (Raine, Lencz, and Benishay 1995) and schizophrenia, a debilitating psychological disorder characterized by impairment in cognitive processes, social withdrawal, and personality disintegration (Ohman 1981;

Bernstein et al. 1982). Additionally, Raine, Reynolds, and Sheard (1991) have shown associations between the number of SC orienting responses and the prefrontal cortical area in normal subjects; fewer orienting responses were related to a reduced prefrontal area as measured by Magnetic Resonance Imaging (MRI). As will be discussed in the section on neuropsychology, the prefrontal area is the anterior part of the frontal lobe and is believed to be involved in planning and flexibility in behavioral strategies. Prefrontal structural and functional deficits are believed to play an important role in the genesis of antisocial behavior. Based on the finding of reduced SC orienting in a subgroup of antisocial subjects with concomitant schizoid features, Raine (1993) has hypothesized that frontal dysfunction may be a defining feature of this subgroup of antisocials.

Skin Conductance Responses to Aversive Stimuli

In order to test the view that antisocial individuals are not responsive to negative stimuli, such as punishment, several studies have assessed SC responding to aversive stimuli. As noted previously, aversive stimuli such as loud tones are expected to elicit orienting responses. If antisocial individuals are indeed not responsive to aversive stimuli, they would evidence reduced SC responding to aversive tones relative to groups of normal individuals. A comprehensive review of this material was conducted by Hare (1978) in which he concluded that psychopaths evidenced reduced SC responses to aversive but not neutral tones. Raine (1993) has summarized the findings from studies conducted since 1978 and reported that only two of eight studies found evidence of lower SC response amplitudes to aversive stimuli (auditory stimuli ranging from 90 to 120 decibels) in psychopathic and nonpsychopathic antisocial groups. Thus, more recent studies fail to replicate previous findings of reduced responsiveness to aversive stimuli in psychopathic subjects.

Classical Conditioning

Poor classical conditioning has been proposed as one of the fundamental deficits among antisocial groups (Eysenck 1964, 1977). Classical conditioning is an associative learning process whereby a neutral stimulus (the conditioned stimulus, CS) takes on the properties of an unconditioned stimulus (UCS) and comes to elicit a conditioned response (CR) following repeated pairings of the neutral stimulus (CS) with the UCS. The process of classical conditioning was discovered by the Russian physiologist Ivan Pavlov, who found that his laboratory dogs could learn to salivate to the sound of a bell. The presentation of food (UCS) normally elicits salivation in dogs (UCR, unconditioned response). When the sound of a bell (CS) was repeatedly paired with the presentation of food (UCS), the sound of the bell (CS) eventually elicited salivation (CR) in the dogs. Similarly, punishment (UCS) naturally causes feelings of distress, an unconditioned response (UCR) for most children. Each time a child is caught stealing, he is presumably punished, thereby leading to feelings of distress. According to classical conditioning theory, the repeated pairing of stealing with punishment will eventually cause the child to feel distress when thinking about stealing something. In this example, stimuli associated with stealing become the CS that will eventually elicit the same response as the UCS (punishment), distress. It is the association between stealing and feelings of distress caused by punishment that will deter most children from stealing. However, if a child shows deficient conditioning, the process by which the association between stealing and distress is made is either weak or largely absent. In such a scenario, stealing will not be inhibited because the consequences of engaging in that act are not salient to the child.

Skin conductance responding has been used as a measure of classical conditioning. In this paradigm, a neutral stimulus is presented to a subject followed by an UCS, generally a loud aversive tone. After a number of such CS-UCS pairings, the CS (the formerly neutral stimulus) is presented to the subject and the subject's subsequent SC response to the CS is measured. If conditioning has occurred, the CS takes on the properties of the UCS through repeated pairings, and the subject will demonstrate a conditioned orienting response to the CS alone. The amplitude (size) of the response is used as a measure of classical conditioning, such that lower SC amplitudes are seen as evidence of poor conditioning while larger response amplitudes indicate good conditioning.

Several studies indicate that antisocial individuals show poor classical conditioning. Raine (1993) reviewed six studies of SC classical conditioning conducted since 1978 and reported that all six indicate some form of conditioning deficit in the antisocial groups.

Despite the various conditioning paradigms employed and the different subtypes of antisocial populations assessed (ranging from conduct disordered children to psychopaths), each study obtained significant effects, indicating the strength and generality of the relationship between poor conditioning and antisocial behavior.

In addition to revealing deficient classical conditioning in antisocials, a biosocial interaction has been demonstrated (Raine et al. 1981; Raine et al. 1997d). Poorer conditioning appears to be most characteristic of antisocials from better social backgrounds. Raine (1993) argues that if an individual lacks the "social push" for antisocial behavior (by virtue of coming from a benign home background), yet still exhibits antisocial behavior, then the causes of this antisociality are more likely to be biologically based than socially based. In contrast, antisocial individuals from poorer social backgrounds may be predisposed to crime by virtue of their social environment, with biological influences assuming a less important role.

Summary of Psychophysiological Research

Research conducted on SC activity among various antisocial populations generally reveals that such individuals are electrodermally underaroused (i.e., have a reduced frequency of NSFs) and have orienting deficits. This latter finding is particularly characteristic of antisocial individuals with schizotypal and schizoid features. When assessing SC responding to aversive stimuli,

earlier studies found reduced responsiveness in antisocials. However, studies conducted in the past two decades have failed to replicate these findings. In contrast, strong evidence exists demonstrating deficient classical conditioning among various antisocial groups.

Heart Rate and Crime

Similar to SC activity, which is measured both during resting states to assess general arousal and also in response to the presentation of stimuli, two basic measures of HR activity exist. Tonic (or resting) HR levels are assessed most frequently in offender and antisocial groups because of the relative ease with which they can be recorded (e.g., using portable equipment or taking a pulse). Tonic HR, like SC, is used to assess autonomic arousal. Similar to SCORs, phasic changes in HR occur in response to neutral or aversive environmental stimuli. Phasic activity is somewhat more difficult to assess relative to tonic HR due to movement artifacts and respiration changes in response to stimuli. Consequently, fewer studies have assessed phasic HR or HR reactivity.

Phasic Heart Rate and Crime

As noted above, few studies have assessed phasic HR in relation to antisocial activity. Briefly, "deceleratory" responses, in which the heart slows down for a short period of time, occur following the presentation of neutral stimuli. This type of response is believed to reflect greater sensitivity and openness to the environment. "Acceleratory" responses commonly occur following aversive stimuli. Acceleratory responses, which involve faster HR, are perhaps reflective of the organism's attempt to shut out the harmful environment cues (cf. Raine 1993). Therefore, larger acceleratory responses may characterize individuals who are effectively able to reject aversive stimuli and, thus, have well-functioning coping mechanisms. Conversely, larger deceleratory responses indicate greater attentional processing and orienting rather than shutting out environmental events.

Raine (1993) describes studies that have demonstrated larger anticipatory HR acceleratory responses in psychopathic groups followed by reduced SC orienting responses to the aversive tone that ensues. According to Hare (1978), these findings demonstrate proficient coping and an enhanced ability to "tune out" aversive events among the psychopathic groups.

Phasic HR measures have also demonstrated predictive utility. Raine, Venables, and Williams (1990b) have shown that reduced HR orienting measured at age 15 predicted a criminal outcome at age 24 in a sample of noninstitutionalized schoolboys. Criminal outcomes at age 24 were also marked by reduced SC responding at age 15 in this same sample (Raine, Venables, and Williams 1990a).

Resting Heart Rate and Crime

Research studies have shown that while investigations using institutionalized offenders have failed to demonstrate significant effects for resting HR, robust associations between lower resting HR and increased antisocial behavior have been demonstrated among noninstitutionalized, younger antisocial samples.

The strength of this finding is indicated by the nonstandardized nature of the various studies that have demonstrated this effect (Wadsworth 1976; West and Farrington 1977; Raine and Venables 1984b; Maliphant, Hume, and Furnham 1990). Despite the use of populations ranging from 7 to 18 years of age, the various methods of measuring HR and assessing antisocial behavior, and samples from different cultures and both genders, the majority of these studies have found lower resting HR in the antisocial groups. Among all psychophysiological studies of antisocial behavior, the best replicated finding appears to be that of lower resting HR in noninstitutionalized antisocial populations (Raine 1993).

Explaining Lower Resting Heart Rate Levels in Antisocials: Fearlessness and Stimulation Seeking

Two theories have been developed to explain how lower resting HR levels influence antisocial behaviors. HR is an index of anxiety and fearfulness. Children with low HR levels have been shown to exhibit a lack of anxiety and are temperamentally fearless (Scarpa, Raine, Venables, and Mednick 1997). Reduced fear is thought to predispose to violence because fearless individuals are less concerned about negative consequences of fighting (e.g., injury or punishment). Consistent with this theory is the finding of low HR levels in decorated bomb disposal experts (Cox et al. 1983), indicating that reduced HR indexes a lack of fear. Fearlessness in children would also reduce the effectiveness of punishment and impede conditioning because without fear, the learned association between antisocial behavior and punishment would be inconsequential (Mednick 1977).

An alternative theory developed to interpret lower resting HR in antisocials is based on optimal arousal levels and stimulation seeking. According to this theory, there is an optimal level of arousal which people seek to attain and maintain. The amount of stimulation required to maintain this optimal arousal level varies among different individuals. The differential need for stimulation is thought to arise from functional differences in the brain's reticular activating system (RAS), cells in the brainstem that control attentiveness and wakefulness. One of the primary functions of the RAS is alerting the cerebral cortex to incoming information. Sensory input from all over the body travels through the brainstem before entering the cortex, where higher level processing takes place. The RAS is responsible for activating the cortex and keeping it alert to enable the processing of incoming sensory stimuli (Carlson 1994).

In addition to activating the cortex, the RAS is also responsible for de-activating the cortex when the incoming sensory information is no longer relevant. Thus, a feedback loop travels from the cortex back to the RAS, enabling the RAS to know when to filter out irrelevant or repetitive information. The filtering process of the RAS is called *habituation*, which prevents the cortex from becoming overloaded.

Antisocials are physiologically underaroused, as evidenced by lower resting HR levels (Wadsworth 1976; West and Farrington 1977; Raine and Venables 1984b; Maliphant, Hume, and Furnham 1990) and fewer nonspecific SC fluctuations (see Raine 1993). It has been hypothesized that such individuals actively seek out thrilling and exciting activities to compensate for physiological underarousal. Thus, a child who is physiologically underaroused may begin cheating in class, fighting, or eventually shoplifting simply for the thrill of avoiding getting caught. On the other hand, individuals with optimal arousal levels tend not to seek out exciting or dangerous lifestyles.

Although the exact neurophysiological mechanism underlying underarousal is not yet known, it is hypothesized that underarousal results from two possible circumstances. In the first scenario, the cortex is unable to completely process the full extent of incoming sensory information due to insufficient activation by the RAS. In a sense, the individual is left somewhat deprived of sufficient sensory stimulation. Alternatively, the RAS may provide sufficient cortical activation initially, yet may begin to filter out too much information (i.e., habituate rapidly), thus cutting off activation to the cortex. In each of these cases, the individual is not sufficiently aroused and therefore seeks to attain an optimal arousal level by engaging in antisocial and thrill-seeking behaviors.

Are Psychophysiological Underarousal and Reduced Orienting Specific to Violent Offenders?

Currently, there is a paucity of research on autonomic activity in violent offenders versus nonviolent antisocial populations. Although three studies have found that HR is particularly low in violent offenders relative to nonviolent offenders (Wadsworth 1976; Farrington, 1987), and in aggressive versus nonaggressive children (Raine et al. 1997b), specificity for violence has not yet been shown for SC measures. In addition, a reanalysis of data from a previous study by Raine, Venables, and Williams (1990a) revealed that when offenders were subdivided into violent and nonviolent groups, the violent group had the lowest HRs. Given the small sample sizes used in this study (5 violent offenders and 12 nonviolent offenders), these results must be treated with due caution (Raine 1996). Additional research with larger numbers of participants is needed to establish whether psychophysiological correlates differ among violent and nonviolent offenders.

Central Nervous System Psychophysiology and Antisocial Behavior

Electroencephalography

Electroencephalography (EEG) is the method used to record the electrical activity of the brain. EEG measures are obtained by placing electrodes in standardized positions on various parts of the scalp and recording the activity of large groups of neurons. Researchers are still unsure whether EEG reflects cerebral cortical activity or is controlled by processes occurring in subcortical brain regions (i.e., in regions located within the brain, beneath the cortical surface) (cf. Ray 1990). Nevertheless, EEG data provide valuable information about central nervous system arousal.

Once EEG chart records are obtained, they are scored in one of two ways. The more qualitative, clinical method involves a visual assessment of normality and subsequent classification of the EEG as normal or abnormal. For example, an EEG chart may be labeled abnormal if excessive theta activity is present. While this method is simple, its subjectivity remains an important drawback. The second scoring method involves a more reliable computerized analysis of the EEG record. This quantitative approach objectively quantifies the EEG chart record into different frequency components.

EEG is delineated into different frequency components that reflect differing degrees of consciousness. Delta (0–4 Hz) is the frequency range generally associated with sleep. Theta (4–8 Hz) is associated with low levels of alertness or drowsiness. Alpha and beta are the two frequencies that are subdivided into fast and slow components. Alpha is found in the 8–12 Hz frequency range and is associated with relaxed wakefulness, while beta is found in the 13–30 Hz frequency range and represents alertness and vigilance. Despite the presence of all frequency bands in the awake individual, individual differences exist in the power of each of these frequency bands. Thus, the EEG profiles of individuals with high levels of cortical activity include all four frequency bands with a predominance of fast alpha (10–12 Hz) and beta waves. Likewise, individuals with lower levels of cortical activity would have more theta and delta activity and relatively less fast alpha and beta activity.

The majority of studies that have assessed cortical activity levels among antisocial populations have relied on visual scoring rather than quantitative computerized analyses. Using this type of scoring, 10 to 15 percent of *normal* individuals appear to have *abnormal* EEGs. This figure should be kept in mind when discussing rates of abnormalities for violent offenders.

In studies of violent offenders, 25 to 50 percent demonstrate EEG abnormalities (Mednick et al. 1982). These abnormalities have been localized in the temporal lobes, a region of the brain involved in audition, visual perception, sexual behavior, and social behaviors (Volavka 1995) and in the anterior (forward) regions of the brain (Mednick et al. 1982). Although the EEG literature on psychopathy reveals mixed findings, clear evidence does exist for various types of EEG abnormalities among murderers and violent recidivistic offenders. The chief abnormality appears to be EEG slowing and is seen among children and adolescents as well as aggressive adults. Volavka (1995) reports a predominance of slow alpha activity and excessive theta activity among "violent youngsters." While these same abnormalities characterized aggressive adults, increased delta activity was also found among the violent adults. Even though the exact nature of these abnormalities is not known, several possible

causes have been proposed (e.g., developmental immaturity, brain injuries, or cortical disinhibition). Volavka (1995) hypothesizes that brain injuries sustained at an early age may have interfered with normal developmental trajectories, thus contributing to EEG slowing.

Prospective Longitudinal Studies

While the evidence reported thus far indicates psychophysiological anomalies in various response systems (cardiovascular, cortical, and electrodermal) among different antisocial populations, these studies provide limited information about causality. Given the cross-sectional nature of these studies, in which the assessment of psychophysiological variables and criminal conduct occurs simultaneously, it is not possible to infer cause-effect relationships. However, prospective longitudinal studies partly overcome this obstacle by allowing assessments to be made at various points in time. In the following studies that we discuss, the assessment of psychophysiological functioning has taken place many years prior to the onset of criminal or antisocial behavior. Thus, it is feasible to conclude that any psychophysiological anomalies that may exist preceded the behavioral outcomes being studied, rather than being a consequence of antisocial behavior.

Although prospective longitudinal studies have the advantage of elucidating cause-effect relationships, few such studies have been conducted due to practical issues and difficulty executing such research. Raine, Venables, and Williams (1990a, 1990b) have conducted a series of prospective analyses of a random sample of 101 15-year-old male school children whose official records of criminal offenses were investigated nine years later. At that time, 17 of the original sample of 101 subjects had been found guilty of crimes ranging from theft to wounding and had been sentenced in court. Of the 17 subjects who had criminal records, five had been imprisoned at some point in time between the ages of 15 and 24.

In the first of these analyses (Raine et al. 1990a), electrodermal, cardiovascular, and cortical measures taken at age 15 were compared between the criminal and noncriminal subjects. Relative to the noncriminal group, subjects with criminal records at age 24 demonstrated lower resting HR, fewer non-specific skin conductance fluctuations (NSFs) during rest, and EEG slowing as evidenced by increased slow-frequency theta activity. This study provides evidence of psychophysiological underarousal in three response systems in adolescents who go on to develop criminal behavior in adulthood.

The second analysis (Raine et al. 1990b) involved skin conductance and HR orienting responses. To review, orienting responses are indirect measures of how an individual allocates attentional resources to the processing of external stimuli. The results indicated that relative to noncriminals, subjects with criminal records at age 24 were characterized by fewer skin conductance orienting responses (SCORs) to a series of neutral tones. The authors also examined SC nonresponding and found that 31 percent of criminals did not respond at all to the orienting stimuli. The rate of nonresponse among the noncriminals was 10 percent. In terms of cardiovascular responding, the criminal group evidenced smaller HR orienting responses when compared to their noncriminal counterparts. These findings are consistent with some of the cross-sectional findings we have already presented and can be interpreted as evidence of deficient allocation of attentional resources to external stimuli (Raine et al. 1990b).

The combined result of this series of prospective studies is electrodermal, cardiovascular, and cortical underarousal and deficient orienting to external stimuli. It is important, however, to keep in mind that these results were obtained from one population of subjects whose "criminal" activity was limited to theft and wounding. These findings may not generalize to more serious offenders.

Protective Factors

Whereas the majority of studies of antisocial behavior have focused on psycho-physiological correlates as *risk factors*,

Raine, Venables, and Williams (1995, 1996) examined psychophysiological correlates that serve *protective* roles. In prospective longitudinal analyses of the sample described above, they found that 15-year-old antisocial adolescents who did not go on to become criminals by age 29 had higher HR levels, higher SC arousal, and better SC conditioning when compared to their antisocial counterparts who became adult criminals. The authors suggest that higher arousal levels reflect fearfulness and better conditioning indicates the ability to learn the association between crime and punishment faster. As such, high levels of arousal and better conditioning may operate to reduce the tendency to engage in crime.

Similar findings were also obtained by Brennan et al. (1997), who found that subjects at high risk for antisocial outcomes (by virtue of having criminal fathers), who nevertheless desisted from crime, were characterized by higher SC and HR orienting reactivity relative to individuals with criminal fathers who became criminals themselves and individuals (both criminal and noncriminal) whose fathers were not criminals. Thus, heightened autonomic nervous system responsiveness, indexed by SC and HR reactivity, is another biological protective factor that reduces the risk of antisocial outcomes in high-risk individuals.

Brain Imaging and Crime

In recent years, important technological advances have been made in the field of brain imaging. These developments have permitted scientists to visualize both structural and functional properties of the brain. Thus, scientists now have a better understanding both of how the brain is organized and how the brain works. In addition to a wide range of medical applications, neuroimaging technology has begun to be applied to the field of crime and violence research. By directly indexing brain structure and function, brain-imaging techniques hold the promise of adding exponentially to what is currently known about the biological underpinnings of antisocial and violent behavior.

The most common methods of obtaining structural information about the brain include CT (Computerized Tomography) and MRI scanning, both of which allow scientists to see a "picture" of the brain and its structures. Raine (1993) reviews brain imaging studies that have found associations between temporal lobe abnormalities and violent behavior. The temporal lobes are the portions of the cerebral cortex that lie below the frontal and parietal lobes and are involved in emotion regulation, sexual behaviors, audition, and speech perception (Heilman and Valenstein 1993; Carlson 1994). The temporal lobes also include aspects of the limbic system, which is a collection of many structures including the amygdala and the hippocampus (Carlson 1994). In addition to learning and memory, motivation and emotion are among the primary functions of the limbic system.

Although CT and MRI studies provide useful information about structural abnormalities associated with violence, neuroimaging techniques, such as PET (Positron Emission Tomography), which measures glucose uptake, reveal the *functional* properties of the brain. Thus, while structural imaging involves seeing "pictures" of the brain, functional imaging reveals information about which parts of the brain are relatively more active at various times. When a region of the brain becomes activated (such as when performing a particular task), that region requires more "fuel," or glucose. Functional imaging provides information about how much glucose is metabolized in various parts of the brain. Based on rates of glucose metabolism, scientists can infer which regions of the brain are more or less active. This strategy has been used to compare rates of glucose metabolism among criminal and noncriminal populations.

Evidence from PET studies of violence and aggression support a prefrontal dysfunction theory of antisocial behavior (Raine 1997). According to this hypothesis, damage or dysfunction to the frontal lobe can predispose to antisocial and violent behavior. The frontal lobe has been implicated in higher cognitive functions, such as abstraction, planning, devising behavioral strategies, assessing progress made toward goals, and judgment (Carlson 1994). Thus, frontal dysfunction may have far-reaching effects, ranging from personality changes (e.g., high impulsivity and thrill-seeking) to cognitive manifestations (e.g., poor judgment, intellectual slowing) to impaired social skills.

Prefrontal dysfunction may also explain previously reviewed arousal and orienting deficits among antisocials. As we have noted, Raine et al. (1991) have shown that the area of the prefrontal cortex is positively correlated with a number of SC orienting responses. That is, reduced prefrontal cortical area as measured by MRI is associated with reduced orienting. Several other brain-imaging and neurological studies suggest that the source of orienting deficits in antisocials may be dysfunction of the prefrontal cortex (Damasio et al. 1990; Hazlett et al. 1993; Tranel and Damasio 1994). The prefrontal cortex lies in the anterior part of the frontal lobe. It makes up most of the frontal cortex.

In support of a prefrontal dysfunction hypothesis, Raine and colleagues (1994) have demonstrated that a sample of murderers pleading not guilty by reason of insanity are characterized by reduced glucose metabolism in the prefrontal cortex when compared to a comparison group. Reduced glucose metabolism is also observed in several other regions of the brain, specifically the posterior parietal cortex (bilateral superior parietal gyrus and left angular gyrus) and the corpus callosum, a fiber tract that connects the right and left hemispheres of the brain (Raine, Buchsbaum, and LaCasse 1997d).

Abnormal asymmetries of function can be found in the amygdala, hippocampus, and the thalamus. Neuroanatomists generally describe these three regions as consisting of two parts—right and left. Thus, one can speak of the right hippocampus and left hippocampus. Although it is expected that both parts will metabolize glucose relatively equally, the study by Raine and colleagues indicates that in murderers there is sometimes an imbalance in the amount of glucose metabolism that occurs in the right and left portions of these structures. Reduced prefrontal glucose metabolism is particularly characteristic of the murderers who had experienced *less* psychosocial deprivation than the murderers with deprived early backgrounds, suggesting that biological predispositions to violent offending are more salient in murderers who lack social predispositions to engage in violence (Raine, Stoddard, Bihrle, and Buchsbaum 1998).

Functional deficits in these regions have important implications for violent behavior. Prefrontal deficits have been associated with behavioral disinhibition, increased risk-taking, and impulsivity. The parietal region of the brain, which contains the somatosensory cortex, is involved in the integration of sensory input. Abnormalities in various regions of the parietal cortex, including the left angular gyrus, have been associated with cognitive dysfunction, including impaired verbal fluency and reading and arithmetic skills, which may present problems in schooling. Finally, the corpus callosum is a large fiber tract that interconnects the two hemispheres of the brain. Callosal dysfunction may result in less left hemisphere regulation over emotions generated by the right hemisphere.

In addition to a sample of murderers, evidence of reduced glucose metabolism has been found in a sample of violent psychiatric patients. Volkow et al. (1995) demonstrated lower glucose metabolism in medial temporal and prefrontal cortices in violent psychiatric patients relative to normal control subjects. Goyer and Semple (1996) have also demonstrated that inpatients with problems controlling aggressive impulses demonstrate lower rates of glucose metabolism in orbital frontal, upper prefrontal, and left insular temporal-parietal regions. These patients were also characterized by Axis-II personality disorders, which involve inflexible and maladaptive behavioral patterns. Taken together, the above findings provide significant evidence for both structural and functional brain abnormalities in various groups of subjects including murderers, violent psychiatric patients, and aggressive personality-disordered inpatients.

While it is clear that brain abnormalities underlie violent behavior, the specific mechanisms of these relationships are not yet completely understood. However, based on the functions performed by various brain structures, it is possible to speculate about how certain types of brain dysfunction may influence violent behavior. For example, cognitive dysfunction resulting from brain injury may lead to academic and occupational failure that, in turn, predisposes one to delinquent lifestyles. Prefrontal deficits may lead to the inability to foresee the consequences of violent acts, while deficient auditory or speech perception may lead one to misperceive and misinterpret innocuous stimuli as threatening, thus eliciting a paranoid-aggressive reaction. Even though scenarios such as these are speculative, they help illustrate how brain abnormalities may render certain individuals more susceptible to engaging in violence and highlight the contribution of brain imaging to the study of violent behavior.

Cognitive Deficits and Crime

Intelligence levels among criminals and delinquents have been assessed in many studies, and numerous reviews have been conducted of this extensive area of research. These reviews conclude that, overall, criminals and delinquents have lower IQ scores than noncriminals (Hirschi and Hindelang 1977; Wilson and Herrnstein 1985; Quay 1987). The extent of this deficit ranges from 8 to 10 IQ points.

The most frequently used measure for the assessment of intelligence is the Wechsler Adult Intelligence Scale-Revised (WAIS-R), which includes 11 different subtests, each tapping different domains of intellectual functioning. General IQ scores are broken down into Verbal and Performance IQ scores. The verbal subtests assess an individual's verbal fluency, verbal memory, ability to work with abstract symbols, and general fund of accumulated knowledge. The performance scales assess spatial abilities—the ability to integrate perceptual stimuli with relevant motor responses, analysis and synthesis of spatial relations, an individual's understanding of interpersonal situations, visual acuity, and manipulative and perceptual speed (Groth-Marnat 1990).

Reviews of specific IQ deficits have shown that delinquents' verbal IQ scores are lower than their performance IQ scores, particularly among aggressive, psychopathic individuals. The degree of the verbal-performance IQ discrepancy ranges from 8 to 12 IQ points (Wilson and Herrnstein 1985; Quay 1987). Several hypotheses have been put forth to explain precisely how low IQ can be related to crime. Low IQ can impede successful school performance, which in turn could limit employment opportunities and bring on poverty and alienation. Under these circumstances, a criminal lifestyle may become more appealing to certain individuals (Raine 1993).

Returning to the issue of causality discussed previously, the results of a 17-year longitudinal study show that cognitive deficits lead to conduct disorder at age 17, that is, cognitive deficits *precede* conduct disorder (Schonfeld et al. 1988). However, Raine (1993) proposes that early brain dysfunction may be a "third factor" underlying both cognitive deficits and delinquency and crime. Early brain dysfunction resulting from birth complications (discussed in further detail below), environmental toxins, pregnancy complications, or head injury, among other causes, may lead directly and independently to both antisocial behavior and low IQ. Alternatively, early brain damage may indirectly affect antisocial outcomes by causing cognitive deficits that hinder academic success. To test the "third factor" hypothesis, longitudinal studies that assess early brain dysfunction are needed.

A biological explanation also exists for the link between verbal-performance IQ deficits and crime. The left hemisphere of the brain is thought to be specialized in verbal abilities that are reflected in verbal IQ scores. In contrast, the right hemisphere of the brain is specialized in spatial abilities that are reflected in performance IQ scores. Thus, damage to the left hemisphere would impact verbal functioning, while damage to the right hemisphere would be consistent with performance IQ deficits. Raine (1993) suggests that lower verbal IQ scores in delinquent populations would be consistent with left hemisphere dysfunction, possibly due to

head injury or delivery complications. Evidence of left hemisphere dysfunction was briefly reviewed in the section on brain-imaging studies of crime. Verbal deficits, however, may also be genetically determined, as verbal IQ has a heritable component.

An important methodological consideration of studies that assess IQ in delinquents and criminals involves the extent to which the sample being studied is representative of all criminals and delinquents. That is, the criminals and delinquents who make up the subject populations of research studies may be biased by virtue of having failed to elude detection. These individuals may have low IQ scores, which are partly responsible for their having been caught by the police. In order to rule out the possibility that the criminals who have successfully avoided detection might have higher IQ scores, self-report measures of crime and delinquency are necessary. By using self-report measures of crime, it is more likely that a representative population of people who have committed crimes will be examined, including criminals who have not been caught and therefore have no official record of criminal activity. This helps to rule out the possibility that only criminals with low IQs are assessed. Two studies that have utilized both self-report measures of criminal activity or delinquency and official records (Moffitt and Silva 1988; Farrington 1989) have also found a link between self-reported crime and low IQ scores, thus ruling out the possibility that the link between low IQ and crime is an artifact of biased samples that have failed to elude the police.

Birth Complications

It has been suggested that birth complications may predispose one to violence (Reiss and Roth 1993). In this context, in a sample of 4,269 male Danish births, Raine et al. (1994) have shown that birth complications (e.g., breech birth, anoxia) interact with early maternal rejection in the first year of life to predispose to adult violent crime by age 18 years. Because possession of birth complications alone or early maternal rejection alone were not associated with greater adult violent offending, this study highlights the necessity of examining the interactions between biological and social and environmental risk factors. In a follow-up study of this sample, Raine et al. (1997c) showed that the same biosocial interaction effect was significant in predicting violent crime at age 34 years. This study also showed that:

(a) The interaction was specific to violent forms of offending.

(b) The interaction predicted early but not late onset violent offending.

(c) Institutionalization in the first year of life and the mother's attempt to abort the fetus were the two key elements of "maternal rejection" that interacted with birth complications in predicting violent crime.

Precisely how this interaction is translated into adult crime is still unknown. It is likely that maternal rejection before the age of 1 year has implications for the formation of early mother-child bonding processes that subsequently influence the formation of appropriate interpersonal relationships in adulthood. Volatile adult relationships increase the likelihood of violent interactions (Raine and Liu 1998).

Birth complications, in turn, may serve as a primary source of brain dysfunction, and neurological and neuropsychological deficits. The associations between brain dysfunction and antisocial and violent behavior have already been discussed. Brain dysfunction, which is likely to be exacerbated by negative psychosocial factors (e.g., maternal rejection), may trigger a chain of negative events (e.g., cognitive deficits, school failure, unemployment, crime) or contribute to the lack of behavioral inhibition, resulting in aggressive outcomes (Raine and Liu 1998).

Conclusions and Policy Implications

It has been shown that various biological markers exist that differentiate criminals and delinquents from noncriminals. Antisocial individuals show tendencies towards low electrodermal arousal, as indicated by fewer SC nonspecific fluctuations. SC and HR orienting deficits have also been indicated, reflecting dysfunctional processing of external stimuli. Psychophysiological studies also provide evidence of lower resting HR levels and cortical underarousal among antisocials, while brain imaging studies reveal structural deficits and reduced glucose metabolism in various offender groups relative to control subjects. Studies that have adopted a prospective, longitudinal approach have demonstrated the utility of psychophysiological measures in predicting adult offending as well as identifying factors that serve a protective role among high-risk adolescents. In the area of cognitive functioning, deficits are found more often among antisocials than controls, particularly deficits in verbal IQ. Finally, the interaction between birth complications and early maternal rejection predisposes to adult violent crimes, suggesting that biological predispositions can be exacerbated by negative social environments.

Even though biological research in the area of crime and antisociality has contributed largely to current formulations about the genesis of crime, biological factors alone cannot account for criminal behavior. If one aims to completely understand the phenomenon of violence, social influences must inevitably be considered alongside biological influences. Furthermore, the study of biological risk factors and social risk factors in isolation only partially describes the process of violence. Clearly, humans are born with a particular genetic makeup, but they are continuously influenced by their surrounding environment even prenatally. It is the constant interaction between one's genetic composition and environmental factors that determines one's behavior. Thus, the singular approach to gaining a thorough understanding of why one commits criminal acts must account for both biological and social factors, the "biosocial" approach (Raine et al. 1997c).

Evidence for the contribution of one's environment to eventual antisocial behavior was reviewed in the section on classical conditioning and crime. Briefly, Raine et al. (1981) found that poor conditioning was characteristic of antisocials from good home backgrounds. In contrast, a conditioning deficit was not detected for antisocials from poor home environments, indicating better conditioning among this subgroup of antisocials. Careful consideration of this latter result raises the possibility that children growing up in poor home environments who nevertheless condition well might condition into antisocial lifestyles. In contrast, children living under more privileged circumstances, where the "prosocial" way of life is the norm, may not adopt this lifestyle even if they are unable to condition well (Raine and Dunkin 1990). These findings provide an example of how environmental factors affect the expression of a biological predisposition and play a central role in determining a child's outcome as an adult. Further evidence of how one's environment influences behavior is provided by the interaction between early maternal rejection and birth complications in predisposing to criminal outcomes. This biosocial interaction has important implications for prevention as we will show.

In the discussion of SC and resting HR findings, fearlessness and stimulation seeking were put forth as possible explanations for the translation of psychophysiological underarousal into antisocial or criminal behavior. Stimulation-seeking theory has possible implications for treatment and prevention. If a class of children exists who are physiologically underaroused and fearless, and prone to engaging in dangerous activities to attain optimal arousal, early intervention strategies could focus on directing their stimulation-seeking tendencies towards more prosocial activities. Such redirection might obviate the need for antisocial behaviors that are hypothesized to offset the discomfort that arises from physiological underarousal.

Evidence for brain dysfunction among aggressive individuals and criminals has raised the possibility that the source of brain damage may lie externally. Thus, an additional preventive route would involve efforts to reduce the incident of brain damage resulting from child abuse, head injury, environmental toxins, or birth complications. Better antenatal and perinatal health care services could be an important step toward this goal (Raine and Liu 1998). Educational programs aimed at informing women about the deleterious effects of drugs and alcohol on the fetus as well as providing information about proper nutrition during pregnancy may also serve to reduce the likelihood of birth complications. Such programs may indirectly reduce the incidence of crime later in life by decreasing birth complications and resulting brain damage, which in turn has both direct (e.g., increased inhibition) and indirect influences (e.g., improved cognitive functioning) on the reduction of crime and violence. Raine et al. (1994) showed that while only 4 percent of the sample of 4,269 had both birth complications and maternal rejection, this small group accounted for 18 percent of all the violent crime committed by the entire sample. By reducing rates of either birth complications or maternal rejection, they argued that rates of violence in society could be reduced 18 percent.

The efficacy of crime prevention programs may also be improved by intervening at the social level. For example, the reduction of maternal rejection may suppress the biological predisposition to crime stemming from birth complications and brain damage. Interventions can be aimed at helping foster stronger mother-infant bonding behaviors. These measures may prove to be especially effective when dealing with teenage mothers or births resulting from unwanted pregnancies. Parenting classes may also improve caregiving skills and thus promote stronger mother-infant bonds (Raine and Liu 1998).

Lastly, efforts to integrate biological findings into prevention policies may involve directly altering one's biological functioning. Even though highly controversial, the use of biofeedback training and psychotropic medication may increase arousal to optimal levels. Several investigators have examined the efficacy of psychotropic medication in treating symptoms of attention-deficit hyperactive disorder (ADHD) and comorbid (co-existing) conduct disorder in children. These studies seem to suggest that psychopharmacological interventions for ADHD may enhance effective treatment of behavior problems, including conduct disorder (Connor and Steingard 1996; Riggs 1998; Riggs et al. 1998; Hendren 1999). Given the numerous factors that influence antisocial behavior, the most effective treatment programs will undoubtedly rely on the integration of treatment from several different modalities including social-environmental, prenatal, and psychopharmacological.

References

Bernstein, A.S., C.D. Frith, J.H. Gruzelier, T. Patterson, E. Straube, P.H. Venables, and T.P. Zahn. (1982). "An analysis of the skin conductance orienting response in samples of American, British, and German schizophrenics." *Biological Psychology*, 14:155–211.

Blackburn, R. (1979). "Cortical and autonomic response arousal in primary and secondary psychopaths." *Psychophysiology*, 16:143–150.

Brennan, P.A., A. Raine, F. Schulsinger, L. Kirkegaard-Sorensen. (1997). Psychophysiological protective factors for male subjects at high risk for criminal behavior. *American Journal of Psychiatry*, 154(6):853–855.

Carlson, N.R. (1994). *Physiology of Behavior*, Fifth Edition. Boston, MA: Allyn and Bacon.

Connor, D.F. and R.J. Steingard. (1996). "A clinical approach to the pharmacotherapy of of aggression in children and adults." Pp. 290–307 in C.F. Ferris, T. Grisso, et al. (eds.), "Understanding aggressive behavior in children." *Annals of the New York Academy of Sciences*, 794. New York: New York Academy of Sciences.

Cox, D., R. Hallam, K. O'Connor, and S. Rachman. (1983). "An experimental study of fearlessness and courage." *British Journal of Psychology*, 74:107–117.

Damasio, A.R., D. Tranel, and H. Damasio. (1990). "Individuals with sociopathic behavior caused by frontal damage fail to respond autonomically to social stimuli." *Behavioral Brain Research*, 41:81–94.

Dawson, M.E., D.L. Filion, and A.M. Schell. (1989). "Is elicitation of the autonomic orienting response associated with the allocation of processing resources?" *Psychophysiology*, 26:560–572.

Dawson, M.E. and K.H. Nuechterlein. (1984). "Psychophysiological dysfunction in the developmental course of schizophrenic disorders." *Schizophrenia Bulletin*, 10:204–232.

Eysenck, H.J. (1964). *Crime and Personality*, First Edition. London: Methuen.

Eysenck, H.J. (1977). *Crime and Personality*, Third Edition. St. Albans, England: Paladin.

Farrington, D.P. (1987). "Implications of biological findings for criminological research." Pp. 42–64 in S.A. Mednick, T.E. Moffitt, and S.A. Stack (eds.). *The Causes of Crime: New Biological Approaches*, New York: Cambridge University Press.

Farrington, D.P. (1989). "Early predictors of adolescent aggression and adult violence." *Violence and Victims*, 4:79–100.

Goyer, P.F., W.E. and Semple. (1996). "PET studies of aggression in personality disorder and other nonpsychotic patients." Pp. 219–235 in D.M. Stoff and R.B. Cairns (eds.), *Aggression and Violence: Genetic, Neurobiological, and Biological Perspectives*, Hillsdale, NJ: Erlbaum.

Groth-Marnat, G. (1990). *Handbook of Psychological Assessment*, Second Edition. New York: Wiley and Sons.

Hare, R.D. (1978). "Electrodermal and cardiovascular correlates of psychopathy." Pp. 77–105 in D.C. Fowles (ed.), *Clinical Applications of Psychophysiology*. New York: Cambridge University Press.

Hazlett, E., M. Dawson, M.S. Buchsbaum, and K. Nuechterlein. (1993). "Reduced regional brain glucose metabolism assessed by PET in electrodermal nonresponder schizophrenics: A pilot study." *Journal of Abnormal Psychology*, 102:39–46.

Heilman, K.M. and E. Valenstein. (1993). *Clinical Neuropsychology*, Third Edition. New York: Oxford University Press.

Hendren, R.L. (1999). *Disruptive Behavior Disorders in Children and Adolescents*. Washington DC: American Psychiatric Press.

Hirschi, T. and M.J. Hindelang. (1977). "Intelligence and delinquency: A revisionist review." *American Sociological Review*, 42:571–587.

Kruesi, M.J., E.D. Hibbs, T.P. Zahn, and C.S. Keysor. (1992). "A 2-year prospective follow-up study of children and adolescents with disruptive behavior disorders: Prediction by cerebrospinal fluid 5-hydroxyindoleacetic acid, homovanillic acid, and autonomic measures?" *Archives of General Psychiatry*, 49:429–435.

Maliphant, R., F. Hume, and A. Furnham. (1990). "Autonomic nervous system (ANS) activity, personality characteristics and disruptive behavior in girls." *Journal of Child Psychology and Psychiatry*, 31:619–628.

Mednick, S.A. (1977). "Autonomic nervous system recovery and psychopathology." *Scandinavian Journal of Behavior Therapy*, 4:55–68.

Mednick, S.A., J. Volavka, W.F. Gabrielli, and T. Itil. (1982). "EEG as a predictor of antisocial behavior." *Criminology*, 19:219–231.

Moffitt, T.E. and P.A. Silva. (1988). "IQ and delinquency: A direct test of the differential detection hypothesis." *Journal of Abnormal Psychology,* 97:227–240.

Ohman, A. (1979). "The orienting response, attention, and learning: An information processing perspective." Pp. 443–471 in H.D. Kimmel, E.H. van Olst, and J.F. Orlebeke (eds.), *The orienting reflex in humans,* Hillsdale, NJ: Erlbaum.

Ohman, A. (1981). "Electrodermal activity and vulnerability in schizophrenia: A review." *Biological Psychology,* 12:87–145.

Ohman, A. (1985). "Face the beats and fear the face: Animal and social fears as prototypes for evolutionary analyses of emotion." *Psychophysiology,* 23:123–145.

Quay, H.C. (1965). "Psychopathic personality as pathological stimulation-seeking." *American Journal of Psychiatry,* 122:180–183.

Quay, H.C. (1987). "Intelligence." Pp. 106–117 in H.C. Quay (ed.). *Handbook of juvenile delinquency,* New York: Wiley.

Raine, A. (1987). "Effect of early environment on electrodermal and cognitive correlates of schizotypy and psychopathy in criminals." *International Journal of Psychophysiology,* 4:277–287.

Raine, A. (1989). "Evoked potentials and psychopathy." *International Journal of Psychophysiology,* 8:1–16.

Raine, A. (1993). *The Psychopathology of Crime: Criminal Behavior as a Clinical Disorder.* San Diego: Academic.

Raine, A. (1996). "Autonomic nervous system activity and violence." Pp. 145–168 in D.M. Stoff and R.F. Cairns (eds.). *The neurobiology of clinical aggression,* Hillsdale, NJ: Erlbaum.

Raine, A. (1997). "Antisocial behavior and psychophysiology: A biosocial perspective and a prefrontal dysfunction hypothesis." In D.M. Stoff, J. Breiling, and J.D. Maser (eds.), *Handbook of Antisocial Behavior.* New York: Wiley and Sons.

Raine, A., P.A. Brennan, D.P. Farrington, and S.A. Mednick. (1997). *Biosocial Bases of Violence.* New York: Plenum.

Raine, A., P.A. Brennan, and S.A. Mednick. (1994). "Birth complications combined with early maternal rejection at age 1 year predispose to violent crime at age 18 years." *Archives of General Psychiatry,* 51:984–988.

Raine, A., P.A. Brennan, and S.A. Mednick. (1997). "Interaction between birth complications and early maternal rejection in predisposing individuals to adult violence: Specificity to serious, early-onset violence." *American Journal of Psychiatry,* 154(9):1265–1271.

Raine, A., M.S. Buchsbaum, and L. LaCasse. (1997). "Brain abnormalities in murderers indicated by positron emission tomography." *Biological Psychiatry,* 42:495–508.

Raine, A., M.S. Buchsbaum, J. Stanley, S. Lottenberg, L. Abel, and J. Stoddard. (1994). "Selective reductions in prefrontal glucose metabolism in murderers." *Biological Psychiatry,* 36:365–373.

Raine, A. and J.J. Dunkin. (1990). "The genetic and psychophysiological basis of antisocial behavior: Implications for counseling and therapy." *Journal of Counseling and Development,* 68:637–644.

Raine, A., T. Lencz, and D.S. Benishay. (1995). "Schizotypal personality and skin conductance orienting." Pp. 219–249 in A. Raine, T. Lencz, and S.A. Mednick (eds.), *Schizotypal Personality.* New York: Cambridge University Press.

Raine, A. and J. Liu. (1998). "Biological predispositions to violence and their implications for biosocial treatment and prevention." *Psychology, Crime and Law,* 4:107–125.

Raine, A., G. Reynolds, and C. Sheard. (1991). "Neuroanatomical mediators of electrodermal activity in normal human subjects: A magnetic resonance imaging study." *Psychophysiology,* 28:548–558.

Raine, A., J. Stoddard, S.E. Bihrle, and M.S Buchsbaum. (1998). "Prefrontal glucose deficits in murderers lacking psychosocial deprivation." *Neuropsychiatry, Neuropsychology, and Behavioral Neurology,* 11(1):1–7.

Raine, A. and P.H. Venables. (1981). "Classical conditioning and socialization—A biosocial interaction?" *Personality and Individual Differences,* 2:273–283.

Raine, A. and P.H. Venables. (1984a). "Electrodermal nonresponding, schizoid tendencies, and antisocial behavior in adolescents." *Psychophysiology,* 21:424–433.

Raine, A. and P.H. Venables. (1984b). "Tonic HR level, social class, and antisocial behavior." *Biological Psychology,* 18:123–132.

Raine, A., P.H. Venables, and S.A. Mednick. (1997). "Low resting HR at age 3 years predisposes to aggression at age 11 years: evidence from the Mauritius child health project." *Journal of the American Academy of Child and Adolescent Psychiatry,* 36(10):1457–1464.

Raine, A., P.H. Venables, and M. Williams. (1990a). "Autonomic orienting responses in 15-year-old male subjects and criminal behavior at age 24." *American Journal of Psychiatry,* 147(7):933–937.

Raine, A., P.H. Venables, and M. Williams. (1990b). "Relationships between central and autonomic measures of arousal at age 15 years and criminality at age 24 years." *Archives of General Psychiatry,* 47:1003–1007.

Raine, A., P.H. Venables, and M. Williams. (1995). "High autonomic arousal and electrodermal orienting at age 15 years as protective factors against criminal behavior at age 29 years." *American Journal of Psychiatry,* 152:1595–1600.

Raine, A., P.H. Venables, and M. Williams. (1996). "Better autonomic conditioning and faster electrodermal half-recovery time at age 15 years as protective factors against crime at age 29 years." *Developmental Psychology,* 32:624–630.

Ray, W.J. (1990). "The electrocortical system." Pp. 385–412 in J.T. Cacioppo and L.G. Tassinary (eds.). *Principles of psychophysiology,* Cambridge: Cambridge University Press.

Reiss, A.J. and J.A. Roth. (1993). *Understanding and Preventing Violence.* Washington, DC: National Academy Press.

Riggs, P.D. (1998). "Clinical approach to the treatment of ADHD in adolescents with substance use disorders and conduct disorder." *Journal of the American Academy of Child and Adolescent Psychiatry,* 37(3):331–332.

Riggs, P.D., S.L. Leon, S.K. Mikulich, and L.C. Pottle. (1998). "An open trial of bupropion for ADHD in adolescents with substance abuse disorders and conduct disorder." *Journal of the American Academy of Child and Adolescent Psychiatry,* 37(12):1271–1278.

Scarpa, A., A. Raine. P.H. Venables, and S.A. Mednick. (1997). "Heart rate and skin conductance in behaviorally inhibited Mauritian children." *Journal of Abnormal Psychology,* 106(2):182–190.

Schonfeld, I.S., D. Shaffer, P. O'Connor, and S. Portnoy. (1988). "Conduct disorder and cognitive functioning: Testing three causal hypotheses." *Child Development,* 59:993–1007.

Tranel, D. and H. Damasio. (1994). "Neuroanatomical correlates of electrodermal skin conductance responses." *Psychophysiology,* 31:427–438.

Venables, P.H. (1974). "The recovery limb of the skin conductance response." Pp. 110–136 in S.A. Mednick, F. Schulsinger, J. Higgins, and B. Bell (eds.). *Genetics, Environment, and Psychopathology.* New York: Cambridge University Press.

Volavka, J. (1995). *Neurobiology of Violence.* Washington, DC: American Psychiatric Press.

Volkow, N.D., L.R. Tancredi, C. Grant, H. Gillespie, A. Valentine, N. Mullani, G. Wang, and L. Hollister. (1995). "Brain glucose metabolism in violent psychiatric patients: A preliminary study." *Psychiatry Research: Neuroimaging,* 61:243–253.

Wadsworth, M.E.J. (1976). "Delinquency, pulse rate and early emotional deprivation." *British Journal of Criminology,* 16:245–256.

West, D.J. and D.P. Farrington. (1977). *The Delinquent Way of Life.* London: Heinemann.

Wilson, J.Q. and R. Herrnstein. (1985). *Crime and Human Nature.* New York: Simon and Schuster.

Acknowledgments: This chapter was written while the first author was supported by a National Research Service Award from NIMH (1 F31 MH11761-01).

4
Control Theories of Crime

Introduction

The two essays in this chapter share some common conceptual ground in that they are both variations of what are called *control* theories of crime. Control explanations of crime uniquely reverse the usual question about criminal offending. Rather than asking the question "What causes people to break rules and commit criminal offenses?" control theorists ask "What causes people to conform to rules and criminal laws?" Control theories, in other words, generally take deviant motivation for granted and as nonproblematic. What this perspective must therefore explain is conformity or compliance. That is, instead of explaining the causes of crime, control theorists attempt to explain the reasons why people do *not* commit crimes. There is, however, some variation in how strictly this assumption is adhered to. For example, some control theories also include a discussion of the factors that might attract someone to commit crime. Thus, it is probably safe to say only that control theories minimize the importance of criminal motivation, with some versions virtually silent on the issue, while others have more fully developed accounts of criminal motives.

With some variation, then, the distinctive feature of control theories is the assumption that the motivation to break rules and commit crimes is evenly distributed throughout society. In other words, no one person is more highly motivated to commit crime than another—we would all commit crimes if it were in our interest to do so. If you assume that deviant motivation is generally constant across individuals, then criminal conduct must be due to variations in con-

trols or restraints that people have over their deviant impulses. Travis Hirschi (1969, 34), a notable control theorist, succinctly describes the control theory position: "The question 'Why do they do it'? Is simply not the question the [control] theory is designed to answer. The question is 'Why don't we do it'? There is much evidence that we would if we dared." In assuming that deviant motivation is generally uniform, then, control theories are theories of compliance or crime inhibition rather than theories of criminal motivation. Crime occurs when restraints or controls over naturally occurring deviant impulses are either not formed, break down, or are weakened.

Historical Roots of Control Theory

Durkheim on Human Nature and Social Order

Control theories of crime have a long history. We can see the seeds of later control theory explanations of crime in the work of the late nineteenth century sociologist Emile Durkheim. Durkheim was concerned with the very broad question of social control in emerging modern societies. What made social control generally problematic was that human beings are unique in the animal world for having the power of "reflection" (Durkheim [1897] 1951, 246). The power of reflection is the distinctly human characteristic of imagining more of something. Lower animals, Durkheim argued, have basic biological drives and biological limitations to their appetites spurred by those drives. For example, a dog can only eat or drink until she is full and the drive is satisfied; eating more will only prompt vomiting rather than additional satisfactions.

In addition to basic biological drives for food, water, and sex, Durkheim argued, human beings have socially created desires. They crave not simply shelter and sustenance, but better and larger homes, faster and more exotic cars, expensive meals and wines, and things like social status, prestige, money and power, and sexual access to desirable partners. Because of the power of reflection, humans have no naturally occurring restraints over their appetites—whatever they currently possess, they can always imagine more. Their wants and desires, Durkheim ([1897] 1951) argued, neither recognize nor yield to a natural limit:

> In the animal, at least in a normal condition, this equilibrium is established with automatic spontaneity because the animal depends on purely material conditions. . . . When the void created by existence in its own resources is filled, the animal satisfied, asks nothing further. Its power of reflection is not sufficiently developed to imagine other ends than those implicit in its physical nature. . . . This is not the case with man, because most of his needs are not dependent on his body or not to the same degree. . . . But how determine the quantity of well-being, comfort or luxury legitimately to be craved by a human being? Nothing appears in man's organic nor his psychological constitution which sets a limit to such tendencies. . . . It is not human nature which can assign the variable limits necessary to our needs. They are thus unlimited so far as they depend on the individual alone. Irrespective of any external regulatory force, our capacity for feeling is in itself an insatiable and bottomless abyss. (246–247)

The assumption of human nature that Durkheim presents is of beings whose appetites are limited only by their own self-interest. Driven by socially defined goals that seem to know no bounds or satisfaction, Durkheim ([1897] 1951) further argued, human beings live a miserable existence:

> But if nothing external can restrain this capacity, it can only be a source of torment to itself. Unlimited desires are insatiable by definition and insatiability is rightly considered a sign of morbidity. . . . To pursue a goal which is by definition unattainable is to condemn oneself to a state of perpetual unhappiness. (247–248)

The key to human happiness, therefore, is that their appetites must be regulated or controlled. Because these appetites are socially driven and know no biological limit, and self-regulation is impossible because of the power of reflection, the only possible source of regulation or restraint must be so-

cial. The satisfaction of human desires, in other words, must be limited and controlled by a force external to the individual—society:

> To achieve any other result, the passions first must be limited. Only then can they be harmonized with the faculties and satisfied. But since the individual has no way of limiting them, this must be done by some force exterior to him. . . . Either directly and as a whole, or through the agency of one of its organs, society alone can play this moderating role; for it is the only moral power superior to the individual, the authority which it accepts. (248)

And so Durkheim would have society regulate the goals that persons desire; otherwise, there will be no limit to their appetite and without limits, humans face the prospect of unhappiness. What will provide this regulation or limit are the connections individuals have to social groups and institutions. That is, control over human appetite is achieved when the individual is connected to a social group. This is the import of Durkheim's ([1925] 1961, 64) proclamation that "we are moral beings only to the extent that we are social beings." Hence, Durkheim ([1925] 1961) argued, what society gives us when we are attached to it through its institutions is moral discipline, and moral discipline provides the only restraint over individual appetites:

> Morality, we have said, is basically a discipline. All discipline has a double objective: to promote a certain regularity in people's conduct, and to provide them with determinate goals that at the same time limit their horizons. . . . In molding us morally, society has inculcated in us those feelings that prescribe our conduct so imperatively; and that kick with such force when we fail to abide by their injunctions. Our moral conscience is its product and reflects it. When our conscience speaks, it is society speaking within us. The tone with which it speaks is the best demonstration of its remarkable authority. Not only is society a moral authority, but there is every reason to consider it the type and source of all moral authority. (47, 90)

In Durkheim's work, morality, achieved through a union or bond with society, provides restraint on potentially insatiable needs.

We have presented this somewhat lengthy review of Durkheim's writings because a substantial body of subsequent control theory in the study of crime is simply an elaboration of his basic argument. Human beings are portrayed as essentially asocial in the sense that in the absence of some form of restraint their natural inclination is to bend and break rules in pursuit of the elusive satisfaction of their desires. In sum, deviance requires no explanation; it is taken for granted. What must be accounted for, then, is conformity and compliance. In Durkheim's work, the basis of social control is the connection between the individual and society.

Early Control Theories of Crime

In what may be the first appearance of a control theory of criminal offending, the sociologist Albert J. Reiss, Jr., published a paper in 1951 titled "Delinquency as the Failure of Personal and Social Controls." Without ever making it explicit, Reiss presumes that delinquency will naturally occur, and that a theory of offending must provide an account of why it does not happen. There is, therefore, no explanation as to delinquent motivation in his paper; it is assumed. More specifically, he states that delinquency will arise *in the absence of restraints or controls against it.* The presumption that rule breaking will occur unless there is something to stop it is the defining characteristic of a control theory.

Reiss argued that there are several social sources of restraint. One of the most important sources of control is the family. The family restrains the deviant impulses of its children by meeting their basic economic needs and by providing a strong emotional relationship. Children who are strongly attached to conventional parents are more likely to internalize nondelinquent values. Strong attachment on the part of the parent includes such behaviors as providing close supervision over the actions of the child, staying married, and providing firm and consistent discipline. In addition to the family, the community or neighborhood plays a role in providing social controls. Neighborhoods that have informal groups, that have a higher percentage of owner-occupied dwellings, and where residential mobility is low are more effective in controlling the conduct of the children who live there. Finally, a strong attachment of the child to the school is an effective source of social control. Personal controls include the capacity to defer gratification and to keep one's impulses in check. In sum, Reiss argued that rule breaking is likely when the child is not emotionally involved with and attached to a strong family unit, when community controls are weakened by population mobility, and when internal discipline is lacking.

Writing just six years after Reiss, Jackson Toby presented a very similar control theory argument about the causes of what would now be called *gang delinquency.* In trying to account for high rates of crime, particularly property crime, in a nation of affluence, Toby (1957) began with the classic control theory statement about the ultimate source of crime—the absence of restraint: "people are more prone to act upon their anti-social impulses when external controls over them are weak" (12). Presuming, rather than explaining, the origins of "anti-social impulses," Toby (1957) argued that such impulses are uniformly distributed in American society, and that one is free to act on them when there is no "stake in conformity":

> . . . the difference between the law-abiding adolescent and the hoodlum is not that one has impulses to violate the rules of society while the other has not. Both are tempted to break laws at some time or other—because laws prohibit what circumstances may make attractive: driving an automobile at 80 miles an hour, beating up an enemy, taking what one wants without paying for it. The hoodlum yields to these temptations. The boy living in a middle-class neighborhood does not. How can this difference be accounted for? . . . In short, youngsters vary in the extent to which they feel a stake in American society. (16)

In other words, while the motivation to commit crimes does not vary across persons, the extent to which youths have something to lose does. Those who have family members who love and respect them, who do well in school and are attached to teachers, and who have aspirations of going to college, getting a good job, and finding the right spouse are less likely to succumb to the immediate temptations of crime than those with fewer incentives or anchors in conformity.

One of the most comprehensive versions of early control theory was developed by F. Ivan Nye. According to Nye (1958), the problem for theorists was to develop explanations of conformity. Like all control theorists, he took the problem of deviant motivation for granted—deviance does not need any explanation because the immediate benefits are clear, and it frequently gets us what we want with minimal effort:

> It is our position, therefore, that in general, behavior prescribed as delinquent or criminal need not be explained in any positive sense, since it usually results in quicker and easier achievement of goals than the normative behavior. (5)

As a classic statement of control theory, Nye proclaims that the real issue is a theory of conformity rather than a theory of deviance.

Nye (1958) pointed out three sources of control: (1) direct, (2) internalized, and (3) indirect. *Direct control* includes a wide variety of possible restraints on one's deviant impulses and includes formal punishment through the legal system, informal sanctions, such as shame and ridicule, or limiting the opportunity for deviant acts by the direct supervision of parents. *Internal control* occurs when persons have been effectively socialized and have internalized the normative system of their society. Internal control, therefore, consists of moral restraints on conduct because of an internalized belief system or the conscience. *Indirect control* occurs when children have a warm and affectionate relationship with their parents or other conventional adult. For Nye, the institution most suited for the creation of effective controls is the family. Not only is the

family the first social institution that individuals experience, it is the locus of the most intense emotional relationships. If families do their job well, a strong conscience or internal source of control will be created, and other controls will be unnecessary. Even though other social institutions, such as the school and the legal system, can provide some measure of control in the face of weak familial controls, these institutions are much less effective in establishing and maintaining conforming conduct, Nye argued.

We have suggested that control theories of crime are frequently silent with respect to deviant motivation because they assume that humans are asocial beings who need to be taught to conform. Indeed, we have stated that because of this assumption, perhaps the most distinctive feature of control theories is that they are theories of restraint and conformity rather than deviance. However, Nye's perspective breaks somewhat with this tradition (as does the next theory discussed). Nye (1958) proposed that the family may indeed be a source of deviant motivation as well as restraint. If the family is effective in satisfying the needs of the child, he suggested, then "there is less pressure to achieve [these needs] through delinquent behavior" (7–8). The introduction of this remark implies that sometimes youths are motivated to break rules when their needs and wants are not satisfied within the family. That is, unsatisfied wants or desires may provide the motivation for antisocial conduct. (We are soon going to see that the creation of deviant motivation by the failure to meet expected needs and wants is a characteristic of another class of criminological thought—strain theories of crime.) Because we can assume that families have varying abilities to meet the needs of their children (due to things like the attentiveness of parents, their stock of resources, and the number of children), then deviant motivation must not be uniformly distributed. Hence, when the pressure to break rules becomes too much, the kinds of direct and indirect controls alluded to by Nye must spring into action to forestall delinquent behavior.

In the mid-1960s, Walter C. Reckless proposed a control-based theory of crime and deviance that he termed *containment theory* (Reckless 1967, 468–483). Reckless' theory is actually a combination of controls and deviant motivation. He argued that motivation to commit deviant acts could be provided by different "pushes" or "pulls." One could be pushed toward delinquent conduct by psychological factors such as restlessness, rebelliousness, inner tension, impulsivity, or aggressiveness. Pushes toward delinquency can also come from one's social environment and include poverty or a lack of legitimate opportunities. One can be pulled toward delinquency by such factors as media portrayals of crime, the level of crime in one's neighborhood, and the presence of delinquent companions.

Reckless assumed that the pushes and pulls of delinquency are sufficiently strong to produce delinquent behavior unless there is some countervailing source of restraint. To Reckless these controls provide the "containment" of delinquent motivation. Much like Reiss' earlier notion of personal and social controls, Reckless argued that there are two types of restraint or control over deviant inclinations, *inner containment* and *outer containment*. Inner containment is similar to impulse management in that it refers to the capacity of the individual to control themselves by resisting the temptations of crime and deviance and give the self positive direction. One of the most important components of inner containment is the favorable self-concept. Other components include being focused on conventional goals, having realistically high aspirations, having high frustration tolerance, and believing in the legitimacy of norms and laws. Outer containment consists of the capability of social institutions to restrain the conduct of individuals. Social institutions provide effective control to the extent that they have clear and reasonable expectations for the conduct of members, provide them with meaningful and fulfilling roles, and provide nurturing and emotionally supportive relationships. According to Reckless, inner and outer containment are complementary restraining factors. For example, strong inner containment can prevent crime in the presence of

delinquent motivation even when outer containment is weak.

Although there was a rich history of control theories of crime by the mid-1960s, these were eclipsed by the work of Travis Hirschi (1969), whose theory of the social bond quickly became the most prominent form of control theory. By the early 1970s, Hirschi's own version became virtually synonymous with control theory. Hirschi realized, of course, that he was not writing on a clean slate when he devised his theory of the social bond. Explicitly drawing on Durkheim, Toby, Nye, and Reckless, Hirschi (1969) adopted the assumption that the work of delinquency theory was not to explain why delinquency occurs, because "there is much evidence that we would [do it] if we dared." As a control theorist, the question for Hirschi was still "Why don't we do it?" (34)

Very much in the tradition of Durkheim, Hirschi said that what restrains a natural inclination to commit delinquent acts is the social bond that is formed between the individual and society. That is, what controls deviant impulses is the connection one has with a conventional social group. Deviance and crime are more likely when this bond between the individual and society is not formed, is not formed well, or is weakened. The stronger the bond, the tighter the control and the less likely is delinquent behavior. There are four specific elements to Hirschi's social bond: (1) attachment, (2) commitment, (3) involvement, and (4) belief.

Attachment to others can be thought of as the affective element of the social bond. One of the forces that keeps us from committing crimes is that we may lose the good opinion of those near and dear to us. To the extent, then, that we have established close relationships with conventional others (e.g., parents, teachers, neighbors, coaches, conventional peers), and we both admire them and care about their opinions of us, we are less likely to break rules. When we lack this attachment to others, we are not restrained by their censure of our conduct and are more likely to do what we wish.

Commitment can be thought of as the material element of the social bond. It consists of highly prized objects, experiences, or aspirations that we risk losing when we commit delinquent acts. Essentially, commitment represents what Toby (1957) called our stake in conformity. The more commitments one has, the more one has to lose by breaking rules, and the more restrained one is likely to be. Commitments can include things like investing yourself in getting good grades in school, aspiring to college, or planning a career in the armed services. It can also include more mundane things like wanting an allowance or access to the family car. When we have few commitments, we have little to lose, and there is less incentive for us to behave. In the words of the songwriter Bob Dylan, "When you've got nothing, you've got nothing to lose."

Involvement can be thought of as the temporal element of the social bond. Committing criminal acts takes time and energy. As zero sum resources, time and energy are limited, and if we spend them doing one thing, we cannot use them to do another. For example, in doing conventional things like studying, playing sports, engaging in extracurricular activities, and doing volunteer work, we have less time and energy to do deviant things. One of the restraints on our inclination to be "involved" in an antisocial manner is that we are simply too busy being conventional. The logic of involvement confirms the notion, "idle hands are the devil's workshop." In other words, rule breaking is more likely for those with more unstructured free time on their hands.

Belief represents the moral element of the bond. Hirschi argued that one of the things that restrains us from breaking rules is that we believe the rule itself to be legitimate, and that one has a moral obligation to comply with it. To the extent that one has internalized a conventional moral code and believes that it is right to obey the laws, then delinquency and crime are less likely. When the moral legitimacy of norms and laws is in question, however, rule breaking is more likely. For example, we may abstain from stealing other people's property partly because we believe that it is wrong to take things that are not ours. Similarly, we may refrain from substance use simply because

we think that it is wrong to use drugs. On the other hand, I may think that drug use is a "victimless crime," and that the state has no business telling me what I may or may not do to my own body. Rule breaking is more likely in the latter case because the law has no moral authority. Belief about the legitimacy of rules and laws, therefore, operates much like a conscience or superego. It consists of internalized conventional teachings from parents, schools, and other conventional institutions and prevents us from acting in ways that are contrary to prevailing norms.

In his original formulation of the theory, Hirschi (1969) argued that these four elements of the bond are interrelated. The stronger one's conventional attachments are, the more likely one is to have a stock of conventional commitments; the more one is committed to a conventional goal, the more one is involved in conventional activities; and the more one is enmeshed in a network of conventional others and commitments, the more likely one will have internalized a conventional belief system. This also implies that a weakness in one link of the bond will be spread to other dimensions (i.e., one with weak attachments with conventional others is less likely to have developed other elements of the bond). In sum, strengthening one element of the bond will strengthen others, and a weakening of one will lead to a weakening of other elements.

Since its appearance in 1969 with the publication of Hirschi's book, *Causes of Delinquency*, the theory of the social bond has been one of the most prominent theories of crime, and as we suggested, certainly the most dominant version of control theory. There have been numerous attempts to extend and refine Hirschi's original formulation, and it has been one of the most empirically tested theories of delinquent and criminal offending (see reviews in Akers 1997).

Later Control Theories

From 1969, with the publication of *Causes of Delinquency*, until 1990, scholarly work within the control theory tradition generally took the form of empirical tests of extant theory, rather than the development of new theory. In 1990, Travis Hirschi joined with Michael Gottfredson to publish a book, *A General Theory of Crime* (Gottfredson and Hirschi 1990), that presented a different kind of control theory. A statement of that theory by Professors Hirschi and Gottfredson appears as the first essay in this chapter. Basically, they argue that rather than four elements of social control there is one—self-control. Self-control is the capacity that persons have to resist immediate and easy gratification. Those with low self-control are less able to resist the temptation of crime as well as other behaviors that, like crime, provide immediate and easy satisfaction of wants. Self-control is established early in life, is the product of effective child-rearing, and once formed, is relatively stable over time. By "relatively stable," they mean that although a strengthening of self-control may occur over time as one becomes older, those who rank lower than others in self-control early in life will generally rank low in self-control compared with others later in life. Self-control is not, however, the only factor related to crime. Gottfredson and Hirschi argue that there must be available criminal opportunities that can be taken advantage of.

The theory of self-control is fundamentally different from Hirschi's theory of the social bond in a number of dimensions. First, even though in the earlier version of control theory the source of restraint was thought to lie in the relationship between the individual and society, by 1990 he and Gottfredson proposed that the source of inhibition (self-control) lies within the individual. Second, while the theory of the social bond is primarily a theory of delinquency, self-control theory is a general theory of crime. That is, low self-control can account for delinquency during adolescence and criminality as an adult, and that it can account for all crime—property, violent, drug, white-collar, and others. Moreover, those with low self-control are unable to resist any temptation that involves immediate and easy gratification. They are at risk for other deviant and self-destructive acts as well, such as unemployment, sexual promiscuity, obesity, alcoholism, heavy smoking, and gambling. Thus,

the theory of self-control is not only a general theory of crime, but also a general theory of deviance.

Although Hirschi (and Gottfredson along with him) has moved away from the theory of the social bond, two other scholars, Robert J. Sampson and John H. Laub (1993), have attempted to extend classic control theory in an important way. Hirschi (1969) had originally indicated that the social bond was important in controlling delinquency during adolescence. However, Professors Sampson and Laub argue that the social bond is relevant for controlling adult crime as well. In the second essay of this chapter, they (along with Leana C. Allen) present a control theory that they have characterized as an age-graded theory of informal social control.

Their argument is that any theory of crime must account not only for the fact that there is stability in offending over time, but also for the fact that there is a nontrivial amount of change. Not all who commit crimes when young commit crimes as adults. This means that some who have committed crimes in the past subsequently drop out of crime or desist from offending later on. Similarly, some others who may have committed no offenses or only minor ones may initiate or accelerate their involvement in crime later in life. What leads to continuity and change in crime, you may ask? Their answer is that the social bond is not just relevant during adolescence; it is also an important factor for adults. Their position is that criminal behavior can erode an existing social bond, making things worse and leading to additional crime. They also argue, however, that some kinds of noncriminal activity, like having a satisfying marriage and maintaining a stable job, lead to a strengthening of the social bond. This strengthening of the bond can lead to desistance from crime. People can, therefore, change their lives—sometimes for the worse, sometimes for the better.

There is a critical point of difference between Gottfredson and Hirschi's self-control theory and Sampson and Laub's theory of informal social control. Gottfredson and Hirschi would argue that events occurring later in life (e.g., a successful marriage, job stability) have no causal impact on adult criminality because those low in self-control either miss out on or mis-play opportunities for self-improvement. Because they behave impulsively and with little regard for the long-term consequences of their actions, those with low self-control tend to get involved in destructive relationships, have long-term bouts of unemployment, and generally are unable to substantially improve their lot in life. Although a correlation may exist between good jobs, satisfying marriages, and adult criminality (and, correspondingly, between bad jobs, unhappy marriages, and crime), the correlation is spurious rather than causal, they argue. Those with different levels of self-control sort themselves over time into good or bad adult roles and experiences. In other words, it is because of what they are like that those with low self-control fail at marriages, find themselves unemployed, and thus are attracted to the immediate benefits of crime. Low self-control causes a wide range of self-destructive behaviors later in life.

Sampson and Laub would take exception to this. They argue that genuine change is possible, that even the worst offenders (those with the lowest levels of self-control) can nonetheless alter their life course when they are able to strengthen their investment in conformity. Their reanalysis of some older data collected by Sheldon and Eleanor Glueck convinced them that even delinquents committed to crime can turn their lives around. Their position would be that even taking into account initial differences in self-control, those who fall into good marriages or land good jobs, or both, are able to get themselves out of a life of crime. In other words, they believe what Hirschi and Gottfredson do not—that adult events and experiences can serve as turning points in life.

There is now accumulating a great deal of rather technical empirical research directed at determining whether later life events affect criminal behavior after one's initial propensity to offend is taken into consideration. The two essays in this chapter, one by Professors Hirschi and Gottfredson and the other by Professors Laub, Sampson, and Allen, directly spell out these two respective control theory positions.

References

Akers, Ronald L. (1997). *Criminological Theories: Introduction and Evaluation,* Second Edition. Los Angeles: Roxbury.

Durkheim, Emile. [1897] (1951). *Suicide.* Reprint. New York: Free.

——. [1925] (1961). *Moral Education.* Reprint. New York: Free.

Gottfredson, Michael and Travis Hirschi. (1990). *A General Theory of Crime.* Palo Alto, CA: Stanford University Press.

Hirschi, Travis. (1969). *Causes of Delinquency.* Berkeley: University of California Press.

Nye, F. Ivan. (1958). *Family Relationships and Delinquent Behavior.* Westport, CT: Greenwood.

Reckless, Walter C. (1967). *The Crime Problem,* Fourth Edition. New York: Appleton-Century-Crofts.

Reiss, Albert J., Jr. (1951). "Delinquency as the failure of personal and social controls." *American Sociological Review,* 16:196–207.

Sampson, Robert J. and John H. Laub. (1993). *Crime in the Making: Pathways and Turning Points Through Life.* Cambridge, MA: Harvard University Press.

Toby, Jackson. (1957). "Social disorganization and stake in conformity: Complementary factors in the predatory behavior of hoodlums." *Journal of Criminal Law, Criminology, and Police Science,* 48:12–17.

Self-Control Theory

Travis Hirschi
University of Arizona

Michael R. Gottfredson
University of Arizona

In the summer of 1998, three white men in east Texas chained a black man to the rear of a pickup truck and dragged him for several miles along the backroads near his hometown. The victim's remains were found strewn along the road the next morning. When arrested that same day, the three men had in their possession a large quantity of meat they had stolen during a burglary of a packing plant. According to media reports, all had served time in prison and all had been drinking heavily at the time the crimes were committed. In federal law, murder involving race hatred is punishable by death. In Texas law, murder involving kidnapping (forcing the movement of the victim) is also subject to the death penalty. Many calls for speedy execution of the offenders were heard in the days that followed. These calls were not limited to one area of the country or to one ethnic group. In fact, a good guess would be that about 95 percent of the U.S. population favored the death penalty in this case. Through his lawyer, one of the arrested men quickly denied participation in the act.

A theory of crime should be able to make sense of these facts, however rare and horrible they may be. A general theory should also make sense of the far more common crimes and delinquencies at the other end of the seriousness scale: truancy, shoplifting, underage smoking, bicycle theft, cheating on tests.

What are "the facts" in this case? You may have heard that theories favor some facts and ignore others. If so, what you have heard is true. Facts accepted by one theory may be rejected or ignored by other theories. Self-control theory focuses on the typical features of criminal acts and on the criminal record of the offender. In the case in question, self-control theory would emphasize the following: (1). The offenders had long records of involvement in criminal and deviant acts. (2). They did not limit themselves to one kind of crime, but engaged in a wide variety of criminal and deviant acts, even in a short period of time (burglary, murder, kidnapping, drinking excessively, driving under the influence). (3). Everyone believes that these acts are criminal or deviant and that some of them deserve severe punishment. (4). The potential costs to the offenders of the crimes described are considerable and long term; the benefits are minimal and of short duration. (5). Despite the enormity of the crimes described, no special skill or knowledge is required to commit them. (6). Although three offenders were involved in these crimes, they did not act as an organized group. Indeed, one offender took the first opportunity to claim that he did not participate in the most serious offense.

Self-control theory would largely ignore the two features of the homicide that made it so newsworthy: its unusual brutality and its element of race hatred. Self-control theory pays little attention to the seriousness of crimes and is not interested in the motives of offenders. It is also relatively uninterested in the social or economic backgrounds of the perpetrators. The theory would lead us to guess that the offenders in this case were uneducated and unskilled, but it would do so because it assumes that people committing such crimes are unlikely to have exerted the effort required to obtain an education or a high level of occupational skill, not because poverty forced them into the acts in question. In short, self-control theory takes the social and economic conditions of offenders as a reflection of their tendency to offend, not as a cause of their offending. By the same token, the theory would pay little attention to the time and place of the crime. In its view, there is nothing special with respect to crime about east Texas or the end of the twentieth century.

Which of the facts listed is most important? We begin to answer this question by asking another: What fact best predicts crime? The answer is previous crime. If you want to know the likelihood that a person will commit criminal or deviant acts in the future, you can do no better than count the different kinds of criminal and deviant acts he or she has committed in the past. This is the central fact on which self-control theory is based. It says to the self-control theorist that all criminal and deviant acts, at whatever age they are committed, whatever their level of seriousness, have something in common. It says also that people differ in the degree to which they are attracted to or repelled by whatever it is crime and deviance have to offer.

We know that criminal and deviant acts have something in common because participation in any one of them predicts participation in any one of the others. People who smoke and drink are more likely than people who do not smoke or drink to use illegal drugs, to cut classes, to cheat on tests, to break into houses, to rob and steal. People who rob and steal are more likely than people who do not rob and steal to smoke and drink, use illegal drugs, break into houses, and cheat on tests. What do robbery, theft, burglary, cheating, truancy, and drug use (and the many forms of criminal and deviant behavior not listed) have in common? They are all quick and easy ways of getting what one wants. They are all also, in the long run, dangerous to one's health, safety, reputation, and economic well-being.

The features common to various crimes and deviant acts would not cause them to predict one another unless these features were reflected in some relatively enduring tendency of individuals. People must differ in the likelihood that they will take the quick and easy way regardless of long-term consequences. This enduring difference between people the theory calls *self-control*. Those who have a high degree of self-control avoid acts potentially damaging to their future prospects, whatever the current benefits these acts seem to promise. Those with a low degree of self-control are easily swayed by current benefits and tend to forget future costs. Most people are between these extremes, sometimes doing things they know they should not do, other times being careful not to take unnecessary risks for short-term advantage.

So, a *fact* at the heart of the theory is the ability of previous criminal and deviant acts to predict future criminal and deviant acts. The *concept* at the heart of the theory is self-control, defined as the tendency to avoid acts whose long-term costs exceed their immediate or short-term benefits. This concept, in our view, accounts for the important facts about crime. In our view, it also questions the meaning of the facts claimed by competing theories. Where did our version of self-control theory come from?

Background and History

For a hundred years or so, criminologists, social workers, and ordinary citizens have tried to draw a clear line between the delinquencies of children and the crimes of adults. As a result, juveniles and adults have separate justice systems, universities offer separate courses in juvenile delinquency and criminology, and theories continue to focus on the activities of one group and to ignore the other. Beginning in the 1960s, academics became interested in the connection between juvenile delinquency and adult crime, often called the *issue of maturational reform*. It was then widely believed that most delinquents quit delinquency as they enter adulthood, with only a small number going on to criminal careers. Although reform was thought to be common, explanations of it tended to be vague and unsatisfactory. In most accounts, the justice system was given little credit. Indeed, before Robert Martinson (1974a) popularized the view that "nothing works" in the justice system, two famous delinquency researchers, Sheldon and Eleanor Glueck (1940), had concluded that reform was simply the work of Mother Nature and Father Time.

Because reform was thought to be common, it was seen as a serious problem for the delinquency theories popular at the time. The most popular was what is now called *strain theory*, the theory behind the Great Society and War on Poverty programs of the 1960s and 1970s. This theory said that people turn to crime because they cannot realize the American Dream through conventional means. So, according to the theory, poverty, discrimination, and lack of opportunity are major causes of crime. This sounded plausible to many Americans and to most academics. But the theory had an obvious flaw. It could perhaps explain why some kids become delinquent, but it could not explain why they stop being delinquent. It predicted too much delinquency. Poverty, discrimination, and lack of opportunity do not go away in the middle teens. They are still there when delinquency begins to decline.

Social control theory was developed in part to remedy this defect. This theory says that delinquent acts result when an individual's bond to society is weak or broken. In one version (Hirschi 1969), the bond to society, the individual's ties to institutions and other people, is made up of four elements: (1). *Attachment,* the bond of respect, love, or affection. The more the adolescent cares for the opinion of others, the less likely he or she is to commit delinquent acts. (2). *Commitment,* the bond of aspiration, investment, or ambition. The greater the individual's stake in conformity (Toby 1957), the greater the individual's social and personal capital (Coleman 1990), the more he or she has to lose by the commission of delinquent acts. (3). *Involvement,* the restriction of opportunity to commit delinquent acts by engaging in conventional activities. (4). *Belief,* the bond to conformity created by the view that criminal and delinquent acts are morally wrong. Hirschi assumed that these causes could change over the life course, and could thus account for corresponding changes in delinquency.

Social control theory was testable in ways not true of earlier theories. When tested, it worked reasonably well. Kids attached to their parents, kids attached to school, ambitious and diligent kids were less likely to commit delinquent acts whether delinquency was measured by self-reports or police records. Initial research on the theory did not, however, test its ability to account for change in delinquency over time.

Hirschi's exposition and test of social control theory was published in 1969 as *Causes of Delinquency.* In 1974, Robert Martinson published his famous article just mentioned, "What Works—Questions and Answers about Prison Reform," concluding that indeed nothing works. In the same year, he delivered at a conference a paper titled "The Myth of Treatment and the Reality of Life Process." The second paper attempted to deal with issues raised by his first paper and by social control theories of delinquency.

Martinson saw that the failure of treatment said something important about the theories of crime then dominant in the social and behavioral sciences. Put bluntly, the failure of treatment said there was something wrong with the theories of crime on which the treatment enterprise was based. To illustrate this inadequacy, Martinson turned to the relation between age and crime: 140 years earlier, the French statistician Quetelet (1833) had said: ". . . among all the causes that influence the growth and abatement of the penchant for crime, age is without question the most energetic."

Martinson admitted that we did not know the shape of the entire age-crime curve, but he thought we knew enough to use it to judge theories. We knew when crime tends to begin and we knew something about the peak age. We also knew that what he called *drop out* after the peak age is quite common, and that complete remission usually takes place sometime before the end of life. Another thing we knew, he said, was that there are chronic or persistent offenders. This "knowledge" allowed Martinson to sketch a hypothetical age-crime curve for two societies (see Figure 1).

Martinson then applied the major theories of delinquency to these facts, quickly concluding that none of them was adequate to the task. He then introduced a theory he thought might be useful in this effort, which he called "A New Beginning" and "commend[ed] to the attention" of his audience. This was social control theory. The question was whether the concepts of attachment, commitment, involvement, and belief could actually account for the hypothetical age curves Martinson had before him.

Figure 1
Hypothetical Curves of the Age Distributions of Acts
Definable as Deliquency or Crime in Birth Cohorts in Two Societies

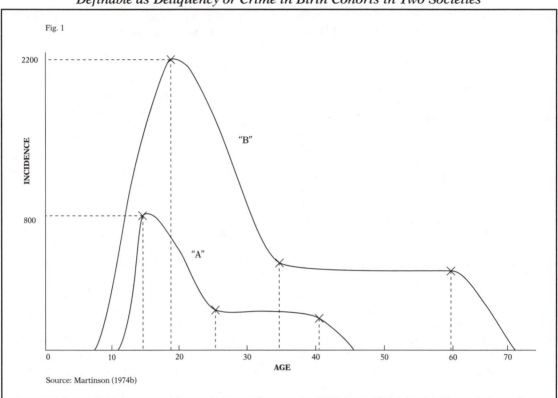

Source: Martinson (1974b)

After much effort, he concluded that they could not. Martinson's (1974b) conclusions deserve repeating here.

(1) The idea that criminal offenders may be induced to desist from offending through correctional treatment is a myth.

(2) The failure of correctional treatment is a failure of the idea that crime is analogous to a disease which may be cured by appropriate treatment of the individual.

(3) An adequate theory of. . . crime must be able to account for the complex relationship between crime and age, and should therefore include variables reflecting variations in the life course of both offenders and nonoffenders.

(4) No existing sociological theory is able to account for such age distributions, although control theory has the potential to do so.

(5) Control theory must be expanded to include: a) the deterrent effect of the threat of legal punishment; and b) a notion of social damage which is adequate to account for the persistence of offenders in crime. (16–17)

Martinson himself later expanded on the idea of social damage, arguing in a book-length unpublished work that prison may in fact delay maturation by shielding offenders from ordinary social processes. Attempts at treatment, therefore, extend the criminal career beyond its normal age limits.

We did not agree with Martinson's idea of delayed maturation, arguing that such an effect of treatment was contrary to his position that treatment does not work, one way or the other. (If treatment does not make offenders better, it also does not make them worse [Hirschi 1975].) We did agree, however, that no evidence had shown that change in the strength of social bonds actually accounts for the reformation of juvenile delinquents. It seemed necessary to look more closely at the connection between age and crime. Does crime follow the path described by Martinson?

In 1983, we published our answer to this question in a paper titled "Age and the Explanation of Crime." This paper rediscovers what Quetelet 150 years earlier had called the most "energetic" cause of crime, and what the English physician Charles Goring 70 years earlier (1913) had called "a law of nature."

This law of nature is illustrated in Figure 2, which shows that the facts are more dramatic but less complex than Martinson guessed them to be. Crime rates vary from group to group and from one society to another, and they often change over time. But wherever the place and whatever the time, they are highest in adolescence and early adulthood, decline rapidly from peak levels, and continue to decline throughout life. This appears to be true for all, or almost all, crimes. It appears to be true as well for behavior similar to crime: accidents, legal drug use, promiscuous sexual activity. It appears to be true for all groups and societies, at all times and places, even in prisons. It is true whether crime is measured by police records or by asking people to report their own delinquent acts.

At the time we published our article, we were restricted largely to measures of crime based on police, court, or prison records—so-called official data. Although self-report measures of crime and delinquency had been in use for some time, they had not yet been applied in a convincing way to the age question. This allowed doubters to argue that the decline in crime with age shown in official data was evidence only that the abil-

Figure 2
Arrests for Burglary by Age, United States, 1970, 1974, 1983

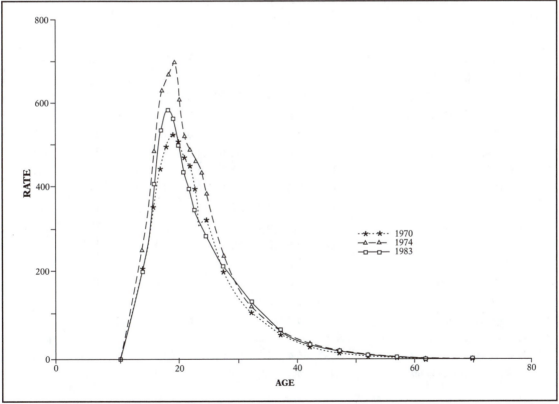

ity of offenders to avoid detection improves as they get older. We believed facts already available undermined such skepticism. Criminal, deviant, and reckless acts differ greatly in the likelihood that they will be observed or recorded, yet almost all decline with age. Automobile accidents, for example, are in important ways analogous to crimes. They may result from short-term advantage (speeding, drinking, inattention) and may produce long-term ill effects. Precisely because they are considered accidents, those involved feel no need to conceal them—and could not even if they wished to do so. The decline in automobile accidents with age, which is much like the decline in crime with age, could not be accounted for by a quirk of measurement. We therefore predicted that self-report measures would confirm the age-crime relation described by official data. Our prediction turned out to be true, something all too rare in social science (see Table 1).

Once recognized, these facts changed everything. It was no longer meaningful to ask, why do delinquents quit? because they do not. Active, high-rate offenders slow down with age, but so does everyone else. Differences between people in their criminal and deviant behavior seen early in life are still present long after the peak ages of crime are behind them. It was no longer meaningful to ask how the criminal justice system changes, for good or for ill, the tendency to offend—because it does not. It was no longer meaningful to require sociological theories to explain the decline in crime with age. The decline is found everywhere. It, therefore, cannot be explained by factors that differ from one society to another.

Table 1
Self-reported Illegal Behavior by Age and Sex: Percent Reporting One or More Offenses

Offense	17	18	19	20	21	22	23	Chi²	Gamma
Males									
Hit Supervisor	3.8	1.8	.1	1.1	.7	2.5	1.3	18.2*	−.38
Fight at Work/School	16.2	14.1	7.9	10.2	5.3	8.7	6.2	32.7*	−.27
Gang Fight	20.3	15.9	11.6	12.0	7.5	8.7	3.1	47.7*	−.32
Hurt Someone Badly	15.6	14.8	9.7	6.4	4.5	4.1	1.6	53.6*	−.38
Robbery	4.2	3.0	1.5	1.2	.0	1.1	.3	21.7*	−.52
Steal < $50	41.2	39.9	37.3	32.1	31.3	24.3	21.7	31.8*	−.18
Steal > $50	8.9	7.3	4.2	7.5	5.7	6.2	2.1	12.1	−.17
Shoplift	39.0	28.8	22.8	16.4	19.4	10.4	11.5	102.8*	−.36
Joyride	5.2	4.2	3.2	2.8	1.2	.5	.0	18.2*	−.39
Steal Car Parts	11.5	10.2	6.0	6.3	3.7	3.3	2.3	31.0*	−.33
Trespass	34.0	25.8	16.4	19.3	9.2	10.4	5.7	111.3*	−.40
Arson	3.2	2.2	.5	.7	.1	.5	.0	20.3*	−.59
Damage School Property	19.5	14.5	4.9	4.3	3.1	2.7	.8	113.0*	−.56
Damage Work Property	10.4	10.7	5.5	6.7	3.1	4.4	3.1	25.4*	−.29
Any Aggressive Offense	34.9	28.0	21.8	20.6	13.8	17.0	8.7	77.2*	−.32
Any Property Offense	68.5	59.6	47.8	46.4	42.1	31.0	27.7	140.2*	−.36
Any Offense	74.3	65.4	54.6	53.1	45.7	40.7	29.7	149.8*	−.38
Sample Size (Weighted)	593	289	246	269	241	122	127		

Table
(continued)

Offense	17	18	19	Age 20	21	22	23	Chi²	Gamma
Females									
Hit Supervisor	1.6	.1	.2	.0	.2	.0	.0	18.8*	−.80
Fight at Work/School	9.9	7.2	7.1	6.3	6.1	3.2	7.4	11.4	−.16
Gang Fight	10.9	9.1	8.6	3.0	3.2	2.7	1.6	45.3*	−.38
Hurt Someone Badly	2.8	1.9	1.0	1.1	.5	.6	.7	12.3	−.41
Robbery	.7	1.0	1.0	.2	.1	.2	.0	5.6	−.34
Steal < $50	23.2	23.0	19.3	19.2	13.3	16.4	11.2	23.5*	−.17
Steal > $50	1.6	1.0	1.1	.6	2.3	1.1	1.6	4.0	−.01
Shoplift	26.6	18.2	15.4	12.7	8.0	11.8	7.0	80.4*	−.35
Joyride	2.3	1.9	2.0	.8	.4	.0	.9	9.8	−.36
Steal Car Parts	1.9	1.0	1.3	.1	.6	.0	1.3	9.5	−.35
Trespass	18.8	9.6	10.5	8.2	6.1	4.4	2.9	69.6*	−.38
Arson	.3	.0	.4	.1	.0	.0	.2	3.2	−.30
Damage School Property	6.4	3.3	2.5	1.5	1.4	1.1	.2	34.7*	−.50
Damage Work Property	1.9	1.7	1.1	2.0	1.1	1.7	1.1	2.0	−.09
Any Aggressive Offense	19.5	15.0	14.6	9.3	8.5	5.4	9.3	44.7*	−.28
Any Property Offense	45.0	34.7	29.3	28.3	18.9	22.7	16.8	104.1*	−.31
Any Offense	50.8	40.1	35.9	32.1	25.3	25.2	24.3	98.3*	−.29
Sample Size (Weighted)	676	318	304	314	306	157	147		

* p < .05

Source: Osgood et al. (1989, 398)

So, we began with the idea that a theory of crime must explain the tendency of offenders to reform with age. We ended up with facts suggesting that reform is not the issue. Criminal activity declines with age, but it declines for everyone. True reform is too rare to show itself in statistics on crime. What was needed was a theory capable of explaining persistent differences in the tendency to offend over the life course.

The Theory

To construct such a theory, it was first necessary to distinguish between crime and criminality, a distinction forced upon us by the age distribution of crimes. Crimes rise and fall during the life course, but *differences* in the tendency to commit criminal acts do not follow this pattern. Children in trouble with teachers in the 2nd and 3rd grades are more likely to be in trouble with juvenile authorities at 15 and 16; they are more likely to serve prison terms in their 20s; they are more likely to have trouble with their families and jobs at all ages.

So, to discuss the facts sensibly, we need something that may change with age and something that may not. The changeable element is crime. Crimes are acts or events that take place at specific points in space and time. We began this chapter describing an event in east Texas in the summer of 1998. Three men tied another man to a battered pickup truck and dragged him to his death.

That is a crime: murder. A witness in a criminal trial lies under oath. That is a crime: perjury. A man drives after drinking ten cans of beer. That is a crime: driving under the influence. Crimes are very common. Each year in the United States, the police report about 15 million arrests to the Federal Bureau of Investigation (FBI).

The unchangeable element is criminality, the tendency of people to engage in or refrain from criminal acts. Because criminality is a propensity or tendency, it cannot be counted, but it can be observed or measured. From such observation, we know that few people would allow themselves to be involved in the murder of a stranger. (In context, the oft-repeated statement that "everybody does it" is obviously foolish. It is usually foolish elsewhere as well.) We know that more people might, under the right circumstances, commit perjury. And we know that many would and do drive after drinking more than the law allows. In fact, experience shows that everyone is capable of criminal or deviant acts. More meaningfully, however, it shows that some are more likely than others actually to commit them. Criminality is a matter of degree.

With this distinction, the task of theory is clear: It is to identify and explain criminality and to relate it to the commission of criminal acts.

We begin by looking more closely at crimes and deviant acts. What do murder, perjury, and driving under the influence (and theft, assault, cheating on tests, burglary, robbery, forgery, and fraud) have in common? The Chinese have a saying: "Crime is as easy as falling down a mountain." Indeed, most crimes require no special learning or knowledge. Children invent them without help. Young people are their major practitioners. A fiendish and relatively complex murder may be committed by (1). wrapping a chain around an outnumbered man; (2). hooking it to a pickup bumper; (3). driving away. Most people know or could learn on the spot how to wrap and hook a chain, and most adults know how to drive. Perjury may be accomplished by saying "No" when what actually happened would require "Yes." The capacity for perjury is thus present the mo-

ment the child is able to affirm or deny the occurrence of an event. Driving drunk requires only the ability to drink and the ability to drive. The highest rates of drunk driving are found among those still learning these skills.

Most crimes take little time or effort. They are rarely the product of lengthy and elaborate preparation. Among our examples, drunk driving appears to be the most time-consuming but would not normally be considered hard work. In the United States, homicide is most often committed with a gun. In the typical case, the decision to aim and fire is made instantaneously, on the spot. Compared to this, our east Texas homicide was unusually difficult, possibly requiring several minutes to accomplish. Perjury too may take only a split second. The consequences of perjury may be complicated, but the difficulties following the commission of a criminal or deviant act should not be confused with the act itself.

Indeed, another characteristic of criminal and deviant acts is that they entail just such long-term complications, difficulties, or costs. These costs or penalties are called *sanctions*. Following the British philosopher Jeremy Bentham ([1789] 1970), we identify four kinds of sanctions. *Physical* sanctions are those that follow naturally from the act, without the active intervention of others. Examples include hangovers and diminished health from the consumption of drugs, disease from promiscuous sexual activity, injuries from the actions of victims attempting to defend their persons or property, and diminished earning capacity from repeated truancy. *Moral* or *social* sanctions are those imposed by family, friends, neighbors, employers, clients, and constituents in the court of public opinion. They include divorce, shaming, shunning, and reduced responsibility and trust. *Political* or *legal* sanctions are those imposed by governments and organizations for violations of law. They include fines, imprisonment, and even execution. They also include expulsion and impeachment. *Religious* sanctions are those imposed by supernatural authorities, now and in the hereafter. Their form varies from one religion to another, but they are usually pictured as long-term and serious.

We often refer to the *risk* of legal and moral sanctions because they cannot be imposed unless the offender is convicted or caught in the act. This suggests the possibility of cost-free crime and deviance, depending on the luck of offenders or their ability to avoid detection. Indeed, religious sanctions are sometimes explained as an effort to solve this problem, as devices that punish deviant behavior whether or not it is seen by others. Self-control theory does not require supernatural or religious sanctions for several reasons: (1). It emphasizes often serious physical or natural sanctions whose application does not require third-party knowledge or intervention; (2). It emphasizes the generality of deviance, the tendency of people to repeat offenses and to be involved in a wide variety of them. As the level and variety of deviant activity increase, detection and automatic penalties become more and more certain; (3). It emphasizes the spontaneous and unplanned nature of criminal and deviant acts, a characteristic inconsistent with successful long-term concealment.

We now see another reason that reckless, deviant, criminal, and sinful acts tend to go together, to be committed by the same people: They all produce potentially painful consequences. Distinctions among deviant acts on the basis of the sanction system most concerned with them are to some extent arbitrary and misleading. Murder is a crime punished by the legal system, but it is also reckless, deviant, and sinful. In fact, one reason it is judged a crime is to control the natural tendency of the victim's family and friends to seek their own revenge. Perjury (lying under oath) is sometimes said to be the quintessential criminal act, but lying in other contexts is also subject to natural, social, and religious penalties. Driving under the influence of alcohol has only recently become a major concern of the criminal justice system. Not long ago, it was widely practiced and considered only mildly deviant. This should not be taken to mean that it was not punished. Whatever its legal or moral status, few acts are more reckless than drunk driving. Since the invention of the automobile, in the

United States alone, drunk driving has killed hundreds of thousands of its practitioners (as well as countless others).

The idea that murder, perjury, drunk driving, and marijuana smoking (and all other criminal and delinquent acts) have something in common is sometimes met by such statements as: "Marijuana smoking is not murder!" "Sex is not shoplifting!" "Perjury is not driving under the influence!" Self-control theory does not say these acts are the same thing. It says they have something in common. This common element may be identified more clearly by focusing on the logical structure of criminal and deviant acts.

The logical structure of an act is the set of conditions necessary for it to occur. Each distinct criminal or deviant act has a unique set of necessary conditions. For example, smoking marijuana requires attractive (for reasons of cost, quality, and reputation) and available marijuana. It also requires an offender unrestrained by the consequences of marijuana use. Homicide is more complex. It requires interaction between an offender and a victim, an offender with the means of taking the life of another, an offender insufficiently restrained to prevent the crime, a victim unable to remove himself from the scene, and absence of life-saving third-party intervention. (Life-saving intervention would make the crime attempted murder or aggravated assault.) Perjury is ultimately simple. It requires only a question asked of a person who has sworn to tell the truth, where that person is insufficiently restrained to prevent the crime. Driving under the influence combines the logical structure of two distinct acts. It requires a drug (usually alcohol) that is available and attractive to the offender, a vehicle that is accessible to the offender, an offender capable of operating the vehicle while intoxicated, and an offender insufficiently restrained to prevent the crime.

The element common to these acts (and all other criminal and deviant acts) is an unrestrained offender, a person willing to risk long-term costs for immediate personal benefits. Self-control theory says there is nothing extraordinarily attractive about the benefits of crime, that they may be found in non-criminal activities as well, and that in practice crime is not an efficient method of producing them. It says further that awareness and appreciation of the benefits of crime are not restricted to offenders. Everyone enjoys money, sex, power, excitement, ease, euphoria, and revenge. Everyone can see that crime provides a direct and easy way of obtaining them. So, according to the theory, the difference between offenders and nonoffenders is in their awareness of and concern for the long-term costs of crime—such things as arrest, prison, disgrace, disease, and even eternal damnation.

The idea that crime satisfies special needs and that offenders are strongly motivated to accomplish their purposes is accepted in many theories of crime and discussions of crime control policy. The source of this idea may be the obvious imbalance between the short-term and uncertain rewards of crime and its long-term and more certain penalties. Offenders often appear to trade a cow for a bag of beans, to risk powerful positions for brief sexual pleasures or small monetary gains. To strike such bargains, the logic goes, offenders must be driven by emotions (seductions and compulsions) of considerable strength. Self-control theory solves this "problem" by reducing the offender's awareness of or concern for the long term. What distinguishes offenders from others is not the strength of their appetites but their freedom to enjoy the quick and easy and ordinary pleasures of crime without undue concern for the pains that may follow them.

From the nature of crime, and acts analogous to crime, we thus infer the nature of criminality. People who engage in crime are people who tend to neglect long-term consequences. They are, or tend to be, children of the moment. They have what we call low self-control.

Where does low self-control come from? All of us, it appears, are born with the ability to use force and fraud in pursuit of our private goals. Small children can and do lie, bite, whine, hit, and steal. They also sometimes consider horrendous crimes they are too small to carry off. By the age of 8 or 10, most of us learn to control such tendencies

to the degree necessary to get along at home and school. Others, however, continue to employ the devices of children, to engage in behavior inappropriate to their age. The differences observed at ages 8 to 10 tend to persist from then on. Good children remain good. Not so good children remain a source of concern to their parents, teachers, and eventually to the criminal justice system. These facts lead to the conclusion that low self-control is natural and that *self-control* is *acquired* in the early years of life.

Children presumably learn from many sources to consider the long-range consequences of their acts. One important source we previously called natural sanctions, penalties that follow more or less automatically from certain forms of behavior. The list is long. It include burns from hot stoves, bruises from falling down stairs or out of trees, and injuries from efforts to take things thought by others to belong to them. Obviously, natural sanctions can be dangerous and painful. In fact, the natural system is so unforgiving that parents and other adults spend a lot of their time protecting children from it.

But the major sources of self-control, in our view, are the actions of parents or other responsible adults. Parents who care for their children watch them as best they can. When they *see* their children doing something they should not do, they correct, admonish, or punish them. The logical structure of successful socialization thus has four necessary conditions: care, monitor, recognize (deviant behavior), and correct. When all of these conditions are present, the child presumably learns to avoid acts with long-term negative consequences, whatever their legal or moral status. When any one of them is missing, continued low self-control may be the result. Delinquency research provides strong support for these conclusions. It shows that the greater the attachment of the parent to the child, the lower the likelihood of delinquency. It shows that careful supervision and adequate discipline are among the most important predictors of nondelinquency. By extension, this child-rearing model goes a long way toward explaining all of the major family factors in crime: neglect, abuse, single parents, large number of children, parental criminality. All of these are measures of the extent of parental concern for the child or are conditions that affect the ability of the parent to monitor and correct the child's behavior. As would be expected, they are also major predictors of behaviors we call analogous to crime: truancy, quitting school, smoking, excessive drinking, and job instability.

We are now ready to use the theory to explain criminal, deviant, and reckless acts. Persons deficient in self-control are attracted to acts that provide immediate and apparently certain pleasure with minimal effort, whatever their collateral consequences. Criminal, deviant, and reckless acts fit this definition. In many, force and fraud speed up the process and reduce the effort required to produce the desired result. In others, mind-altering chemicals provide shortcuts to happiness. In still others, the pleasure inheres in the act itself or in the risks it entails.

Persons sufficient in self-control avoid such acts because they find that their collateral consequences outweigh their benefits. Force and fraud in the service of self-interest are opposed by the law and by most people (including those lacking self-control). Drugs entail risks to self and others inconsistent with long-term goals. And reckless behavior gains its charm from the very possibility that it may put an end to future prospects, whatever they may be.

Theories explain facts by stating general propositions from which specific facts may be derived. For example, in Newton's theory, apples fall to earth *because* every particle of matter in the universe is attracted by every other particle. The larger the particle, the stronger the attraction. We often condense this explanation into one word, *gravity,* but the truth and value of the explanation are not reduced by this practice. By the same logic, in self-control theory, people commit criminal acts because they fail to consider their long-term consequences. This explanation, too, may be condensed into a single concept, (low) self-control, but its truth and value are not reduced by this practice.

Other theories of course also explain crime by stating general principles from which specific acts can be derived. For example, traditional strain theory would say that people commit criminal acts because they have been blocked from attaining success by noncriminal or conventional means. And social learning theory might explain crime by saying that people commit criminal acts because they have learned such behavior from their peers. Choosing among theories is not, then, so much a matter of their logic as of their relative ability to predict the facts about crime and criminals.

Tests of Self-Control Theory

Our version of self-control theory was published in 1990, which makes it a new or contemporary theory. Given the traditions of the field, new theories are by definition untested. They are hypotheses or conjectures whose fate depends on the results of research not yet conducted. This suggests that new theories are more problematic than theories that have withstood efforts to test or falsify them. Actually, the reverse should be true. If theories are logical systems based on current understandings of the facts, new theories should be especially consistent with the results of current research. And the use of old theories to explain facts they once ignored or denied should be viewed with considerable suspicion.

Self-control theory is based on and, therefore, "predicts" the following facts:

- Differences between high- and low-rate offenders persist over the life course. Children ranked on the frequency of their delinquent acts will be ranked similarly later in life. This is not to say "once a criminal always a criminal." It is to say that differences in tendencies to commit crime, like differences in height, maintain themselves over long periods of time. This is among the best-established facts in criminology (Nagin and Paternoster 1991; Gendreau, Little, and Goggin 1996).

- Efforts to treat or rehabilitate offenders do not produce the desired results. The search for effective treatment programs of course continues. But research continues to show that once tendencies to engage in crime and delinquency have been established, successful treatment is, at a minimum, extraordinarily difficult (Martinson 1974a; Sechrest et al. 1979. For a strongly contrary view, see Andrews et al. 1990).

- Intervention efforts in childhood offer the greatest promise of success in crime reduction (Tremblay et al. 1992).

- The law enforcement or criminal justice system has little effect on the volume of criminal behavior. Offenders do not attend to increases in the number of police or in the severity of penalties for violations of law (Andrews et al. 1990).

- Crimes may be prevented by increasing the effort required to commit them (Murray 1995).

- Crime declines with age among all groups of offenders and in almost all types of offending (Cohen and Land 1987; Gottfredson and Hirschi 1990).

- Offenders do not specialize in particular forms of crime. Career criminals are extremely rare (Wolfgang et al. 1972; Britt 1994).

- Offenders have higher accident, illness, and death rates than nonoffenders (Farrington and Junger 1995).

- Offenders are more likely than nonoffenders to use legal and illegal drugs (Boyum and Kleiman 1995).

- Offenders are more frequently involved in noncriminal forms of deviance (Evans et al. 1997).

- Offenders are more weakly attached than nonoffenders to restrictive institutions and long-term careers—families, schools, jobs (Glueck and Glueck 1968).

- Compared to nonoffenders, offenders are disadvantaged with respect to intellectual or cognitive skills (Hirschi and Hindelang 1977).

- Family structure, family relations, and childrearing practices are important predictors of deviant behavior (Glueck and Glueck 1950; Loeber and Stouthamer-Loeber 1986).

In our view, these facts have been repeatedly confirmed by research. In our view, self-control theory is consistent with all of them, something that cannot be said for any of its competitors.

Policy Implications of the Theory

The control theory approach to policy is to analyze the features of the criminal act and the characteristics of offenders and to pattern prevention efforts accordingly. The major relevant characteristics of offenders are youthfulness, limited cognitive skills, and low self-control. Because the rates of such important crimes as burglary, robbery, theft, shoplifting, and vandalism all peak in mid- to late adolescence and fall to half their peak levels as early as the mid-twenties, effective crime control policies will naturally focus on the interests and activities of teenagers. Because the cognitive skills of offenders are relatively limited, their criminal acts are typically simple and easily traced. As a result, policies targeting sophisticated offenders or career criminals are unnecessarily complex and inefficient. Because offenders have low self-control, they are easily deterred by increasing the immediate difficulties and risks of criminal acts and are generally unaffected by changes in the long-term costs of criminal behavior. Consequently, steering wheel locks are more effective than increased penalties in reducing auto theft, and moving in groups is more effective than increased police presence in preventing robbery.

The characteristics of criminal acts relevant to their prevention have been listed earlier. Crimes provide immediate, obvious benefit, are easily accomplished, and require little skill, planning, or persistence. They involve no driving force beyond the satisfaction of everyday human desires. Because people do not suffer when criminal opportunities are unavailable to them, crimes can be prevented by making them more complex or difficult. For example, increasing the cost of alcohol or banning its use in particular settings will often produce the desired result with little effort. Guarding parking lots or apartment complexes can also be effective in preventing theft and vandalism.

Although it focuses on an element common to all forms of crime and deviance, low self-control, self-control theory actually supports an offense-specific approach to crime prevention. Procedures for preventing one type of crime may be inapplicable to others. Effective efforts to control hijacking have no impact on vandalism or burglary. Offense-specific approaches begin by analyzing the conditions necessary for a particular act to occur. Graffiti, for example, requires spray paint and large, accessible, paintable, generally observable surfaces that are unguarded for a predictable period of time. It also requires an unrestrained offender. Graffiti may be controlled by removing any one of its necessary physical conditions or by altering the behavior of unrestrained offenders. Clearly, efforts directed at offenders—treatment, deterrence, incapacitation—will be highly inefficient compared to programs that restrict access to paint and to paintable surfaces.

Self-control theory is based on the idea that behavior is governed by its consequences. As we have seen, this idea is also central to the criminal justice system, according to which crime may be reduced by increasing the likelihood and severity of such legal sanctions as fines and imprisonment. Nevertheless, self-control theory leads to the conclusion that the formal criminal justice system can play only a minor role in the prevention and control of crime. Because potential offenders do not consider the long-term legal consequences of their acts, modification of these consequences will have little effect on their behavior. Because criminal acts are so quickly and easily accomplished, they are only rarely directly observed by agents of the criminal justice system. As a result, even large increases in the number of such agents would have minimal effect on the rates of most crimes.

These and other considerations led us to advance the following recommendations for crime control policy (from Gottfredson and Hirschi 1995):

(1). Do not attempt to control crime by incapacitating adults. A major factor in the decision to incarcerate offenders is the number of prior offenses they have committed. The result is that adults are much more likely to be imprisoned than adolescents. Most people would agree that prior records should be considered, but the age distribution of crime (see Figure 2) shows us that putting adults in prison is ineffective because by then it is too late. They are too old. The average age of persons sentenced to prison is the late twenties, more than ten years after the peak age of crime.

(2). Do not attempt to control the crime rate by rehabilitating adults. As has been shown above, there are two very good arguments against treatment programs for adult offenders. The first is the age effect, which makes treatment unnecessary. The second is that no treatment program for adults has been shown to be effective. If nothing but time works, it seems ill-advised to pretend otherwise.

(3). Do not attempt to control crime by altering the penalties available to the criminal justice system. Legal penalties do not have the desired effect because offenders do not consider them. Increasing their certainty and severity may make citizens and policymakers feel better about the justice system, but it will have a highly limited effect on the decisions of offenders.

(4). Restrict the unsupervised activities of teenagers. Crime requires opportunity and unrestrained individuals. Much can be gained from limiting access of teenagers to guns, cars, alcohol, unwatched walls, unattended houses, and to each other. One of the great success stories of the last quarter of the century was the reduction in fatal auto accidents that followed increases in the drinking age. Curfews, truancy prevention programs, school uniforms, and license restrictions—all of these have potential value for the same reason.

(5). Limit proactive policing including police sweeps, police stings, intensive arrest programs, and aggressive drug policies. Control theory sees crime as a product of human weakness. It sees no point in creating opportunities for crime in order to identify those suffering from such weakness. It sees no point in exploiting such weakness merely for the benefit of the law enforcement establishment.

(6). Question the characterization of crime offered by agents of the criminal justice system and uncritically repeated by the media. The evidence suggests that offenders are not the dedicated, inventive, and clever professionals law enforcement and the media often make them out to be. In fact, control theory questions the very existence of huge juvenile gangs and highly organized criminal syndicates. Where, the theory asks, do people unable to resist the pleasures of drugs and theft and truancy and violence find the discipline to construct organizations that force them to resist such pleasures?

(7). Support programs designed to provide early education and effective child care. Programs that target dysfunctional families and seek to remedy lack of supervision have been shown to have promise. This does not contradict the control theory notion that self-control is acquired early in life. The finding that nothing works in the treatment area may be limited to programs focusing on adolescents and adults.

(8). Support policies that promote and facilitate two-parent families and that increase the number of caregivers relative to the number of children. Large families and single-parent families are handicapped with respect to monitoring and discipline. As a consequence, their children are more likely to commit criminal acts and are especially more likely to become involved with the criminal justice system. A major source of weak families is unmarried pregnancy among adolescent girls, which is itself important evidence of low self-control. Programs to prevent such pregnancies should therefore be given high priority.

Criticisms of the Theory

Self-control theory is among the most frequently tested theories in the field of crime and delinquency. It is also frequently criticized. These criticisms are concentrated around three more or less traditional issues: (1) the definition of the dependent variable—crime and deviant behavior; (2) the logical structure of the theory; and (3) the ability of the theory to deal with particular offenses.

The Dependent Variable

Self-control theory attempts to explain short-term self-interested behavior that entails the risk of long-term sanctions. Because it is framed without regard to the law, this definition includes acts that may not be defined as criminal and may exclude acts defined as criminal by the jurisdiction in question. Examples of the first are behaviors we have labeled "analogous to crime" (e.g., premarital pregnancy, divorce, job-quitting, accidents). Examples of the second are terrorism and espionage, acts committed on behalf of political organizations. The definition also excludes the use of force or fraud in the public interest or as required by the legal system (e.g., killings by soldiers, undercover activities by police, forced removals of property owners by university officials).

This definition of crime is very different from the traditional definition, according to which crime is restricted to and includes all behavior "in violation of law." How can we exclude behavior that is clearly criminal by the laws or norms of all societies (terrorism) and include behavior that is rarely if ever punished by the state (accidents)? The answer is that we have no choice in this matter. Theories define the behavior they explain and their definition cannot be changed without changing them. Terrorist acts are excluded from self-control theory because they are assumed to reflect commitment to a political cause or organization. Terrorists do not act without regard for the broad or long-term consequences of their acts. On the contrary, their purpose is to alter the status quo. However heinous the consequences of their acts, and however severely they are punished by the state, they do not meet the requirement common to acts explained by control theory—that they be committed by an unrestrained offender.

The seriousness of this criticism of self-control theory will depend on the range and frequency of acts it fails to cover. As far as we can see, this number is small, especially when compared to the theory's coverage of the very large number of acts ignored by traditional definitions of crime.

Logical Structure

Self-control theory says that crime is the best predictor of crime and that self-control is the element common to the crimes of interest. These statements are often described as tautological, a serious criticism of the theory in the eyes of many social scientists. One meaning of *tautology* is "repetition; saying or, by extension, doing the same thing again." The *Oxford Universal Dictionary* lists an example from 1687: "Our whole Life is but a nauseous Tautology." This statement introduces another meaning of the term: The repetition described is trivial, pointless, or worse.

That crimes repeat themselves may be tautological, and some criminologists have indeed labeled this fact "trivial and theoretically pointless" (Akers 1998, 168–169). But such repetition is neither logically nor empirically necessary. It cannot therefore possibly be a valid criticism of control theory. Theories are not responsible for the nauseousness of the behavior they attempt to explain.

Another meaning of *tautology* is that the logical relations among concepts may be derived from their definitions. Thus, if low self-control is defined by willingness to engage in behavior with long-term negative consequences, and *crime* is defined as behavior with long-term negative consequences, a relation between low self-control and crime is logically necessary or tautological. The theory repeats the definition and vice versa. We do not deny the tautological or circular nature of self-control theory. On the contrary, we believe that pure theory is always tautological in this sense of the term (Hirschi and Selvin [1967] 1994). Definitions entail theories. Theories entail definitions. It cannot be otherwise. The source of confusion appears to be the belief among social scientists that tautological theories cannot be falsified. This belief, in our view, is demonstrably false.

Applicability of the Theory to Particular Crimes.

In constructing self-control theory, we tried to concentrate on the characteristics of ordinary crimes. This led us to emphasize their triviality and predictability, the ease and speed with which they are committed, the small losses and smaller gains they typically involve. The purpose was to avoid the distractions that come from looking first or mainly at large, serious, or apparently bizarre crimes, crimes that attract the attention of the media and criminal justice system. This strategy has led some critics of the theory to the conclusion that it applies only to the ordinary, mundane crimes from which it was constructed. We believe this conclusion ignores the success of our strategy in revealing features shared by rare and common, serious and trivial offenses. Indeed, we began this essay with a rare and most serious offense to show that it fell easily within the scope of the theory.

Other crimes said at one time or another to fall outside the scope of the theory include income tax evasion, white-collar crime, corporate crime, organized crime, and gambling. Tests of these alleged exceptions seem to us straightforward. Those involved in crimes where self-control is not a factor should be otherwise indistinguishable from the law-abiding population. As of now, it seems to us, the evidence on these matters points in directions favorable to the theory. Those involved in such apparently exceptional crimes tend to have been involved in other forms of crime and deviance as well (Le Blanc and Kaspy 1998).

References

Akers, Ronald. (1998). *Social Learning and Social Structure: A General Theory of Crime and Deviance*. Boston: Northeastern University Press.

Andrews, D.A., Ivan Zinger, Robert D. Hoge, James Bonta, Paul Gendreau, and Francis T. Cullen. (1990). "Does correctional treatment work? A clinically relevant and psychologically informed meta-analysis." *Criminology*, 28:369–404.

Bentham, Jeremy. [1789] (1970). *An Introduction to the Principles of Morals and Legislation*. Reprint. London: The Althone.

Boyum, David and Mark A. R. Kleiman. (1995). "Alcohol and other drugs." Pp. 295–326 in J.Q. Wilson and J. Petersilia (eds.), *Crime*. San Francisco: ICS.

Britt, Chester L. (1994). "Versatility." Pp. 173–192 in T. Hirschi and M.R. Gottfredson (eds.), *The Generality of Deviance*. New Brunswick, NJ: Transaction.

Cohen, Lawrence C. and Kenneth C. Land. (1987). "Age structure and crime: Symmetry versus asymmetry and the projection of crime rates through the 1990s."*American Sociological Review*, 52:170–183.

Coleman, James. (1990). *Foundations of Social Theory*. Cambridge, MA: Belknap.

Evans, T., F. Cullen, V. Burton, R. Dunaway, and M. Benson. (1997). "The social consequences of self-control: Testing the general theory of crime." *Criminology*, 35:475–504.

Farrington, David P. and Marianne Junger (eds.). (1995). *Criminal Behavior and Mental Health*, 5(4): Special Issue.

Gendreau, Paul, Tracy Little, and Claire Goggin. (1996). "A meta-analysis of the predictors of adult offender recidivism: What works!" *Criminology*, 34:575–607.

Glueck, Sheldon and Eleanor Glueck. (1940). *Juvenile Delinquents Grown Up*. New York: Commonwealth Fund.

——. (1950). *Unraveling Juvenile Delinquency*. Cambridge, MA: Harvard University Press.

——. (1968). *Delinquents and Nondelinquents in Perspective*. Cambridge, MA: Harvard University Press.

Goring, Charles. (1913). *The English Convict*. Montclair, NJ: Patterson Smith.

Gottfredson, Michael R. and Travis Hirschi. (1990). *A General Theory of Crime*. Stanford, CA: Stanford University Press.

——. (1995). "National crime control policies." *Society*, 32:30–37.

Hirschi, Travis. (1969). *Causes of Delinquency*. Berkeley: University of California Press.

——. (1975). "Labeling theory and juvenile delinquency: An assessment of the evidence." Pp. 181–203 in Walter Gove (ed.), *The Labeling of Deviance*. Halsted.

Hirschi, Travis and Michael Gottfredson. (1983). "Age and the explanation of crime." *American Journal of Sociology*, 89:552–584.

Hirschi, Travis and Michael J. Hindelang. (1977). "Intelligence and delinquency: A revisionist review." *American Sociological Review*, 42:571–187.

Hirschi, Travis and Hanan C. Selvin. [1967] (1994). *Delinquency Research: An Appraisal of Analytic Methods*. New Brunswick, NJ: Transaction.

Le Blanc, Marc and Nathalie Kaspy. (1998). "Trajectories of delinquency and problem behavior: Comparison of social and personal control characteristics of adjudicated boys on synchronous and nonsynchronous paths." *Journal of Quantitative Criminology*, 14:181–214.

Loeber, Rolf and Magda Stouthamer-Loeber. (1986). "Family factors as correlates and predictors of juvenile conduct problems and delinquency." Pp. 29–149 in M.H. Tonry and N. Morris (eds.), *Crime and Justice: A Review of Research*. Chicago: University of Chicago Press.

Martinson, Robert. (1974a). "What works? Questions and answers about prison reform." *The Public Interest*, Spring, 35:22–54.

——. (1974b). The myth of treatment and the reality of life process. April. Paper delivered at the Eastern Psychological Association, Philadelphia.

Murray, Charles. (1995). "The physical environment." Pp. 349–361 in J.Q. Wilson and J. Petersilia (eds.), *Crime*. San Francisco: ICS.

Nagin, Daniel S. and Raymond Paternoster. (1991). "On the relationship of past to future participation in delinquency." *Criminology*, 29:163–189.

Osgood, D. Wayne, Patrick M. O'Malley, Jerald G. Bachman, and Lloyd D. Johnston. (1989). "Time trends and age trends in arrests and self-reported illegal behavior." *Criminology*, 27:389–417.

Quetelet, Lambert A.J. [1833] (1969). *A Treatise on Man*. Gainesville, FL: Scholars' Facsimiles and Reprints.

Sechrest, Lee, Susan O. White, and Elizabeth Brown (eds.). (1979). The *Rehabilitation of Criminal Offenders: Problems and Prospects*. Washington, DC: National Academy of Sciences.

Toby, Jackson. (1957). "Social disorganization and stake in conformity: Complementary factors in the predatory behavior of hoodlums." *Journal of Criminal Law, Criminology, and Police Science*, 48:12–17.

Tremblay, Richard E., Frank Vitaro, Lucie Bertrand, Marc LeBlanc, Helene Beauchesne, Helene Boileau, and Lucille David. (1992). "Parent and child training to prevent early onset of delinquency: A Montreal Longitudinal-Experimental Study." Pp. 117–138 in J. McCord and R. Tremblay (eds.), *Preventing Antisocial Behavior*. New York: Guilford.

Wolfgang, Marvin, Robert Figlio, and Thorsten Sellin. (1972). *Delinquency in a Birth Cohort*. Chicago: University of Chicago Press.

Explaining Crime Over the Life Course

Toward a Theory of Age-Graded Informal Social Control

John H. Laub
University of Maryland, College Park

Robert J. Sampson
University of Chicago

Leana C. Allen
University of Maryland, College Park

One of the major developments in criminology over the last 25 years is the recognition that there is no single cause or risk factor for crime and violence; instead, there are multiple pathways to crime and violence. Chronic offenders, in particular, have multiple risk factors in their background, including individual factors such as hyperactivity, impulsivity, and attention deficit; family characteristics, especially poor family functioning and childrearing practices; school factors like poor school achievement and low commitment to school; and peer factors, especially associating with delinquent peers and gang membership. Moreover, these factors tend to be cumulative and interact with one another over time.

Given such considerations, the field of criminology may well turn to developmental approaches to better understand the onset of criminal behavior and its continuation or cessation over the life span. Developmental approaches are inextricably tied to dynamic concerns and the unfolding of biological, psychological, and sociological processes through time. Rutter and Rutter (1993) propose a useful, although fuzzy, definition of *development* as "systematic, organized, intra-individual change that is clearly associated with generally expectable age-related progressions and which is carried forward in some way that has implications for a person's pattern or level of functioning at a later time" (64). Development is thus focused on systematic change, especially how behaviors set in motion dynamic processes that alter future outcomes.

With respect to crime, Loeber and LeBlanc (1990) argue that "developmental criminology" recognizes both continuity and within-individual changes over time, focusing on "life transitions and developmental covariates. . . which may mediate the developmental course of offending" (451). This strategy has been referred to as a *stepping stone approach* in which factors are time ordered by age and assessed with respect to outcome variables (see Farrington 1986). A similar orientation can be found in interactional theory (Thornberry 1987), which embraces a developmental approach and asserts that causal influences are reciprocal over the life course.

Fortunately, there is a growing body of developmental theories in criminology. For instance, Terrie Moffitt's theory of life-course persistent offending and adolescent-limited offending (1993); Gerry Patterson's theory of antisocial behavior, including what he calls *early* and *late starters* (see Patterson 1993; Patterson, DeBaryshe, and Ramsey 1989; and Patterson and Yoerger 1993); and Sampson and Laub's (1993) age-graded theory of informal social control over the life course come to mind in this regard. A good overview of this body of theory and research can be found in *Developmental Theories of Crime and Delinquency*, edited by Terence P. Thornberry (1997).

The focus of this chapter is Sampson and Laub's (1993) theory of informal social control. This theory attempts to unite continuity and change within the context of a sociological understanding of crime in the life course. As will be illustrated below, by drawing attention to the significance of both pathways and turning points in the life course, Sampson and Laub's theory has the potential to unify divergent conceptions of stability and change in the field of human development and criminology.

Background

For over 40 years, Sheldon Glueck (1896–1980) and Eleanor Touroff Glueck (1898–1972) performed fundamental research in the field of criminology at the Harvard Law School. Of their four pioneering studies, the Gluecks are best known for their *Unraveling Juvenile Delinquency* study which was published in 1950. This study of the formation and development of criminal careers is considered to be one of the most influential studies in the history of criminological research. However, the original case files were stored away in a dusty, dark sub-basement of the Harvard Law School Library until they were uncovered again by Robert Sampson and John Laub in 1987. The recovery, restoration, and reanalysis of this very rich data source has, in part, led to the development of a new theory of the initiation, continuation, and cessation of delinquency throughout an individual's life, Sampson and Laub's (1993) age-graded theory of informal social control.

The Gluecks' *Unraveling Juvenile Delinquency* study involved a comparison of 500 officially defined delinquents from two Massachusetts reform schools for boys and 500 nondelinquent boys from the Boston public schools. Nondelinquent status was determined on the basis of official record checks and interviews with teachers, parents, and the boys themselves. A unique aspect of this study was the matching design. Specifically, the delinquents and the nondelinquents were matched case by case on age, race/ethnicity, measured intelligence, and neighborhood socioeconomic status (see also Glueck and Glueck 1950). The two groups grew up in similar high-risk environments of poverty and exposure to antisocial conduct. That 500 of the boys were persistent delinquents and the other 500 avoided delinquency in childhood thus cannot be attributed to age differences, ethnicity, IQ, or residence in slum areas.

Begun in 1940, the initial period of data collection took eight years. The original sample of 1,000 boys was followed up at two different points in time—at the age of 25 and again at the age of 32 (see also Glueck and Glueck 1968). As a result, extensive data are available for nearly 90 percent of the original sample at all three age periods. The Gluecks collected a wide range of data for analysis relating to criminal career histories, criminal justice interventions, family life, school and employment history, and recreational activities for the subjects in childhood, adolescence, and young adulthood. The following life histories of Jimmy and Charlie provide examples of the rich and extensive data included in the Gluecks' study.

Jimmy was born in Boston on August 8, 1926. He had an extensive record of criminal behavior as an adolescent and as an adult, totaling 35 arrests up to his death at the age of 58. Although his first arrest occurred when he was 12, Jimmy began stealing much earlier, at the age of 8. He was eventually committed to a juvenile correctional facility one month before his 14th birthday. As an adolescent, Jimmy was incarcerated three times, serving a total of 19 months. As a young man, he was arrested for assault and battery, robbery, larceny, reckless driving including leaving the scene of an accident, and public drunkenness.

Jimmy grew up in a poor neighborhood of Boston. He was one of eight children, and there was little parental control or supervision in the household. At the age of 6, Jimmy began staying out late at night and skipping school on a regular basis. Although his IQ scores were relatively high, he refused to attend school, repeated grades, and eventually dropped out in the ninth grade. Throughout his childhood and early adolescence, Jimmy's best friends were juvenile delinquents like him.

Jimmy's problems continued as he grew up. He began working as an "unskilled laborer" at age 16. While on parole at 17, Jimmy enlisted in the Navy. Although he served 28 months, he eventually received a "Bad Conduct Discharge"—the result of a General Court Martial for being AWOL. He also overstayed his leave several times, "engaging in wild drinking bouts." At the age of 25, he was employed as a steel worker. He made no effort to improve his occupational status and seemed content to just drift from job to job. Jimmy's poor work habits appeared to be related to his drinking.

Jimmy's problems with alcohol, a major source of difficulty in his work life, also affected his family life. At age 24, Jimmy married, and he lived with his wife and children in the Boston area. During his first year of marriage, there were domestic difficulties, and the couple separated and reunited a number of times. There were also indications of domestic violence, with Jimmy repeatedly threatening his wife with violence. He was later arrested for assault and battery on his wife as well as child neglect, but the case was dismissed because his wife was reluctant to move forward on the charges. The source of trouble was that Jimmy drank excessively and stayed out late at night to spite his wife. This led to much arguing in the home.

Jimmy did not change very much in later adulthood. At age 32, he was being sought as a fugitive from justice. He was formally divorced but had lived with his former wife again, and they had a second child two years after the divorce. Jimmy's cruel and abusive treatment of his wife and children continued, as did his drinking. Although employed as an iron worker, Jimmy frequently did not work to avoid paying financial support to his wife and children. Overall, Jimmy's antisocial behavior and related problems with family and work revealed remarkable stability over his life span, including two arrests for driving under the influence of alcohol at the ages of 50 and 54.

In many ways, Charlie's early life was like Jimmy's. Charlie was born in Boston on June 13, 1928. He had ten arrests as a juvenile, primarily for larcenies and burglaries. Charlie's first arrest occurred at the age of 8. Moreover, he was incarcerated three times (his first commitment took place when he was 11), and he spent a total of 30 months confined in reform schools. Despite this background of juvenile delinquency, Charlie had no record of criminal behavior as an adult.

Like Jimmy, Charlie grew up in a poor neighborhood of Boston. He also came from a large family, one of seven children, and he was not well supervised by his parents. Al-

though his IQ scores were much lower than Jimmy's, Charlie's school experiences were much the same. He was frequently truant, repeated grades, and dropped out in the ninth grade. Charlie's best friends growing up were also involved in delinquent activities and included his older brother and cousin.

At the age of 18, Charlie joined the U.S. Merchant Service. He remained with the same shipping line for two and a half years and returned home once every three months. He gave virtually all of his earnings to his mother to bank for him. During this same period, Charlie began a relationship with a woman who would eventually become his wife. At the age of 25, Charlie remained devoted to his wife, and the couple appeared especially united in their mutual desire to advance economically and to build their own home.

During his early 20s, Charlie held a variety of factory jobs and appeared to be a solid, industrious worker. This portrait of Charlie did not change very much in later adulthood. At age 32, he was living with his wife and two children in a suburb of Boston. He appeared happy with his marriage and family, and in his spare time, he worked on home improvement. Charlie worked at a factory and was eventually promoted to foreman. As of age 65, Charlie had no record of criminal behavior in adulthood.

These life histories demonstrate the amount of information available in the Gluecks' data, and raise a number of questions about criminal behavior which a criminological theory should be able to answer. What accounts for the different life patterns illustrated in these stories? How is it that some juvenile delinquents like Charlie are able to turn their lives around and change their criminal behavior so dramatically, while others like Jimmy display a pattern of continuous antisocial behavior from childhood through adulthood? Can pathways to delinquency be explained? Once formed, can delinquent pathways be altered? In other words, are there "turning points" in life? By integrating a life-course perspective with a social control theory of delinquency, Sampson and Laub's (1993) age-graded theory of informal social control is able to answer these questions.

The Life-Course Perspective

The life-course perspective encompasses a number of different themes and has been applied to human behavior, particularly crime, in a variety of ways. Cohen and Vila (1996) contend that life-course studies attempt to understand human behavior by understanding 1) how lives and societal or historical change both influence each other, and 2) how early events and influences in an individual's life may influence behavior and other outcomes throughout the life-course. That is, the life-course perspective is concerned with both the effects of macro-level events (e.g., the Great Depression, World War II) on individual life histories, as well as the study of patterns of continuity and change between childhood behavior and later adult outcomes.

The life course may be defined as pathways through the life span, involving a sequence of culturally defined, age-graded roles and social transitions enacted over time and throughout an individual's life (Elder 1985). For example, in American culture, one dominant pathway for an individual to follow is to attend school, often through college and possibly beyond, to find employment which may develop into a career, to marry, and to have children. Though variation is possible in both the order of these events and the age at which an individual may experience them, the described sequence is, for the most part, the traditional, culturally defined pathway for many individuals. Some life-course events may be characterized as age-graded, while others are not. In the United States, for example, states have passed laws specifying the minimum age at which individuals may legally be married or employed. Thus, these events are age-graded in the sense that the opportunity to experience them is defined by age.

Two central concepts underlie the analysis of life-course dynamics; trajectories and transitions (Elder 1985). *Trajectories* may be described as pathways or lines of development throughout life. These long-term patterns of behavior may include work life, marriage, parenthood, or even criminal behavior. *Transitions,* on the other hand, are short-term events embedded in trajectories, which may include starting a new job, getting married, having a child, or being sentenced to prison. Because transitions and trajectories are so closely connected, transitionary events may lead to *turning points,* or changes in an individual's trajectory or life course. For example, getting married may have a great influence on one's life and behavior, from changing where a person lives or works to changing the number and type of friends with whom one associates. Turning points are closely linked to role transitions and are helpful in understanding change in human behavior over the life course. Despite the connection between childhood events and experiences in adulthood, turning points can modify life trajectories—they can "redirect paths."

One major objective of the life-course perspective is to link social history and social structure to the unfolding of human lives. Elder (1985) argues that social or historical change may be consequential in altering the life course of individuals and groups. Many changes in life result from chance or random events, while other changes stem from macro-level events largely beyond the pale of individual choice (e.g., war, depression, natural disasters, revolutions). Turning points and developmental changes are bounded by historical context as well. At the macro-level, different groups of individuals may experience historical events differently. For example, the European experience of World War II was much different than the American experience. Similarly, those who were working adults during the Great Depression were affected more negatively than those who were very young at the time.

At the individual level, the life-course perspective emphasizes the extent of stability and change in behavior and personality attributes over time through the connection of trajectories and transitions. While the long-term view embodied by the life-course focus on trajectories implies a connection between childhood events and experiences in adulthood (continuity), the simultaneous shorter-term view implies that transitions or turning points can modify (change) the course of life trajectories, redirecting pathways. To address these phenomena, individual lives are studied through time. This may be one of the most complex themes of the life-course perspective as well as one of the most hotly debated and controversial issues in the social sciences.

Age-Graded Theory of Informal Social Control

For many years, Sampson and Laub have been recoding, recasting, and reanalyzing the Gluecks' longitudinal data on juvenile delinquency and adult crime. The overriding goal of this project was to examine crime and deviance in childhood, adolescence, and adulthood in a way that recognized the significance of both continuity and change over the life course. To do so, they synthesized and integrated the criminological literature on childhood antisocial behavior, adolescent delinquency, and adult crime with theory and research on the life course. By uniting a developmental, life-course perspective with research on antisocial and criminal behavior and social control theory, Sampson and Laub (1993) have developed a new theory of crime and delinquency over the life course, the age-graded theory of informal social control.

The organizing principle of Sampson and Laub's (1993) theory is social control—the idea that delinquency is more likely when an individual's bond to society is weak or broken. Somewhat different from Hirschi's (1969) traditional social control theory, Sampson and Laub focus more on social bonding over the life course, suggesting that the institutions of both formal and informal social control vary throughout life. Particularly important to this theory are informal social controls, which are reflected in the structure of interpersonal bonds that link members of society to each other and to larger social institutions, such as school, work, and family. These social relations between individuals (e.g., parent-child, teacher-student, employer-employee) at each stage of the life course are character-

ized as a form of social investment or social capital. In other words, strong social capital derives from strong social bonds, which provide social and psychological resources that individuals may draw on as they move through life transitions. The concept of social capital also conveys the sense that the stronger an individual's bond to others and to societal institutions, the more that person jeopardizes by engaging in delinquent or criminal behavior.

In addition to the central concept of informal social control, this theory also draws from a large body of literature on continuity and change in delinquent and criminal behavior over the life course. From these various sources, Sampson and Laub's (1993) theory recognizes the importance of both stability and change in the life course and proposes three thematic ideas regarding age-graded social control. The first concerns the mediating effect of structural and bonding variables on juvenile delinquency; the second centers on the consequences of delinquency and antisocial behavior for adult outcomes; and the third focuses on the explanation of adult crime and deviance in relation to adult informal social control and social capital.

Structure and Process in Adolescent Delinquency

In explaining the onset of delinquency, criminologists have typically embraced either structural factors (e.g., Shaw and McKay's [1942] social disorganization theory) or process variables (e.g., Hirschi's [1969] social control theory). The age-graded theory suggests that such a separation is a mistake and joins structural and process variables along with individual characteristics, like temperament and early conduct disorder, into a single theoretical model (see Figure 1 for an illustration with respect to family variables). Thus, the first building block of the theory focuses on both structural factors, such as poverty or broken homes, and process variables, including attachment to family or school. Specifically, this theoretical model proposes that structural context influences dimensions of informal social controls by the family and school, which in turn explain variations in delinquency.

Recently, research in criminology has begun to refocus its attention on the role of the family in explaining delinquency. Consistent with a theory of informal social control, Sampson and Laub (1993) suggest that delinquency in childhood and adolescence results from weak bonds to the family. Informal social controls derived from the family include the consistent use of discipline and monitoring by parents and attachment to the family. The key to these three components is the extent to which they facilitate linking the child to the family and ultimately to society through emotional bonds of attachment and direct forms of control, monitoring, and punishment. Like the family, the school is also considered to be an important socializing institution in the prevention of delinquency. Therefore, this theory proposes that weak attachment to school and poor school performance increase delinquency.

In addition to the direct effects of social bonds to family and school, this theory proposes that social structural factors, such as family disruption, unemployment, residential mobility, and socioeconomic status, play an indirect role in delinquency by influencing social bonds. These factors are considered to be structural because they reflect characteristics of the structure of society. For example, a person's position in the class structure may be represented by his or her lack of employment or socioeconomic status. Sampson and Laub (1993) contend that previous research on delinquency has failed to account for this social structural context and how it influences family life and social bonds. Some authors have argued that socioeconomic disadvantage has potentially adverse effects on parents, such that parental difficulties are more likely to develop and good parenting is impeded (McLoyd 1990). Similarly, factors related to socioeconomic disadvantage, such as poverty and household crowding, may disrupt bonds of attachment between the child and school and may lead to educational deficiencies. If true, one would expect poverty and disadvantage to have their effects on delinquency transmitted through parenting and education. There-fore, this theory predicts that the effects of structural background factors on delinquency will be mediated by family and school bonding.

The Importance of Continuity Between Childhood and Adulthood

Sampson and Laub's (1993) theory also incorporates the considerable evidence that antisocial behavior is relatively stable across stages of the life course. The second proposition contends that childhood and adolescent antisocial behavior, like delinquency, conduct disorder, and violent temper tantrums, extends throughout adulthood across a variety of life's domains, such as crime, deviance, and drug or alcohol abuse. In other words, antisocial behavior in childhood predicts a wide range of troublesome adult outcomes as well as dimensions of adult social bonding (e.g., economic dependency, educational attainment, attachment to the labor force, and quality of marital experiences). Finally, these outcomes occur independent of traditional sociological and psychological variables, such as social class background, ethnicity, IQ, and even the family and school factors suggested to predict the onset of delinquency.

There are many explanations for the link between delinquency and crime over time. The population heterogeneity perspective suggests that childhood delinquency has no causal influence on adult crime; instead, both are caused by an underlying criminogenic trait (see, for example, Gottfredson and Hirschi 1990). The state dependence perspective, on the other hand, points to a causal influence of prior delinquency in facilitating future crime (Nagin and Paternoster 1991). State dependence may occur in many ways; however, Sampson and Laub (1993; Sampson and Laub 1997) emphasize a developmental model of cumulative continuity. This process suggests that delinquency continues into adulthood because of its negative consequences for future life chances. For example, arrest, official labeling, incarceration, and other negative life events associated with delinquency may lead to decreased opportunities, including failure in school and unemployment. Delinquent

Figure 1
Theoretical Model of Structural Background Factors, Child Characteristics, Family Process, and Delinquency. Broken Line Indicates Hypothesized Weak or Insignificant Effect; Solid Line Signifies Hypothesized Strong Effect.

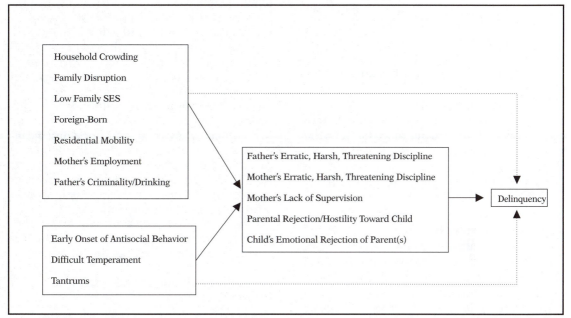

activities are also likely to sever informal social bonds to school, friends, and family and to jeopardize the development of adult social bonds. In this way, childhood delinquency has an indirect effect on adult criminal behavior through the weakening of social bonds. Thus, the theory proposes that crime, deviance, and informal social control are intimately linked over the full life course.

The Significance of Change in the Life Course

The concept of change has not received the same attention in the social sciences as its counterpart, continuity. Sampson and Laub's (1993) theory recognizes that the two concepts are not mutually exclusive, and the third focus of the theory is change in deviance and offending throughout the life course. Despite significant continuity in behavior, Sampson and Laub argue that salient life events and social bonds in adulthood, especially attachment to work and to a spouse, can counteract, at least to some extent, the trajectories of early child development. These events and the social capital they pro-

vide can change an individual's path from a delinquent trajectory to a nondelinquent one or vice versa. In other words, pathways to both crime and conformity are modified by key institutions of social control in the transition to adulthood independent of prior differences in criminal propensity.

Contrary to the emphasis of many life-course researchers, Sampson and Laub argue that the mere occurrence of an event (e.g., getting married or getting a job) or the timing of that event are not the determining factors. Rather, the changes in social bonds and social capital that occur in conjunction with a transition may cause the change in behavior. Similarly, the mere presence of a relationship between adults is not sufficient to produce social capital. Instead, adult social ties are important insofar as they create interdependent systems of obligation and restraint that impose significant costs for translating criminal propensities into action. For example, marriage per se may not increase social control, but close emotional ties and mutual investment increase the social bond between individuals and, all else being equal, should lead to a reduction in criminal behavior. Sampson and Laub (1993) believe that adults, regardless of delinquent background, will be inhibited from committing crime to the extent that they have social capital invested in their work and family lives. By contrast, those subject to weak informal social control as an adult are freer to engage in deviant behavior, even if nondelinquent in youth.

Though this focus on change may seem to be at odds with the earlier discussion of the stability of criminal behavior over time, evidence indicates that continuity is far from perfect. Additionally, lives are often unpredictable, and change is ever present. Sampson and Laub (1993; Laub and Sampson 1993) propose a dynamic theory of social capital and informal social control that at once incorporates stability and change in criminal behavior. This theoretical framework implies that adult social ties can modify childhood trajectories of crime despite general stability. Specifically, adult social bonds are suggested to have a direct negative effect on adult criminal behavior, controlling for childhood delinquency.

In sum, the age-graded theory of informal social control brings together a focus on continuity and change. A major concept in this theoretical framework is the dynamic process whereby the interlocking nature of trajectories and transitions generates turning points or changes in the life course. Sampson and Laub (1993) found that some positive turning points in the life course were a cohesive marriage, meaningful work, and serving in the military. A clear negative turning point was prolonged incarceration and subsequent job instability during the transition to young adulthood. Although the theory was developed in the ongoing context of an analysis of the Gluecks' data described previously, the theoretical notions have wider appeal and are not solely bound by these data. This assertion and general support for the theory will be demonstrated with a discussion of the empirical literature.

Empirical Literature

The age-graded theory of informal social control includes a variety of propositions, which may be examined in the empirical literature. Sampson and Laub (1993) propose that bonds to family and school directly influence delinquency and that structural factors indirectly influence delinquency through those bonds. The theory also suggests that childhood delinquency and deviance will continue into adulthood through a process of cumulative continuity, resulting in criminal behavior in adulthood and weakened adult social bonds. Finally, despite a history of delinquency, those who develop strong adult social bonds will be less likely to engage in criminal or deviant behavior in adulthood. Empirical support for these propositions is derived from a number of different sources, including previous criminological research and direct tests of the theory.

Explaining Childhood and Adolescent Delinquency

The theoretically predicted relationship between social bonds to family and school and delinquent behavior in childhood is supported by a great deal of research. Some evidence has indicated that social bonds in childhood, as determined by parenting variables, consistently predict delinquency. In an extensive review, Loeber and Stouthamer-Loeber (1986) report that the strongest family predictors of delinquency were parental involvement, monitoring, discipline, and rejection. Moreover, parenting variables continue to have a direct effect even after controlling for other predictors found to be important determinants of delinquency. Results from Sampson and Laub's (1993) analysis of the Gluecks' data also suggest that when bonds to family or school are weak or broken, delinquency is more likely. Regardless of early childhood propensity, parental discipline, supervision, and attachment consistently influence delinquent conduct. Additionally, school attachment is found to be an important inhibitory force in delinquency causation.

In addition to the importance of ties to family and school, the theoretical prediction of an indirect effect of structural factors also finds support in the empirical literature. A study by Larzelere and Patterson (1990) showed that the effect of socioeconomic status on delinquency is mediated entirely by parental discipline and monitoring. Analysis of the Gluecks' data also revealed that structural factors, such as residential mobility, socioeconomic status, and family disruption, influence delinquency primarily through family bonds. In other words, structural factors affect how parents and children relate and how families function (Sampson and Laub 1994). These family relationships then influence delinquency such that children are more likely to be delinquent if they are poorly monitored by, supervised by, or attached to their parents. Overall, the empirical evidence is consistent with Sampson and Laub's first theoretical prediction that both structural factors and bonds to family and school predict childhood and adolescent delinquency and that the influence of structural factors is primarily mediated by family bonding.

Continuity of Behavior into Adulthood

The second theoretical prediction, that there is continuity in delinquent and antisocial behavior from childhood to adulthood, also receives support from the empirical literature. Research spanning several decades indicates a great deal of stability and continuity in criminal behavior over time. In fact, Robins (1978) demonstrated that childhood delinquency is almost a prerequisite for adult offending. A review of several research studies revealed substantial stability between early aggressive behavior and later criminality (Olweus 1979). More recently, Caspi and Moffitt (1995) note that continuities in antisocial behavior have also been replicated in nations other than the United States (e.g., Canada, England, Finland, New Zealand, and Sweden) and with multiple methods of assessment (e.g., official records, teacher ratings, parent reports, peer nominations). Taken as a whole, these different studies across time, space, and method yield an impressive generalization that is rare in the social sciences. Results from the Gluecks' data also demonstrated that inde-

pendent of age, IQ, socioeconomic status, and ethnicity, both the delinquents and the nondelinquents displayed behavioral consistency well into adulthood (Sampson and Laub 1993). Overall, a large body of research supports Sampson and Laub's contention that childhood delinquency leads to adult criminal behavior.

Research has also demonstrated that childhood and adolescent delinquency are related to a variety of other troublesome adult outcomes including economic dependence and marital instability. Robins (1966) found strong relationships between childhood antisocial behavior and adult occupational status, job stability, income, and residential mobility. Analysis of the Gluecks' data also indicated that childhood delinquency predicts educational, economic, employment, and family status well into adulthood (Sampson and Laub 1993).

Continuity may also be fueled by the negative effects of official sanctions on opportunities in adulthood, and research supports this contention. Specifically, analysis of the Gluecks' data found that adult social ties to work and family were influenced by prior delinquency and official sanctions. Incarceration as a juvenile and as a young adult was negatively related to later job stability, which in turn was negatively related to continued involvement in crime over the life course (Laub and Sampson 1995). Although this analysis found little direct effect of incarceration on subsequent criminality, the indirect criminogenic effects through job stability appear substantively important. Recent research also supports the cumulative continuity thesis, finding a detrimental effect of delinquent behavior on the labor market prospects of young males (Hagan 1993). Overall, the evidence suggests that delinquent behavior is relatively stable across stages of the life course and that antisocial behavior predicts a wide range of troublesome adult outcomes.

Change in Behavior Through Adult Social Bonds

The stability of criminal behavior patterns, especially aggression, throughout the life course is one of the most consistently documented patterns found in longitudinal research. However, not all delinquent children grow up to be criminal or antisocial as adults. Somewhat paradoxically, although studies show that antisocial behavior in children is one of the best predictors of antisocial behavior in adults, most antisocial children do not become antisocial adults. In a review of the literature, Loeber and LeBlanc (1990) reported that despite continuity, studies also show great change in behavior across the life course. Sampson and Laub's (1993) theory suggested that this change is the result of important life events and social bonds in adulthood, particularly job stability and attachment to a spouse. There is evidence supporting this prediction as well. Strong adult bonds to work are predicted to decrease the likelihood of offending. Farrington and colleagues (1986) found that individuals are more likely to commit property crimes during periods of unemployment. Sampson and Laub's (1993) study of the Gluecks' data demonstrates that job stability is consistently and negatively related to crime and deviance.

Similarly, Sampson and Laub (1993) predicted that strong marital attachment decreases offending. In a study of incarcerated offenders, Horney, Osgood, and Marshall (1995) reported that regardless of their overall level of offending, men were less likely to be involved in crime when they were living with a wife or attending school. Farrington and West (1995) also found that staying married and having children, indicators of a strong marital bond, were related to decreased offending; however, separation from a spouse led to increased offending. Sampson and Laub's (1993) analysis of the Gluecks' data also supported this prediction, finding that strong marital attachment was related to changes in adult crime despite differences in early childhood delinquency (see also Laub, Nagin, and Sampson 1998). Warr (1998) found a similar relationship between marital attachment and crime, though his interpretation differed somewhat. As demonstrated in the life histories of Jimmy and Charlie, some delinquents develop social ties to work and family in adulthood and discontinue their offending, while others do not develop these ties and continue offending throughout their life course.

Overall, a growing body of empirical literature supports the age-graded theory of informal social control. Research suggests that the strongest and most consistent effects on delinquency flow from the social bonds derived from family and school. At the same time, structural background factors have little direct effect on delinquency, but instead are mediated by intervening sources of informal social control. Additionally, individuals display behavioral consistency in offending or nonoffending patterns well into adulthood, and some evidence indicates that this occurs through a process of cumulative continuity. Consistent with the predictions of Sampson and Laub's (1993) theory, however, social ties in adulthood, especially job stability and marital attachment, are related to changes in adult criminal behavior. These results overall support the theoretical explanation of the onset of delinquency as well as the dual concern of the theory with continuity and change in behavior over the life course.

Contradictory Evidence

Though much evidence supports Sampson and Laub's (1993) theory, some authors contradict some of their theoretical propositions. Hirschi and Gottfredson (1995) argued that the demonstrated continuity in behavior from childhood to adulthood is not due to cumulative continuity, as Sampson and Laub (1993) suggested. Rather, childhood delinquency, adult criminal behavior, and other troublesome adult outcomes are all the result of an underlying criminogenic trait, namely low self-control (see Gottfredson and Hirschi 1990). These authors suggested that adult criminal behavior and other outcomes are the result of *self-selection*. In other words, because of this underlying trait, individuals choose certain events and environments. For example, delinquent individuals may be less likely to choose stable employment or marriage, so the benefits of those institutions would not apply to them.

Sampson and Laub (1995) recognized this argument and suggested that self-selection and cumulative continuity do not negate one another. To argue that individual differences influence the choices one makes in life, which they certainly do, does not mean that social mechanisms emerging from those choices can then have no causal significance. In other words, individuals may choose certain situations, and those events can then exert some influence in their lives. Although delinquents may be less likely to choose stable employment and marriage, sometimes they do make those choices, and as a result, they will be less likely to continue their criminal behavior.

Another argument in contradiction to Sampson and Laub's (1993) theory is the contention that social bonds and social capital are not the important causal mechanisms. Instead, some authors suggest that the effects of marriage and employment may be due to a differential association or social learning mechanism, the reduction of delinquent peers (see Akers 1998, 351 and Warr 1998). The number of delinquent friends an adolescent has is one of the strongest predictors of delinquency (Warr and Stafford, 1991). Though Warr (1998) found that marital cohesion does result in a reduction in criminal behavior, he argued that this relationship is the result of reduced interactions with peers, particularly delinquent peers. Marriage is often a transition in which individuals spend more time with their spouse and family rather than their friends. For those with a history of delinquency who presumably have delinquent friends, this change will result in fewer delinquent associations and fewer opportunities to commit crime. However, as Warr himself pointed out, these results may also be explained by social control theory. It may be that friendships change as the result of spouses exerting informal social control on their marital partners.

Rethinking Crime Policy

Some authors suggest that one important function of criminological theory is to provide some direction for controlling or preventing crime (Wellford 1997). A life-course perspective and Sampson and Laub's (1993)

theory offer new ways of thinking about crime control policy. Since the mid-1970s, the United States has embarked on a policy of unprecedented incarceration (MacKenzie 1997). From all appearances, the major thrust of current crime control policy, whether aimed at drugs or violence, is to lock up offenders regardless of age. For those offenders with extensive prior records, even longer sentences of incarceration are being recommended for (e.g., Three Strikes policies, mandatory sentences). Such policies assume that either individual deterrence (the idea that individuals will not commit crimes because they fear criminal sanctions) or incapacitation (the idea that confinement in prison will physically prevent people from offending) will reduce further violence. However, there is little evidence that the increased use of incarceration has reduced crime (Cullen 1994).

The age-graded theory of informal social control makes it apparent that it is time to take a renewed look at social policies that focus on prevention as opposed to reactive approaches like incarceration (Laub et al. 1995). Our current retributive policies ignore the structural context of crime and neglect the basic institutions of society like family, school, and work that provide informal social control and social capital. This is not to say that imprisonment is unnecessary or undeserved, or even that it has no deterrent effect on crime. Rather, some evidence suggests that these policies may not reduce crime and may in fact be counterproductive in the long run. It is time for a broader crime policy that focuses on more than formal social control by the criminal justice system. A more complex and long-term perspective that recognizes the linkages among crime policies, employment, family cohesion, and the social organization of inner-city communities is needed. Although these more complex crime policies are not easily translated into specific programmatic initiatives, they may provide a more cost-effective and long-lasting alternative to current policies. Some promising programmatic initiatives and policies are presented below.

Parent Training Programs

The central theme of crime policy should focus on developing and strengthening an individual's bonds to society. The foundation of sound policy on crime is that strong social bonds provide informal social control, and this holds at each stage of the life course. In addition, the ideas of pathways and turning points, which stem from a life-course perspective, are useful metaphors in the development of crime policy. The concept of pathways suggests that some individuals are set on an often predictable and stable track toward delinquency and adult criminality through the combined negative influence of poor parenting and weak school and peer attachments. At the same time, the notion of turning points suggests that these pathways could be deflected or redirected by positive developments that strengthen social bonds to key institutions in society.

Sampson and Laub's theory and the empirical support for its propositions urge us to seriously consider the role that families play in crime causation. Intervention programs that focus on the ability of parents to monitor, recognize, and discipline the misbehavior of their children appear to be most promising in reducing antisocial behavior and delinquency. A starting point in the development of effective crime control policy then is the development of parent training programs in which parents learn skills that are conducive to successful childrearing. Sherman (1997) reported that the current research indicates that home visits focusing on parent training appear to be successful in preventing delinquency.

One example of a program along these lines, which has been demonstrated to be effective, is the Prenatal and Early Childhood Nurse Home Visitation Program, developed by David Olds and his colleagues (1998). This program is designed "to help low-income, first-time parents start their lives with their children on a sound course and prevent the health and parenting problems that can contribute to the early development of antisocial behavior" (Olds, Hill, and Rumsey 1998, 1). Trained, experienced nurses visit new mothers every one or two weeks beginning during pregnancy and continuing for the first two years after the child is born. Parents are taught how to care for their children, including how to provide safe and consistent discipline. Results from a 15-year follow-up study of this program indicate that children whose mothers participated in this program were much less likely to have been arrested or to have been convicted of a crime. These findings suggest that programs that focus on parent training can be successful in preventing future delinquency and antisocial behavior.

Job Training Programs

A recent review of the research on job training programs suggests that certain programs aimed at high-risk youth appear to be promising in the prevention of delinquency (Bushway and Reuter 1997). One particular program, Job Corps, is a residential program with intensive training. Extremely disadvantaged youth are "resocialized" by presenting them with prosocial role models and by providing vocational and educational training in connection to the labor market. Four years after graduation from the program, individuals demonstrate increased earnings and educational achievement and decreased arrests for serious crimes (Bushway and Reuter 1997).

Incarceration and Alternative Sanctions

One clear implication of the age-graded theory of informal social control is that current policies may produce unintended criminogenic effects. Sampson and Laub's (1993) research offers some pointed findings on the negative effects of lengthy prison sentences. In their reanalysis of the Gluecks' data, Sampson and Laub (1993) demonstrated that social bonds to employment were directly influenced by state sanctions (see also Laub and Sampson 1995). That is, incarceration as a juvenile and as an adult had negative effects on later job stability, and job instability in turn increased the likelihood of continued involvement in crime over the life course. Simply put, lengthy prison terms severely damage the future job prospects of offenders.

Two strategies for ameliorating this situation are required. First, those who must be imprisoned should be able to update their education and participate in occupational programs in prison to align with current labor market realities so that the potential for postrelease employment is maximized. Sampson and Laub's (1993) analysis revealed that individual change is possible, and therefore it is critical that individuals have the opportunity to reconnect to institutions (e.g., family, school, and work) after a period of incarceration. Second, we must seriously rethink our current overreliance on prison terms for property and drug offenders and examine the possibility that credible, strict punishments may be available in the community. Community based sentences can satisfy the important principle of just deserts without the devastating impact on employability that comes with a prison sentence.

Sampson and Laub (1993) have argued that despite strong continuities between delinquency and adult antisocial behaviors, change is possible largely through adult attachments to the labor force and cohesive marital bonds. The key concept here is development of social capital in interpersonal relations in adulthood, social bonds to a spouse, or to work. Thus, it is not enough to have a spouse or a job; more important is the quality of interpersonal ties. The policy implications of these findings are, by necessity, indirect. There is little within the realm of criminal justice or social policy that can be done about finding the right spouse or job. These challenges, however, can be made less burdensome through changes in criminal justice and social policy. For example, in the correctional setting, counseling—especially regarding marital responsibility and the importance of commitment, education, and job training—could be of assistance to those who sincerely participate in them.

Some evidence indicates that vocational training programs provided in prison or in a residential setting are effective in reducing recidivism (Bushway and Reuter 1997; MacKenzie and Hickman 1998). Additionally, some studies suggest that education programs may be effective in changing criminal trajectories. Harer (1995) reported that participation in a general education program resulted in lower rearrest rates upon release from prison. Similarly, participation in GED programs appears to result in lower rates of reincarceration during the first two years after release (MacKenzie and Hickman 1998).

Another recommendation is the reduced use of incarceration and the greater use of community based corrections. These may take the form of traditional or intensive-supervision probation, use of electronic monitoring, and greater use of furloughs and parole to assist the inmate in his or her reintegration into the "normal" world. Some research has indicated that intensive probation combined with treatment reduces rearrests (MacKenzie 1997). One study of a juvenile intensive-supervised probation program in Pennsylvania reported that with intensive aftercare for serious juvenile offenders, the rearrest rate was reduced by 50 percent (Sontheimer and Goodstein 1993). Transitional assistance to help offenders with their release from prison may also reduce criminal behavior. Studies of these programs have produced some mixed results; however, they report that ex-offenders with jobs commit fewer crimes than those without jobs (Bushway and Reuter 1997). Thus, these programs may prove to be successful in reducing recidivism due to their emphasis on developing social bonds in adulthood.

Conclusion

The age-graded theory of informal social control has been driven by the following challenge: is it possible to develop and test a theoretical model that explains crime and deviance in childhood, adolescence, and adulthood? To answer this question, Sampson and Laub (1993) first synthesized and integrated the criminological literature on childhood antisocial behavior, adolescent delinquency, and adult crime with theory and research on the life course. This theoretical framework has three major themes. The first is that structural context is mediated by informal family and school social controls, which in turn explain delinquency in childhood and adolescence. The second theme is that there is strong continuity in antisocial behavior running from childhood through adulthood across a variety of life domains. The third theme is that informal social control emerging from social bonds and social capital in adulthood explains changes in criminal behavior over the life span, regardless of prior differences in delinquency.

Overall, the empirical literature supports the propositions of Sampson and Laub's (1993) theory. When the bonds linking youth to society, whether through family or school, are weakened, the probability of delinquency is increased. Negative structural conditions, such as poverty or family disruption, also affect delinquency, but largely through family and school bonding variables. Delinquency and other forms of antisocial conduct in childhood strongly predict troublesome adult behavior including crime, economic dependence, and marital discord. At the same time, research findings suggest that social ties in adulthood, such as marital attachment and job stability, explain variations in adult criminal behavior.

This theoretical and empirical framework also provides new ways to think about crime control policies and crime prevention. Public discourse on crime has been shortsighted, and debates have largely centered on increasing punishment and getting tougher on crime. The debates have little connection to realistic policies for crime control. It is time for broader crime policy that focuses on more than formal social control by the criminal justice system. Sampson and Laub's theory provides a rationale for a movement towards policies that prevent crime rather than merely controlling it. Several current programs that appear to be successful in preventing criminal behavior in adolescence and in adulthood have been presented, and many others exist throughout the country. Instead of focusing on punishing those who have already committed crimes, these programs allow us to try to prevent crime from occurring in the first place. Because of its focus on a life-course perspective and the simultaneity of continuity and change in behavior, the age-graded theory of informal social control provides a sound theoretical framework that is empirically supported and provides realistic directions for successful crime policy.

References

Akers, Ronald L. (1998). *Social Learning and Social Structure: A General Theory of Crime and Deviance.* Boston, MA: Northeastern University Press.

Bushway, S. and P. Reuter. (1997). "Labor markets and crime risk factors." Pp. 6–59 in L.W. Sherman, D. Gottfredson, D. MacKenzie, J. Eck, P. Reuter, and S. Bushway (eds.). *Preventing crime: What works, what doesn't, what's promising.* Report to the United States Congress. Prepared for the National Institute of Justice.

Caspi, A. and T.E. Moffitt. (1995). "The continuity of maladaptive behavior: From description to understanding in the study of antisocial behavior." Pp. 472–511 in D. Cicchetti and D. Cohen (eds.). *Manual of developmental psychopathology.* New York: Wiley.

Cohen, L.E. and B.J. Vila. (1996). "Self-control and social control: An exposition of the Gottfredson-Hirschi/Sampson-Laub debate." *Studies on Crime and Crime Prevention,* 5:125–150.

Cullen, F.T. (1994). "Social support as an organizing concept for criminology: Presidential address to the Academy of Criminal Justice Sciences." *Justice Quarterly,* 11:527–559.

Elder, G.H. (1985). "Perspectives on the life course." Pp. 23–49 in G.H. Elder (ed.). *Life Course Dynamics.* Ithaca, NY: Cornell University Press.

Farrington, D.P. (1986). "Stepping stones to adult criminal careers." Pp. 359–384 in D. Olweus, J. Block, and M. Radke-Yarrow (eds.). *Development of Antisocial and Prosocial Behavior.* New York: Academic.

Farrington, D.P., B. Gallagher, L. Morley, R.J. St. Ledger, and D.J. West. (1986). "Unemployment, school leaving, and crime." *British Journal of Criminology,* 26:335–356.

Farrington, D.P. and D.J. West. (1995). "Effects of marriage, separation, and children on offending by adult males." Pp. 249–281 in Z.S. Blau and J. Hagan (eds.). *Current Perspectives on Aging and the Life Cycle, Vol. 4: Delinquency and Disrepute in the Life Course.* Greenwich, CT: JAI.

Glueck, S. and E. Glueck. (1950). *Unraveling Juvenile Delinquency.* New York: The Commonwealth Fund.

Glueck, S. and E. Glueck. (1968). *Delinquents and Nondelinquents in Perspective.* Cambridge, MA: Harvard University Press.

Gottfredson, M.R. and T. Hirschi. (1990). *A General Theory of Crime.* Stanford, CA: Stanford University Press.

Hagan, J. (1993). "The social embeddedness of crime and unemployment." *Criminology,* 31:465–491.

Harer, M.D. (1995). "Recidivism among federal prisoners released in 1987." *Journal of Correctional Education,* 46:98–127.

Hirschi, T. (1969). *Causes of Delinquency.* Berkeley: University of California Press.

Hirschi, T. and M. Gottfredson. (1995). "Control theory and the life-course perspective." *Studies on Crime and Crime Prevention,* 4:131–143.

Horney, J., D.W. Osgood, and I.H. Marshall. (1995). "Criminal careers in the short-term: Intra-individual variability in crime and its relation to local life circumstances." *American Sociological Review,* 60:655–673.

Larzelere, R.E. and G.R. Patterson. (1990). "Parental management: Mediator of the effect of socioeconomic status on early delinquency." *Criminology,* 28:301–323.

Laub, J.H., D.S. Nagin, and R.J. Sampson. (1998). "Trajectories of change in criminal offending: Good marriages and the desistance process." *American Sociological Review,* 63:225–238.

Laub, J.H. and R.J. Sampson. (1993). "Turning points in the life course: Why change matters in the study of crime." *Criminology,* 31:301–325.

Laub, J.H. and R.J. Sampson. (1995). "The long-term effect of punitive discipline." Pp. 247–258 in J. McCord (ed.). *Coercion and Punishment in Long-Term Perspective.* Cambridge: Cambridge University Press.

Laub, J.H., R.J. Sampson, R.P. Corbett, and J.S. Smith. (1995). "The public policy implications of a life-course perspective on crime." Pp. 91–106 in H.D. Barlow (ed.). *Crime and Public Policy: Putting Theory to Work.* Boulder, CO: Westview.

Loeber, R. and M. LeBlanc. (1990). "Toward a developmental criminology." Pp. 375–451 in M. Tonry and N. Morris (eds.). *Crime and Justice,* Vol. 12. Chicago: University of Chicago Press.

Loeber, R. and M. Stouthamer-Loeber. (1986). "Family factors as correlates and predictors of juvenile conduct problems and delinquency." Pp. 29–149 in M. Tonry and N. Morris (eds.). *Crime and Justice,* Vol. 7. Chicago: University of Chicago Press.

MacKenzie, D.L. (1997). "Criminal justice and crime prevention." Pp. 9–76 in L.W. Sherman, D. Gottfredson, D. MacKenzie, J. Eck, P. Reuter, and S. Bushway (eds.). *Preventing crime: What works, what doesn't, what's promising.* Report to the United States Congress. Prepared for the National Institute of Justice.

MacKenzie, D.L. and L.J. Hickman. (1998). *What Works in Corrections? An Examination of the Effectiveness of the Type of Rehabilitation Programs Offered by Washington State Department of Corrections.* Report to the State of Washington Legislature, Joint Audit and Review Committee.

McLoyd, V.C. (1990). "The impact of economic hardship on black families and children: Psychological distress, parenting, and socioemotional development." *Child Development,* 61:311–346.

Moffitt, T.E. (1993). "Adolescence-limited and life-course persistent antisocial behavior: A developmental taxonomy." *Psychological Review,* 100:674–701.

Nagin, D. and R. Paternoster. (1991). "On the relationship of past and future participation in delinquency." *Criminology,* 29:163–190.

Olds, D., P. Hill, and E. Rumsey. (1998). *Prenatal and Early Childhood Nurse Home Visitation. Juvenile Justice Bulletin.* Washington, DC: U.S. Department of Justice, Office of Juvenile Justice and Delinquency Prevention.

Olweus, D. (1979). "Stability of aggressive reaction patterns in males: A review." *Psychological Bulletin,* 86:852–875.

Patterson, G.R. (1993). "Orderly change in a stable world: The antisocial trait as a chimera." *Journal of Consulting and Clinical Psychology,* 61:911–919.

Patterson, G.R., B.D. DeBaryshe, and E. Ramsey. (1989). "A developmental perspective on antisocial behavior." *American Psychologist,* 44:329–335.

Patterson, G.R. and K. Yoerger. (1993). "Developmental models for delinquent behavior." Pp. 140–172 in S. Hodgins (ed.). *Mental Disorder and Crime.* Newbury Park, CA: Sage.

Robins, L.N. (1966). *Deviant Children Grown Up.* Baltimore, MD: Williams and Wilkins.

Robins, L.N. (1978). "Sturdy childhood predictors of adult antisocial behavior: Replications from longitudinal studies." *Psychological Medicine,* 8:611–622.

Rutter, M. and M. Rutter. (1993). *Developing Minds: Challenge and Continuity Across the Life Span.* New York: Basic.

Sampson, R.J. and J.H. Laub. (1993). *Crime in the Making: Pathways and Turning Points Through Life.* Cambridge, MA: Harvard University Press.

Sampson, R.J. and J.H. Laub. (1994). "Urban poverty and the family context of delinquency: A new look at structure and process in a classic study." *Child Development,* 65:523–540.

Sampson, R.J. and J.H. Laub. (1995). "Understanding variability in lives through time: Contributions of life-course criminology." *Studies on Crime and Crime Prevention,* 4:143–158.

Sampson, R.J. and J.H. Laub. (1997). "A life-course theory of cumulative disadvantage and the stability of delinquency." Pp. 133–161 in T.P. Thornberry (ed.). *Developmental Theories of Crime and Delinquency.* New Brunswick, NJ: Transaction.

Shaw, C.R. and H. McKay. (1942). *Juvenile Delinquency and Urban Areas.* Chicago: University of Chicago Press.

Sherman, L.W. (1997). "Family-based crime prevention." Pp. 8–58 in L.M. Sherman, D. Gottfredson, D. MacKenzie, J. Eck, P. Reuter, and S. Bushway (eds.). *Preventing crime: What works, what doesn't, what's promising.*

Report to the United States Congress. Prepared for the National Institute of Justice.

Sontheimer, H. and L. Goodstein. (1993). "Evaluation of juvenile intensive aftercare probation: Aftercare versus system response effects." *Justice Quarterly,* 10:197–227.

Thornberry, T.P. (1987). "Toward an interactional theory of delinquency." *Criminology,* 25:863–891.

Thornberry, T.P. (ed.). (1997). *Developmental Theories of Crime and Delinquency.* New Brunswick, NJ: Transaction.

Warr, M. (1998). "Life-course transitions and desistance from crime." *Criminology,* 36:183–216.

Warr, M. and M. Stafford. (1991). "The influence of delinquent peers: What they think or what they do?" *Criminology,* 29:851–866.

Wellford, C.F. (1997). "Controlling crime and achieving justice—the American society of criminology 1996 presidential address." *Criminology,* 35:1–11.

5
Social Disorganization and Crime

Introduction

One of the first things you may have noticed about crime, even before taking a single course in criminology, was that there were "bad parts" of your town. You knew a lot of crime was being committed there, so you avoided walking, parking, or even driving a car through such areas. You also sensed that crime was not the only social problem in those areas. In addition to high levels of crime, you saw that these areas also had high levels of unemployment, drug addiction, alcoholism, domestic violence, mental illness, poverty, and run-down housing. You were aware of the "good parts" of your town as well. These "good parts" had low rates of crime and the residents were not afflicted by the numerous social ills found in bad areas. With a little more thought, you may have realized that still other parts of town fell in between these two extremes in terms of the amount of crime and social problems.

In thinking about where crime is high and where it is low, one is really interested in how crime is distributed within a given geographical area, that is, within a particular space. Therefore, scholars of crime are concerned with the *spatial distribution* of crime. For example, from thinking about your own town, you know that crime and other social problems do not seem to be randomly distributed. If they were, there would be no pattern or "rhyme and reason" as to their appearance. The distribution of crime over geographical areas would be due to chance or luck under a random scheme. Rather, you detect a definite pattern to crime and other

social problems. They seem to appear together—that is, they are highly correlated. Moreover, they seem related, so there may be some connection between the high rates of crime and the high rates of other social ills in these areas.

This chapter provides some insight into a school of criminological thought whose focus is explaining the geographic or spatial distribution of crime rates. These scholars have noticed the same things you have. They have also empirically documented the spatial distribution of crime and social problems. Rather than being concerned with the criminality of individuals, however, they are generally interested in the criminality of groups of individuals in units like neighborhoods, cities, counties, states, or countries. For example, they want to know why the rate of crime is higher in some neighborhoods than others. The specific question they want to address is, "Are observed neighborhood differences in crime rates due solely to the kinds of people who live in them, or is there something about the characteristics of these neighborhoods themselves that fosters a particular amount of crime?"

Historically, several terms have been used to describe these scholars and their work. Sometimes they are referred to as *social disorganization theorists*, after one of their principal explanatory variables. Sometimes they are called environmental criminologists. Sometimes they are referred to as the *school of social ecology* because the science of ecology concerns the relationship between organisms and their environments. Perhaps most often, this tradition of thought is simply referred to as the *Chicago School*, due to the fact that the most comprehensive empirical and theoretical work was initially done at the University of Chicago. Whatever name is used to refer to them, what makes this group distinctive is their interest in explaining aggregate *rates of crime* across geographical units (see Bursik 1988).

Next, we would like to lay a foundation that provides a brief history of this school of thought. The essay by Professor Ralph B. Taylor that follows builds on this foundation by presenting some of the key concepts of this school, some of the major empirical findings to date, and the policy implications that flow from the theories. This chapter comes immediately after the chapter on control theory because both chapters emphasize the idea that crime appears in the absence of control. In fact, the key theoretical construct, social disorganization, is premised on the idea that crime and deviance occur in the absence of concerted community activity to prevent it. That is, crimes take place whenever community institutions that foster social control break down because of social disorganization. The fact that a lack of community control makes crime possible means that the explanation is a control theory of crime.

Early Interest in the Spatial Distribution of Crime

Interest in the spatial distribution of crime goes way back. Perhaps the first systematic attempt to assemble and publish crime data on geographical units was conducted by the French government around the beginning of the nineteenth century (Beirne 1993). One of the most important of these early crime publications was the annual *Compte general de l'administration de la justice criminelle en France*, first published in 1827 (Beirne 1993, 73). The *Compte* was an early forerunner of the FBI's Uniform Crime Reports. It consisted of crime reports compiled by local French prosecutors who mailed in quarterly reports to a central administration in Paris. The data included such information as the location of the crime, the type of crime committed, whether a suspect was arrested, and if arrested, convicted, and the punishment received. The statistical data printed in the *Compte* were soon analyzed by a group of scholars, perhaps the most influential of whom was the Belgian astronomer and mathematician Adolphe Quetelet.

Though formally trained in mathematics and astronomy, Quetelet became one of the leading intellectuals who applied statistical knowledge to social and public problems, which became known as *social mechanics*, *social physics* (Beirne 1993, 76), or *moral statistics* (Taylor et al. 1974, 37). One of the first things that Quetelet noticed about French criminal statistics was their regularity. Although mindful that human behavior would not likely follow the same determinate laws as natural phenomena, Quetelet was impressed with the fact that within geographical areas (in this case, French provinces) crime rates were quite stable over time, but crime rates across geographical areas were quite different. The stability of the crime data convinced Quetelet that the cause of crime also had to be regular and could not, therefore, be entirely due to individual factors. He suspected that some consistent feature of society or the social structure might lead to crime with some degree of regularity. The contribution of Quetelet, then, was to acknowledge that existing social arrangements may be responsible for crime. Quetelet never fully developed his theory of social organization and crime, however, and it was left to others at a later time in a different place to do this important work.

Early Chicago Theorists and the Theory of Social Disorganization

Research Findings from the Chicago School

The Department of Sociology at the University of Chicago in the early 1900s had a group of faculty who were interested in the process by which urban areas grow and develop. Two of the most prominent of these sociologists were Robert E. Park and Ernest W. Burgess. Park and Burgess likened the growth of a city to a natural ecological competition. Just as there is a natural ecology where animals and plants compete for space and existence, so there is a social ecology where humans compete for scarce and desirable space. The "laboratory" where Park, Burgess, and their colleagues first studied the human competition over space was the city of Chicago. During the late nineteenth and early twentieth centuries, this was a perfect laboratory to study urban growth. Chicago began as a small and bucolic town of approximately 4,000 residents in 1833, but by 1910 it numbered two million (Palen 1981). This rapid population expansion was principally brought on by the migration of outsiders, notably foreign-born immigrants, rather than by natural fertility.

With the increase in numbers, therefore, came heightened cultural, religious, and ethnic heterogeneity in the city's population. Because of an explosion in immigration, Chicago became populated with people who spoke different languages and had different customs, histories, and religions. During this growth in population size and heterogeneity, the area's industry expanded as well as its hunger for cheap labor. Chicago became the nation's slaughterhouse and was also a key site for heavy industry, like Pullman train cars. In a short time, therefore, Chicago was rapidly changed by the forces of urbanization, immigration, and industrialization. The sociologists at the University of Chicago wanted to understand the effects of these rapid social changes, particularly their moral effects or their implications for social order.

The essence of Park and Burgess' theory of urban ecology was that when cities grow, they typically extend outward from the oldest area into the newest (Park et al. 1928; Park 1936). The expansion occurs as newer (generally better) areas are "invaded" by the residents of older (generally worse) areas. This theory posited that urban areas could be characterized by a series of adjacent circles or *concentric zones*. The innermost zone is the oldest part of the city and is the site of business and industry. The next zone out is referred to as the *zone of transition*. This is a residential area adjacent to the industrial zone. It is unattractive, sooty, odorous, and noisy, where housing is inexpensive and unattractive. It is a very unpleasant residential area inhabited by the poorest, who are attracted to the menial jobs and cheap housing nearby.

The residential area in this zone is changing, or is in a state of transition. It is being invaded by business and manufacturing interests from the central business district and slowly converting from a residential to a commercial zone. The next zone out is "fitted with workingmen's homes." This zone contains better communities and more attractive, though still relatively inexpensive, housing. This zone is "invaded" by the residents of the zone of transition, who leave as soon as they can afford better housing. The next zone is the *residential zone* followed by the *commuter zone*. These latter two areas are physically far removed from the industrial zone. They contain attractive housing, good schools and neighborhoods, and the appearance of a successful adjustment to urban life. Essentially, the greatest competition over space occurs when residents from the zone of transition try to move out to better areas as their economic lot in life improves. Those unable to compete stay behind and those who successfully escape are replaced by newer poor residents in the zone of transition.

Park and Burgess were urban sociologists and were not really interested in the study of crime. However, two other sociologists, Clifford R. Shaw and Henry D. McKay, who worked at the Illinois Institute for Juvenile Research in Chicago, were keenly interested in crime and applied the Park-Burgess concentric zone theory to the study of delinquency in Chicago. Beginning in 1921, Shaw embarked on a large-scale research and data collection project that would provide the empirical platform for the important theoretical work he was to do over the next several decades with McKay and others (Shaw 1929; Shaw and McKay 1942, 1969; Bursik and Grasmick 1993). These researchers collected official data on delinquents and marked the home address of each delinquent with a pin on a map of the city of Chicago. They used various definitions of what a delinquent was—one who was contacted by police, referred to juvenile court, or sent to reform school. Essentially, Shaw and McKay had an enormous map in their office which was covered with pins. They collected, tabulated, and mapped their information for several decades. From these pin maps, Shaw and McKay then calculated the rates of delinquency for various geographic areas or zones of Chicago. With this massive amount of data, they discovered several things about the spatial distribution of delinquency in Chicago:

- The area with the highest rate of delinquency was directly next to the central business district.

- The area with the lowest rate of delinquency was the farthest from the central business district.

- Rates of delinquency declined steadily as one moved out from the poorest zone of transition to the most affluent commuter zone.

- This distribution of delinquency within a given geographical area was fairly consistent over a forty-year period.

- No matter which immigrant group lived there, the delinquency rates of the children were among the highest in the city when they lived in the zone of transition, but declined as they moved out to better areas.

- Immigrant children left behind had the delinquency rates of the area where they lived; those who moved out adopted the delinquency rates of their new neighborhood.

- No matter which ethnic group lived in the zone of transition, their delinquency rates were the highest in the city. In other words, although the ethnic make-up of the zone of transition changed over time, rates of delinquency were consistently high there.

- In addition to delinquency, rates of other social ills (poverty, poor housing, mental illness, alcoholism, tuberculosis, population mobility, and heterogeneity) evidenced the same pattern. They were highest in the zone adjacent to the central business district and declined steadily as one moved outward.

Shaw and McKay also compiled similar maps of other cities (Philadelphia, Boston, Cincinnati, Cleveland, Richmond) and observed the same thing.

The consistencies in their data led Shaw and McKay to conclude that delinquency and crime could not be due to the fact that the children of immigrants were biologically (and, therefore, morally) inferior, as some had argued, because while their biological make-up remained the same, their rates of crime declined as they moved to better areas. That is, the delinquency rate of the neighborhood did not seem to be due to the individual characteristics of those who lived in those neighborhoods. If it were, they concluded, delinquency rates would not be so consistent within neighborhoods over such long time periods (decades), nor would the delinquency rates of ethnic groups change as they moved into different neighborhoods. Shaw and McKay also concluded that delinquency and crime could not be due to the fact that the city was invariably corrupt and pathological, as others had argued, because high delinquency rates were not uniform. High rates of delinquency were concentrated in certain areas of the city. Other areas not only had low rates of delinquency, they had low levels of other social problems as well. This convinced Shaw and McKay that the cause of high crime rates for some areas was rooted in characteristics of particular *types of neighborhoods*, and was not due to the kind of people who resided in those neighborhoods. Moreover, because some neighborhoods had high rates of delinquency that spanned decades, there must be something about the social arrangements or conditions in those neighborhoods themselves that lead to crime.

What was it about these neighborhoods that consistently bred high levels of crime? Shaw and McKay's key theoretical concept in explaining high-crime areas was the notion of *social disorganization*. Remember that high-crime areas also had high concentrations of families living in poverty, diverse ethnic groups, and rapid population mobility and transience. These areas were the most undesirable areas of the city. Hence people were eager to leave them, did not view their residence as permanent, and left as soon as they were economically able. These conditions of poverty, population heterogeneity, and residential impermanence produced social disorganization, and social disorganization in turn produced high rates of crime. Notice that Shaw and McKay did not say that poverty, heterogeneity, and residential mobility are the direct causes of crime, nor did they argue that these factors comprise or are the elements of social disorganization. Rather, their position was that these conditions indicated the presence of socially disorganized communities. They are, then, indicators of social disorganization (Kornhauser 1978). Poverty, population heterogeneity, and mobility produce social disorganization which in turn leads to consistent and stable rates of neighborhood crime. But what exactly is social disorganization?

One way to think of social disorganization is to view it as a form of community disruption that occurs in the presence of transient and diverse residents. The disruption manifests itself in the inability of residents to solve their own problems and secure their own needs. Normally, community residents are organized to achieve the goals of the neighborhoods where they live—they have clean sidewalks, effective and pleasant schools for their children, regular garbage pick-up, safe streets, and most importantly, adults who both effectively socialize their own children to behave and who intervene and assist when problems in the community arise. The achievement of community goals and needs is easy when there are neighbors who share common values and interact with one another on a repeated basis. However, when families are dysfunctional, neighbors are inattentive to the needs of one another, and families are frequently moving in and out of the area, organized groups within the community are either nonexistent or ineffective in achieving the interests of their residents. When this occurs, social disorganization is said to exist, and the natural controls of the community break down. In the absence of these informal community controls, crime is more likely. Shaw and McKay (Shaw 1929) put it this way:

> Under the pressure of the disintegrative forces which act when business and industry invade a community, the community thus invaded ceases to function effectively as a means of social control. Traditional norms and standards of the conventional community weaken and disappear. Resistance on the part of the community to delinquent and criminal behavior is low, and such behavior is tolerated and may even become accepted and approved. (204–205).

Moreover, because social disorganization is a property of neighborhoods or communities rather than individuals, it persists over time even when residents come and go. As a result, crime rates are stable in the same neighborhoods over long periods of time.

We can all understand that a common goal that residents of a given neighborhood would have is the goal of living free from crime. Community members can work together to achieve this common goal by both collective and individual action. They can effectively socialize their own children, they can intervene when neighbors' children seem to be going astray, they can watch others' homes and call police if something looks suspicious, they can organize youths into athletic clubs, and they can form community organizations to lobby city government to provide better services to the neighborhood. When organized, then, communities can do a lot of things to help them achieve the goal of minimizing crime. Notice, however, that this organization requires that parents care about the effective rearing of children (theirs and others'), that they care about and frequently interact with other neighbors, that they feel some connection or affinity with the neighborhood. Communities whose members share these characteristics are socially organized and are able to mobilize their resources to achieve group goals. Communities lacking these characteristics, whose residents are not concerned about how children are raised, about proper upkeep of their home or streets, who do not interact with others in the neighborhood, and in fact who do not identify with the neighborhood but are only counting the days until they leave are said to be socially disorganized.

This theory of social disorganization would seem to explain the spatial distribution of crime and delinquency that Shaw and McKay observed in their pin maps. Social disorganization was highest in the zone of transition around the central business district. As one moved beyond this area, however, the sources of social disorganization (poverty, ethnic homogeneity, residential mobility) decreased in intensity. In the outer areas in the commuter zone, communities were well organized to meet their needs, and the rates of crime and delinquency were low. You can also perhaps see why Shaw and

McKay's theory of social disorganization is a kind of control theory. The consequence of social disorganization is a breakdown in informal control, which leads to crime. The explanation that crime arises in the absence or weakness of restraint, you will recall from the last chapter, is a control theory explanation.

The Methodological Contribution of Shaw and McKay

Shaw and McKay were empirical scientists, as seen in their systematic attempt to collect, record, and statistically analyze delinquency data. By prevailing standards, their quantitative work in the study of crime was impressive. In addition to this quantitative work, however, Shaw and McKay employed more qualitative methodologies. They collected data from several individual residents of high-crime communities in the form of case studies or "life histories." These life histories were gathered in the course of extensive interviews and consisted of narratives from youths who resided in Chicago's socially disorganized communities. A good part of each of these life histories was in the form of a first-person narrative, with the subject telling his own story. The purpose was to vividly demonstrate the process by which one becomes delinquent in a high-delinquency area at the level of the individual rather than the community (Finestone 1976). The process at the individual level was reflected as a disruption in the communication and connection between youths in an area and conventional adults (parents, teachers, employers, police). The dissolution of the connection between the individual and representatives of conventional society put youths in high-delinquency areas at risk for recruitment into crime. This breakdown in conventional controls that gives way to deviant impulses among particular youths is the manifestation of social disorganization at the level of the individual.

There are three prominent examples of the qualitative approach Shaw and McKay took in their study of crime. The first of these is the life history of "Stanley" found in *The Jack-Roller* (Shaw 1930). Stanley grew up in a large Polish neighborhood in Chicago near the stockyards. Stanley's neighborhood was very poor and deteriorated, had a high proportion of foreign-born residents, and had a transient population. It manifested all the characteristics of a socially disorganized community—poor, high-population heterogeneity, substantial mobility, and a clustering of diverse social ills. Stanley's criminal career started at an early age, was punctuated with several stays in a reform school, and continued well into adolescence.

In accounting for his own conduct, Stanley described his home life as miserable. His mother died when he was 4 years old, and his emotionally distant father remarried a cruel woman who favored her own seven children when she and Stanley's father joined their families. With an unhappy home life, Stanley soon found the company of delinquent companions on the streets. Stanley and his friends were active thieves, and he reported that his step-mother approved of his stealing, so long as he brought some of his loot home. In fact, Stanley reported that theft was approved by all parents in his neighborhood. He observed no strong neighborhood norms against delinquency of most kinds. Beginning with theft, Stanley continued his life of crime. In sum, Stanley's own life corresponds to social disorganization on the individual level. Both his family and neighborhood were unable to restrain his tendency to commit crimes. The only relationships he found satisfying were those with other delinquents. Unable to forge emotionally close bonds with his parents or other conventional people, no controls or restraining forces influenced his conduct. In the absence of personal controls, Stanley resorted to a life of crime.

A second example of the life history is found in *The Natural History of a Delinquent Career* (Shaw 1931), which details the life of Sidney Blotzman, a Polish-American youth, who was raised in a high-delinquency neighborhood just west of the "loop" in Chicago. Like Stanley, Sidney had a very active delinquent career that began at age 7 and eventually included arrests for truancy, shoplifting, burglary, auto theft, armed robbery, and rape. In accounting for Sidney's prolific criminal career, Shaw (1931) makes reference to the fact that he "lived in one of the most deteriorated and disorganized sections of the city . . .[where] conventional traditions, neighborhood institutions, and public opinion, through which neighborhoods usually effect a control over the behavior of the child, were largely disintegrated" (229). The restraining influence of conventional culture did not, therefore, filter down into Sidney's neighborhood.

Shaw also points out that Sidney, like Stanley, came from a dysfunctional family. His father was an emotionally cold and abusive alcoholic who frequently deserted the home. Although Sidney was not strongly attached to his mother or father, he did maintain strong emotional ties to a few of the neighborhood boys. These boys, however, were active delinquents and provided Sidney's initiation into delinquency. Shaw (1931) concluded that Sidney's only social contacts were with criminal and deviant groups, and "he was never incorporated into a conventional group through which he might assimilate the conventional attitudes and moral values of society" (233). In other words, Sidney's own disaffiliation from conventional groups prevented him from learning moral restraints on his own behavior, just as his neighborhood's social disorganization prevented it from being influenced by the moral standards of the larger society.

The third life history, in *Brothers in Crime* (Shaw 1938), tells the story of the Martin brothers—John, Edward, James, Michael, and Carl. Like the other life histories, this contains the boys' own first-person accounts of the process that led to their delinquent career. The Martin family resided in a section of Chicago that was adjacent to an industrial site. It was an unattractive community that traditionally had a high level of delinquency. By all accounts, the Martins were good parents. However, both Mr. and Mrs. Martin had to work outside the home for long hours in order to make ends meet. This left the boys unsupervised and eventually in the streets in the company of delinquent peers. A great deal of conflict was caused by the tension between the conventional and religious views of the parents (especially Mrs. Martin) and the life of crime favored by the boys and their

friends. This tension, poor supervision, and the emotional distance between children and parents became greater because of repeated terms of confinement for the boys in reform schools. There they cemented their bonds with the criminal life. Not only did the boys not have a strong family to restrain their conduct, but given the massive problems in the community, few neighborhood groups or institutions were available to provide guidance and assistance to parents. In sum, there was very little restraint over the conduct of the boys because their family life had too much conflict and their neighbors were too disinterested.

In each of these three life histories, Shaw and McKay describe the process by which individuals within high-crime areas become delinquent. In each case, this process reflects on a micro- or individual level the failure of conventional institutions (family, school) to effectively control the conduct of youths. Just as the disorganization of neighborhoods prevented conventional norms from filtering into some communities, the disaffiliation of boys from conventional people allowed them to wriggle free of any control that others would normally have placed over their conduct. That is, for both neighborhoods and the youths who live in them, criminal conduct becomes more likely in the absence of control.

The Crime Prevention Program of the Chicago School

We would like to make one more point about the early Chicago theorists. In the first chapter of this book, we argued that not all criminological theorists are entirely explicit about the policy implications of their theories. These policy implications are always present but often not articulated. The theory that Shaw and McKay developed is an exception. Unlike perhaps any other theorists, Shaw and McKay (particularly Clifford Shaw) were very clear in drawing the policy implications of their work and were actively involved in criminal justice policy. Based on the theory of social disorganization, Clifford Shaw initially developed and supervised a crime prevention and treatment program in

Chicago neighborhoods called the Chicago Area Projects.

The Chicago Area Projects was designed to strengthen and mobilize local community residents to care about and improve the conditions within their neighborhoods. That is, if crime and other social ills were due to the fact that communities were incapable of organizing and working toward solving their own problems, then community residents could be taught and assisted in doing so. The Area Projects identified and trained community members to be active advocates for their own neighborhoods. Under the guidance of the Area Projects, community members were assisted in the development of recreation programs for youths in their neighborhoods and in their attempt to make local politicians more responsive to their needs and demands. Neighborhood leaders were assisted in attempts to have their streets cleaned, street lights repaired, garbage picked up regularly, and regular police patrols on duty. Have the Chicago Area Projects (which are still going on) been successful? In a comprehensive evaluation that was conducted some fifty years after the Projects were started, Schlossman and his colleagues (Schlossman and Sedlak 1983; Schlossman et al. 1984) noted that the evidence was mixed. There was evidence of some increase in how well communities were organized against delinquency, but there was a substantial amount of variation from neighborhood to neighborhood. In other words, even with the direct attempt to organize their neighborhood by the Chicago Area Projects, it was difficult for some communities to develop a grassroots base of support and community-run delinquency prevention programs. In terms of delinquency reduction, some neighborhoods did seem to have lower rates of delinquency than in the past. However, in spite of this apparent success, it was not clear that the reduced delinquency was due to the efforts of the Chicago Area Projects or some other source, and other communties where the Projects were operating had higher than expected levels of delinquency. The whole idea of the Chicago Area Projects was to create social organization and community involvement and participation in what had been isolated and disorganized neighborhoods.

The Revival of the Chicago Tradition in Crime and Ecology

At the time, the work of Shaw and McKay had a profound impact on the field of criminology and the study of crime generally. However, interest in the relationship between community characteristics and rates of crime began to ebb beginning in the 1950s. At this time, the field's center of gravity moved toward individual theories of crime causation (i.e., the *micro-level*). Over the next several decades, scholars of crime were influenced by strain, social learning, labeling, and social control theories. As an indication of the fact that the work of the Chicago School was losing its influence over the field, little systematic theorizing or empirical research was conducted pertaining to crime and social ecology or human communities from approximately 1950 to 1980. Beginning in the 1980s, however, scholars showed a revival of interest in ecological studies of crime and the relationship between characteristics of communities and crime rates. Although theoretical interest in the concept of social disorganization was not as strong as in the past, scholars were again interested in the relationship between what is referred to as *macro-level* factors and crime rates.

Prominent in this renewed interest in community studies of crime was the work of Robert Sampson, Robert Bursik and Harold Grasmick, and Ralph Taylor. In 1986, the prestigious *Annual Review of Research* published by the University of Chicago Press produced a volume titled *Communities and Crime*, thereby formally announcing the reemergence of interest in ecological studies of crime (Reiss and Tonry 1986). In a paper in that volume, Sampson (1986) argued that variation in homicide and robbery rates across U.S. cities could be attributed to differences in both formal and informal social control. He found that crime rates were affected by official sanction policies (how aggressive city police were in responding to crime and the risk of local jail incarceration) and by the condition of the family within cities (divorce and the proportion of "two-parent families"). Some cities have high rates of homicide and robbery, he argued, because formal controls are weak, and disrupted families make it difficult for communities to assert informal controls.

In a subsequent paper, Sampson and Groves (1989) extended the work of the early Chicago theorists. Recall that Shaw and McKay argued that communities stricken with high rates of poverty, population heterogeneity, and mobility were unable to sustain informal controls over the behavior of unsupervised youths. Using the British Crime Survey, Sampson and Groves confirmed this link. They found that structural factors (poverty, mobility) were connected to community rates of criminal victimization through three indicators of social disorganization: community supervision of teenage peer groups, local friendship networks, and the rate of participation in community organizations. In his most recent work, Sampson and colleagues (1997) confirmed the prediction from Shaw and McKay that strong communities can resist crime. They found that "disadvantaged communities" (those characterized by poverty, a concentration of young racial minorities, and family disruption) have higher levels of violent crime. Most importantly, they found that the effect of disadvantage was primarily felt through what they called *collective efficacy*, which is the ability of community members to trust and informally assist one another. As the early Chicago theorists predicted, disadvantaged communities had higher rates of violent crime because it disrupted their ability to foster and effectively utilize informal mechanisms of control.

In 1993, Bursik and Grasmick published an important theoretical extension of the Chicago School, which they called a *systemic reformulation* of social disorganization theory. Drawing on the work of Albert Hunter (1974, 1985), they argued that the population instability and heterogeneity that were central to the Chicago School affected the rate of neighborhood crime through three levels of social control: (1) the private level, (2) the parochial level, and (3) the public level.

Private control occurs when parents care about and effectively socialize their children, and when neighbors care about and are influenced by the opinions of others. For example, if I keep my yard tidy and free of garbage and make sure that my children do not vandalize property, in part because I want my acquaintances in the neighborhood to think well of me, I am under private control. Private control, therefore, is based on social censure, embarrassment, and gossip. In order for private control to work, therefore, the connections between persons must be based on sentiment or emotions (i.e., persons must interact with and personally care about one another).

Parochial control is more general and less effective than private control. It refers to the control exercised by community members and community institutions and organizations such as schools, churches, and voluntary groups. Parochial control occurs when neighbors watch and supervise other children in the community, when they question strangers who enter the neighborhood, and when schools are effectively used as the focal point of community activities.

Finally, *public control* refers to the capacity of the neighborhood to successfully secure goods and services from larger political entities (for example, city government) that will directly benefit them. Public control is exercised, for example, when a community wins approval from the police to have a local district office with foot patrols in their neighborhood, or when they defeat the attempts of the state department of corrections to place a drug treatment program for ex-offenders within the community. Bursik and Grasmick's (1993) point was that population instability and heterogeneity affect the exercise of private, parochial, and public control. Communities with substantial population turnover and a diverse make-up find it difficult to exercise each of the three levels of control. As a result, they are unable to organize themselves to achieve a common goal, such as a crime-free neighborhood.

Professor Ralph Taylor has conducted some important research over a number of years linking community characteristics and levels of crime. He and Stephen Gottfredson found that the recidivism of a sample of prison releasees depended upon the kind of neighborhood into which they were released (Gottfredson and Taylor 1986). In a series of research projects conducted in the city of Baltimore, Taylor also found that communities where neighbors socialize with one another and interact more frequently have lower levels of crime, in part because they are better able to organize, react, and effectively respond to crime and other social problems than communities where the social bonds and connections among neighbors are weaker (Taylor et al. 1985; Taylor 1986). You will learn more about ecological studies of crime in Professor Taylor's essay that follows.

References

Beirne, Piers. (1993). *Inventing Criminology: Essays on the Rise of "Homo Criminalis."* Albany: State University of New York Press.

Bursik, Robert J., Jr. (1988). "Social disorganization and theories of crime and delinquency." *Criminology,* 26:519–551.

Bursik, Robert J., Jr. and Harold G. Grasmick. (1993). *Neighborhoods and Crime: The Dimensions of Effective Community Control.* New York: Lexington.

Finestone, Harold. (1976). "The delinquent and society: The Shaw and McKay tradition." Pp. 23–49 in *Delinquency, Crime and Society,* J.F. Short, Jr. (ed.). Chicago: University of Chicago Press.

Gottfredson, Steven D. and Ralph B. Taylor. (1986). "Person-environment interactions in the prediction of recidivism." Pp. 221–228 in *The Social Ecology of Crime.* J.M. Byrne and R.J. Sampson (eds.). New York: Springer-Verlag.

Hunter, Albert J. (1974). *Symbolic Communities.* Chicago: University of Chicago Press.

——. (1985). "Private, parochial, and public school orders: The problem of crime and incivility in urban communities." Pp. 230–242 in *The Challenge of Social Control: Citizenship and Institution Building in Modern Society.* G.D. Suttles and M.N. Zald (eds.). Norwood, NJ: Ablex.

Kornhauser, Ruth Rosner. (1978). *Social Sources of Delinquency.* Chicago: University of Chicago Press.

Palen, John J. (1981). *The Urban World,* Third Edition. New York: McGraw-Hill.

Park, Robert E. (1936). "Human ecology." *American Journal of Sociology,* 3–15.

Park, Robert E. and Ernest W. Burgess. (1925). *The City.* Chicago: University of Chicago Press.

Park, Robert E., Ernest W. Burgess, and Roderick D. McKenzie. (1928). *The City.* Chicago: University of Chicago Press.

Reiss, Albert J., Jr. and Michael Tonry. (1986). *Communities and Crime, Vol. 8, Crime and Justice: An Annual Review of Research.* Chicago: University of Chicago Press.

Sampson, Robert J. (1986). "Crime in cities: The effects of formal and informal social control." In *Communities and Crime, Vol. 8, Crime and Justice: An Annual Review of Research.* Chicago: University of Chicago Press.

Sampson, Robert J. and W. Byron Groves. (1989). "Community structure and crime: Testing social-disorganization theory." *American Journal of Sociology,* 94:774–802.

Sampson, Robert J., Stephen W. Raudenbush, and Felton Earls. (1997). "Neighborhoods and violent crime: A multi-level study of collective efficacy." *Science,* 277:918–924.

Schlossman, Steven and Michael Sedlak. (1983). "The Chicago area projects revisited." *Crime and Delinquency,* 29:398–462.

Schlossman, Steven, and Michael Shavelson with Michael Sedlak and Jane Jacob. (1984). "Delinquency prevention in South Chicago: A fifty-year assessment of the Chicago area projects. Santa Monica, CA: Rand.

Shaw, Clifford R. (with the collaboration of Frederick M. Zorbaugh, Henry D. McKay, and Leonard S. Cottrell). (1929). *Delinquency Areas.* Chicago: University of Chicago Press.

Shaw, Clifford R. (1930). *The Jack-Roller: A Delinquent Boy's Own Story.* Chicago: University of Chicago Press.

Shaw, Clifford, R. (in collaboration with Maurice E. Moore). (1931). *The Natural History of a Delinquent Career.* Chicago: University of Chicago Press.

Shaw, Clifford R. (with the assistance of Henry D. McKay and James F. McDonald). (1938). *Brothers in Crime.* Chicago: University of Chicago Press.

Shaw, Clifford R. and Henry D. McKay. (1942). *Juvenile Delinquency and Urban Areas.* Chicago: University of Chicago Press.

——. (1969). *Juvenile Delinquency and Urban Areas* (Revised Edition). Chicago: University of Chicago Press.

Taylor, Ian, Paul Walton, and Jock Young. (1974). *The New Criminology.* New York: Harper and Row.

Taylor, Ralph S. (1986). "Environmental design, crime, and prevention: An examination of community dynamics." In *Communities and Crime, Vol. 8, Crime and Justice: An Annual Review of Research.* Chicago: University of Chicago Press.

Taylor, Ralph, S.A. Schumaker, and Stephen D. Gottfredson. (1985). "Neighborhood-level link between physical features and local sentiments: Deterioration, fear of crime, and confidence." *Journal of Architectural Planning and Research,* 2:261–275.

The Ecology of Crime, Fear, and Delinquency

Social Disorganization Versus Social Efficacy

Ralph B. Taylor
Temple University

Some Background

The Eighteenth Century

Napoleon was a pretty big guy, even though vertically challenged. He knew how to get things done. He ran into a few problems outside Moscow and had a really bad day at Waterloo, but when he wasn't busy trying to take places over, he was initiating reforms at home. In France, he centralized local governments; rewrote civil, commercial and criminal law codes; and even balanced the budget, among other things. As a result of his efforts, in the years that followed, local officials and local arms of government agencies started collecting data about how the country was running.[1] And, as often happens with data, when researchers are hanging around, someone starts looking at them. Even back then, some people didn't get out enough.

Officials were particularly interested in seeing the effects of their new criminal laws. How many people were being arrested, imprisoned, flogged, or hung in different parts of the country? (Radzinowicz 1966). Using a lot of ink and addition, researchers like Guerry and Quetelet in France found *spatial variation* in the rate at which people were being arrested for crime in different parts of the country (Brantingham and Brantingham 1991).

The specifics of the patterns they observed still hold true for researchers looking at spatial differences in crime rates today:

(1) There were 86 "departments" in France; a few had very high rates, a few had very low rates, and many places were in between. (2) These differences between regions appeared relatively stable over time. (3) The rates varied widely; for example, the rate of people accused of crimes against persons for the period 1826–1830 ranged from 1/2,199 in Corse to 1/37,014 in Creuse.[2] (4) Patterns for violent and property crimes differed. Violent crimes were highest in southern rural areas; property rates were highest in industrialized, northern, urbanized departments. Each of these features of local crime rates has proven true in most subsequent research over the past 150 years.

Researchers in Britain around the same time found comparable patterns when they examined data at the county level and below: marked spatial variation in the crime rates (e.g., Glyde 1856). But the differences were not always what they expected. In the mid-1850s in Suffolk County, England, the highest crime rates were in the rural part of the county.

Complementing these statistical efforts were investigations by nineteenth-century British social workers going into some of these "bad" areas (Morris 1957). They saw deplorable conditions right out of a Charles Dickens novel. Their reports led to some widespread slum-clearing efforts. Nonetheless, some of these same locations, populated largely by "thieves and pickpockets and prostitutes," remained high-crime areas in the late 1880s, at the turn of the century, and through to the 1960s (Brantingham and Brantingham 1991, 11).

By the end of the nineteenth century, environmental criminologists had discovered the following fundamental features about spatial and temporal distributions of crime:

- There is spatial variation in rates of reported crime. This variation shows up no matter the level of resolution. It is higher in some places than in others, regardless of whether one is looking at large-scale units, such as counties, or areas within counties, like different towns or different cities or different sections of a city.

- The spatial variation is persistent. Areas that are high on offense or offender or delinquency rates might stay high for a decade, or even generations, regardless of the physical changes made in the locale.

- Sometimes the spatial patterns are not what you would expect. High violence in rural areas represents one case in point. In 1980, 71 out of the 100 highest homicide-rate counties in the United States were rural counties (Kposowa, Breault, and Harrison 1995).

The challenge for environmental criminologists is to explain why the rates are higher in some places than others, why they stay higher, and what can be done about this. In the field called *environmental criminology*, researchers seek to understand three fundamentally distinct yet interrelated questions:

- Why are crime or victimization rates higher in some places than others?

- Why are the rates at which people commit crimes, or become delinquent, higher in some places than others?

- How do offenders "travel to work"—going from work, or home, or a place where they are at leisure to a site where they commit their offense?

The Twentieth Century

The Pattern

In the twentieth century, researchers continued to examine regional variation in crime rates (e.g., Cohen and Nisbett 1994). But they also turned their attention to understanding the spatial variation at a lower level—how did it vary across communities in a city, for example? Most of the work we will discuss was domestically produced. But before we get to the United States, you might want to hear about one more European. Sir Cyril Burt, an influential British psychologist (1883–1971), was the only psychologist ever to be knighted; he also published with a fictitious female coauthor, was reputed to have demolished any colleagues opposing him, may have falsified some of his data later

in his career and, most importantly for you, is one of the godfathers of the SATs and the GREs (Dorfman 1978).

But when Sir Burt was not making up standardized tests, he was researching topics like genetics and IQ, or, of more interest here, delinquency and class. In 1925 he published *The Young Delinquent* (Burt 1925).[3] He looked up the addresses of boys and girls reported as "industrial school cases" in London. Then he looked up where they lived and made up a *delinquency rate*.[4] For every 1,000 people living in the district between ages 9 and 15, how many had become industrial school cases?

A pattern emerged that is now quite familiar to ecological crime researchers in this country. In London, in the early part of this century, delinquency rates were highest in the areas right near the central business district (CBD), and they declined as you moved toward the edge of the city. In addition, the areas of highest delinquency were also the areas of highest poverty. Burt concluded that a relationship existed between social class and delinquency. Furthermore, even though his data were cross-sectional, he concluded that the relationship was causal.[5]

Even though later research of individuals continued to find connections between delinquency and social class (e.g., Hindelang, Hirschi, and Weis 1981), Burt made two mistakes in interpreting his data. First, he committed or at least came very close to committing the *ecological fallacy*. He presumed that the relationships he described connecting features of areas also described connections between attributes of individuals. In 1939, E. L. Thorndike, another psychologist, in a two-page journal article showed why this is not necessarily true computationally (Thorndike 1939). It also does not have to hold logically. If poorer areas have higher delinquency rates, this does not mean that because I am poor, or that because I live in a low-income neighborhood, I am necessarily more likely to become delinquent. In short, the connections we find between characteristics of areas do not necessarily tell us about connections between the characteristics of individuals.

In addition, Burt presumed that correlations implied causality. If I find that low-income areas have higher delinquency rates, this does not mean that their low-income status caused them to have higher delinquency rates. The higher delinquency rates could have caused the lower income level over time, as households with the means to move left the neighborhood to provide a better setting for their children or left so that they would have a safer, victimization-free setting for their golden years. Alternatively, each could have been caused by some third factor, making their relationship spurious. For example, the racial composition of the neighborhood may have led to a withdrawal of city services over time, such as policing and quality education, or declining commercial interest in the locale, resulting over time in both a lower-income neighborhood and a higher delinquency-rate neighborhood (see Figure 1).

Let us cross the pond and talk about U.S. cities. Sociologists at the University of Chicago in the first half of the twentieth century investigated a wide array of urban social problems: delinquency, petty theft, dance halls, gambling, and immigrants' "culture shock," to name a few. These researchers in the Chicago School of Human Ecology not only carried out research, but also tried to get programs going, based on their work, to solve some of the city's problems.

Two of these sociologists, Clifford Shaw and Henry McKay, investigated delinquency (Shaw and McKay [1942] 1969). They collected data not only from Chicago, but from other cities as well: Philadelphia, Richmond, Cleveland, Birmingham, Denver, and Seattle.

Shaw and McKay went to juvenile courts and collected data about the number of juveniles who had been adjudicated delinquent.[6] They collected a lot of data about delinquents over a number of decades.[7]

Shaw and McKay's underpaid graduate students at the University of Chicago then used the addresses of these juveniles found delinquent to plot their location on a map of Chicago.[8] Some of these maps can be found today on display at the University.

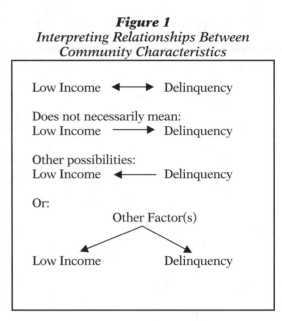

Figure 1
Interpreting Relationships Between Community Characteristics

Low Income ⟷ Delinquency

Does not necessarily mean:
Low Income ⟶ Delinquency

Other possibilities:
Low Income ⟵ Delinquency

Or:
Other Factor(s)
Low Income ↙ ↘ Delinquency

Other researchers at the University of Chicago had used information about natural physical boundaries in the city (rivers, railroad tracks, large blocks of nonresidential land use, dramatic shifts in housing quality, main thoroughfares) and current ethnic, racial, and class variations in settlement patterns, to carve up the entire city into 75 *natural areas* (Hunter 1974).[9] Because they knew from U.S. Census data how many people lived in each natural area at the end of each decade, and how many of those were of the same age as those youth whose records they had unearthed in family court, they were able to construct *delinquency rates:* for every 1,000 youth living in the community between the ages of 9 and 15, how many had officially been adjudicated delinquent by the court? They also constructed rates using other spatial units, such as one-square-mile areas.

Shaw and McKay collected these delinquency data for many years in Chicago. In addition, they collected delinquency data for the other cities mentioned above and likewise plotted those data on maps, constructing rates for various areas within each city. Not only that, they also spatially plotted other features of the communities in which they were interested, such as the number of housing structures demolished.

With these data in hand, Shaw and McKay, like Burt had earlier, linked delinquency with community characteristics. In contrast to Burt, however, they clearly stated that their interest was in *communities*, not individual delinquents. They hoped to identify the community characteristics linked to high juvenile delinquency rates.

The Theory

"Classic" Social Disorganization Theory

The Context Pre-World War II. As had Burt, Shaw and McKay (1942, 18) found higher delinquency rates closer to the center of the city, the *central business district* (CBD), than they did farther away from the city center. Indeed, they observed that the further away a community was from the city center, the lower its delinquency rate. This pattern appeared not just in Chicago, but in each of the other cities they examined as well, such as Philadelphia.

As is often true in cities, spatial differences link to social and economic differences. At the time Shaw and McKay were writing, populations were increasing in older cities. This "engine" of city growth led to economic differences across communities at varying distances from the city center. More specifically, because of city growth, the CBD was expanding to keep up and "serve" the growth in the broader city. This, of course, had happened in the past as well. Given this historical and ongoing pattern, more desirable locations were always at the outer edge of the expanding city. Land use closer to the city center was often converted to nonresidential land uses, such as large industries, stockyards (in the case of both Chicago and Baltimore), and large commercial concerns. The dominant modes of transport from the mid-nineteenth to the mid-twentieth century for heavy goods were railways and shipping. Those two modes often converged near a city center. So the easiest way to get the hogs (Baltimore) or the cattle (Chicago) off the railroads, slaughtered, and shipped out by rail or water or both was to locate all of this near the city center. Not surprisingly, not too many people wanted to live near slaughtering houses or heavy manufac-

turing or the congestion, soot, and noise that generally surrounded the activities found in central-city locations.

Not only were more central locations less desirable per se, they also were the sites of older housing. For the most part, older housing is also more worn-out housing. Given these less desirable locations and more dilapidated housing stock, housing in these areas tended to be less expensive. The further you got from the city center, the more likely you were to encounter newer housing and more desirable neighborhoods. So house prices and apartment rents increased as you progressed away from downtown.

As you might expect, as prices shifted, so too did the types of households living there. Poorer households were more likely to locate close to the city center, where housing was least expensive. Farther away, you would find housing occupied by low-wage or blue-collar workers. More distant, you would find middle-income households. And finally, even farther away, in an outer city or perhaps in a more distant suburban location, you would find the highest-income households.

These economic differences in house values and rents were exacerbated by the threat of invasion from the expanding CBD. People were constantly trying to "trade up" in their housing and move to a slightly better location. But, because the CBD was growing at the time, residents from each inner zone would be "invading" the zones just beyond.[10] In the innermost zone, the residential areas were in transition, converting from residential to commercial or industrial. This zone was thus labeled the *transition zone*. These impending changes led those residents who could get out to do so, and led those who owned properties there to stop maintaining them and to maximize their return by converting these units to apartments. Left living in these sites were low-income individuals and households who could not afford housing anywhere else. The residential environment here was rather chaotic.

Linked to the economic differences were ethnic ones. It is generally true, with some exceptions (Massey and Denton 1993) that the newest immigrants to a city are predominantly lower-income households. This is still true today in large U.S. cities even though the immigrant groups in question are different now than they were then.[11] Consequently, many members of these immigrant groups, when they first arrived in U.S. cities, were limited to central-city, low-income neighborhoods where housing was cheap.

Figure 2
Spatially-Linked Socioeconomic Dynamics Underlying Shaw and McKay's Model Explaining Delinquency Differences

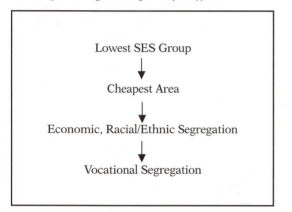

In short, Shaw and McKay's basic model was an *economic* one; location-based dynamics were set in motion based on the socioeconomic status of the group in question. The physical dilapidation of an area matched the segregation of the population on an economic basis (see Figure 2).

The Post-World War II Context. Of course, the spatial pattern described above has shifted markedly in large cities in the post-World War II era. Consider the following (Bursik, 1986; 1989): (1) Centralized city planning increased in the years following World War II. Urban renewal initiatives destroyed vast tracts of older, worn-out housing in older cities and replaced them with large numbers of public-housing communities, built in only small numbers before the war. Many of those displaced from older "slum" locations lost many friends in the process (Frey 1984; Gans 1962). The siting of these communities influenced the surrounding locations, sometimes destabilizing them (Bursik 1989). (2) Suburbanization in-

creased as federal highway initiatives, especially under Eisenhower, provided drastically improved road access to cities. (3) But, for a number of reasons, the suburbanization of African-American households proceeded more slowly than the suburbanization of white households. Consequently, the larger, older cities themselves became increasingly African-American in composition. (4) Passage of various fair housing laws, and related court cases in the 1950s and 1960s, increased African-Americans' access to housing. In cities where African-Americans had historically been limited to specific sections of the city, pent-up demand resulted in rapid racial turnover in large numbers of neighborhoods.

Since about 1970, additional changes in cities have further modified the spatial pattern described above (Gottdiener 1994). Most importantly, large numbers of manufacturing jobs have left, migrating from central-city locations first to southern locations, then abroad, making it increasingly difficult for those with relatively low education levels to secure employment. Receiving more media attention than has perhaps been warranted given the relatively small number of locations where it has occurred, central-city neighborhoods in many urban locations have become partially gentrified. Lower-income households were partially replaced by middle- or upper-income households that moved in and improved the housing stock.

Given these shifts seen in the last fifty years in cities, we would not necessarily expect to see the same spatial pattern for delinquency rates, or crime rates, as were reported for the years prior to World War II. Nonetheless, we still might expect community characteristics to link to these outcomes in a similar way.

The Central Process

At the heart of the human ecological model of offense and delinquency rates is a constellation of processes: *social disorganization*. Its opposite is *collective efficacy*. A locale is socially disorganized if several things are true: residents do not get along with one another; residents do not belong to local organizations geared to bettering the community and thus cannot work together effectively to address common problems; residents hold different values about what is and what is not acceptable behavior on the street; and residents are unlikely to interfere when they see other youths or adults engaged in wrongdoing (Bursik 1988; Maccoby, Johnson, and Church 1958). As you can see, the social disorganization idea contains several themes.

By contrast, if collective efficacy is high in a locale, residents will work together on common, neighborhood-wide issues, will get along somewhat with one another, and will take steps to supervise activities of youth or teens taking place in the immediate locale. *Collective efficacy* refers to several features of community social life including organizational participation (Do you belong to the local improvement association? Does your neighbor?) (Logan and Rabrenovic 1990; Portney and Berry 1997; Unger and Wandersman 1983; Zimmerman and Rappaport 1988); informal social control (If your neighbor saw a young teen spray painting the side of a building about midnight, would he do something about it?) (Hackler, Ho, and Urquhart-Ross 1974); and local social ties based on physical proximity (How many of the people living on your block do you know by name? How many can you recognize when you see them? If you needed to borrow a tool, could you do so from a close neighbor?) (Fischer 1982; Hummon 1990).

Researchers have suggested that three levels of resident-based control shape the level of social disorganization versus collective efficacy in a locale (Bursik and Grasmick 1992; Hunter 1985). *Private control* refers to dynamics within families and between close friends. If junioretta extorts school lunch money from two other neighbors while walking to school and her parents find out about it, will they punish her appropriately? *Parochial control* refers to supervisory efforts made by neighbors and acquaintances. If a neighbor while gardening out back sees junioretta walking down the alley threatening two other children and demanding their lunch funds, will she grab junioretta by the ear and walk her home to her dad, or will she, the neighbor, just shrug her shoulders

and go about planting her tomatoes? How much parochial control is exercised varies from block to block in a neighborhood (Taylor 1997b). *Public control* refers to the neighborhood leadership's ability to garner resources from public and private agencies outside the neighborhood. Can the community association's leaders effectively lobby "City Hall" for resources for neighborhood improvements and programs? For example, can they obtain funding for more school crossing guards on well-traveled routes leading to and from the local school? Can they work collaboratively with other neighborhood organizations on issues affecting their part of town?

High delinquency rates occurred in low-income, ethnically heterogeneous, unstable locations because those ecological characteristics made social disorganization more likely. In lower-income locales residents' concerns are more spatially circumscribed than in higher-income locales (Suttles 1972; Taylor 1988). In some low-income neighborhoods, residents feel safe only within their own dwelling (Rainwater 1966). As ethnic heterogeneity increases, it becomes increasingly difficult for residents to "decode" what other residents are doing. There are language barriers, and increasing intercultural distance just makes it harder to figure out what is going on (Merry 1981). A Cambodian woman looking out her window at a group of ten teen African-Americans on the corner standing around, shouting, and punching one another may not be sure if a fight is starting or if they are just celebrating Sammy Sosa's setting a new all-time home run record. As instability increases, residents have less time to get to know their neighbors; it is harder to figure out who belongs on the block and who does not.

In other words, these structural attributes of the community either increased or decreased the chances that residents would exert some control over what took place in their community; these dynamics in turn would influence outcomes like delinquency, the local offending rate, and local victimization rates.

Note that social disorganization *mediates* the impacts of community structure on the

Figure 3

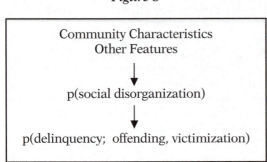

outcomes. It represents a crucial link connecting community fabric with the outcomes (see Figure 3).

Social disorganization was likely to be strongest, and collective efficacy weakest, when a community was in the midst of an *invasion-succession* cycle. In such a cycle, a neighborhood "turns over," with one type of resident replacing another. In the midst of such a cycle, residents are unlikely to know their neighbors, and the local population will be quite heterogeneous in makeup.

Neighborhood residents are always changing: people move in and people move out. But if the two rates are roughly matched, and if the volume is relatively modest, and if those moving in are sociodemographically similar to those moving out, then the neighborhood is stable (Ahlbrandt and Cunningham 1979). But if the volume of in-movers increases beyond a relatively low rate, and if the in-movers are sociodemographically dissimilar from the current residents, then over time the population in the locale would change. There would be an "invasion" of a new type of resident, and eventually that new type of resident would "succeed" the older type of resident.

Such cycles could be seen most clearly in the 1960s and 1970s in urban neighborhoods where racial succession took place, and white populations were replaced in relatively short order by African-American households. Many expected that gentrified neighborhoods would follow the same cycle, but they have not. Even in some of the most reclaimed neighborhoods, higher-income, recent in-migrant owners mingle on the street with lower-income, longer-term renters (Lee and Mergenhagen 1984; Levy and Cybriwsky 1980). The invasion-succession cycle can "stall" before completion.

What the Research Shows

Shaw and McKay's initial research was followed by a wide array of subsequent studies, usually in urban settings. Rather than attempt an exhaustive review of studies, I focus on a few. Each one described supports or develops the theory in question in a particular way.

Shaw and McKay's initial cross-sectional findings have been supported again and again (Baldwin 1975, 1979). Studies routinely find the following:

- Delinquency and offense and offender rates are higher closer to the city center than farther away, although there are exceptions, and although each of these outcomes maps differently onto spatial structure (Baldwin and Bottoms 1976).

- Delinquency and offense and offender rates are higher in lower-income, and/ or less stable, and/or more predominantly African-American communities (Bursik and Grasmick 1993; Harries 1980), although differences have arisen regarding the relative contribution of each attribute and the appropriate labels to apply to some of the dimensions of urban community structure examined (Gordon 1967, 1968; Sampson and Lauritsen 1994). For example, some have argued that relative socioeconomic status in a locale—how poor the residents are, or how poor they are relative to those residents in adjoining neighborhoods—is the most important community correlate of high violent-crime rates (Land, McCall, and Cohen 1990). Others argue that family disruption, and/or family structures that are less stable or provide less supervision of the locale are the most important (Sampson and Lauritsen 1994). This debate is not about to end anytime soon.

Another ecological feature leading away from delinquency and investigated repeatedly is religious context. Work shows negative relationships between religious attendance and delinquency, but only in regions of the country where churchgoing is at least somewhat prevalent (Stark 1996; Stark, Kent, and Doyle 1982). Are boys on the way home from Sunday school as likely to swipe your hubcaps as boys on the way home from the pool hall? On the West Coast it appears they are, but not so in other areas of the country. Religious context may be strengthened through family context, allowing children in extremely economically disadvantaged contexts, and perhaps contexts where collective efficacy is low, to "beat the odds" and avoid becoming delinquent (Furstenberg 1999).

Changes Over Time

In essence, the human ecological theory focuses on a community's position in the larger urban fabric *and how that position changes over time*. It is its relative status, stability, and racial composition, and the changes in those features that determine changes in offense, offender, and delinquency rates. Here are some examples to help you think about the idea of relative change.

In 1990, you might have been living in a neighborhood in Ajax City where the average house value in your neighborhood was $56,000. At that time, 50 percent of the population living in Ajax City lived in neighborhoods where the average housing price was at that value or lower; 50 percent lived in neighborhoods where the average house price was higher. So your neighborhood's house value percentile score was the 50th percentile.[12]

In the year 2000, controlling for inflation, the average house value in your neighborhood might still be $56,000, but that might correspond now to a percentile score of 15. What has happened? Now only 15 percent of the city population live in neighborhoods with an average house value of that amount or lower.

Even though, after controlling for inflation, house values in your neighborhood held steady in the 1990s, they failed to keep

pace with house value increases taking place elsewhere in your city. The other neighborhoods have "moved ahead" faster than your neighborhood did in the intervening decade. Maybe some new businesses moving in created strong demand for housing in several other parts of town. Your neighborhood's position has "slipped" relative to theirs, at least on this feature of community fabric.

Human ecology theory suggests that relative changes in dimensions like this will affect informal social control processes and outcomes like victimization, delinquency, and offending. So over the decade, the increases in delinquency, offending, and victimization in your neighborhood—relative to those rates in other neighborhoods in the city—might increase. Here are some ideas about how these processes might work.

If house values in the neighborhood in question were slipping during the decade, relative to other city neighborhoods, homeowners there may have tried to sell their houses, to get out "while the getting was good." Alternatively, the area may have become less attractive for in-migrating, middle-income residents looking for a place where their housing investment would appreciate over time. If house values were slipping relative to the rest of the city, the area became less attractive for house investment. Consequently, a shift may have taken place in the type of resident looking to move into the locale.

This shift in the type of in-migrating household may have widened background differences, and discrepancies in values as well, between long-term households and those moving in. Longer-term residents may frown on those who leave their children "on the street" during a summer day, locking them out of the house. Single-parent, working moms recently moved into the neighborhood may not think they have any choice other than to lock their kids out, and may reason that someone will look out for their children.

In a series of studies using Shaw and McKay's data on delinquency and census characteristics in Chicago, Bob Bursik examined these connections between community shifts and delinquency shifts from the

1930s through the 1960s (Bursik 1984, 1986; Bursik and Webb 1982; Heitgard and Bursik 1987). He observed, as expected, that more rapid community shifts were connected with more rapid changes in the delinquency rate. The ways in which neighborhoods changed varied across each decade, as did the relative contribution of different types of neighborhood changes to changes in delinquency. What was happening in each decade was conditioned by the historical context. But despite these variations in each decade, community changes were linked to delinquency changes in the expected ways. For example, increasing unemployment and increasing nonwhite racial composition were both tied to increasing delinquency rates in the 1960s.[13]

A Los Angeles study looked at community changes and delinquency changes during some of the same decades (Schuerman and Kobrin 1986). These researchers observed connections in the predicted directions, focusing on "lagged" relationships. For example, they found that neighborhood features in 1960 helped explain the changes in delinquency observed by 1970.

Changes in neighborhood fabric link not only to changes in delinquency but also to changes in violence as well. A Baltimore study of changes in the 1970s found that neighborhoods shifting more dramatically in stability or status experienced more sizable shifts in violence as well (Taylor and Covington 1988). Which particular feature of neighborhood fabric proved important depended on the type of violent crime examined.

Briefly put, one of the major extensions of social disorganization theory in the last two decades has been the application of the model to ecological changes over time. As the theory predicts, neighborhoods whose composition is changing more rapidly, relative to the other neighborhoods in the city, are more likely to experience increasing delinquency or crime problems. Even if the rapid change is in a "positive" direction, such as gentrification, increasing crime may accompany the shift (Covington and Taylor 1989).

Centrality of Social Disorganization Versus Collective Efficacy

The studies mentioned immediately above are limited in an important way. They include the "front end" of the human ecology model—attributes of community and how they shift over time—and the "back end"—the actual crime or delinquency outcomes. However, they leave out the crucial middle—the indicators reporting how much social disorganization or collective efficacy is actually taking place in a neighborhood. Recall that the features of neighborhood structure only predispose, not predict, a neighborhood to have more or less social disorganization (Kornhauser 1978).

Two key studies highlight the central importance of social disorganization versus collective efficacy processes. The first used a national victimization survey conducted every now and then in the United Kingdom, called the British Crime Survey. Sampson and Groves aggregated the survey data to the neighborhood level and then threw away the individual data.[14] Thus, they could concentrate just on community-level dynamics (Sampson and Grove 1989).

Sampson and Groves' analysis confirmed two key parts of the social disorganization model. First, for the most part, elements of community fabric linked in the expected ways to indicators of collective efficacy versus social disorganization. Indicators included local friendship networks, perception of troublesome teen groups, and participation in local organizations. For example, as ethnic heterogeneity of the locale increased, so too did residents' reports about bothersome teen groups.

Second, these indicators of social efficacy versus social disorganization influenced outcomes like offending rates based on self-reports. For example, in neighborhoods where residents reported more problems with unsupervised teen groups, they also reported higher rates of offending. Also, as expected by the model, the impact of community structure on the outcomes was mediated by the indicators of social efficacy versus social disorganization.[15]

A more recent study, done in Chicago by Sampson, Raudenbush, and Earls (1997) not only reexamined the importance of social efficacy versus social disorganization, it also investigated how these dynamics are structured at both the individual as well as the community level. In this project, over 8,000 residents in 343 Chicago neighborhood clusters were interviewed.[16] Researchers joined together indicators of expected informal social control, local social ties, and organizational participation to create a more general measure of social capital.

Attention focused on three violence-related outcomes: (1) respondent estimates of how often various violent events had occurred in the neighborhood in the last six months; (2) violent victimization in the neighborhood—at any time—experienced either by the respondent or by other household members; and (3) police homicide reports with address level information for those murders taking place during the survey field effort were aggregated to the neighborhood cluster level so that homicide rates could be constructed.

Collective efficacy varied significantly from neighborhood to neighborhood, but it also varied between neighbors in the same neighborhood. Perhaps most importantly for the human ecology model, even after researchers controlled for the type of people living in each neighborhood, average neighborhood collective efficacy was linked to features of neighborhood fabric. For example,

it was weaker in poorer, less stable, and more immigrant-dominated neighborhoods.

Collective efficacy in turn, even after controlling for survey respondent characteristics, linked to outcomes like neighborhood-to-neighborhood differences in perceived violence, violent victimization experiences, and recent homicides. Collective efficacy, however, did not completely mediate impacts on neighborhood fabric. Structural features of the neighborhood continued to exert independent impacts on the outcomes even after controlling for collective efficacy. Extreme disadvantage—neighborhoods with lots of poverty, unemployment, African-American households, and female-headed households—continued to strongly influence the outcomes. The authors concluded "that concentrated disadvantage more than race per se is the driving structural force at play" (923). In short, these results suggest a slight modification to the process described by the human ecology model (see Figure 4).

Extending the Model to Fear and Other Reactions to Crime

So far, the human ecology model has expanded from a focus just on delinquency as an outcome to reported violent crime rates, adult offending rates, and victimization rates. Bursik (1988) also has suggested that it might apply to reactions to crime, such as fear of crime, avoiding dangerous places, and staying in more at night.

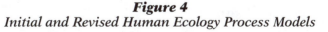

Figure 4
Initial and Revised Human Ecology Process Models

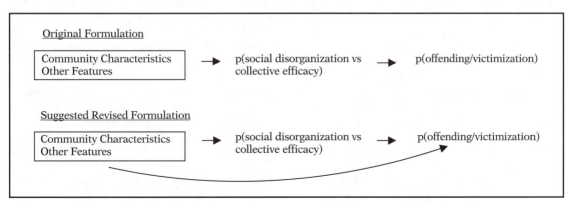

I used data from 66 Baltimore neighborhoods gathered in the early 1980s to test the applicability of the social disorganization model to responses to crime (Taylor 1996). Instead of looking at collective efficacy versus social disorganization, however, I looked at a closely related set of dynamics tapping local social involvement and attachment. I found that the impacts of neighborhood structure on reactions to crime were, as predicted, mediated by the "attached and involved" index. Neighborhoods where residents relied on neighbors more, and felt a stronger connection with their community, were neighborhoods where residents were less fearful and more responsive to potential problems.[17] As predicted by the human ecology model in its initial formulation (Figure 3, top panel), neighborhood makeup affected responses to crime only by way of the effects of neighborhood makeup on the "attached and involved" index.

Other studies have likewise applied a social disorganization perspective to fear of crime or other responses to disorder (e.g., Covington and Taylor 1991; Perkins, Meeks, and Taylor 1992; Perkins and Taylor 1996; Rountree and Land 1996a, b). Although there are some differences from study to study, it does appear that neighborhood structure—especially status and stability—affects these outcomes in ways anticipated by the model, and that indicators of social disorganization versus social efficacy at least partially mediate the relationship.

Extensions to Signs of Disorder

In the last few years, one group of researchers has put the human ecology model through the following changes: they have "psychologized" the basic social disorganization model, added a physical component, and then "re-ecologized" it while adding additional outcomes linked to neighborhood change. Within this family of models are several different variations; they are generally referred to as *broken windows, crime and grime, decline and disorder,* or the *incivilities thesis* (Taylor 1997a).

The kernel of the idea was that some residents are more surrounded by, and more bothered by, disorderly social and physical conditions. The social conditions include the unruly teens we have been talking about, "hey honey" hassles, public drug sales or drug usage, public drinking or drunkenness, and so on. Linked physical conditions include more extensive litter, graffiti, abandoned houses, abandoned cars, weedy vacant lots, and houses in disrepair.

The first theorists paying attention to these conditions suggested that those viewing them would feel vulnerable and at risk of being victimized (Garofalo and Laub 1978). Others suggested it was the lack of repair made to deteriorated physical conditions that sparked residents' concerns—the broken window that wasn't fixed (Perkins, Meeks, and Taylor 1992; Wilson and Kelling 1982).

The theory further evolved to encompass how these dynamics would unfold over time. The window isn't fixed, or the graffiti isn't erased, and residents become more fearful, local rowdies act bolder and vandalize further, and the process spirals onward.

Further, as noted above, the model got "re-ecologized." Researchers began suggesting that the outcomes applied to neighborhoods, not just individuals. So outcomes like neighborhood fear, neighborhood economic decline, increasing neighborhood instability, and neighborhood outmigration became of interest. Some suggested that these disorderly social and physical conditions could independently cause neighborhoods to go down the tubes (Skogan 1990).

The only part of this theory that has received strong, consistent support is the psychological version. Those who, at one point in time, perceive more problems than their neighbors, are indeed more concerned about their personal safety and more desirous of leaving their neighborhood (Perkins, Meeks, and Taylor 1992; Perkins and Taylor 1996; Taylor 1997a). At the neighborhood level, disorderly social behavior and physical deterioration might mediate or carry the impacts of neighborhood structure or changes in structure on fear of crime (Covington and Taylor 1991; Skogan 1990; Taylor and Covington 1993). But deterioration does not make its own independent contribution

(Kurtz, Koons, and Taylor 1998; Taylor 1998). In part, this is because deterioration is so strongly driven itself by the basic structure of the neighborhood (Hope and Hough 1988; Taylor, Shumaker, and Gottfredson 1985).

Implications

Implications for delinquency prevention emerging from the human ecology model prove straightforward. This theoretical approach has been the touchstone for prevention programs for well over fifty years, most notably in the original Chicago Area Projects launched in the 1930s, with assistance from Shaw himself (Lab 1992, 140). Community development programs were launched to increase organizational effectiveness of local groups, strengthen informal supervision of youth, teach youth skills, and provide viable alternatives to troublesome behavior. Numerous programs along these lines continue today (Podolefsky 1983).

Space limitations preclude a full discussion of whether or not community redevelopment programs like these achieve their objectives. But the most important point here is that according to this theoretical perspective, if you want to reduce delinquency in a locale you need to change the locale, to shift it from being socially disorganized to being socially effective, on different levels. This is not a small challenge. But this perspective suggests no point in trying to change the potential delinquent unless you also can shape his or her surround.

A second, perhaps less obvious, policy implication emerging from the perspective is the importance of residential stability. Repeatedly, analyses demonstrate the powerful independent impacts of residential stability on local social efficacy (McKenzie 1921) and, in turn, on crime and delinquency outcomes. Neighborhood redevelopment projects often disrupt local social ties and informal supervision of youth if they displace large numbers of long-term residents. Such projects increase the risk of local youth becoming delinquent. Redevelopment planners would do well to think how their efforts might be accomplished without damaging the neighborhood social fabric dependent upon and emerging from lengthy tenure.

Notes

1. For a pretty humorous perspective on this era, see Danny Kaye in *The Inspector General.*

2. Creuse is an agricultural section in central France. Corse is an island in the Mediterranean 105 miles south of France.

3. The anticipated follow-up volume, *The Old Delinquent*, did not appear.

4. Actually, we're pretty sure it was his coworkers and students who did the actual work.

5. A relationship is cross-sectional if the correlation is between two variables measured at roughly the same point in time. But correlation does not prove causation. Just because beaches near the shore that have higher volumes of ice cream sales have more drownings per month than beaches with low ice cream sales, that does not mean the ice cream sales cause the drownings. Nor does it mean the reverse. A relationship is longitudinal if one variable, the predictor, is measured before the other variable, the outcome. Then, depending on a range of factors, the researcher may be able to make the case that one variable causes the other.

6. If you have not yet had a course in juvenile justice, except for offenses where a juvenile is tried as an adult, juvenile crimes and acts of delinquency are handled through a separate court system, usually called *family court*. A juvenile brought before the court can be "found delinquent" by a master or judge, which means that he or she agrees the juvenile did commit a delinquent act or a crime. Delinquent acts include many activities that are permissible for adults, such as drinking, but also include a special class of actions that make sense only for juveniles, such as defying authority figures. In the Shaw and McKay data, we do not have a breakdown on the specific type of offense for which the juvenile was found delinquent.

7. See Bursik and Grasmick (1993), pp. 30–31, for details.

8. I have never known any graduate student who protested that he or she was paid fairly or was overpaid.

9. These 75 natural areas are larger in size than the neighborhoods typically found in many cities, either at that time or now. For example, Roderick McKenzie, another Chicago sociologist who went on to Ohio State, researched

neighborhood associations in Columbus (OH). He found that four out of the five community groups that he studied comprised just a few blocks along a major street that had a trolley car running on it. Al Hunter and others have suggested that in defining the natural areas in Chicago the researchers tried to impose some uniformity on the variations in community size.

10. Growing CBDs were a feature of large cities in the first half of the twentieth century. This was less true in older cities after World War II as they stopped growing and began losing population, and as automobile and truck transport superseded rail.

11. The important exception here is for African-Americans, who, despite relatively long tenure in many large U.S. cities, remain a highly segregated population, with substantial numbers limited to extremely low-income locations. Some, such as William Julius Wilson, have suggested that their concentration in poor, urban locations has increased since 1970.

12. These percentile scores are just like SAT scores. If your SAT Verbal score put you in the 98th percentile, it means that 98 percent of those taking the test had a score equal to or lower than yours.

13. Bursik (1986), Table 4.

14. For example, suppose I wanted to find out what class in your major was hardest. I could take the grade in each section in each class last semester, save just those class averages, and throw away the individual information around each of those averages. I have aggregated the class grades. I can then use the lowest class average to decide which class was hardest.

15. The researchers know the connection is mediated because they do the following checks. When they put in the community structure indicators by themselves, they have a big impact on the outcome. But when they then add in the mediating variables, like perceptions of annoying teen groups, the influence of the community structure indicators weakens.

   The Sampson and Grove study did not flawlessly support all the predictions of social disorganization theory (see Bursik and Grasmick 1993, 44–45).

16. Neighborhood clusters were smaller than the 75 Chicago "natural areas" often used by Chicago researchers, but also more homogeneous.

17. Even though this study used data from one point in time only, I used statistical techniques to assure myself, as best I could, that the relationship did *not* go the other way. It wasn't because people were afraid that they were unlikely to get locally involved.

References

Ahlbrandt, R. and J. Cunningham. (1979). *A New Public Policy for Neighborhood Preservation.* New York: Praeger.

Baldwin, J. (1975). "British areal studies of crime: An assessment." *British Journal of Criminology,* 15:211–227.

Baldwin, J. (1979). "Ecological and areal studies in Great Britian and the United States." *In Crime and justice: An annual review of research,* 1. N. Morris and M. Tonry (eds.). Chicago: University of Chicago Press.

Baldwin, J. and A.E. Bottoms. (1976). *The Urban Criminal.* London: Tavistock.

Brantingham, P.J. and P.L. Brantingham. (1991). "Introduction: The dimensions of crime." Pp. 7–26 in *Environmental Criminology.* P.J. Brantingham and P.L. Brantingham (eds.). Prospect Heights, IL: Waveland.

Bursik, R.J., Jr. and J. Webb. (1982). "Community change and patterns of delinquency." *American Journal of Sociology,* 88:24–42.

Bursik, R.J., Jr. (1984). "Urban dynamics and ecological studies of delinquency." *Social Forces,* 63:393.

Bursik, R.J., Jr. (1986). "Ecological stability and the dynamics of delinquency." Pp. 35–66 in *Communities and crime.* A.J. Reiss and M. Tonry (eds.). Chicago: University of Chicago Press.

Bursik, R.J., Jr. (1988). "Social disorganization and theories of crime and delinquency." *Criminology,* 26:519–551.

Bursik, R.J., Jr. (1989). "Political decision-making and ecological models of delinquency: Conflict and consensus." Pp. 105–117 in *Theoretical integration in the study of deviance and crime: Problems and prospects.* S.F. Messner and M.D. Krohn (eds.). Albany: State University of New York Press.

Bursik, R.J., Jr. and H.G. Grasmick. (1992). The multiple layers of social disorganization. November. Paper presented at the American Society of Criminology in New Orleans.

Bursik, R.J., Jr. and H.G. Grasmick. (1993). *Neighborhoods and Crime: The Dimensions of Effective Social Control.* New York: Lexington.

Burt, C. (1925). *The Young Delinquent.* London: University of London Press.

Cohen, D. and R.E. Nisbett. (1994). "Self-protection and the culture of honor: Explaining southern violence." *Personality and Social Psychology Bulletin,* 20:551–567.

Covington, J. and R.B. Taylor. (1989). "Gentrification and crime: Robbery and larceny changes in appreciating Baltimore neighborhoods in the 1970s." *Urban Affairs Quarterly,* 25:142–172.

Covington, J. and R.B. Taylor. (1991). "Fear of crime in urban residential neighborhoods: Implications of between- and within-neighborhood sources for current models." *The Sociological Quarterly,* 32:231–249.

Dorfman, D.D. (1978). "The Cyril Burt question: New findings." *Science,* 201:1177–1186.

Fischer, C.S. (1982). *To Dwell Among Friends: Personal Networks in Town and City.* Chicago: University of Chicago Press.

Frey, W.H. (1984). "Lifecourse migration of metropolitan whites and blacks and the structure of demographic change in large central cities." *American Sociological Review,* 49:803–827.

Furstenberg, F.F. (ed.). (1999). *Managing to Make it: Urban Families and Adolescent Success.* Chicago: University of Chicago Press.

Gans, H.J. (1962). *The Urban Villagers.* New York: Free.

Garofalo, J. and J. Laub. (1978). "The fear of crime: Broadening our perspective." *Victimology,* 3:242–253.

Glyde, J. (1856). "Localities of crime in Suffolk." *Journal of Statistical Society of London,* 19:102–106.

Gordon, R.A. (1967). "Issues in the ecological study of delinquency." *American Sociological Review,* 32:927–944.

Gordon, R.A. (1968). "Issues in multiple regression." *American Journal of Sociology,* 73:592–616.

Gottdiener, M. (1994). *The New Urban Sociology.* New York: McGraw-Hill.

Hackler, J.C., K. Ho, and C. Urquhart-Ross. (1974). "The willingness to intervene: Differing community characteristics." *Social Problems,* 21:328–344.

Harries, K.D. (1980). *Crime and the Environment.* Springfield, IL: Thomas.

Heitgard, J. and R. Bursik. (1987). "Extracommunity dynamics and the ecology of delinquency." *American Journal of Sociology,* 92:775–787.

Hindelang, M.J., T. Hirschi, and J.G. Weis. (1981). *Measuring delinquency.* Beverly Hills, CA: Sage.

Hope, T. and M. Hough. (1988). "Area, crime and incivility: A profile from the British Crime Survey." Pp. 30–47 in *Communities and Crime Reduction.* T. Hope and M. Shaw (eds.). London: HMSO.

Hummon, D.M. (1990). *Commonplaces: Community Ideology and Identity in American Culture.* Albany: State University of New York Press.

Hunter, A. (1974). *Symbolic Communities.* Chicago: University of Chicago Press.

Hunter, A. (1985). "Private, parochial and public school orders: The problem of crime and incivility in urban communities." Pp. 230–242 in *The Challenge of Social Control, Citizenship and Institution Building in Modern Society,* G.D. Suttles and M.N. Zald (eds.). Norwood, NJ: Ablex.

Kornhauser, R.R. (1978). *Social Sources of Delinquency.* Chicago: University of Chicago Press.

Kposowa, A.J., K.D. Breault, and B.M. Harrison. (1995). "Reassessing the structural covariates of violent and property crimes in the USA: A county-level analysis." *British Journal of Sociology,* 46:79–105.

Kurtz, E., B. Koons, and R.B. Taylor. (1998). "Land use, physical deterioration, resident-based control, and calls for service on urban streetblocks." *Justice Quarterly,* 15:121–149.

Lab, S.P. (1992). *Crime Prevention: Approaches, Practices and Evaluations,* Second Edition. Cincinnati, OH: Anderson.

Land, K.C., P. McCall, and L.C. Cohen. (1990). "Structural covariates of homicide rates: Are there any invariances across time and space?" *American Journal of Sociology,* 95:922–963.

Lee, B.A. and P.M. Mergenhagen. (1984). "Is revitalization detectable? Evidence from five Nashville neighborhoods." *Urban Affairs Quarterly,* 19:511–538.

Levy, P.R. and R.A. Cybriwsky. (1980). "The hidden dimensions of culture and class: Philadelphia." Pp. 138–155 in *Back to the City.* S. Laska and D. Spain (eds.). New York: Pergamon.

Logan, J.R. and G. Rabrenovic. (1990). "Neighborhood associations: Their issues, their allies, and their opponents." *Urban Affairs Quarterly,* 26:68.

Maccoby, E.E., J.P. Johnson, and R.M. Church. (1958). "Community integration and the social control of juvenile delinquency." *Journal of Social Issues,* 14:38–51.

Massey, D. and S. Denton. (1993). *American Apartheid: Segregation and the Making of the Underclass.* Cambridge, MA: Harvard University Press.

McKenzie, R.D. (1921). "The neighborhood." Pp. 51–93 in *On Human Ecology*. A.H. Hawley and R.D. McKenzie (eds.). Chicago: University of Chicago Press.

Merry, S.E. (1981). *Urban Danger: Life in a Neighborhood of Strangers*. Philadelphia, PA: Temple University Press.

Morris, T. (1957). *The Criminal Area: A Study in Social Ecology*. London: Routledge and Kegan Paul.

Perkins, D.D., J.W. Meeks, and R.B. Taylor. (1992). "The physical environment of street blocks and resident perceptions of crime and disorder: Implications for theory and measurement." *Journal of Environmental Psychology*, 12:21–34.

Perkins, D.D. and R.B. Taylor. (1996). "Ecological assessments of disorder: Their relationship to fear of crime and theoretical implications." *American Journal of Community Psychology*, 24:63–107.

Podolefsky, A. (1983). *Case Studies in Community Crime Prevention*. Springfield, IL: Thomas.

Portney, K.E. and J.M. Berry. (1997). "Mobilizing minority communities: Social capital and participation in urban neighborhoods." *American Behavioral Scientist*, 40:632–644.

Radzinowicz, L. (1966). *Ideology and Crime*. New York: Columbia University Press.

Rainwater, L. (1966). "Fear and house-as-haven in the lower class." *Journal of the American Institute of Planners*, 32:23–31.

Rountree, P.W. and K.C. Land. (1996a). "Burglary victimization, perceptions of crime risk, and routine activities: A multilevel analysis across Seattle neighborhoods and census tracts." *Journal of Research in Crime and Delinquency*, 33:147–180.

Rountree, P.W. and K.C. Land. (1996b). "Perceived risk versus fear of crime: Empirical evidence of conceptually distinct reactions in survey data." *Social Forces*, 74:1353–1376.

Sampson, R.J. and W.B. Grove. (1989). "Community structure and crime: Testing social-disorganization theory." *American Journal of Sociology*, 94:774–802.

Sampson, R.J. and J.L. Lauritsen. (1994). "Violent victimization and offending: Individual, situational- and community-level risk factors." Pp. 1–114 in *Understanding and Preventing Violence* Vol. 3: *Social Influences*. A.J.J. Reiss and J.A. Roth (eds.). Washington, DC: National Academy Press.

Sampson, R.J., S.W. Raudenbush, and F. Earls. (1997). "Neighborhoods and violent crime: A multi-level study of collective efficacy." *Science*, 277:918–924.

Schuerman, L. and S. Kobrin. (1986). "Community careers in crime." Pp. 67–100 in *Communities and Crime*. A.J. Reiss and M. Tonry (eds.). Chicago: University of Chicago Press.

Shaw, C.R. and H.D. McKay. [1942] (1969). *Juvenile Delinquency and Urban Areas*, Second Edition. Chicago: University of Chicago Press.

Skogan, W. (1990). *Disorder and Decline: Crime and the Spiral of Decay in American Cities*. New York: Free.

Stark, R. (1996). "Religion as context: Hellfire and delinquency one more time." *Sociology of Religion*, 57:163–173.

Stark, R., Kent, L., and Doyle, D.P. (1982). "Religion and delinquency: The ecology of a 'lost' relationship." *Journal of Research in Crime and Delinquency*, 19:4–24.

Suttles, G.D. (1972). *The Social Construction of Communities*. Chicago: University of Chicago Press.

Taylor, R.B. (1988). *Human Territorial Functioning*. Cambridge: Cambridge University Press.

Taylor, R.B. (1996). "The systemic model of attachment, neighborhood use value, and responses to disorder." *Sociological Forum*, 11:41–74.

Taylor, R.B. (1997a). "Relative impacts of disorder, structural change, and crime on residents and business personnel in Minneapolis-St. Paul." In *Community Crime Prevention at the Crossroads*. S. Lab (ed.). Cincinnati, OH: Anderson.

Taylor, R.B. (1997b). "Social order and disorder of streetblocks and neighborhoods: Ecology, microecology and the systemic model of social disorganization." *Journal of Research in Crime and Delinquency*, 33:113–155.

Taylor, R.B. (1998). Crime, grime, fear, and decline: A longitudinal look at the impacts of incivilities. November. Paper presented at the annual meetings of the American Society of Criminology, Washington, DC.

Taylor, R.B. and J. Covington. (1988). "Neighborhood changes in ecology and violence." *Criminology*, 26:553–589.

Taylor, R.B. and J. Covington. (1993). "Community structural change and fear of crime." *Social Problems*, 40:374–397.

Taylor, R.B., S.A. Shumaker, and S.D. Gottfredson. (1985). "Neighborhood-level links between physical features and local sentiments: Deterioration, fear of crime, and confidence." *Journal of Architectural Planning and Research,* 2:261–275.

Thorndike, E.L. (1939). "On the fallacy of inputing the correlations found for groups to the individuals in smaller groups composing them." *American Journal of Psychology,* 52:122–124.

Unger, D.G. and A. Wandersman. (1983). "Neighboring and its role in block organizations." *American Journal of Community Psychology,* 11:291–300.

Wilson, J.Q. and G. Kelling. (1982). "Broken windows." *Atlantic Monthly,* 211:29–38.

Zimmerman, M. and J. Rappaport. (1988). "Citizen participation, perceived control, and psychological empowerment." *American Journal of Community Psychology,* 16:725–750.

6
Anomie/Strain Theories of Crime

Introduction

This chapter is concerned with what are called *anomie* and *strain* theories of crime. Some scholars maintain a distinction between strain theories and anomie theories (Cullen and Agnew 1999). This distinction is based on the fact that strain theories are micro-level theories that attempt to explain why given *individuals within a society* commit criminal and deviant acts, while anomie theories are macro-level or structural theories that attempt to explain why some societies (or other collectivities) have higher rates of crime than others. Although the difference in the level of analysis between the two is real, our preference is to combine strain and anomie theories in the same theoretical classification.

We take this position for several reasons: (1) the historical roots of both anomie and strain theory can be traced to a common source (the sociologists Emile Durkheim and Robert K. Merton), and (2) until recently, both sets of theories have found the motivation for criminal conduct in the discrepancy between culturally defined goals and culturally accepted means to attain goals. For this reason, in this chapter we will speak of anomie/strain theory as a common theoretical system, although we will make a distinction between anomie/strain at the individual level and anomie/strain at the macro or structural level. We will refer to the former as *individual* anomie/strain theory and the latter as *institutional* anomie/strain theory.

Another area of agreement between anomie and strain theories is the assumption that is made about human beings. All strain theories assume that humans are basically social and compliant beings. The presumption, then, is that under normal conditions people are naturally inclined to abide by social norms and rules, and, as a result, their inclination is to conform to such rules and norms. If one assumes that people naturally want to comply with rules, then one must account for why rules are sometimes broken. Anomie/strain theorists are neither utopian nor sentimentalists. Even though they presume that people are basically good, they nonetheless recognize that deviance and crime do occur. Because they assume conformity, what anomie/strain theorists must explain is rule-breaking or deviance. They must, then, provide us with a explanation of the motivation to break rules. One way to think of anomie/strain theories, therefore, is that they are motivational theories of crime because they must account for rule-breaking, given an assumption that humans naturally conform.

The easy answer to the question of why naturally conforming beings would ever break rules, then, is that they are under tension, pressure, or "strain" to do so. This is not a particularly satisfying explanation, however, because it does not really reveal the basis or source of the motivation. According to anomie/strain theorists, the key to understanding this motivation is the idea that people are naturally inclined to follow rules *under normal conditions*. The implication here is that sometimes conditions are not "normal." Sometimes persons find themselves confronting abnormal or extraordinary conditions. Under these extraordinary conditions, persons feel pressure or "strain" to break rules with which they would normally comply.

Anomie/strain theories, then, assume that individuals are more inclined to commit crime and deviant acts when they are under extraordinary pressure or strain to do so. Sometimes this tension is felt collectively because a person is a member of a particular society or a particular social class, all or most of whose members are under strain. Crime is unevenly distributed across societies or across social classes, therefore, because some groups experience more strain than others. Unique structural conditions produce varying levels of strain. In other versions of the theory, strain is felt at the level of the individual because of the unique *events* one has experienced. Crime is unevenly distributed across individuals within collective groups, therefore, because some persons experience more strain than others. Whether they are felt at the group or individual level, crime and deviance occur in all anomie/strain theories, when there is sufficient pressure to do so.

Historical Roots of Strain Theory

Durkheim's Contribution

Ironically, we can trace the beginning of strain theory to the work of the French sociologist Emile Durkheim. We say "ironically" for two reasons. First, as we discussed in Chapter 4, control theorists, who adopt the assumption that human beings are naturally inclined to break rules in pursuit of self-interest, also trace their origins to the work of Durkheim (Hirschi 1969). Second, Durkheim never really developed an anomie/strain theory of crime. What he did was to develop a conceptual scheme that eventually formed the foundation for others, who did develop explicit strain theories of crime, such as the sociologist Robert K. Merton.

In his 1897 book, *Suicide,* Durkheim was interested in understanding the causes of self-destruction. Durkheim did not believe that the key to understanding suicide lay within individual pathology (e.g., emotional depression or stress) because suicide rates seemed to follow systematic patterns (e.g., they were consistently lower for married than single and divorced or widowed men and were higher for Protestants than Catholics). Such regularity in the rates of suicide convinced Durkheim that the source must be social rather than individual (Durkheim [1897] 1951). Dismissing a commonly held belief that suicides are the product of poverty, Durkheim showed that rates of suicide increase during periods of both rapid economic prosperity as well as decline. What was important about financial crises, wrote Durkheim, was that they were *crises,* that is, they were sudden dislocations of established

life that thrust people into new and unaccustomed circumstances.

The power of crises that led to suicides, Durkheim concluded, was that it extracted or detached persons from their normal lives, lives which included familiar and accepted limits to their needs and wants. For Durkheim, human beings cannot be happy unless their needs and desires are under some sort of regulation. Recall in our discussion of control theory that according to Durkheim, human beings uniquely have the power of reflection—the capacity to always imagine "more or better." Unless there are limits or restraints placed on their desires, then, human beings will never be able to feel satisfied; they will be miserable. Because they are unable to control their own appetites, Durkheim argued that the restraint on human desire must be social. This restraint consists of the attachment people have to society and to their concomitant roles and role obligations.

What crises do, therefore, is to remove persons from these traditional roles, which include familiar restraints on their desires, and place them in circumstances where they have no clear guides as to how to behave or what they should expect. Unlike the married man, the recently divorced man feels that there are no limits to his sexual appetite, the recently wealthy person feels that there is nothing he cannot buy or accomplish with his newfound wealth, and one made recently poor is similarly confused and unanchored to life as usual. Thrust into new circumstances without sufficient guides or norms as to what is acceptable or attainable, anything seems possible. Unfortunately, in trying to pursue goals that are unattainable, people become miserable and seek comfort from their torment through suicide.

According to Durkheim, the state of normlessness that people find themselves in as a result of a crisis is referred to as *anomie.* The state of anomie, then, is to Durkheim an uncomfortable position produced when human goals are not moderated and appetites are unregulated. Durkheim described anomie as a condition of normlessness—under its spell, people lack norms or guides for their conduct. Sometimes anomie is caused by temporary shocks to a society, such as financial booms and depressions. It also can occur at the death of a spouse or because of divorce. In other situations, a condition of anomie is more stable. For example, Durkheim thought that Protestants are more likely to commit suicide than Catholics because of their respective religious dogmas. Protestantism, he argued, places more reliance on the individual and individual freedom, while Catholicism is more communal in trying to tightly bond individuals to the church. Being more emotionally connected to an entity greater than themselves, he believed that Catholics experience less anomie and normlessness, and experience lower suicide rates than their more individualistic Protestant counterparts. Thus, in Durkheim's version of anomie/strain theory, temporary shocks or more persistent sources of strain in a social system produce anomie (normlessness), which in turn pro-

Figure 1
Durkheim's Anomie/Strain Theory

duces deviant acts such as suicide. We illustrate his anomie/strain model in Figure 1.

If anomie can be brought on only by temporary perturbations or social strains (divorce, sudden poverty), suicide rates would erratically vary up and down in response to such provocations. However, some of Durkheim's data led him to believe that suicide rates (in particular countries and for particular kinds of persons) were fairly stable over long periods of time. This observation then led Durkheim to the important conclusion ([1897] 1951, 254) that anomie could at times be a chronic condition of a society rather than a temporary one. More specifically, he argued that anomie is in a persistent state within the economic realm of modern society.

Merton's Perspective

The twentieth-century social theorist Robert K. Merton (1968) picked up on Durkheim's notion that under some social conditions anomie could be persistent. Merton argued that a society that is healthy or in equilibrium is one with an equal emphasis placed on both the attainment of collectively held goals as well as the use of culturally defined appropriate means to attain those goals. That is, goals and means are integrated in the healthy society, in which *integration* results in an equal emphasis on the importance of both. In such societies, individuals receive satisfaction either because they have obtained culturally defined success goals, or because they have used culturally accepted means to try to achieve those goals (even if without sucess). Societies vary, however, in how well the goals and means of the collective are integrated. Some societies are characterized by an equal emphasis, but others are malintegrated in the sense that there is a greater emphasis on one over the other. Modern American society, Merton argued, is one such malintegrated society.

American society is characterized by the goal of material wealth that all individuals are supposed to strive for. Strain theorists argue that all persons are evaluated in our society by the extent to which they are affluent and possess the objects that wealth brings (beautiful homes, expensive cars and jewelry, fabulous vacations, etc.). This is the "American Dream." In a democratic society that emphasizes open competition, the goal of material affluence is a universal goal—everyone, no matter what their initial position in life, is expected to strive to attain financial wealth. Those who opt out of the game of accumulating wealth or who "trim their sails" by lowering their expectations are denigrated by our culture as "dropouts" or "losers." A society that holds out the accumulation of material wealth to all its citizens is not, by itself, a malintegrated society. It is only when such societies place a great deal of emphasis on goal attainment, with almost no concern for how one attains the goal, that it becomes malintegrated. To Merton, this lack of integration between goals and means is anomie.

In Merton's view, American society is just such a malintegrated and anomic society because we do emphasize goal attainment far more than we emphasize using the approved or correct means to attain goals, such as through education and hard work. He points to examples, such as the fabulously wealthy "robber barons" of the late nineteenth and early twentieth centuries. Men like Andrew Carnegie and Cornelius Vanderbilt built vast industrial and financial empires through greed, dirty business deals, and borderline criminal, if not criminal, activity. In American society, it matters much less how persons become wealthy than the fact that they actually are financially successful. Thus, we idolize as American royalty the Kennedy clan, whose financial empire was built in large part on illegal bootleg liquor during Prohibition. We have even an honored place in our culture for men like Al Capone, who built his wealth on gambling, prostitution, and murder. As a society, therefore, we do not place an equal emphasis on winning and playing fair. Our motto is not "it's not whether you win or lose, it's how you play the game." Rather, our cultural icons are people like the late Green Bay Packer football coach Vince Lombardi, who extolled: "Winning isn't everything—it's the only thing." As for Durkheim, anomie for Merton is a condition of normlessness. However, for Merton, anomie is normlessness with respect to means—anomie is the lack of regulation of people's means.

As a condition of society, anomie is related to crime and deviant behavior because it encourages people to use whatever means necessary, even if they are illegal, to attain monetary wealth. Thus, it places a high personal cost on failure. With respect to crime, an anomic society essentially says, "You have to attain monetary wealth, you cannot substitute another goal of your own choosing, but we don't much care how you acquire wealth so long as you do it." Anomie, in Merton's scheme, puts people under pressure or strain to break rules in order to secure financial goals. For Merton, then, people want to conform to rules. The problem arises in anomic societies where they are under substantial pressure to use any means to secure goals.

Figure 2
Merton's Anomie/Strain Theory

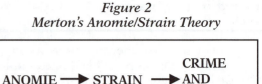

We illustrate Merton's anomie/strain theory in Figure 2.

One way to see the difference in the anomie/strain explanations of Durkheim and Merton, therefore, is that in Durkheim's model, anomie is the failure to regulate the *goals* people aspire to and is the effect of social pressures and strain (see Figure 1), while for Merton, anomie is the failure to regulate the *means* people use to achieve goals, and anomie generates strain (Kornhauser 1978).

A second dimension to anomie in Merton's work relates to the disjunction or malintegration between goals and means (Bernard 1987; Akers 1997). In this second dimension, a healthy society is one wherein the goals and means are in equilibrium, in the sense that persons are expected to strive for only the goals they realistically are able to achieve, given their social position. For example, in Indian caste society, different goals traditionally were held out to the members of different social classes or castes. The upper caste, or Brahmins, had a different set of goals and expectations (more lofty) that they were expected to pursue than those at the bottom of the social ladder, the "untouchables." This was a nonanomic society because the goals and means were in equilibrium—even though the Brahmins had lofty goals, they also had the available means to achieve them; similarly, the untouchables had minimal means and their expected goals were comparably minimal. The result is balance, or equilibrium, and a condition of nonanomie.

In modern American society, however, there is one common set of goals—everyone, no matter what their initial social position, is expected to strive for monetary success. We have a set of folk stories of people going from "rags to riches" to vividly demonstrate that the goals are in fact equally available to all. Unfortunately, these universal goals are not well integrated with the availability of or access to legitimate and culturally approved means. Although the goal of monetary success is held out to all, American society is also a class-stratified society. In reality, access to available legitimate means is restricted or more limited to some groups of people. Those in the lower class, racial and ethnic minorities, and women find themselves "blocked" in their goal attainment because they have limited access to educational and occupational opportunities. For example, schools in lower-class neighborhoods tend to be of poorer quality than those in more affluent communities. Attendance at poor primary and secondary schools is likely to lead to a lack of access to better colleges, or even college at all. These educational limitations are then eventually translated into worse job opportunities.

A society that holds out success goals to all, while limiting the legitimate opportunities for some, is an anomic society. Anomie, then, is also produced by the convergence of universal success goals (the "American Dream") with a social structure that limits and blocks for some their opportunities or legitimate means to achieve those goals. In other words, in response to this second dimension of anomie (high goals and limited legitimate means), persons feel frustration and strain.

Merton then pointed to five different kinds of adaptations to strain:

1. *Conformity*: one accepts both the goals and means of the society and strives to attain goals with the limited means at one's disposal.

2. *Innovation*: one accepts the goals (monetary success) but rejects the available means. Those who innovate improvise by using any means available, even illegal means such as criminal activity, to attain success goals.

3. *Rebellion*: in this adaptation, one responds to strain by rejecting the existing goals and means of society and substituting other goals and means.

4. *Ritualism*: one rejects the goals of society (or realizes that they cannot be attained) and responds to strain with a mindless and slavish conformity to means. In other words, one becomes a bureaucrat or an "organizational fellow" and blindly follows rules for their own sake. One way to think of ritualism, then, is that it is over-conformity.

5. *Retreatism*: One rejects both goals and means. However, unlike the rebel, the one who retreats does not substitute other goals and means; rather, one simply drops out of society into alcoholism, homelessness, mental illness, or drug addiction.

As you can perhaps surmise, most acts of crime and deviance are found among innovators. Innovators adapt to strain by improvising. They employ what might be termed technically efficient but illegal means to reach their goals. Another way to say this is that they respond to the strain of anomie by doings such things as stealing, swindling, selling drugs, and prostituting themselves in order to attain some degree of financial success.

Merton's theory proved to be very popular and was probably the dominant explanation for crime and deviance in the 1950s and 1960s. It did, however, proceed on two somewhat different tracks. Some scholars interpreted anomie/strain as being a characteristic of aggregate bodies, such as societies, and therefore useful in explaining how crime rates varied across these aggregate units (Bernard 1987). As an example, one "branch" of anomie/strain theory is institutional anomie theory. Other scholars interpreted anomie/strain as being a property of individuals, attempting to explain why some people within a society engaged in criminal and deviant acts while others did not (Agnew 1987). The second branch of this theoretical tree is individual strain theory. We will briefly review these two different approaches to strain theory.

Institutional Anomie/Strain Theory

Those who interpret anomie/strain theory as an aggregate-level explanation for variations in crime rates can point to specific language in Merton's own work for support. In the 1957 edition of his book *Social Theory and Social Structure*, Merton (1957) noted that his anomie/strain theory is supposed to explain "why it is that the frequency of deviant behavior varies within different social structures, and how it happens that the deviations have different shapes and patterns in different social structures" (131). In the 1968 edition of the same book, he again emphatically stated that he intended the theory to explain crime at the aggregate or group level rather than at the individual level: "[O]ur perspective is sociological. . . .[W]e look at variation in the rates of deviant behavior, not at its incidence" (186). What could be more clear? In both statements, Merton appears to plainly argue that anomie/strain is a property of collective units and that he wants the theory to explain why some countries, like the United States, seem to have higher levels of crime than other countries and why some social groups have higher rates of crime than others. The theory was thus designed to explain both why the amount of crime is higher in some societies (the United States) than others, and why the amount of crime/deviance is higher in some social groups (the lower class, minority groups) than others within a society (Bernard 1987).

Cohen's Application of Merton's Theory

Those who immediately developed the criminological implications of Merton's theory also understood it as an explanation of variation in crime rates. For example, Albert Cohen (1955) used Merton's framework to explain the origin and content of the delinquent subculture shared by lower-class males. In Cohen's version, however, strain is due to the failure to achieve status rather a failure to reach monetary goals. He argued that because of the way they are raised and socialized, lower-class boys as a group find themselves unprepared for the status competition that occurs in the predominantly middle-class school. That is, because of class differences in childrearing practices, lower-class males are less able to do the things that gain praise within the school—sit quietly in their seats, raise their hands before speaking, or show interest in intellectual and cultural matters. Unfortunately for them, lower-class boys are held to the same "middle-class measuring rod" in school as more privileged boys.

Because they cannot compete on middle-class terms, and rather than accept defeat, some lower-class boys engage in behaviors that they can perform, awarding status to those who perform them well. These behaviors, however, are directly contrary to established middle-class values, such as respect for private property and nonviolence. The acts that earn status points for lower-class males include vandalism, assault, burglary, and other anti-middle-class acts. In fact, Cohen argues that delinquent acts are very malicious and negativistic because they seem to directly attack what the middle class values. These malicious/negativistic acts comprise part of what Cohen called the *delinquent subculture*, which turns middle-class values "upside down."

Cohen accounted for the fact that the delinquent subculture was primarily, if not exclusively, a lower-class male phenomenon. It makes its appearance among lower-class males because lower-class socialization does not prepare males to easily conform to the rules and culture of the middle-class school. Lower-class males, therefore, have a collective problem—status failure. As such, they are in need of a collective solution. One solution is to directly attack those who are denying them status by valuing what is contrary to the middle class. These behaviors are acts that have no utility (destruction of property, senseless stealing, mindless violence) but simply seem to mock middle-class values. The delinquent subculture emerged in the lower class, then, because status strain is most acute there, and took on a negativistic and malicious content because it allowed lower-class boys to directly confront and repudiate those who were rejecting them.

The delinquent solution is not the only one available to lower-class males who feel strain because they have little social status or prestige. They can try to overcome the limitations imposed by their lower-class socialization and pursue status on middle-class terms. That is, they can study hard in school, do their homework after school, get involved in extracurricular activities, stay away from bad companions, show good manners, dress appropriately, and behave in class. Cohen referred to this as the *college boy* solution to the status failure of lower-class boys. This solution comes at a high price, however, because the lower-class boy must essentially leave his past behind. Moreover, given the disadvantage of his upbringing, there is a low probability of success.

The most likely solution to status strain felt by lower-class boys, Cohen argued, was the *corner boy* solution. Corner boys neither buy into middle-class status like the college boy, nor do they directly attack and confront middle-class values as delinquents. The corner boy essentially accepts failure in the eyes of the middle class and structures his life so that he is sheltered by like-minded others. In other words, the corner boy retreats into a stable, lower- and working-class life with other corner boys. This is the most frequent solution to strain. It does not mean, however, that corner boys are not delinquent; indeed they are. But it is not the serious and repetitive delinquency that is fostered by the delinquent subculture.

Cloward and Ohlin Expand Merton's Theory

Drawing upon, and also elaborating, the work of Merton were Richard A. Cloward and Lloyd E. Ohlin (1960). In their book, *Delinquency and Opportunity*, they combined the anomie theories of Merton and Cohen with the notion of the learning of crime by Edwin Sutherland (more about him in the next chapter). According to Cloward and Ohlin, blocked legitimate opportunities do not provide sufficient strain to produce the delinquent subculture described by Cohen. The failure to achieve desired goals, or the discrepancy between one's aspirations and expectations, may be attributed to one's own failures. If that is the case, then, there is little motivation for subcultural delinquency— after all, there is only oneself to blame for one's failure. This is not the case, however, if society is to blame for one's failures. For instance, if one notices that the economic system is not open to free competition but is instead based on personal "connections" (i.e., "it's not what you know, but whom you know that counts"), then one becomes angry and alienated from conventional life and is closer to adopting a delinquent solution.

Even being strained and alienated is not enough to make one a subcultural delinquent, however. Cloward and Ohlin argued that persons cannot become delinquent without access to an environment where they can learn how to do delinquent things. Just as persons may be blocked in their access to a legitimate opportunity system, they may not have access to an illegitimate opportunity system. Without such a learning opportunity, there will be no subcultural delinquency. Only those who are embedded in a social structure where they can learn illegitimate enterprises (i.e., those who are exposed to differential associations with norms favoring the violation of law) will become subcultural delinquents.

In Cloward and Ohlin's scheme, the structure of illegitimate opportunities is based upon the organization of the local neighborhood. Some neighborhoods are organized around crime in that there is an easy movement from criminal to conventional life. This occurs when legitimate businesses are also fronts for illegal criminal activities, when criminals as a result become active role models for the community, and when there is a steady movement of youths into criminal enterprises where they can be taught and mentored by older criminals. Where neighborhoods like these exist, Cloward and Ohlin claim that a criminal subculture emerges. The criminal subculture is a well-organized subculture that supports crime and receives the protection, or at least the toleration, of the neighborhood. Because crime is stable, it can be learned and transmitted from one generation to the next.

When neighborhoods are not so well organized, and there is little integration of criminal and conventional lifestyles, an enduring criminal subculture cannot emerge. Communities that the early Chicago theorists would call *socially disorganized* cannot support an organized criminal subculture that is capable of providing illegitimate opportunities and a stable criminal career. Crime and delinquency do exist in such neighborhoods, but they likely result in disorganized, solitary, and predatory kinds of crime (mugging, strong-armed robbery, assaults). Cloward and Ohlin argued that a conflict or violent subculture is likely to emerge under these conditions.

Finally, Cloward and Ohlin argued that a third subculture exists. Not everyone who is both alienated and strained and has access to illegitimate learning opportunities takes successful advantage of those opportunities. That is, some youths who aspire to the criminal subculture fail. Failures also occur among those in disorganized neighborhoods who cannot meet the requirements of the conflict subculture. What happens to these "double failures?" Cloward and Ohlin argue that they form a loosely knit retreatist subculture. Those in retreatist subcultures often resort to drug and alcohol abuse.

Recent Versions of Institutional Anomie Theory

Although it was perhaps the dominant criminological theory during the 1950s through the early 1960s, anomie/strain theory fell out of favor within the discipline. In part, it had to do with the fact that many empirical attempts to test the theory provided little support for it. It also had to do with the fact that by the mid-1960s a more critical group of theorists (labeling theorists) began to look at the operation of the state and formal control mechanisms and the role that they played in the creation of crime and deviance. Within recent years, however, institutional anomie/strain theory has experienced something of a rebirth. In 1987, Thomas Bernard published a paper in which he argued that anomie/strain theory could only be correctly tested with macro- and not individual-level data. His position, therefore, was that much of the previous empirical literature, which generally showed that strain felt by individuals was not strongly related to crime, cannot be used to question the theory.

Interest in the institutional version of anomie/strain theory received a great shot in the arm with the publication of Professors Steven F. Messner and Richard Rosenfeld's book *Crime and the American Dream* in 1994. Their theory is almost a pure form of Mertonian anomie theory. Like Merton, they are interested in explaining variation in crime rates across countries. Also like Merton, they lay much of the blame for high American crime rates on our own culture, which places an inordinate emphasis on the achievement of monetary success with little regard for the way in which it is achieved. The cultural emphasis on material wealth by whatever means is, then, a major culprit in accounting for high levels of serious crime in America. In an important way, however, they have expanded the notion of anomie that was advanced by Merton. Messner and Rosenfeld (1994) argue that the cultural emphasis on monetary success is not the sole explanation for high rates of serious crime in America. They also note that American society is dominated by the economy. Because of this, economic needs come first, before other institutions such as families, schools, and political institutions. Because our society is overpowered by the economic order, the roles of family, school, church, and other institutions are consequently weakened. These other institutions cannot effectively control the behavior of their members. This theory is an important new addition to the family of anomie/strain theories, and Professors Messner and Rosenfeld have provided an essay that explains in some detail their theory.

Individual Anomie/Strain Theory

Those who argue that anomie/strain is an individual-level theory, whose purpose it is to explain why some individuals commit crimes and others do not, can also point to language in Merton's theory to support their interpretation. With respect to the effects of strain, Merton (1968) seemed to imply that it has a social psychological impact on those who experience it. "Our primary aim is to discover how some *social structures exert a definite pressure upon certain persons in the society to engage in non-conforming rather than conforming conduct"* (186, emphasis added). In this passage, Merton seems to be arguing that while anomie may have its source in the structure of society (emphasis upon goals rather than means and the convergence of universal goals and blocked means), it has its effect on crime via an intervening social psychological trait that is the property of individuals. Similar statements suggesting that anomie/strain operates on an individual social psychological level can be found in the writings of Cohen (1955):

. . . it may confidently be said that the working-class boy, particularly if his training and values be those we have here defined as working-class, is more likely than his middle-class peers to find himself at the bottom of a status hierarchy whenever he moves in a middle-class world, whether it be of adults or children. To the degree to which he values middle-class status, either because he values the good opinion of middle-class persons or because he has to some degree internalized middle-class standards himself, *he faces a problem of adjustment* and is in the market for a "solution." (119, emphasis added)

And Cloward and Ohlin (1960):

The disparity between what lower-class youth are led to want and what is actually available to them is the source of a major problem of adjustment. Adolescents who form delinquent subcultures, we suggest, have internalized an emphasis upon conventional goals. Faced with limitations on legitimate avenues of access to these goals, and unable to revise their aspirations downward, *they experience intense frustrations;* the exploration of nonconformist alternatives may be the result. (86, emphasis added)

The individual version of anomie/strain theory argues that the mediating mechanism between anomie (defined as blocked opportunities or a disparity between what one aspires to and what one can realistically expect to attain) is social psychological strain, frustration, or pressure. This strain or pressure that individuals experience can be alleviated in several ways; one of them is to commit delinquent acts. Delinquent acts may successfully relieve strain because they provide an illegal but efficient way to obtain goals such as money or prestige. If strain is a social psychological characteristic of individuals, then, the way to test the theory would be to collect individual-level data. What constitutes support for the theory would be a finding that variations in strain felt by individuals are related to variations in delinquent offending (i.e., that those who feel more strain should be more delinquent). In other words, *individuals* in certain social circumstances feel strain in the form of pressure to break rules in order to achieve monetary success. Thus, some individuals experience more strain than others, and the theory would predict that they are at a greater risk for criminal/deviant conduct than other individuals who experience less strain.

It is probably safe to say that the individual-level version of anomie/strain theory is the version of the theory that has been most frequently articulated and put to empirical test. Generally, when researchers sought to test anomie/strain theory, they measured strain in terms of a self-reported discrepancy between educational or occupational aspirations (goals) and the expectation that these aspirations would be realized. Those who aspired to advanced education and good jobs, but who felt that they would probably not be able to achieve them, were thought to be experiencing strain. Unfortunately, much of this research did not support the prediction from strain theory. Those who had high aspirations and low expectations of success were no more likely to be delinquent than those with high aspirations and high expectations (for reviews of this literature, see Farnworth and Leiber 1989; Akers 1997). In fact, this research tended to show that youths with high aspirations were less likely to commit delinquent acts than those with low aspirations, regardless of what their expectations were. These findings are more compatible with control theory than they are with anomie/strain theory.

In response to repeated failures to find support for the key individual anomie/strain theory prediction that a discrepancy between occupational or educational aspirations and expectations is related to delinquency, the theory underwent a number of revisions. One revision was to define strain in terms of a discrepancy between aspirations and expectations in realms other than education and occupation. It was argued that youths pursue other goals besides money and prestige, such as popularity, social/sexual partners, athletic success, and good grades. In this revised anomie/strain theory, strain arises when youths aspire to things like popularity and attractive dates, but think it is unlikely that they will be able to attain them. As a result, they experience strain and are motivated to do something about it—like commit delinquent acts (Simon and Gagnon 1976). Another revision was to define strain in terms of relative rather than absolute deprivation. That is, strain occurs when there is a discrepancy between what one has (money or some other goal) relative to others in a comparison group (Passas 1997). Under this scheme, no matter what I have, if I feel that I have less than those in my reference group, I will feel frustration and strain and will be looking for a solution that could include crime and deviance.

Both of these revisions of anomie/strain theory still anchor their conception of strain to the failure to achieve valued goals—affluence, non-monetary goals, relative affluence—and they have not been much more successful in supporting the theory than previous conceptualizations (Cullen and Agnew 1999). In a recent series of papers, however, Professor Robert Agnew has put forth a major revision of individual anomie/strain theory, which he calls *General Strain Theory*. His essay follows that of Professors Messner and Rosenfeld and describes a theory that is general in two senses: (1) he has substantially expanded the sources of strain (strain is now a more general concept), and (2) he applies his revised strain theory to diverse kinds of criminal and delinquent behavior (it is a general theory of crime).

References

Agnew, Robert. (1987). "On testing structural strain theories." *Journal of Research in Crime and Delinquency*, 24:281–286.

Akers, Ronald L. (1997). *Criminological Theories: Introduction and Evaluation*, Second Edition. Los Angeles: Roxbury.

Bernard, Thomas J. (1987). "Testing structural strain theories." *Journal of Research in Crime and Delinquency*, 24:262–280.

Cloward, Richard A. and Lloyd E. Ohlin. (1960). *Delinquency and Opportunity: A Theory of Delinquent Gangs*. New York: Free.

Cohen, Albert K. (1955). *Delinquent Boys: The Culture of the Gang*. New York: Free.

Cullen, Francis T. and Robert Agnew. (1999). *Criminological Theory: Past to Present*. Los Angeles: Roxbury.

Durkheim, Emile. [1897] (1951). *Suicide*. Reprint. New York: Free.

Farnworth, Margaret and Michael J. Leiber. (1989). "Strain theory revisited: Economic goals, educational means, and delinquency." *American Sociological Review*, 54:263–274.

Hirschi, Travis. (1969). *Causes of Delinquency*. Berkeley: University of California Press.

Kornhauser, Ruth R. (1978). *Social Sources of Delinquency*. Chicago: University of Chicago Press.

Merton, Robert K. (1957). *Social Theory and Social Structure*. New York: Free.

——. (1968). *Social Theory and Social Structure*, 1968 Enlarged Edition. New York: Free.

Messner, Steven F. and Richard Rosenfeld. (1994). *Crime and the American Dream*. Belmont, CA: Wadsworth.

Passas, Nikos. (1997). "Anomie and relative deprivation." Pp. 62–94 in *The Future of Anomie Theory*. N. Passas and R. Agnew (eds.). Boston: Northeastern University Press.

Simon, William and John H. Gagnon. (1976). "The anomie of affluence: A post-Mertonian conception." *American Journal of Sociology*, 82:356–378.

An Institutional-Anomie Theory of Crime

Steven F. Messner
SUNY at Albany

Richard Rosenfeld
University of Missouri–St. Louis

Crime in Sociological Perspective

The sociological approach to the study of crime and deviance has a long and venerable tradition. The pioneers of quantitative criminology—Quetelet and Guerry—highlighted the importance of social factors in their studies of official crime statistics in France in the early nineteenth century. Using maps shaded to reflect the varying levels of crime in the provinces of France, these scholars documented the striking regularity in the spatial distributions of crime and related these distributions to other social and economic factors. Quetelet in particular was impressed by the connection between crime rates and features of the larger social environment. In a famous (and somewhat hyperbolic) statement, Quetelet wrote:

> The crimes which are annually committed seem to be a necessary result of our social organization. . . .Society prepares the crime, and the guilty are only the instruments by which it is executed.[1]

Karl Marx, a founding figure in sociology writing later in the nineteenth century, also drew attention to the link between crime and the basic features of the organization of society. As part of his more general critique of the inherent flaws of capitalism, Marx (1859) argued that "there must be something rotten in the very core of a social system which increases its wealth without diminishing its misery, and increases in crimes even more rapidly than in numbers." Whereas Marx directed attention to the economic foundations of society, another of the classic figures in sociology, Emile Durkheim, emphasized the importance of the moral order for understanding deviant behavior. Durkheim explained how the rapid social changes associated with modernization could lead to *anomie*, a weakening of the social norms that restrain individual impulses. Anomie, Durkheim (1966) argued, is conducive to two lethal forms of deviant behavior: suicide and homicide (see especially 346–360).

The sociological approach to the study of crime and deviance continued to develop in the early and middle years of the twentieth century. Following in the footsteps of Quetelet and Guerry, researchers at the University of Chicago used maps to plot rates of juvenile delinquency and other "social pathologies" across different neighborhoods of the city (Liska and Messner 1999). The so-called Chicago School of urban sociology held that high rates of crime and deviance reflect *social disorganization*, a condition wherein the informal social controls in the neighborhood (rooted in relations with family members, neighbors, shopkeepers, and others) have ceased to be effective. Taking a somewhat more macro-level approach, the sociologist Robert K. Merton (1938) linked high crime and deviance to disorganization at the societal level in his famous essay "Social Structure and Anomie." Merton claimed that American culture and social structure are incompatible in a fundamental sense. The culture encourages everyone to succeed (understood largely in monetary terms), while the social structure distributes opportunities for success unequally. This "disconnect" between cultural orientations and structural realities pressures some people to abandon the legitimate means for success and to substitute alternative, sometimes criminal, means.

In short, criminologists have long recognized that a full understanding of criminal behavior requires consideration of the larger social context. The purpose of this chapter is to explicate a contemporary perspective on crime that places primary emphasis on the social context: institutional-anomie theory. This theory is predicated upon the core principle of earlier sociological approaches that crime is to some extent a product of the basic social organization of a society. The theory explains how crime results from the nature and relationships among a society's major institutions, such as the family, economy, education, and political system, and from prevailing cultural orientations. In the pages that follow, we introduce the general concepts used in institutional-anomie theory, present the main substantive arguments of the theory, review relevant evidence, identify key issues for future research, and consider briefly the implications of our arguments for creating a society with relatively low levels of crime.

The General Conceptual Framework

Institutional-anomie theory links crime to the basic features of social organization—*culture* and *social structure*. Culture consists of the values, goals, beliefs, and norms shared by the members of a society. Culture defines "the rules of the game" that distinguish one society from another. Examples of cultural elements within American society include the value placed on individual freedom, equal opportunity for success, and the use of monetary standards for measuring social standing and achievement. These examples point to a core value complex in American culture, the "American Dream," which specifies that economic success is attainable by anyone who works hard, plays by the rules, and is willing to engage in competition with others for jobs, income, and status. We have argued that the American Dream has special relevance for understanding the high crime rates in the United States compared with other developed societies (Messner and Rosenfeld 1997a).

The other dimension of social organization, social structure, refers to the social positions that people occupy and the roles accompanying these positions. For example, the position of "parent" carries with it the role obligation of caring for children; the position of "student" is accompanied by the obligation to attend classes; and so on. Social positions are knit together by their accompanying roles, which specify the legitimate ex-

pectations people have of one another and their obligation to fulfill those expectations. The full range of interconnected positions and roles defines the social structure of a society.

The two dimensions of social organization, culture and social structure, are united through a society's major *social institutions*. It is useful to think of institutions as complexes of positions, roles, values, and norms that constitute the pillars of a society, anchored in the social structure and supporting the culture. The function of an institution is to channel social behavior within the grooves specified by the social structure according to the rules that comprise the culture. All societies of any complexity contain economic, political, educational, religious, and kinship institutions.

Each of the multiple institutions comprising a social structure cannot function properly in isolation from the others. If the family system, for example, is to successfully perform the function of preparing a society's "new recruits" for the demands and opportunities of membership, it must depend on the effective functioning of the economy (to provide sustenance and employment), the political system (to mobilize the resources necessary to achieve collective goals), and in complex societies, the education system (to provide advanced or technical training required for the performance of occupational roles). And, of course, the operation of economic, political, and educational institutions depends upon the "raw material" of individual persons who have been more or less effectively socialized in the family.

The interdependence of social institutions is central to the explanation of crime offered by institutional-anomie theory. It is useful to think about this interdependence as constituting an *institutional balance of power*, which refers to the relations of mutual dependence among social institutions. Societies differ, however, in the particular form the institutional balance of power assumes. In some societies, certain institutions assume dominant positions in the balance of power; in other societies, the same institutions are subordinate and others are dominant. In summary, if in all societies institutions necessarily depend on one another, the relations of mutual dependence need not be, and in fact rarely are, perfectly balanced or equal.

The central proposition of institutional-anomie theory is that a society's distinctive level and form of crime are products of its institutional balance of power. In market capitalist societies, the particular institutional configuration of greatest relevance to crime is that in which the economy dominates the balance of power. Such societies, for reasons explained below, have a strong tendency toward *anomie,* which refers to an overall weakening of the regulatory force of basic values and norms. However, anomic societies are not the only societies with high rates of crime. Societies with differing institutional configurations, for example, those in which political or religious institutions are dominant, also may exhibit high levels of criminal activity, even if the type of crime differs from that observed in anomic societies. We describe the anomic form of the institutional balance of power in greater detail in the following pages and contrast it with other crime-producing institutional forms. Before elaborating on the specifics of institutional-anomie theory, however, we should make a final general observation about our portrait of social organization.

The picture we have drawn of culture, social structure, and institutions is an ideal-typical depiction. Actual societies are hardly as tidy and coherent as the picture implies. In reality, culture and social structure are never perfectly matched: Not all social positions and roles are culturally scripted, and some cultural values and norms are not fully institutionalized. In the United States, for example, the persistence of race and sex discrimination serves as a reminder that the value placed on equal opportunity for all is often honored in the breach.

Our intention in presenting the image of a perfectly organized society is to make a fundamental point about the sociology of crime and deviance, the intellectual home of institutional-anomie theory. Crime and other forms of non-normative behavior are normal and inevitable features of societies, even those in which institutions function smoothly.[2] Neither defective individuals nor malfunctioning social systems are required for crime to occur. The normal pressures and opportunities associated with the nature of social organization itself will always produce some amount and type of deviant conduct, and in those societies with developed legal systems, some of that conduct will be defined as criminal. Institutional-anomie theory seeks to explain the elevated levels and differing types of criminal activity that result from particular forms of institutional imbalance. As a sociological theory of crime, it recognizes that perfectly organized societies are imaginary, if useful, constructs and that crime rates cannot fall to zero. However, by specifying with some precision the institutional sources of crime, it encourages us to imagine the social changes required to move a little closer to perfection.

Social Organization and Crime

Institutional-anomie theory stipulates that an important cultural condition that promotes high levels of crime is *anomie.* The concept of anomie has been used in many different ways in the sociological literature, and scholars continue to debate its various meanings (see, for example, Orru 1987). For our purposes, the distinctive feature of anomie is the *deregulation* of both the goals that people are encouraged to aspire to, and the means that are regarded as acceptable in the pursuit of these goals.

The regulation of goals is particularly challenging in market capitalist societies. That is because a primary feature of everyday life in such societies—the production and exchange of the goods and services required for subsistence—is organized around the principles of profit and loss. Indeed, the pursuit of profit or monetary gain is the driving motivational force underlying a capitalist economy. If people were not motivated to accumulate monetary rewards, the capitalist economy would grind to a halt.

Note, however, that the economic goals of profit and gain are elusive; they have no clear stopping points. No matter how much money one accumulates, there is always more that could in theory be attained. In a real sense, the "sky's the limit" in the pursuit of profit, which means of course that there is no limit at all. The primary goals associated with the market economy, therefore, have an inherently unregulated, anomic quality.

The establishment of restraints on the selection of the means for pursuing goals is also a challenging task in capitalist societies. The capitalist economy is predicated upon competition. Consumers try to purchase items at the lowest price; sellers try to obtain the highest price. Employees fight for high wages; employers maneuver to minimize labor costs. In this ongoing economic struggle, all participants in the market are encouraged to develop a highly calculating orientation to the means that they use to realize their goals. How likely is it that a given course of action will yield maximum gain at minimal cost? From a purely economic standpoint, in other words, what matters is what works. The norms guiding economic action are in this sense what the sociologist Robert Merton (1938) referred to as *efficiency norms*. When behavior is governed exclusively by such standards, the means for pursuing goals lack any *moral* regulation; they are selected on the basis of purely technical considerations without regard for what is right or wrong. Under these conditions, goals are achieved by any means necessary.

Anomie, in the sense of deregulated goals and means, is a natural tendency in market capitalist societies. Not all capitalist societies, however, are anomic. Recall that the economy is only one social institution among many, including the family, the schools, and the political system. These other, noneconomic institutions typically have different operating principles, or *moral codes* (see Wolfe 1989). They provide alternative social goals to those of profit and gain. They employ alternative standards for earning admiration and respect. To the extent, then, that these noneconomic institutions play a vital role in society, they will temper the anomic tendencies inherent in the economic realm of a capitalist society.

Anomie is particularly likely in market capitalist societies, we are suggesting, when the economy assumes dominance in the institutional balance of power. Such economic dominance manifests itself in three important ways (see Messner and Rosenfeld 1997a, Chapter 4). First, the roles of other institutions are *devalued* in comparison with those of the dominant institution. For example, the homeowner accrues more status than the homemaker; the economically successful alumni stand out as the "stars" at the twentieth high school reunion. Second, noneconomic institutional roles must *accommodate* to economic needs and requirements when role demands conflict. To illustrate, parents often worry about finding time for their families, but few workers agonize about finding time for their jobs. Finally, under conditions of economic dominance, noneconomic institutions are *penetrated* by the language and logic of the economy. The market becomes the model for social relationships, and people are thought of as "calculating maximizers" in all their dealings with others; and to some extent, they become so (Schwartz 1994).

Economic dominance and anomie are thus mutually reinforcing social structural and cultural conditions in market capitalist societies. When non-economic institutions lose their vitality, people orient their behavior towards the anomic imperatives of the market economy. And as anomic cultural orientations permeate a society, the economy assumes ever greater importance as the institutional domain governing behavior.

Institutional-anomie theory holds that a society characterized by an anomic culture and economic dominance in the institutional balance of power is likely to exhibit high rates of crime. The lack of effective regulation of goals and means implies that the culture pressures people to strive relentlessly for success, understood with reference to the elusive goal of monetary gain, and to do so with the most technically expedient means at hand. That these means are often criminal in nature should not be surprising because the basic idea of much (if not all) crime is to get things the easy way (Gottfredson and Hirschi 1990; Felson 1997). As a result, some elements of the culture (the pursuit of profit by any means necessary) ironically promote behavior at odds with other elements of the culture (social prohibitions formally codified in the laws).

At the same time, economic dominance in the institutional balance of power implies that noneconomic institutions will have difficulty fulfilling their distinctive functions. These functions include socializing people into the shared moral beliefs of the culture, and regulating behavior by dispensing rewards and punishments in accord with the performance of institutional roles. In short, a society with an anomic culture and an imbalanced institutional structure tilted toward the economy will simultaneously generate cultural pressures for crime while at the same time eroding the cultural and social restraints against crime. High levels of crime are likely to be observed in such a society, reflecting the core features of its social organization.

Institutional-anomie theory not only predicts high *levels* of crime under conditions of anomie and economic dominance, but particular *types* of crime as well. Anomic societies tend to produce distinctively high rates of what can be viewed as "anomic crime." These are crimes with a highly *instrumental* motive, that is, the crime functions as an instrument to secure a specific goal, which usually involves taking something of value from someone. In addition, anomic crimes are likely to involve force or the threat of force. Predatory street crimes such as robbery are a good example of these kinds of offenses, which combine the goal of economic gain with the technically most proficient means of securing the goal, including if necessary the use of violence. Because firearms are highly effective instruments for securing compliance from victims, we should also expect to find high levels of gun-related crime in anomic societies. We draw just such a connection in our study of U.S. crime rates, which attributes high rates of robbery, homicide, and gun-related violence in the United States to the anomic tendencies of the "American Dream" and the dominance of the economy in the American institutional structure (Messner and Rosenfeld 1997a).

High levels of anomic crime are produced when the economy dominates the institutional structure of market capitalist societies. Given the spread of free-market arrangements throughout the world since the demise of the former Soviet Union and Eastern bloc socialist states, from the perspective of institutional-anomie theory, we would expect to observe increasing rates of predatory street crime in societies where such crimes once were relatively rare. In fact, a particularly anomic form of market dominance seems to have taken hold in Russia. A minor journalistic industry has emerged documenting Russia's so-called "dog-eat-dog capitalism" and attendant social dislocations including rising crime rates (Bohlen 1992; Erlanger 1994; Handelman 1995; Gordon 1996; Holmes 1997).

Although economic dominance in societies undergoing rapid social change is an important global development, it is not the only form of institutional imbalance that leads to high levels of crime. The principal claim of institutional-anomie theory is that institutional imbalance *per se*, and not simply dominance of the economy, produces high rates of criminal activity. We should expect, therefore, to find elevated levels and distinctive forms of criminality in societies in which the institutional balance of power is dominated by the political system and in those where so-called "civil" institutions, such as the family and religion, are dominant.

Consider, first, the situation of political dominance. As the state assumes an ever expanding role in regulating everyday life, the opportunities for the exercise of personal agency are diminished. A sense of direct responsibility for the well-being of others accordingly atrophies, and people develop a cynical orientation towards personal responsibility and accountability. This type of moral climate, we suggest, invites corruption on the part of both the powerful and powerless alike (for examples, see Wolfe's [1989, 168–177] discussion of tax avoidance and underground economic activity in Scandinavia).

By contrast, consider the dominance of the institutional balance of power by civil institutions, such as the kinship system or religion. Whereas economic dominance is associated with the cultural condition of anomie, and state dominance with moral cynicism and withdrawal, civic dominance leads to a kind of extreme moral vigilance or *hypermoralism*. People develop a strong sense of interpersonal obligations, but these obligations are restricted to those with whom they share particular social statuses or identities, often based on kin, ethnic, or religious affiliations. In the absence of any universalistic rules of conduct, a sense of obligation to others who are outside of the relevant social groups is virtually nonexistent.

This type of moral code encourages crimes in the defense of the moral order itself, albeit understood in narrow and highly particularistic terms. Such offenses include vigilanteeism, hate crimes, and violations of human rights that might not be crimes in a legalistic sense but are widely regarded as crime-equivalents (cf. Michalowski and Kramer 1987). Because perceived disturbances in the traditional sex-role system are viewed as striking at the heart of civil society, women have been disproportionately victimized by such violations of human rights and crimes of social control (for examples, see Borger 1997; Herbert 1997; *New York Times* 1997).

The common element cutting across the different moral orders associated with the three forms of institutional imbalance discussed above is that they are each "incomplete" in an important sense. They fail to incorporate elements of the moral codes associated with other institutions. A market economy tends to foster respect for individual rights and for voluntary personal choices. Markets also are "universalizing" institutions; they encourage people to venture beyond the confines of local social settings and ties in search of more customers, higher incomes, and lower costs.

These moral orientations associated with markets do not in themselves produce crime. To the contrary, when properly joined with sentiments of mutual obligation, they bolster the norm of "reciprocity" that joins the expectations of some roles to the obligations of others (borrower to lender, landlord to tenant, student to teacher) and thus serve to inhibit criminal victimization. The institutions of civil society and the state foster such sentiments of mutual obligation, the former promoting a sense of interpersonal obligation and the latter sentiments of collective solidarity. However, the institutions of civil society do not embody the univeralism of the market, nor does the state manifest values of individual autonomy.

A full understanding of the social and cultural sources of crime, in summary, must consider not only the values and beliefs that are favored when a particular institution dominates the institutional balance of power but also the consequences for crime when alternative cultural prescriptions are renounced or insufficiently developed. The market promotes crime when the freedom of action that it encourages is left unchecked by considerations of collective order and mutual obligation. These political and social values, likewise, assume degraded forms in the absence of attention to individual rights and liberties, which typically accompany market arrangements. It follows that crime is likely to be minimized when the respective cultural orientations of the three institutional complexes are balanced such that each serves as a continuous reminder of the indispensability of the others.

Evidence in Support of Institutional-Anomie Theory

Our intention in developing institutional-anomie theory has been to stimulate debate and research about the broad cultural and social sources of crime in modern societies. The examples we have offered of different patterns of crime in societies under alternative institutional configurations are just that, examples; and the implied causal relationships require much more systematic attention by researchers. Nevertheless, a body of research has begun to emerge on crime and market dominance that lends some support to the theory. In a study of property crime rates across the United States, Chamlin and Cochran (1995) found that levels of property crime were lower in states with stronger families (measured by the ratio of marriages to divorces), high levels of religious participation (measured by church membership), and high levels of political involvement (measured by voter turnout rates). In other words, consistent with the predictions of institutional-anomie theory, the strength of noneconomic institutions (family, church, and state) appears to be associated with lower levels of criminal involvement in the United States.

These investigators then tested a more subtle implication of the theory, which is that the strength of noneconomic institutions *conditions* the impact of economic deprivation on crime rates. Strong families, churches, and political institutions should, in essence, "soften the blow" of economic hardship, resulting in a weaker association between indicators of deprivation and property crime rates in states where the strength of the noneconomic institutions is greater. The researchers found support for this hypothesis. In states with strong noneconomic institutions, property crime rates are less closely associated with the rate of poverty than in states with weak noneconomic institutions. This test was repeated with different measures of economic deprivation, and the results generally confirmed those produced when the state poverty rate was used to measure deprivation.[3]

Another study, one we conducted, assessed the effect on homicide rates of the strength of the political system (the *polity*) in relation to the market economy for a sample of about forty nations (Messner and Rosenfeld 1997b). The relative strength of the polity was measured by scoring each nation according to its "decommodification of labor" as reflected in the extensiveness of policies that insulate personal well-being from pure market forces (e.g., family support, social security, unemployment insurance).[4] We hypothesized that, other things equal, nations with highly decommodified policies, in the form of broad and generous social welfare and insurance programs, would have lower rates of homicide than those with more restrictive policies. In such societies, we reasoned, the institutional balance of power was less likely to be dominated by the market economy and more likely to reflect the norms of collective support and mutual obligation associated with the state. We found that, controlling for other influences, the level of decom-

modification is in fact related to the homicide rate: In societies with greater decommodification—and, by extension, stronger political institutions—homicide rates are lower than in those where persons are afforded less protection from market forces.

A final line of research that we have been engaged in links anomie and the strength of political and civic institutions to the concepts of social trust and social capital. *Social capital* refers to the capacity of groups to cooperate in the attainment of collective goals and is typically measured with indicators of social trust and civic engagement (Coleman 1990; Brehm and Rahn 1997; Jackman and Miller 1998). In environments with depleted social capital, people are likely to perceive others as untrustworthy and as "out for themselves." Under such conditions, the level of anomie is likely to be very high, because the absence of regulatory standards—the essence of anomie—leaves little basis for trust in others. The other component of social capital, civic engagement, is usually assessed in terms of the extensiveness of organizational membership and political involvement, both indicators of the strength of civic and political institutions.

In an investigation of a national sample of U.S. geographic areas, we found an inverse relationship between an area's homicide rate and a measure of social trust derived from responses to national surveys (Rosenfeld and Messner 1998). In a subsequent analysis based on the same sample, we combined our measure of social trust with indicators of organizational membership and political involvement to assess the level of social capital across communities. We found that areas with high levels of social capital tend to have low homicide rates, controlling for other determinants of homicide. Because it is reasonable to assume that high rates of criminal violence will reduce trust in others and promote withdrawal from the community, we evaluated the *reciprocal* (two-way) relationship between homicide and social capital. That analysis confirmed our earlier finding that the level of social capital in an area influences its homicide rate, even controlling for the presumed effect of homicide on social capital (Messner, Rosenfeld, and Baumer 1999).

Future Research

Institutional-anomie theory has thus received some support in the empirical literature. However, research remains in the beginning stages. Subsequent analysis will almost certainly lead to refinements and modifications in the explanatory framework. In addition, a critical task for future research is to move beyond the situation of market dominance to assess the relationship between crime and institutional imbalance more broadly. It would seem of special importance to analyze critically the zero-sum assumption in our assessment of the institutional balance of power, the idea that a society's institutional structure is "imbalanced" by the domination of a single institution.

Our argument presumes that the institutional balance of power does not function effectively and a specific form of criminality is activated when a single institution is dominant. Yet, the case could be made that two of the major institutions may dominate a society without significant tension between them. Consider a society, such as Singapore, where an authoritarian and seemingly stable national government coexists with an equally strong market economy. China could well emerge into a similar configuration with the continued development of market arrangements. Such instances call attention to the possibility of alternative, complex forms of institutional dominance under differing cultural circumstances. They also serve as a reminder that markets are not universal guarantors of individual freedom or, more precisely, that the relationship between economic and political freedom will vary according to different understandings of the meaning and scope of individual rights.

Another promising avenue for further inquiry is the presumed opposition, in our discussion and elsewhere, between civil society and the state. We have proposed, following Wolfe (1989), that an expansive regulatory state runs the risk of eroding the informal controls and sources of moral vitality of civil institutions. While suggestive, this concep-

tion of the antagonistic relationship between the state and civil society fails to reflect the complex historical interconnections between the two institutional sectors. Skocpol (1996, 22) argues, for example, that in the United States the welfare state and community-based voluntary associations historically "have operated in close symbiosis," each responsible for the continued growth and effectiveness of the other. In a similar vein, Robert D. Putnam has pointed out that his recent research on the decline in voluntary associations and civic involvement in the United States (Putnam 1995) should not be construed as support for a retreat from activist government. "Social capital," he writes, "is not a substitute for effective public policy but rather a prerequisite for it and, in part, a consequence of it" (Putnam 1996, 28). As an example, Putnam (1996) mentions neighborhood crime watch groups, which sprang from government-funded anticrime programs during the 1970s.

While we believe that the ideas presented in this essay require careful empirical scrutiny and conceptual refinement, we hope that the requisite scholarly research is carried out with due regard for the policy implications of our arguments. A major task with respect to crime control confronting both the developed and developing societies is to promote a proper balance among the three major institutional realms of society—market, state, and civil society. We suspect that the most pressing danger for most societies in this era of the "triumph of capitalism" (Teeple 1995) is market dominance. Accordingly, crime control will require concerted efforts to tame the imperatives of an increasingly globalized market, thereby reducing the spread of anomic predatory crime, which is of growing concern throughout the world. However, as indicated in our discussion of the crimes committed in the name of traditional moral codes, the challenge is to strengthen the institutions of the state and civil society without sacrificing the respect for individual rights and the protections against absolutism and fanaticism that socially embedded markets provide.

Notes

1. Quoted in Vold, Bernard, and Snipes (1998, 310). See this source for a general discussion of Quetelet's and Guerry's contributions to criminology.

2. The classic statement of the "normality" of crime is Durkheim's (1964).

3. When the unemployment rate was substituted for the poverty rate, the family indicator did not have the expected effect of reducing the association between deprivation and crime rates. For a discussion of the sensitivity of tests of institutional-anomie theory to differing measures of key theoretical constructs, see Piquero and Piquero (1998).

4. The concept of the *decommodification of labor* is based on Gosta Esping-Andersen's (1990) analysis of national social welfare policies.

References

Bohlen, Celestine. (1992). "The Russians' new code: If it pays, anything goes." *New York Times*, August, 30, 1, 6.

Borger, Julian. (1997). "Women are killed for family honor." *St. Louis Post-Dispatch*, November, 6:A11.

Brehm, John and Wendy Rahn. (1997). "Individual-level evidence for the causes and consequences of social capital." *American Journal of Political Science*, 41:999–1023.

Chamlin, Mitchell B. and John K. Cochran. (1995). "Assessing Messner and Rosenfeld's institutional anomie theory: A partial test." *Criminology*, 33:411–429.

Coleman, James S. (1990). *Foundations of Social Theory*. Cambridge, MA: Harvard University Press.

Durkheim, Emile. [1895] (1964). *The Rules of Sociological Method*. Reprint. New York: Free.

——. [1897] (1966). *Suicide: A Study in Sociology*. Reprint. New York: Free.

Erlanger, Steven. (1994). "Russia's new dictatorship of crime." *New York Times*, May 15.

Esping-Andersen, Gosta. (1990). *The Three Worlds of Welfare Capitalism*. Princeton, NJ: Princeton University Press.

Felson, Marcus. (1997). *Crime and Everyday Life*. Second Edition. Thousand Oaks, CA: Pine Forge.

Gordon, Michael R. (1996). "Slaying tells of Russia's deadly capitalism." *New York Times*, November, 5:A3.

Gottfredson, Michael R. and Travis Hirschi. (1990). *A General Theory of Crime*. Stanford, CA: Stanford University Press.

Handelman, Stephen. (1995). *Comrade Criminal: Russia's New Mafiya*. New Haven, CT: Yale University Press.

Herbert, Bob. (1997). "Algerian Terror." *New York Times*, November, 9(4):15.

Holmes, Stephen. (1997). "What Russia teaches us now." *The American Prospect*, July–August, 30–39.

Jackman, Robert W. and Ross A. Miller. (1998). "Social capital and politics." *Annual Review of Political Science*, 47–73.

Liska, Allen E. and Steven F. Messner. (1999). *Perspectives on Crime and Deviance*, Third Edition. Upper Saddle River, NJ: Prentice Hall.

Marx, Karl. (1859). "Europe: Population, crime, and pauperism." *New York Daily Tribune*, September 16.

Merton, Robert K. (1938). "Social structure and anomie." *American Sociological Review*, 3:672–682.

Messner, Steven F. and Richard Rosenfeld. (1997a). *Crime and the American Dream*, Second Edition. Belmont, CA: Wadsworth.

——. (1997b). "Political restraint of the market and levels of criminal homicide: A cross-national application of institutional anomie theory." *Social Forces*, 75:1393–1416.

Messner, Steven F., Richard Rosenfeld, and Eric Baumer. (1999). "Estimating the reciprocal effects of social capital and homicide rates." Paper presented at the meeting of the American Society of Criminology, Toronto, Ontario, Canada, November 17–20.

Michalowski, Raymond J. and Ronald C. Kramer. (1987). "The space between laws: The problem of corporate crime in a transnational context." *Social Problems*, 34:34–53.

New York Times. (1997). "The Taliban's war on women," November, 5:A26.

Orru, Marco. (1987). *Anomie: History and Meanings*. Boston: Allen and Unwin.

Piquero, Alex and Nicole Leeper Piquero. (1998). "On testing institutional anomie theory with varying specifications." *Studies on Crime and Crime Prevention*, 7:61–84.

Putnam, Robert D. (1995). "Tuning in, tuning out: The strange disappearance of social capital in America." *PS: Political Science and Politics*, December, 64:683.

——. (1996). "Robert Putnam responds." *The American Prospect*, March–April:26–28.

Rosenfeld, Richard and Steven F. Messner. (1998). "Beyond the criminal justice system:

Anomie, institutional vitality, and crime in the United States." Paper presented at the meeting of the American Sociological Association, San Francisco, CA, August 21–25.

Schwartz, Barry. (1994). *The Costs of Living: How Market Freedom Erodes the Best Things in Life*. New York: W.W. Norton.

Skocpol, Theda. (1996). "Unravelling from above." *The American Prospect*, March–April:20–25.

Teeple, Gary. (1995). *Globalization and the Decline of Social Reform*. Atlantic Highlands, NJ: Humanities.

Vold, George B. (1998). *Theoretical Criminology, Fourth Edition*. New York: Oxford University Press.

Wolfe, Alan. (1989). *Whose Keeper? Social Science and Moral Obligation*. Berkeley: University of California Press.

An Overview of General Strain Theory

Robert Agnew
Emory University

The basic idea behind General Strain Theory (GST) is quite simple: when people are treated badly, they may get upset and engage in crime (Agnew 1992, 1995a). For example, they may assault the peers who mistreat them, run away from the parents who abuse them, or take drugs to make themselves feel better. GST builds on this simple idea by 1) describing the types of negative treatment or strains that upset people and 2) describing why some people are more likely to respond to strain with crime than others.

The first part of this essay describes the central ideas of GST and the research on the theory. The second part uses GST to explain certain key issues in criminology, like why adolescents have higher crime rates than adults and children, why males have higher crime rates than females, and why some communities have higher crime rates than others. The third and final part briefly explores the recommendations that GST makes for controlling crime.

General Strain Theory

What Is Strain and How Is It Measured?

GST argues that strain ultimately causes crime. *Strain* refers to negative treatment by others and it may be measured in two ways. The first and most direct way is to ask individuals whether they dislike the ways they are being treated. For example, we may ask a sample of juveniles whether they dislike the ways their teachers treat them. This provides us with information about the individual's *subjective* or perceived level of strain. Second, we may ask individuals whether they

are being treated in v[...] *would be disliked by t[...] group* (or we may *obse[...]* being treated in ways w[...] dislike). For example[...] whether their spouse[...] them or whether th[...] courses at school. This [...] measure of *objective strain*. We assume that they dislike these events. That is, we assume that these objective strains (e.g., getting a failing grade at school) are associated with subjective strain (e.g., disliking one's grades).

Most tests of GST have employed objective measures of strain. Individuals, for example, are asked whether they have been assaulted or had things stolen from them; whether their parents have divorced; whether their parents often complain about them, "blow their tops," try to control whatever they do, et cetera; whether their parents fight with one another a lot; whether they get along with their classmates; whether any of their close friends have died or suffered serious illness or injury; whether their teachers talk down to them and embarrass them; whether their neighborhood has problems like vandalism, winos and junkies, and assaults and robberies; whether their parents can afford to buy them the kinds of clothes they want; whether they have enough money; whether they think they will get the kind of job they want, and so on. Most of these questions focus on the individual's relations with family, friends, people at school and work, and others in the community—because these constitute the major social environments for most people.

It is assumed that most individuals dislike the above types of negative treatment. This is probably a reasonable assumption in most cases, although data suggest that there are some individual and group differences in the reaction to certain objective strains. For example, two individuals may have the same failing grades in school—so they are identical in this measure of objective strain. These individuals, however, may subjectively evaluate his or her grades differently—one may dislike his or her failing grades a lot while the other may not care much about his or her

161

ewise, there is some evidence for
ferences in the evaluation of objec-
rains. For example, evidence suggests
females subjectively evaluate certain
bjective strains more negatively than males
(see Broidy and Agnew 1997). As will be discussed below, GST helps explain why different individuals and groups sometimes react differently to the same objective strains.

What Are the Major Types of Strain or Negative Treatment?

As suggested above, individuals may experience hundreds of different types of strain. GST groups these types of strain or negative treatment into three general categories. In particular, GST focuses on situations where others 1) prevent you from achieving your positively-valued goals, 2) remove or threaten to remove positively-valued stimuli that you possess, and 3) present or threaten to present you with noxious or negatively-valued stimuli. The second and third types of strain are sometimes treated together, because it is often difficult to distinguish between them in practice. For example, suppose one of your friends insults you. From one perspective, that might be viewed as the loss of something you value (harmonious relations with your friend); from another perspective it might be viewed as the presentation of negatively-valued stimuli (the insult).

Several major types of strain are described below, some having to do with the failure to achieve positively-valued goals and some with the loss of positive stimuli and presentation of negative stimuli. Although there are hundreds of types of strain, evidence suggests that some types of strain are more strongly related to crime than other types. GST is still in the process of specifying which types of strain are most strongly related to crime and why, but crime theorists consider the following types of strain to be especially relevant.

The Failure to Achieve Positively-Valued Goals

GST argues that much crime results from the failure to achieve one or more of several positively-valued goals.

Money. Like earlier versions of strain theory, GST argues that crime may result from the failure to achieve the goal of *monetary success* (see Cloward and Ohlin 1960; Cohen 1955; Greenberg 1977; Merton 1938, 1968). Most people in the United States are under a lot of pressure to make money. They are encouraged to make money by those around them—like family, friends, school officials, the media, and even many religious figures. And money is necessary to buy many of the things they want, including the necessities of life and all those luxury items to which they are regularly exposed. At the same time, many of these people are not able to obtain the money they want through legitimate channels, like parents (for young people) and work. They may grow up in troubled families and poor communities. As a consequence, they may not be taught the skills and attitudes necessary to succeed in school and work, they may attend inferior schools, and their family members and friends may not be able to send them to college or help them obtain good jobs. I should note, however, that while the inability to achieve one's monetary goals is more common among the poor, it also affects many in the middle and upper classes. Many middle- and upper-class people in the United States want more money than they have and can obtain through legitimate channels.

The inability to achieve monetary success through legitimate channels is an important type of strain, and data suggest that it sometimes leads to crime. Criminals and delinquents often report that they engage in income-generating crime because they want money but cannot easily get it any other way (e.g., Anderson 1994; Jankowsi 1995; MacLeod 1987; Padilla 1992; Sullivan 1989). Such crimes include theft, drug selling, and prostitution. Further, a few recent studies suggest that crime is more common among people who are dissatisfied with their monetary situation—with such dissatisfaction being higher among lower-class people and people who state that they want "a lot of money" (Agnew 1994; Agnew et al. 1996; Burton and Dunaway 1994). So limited data suggest that monetary strain is related to crime, although more research is needed in this area.

Status and Respect. Most people also desire status and respect: They want to be positively regarded by others and treated in a respectful manner by others, which at a minimum involves being treated in a just and fair manner (see Agnew 1992). Although people have a general desire for status and respect, the desire for *masculine status* is said to be especially relevant to crime (Agnew 1997a; Anderson 1994; Greenberg 1977; Majors and Billson 1992; Messerschmidt 1993). There are class and race differences in views about what it means to be a "man," although most such views emphasize traits like independence, dominance, toughness, competitiveness, and heterosexuality (see Messerschmidt 1993). Many individuals, however, have trouble "accomplishing masculinity" through legitimate channels—like obtaining a powerful, respected job. And they come to feel that others do not view and treat them as "men." This is said to be especially true of juveniles, lower-class individuals, and minority group members. As a consequence, they may attempt to accomplish masculinity through crime. They may engage in crime to demonstrate that they possess traits like toughness, dominance, and independence. And they may attempt to coerce others into giving them the respect they believe they deserve as "real men." In this connection, they may adopt a tough demeanor, respond to even minor shows of disrespect with violence, and occasionally assault and rob others in an effort to establish a tough reputation. There have been no large scale tests of this idea, although several observational studies provide support for it (Anderson 1994; Majors and Billson 1992; Messerschmidt 1993).

Autonomy. Several researchers have also argued that many people have a strong desire for autonomy, with autonomy being defined as power over oneself—the ability to resist the demands of others and engage in action without the permission of others (see Agnew 1984, 1997a; Greenberg 1977; Moffitt 1993, 1997; Tittle 1995). Many people, however, are denied the autonomy they desire. This is especially true of adolescents and lower-class individuals. This denial of autonomy may lead to delinquency and crime for several reasons; delinquency may be a means of asserting autonomy (e.g., sexual intercourse or disorderly conduct), achieving autonomy (e.g., stealing to gain financial independence from parents), or venting frustration against those who deny autonomy. There has not been much research on this issue, although one study found that adolescents with a strong need for autonomy were higher in delinquency (Agnew 1984).

One major category of strain, then, involves the failure to achieve positively-valued goals. I have focused on three major goals that have been linked to crime by theorists and researchers: money, status/respect, and autonomy. *Limited* data suggest that the failure to achieve these goals is linked to crime, but much more research is needed in this area. Also, I should note that crime may result from the failure to achieve other goals. For example, one goal that many college students consider important is good grades. And the failure to achieve good grades is a major type of strain for many students. Some students respond to this strain by engaging in crime or deviance—like underage drinking, cheating, and making negative remarks about their professors. We hope that future work on GST will provide a better idea of those types of goal blockage that are most strongly linked to crime in various groups.

The Loss of Positive Stimuli and Presentation of Negative Stimuli

The failure to achieve positively-valued goals or get what you want is only one of three major categories of strain. Strain may also involve the loss of something you value, like the loss of a romantic partner, the death of a friend, or the theft of a valuable possession. And strain may involve the presentation of noxious or negative stimuli, like verbal insults and physical assaults.

Data suggest that the loss of positive stimuli and the presentation of negative stimuli are often associated with crime. In particular, a large number of studies—some designed to test GST and some not—suggest that crime and delinquency are associated with such things as child abuse and neglect, criminal victimization, physical punishment by parents, negative relations with parents, negative relations with teachers, negative school experiences, negative relations with peers, neighborhood problems, homelessness, and a wide range of stressful life events, such as the divorce or separation of parents, parental unemployment, and changing schools (e.g., Agnew 1985, 1992, 1997a; Agnew and Brezina 1997; Agnew and White 1992; Baron and Hartnagel 1997; Brezina 1998; Hagan and McCarthy 1997; Hoffmann and Cerbone 1999; Hoffmann et al. forthcoming; Hoffmann and Miller 1998; Hoffmann and Su 1997; Landau 1998; Mazerolle and Piquero 1997, 1998; Paternoster and Mazerolle 1994). Many of these studies examine the effect of *prior* strain on *subsequent* delinquency, and they control for variables related to other theories of delinquency. Such studies, then, *suggest* that the association between strain and delinquency is at least partly due to the fact that strain *causes* delinquency.

As an example, Agnew and White (1992) examined the effect of prior strain on subsequent delinquency with data from a sample of New Jersey adolescents. Variables associated with the other leading theories of delinquency were controlled in the analysis. They found that several measures of strain related to the loss of positive stimuli and presentation of negative stimuli had an impact on delinquency. Delinquency was more common for those who a) had experienced a range of negative life events including assault, theft, the death of a close friend, parental divorce, and parental unemployment; b) had reported a number of "life hassles," like not getting along with parents and siblings, not being liked by classmates, and not having enough time to do the things you really wanted to; c) had reported that their parents often complained about them, "blew their tops" when bothered, got cross and angry over little things, acted very strict, et cetera; d) had said that their teachers often talked down to them and embarrassed them for not knowing the right answer; e) had reported that their parents fought with one another a lot; and f) had said their neighborhood was

unsafe and they were afraid to walk alone in it during the day or night.

To give another example, Paternoster and Mazerolle (1994) examined the effect of prior strain on subsequent delinquency with data from a national sample of adolescents. They found that "those who live in neighborhoods beset with many social problems (including crime and physical deterioration), who have in the past year experienced stressful life events, who have problems fitting in with peers and with school, and who have bad relationships with their parents and teachers, commit significantly more delinquent acts than those experiencing less strain" (245).

The data, then, provide a fair degree of support for this part of GST—although it is important to note that not all measures of the loss of positive stimuli and presentation of negative stimuli are related to delinquency. Some evidence, for example, suggests that individuals who report that they are unpopular with members of the opposite sex are less rather than more delinquent (Agnew and Brezina 1997; Agnew and White 1992). GST needs to better describe why some types of strain are related to delinquency and others are not. As a beginning, I might note that some types of strain are associated with expressive social control and a reduction in criminal opportunities. This might offset the influence of these types of strain on crime. For example, unpopular peers may be lower in delinquency because they have fewer opportunities for delinquency—because they date less and engage in fewer social activities with peers. Or mothers burdened with the excessive demands of children might be lower in many types of crime because they have fewer opportunities for crime, feel a strong obligation to their children, and know that criminal behavior on their part would be strongly condemned (see Agnew 1998 for a fuller discussion).

Why Does Strain Increase the Likelihood of Crime?

So there are three major categories of strain: you do not get what you want, you lose something good, you get something bad. Why are individuals who experience these types of strain more likely to engage in crime?

According to GST, strain makes people feel bad—angry, frustrated, depressed, anxious, and so on. These negative feelings may be temporary, such as the anger you experience when someone cuts you off in traffic or insults you. But individuals who experience high levels of negative treatment or strain over a period of time may become angry or irritable on a regular basis. These negative feelings, in turn, create pressure for corrective action. You feel bad and want to do something about it. This is especially true of anger and frustration, which energize the individual for action, create a desire for revenge, and lower concern with inhibitions. There are several possible ways to cope with strain and these negative emotions, some of which involve crime.

Crime may be a method for reducing strain, that is, for achieving positively-valued goals, for protecting or retrieving positive stimuli, or for terminating or escaping from negative stimuli. For example, people who are unable to achieve their monetary goals through legitimate channels may seek money through theft. People threatened with the loss of a romantic partner may attempt to coerce the partner into remaining. And juveniles abused by parents may attack parents in an effort to end the abuse or may run away from home to escape from the abuse.

Crime may also be a method for seeking revenge; data suggest that vengeful behavior often occurs even when there is no possibility of eliminating the strain that stimulated it (Berkowitz 1982). And crime may occur as people try to reduce their negative emotions through illicit drug use (see Pandina et al. 1992).

In support of the above arguments, several studies indicate that measures of negative affect—most often anger—explain part of the effect of strain on crime (Agnew 1985; Baron and Hartnagel 1997; Brezina 1998; Mazerolle and Piquero 1997). That is, these studies suggest that one of the reasons strain leads to crime is that it increases anger. More studies are needed in this area, however, including studies that examine both short- and long-term anger and frustration and examine a broader range of negative emotions.

Are There Other Ways to Respond to Strain and Negative Emotions Besides Crime?

Even though crime is a way to cope with strain and negative emotions, it is not the only way. In fact, criminal responses to strain are relatively uncommon. Most people cope with strain in ways that do not involve crime.

Sometimes people employ *cognitive coping strategies;* that is, they cognitively reinterpret the strain they experience so as to minimize its effect. Three major cognitive coping strategies are summarized in the phrases "it's not that important," "it's not that bad," and "I deserve it." Imagine, for example, a person who is unable to achieve her monetary goals. She may minimize strain by claiming that money is not that important, perhaps claiming that other goals—like family and health—are more important. Or he may exaggerate his level of monetary success, claiming he is financially well off when in fact he is not. Or the person may claim that he or she is to blame for the lack of money. This may not reduce feelings of depression, but it is likely to reduce anger at others. All of these cognitive coping strategies reduce the likelihood that individuals will react to strain with crime.

People may also employ *behavioral coping strategies* of a noncriminal nature. That is, they may act in noncriminal ways that reduce the strain they are experiencing. Adolescents, for example, may attempt to avoid the peers who harass them or negotiate with the teachers who frustrate them. Abused individuals may divorce the spouse who beats them or sue the employer who harasses them.

Finally, people may engage in *emotional coping* of a noncriminal nature. That is, rather than trying to reduce their strain or cognitively reinterpret it, they may act directly on the negative emotions that result from strain. But, rather than taking illicit drugs, they do such things as exercise, listen to relaxing music, or employ deep breathing techniques.

Why Are Some People More Likely to Respond to Strain with Crime?

So, strain, in most cases, does not result in crime. This raises a crucial question: why are some people more likely to respond to strain with crime than others? According to GST, several factors influence whether or not people respond to strain with crime (see Agnew 1992).

Strain is more likely to lead to crime when it *involves areas of life that the person considers important*. For example, financial problems are more likely to result in crime among people who attach high absolute and relative importance to money (i.e., they state that money is very important to them and that it is more important than other goals). Likewise, challenges to masculinity are more likely to result in crime among people who attach great importance to their masculine identity. If strain affects a central area of a person's life, it will be more difficult to ignore it or define it away using one of the cognitive strategies described above.

Strain is more likely to lead to crime among people with *poor coping skills and resources*. Some individuals are better able to legally cope with strain than others. For example, they have the verbal skills to negotiate with others. Or, they have a high level of "self-efficacy," believing that they have the ability to solve their problems. A variety of factors influence coping including intelligence, problem-solving skills, interpersonal or social skills, self-efficacy, and financial resources.

Strain is more likely to lead to crime among people with *few conventional social supports*. Family, friends, and others often help us cope with our problems, providing advice, direct assistance, and emotional support. Many of your parents, I suspect, provided you with assistance when you were experiencing problems, such as problems with peers, teachers, neighbors, and schoolwork. Or perhaps there was some other adult or person you could turn to for help. Such help or support reduces the likelihood of criminal coping.

Strain is more likely to lead to crime if *the costs of crime are low*. Many of us do not engage in crime because the costs are too high. We would feel guilty and we might be punished by others—including family, friends, school officials, employers, neighbors, and police. Many people, however, have little to lose by engaging in crime. Crime does not make them feel guilty, their parents seldom punish them for criminal acts, they do not care if they are expelled from school, they do not have a job to lose, and so forth. Also, they may be in a situation where the likelihood of being caught and punished appears low. Such people are more likely to react to strain with crime.

Finally, strain is more likely to lead to crime among *people who are disposed to crime*. The individual's disposition to engage in crime is influenced by a number of factors, most of which are discussed in other chapters in this book. These factors include certain individual traits, like irritability and impulsivity. Another key factor is whether the person blames his or her strain on the deliberate behavior of someone else. Such blame makes the individual feel angry, which increases the likelihood of crime, as discussed above. People are also more likely to be disposed to crime if they hold beliefs that justify crime, if they have been exposed to criminal models, and if they have been reinforced for crime in the past (see the chapter on social learning theory). This is especially likely to be the case if the individual has delinquent friends.

A variety of factors, then, may influence whether people respond to strain with crime. Unfortunately, not much research is available in this area, and the research results so far show mixed results. Some studies find that the above sorts of factors increase the likelihood that people will respond to strain with crime, while others do not (see Agnew and White 1992; Hoffmann and Cerbone forthcoming; Hoffmann et al. forthcoming; Hoffmann and Miller 1998; Hoffmann and Su 1997; Mazerolle and Piquero 1997; Paternoster and Mazerolle 1994). The reasons for these mixed results are now currently being explored (see Agnew 1998).

Summary

The core idea of GST is rather simple: strain makes you upset and you *may* respond with crime. As you can see, however, this simple idea has been the subject of much elaboration. In particular, there has been much discussion of the major types of strain that contribute to crime and the factors that condition the effect of strain on crime. The data provide some support for GST, although certain parts of the theory have not been well tested. A fair amount of data indicate that many events having to do with the loss of positive stimuli and the presentation of negative stimuli increase the likelihood of crime. There are less data, however, on whether the inability to achieve positively-valued goals leads to crime. Likewise, there are little data on the extent to which the effect of strain on crime is conditioned by the factors listed above. So GST might be described as a promising theory with some support.

Applying GST to Certain Key Issues in Criminology

GST was originally developed to explain why some individuals are more likely to engage in crime than other individuals, but it can also be used to explain group differences in crime rates. In particular, the theory has recently been used to explain why adolescents have higher crime rates than children and adults (see Agnew 1997a) and why males have higher crime rates than females (Broidy and Agnew 1997). As you may know, age and sex are among the best predictors of crime—with most crime being committed by young males. The theory has also been used to help explain why some communities have higher crime rates than other communities (Agnew 1997b), a topic that was neglected for many years but has attracted renewed attention since the mid-1980s. This section briefly describes what GST has to say about these issues. I should note, however, that GST is in the process of being applied to the explanation of still other group differences in crime, such as race and ethnic differences in serious violence (see Rebellon et al. 1998).

Why Do Adolescents Have a Higher Crime Rate than Children and Adults?

GST explains the higher crime rate of adolescents by arguing that adolescents are higher in both objective and subjective strain and are less able to cope with such strain in legitimate ways (Agnew 1997a).

Adolescents develop a strong desire for things such as money, status and respect, and autonomy; but they often have difficulty achieving these goals through legitimate channels. Children are not as interested in these goals, while adults are better equipped to achieve them through legitimate channels. In particular, adolescents are less able to earn money through legitimate employment and their needs for status and respect and autonomy are often severely frustrated by family members, school officials, and others. Some evidence also suggests that adults are better able to adjust their goals in line with reality.

Adolescents live in a larger, more demanding social world than children and adults, which increases the likelihood that they will be negatively treated by others. They leave elementary school and enter larger, more impersonal, and more diverse secondary schools. They typically change teachers and classmates several times during the day in such schools. And they are subject to more rules, given more work, and graded in a more challenging manner. They spend more time away from home, especially in the evening and on weekends. And there is an increase in the size of their peer group, their contact with the opposite sex, their level of intimacy with same- and opposite-sex peers, and their association with delinquent peers. This dramatic increase in the size and complexity of their social world is likely to be stressful in and of itself. But, it also increases the likelihood of negative treatment, because adolescents are interacting with many more people—often people they do not know well and often in unsupervised settings. As adolescents become adults, however, their social world begins to narrow again and they have more control over the nature of this world (e.g., they have some choice over where they live and work).

Some data support these arguments, suggesting that adolescents experience more objective strains or stressors than children or adults. For example, grades become worse during adolescence, victimization increases, association with delinquent peers increases (such peers are more likely to get into conflicts with one another), and a variety of stressful life events seem to peak during adolescence. Further, data suggest that adolescents are not only higher in objective strain, but that they may also be more susceptible to subjective strain. In particular, adolescents may be more likely to notice and get upset over certain objective strains than are children and adults. There are several reasons for this, including certain cognitive changes that accompany adolescence (e.g., egocentrism and a tendency to blame others for one's problems). Related to this, data suggest that adolescents experience higher levels of emotional distress than children and adults.

There is good reason to believe, then, that adolescents are higher in strain and the negative emotions that accompany strain than adults and children. At the same time, adolescents are less able to cope with this strain and emotional distress through legitimate channels. Children are usually under the protection of adults, who cope on their behalf and provide them with much social support. This protection frequently ends at adolescence, however, with adolescents being expected to handle many of their own problems. Unfortunately, adolescents have little experience with coping and they are often reluctant to turn to adults for assistance. Also, adolescents have little power. They are "compelled to live with their family in a certain neighborhood, to go to a certain school; and, within limits, to interact with the same group of peers and neighbors" (Agnew 1985, 156). If any of these contexts is aversive, there is often little the adolescent can do to legally cope. Finally, adolescents are often more disposed to delinquency. They are more likely to associate with delinquent peers, for example, who provide delinquent models, teach beliefs favorable to delinquency, and reinforce delinquency. For all these reasons, then, adolescents are more

likely to cope with strain through delinquency than are children and adults.

Why Do Males Have a Higher Crime Rate than Females?

You might be tempted to answer this question by stating that males have higher levels of strain than females. Certain of the early strain theorists made this argument. As Naffine (1987, 23) states, they claimed that "women are insulated from the pressures of public life. . . their role is less demanding than the male role and they thus do not experience pressures causing them to deviate." Much recent data, however, suggest that females experience as much or more strain than males (see Broidy and Agnew 1997). Further, certain data suggest that females may not only be higher in objective strain, but that they may also be more likely to experience many objective strains as upsetting. The specific strains experienced by females fall into the three general categories of strain listed above. They include the failure to achieve many positively-valued goals, including monetary goals, status and respect, and what are sometimes called *relational* goals (e.g., establishing close relationships with others). They include the loss of positively-valued stimuli, including romantic partners, friends, and the opportunity to engage in a range of valued behaviors (e.g., dressing and acting in certain ways). And they include the presentation of negative stimuli (e.g., verbal, physical, and sexual abuse; the excessive demands of family members and others; and other aversive conditions at home, work, and in their neighborhoods).

So GST cannot explain the higher rate of male crime by arguing that males experience more strain. Nevertheless, even though differences in the *amount* of strain cannot explain gender differences in crime, perhaps differences in the *type* of strain can. Males experience somewhat different types of strain than females, and perhaps these types of strain are more likely to lead to crime. Some evidence suggests that males are more concerned with material success and extrinsic achievements, while females are more concerned with the establishment and maintenance of close relationships and with meaning and purpose in life. This may help explain the greater rate of property crime among males. Crime is a convenient way to obtain money. Crime, however, is not an effective vehicle for establishing close ties to others. (Females have come to experience increased financial strain in recent decades and some evidence suggests that their rates of property crime have increased.)

Some evidence also suggests gender differences in the loss of positive stimuli and presentation of negative stimuli. Females are more likely to experience strains like the excessive demands of family members and restrictions on their behavior, with females being more likely to be confined to the "private sphere." These types of strain involve a restriction of criminal opportunities and excessive social control. It is difficult to engage in serious violent and property crime when one spends little time in public, feels responsible for children and others, is burdened with the demands of others, and is under much pressure to avoid behaving in an aggressive manner. These types of strain, however, may be conducive to self-destructive forms of behavior and family violence, two areas of deviance where male/female differences are relatively small. Males are more likely to report conflict with peers and criminal victimization by others. These forms of strain may be conducive to violence. Gender differences in the type of strain, then, may help explain why males are more likely to engage in most types of crime.

Not only do males and females experience different types of strain, but they may also differ in their emotional response to strain. Males, in particular, may be more likely to respond to strain in ways that are conducive to serious crime. GST argues that strain leads to certain negative emotions, which in turn create pressure to take corrective action—like crime. According to GST, the emotional reactions of anger and frustration are especially conducive to a criminal response because they energize the individual for action, lower inhibitions, and often create a desire for revenge. Several researchers have argued that men tend to respond to strain with anger and hostility, while women tend to re-

spond with depression. If so, this would help explain gender differences in crime.

The data in this area, however, suggest that things are not so simple. Females appear just as likely or more likely to respond to strain with anger than males. However, the anger experienced by females seems to be of a different sort than that experienced by males. The anger of females is often accompanied by emotions like fear, anxiety, shame, and depression; while the anger of males is more often characterized by moral outrage. Several possible reasons for this difference have been suggested, most linked to gender differences in the socialization process: females are more likely to blame themselves when negatively treated by others, are more likely to worry that their anger might lead them to harm others and jeopardize valued relationships, and more often view their anger as inappropriate and a failure of self-control. Males, however, are quicker to blame others for their negative treatment and to interpret such treatment as a challenge or deliberate insult; they are less concerned about hurting others or disrupting relationships, and they often view their anger as an affirmation of their masculinity. These gender differences may help explain gender differences in crime. The moral righteousness of the angry male may propel him into serious violent and property crime, while the depression and serious misgivings of the angry female may lead her into more self-destructive forms of deviance (e.g., drug use, eating disorders).

Finally, males may be more likely to respond to strain and anger with crime. So even if males and females experience the same emotional reactions to the same types of strain, males may still be more likely to respond with crime—especially serious crime. As indicated earlier, the effect of strain on crime is conditioned by a number of factors (e.g., coping resources and skills, social support, the costs of crime, and one's disposition to crime). Strained males may be more likely to engage in crime because of gender-related differences in these factors. For example, data suggest that males have more opportunities than females for at least certain types of crime, the costs of crime are lower for males, males are more likely to possess certain individual traits that are conducive to crime, and males are more likely to associate with deviant others.

A few studies have examined the impact of strain among males and females (Agnew and Brezina 1997; Hoffmann and Cerbone 1997; Hoffmann and Su 1997). Contrary to certain of the above arguments, some find that strain has a similar impact on crime among males and females. However, these studies examine only certain types of strain and tend to focus on minor forms of aggression and crime. More research is needed in this area.

Why Do Some Communities Have Higher Crime Rates than Other Communities?

Some communities have crime rates many times higher than those of other communities. We now have a reasonably good idea of the characteristics of these high-crime communities. They tend to be low in economic status. That is, the average income in such communities is relatively low and rates of poverty, unemployment, and welfare assistance are high. High-crime communities also tend to be located in urban areas, dense and overcrowded, high in residential mobility (people frequently move into and out of the community), and populated by nonwhites and disrupted families. (The relationship between racial composition and crime rates tends to disappear when we take account of the economic and family characteristics of the community. So poor white communities have crime rates similar to poor African-American communities). A closer examination of high-crime communities also reveals that they are lower in social cohesion and trust and that they are plagued by a range of problems, such as unsupervised teenage peer groups that engage in much crime and deviance (for summaries, see Agnew 1997b; Bursik and Grasmick 1993; Sampson 1995; Sampson and Lauritsen 1993; Sampson and Wilson 1995).

How might we explain the higher rate of crime in these communities? Several answers have been suggested, the most popular of which draws on social control theory and argues that the residents of high-crime communities are unable to effectively socialize young people and supervise the behavior of local residents (see the sources cited above). GST, however, argues that such communities are also higher in crime because community residents are higher in strain and less able to cope with strain through legitimate channels (Agnew 1998).

The residents of high-crime communities are less able to achieve their goals—particularly their economic and status goals. Among other things, they have less access to jobs in general and to stable, well-paying jobs in particular. Manufacturing and service-sector jobs are often located at a distance from deprived communities, so they are less accessible; relatively few individuals in the community have job contacts or job information; and there are relatively few individuals in the community to teach and model those skills and attitudes necessary for successful job performance. The employment problems faced by community residents create a host of additional problems that serve to further reduce legitimate opportunities for goal achievement. Such problems include poor pre- and post-natal care, family disruption (along with its negative impacts on child care), inadequate preparation for school, and low-quality schools.

The residents of deprived communities are also more likely to experience the other two categories of strain: the loss of positive stimuli and the presentation of negative stimuli. Among other things, they are more likely to experience class, race, and ethnic discrimination; unpleasant working conditions; family disruption and related problems (e.g., family conflict and child abuse); and neighborhood problems like garbage on the streets, abandoned buildings and houses, street harassment, and conflict with neighbors. Further, they are more likely to have family and friends who have experienced these and other problems. So they are also higher in vicarious strain. Finally, it has been argued that the residents of deprived communities may be more sensitive to certain objective strains, such as disrespectful treatment by others. Among other things, it is said that the continued experience with strain heightens one's sensitivity to slights.

That is, individuals come to develop a "short fuse" (see Bernard 1990).

Not only are the residents of high-crime communities higher in strain, they are also less able to cope with such strain through legitimate channels. There are several reasons for this, including the fact that they have limited coping resources and skills (e.g., money, power, and problem-solving skills); they are less likely to receive effective social support from others; the costs of crime are lower in such communities; and individuals in such communities may be more disposed to crime, partly due to the increased presence of criminal others and groups.

Even though extensive data are compatible with these arguments, the GST explanation of community differences in crime rates has not been directly tested. A full test would require that we determine whether community characteristics (e.g., economic deprivation and family disruption) influence levels of negative affect in the community, and whether such levels of negative affect influence community crime rates.

Policy Recommendations from General Strain Theory

GST argues that the ultimate source of crime is negative treatment by others. And GST makes two simple recommendations for controlling crime. First, reduce the likelihood that people will treat one other badly. This may seem like an unrealistic goal, but much data suggest that we can make some progress in this area. It is unlikely, however, that we can entirely eliminate negative treatment. Therefore, a second policy recommendation is that we reduce the likelihood that people will respond to negative treatment with crime (see Agnew 1995b).

How Can We Reduce the Likelihood that People Will Treat One Another Badly?

A number of programs have reduced the likelihood of negative treatment. None of these programs is explicitly based on GST. And many do not deliberately try to reduce negative treatment. Rather, they try to accomplish other goals, such as improving parental discipline or increasing the juvenile's attachment and commitment to school. The reduction in negative treatment is an unintended consequence of trying to achieve these other goals. Nevertheless, all of these programs are compatible with GST. And all have shown some signs of success in reducing crime and delinquency (for overviews, see Agnew 1995b; Catalano et al. 1998; Wasserman and Miller 1998).

Many of these programs focus on the family. The families of delinquent children are often characterized by much adversity including high levels of interpersonal conflict, harsh discipline, abuse and neglect, low rates of positive reinforcement and high rates of punishment, and ineffective communication patterns. A number of family training programs attempt to deal with these problems. Family members are taught how to better resolve interpersonal conflicts. For example, parents and children are taught how to negotiate agreements when conflicts arise. Parents are taught how to more effectively discipline their children. Among other things, they are taught to make greater use of positive reinforcements like praise and attention and less use of punishments like criticism, yelling, and hitting. Certain of these family programs focus explicitly on the reduction of abuse and neglect.

Other programs focus on the school. Delinquency is related to a range of negative school experiences, like school failure, boredom with school, negative relations with teachers, and unfair disciplinary practices. Many school-based programs attempt to deal with these problems. Most programs attempt to boost school performance, with an example being preschool programs focusing on children in disadvantaged communities. Other programs attempt to improve classroom teaching, provide more opportunities for students to be successful, make school less impersonal and more satisfying, and improve disciplinary practices in the classroom and the school as a whole—with greater use of praise and less use of punishment.

Still other programs have focused on peer relations within the school and larger community. Negative relations with peers is a major—perhaps the major—source of strain among juveniles. Some programs employ teaching strategies that encourage cooperation rather than competition between students. Antibullying programs attempt to stop students from victimizing one another. Recreational programs attempt to increase adult supervision over peer activities. And other programs attempt to place delinquent youth in prosocial peer groups.

Most of the above programs attempt to alter the individual's social environment in ways that reduce the likelihood of negative treatment by others. If we want to fully reduce negative treatment by others, however, we must also alter the behavior of individuals. Individuals play a role in creating their own social environment. Many people, in particular, act in ways that provoke negative reactions from others. This appears to be more true of delinquents, who often lack many social skills. It is possible, however, to alter the behavior of these people in ways that reduce the likelihood of such negative reactions. Several "social skills" training programs have been developed to this end. These programs teach juveniles skills like negotiating with others, making a complaint, responding to testing, and dealing with someone else's anger. It is important to emphasize that these programs do *not* teach juveniles to be submissive or passive. They teach juveniles to express themselves when problems arise, but to express themselves in ways that are less likely to elicit negative reactions from others.

How Can We Reduce the Likelihood that People Will Respond to Negative Treatment with Crime?

Although we may reduce the extent to which people treat one another badly, it is unlikely that we can eliminate negative treatment or strain. As such, it is important that we increase the ability of people to cope with strain through noncriminal means (although we do not want to encourage the passive acceptance of negative treatment).

Several programs attempt to increase the coping skills and resources of people. The social skills programs described above try to do this. For example, they teach juveniles how to best respond to teasing or insults, how to deal with teachers' criticisms, how to

behave during police encounters, and how to keep out of fights. Juveniles are taught to be *assertive* rather than *aggressive*. Other programs are more general in nature and attempt to teach juveniles a set of problem-solving skills that can be applied to a broad range of difficulties. Still other programs focus on the anger and frustration that often result from strain, and people are taught how to better manage or control their anger.

While the above programs attempt to help people cope on their own, other programs attempt to provide people with increased social support. These programs sometimes teach family members and teachers to provide more effective social support to juveniles. They sometimes provide juveniles with mentors who provide support. And they sometimes provide juveniles with trained professionals, who directly assist juveniles and refer them to appropriate social service agencies if necessary. Also, mediation and conflict resolution programs may be viewed as a form of social support because they assist people in resolving conflicts through noncriminal means.

Conclusion

GST is rather different from the other leading theories of crime. It focuses explicitly on negative treatment by others and it argues that such treatment causes crime primarily through its effect on the individual's emotional state.

The central ideas of GST have received a moderate degree of support. A good number of studies suggest that many types of strain or negative treatment increase the likelihood of crime. Further, several studies suggest that negative treatment increases crime partly because it increases anger and other negative emotions. Data, however, suggest that some types of strain may be more strongly related to crime than other types, and one of the challenges for GST is to better specify which types of strain will be most strongly related to crime. Other aspects of GST have less support. In particular, studies examining the factors that condition the effect of strain on crime have produced mixed results. It is not clear why this is the case and more research is needed in this area.

GST was originally developed to explain why some individuals are more likely to engage in crime than others. As indicated above, however, it also has the potential to explain why some groups have higher crime rates than other groups. The arguments of GST in these areas, however, are quite recent and have yet to receive an adequate test. Overall, GST may be characterized as a promising theory that is in need of further development and testing.

References

Agnew, R. (1984). "Autonomy and delinquency." *Sociological Perspectives*, 27:219–240.

——. (1985). "A revised strain theory of delinquency."*Social Forces*, 64:151–167.

——. (1992). "Foundation for a general strain theory of crime and delinquency." *Criminology*, 30:47–87.

——. (1994). "Delinquency and the desire for money." *Justice Quarterly*, 11:411–427.

——. (1995a). "The contribution of social-psychological strain theory to the explanation of crime and delinquency." Pp. 113–137 in *The Legacy of Anomie Theory, Advances in Criminological Theory*. F. Adler and W.S. Laufer (eds.). Vol. 6. New Brunswick, NJ: Transaction.

——. (1995b). "Controlling delinquency: Recommendations from general strain theory." Pp. 43–70 in *Crime and Public Policy*. H.D. Barlow (ed.). Boulder, CO: Westview.

——. (1997a). "Stability and change in crime over the life course: A strain theory explanation." Pp. 101–132 in *Developmental Theories of Crime and Delinquency, Advances in Criminological Theory*. T.P. Thornberry (ed.). Vol. 7. New Brunswick, NJ: Transaction.

——. (1997b). "A general strain theory of community differences in crime rates." Paper presented at the annual meeting of the American Society of Criminology, San Diego, November.

——. (1998). "Building on the foundation of general strain theory." Paper presented at the annual meeting of the Academy of Criminal Justice Sciences, Albuquerque, March.

Agnew, R. and H.R. White. (1992). "An empirical test of general strain theory." *Criminology*, 30:475–499.

Agnew, R., F.T. Cullen, V.S. Burton Jr., T.D. Evans, and R.G. Dunaway. (1996). "A new test of classic strain theory 13:681–704.

Agnew, R. and T. Brezin... problems with peer... quency." *Youth and Soc...*

Anderson, E. (1994). "Th... *Atlantic Monthly*, May, ...

Baron, S.W. and T.F. Hart... tions, affect, and crim... tions to unemployment." *Criminology*, 35:409–434.

Berkowitz, L. (1982). "Aversive conditions as a stimuli to aggression." Pp. 249–288 in *Advances in Experimental Social Psychology*. L. Berkowitz (ed.). Vol. 15. New York: Academic.

Bernard, T.J. (1990). "Angry aggression among the 'truly disadvantaged.'" *Criminology*, 28:73–96.

Brezina, T. (1996). "Adapting to strain: An examination of delinquent coping responses." *Criminology*, 34:39–60.

——. (1998). "Adolescent maltreatment and delinquency: The question of intervening processes." *Journal of Research in Crime and Delinquency*, 35:XX.

Broidy, L. and R. Agnew. (1997). "Gender and crime: A general strain theory perspective." *Journal of Research in Crime and Delinquency*, 34:275–306.

Bursik, R.J., Jr. and H.G. Grasmick. (1993). *Neighborhoods and Crime*. New York: Lexington.

Burton, V.S., Jr. and R.G. Dunaway. (1994). "Strain, relative deprivation, and middle class delinquency." Pp. 79–95 in *Varieties of Criminology*. G. Barak (ed.). New York: Praeger.

Catalano, R.F., M.W. Arthur, J.D. Hawkins, L. Berglund, and J.J. Olson. (1998). "Comprehensive community- and school-based interventions to prevent antisocial behavior." Pp. 248–283 in *Serious and Violent Juvenile Offenders*. R. Loeber and D.P. Farrington (eds.). Thousand Oaks, CA: Sage.

Cloward, R.A. and L.E. Ohlin. (1960). *Delinquency and Opportunity*. New York: Free.

Cohen, A.K. (1955). *Delinquent Boys*. New York: Free.

Greenberg, D.F. (1977). "Delinquency and the age structure of society." *Contemporary Crises*, 1:189–223.

Hagan, John and Bill MCCarthy. (1997). *Mean Streets*. Cambridge, England: Cambridge University Press.

Hoffmann, John P. and Felicia G. Cerbone. (1997). "A cumulative stress model of delinquency escalation in early adolescence." Paper presented at the annual meeting of the

Society of Criminology, San Diego, ...ber.

...n, John P. and Felicia G. Cerbone. (1999). ...tessful life events and delinquency escala-tion in early adolescence." *Criminology*, 37:343–374.

Hoffmann, John P., Felicia G. Cerbone, and S. Susan Su. (1998). "A growth curve analysis of stress and adolescent drug use." Unpublished manuscript.

Hoffmann, John P. and Alan S. Miller. (1998). "A latent variable analysis of general strain theory." *Journal of Quantitative Criminology*, 14:83–110.

Hoffmann, John P. and S. Susan Su. (1997). "The conditional effects of stress on delinquency and drug use: A strain theory assessment of sex differences." *Journal of Research in Crime and Delinquency*, 34:46–78.

Jankowski, Martin S. (1995). "Ethnography, inequality, and crime in the low-income community." Pp. 80–94 in *Crime and Inequality*. J. Hagan and R.D. Peterson (eds.). Stanford, CA: Stanford University Press.

Landau, Simha F. (1998). "Crime, subjective social stress and support indicators, and ethnic origin: The Israeli experience." *Justice Quarterly*, 15:243–272.

MacLeod, Jay. (1987). *"Ain't No Makin' It*. Boulder, CO: Westview.

Majors, Richard and Janet M. Billson. (1992). *Cool Pose*. New York: Lexington.

Mazerolle, Paul and Alex Piquero. (1997). "Violent responses to strain: An examination of conditioning influences." *Violence and Victims*, 12:323–343.

——. (1998). "Linking exposure to strain with anger: An investigation of deviant adaptations." *Journal of Criminal Justice*, forthcoming.

Merton, Robert K. (1938). "Social structure and anomie." *American Sociological Review*, 3:672–682.

——. (1968). *Social Theory and Social Structure*. New York: Free.

Messerschmidt, James W. (1993). *Masculinities and Crime*. Lanham, MD: Rowman and Littlefield.

Moffitt, Terrie E. (1993). "'Life-course persistent' and 'adolescent-limited' antisocial behavior: A developmental taxonomy." *Psychological Review*, 100:674–701.

——. (1997). "Adolescent-limited and life-course persistent offending: A complementary pair of developmental theories." Pp. 11–54 in *Developmental Theories of Crime and Delinquency, Advances in Criminological Theory*. T.P. Thornberry (ed.). Vol. 7. New Brunswick, NJ: Transaction.

Naffine, Ngaire. (1987). *Female Crime: The Construction of Women in Criminology*. Sydney: Allen and Unwin.

Padilla, Felix. (1992). *The Gang as an American Enterprise*. New Brunswick, NJ: Rutgers University Press.

Pandina, Robert J., Valerie Johnson, and Erich W. Labouvie. (1992). "Affectivity: A central mechanism in the development of drug dependence." Pp. 179–210 in *Vulnerability to Drug Abuse*. M. Glantz and R. Pickens (eds.). Washington, DC: American Psychological Association.

Paternoster, Raymond and Paul Mazerolle. (1994). "General strain theory and delinquency: A replication and extension." *Journal of Research in Crime and Delinquency*, 31:235–263.

Rebellon, Cesar, Sherod Thaxton, Joanne Kaufman, and Robert Agnew. (1998). "Race, crime and general strain theory." Paper presented at the annual meeting of the American Society of Criminology, Washington, DC.

Sampson, Robert J. (1995). "The community." Pp. 193–216 in *Crime*. J.Q. Wilson and J. Petersilia (eds.). San Francisco: ICS.

Sampson, Robert J. and Janet L. Lauritsen. (1993). "Violent victimization and offending: Individual-, situational-, and community-level risk factors." Pp. 1–114 in *Understanding and Preventing Violence*. Vol. 3, *Social Influences*. Washington, DC: National Research Council.

Sampson, Robert J. and William Julius Wilson. (1995). "Toward a theory of race, crime, and urban inequality." Pp. 37–54 in *Crime and Inequality*. J. Hagan and R. Peterson (eds.). Stanford, CA: Stanford University Press.

Sullivan, Mercer L. (1989). *Getting Paid*. Ithaca, NY: Cornell University Press.

Tittle, Charles R. (1995). *Control Balance: Toward a General Theory of Deviance*. Boulder, CO: Westview.

Wasserman, Gail A. and Laurie S. Miller. (1998). "The prevention of serious and violent juvenile offender." Pp. 197–247 in *Serious and Violent Juvenile Offenders*. R. Loeber and D.P. Farrington (eds.). Thousand Oaks, CA: Sage.

7
Differential Association and Social Learning Theories

Introduction

Let's admit it, before we had even taken a course where the different causes of crime were discussed, many, if not most, of us had a stereotypical conception of the criminal as a person who is somewhat impulsive, "out of control," and compelled by pathological drives and motivations—a "need to steal," a "drive" to obtain drugs, a "mental problem" that leads to rape or murder. Most likely, we did not take seriously the notion that criminal behavior might be similar to brick laying, rock climbing, or driving a car in that we had *to learn* how to do these things before we could actually do them. The notion that criminal behavior is learned like any other kind of behavior we have to learn is a central theme in the two essays in this chapter. Both presume that criminal conduct is due to personality traits, or biological drives, but is influenced by its own consequences. Both essays in fact derived from a common source, so it is probably pretty safe to think of them as at least very similar (Akers 1998).

The position that criminal behavior is learned by the same mechanisms that other behavior is learned is hostile to theories (e.g., biological or psychodynamic theories) that imply that criminals are fundamentally different from nonoffenders. The two theories in this chapter, differential association and social learning theory, presume that what explains behavior in general also explains criminal behavior. To be clear, the argument made is that the process of learning criminal and noncriminal behavior is comparable; what differs, of course, is simply the

content of what is being learned. The first essay is about differential association theory, one of the first "learning theories" of crime developed in criminology. This essay was prepared by Professor Mark Warr, one of the leading experts on the theory. The second essay is about social learning theory and was written by its developer, Professor Ronald L. Akers. As you will see, although social learning initially came from differential association theory, it is a more general theory in that it considers wider sources of learning. We will first briefly provide some background and issues with respect to these two theories.

Differential Association Theory

Differential association theory was initially developed by Edwin H. Sutherland, a University of Chicago trained sociologist who received his Ph.D. degree there in 1913 (for a detailed discussion of the life and work of Sutherland, see Schuessler 1973; Gaylord and Galliher 1988; Laub and Sampson 1991). You will recall from Chapter 5 that it was around that same time period at the University of Chicago that Clifford Shaw and Henry McKay developed their theory of social disorganization, which argued that some communities lacked the organizational capacity to meet the needs of their residents (e.g., creating a crime-free environment). Disorganized communities were characterized by, among other things, cultural and normative heterogeneity. This simply means that immigrant communities had retained many of the values of the "old country" that at times clashed with American standards of conduct. The idea that communities experience culture conflict was to influence Sutherland's own thoughts and theorizing about crime.

Although Sutherland was made famous by his theory of differential association, this was not his first theoretical perspective on the causes of crime. In the first edition of his textbook on crime, *Criminology* (which later became *Principles of Criminology*), Sutherland (1924) set forth a theory which located the causes of crime at the individual level, implied that there were important differences between offenders and nonoffenders, and attributed criminality to multiple causal factors (see also Schuessler 1973; Gaylord and Galliher 1988; Laub and Sampson 1991; Akers 1998). At least in Sutherland's early foray into criminological theory, then, he laid the causes of crime on the doorstep of such factors as dysfunctional personalities, poor family socialization, low intelligence, and the biological deficiencies of criminals. Sutherland's original theory of crime, then, was both individual-centered and multi-factored. There is no small amount of irony in this. In his later writings, Sutherland was skeptical if not scornful of multi-factored theory that sought the explanation for crime in individual differences between offenders and nonoffenders.

It was not until the second edition of his criminology textbook, published in 1934, that Sutherland's thoughts began to move toward a position that focused the cause of crime external to the individual, and one that was parsimonious in that it involved fewer explanatory variables. In this edition, the theory of differential association was not formally developed, though its seeds were planted, and Sutherland (1934, 51–52) emphasized both the role of learning in crime (he implied that persons can be "trained" to commit any behavior, including criminal behavior) and the importance of cultural conflict in the creation of crime.

The movement of Sutherland's theory at this point was incremental, but nonetheless very profound. He was moving away from a theory that posited a diverse mix of causal factors that primarily resided within the individual and one that was harmonious with the differentiation between criminals and noncriminals, toward one that stressed the importance of social processes and the similarity between offenders and nonoffenders. The transformation of Sutherland's thinking was virtually complete with the 1939 publication of the third edition of *Principles of Criminology*, where, in the very first chapter, he formally articulated the theory of differential association in a set of seven propositions. The seven propositions were expanded to nine in the fourth edition of the book that appeared in 1947 and remained unchanged in subsequent editions. In the

1947 edition of the text, Sutherland dropped the references to culture conflict in his theory but retained the notion in the term *differential social organization*. According to Sutherland, communities are not disorganized or organized, but can be differentiated in terms of the content of their criminal and noncriminal associations. Differential social organization explains why persons are exposed to the kinds of associations they experience (an enjoyable read of the history of differential association theory can be found in Akers 1998, Chapter 2). Think of differential social organization as explaining variation in group or community crime rates, and differential association as explaining variation in individual levels of crime (Akers 1998).

The theory of differential association is described with remarkable clarity by Professor Warr in the first essay of this chapter. Essentially, we can summarize Sutherland's theory with a few statements that capture, but do not directly correspond to, his nine propositions:

- Criminal behavior is learned behavior.
- The learning of criminal behavior is no different than the learning of noncriminal behavior.
- The learning occurs through a social process, taking place in intimate, small, primary groups.
- What is learned are specific techniques for committing crimes and motivations, attitudes, and rationalizations for crimes.
- In addition to learning techniques and motivations for criminal behavior, people learn techniques and motivations for noncriminal behavior.
- Crime is more likely to occur when the collective weight of criminal patterns and thoughts exceeds those associated with noncriminal patterns and thoughts.
- The associations with criminal and noncriminal patterns and thoughts are not equally important, they vary in terms of such characteristics as the prestige or degree of emotional bond

with the source and how frequent and how long the association.

Crime occurs, then, when there is a specific type of differential association—when one is exposed to or associates with those who communicate criminal patterns and thoughts to a greater extent than with those who communicate noncriminal patterns and thoughts. It should be understood that when persons are exposed to both criminal and noncriminal associations, the risk of crime increases when the former exceeds the latter.

It should also be clear that in asserting that criminal behavior is learned, and that it involves the same mechanisms (but different content) of learning as noncriminal behavior, Sutherland was unambiguously distancing himself both from his earlier theoretical stance and from other very prominent criminological theories of the day. In putting his stake in the ground that crime is learned behavior and that criminal offenders might not be so different from nonoffenders, Sutherland squarely put himself at odds with biological and psychological positivists, such as Sheldon and Eleanor Glueck (Laub and Sampson 1991). Although he may once have agreed with their multi-factor, biopsychological approach, Sutherland's work on differential association represented a clean break with this thinking, and both his work and his influence were to eventually place the study of crime in sociology departments on American campuses (see Laub and Sampson 1991).

The idea that persons are profoundly affected by the kinds of associates they have is, of course, not terribly new. Here is just a sample of previous observations about the link between one's character and the character of one's "associations":

A wise man associating with the vicious becomes an idiot; a dog traveling with good men becomes a rational being.

—Arabic proverb

A man is known by the company he organizes.

—Ambrose Bierce (1881)

Tell me thy company, and I'll tell thee what thou art.

—Cervantes (1605)

Every man is like the company he is wont to keep.

—Euripides (425 BC)

If you live with a cripple, you will learn to limp.

—Plutarch (AD 100)

By associating with good and evil persons, a man acquires the virtues and vices which they possess, even as the wind blowing over different places takes along good and bad odours.

—Panchatantra
(Fifth Century)

It is not fair to Sutherland, however, to characterize his theory as a simple "we become the company we keep" hypothesis. Although clearly the most important source of learning, face-to-face interactions were not the only source for Sutherland's learning of differential associations. We can learn criminal (and noncriminal) techniques and associations from others we have no long-standing social relationship with (though such associations are likely to be infrequent and lack intensity) and from nonhuman agents, such as television shows, movies, and music. Nevertheless, Sutherland clearly emphasized the importance of close-knit personal associations, such as friends, family, and neighbors.

Although the theory of differential association refers to several different mechanisms through which the learning of criminal and noncriminal motivations can possibly take place, when researchers have actually tested the theory, they have almost exclusively restricted their attention to the role of criminal peers. As Professor Warr indicates in the opening paragraphs of his essay, what researchers have found is one of the most robust correlations with crime and delinquency in the literature. In other words, one of the best predictors of our behavior is the behavior of our friends and associates. The positive correlation between our behavior and that of our peers is so strong and so consistently found that any failure to find such an effect would be immediately suspect. However, even though there is virtual unanimous agreement about the existence of a positive relationship between our criminality and that of our peers, there is an equally persistent controversy about what this positive relationship actually means. Does the fact that our behavior is strongly related to that of our close associations mean that we learned those behaviors from them, and that they influenced our own conduct, as differential association theory would predict? Or does it mean that we simply select those people as friends whose attitudes and behaviors closely resemble ours, in a way that "birds of a feather flock together?" We believe there is no real consensus in the field about this issue, although you would probably not be wrong to suspect that both processes are at work. Our friends do influence us in subtle and not-so-subtle ways, and we tend to select as companions those who are most like ourselves.

There have been a number of controversies surrounding differential association theory. One controversy concerns the testability of the theory. In the first chapter of this book, we argued that one thing a good theory must provide is an accurate depiction of reality. A theory must "fit the facts" or have sound empirical validity. One of the criticisms of differential association theory has been that, as stated, it is essentially untestable (Gibbs 1987; Hirschi 1969; see also Matsueda 1988). Critics have noted that the key theoretical construct in differential association theory, an excess of definitions favorable to the violation of law over those unfavorable to the violation of law, is exceptionally vague. They ask, "Precisely how does one measure the ratio of favorable to unfavorable definitions of the law?" Moreover, other key constructs such as the duration, priority, intensity, and frequency of definitions are also vaguely defined and, therefore, difficult to empirically measure. Sup-

porters of the theory note that the abstract nature of any theory means that theoretical constructs are not always precisely defined, but that key differential association hypotheses can nevertheless be put to empirical test (Matsueda 1988).

Another persistent controversy surrounding the theory is whether it is a "cultural deviance" theory. In a critique of differential association theory, Kornhauser (1978) observed that cultural deviance theories of crime assume the following: (1) that society has no normative or cultural consensus but is instead characterized by great cultural diversity, (2) there is, therefore, no agreement within such culturally heterogeneous societies as to what is and is not appropriate conduct (i.e., each distinct culture has it own "rules"), (3) each culture within a multi-cultural society successfully socializes its members into its own culture, (4) this socialization is always perfect, so persons within a given culture conform to its rules, (5) the rules of any one culture may or may not be those captured by the criminal law, (6) if the rules of one's own culture are not captured by the criminal law, by conforming to that culture one will inevitably break the law, (7) rule breaking, therefore, is due to conformity, but conformity to the wrong set of rules, (8) there are no deviant or criminal individuals, only deviant or criminal cultures. Kornhauser claimed that differential association was a cultural deviance theory because Sutherland claimed that cultural diversity was rampant in modern society (his notion of differential social organization), that persons learn definitions of rule breaking within their own culture, and they always conform to these definitions. Essentially, she accused Sutherland of being a cultural determinist—one is always perfectly socialized into a culture and the definitions of that culture may conflict with those in the criminal law (see also Hirschi 1969, 11–15; Hirschi 1996).

Numerous other scholars, however, have countered Kornhauser's accusation of cultural determinism by noting that none of the criticisms she levels at Sutherland are true and that the theory of differential association is not a cultural deviance theory.

Matsueda (1988) and Akers (1996) argue that Kornhauser has greatly misinterpreted or at least inaccurately exaggerated components of Sutherland's theory. They state that Sutherland never claimed that definitions about crime are completely relative, so that there may be some cultures within a given society that tolerate or even require behaviors like murder, rape, armed robbery, or burglary. They also assert that Sutherland never claimed that socialization was always perfect, and that one always obeyed the definitions that one happened to be exposed to. Rather, they argued that Sutherland's point was that modern society is not homogeneous with respect to approval for certain kinds of unlawful conduct, that even with the same group, one is constantly exposed to definitions that permit and forbid criminal conduct, that learning these definitions is never perfect but is in a constant state of flux, and that other factors besides criminal definitions (e.g., opportunities) affect whether or not someone commits a crime. The controversy about Sutherland's differential association theory and cultural deviance theory is currently an unsettled dispute and continues to rage in the discipline (see Akers 1996; Bernard and Snipes 1996; Hirschi 1996).

Social Learning Theory

As its chief architect and spokesperson, Professor Ronald L. Akers argues in the second essay of this chapter that social learning theory is a child of differential association theory. Even in the 1960s, the theory of differential association that Sutherland left in the 1947 edition was the object of a great deal of empirical work and additional theorizing about the learning of criminal behavior. DeFleur and Quinney (1966) took on the task of confronting the internal consistency of the theory, and they reported that the nine propositions of differential association theory could be described in the formal logic of set theory, from which specific hypotheses could be deduced. In that same year, Akers and his colleague at the time, Robert Burgess, published a paper in which they sought to explain the precise learning mechanisms behind differential associations. Although Sutherland had clearly spelled out his theoretical position that, like other behavior, criminal conduct is learned, he had not specified in any detail how this learning occurs. This is what Burgess and Akers sought to do.

In their reformulation of differential association, however, Burgess and Akers (1966) did more than restate the theory with the vocabulary of modern learning theory. They also began the process of generalizing it and transforming it into what was to become social learning theory. It is important to remember, however, that social learning theory is not a rival to differential association theory. As Akers (1997, 1998) himself repeatedly argues, the principles of social learning are simply more general than and, therefore, include all those described by differential association theory. The theory of differential association is, then, a specific case of social learning and is subsumed under that more general theory. In fact, even in the most comprehensive presentation of social learning theory, Akers (1998, 47) claimed that "it is still accurate to call the theory differential association-reinforcement [theory]."

The transformation was achieved by linking differential association with the learning processes described by operant conditioning theory in behavioral psychology. Operant learning theory provided the terminology that described how the actual learning of criminal and deviant behavior takes place. One of the principal learning mechanisms that Burgess and Akers borrowed from operant conditioning is the notion that behavior is influenced by its consequences. Acts that reap rewards or reinforcements for the one committing them are likely to be repeated, while those that result in pain or punishment are likely to be extinguished. The obvious implication is that criminal behavior, like any other behavior, is a product of the kinds and magnitudes of reinforcements and punishments that it supplies. Burgess and Akers combined the notion that behavior is influenced by its consequences with Sutherland's earlier work to develop what they called a *differential association-reinforcement* theory of crime, which was initially restated in seven propositions that paralleled Sutherland's original theory. This differential association-reinforcement theory was the seed for what was to become Akers' social learning theory. Professor Akers will provide his own discussion of his theory in the second essay of this chapter. We will here briefly review some major points.

We argued above that in his theory, Sutherland put forth the notion that criminal behavior was learned, but he provided no detail as to how the learning actually occurs. He did say that the learning of criminal behavior involved the same mechanisms as the learning of noncriminal behavior, and in his eighth proposition he was clear that this learning involved more than simple imitation and included "all other processes of learning" (Schuessler 1973, 22). But exactly how one learns about criminal and noncriminal associations was left unspecified. In the development over time of his social learning theroy, Akers (1973, 1977, 1985, 1997, 1998) has argued that there are four principal components in the learning of crime and noncrime: (1) differential association, (2) differential reinforcement, (3) imitation, and (4) definitions.

These four learning processes are woven together into the theory, of which Akers (1998) has recently provided a very succinct statement:

> The probability that persons will engage in criminal and deviant behavior is increased and the probability of their conforming to the norm is decreased when they differentially associate with others who commit criminal behavior and espouse definitions favorable to it, are relatively more exposed in-person or symbolically to salient criminal/deviant models, define it as desirable or justified in a situation discriminative for the behavior, and have received in the past and anticipate in the current or future situation relatively greater reward than punishment for the behavior. (50)

In a nutshell, then, according to social learning theory, persons are at risk for criminal or deviant behavior under the following conditions:

- When they associate with those who are criminals and deviants to a greater degree and intensity than they associate with conforming others (i.e., one is more likely to become a drug user when one associates more with drug users than abstainers);

- Persons who associate with deviant others are at high risk for criminal and deviant behavior because those who commit such acts provide a model to imitate or copy, and because they more than likely hold and espouse beliefs that support such behavior (i.e., one can learn from drug users how to easily and with low risk obtain the drug, how one can best prepare it for ingestion, and how one interprets the effects or stimulation provided; one can also learn from drug users the lore that drug use is no different than alcohol consumption, that any possible side effects can be "handled," that drug use is a bohemian expression and "cool," and that one can be a long-term drug user and still lead a "normal" life); and

- Such persons are at high risk for criminal and deviant behavior because the pleasure they receive from the act outweighs both the costs involved and the anticipated pleasures from nonuse (drug users develop not only a "craving" for the drug, but an appreciation or "taste" for it; they find it pleasurable and find nondrug life tedious and empty, and learn how to minimize or discount the costs involved).

As Professor Akers himself points out in the second essay of this chapter, the learning of both criminal and noncriminal behavior involves a complex interplay of the differential reinforcement and punishment of behavior, the context of social reinforcers and sanctions provided by one's close associations, the available stock of role models to copy, and various cues and stimuli in one's immediate situation. Students of psychology will note that Akers' theory blends two kinds of learning mechanisms: the operant learning theory of B.F. Skinner (1953), which emphasizes the connection between the consequences of behavior (rewards and punishments) and the probability of that behavior, and the more cognitive psychology or social learning theory of Albert Bandura (1977, 1986), which focuses on the symbolic interaction between persons and their environments. When persons anticipate the kinds of rewards they will reap from some behavior or provide self-reinforcement, they are being far more cognitive than "hard behaviorists" such as Skinner would give them the credit or capacity for.

References

Akers, Ronald L. (1973). *Deviant Behavior: A Social Learning Approach*. Belmont, CA: Wadsworth.

——. (1977). *Deviant Behavior: A Social Learning Approach*, Second Edition. Belmont, CA: Wadsworth.

——. (1985). *Deviant Behavior: A Social Learning Approach*, Third Edition. Belmont, CA: Wadsworth.

——. (1996). "Is differential association theory/social learning theory cultural deviance theory?" *Criminology*, 34:229–247.

——. (1997). *Criminological Theories*, Second Edition. Los Angeles: Roxbury.

——. (1998). *Social Learning and Social Structure: A General Theory of Crime and Deviance*. Boston: Northeastern University Press.

Bandura, Albert. (1977). *Social Learning Theory*. Englewood Cliffs, NJ: Prentice Hall.

——. (1986). *Social Foundations of Thought and Action: A Social Cognitive Theory*. Englewood Cliffs, NJ: Prentice Hall.

Bernard, Thomas J. and Jeffrey B. Snipes. (1996). "Theoretical integration in criminology." Pp. 301–348 in *Crime and Justice: A Review of Research*, M. Tonry (ed.). Vol. 20. Chicago: University of Chicago Press.

Burgess, Robert and Ronald L. Akers. (1966). "A differential association-reinforcement theory of criminal behavior." *Social Problems*, 14:128–147.

DeFleur, Melvin L. and Richard Quinney. (1966). "A reformulation of Sutherland's differential association theory and a strategy for empirical verification." *Journal of Research in Crime and Delinquency*, 3:1–22.

Gaylord, Mark S. and John F. Galliher. (1988). *The Criminology of Edwin Sutherland*. New Brunswick, NJ: Transaction.

Gibbs, Jack P. (1987). "The state of criminological theory." *Criminology*, 25:821–840.

Hirschi, Travis. (1969). *Causes of Delinquency*. Berkeley: University of California Press.

——. (1996). "Theory without ideas: Reply to Akers." *Criminology*, 34:249–256.

Kornhauser, Ruth R. (1978). *Social Sources of Delinquency*. Chicago: University of Chicago Press.

Laub, John H. and Robert J. Sampson. (1991). "The Sutherland-Glueck debate: On the sociology of criminological knowledge." *American Journal of Sociology*, 96:1402–1440.

Matsueda, Ross L. (1988). "The current state of differential association theory." *Crime and Delinquency*, 34:277–306.

Schuessler, Karl. (1973). *Edwin Sutherland: On Analyzing Crime*. Chicago: University of Chicago Press.

Skinner, B.F. (1953). *Science and Human Behavior*. New York: Macmillan.

Sutherland, Edwin H. (1924). *Criminology*. Philadelphia: Lippincott.

——. (1934). *Principles of Criminology*, Second Edition. Philadelphia: Lippincott.

——. (1939). *Principles of Criminology*, Third Edition. Philadelphia: Lippincott.

——. (1947). *Principles of Criminology*, Fourth Edition. Philadelphia: Lippincott.

The Social Origins of Crime: Edwin Sutherland and the Theory of Differential Association

Mark Warr
University of Texas at Austin

Imagine for a moment that you are standing in a large room filled with several hundred people who have been randomly selected from the population of the United States. As you would expect from such a sample, the individuals in this room vary considerably in their age, occupation, appearance, income, ethnicity, educational attainment, and many other characteristics. Now suppose that your task as an investigator is to identify those persons in the room who are most likely to have a history of criminal behavior. To accomplish this task, you may acquire any information you want from these individuals, but you may obtain only *one* piece of information from each person beyond what is obvious from his or her appearance (for example, age or sex).

Given this situation, what would you wish to know about each of these individuals? Their family structure? Their religious beliefs? Their educational background? Their genetic history? Their wealth? Their television habits? Where they live?

A powerful answer to this problem comes from one of the most famous and compelling theories of crime of the twentieth century, Edwin Sutherland's theory of differential association. Under Sutherland's theory, the critical question to be answered is this: *With whom do each of these people associate?* To understand human behavior, Sutherland argued, one must examine the primary groups to which individuals belong, for it is in such groups, he believed, that the direction of human behavior is ultimately determined. This quintessentially sociological perspective on human behavior set Sutherland's theory apart from others of its time and was destined to have a profound impact on the development and direction of the field of criminology. We will see how Sutherland's theory has altered the course of criminology as we explore the evolution of and evidence for his theory.

Origins of the Theory

Born in Gibbon, Nebraska, in 1883, Edwin Sutherland was the son of a strict and forceful Baptist clergyman whose devout practices and beliefs were not embraced by Edwin during his adult life, but whose influence may account for the ethical, professional, and gentlemanly behavior for which Sutherland was noted throughout his career, and for his self-discipline and interest in social reform.[1] After receiving a bachelor of arts degree from Grand Island College (where his father was president) in 1904, and a doctorate in sociology and political economy from the University of Chicago in 1913, Sutherland spent six not wholly satisfying years as a professor at William Jewell College in Missouri (a Baptist college for men) before joining the sociology department at the University of Illinois in 1919. It was there, at the urging of his chair, that he wrote the first of several editions of his famous textbook *Principles of Criminology,* initially published in 1924. Sutherland's decision to write this textbook was surely the pivotal event in his career, for it sealed his commitment to criminology, and it was in that textbook that the theory of differential association appeared and evolved.

In the early years of his career, Sutherland relied on what was then known as *multiple-factor theory* to explain the causes of crime. Under this theory, crime has many causes—poverty, broken homes, alcoholic parents, bad housing, mental deficiency—any of which may account for the appearance of criminal behavior in a particular individual. Sutherland's desire for a more parsimonious and coherent account of criminal behavior was spurred by several events during his career. One was the release in 1932 of the Michael-Adler report, a document prepared under the auspices of the Columbia University School of Law. That report severely criticized American criminology as unscientific and incompetent, and recommended the establishment of an American institute of criminology comprised of physicists, a mathematician, a logician, and others. Sutherland, now a professor of sociology at the University of Chicago, initially reacted to the report with anger, but he eventually conceded many of its arguments.

At about the same time, an eminent dean at the University of Chicago brought together several persons interested in criminology and asked them to describe the current state of knowledge about criminal behavior. As he later described it, Sutherland replied—no doubt with some unease:

> The best I could say was that we had certain facts about the incidence of high crime rates and that we had proved that certain propositions were false. I could state no verified positive generalizations. (1956, 16)

Sutherland was also heavily influenced by the groundbreaking research and ideas that were emerging at the University of Chicago in an intellectual movement that would come to be known as the Chicago school of sociology (see Chapter 5). For example, Shaw and McKay, in one of the most famous empirical findings ever presented in the field, demonstrated that delinquency rates in areas of Chicago remained unchanged over time despite nearly complete turnover in the population and ethnic composition of those areas. This finding strongly suggested that the foundation of crime lay, not in characteristics of individuals *per se,* but in cultural traditions that inhered in neighborhoods and that were assimilated by those who moved into the area. Similarly, the great urbanist Louis Wirth wrote about the "culture conflict" that was arising in U.S. cities

as a consequence of large-scale European immigration. This culture conflict meant that Americans, unlike those in many other societies, were often exposed to differing and sometimes conflicting standards of behavior in their own society.

The Theory

Prompted by these developments, and with the encouragement of his colleagues at Indiana University (where he became chair of the sociology department in 1935), Sutherland pursued a general theory of crime during the 1930s. In 1939, the first explicit statement of differential association appeared in the third edition of *Principles of Criminology,* and a revised and final version appeared in the fourth edition in 1947, three years before Sutherland's death. The latter statement of the theory took the form of nine propositions, each followed by brief elaborations or clarifications. The nine propositions were as follows:

1. Criminal behavior is learned.

2. Criminal behavior is learned in interaction with other persons in a process of communication.

3. The principal part of the learning of criminal behavior occurs within intimate personal groups.

4. When criminal behavior is learned, the learning includes (a) techniques of committing the crime, which are sometimes very complicated, sometimes very simple; and (b) the specific direction of motives, drives, rationalizations, and attitudes.

5. The specific direction of motives and drives is learned from definitions of the legal codes as favorable or unfavorable.

6. A person becomes delinquent because of an excess of definitions favorable to violation of law over definitions unfavorable to violation of law.

7. Differential associations may vary in frequency, duration, priority, and intensity.

8. The process of learning criminal behavior by association with criminal and anticriminal patterns involves all of the mechanisms that are involved in any other learning.

9. While criminal behavior is an expression of general needs and values, it is not explained by those general needs and values because noncriminal behavior is an expression of the same needs and values.

To modern students of social science, these statements may seem simple, even quaint, but in fact they constituted a radical departure from earlier (and even some contemporary) criminologies. An exhaustive analysis of the theory is impossible here, but it is important to understand some of the major ideas contained in these propositions.

The four words in proposition 1 ("Criminal behavior is learned") are an explicit rejection of the dominant causal theories of crime of the late nineteenth and early twentieth centuries, theories that primarily came to this country from Europe and that emphasized (especially in the work of Lombroso) physiological or hereditary factors in the etiology of crime (see Jones 1986). These theories were still prominent during Sutherland's early career, and one need not necessarily agree with Sutherland to appreciate the clarity and forthrightness with which he stated his position. At a deeper philosophical level, Sutherland's assertion that criminal behavior is learned forsook the inevitability that attaches to biological theories of crime and distanced criminology from the reactionary movements (eugenics, social Darwinism) that had followed Darwin and which ultimately showed their worst excesses in Nazi Germany during Sutherland's own lifetime.

The second proposition, which augments the first, asserts that learning is not a solitary or isolated process, but a *social* process. Persons come to crime not through purely personal or private experience, but rather through contacts with *others*. This bedrock tenet of Sutherland's theory placed it squarely within the mainstream of sociological thought, where it remains today. The

third proposition narrows the field of "others" to intimate associates. This qualification illustrates the strong emphasis placed on primary groups (e.g., families, friends, neighbors, coworkers) and face-to-face communication in sociological thought, and appears to reflect the influence of Charles Horton Cooley's writings on Sutherland's thinking (Gaylord and Galliher 1988).

In proposition 4, Sutherland asserts that the process of learning crime includes not only the acquisition of motives to commit crime but also knowledge about *methods* of committing crime. Some crimes, he noted, require little or no specialized training or techniques, while others require a considerable degree of sophistication. Sutherland's attention to methods or techniques of crime evidently arose from his investigation of professional thieves, one that resulted in a classic work of criminology, *The Professional Thief* (1937). Though not widely recognized, the screenplay for the Robert Redford/Paul Newman movie *The Sting* relied on this book for details about confidence games (see Gaylord and Galliher 1988).

Proposition 5 reveals the influence of Sutherland's graduate studies with W.I. Thomas and George Herbert Mead. These influential scholars argued that human behavior is affected by the meanings or *definitions* (Mead's term) that individuals place on objects, events, or acts, and they further asserted that these meanings are acquired through social interaction. In accordance with this view of human behavior, Sutherland proposed that it is the favorable or unfavorable meanings that individuals place on legal rules that constitute the critical content of learning when it comes to crime. In elaborating on this proposition, Sutherland (clearly influenced by Wirth) observed that "In some societies an individual is surrounded by persons who invariably define the legal codes as rules to be observed, while in others he is surrounded by persons whose definitions are favorable to the violation of the legal codes. In our American society these definitions are almost always mixed and consequently we have culture conflict in relation to the legal codes" (1947, 6).

Proposition 6 is the heart of Sutherland's theory, so much so that it is sometimes referred to *as* the theory of differential association. The proposition sets forth the mechanism by which a person becomes delinquent: "A person becomes delinquent because of an excess of definitions favorable to violation of law over definitions unfavorable to violation of law." Although it is usually taken literally, it is not clear whether Sutherland actually meant the word *excess* to be understood in a mathematically literal way, as in a positive difference between two quantities. Although at times he seemed to use the word in that fashion, such exactitude seems out of place for a theory described by its author as only "tentative" and from a man who was skilled in empirical research and statistical analysis (at least for the time) and was familiar with the inexactitude of much social scientific data. It may be that, in choosing his words, Sutherland was merely trying to draw attention to the balance between favorable and unfavorable beliefs toward crime.

Proposition 7 attempts to identify the properties of relationships that are critical to differential association. By *priority* Sutherland meant the age at which associations occur, and he suggested that childhood associations are more influential than later ones. This somewhat Freudian point of view of behavior was common in his time but is at odds with modern learning theory and evidence (see Warr 1993a). The meanings of *frequency* and *duration*, Sutherland stated succinctly, "are obvious and need no explanation" (1947, 7). Yet it is not entirely clear what these terms mean in the context of his theory or how these concepts ought to be measured. For example, when exactly does an association end? Or begin? Unless questions like these can be answered precisely, the notion of duration has no clear meaning. *Intensity* was only vaguely defined by Sutherland as having to do with "such things as the prestige of the source of a criminal or anticriminal pattern and with emotional reactions related to the associations" (1947, 7). Apparently, Sutherland had in mind the degree to which a person (i.e., the source of definitions) is liked and respected by his associates.

Sutherland believed that these properties of associations—priority, frequency, duration, and intensity—could ultimately be linked to behavior through a precise formula, although he admitted that "the development of such a formula would be extremely difficult" (1947, 7). He himself offered no such formula, and he was silent when it came to some of the more obvious questions about these properties of relations. For example, which is more consequential for individuals, a short but extremely intense association or a prolonged but less intense relationship?

In some ways, proposition 8 is the most philosophically profound of all the propositions in the theory of differential association. Evidently, Sutherland's primary intention with this proposition was to answer critics' charges that his theory was merely a restatement of Tarde's theory of imitation (see Gaylord and Galliher 1988) and, in fact, Sutherland immediately followed this proposition with the statement that "the learning of criminal behavior is not restricted to the process of imitation" (1947, 7). Whatever its inspiration may have been, however, the proposition says something of great consequence: Criminal behavior is learned in the same way that all human behavior is learned.

In adopting this position, Sutherland rejected the tendency of many amateur criminologists (and even some professional criminologists) to assume that criminals are an ontologically distinct category of human beings whose behavior requires separate or unique explanation from other forms of human behavior. Sutherland avoided this point of view, even using as examples of his theory behavior that was not even remotely criminal ("a Southerner does not pronounce 'r' because other Southerners do not pronounce 'r'" (1947, 6). More generally, he observed that "criminal behavior is part of human behavior . . .and must be explained within the same general framework as any other human behavior" (1947, 4). So strong was Sutherland's commitment to this point of view that he introduced the first published version of his theory with this statement:

The processes which result in systematic criminal behavior are fundamentally the same in form as the processes which result in systematic lawful behavior. . . .Criminal behavior differs from lawful behavior in the standards by which it is judged but not in the principles of the genetic [causal] processes. (1939, 4)

Sutherland is not the only criminologist to insist on a general theory of human behavior to explain crime, but his stance was among the earliest and most forceful declarations of that position.

At first glance, the final proposition (number 9) seems almost to contradict the foregoing position because it maintains that the causes of criminal behavior cannot be the causes of noncriminal behavior. But there is no contradiction, for Sutherland's theory holds that it is the *mechanism* of learning—not the *content* of what is learned—that is the same for all forms of behavior. What differentiates criminal and lawful behavior is not how definitions are learned but *which* definitions are learned.

One general point about Sutherland's theory requires clarification because it is not stated in the propositions above. If individuals acquire definitions favorable to violation of law from others, where do those *other* individuals acquire these definitions? In other words, where do those definitions ultimately originate? As we saw earlier, Sutherland agreed with Wirth that the United States, a diverse land of immigrants, contains a variety of cultural traditions, some more favorable to or tolerant of crime than others. This mixture produces a state of *culture conflict,* or a society where different subgroups have different normative standards of behavior and where, as Sutherland (1939, 7) put it, "the criminal culture is as real as lawful culture and is much more prevalent than is usually believed." Viewed from the perspective of individuals, then, the proximate cause of criminal behavior is differential association. From a societal point of view, however, the ultimate cause of crime is culture conflict, for individuals are unlikely to adopt cultural standards that are not to be found in their society. In Sutherland's words, "Differential as-

sociation is possible because society is composed of various groups with varied cultures. . . .It was possible to predict with almost complete certainty how a person reared in a Chinese village fifty years ago would behave because there was only one way for him to behave. The attempts to explain the behavior of a particular person in a modern city have been rather unproductive because the influences are in conflict and any particular influence may be very evanescent " (1939, 7–8).

In the end, then, it is fair to say that Sutherland approached crime as both a comparative sociologist and a cultural relativist. *Crime* is a social and political label placed on certain behaviors, and what is crime in one society or in one subculture may not be crime in another. Crime increases or decreases in a society as the cultural standards of one social group are adopted—or rejected—by another.

Research Aspects of Differential Association

No causal theory of crime has received more attention from researchers over the last half-century than differential association, and the literature on the subject is somewhat daunting in its size and scope. Consequently, it is more fruitful to characterize the general direction of research results than to review individual studies.

The single strongest piece of evidence in favor of differential association can be stated succinctly: No characteristic of individuals known to criminologists is a better predictor of criminal behavior than the number of delinquent friends an individual has. The strong correlation between delinquency and delinquent friends has been documented in scores of studies dating from the 1950s up to the present day (for reviews, see Matsueda 1988; Warr 1996; Matsueda and Anderson 1998), using alternative kinds of criminological data (self-reports, official records, perceptual data) on subjects and friends, alternative research designs, and data on a wide variety of criminal offenses. Few, if any, empirical regularities in criminology have been documented as often or for as long as the association between delinquency and delinquent friends.

The correlation between delinquency and friends certainly supports the theory of differential association, but it is not sufficient to settle the question. Critics of differential association (or, more accurately, proponents of other theories) do not question the correlation between delinquency and friends. Instead, they question its meaning. Drawing on the venerable sociological principle of homophily (people make friends with people who are similar to themselves), they argue that the causal direction between delinquency and friends runs in the opposite direction from that proposed in differential association. In other words, people do not become delinquent because they acquire delinquent friends; they acquire delinquent friends after they have themselves become delinquent.

The question of causal direction remains a contentious issue in criminology today, but several longitudinal studies of criminal careers support the causal direction stipulated by differential association or suggest a reciprocal process supporting both points of view: having delinquent friends leads to delinquency, which increases the subsequent probability of acquiring still more delinquent friends (see Matsueda and Anderson 1998 for a review of the literature on causal direction). The evidence to date is not yet sufficient to settle the issue one way or the other, but it is not an exaggeration to say that the question remains among the most important unresolved issues in criminology today.

Another piece of evidence in favor of differential association is the fact that adolescents (who commit a disproportionate share of all crimes) ordinarily commit offenses in groups, usually groups of the same sex that range in size from two to four individuals. The group nature of delinquency is one of the most solidly established features of delinquent behavior and has been repeatedly noted by criminological researchers since the 1930s (Reiss 1986; Warr 1996). The fact that most offenders commit offenses with companions rather than alone can be construed as evidence that individuals acquire

the motivation and knowledge to engage in crime through interaction with others.

Critics of differential association often respond to the group nature of delinquency by arguing that adolescents are notoriously gregarious people; they do everything in groups including breaking the law. Consequently, "groupiness" does not differentiate legal and illegal behavior. Even if that is true, however, it is not clear that it is a damning criticism of differential association. Young people may be influenced by their peers in all categories of behavior—music, speech, dress, sports, and *delinquency*—and it should be remembered that Sutherland specifically held that criminal behavior is learned in the same way as other human behavior.

At the same time, however, there is nothing in Sutherland's theory that specifically *requires* delinquency to be group behavior. Although Sutherland stressed that delinquency is learned from others, at no point did he argue that others must be present during criminal events, and it is difficult to imagine that propinquity of that sort is absolutely essential to his theory. For example, who would argue that parents have an influence on their children only when they are physically together? Admittedly, the ability of parents to control their children is greatest when they are in their presence, but there is surely more to parental influence than mere physical control, and Sutherland clearly had more in mind than this kind of influence.

Perhaps the best that can be said about the group nature of delinquency at this point is that it is not inconsistent with differential association and that it is potentially important for the theory if it can be shown that learning methods or motivation for crimes ordinarily takes place within offending groups (for some evidence for this when it comes to smoking marijuana, see Becker 1953). In the end, however, there is no denying that it would be easier to dismiss differential association as a theory *if* delinquent behavior were entirely the work of lone individuals.

Definitions or Other Mechanisms?

Notwithstanding the evidence in favor of differential association, one aspect of Sutherland's theory has consistently failed to receive support from research. Recall that Sutherland argued that individuals become delinquent because they acquire "definitions" (or attitudes) favorable to the violation of law through differential association. In essence, Sutherland was arguing that delinquency is the result of attitude transference, whereby the attitudes of one individual are adopted or absorbed by another. A number of studies over the last three decades, however, have consistently indicated that attitude transference is *not* the process by which differential association operates. For example, after noting that behavior and attitudes are not always consistent, Warr and Stafford (1991) reported that the effect of friends' attitudes on adolescents is small in comparison to that of friends' behavior, and the effect of friends' *behavior* is largely direct, meaning that it does not operate through changing attitudes (see also Matsueda and Anderson, 1998). Consequently, it seems that adolescents are much more sensitive to the behavior of their friends than to their attitudes.

If differential association is not a consequence of attitude transference, how then are people influenced by their associates? What precisely is the mechanism, if any, of differential association? One possible answer comes from modern social learning theory, which emphasizes processes, such as imitation and direct and vicarious reinforcement in the acquisition of behaviors. To use an illustration, an adolescent may imitate the delinquent behavior of his friends (e.g., smoking, theft, drug sales) because he observes the adult status it confers on them in the eyes of others his age (along with additional rewards like sexual attractiveness and money) and because participating in those activities gains him the loyalty and respect of his peers. Some years ago, Burgess and Akers (1966) reformulated Sutherland's theory using the principles of operant conditioning, and Akers and his collaborators have continued this work in subsequent years by applying modern social learning theory to the explanation of crime (see Akers 1998). Ultimately, it may prove to be the case that differential association can be wholly or partially subsumed under social learning theory. If so, it would not diminish the historical impact of Sutherland's work on criminology or sociology, and it would be consistent with Sutherland's search for a general theory of human behavior that would explain legal behavior as fully as illegal behavior.

Other Issues

Virtually all research on differential association during the last five decades has concentrated on the influence of delinquent peers. The reasons for this seem to have more to do with tradition or historical accident than logic, for there is nothing in Sutherland's theory that limits its scope to peer influence. On the contrary, the influence of parents, teachers, employers, clergymen, and others is in no way excluded by the theory, and Sutherland even acknowledged (albeit reluctantly) the potentially powerful influence of movies and other media of mass communication. (Note that Sutherland died before television became widely available.) One of the remaining questions to be answered about differential association is how well the theory applies to persons *other* than peers. For example, there is considerable empirical evidence linking delinquency to parental behavior, but the association between the two is generally interpreted from the vantage point of control theory or other etiological theories of crime rather than from the perspective of differential association.

Turning to another matter, a number of investigators in recent years have attempted to integrate differential association with other causal theories of crime, especially Hirschi's (1969) control theory. A key element of Hirschi's theory is the relation between children and their parents; children with weak attachment or bonds to their parents, Hirschi argued, are most likely to engage in crime. Proponents of integrated theories agree, but argue that this occurs because kids with weak bonds to their parents are precisely those kids who are most likely to acquire delinquent friends. If differential association and control theory are integrated through this common element, then the process of differential association can be viewed as the proximate cause of delinquency in a longer causal chain of variables. There is in fact substantial evidence for this integrated theory, and some of its advocates (see especially Elliott et al. 1985) regard it as the single best empirically-substantiated theory of crime that can be offered by modern criminology.

Policy Implications

Theories about the causes of crime are intrinsically interesting to most people, but in a nation beset by the hard realities of crime, a theory of crime causation ought to be something more than an intellectual exercise or mere armchair speculation. It should be pressed to offer some means to prevent or control crime in the real world. Controlling crime, of course, does not necessarily require an understanding of its causes; prisons and the death penalty are proof enough of that. But just as a physician would rather prevent a disease than attempt to cure it after it is established (many diseases are seemingly incurable once underway), stopping crime *before* it happens by understanding and altering its causes is surely the most defensible and profitable course of action. Unfortunately, because it is intrinsically a long-term strategy, prevention is a difficult policy to sell to a skeptical and frightened public and to politicians interested only in the short term. Worse still, the very evidence that prevention is working is the fact that *nothing happens*. Demonstrating that something did not happen today because of strategies that were adopted years ago is an empirically and politically difficult task. American culture, it would seem, has neither the patience nor the foresight to implement and monitor serious prevention programs.

When it comes to preventing or reducing crime, it is difficult to imagine a theory of crime that has clearer or more direct policy implications than differential association: *To reduce the probability that an individual will engage in criminal conduct, one must limit or control his or her exposure to delinquent associates.* Many policies and programs designed to reduce crime do in fact draw from the theory of differential association, if not always consciously or carefully. For example, after-school and summertime recreational programs for adolescents are designed to provide an alternative to hanging out with the "wrong crowd." Parents often encourage their children to participate in sports, scouting, or church activities on the grounds that their children will make friends with "good kids." Parents are themselves often urged to supervise their children closely and to pay special attention to those with whom they spend their time.

Do such programs or policies work? Not necessarily, though for reasons that are not inconsistent with differential association. For example, parents of high-school students sometimes encourage their children to get a job in order to fill their time and keep them away from the wrong kinds of kids. Ironically, though, employment is *positively* correlated with delinquency among adolescents, and one of the reasons seems to be that adolescents often work in settings where they are with many of their age-peers and have little or no adult supervision (Ploeger 1997). In a similar way, keeping a child away from other children only to put him or her in front of a television set brimming with violent programs may not result in the intended effect.

Nevertheless, there are reasons to believe that differential association offers an effective strategy for delinquency prevention. Warr (1993b) found that adolescents who reported spending much of their time each week with their family had low rates of delinquency *even when they had delinquent friends*. This finding strongly suggests that the family is ultimately capable of counteracting or overcoming peer influence. This may occur merely because spending time with the family limits opportunities to engage in delinquency, but the effect remains the same. Summarizing his and other research, Warr (1993b) also found that adolescents who are close to their parents are less likely to report having any delinquent friends in the first place. This may be true because their parents monitor their friendships or because such children do not want to displease their parents, but in either case the point is that parents can reduce the chances that their children will have delinquent friends by remaining emotionally close to their children. Where this proves difficult or impossible to achieve, differential association implies that, at the very least, prohibiting or minimizing contact with delinquent friends ought to be an effective means of delinquency control.

Conclusion

Edwin Sutherland's theory of differential association has been described as a "watershed in criminology" (Matsueda 1988, 277), the "preeminent sociological theory of criminology" (Gaylord and Galliher 1988, 165), and a theory that has had "a massive impact on criminology" (Vold and Bernard 1986, 225). In his search for a general theory of crime, Sutherland strove to apply sociological reasoning to the study of crime, and his success in doing so is one of the reasons that criminology has been found primarily in departments of sociology for most of the last century (Gaylord and Galliher 1988). Some contemporary criminologists may lament that fact, but there is no denying Sutherland's immense impact on modern criminology.

Perhaps the essence of Sutherland's approach to crime was his belief that criminal behavior should not be studied as an isolated category of human behavior, but rather as behavior that is not different in its origins from other forms of human social behavior. From a historical point of view, Sutherland's theory stands out for other reasons as well. In sharp contrast with the reigning theories of his day, Sutherland believed that the causes of criminal behavior are *extrinsic* to the individual rather than intrinsic, and his theory openly acknowledged—indeed, asserted—the possibility that criminal behavior can be learned by *anyone*. Vold and Bernard (1986, 225) are thus correct when they observe that

> Sutherland's theory, more than any other, was responsible for . . . the rise of the view

that crime is the result of environmental influences acting on biologically and psychologically normal individuals.

Although his theory of learning was crude by contemporary standards, Sutherland's assumptions about the plasticity of human nature (which he may have acquired as a graduate student from John Broadus Watson) anticipated modern learning theory, and his emphasis on the social environment as the key to explaining crime laid the foundation for most major contemporary theories of criminal behavior.

No less important to Sutherland's thinking and career was his intense commitment to the principles and ideals of science. More than many of his time, Sutherland was concerned with the application of scientific method to the study of criminal behavior and social behavior in general, and he remained committed to empirical research as a means of sorting out competing claims about the causes of crime (Cohen, Lindesmith, and Schuessler 1956). His scientific skepticism and critical skills were finely honed, and he passed them on to his graduate students in part by asking them to critique his very own creation, the theory of differential association.

Sutherland's work on differential association was surely the centerpiece of his career, but it was merely a part of the work for which he is remembered today. (Anyone who uses the phrase *white-collar crime*, for example, is using Sutherland's words). Perhaps the greatest testament to Sutherland's theory of differential association is the simple fact that it continues to be taken seriously by criminologists more than a half-century after its publication.

Note

1. Biographical information on Sutherland is scarce, and I rely here primarily on the fine book by Gaylord and Galliher (1988) and on an essay by Schuessler (1973), who was a student and colleague of Sutherland. A less charitable—but minority—view of Sutherland's professional behavior can be found in Laub and Sampson (1991).

References

Akers, Ronald L. (1998). *Social Learning and Social Structure: A General Theory of Crime and Deviance.* Boston: Northeastern University Press.

Becker, Howard S. (1953). "Becoming a marihuana user." *American Journal of Sociology,* 49:235–242.

Burgess, Robert L. and Ronald L. Akers. (1966). "A differential association-reinforcement theory of criminal behavior." *Social Problems,* 14:128–147.

Cohen, Albert, Alfred Lindesmith, and Karl Schuessler. (1956). *The Sutherland Papers.* Bloomington: Indiana University Press.

Elliott, Delbert S., David Huizinga, and Suzanne S. Ageton. (1985). *Explaining Delinquency and Drug Use.* Newbury Park, CA: Sage.

Gaylord, Mark S. and John F. Galliher. (1988). *The Criminology of Edwin Sutherland.* New Brunswick: Transaction.

Hirschi, Travis. (1969). *Causes of Delinquency.* Berkeley: University of California Press.

Jones, David A. (1986). *History of Criminology: A Philosophical Perspective.* New York: Greenwood.

Laub, John H. and Robert J. Sampson. (1991). "The Sutherland-Glueck debate: On the sociology of criminological knowledge." *American Journal of Sociology,* 6:1402–1440.

Matsueda, Ross L. (1988). "The current state of differential association theory." *Crime and Delinquency,* 34:277–306.

Matsueda, Ross L. and Kathleen Anderson. (1998). "The dynamics of delinquent peers and delinquent behavior." *Criminology,* 36:269–308.

Ploeger, Matthew. (1997). "Youth employment and delinquency: Reconsidering a problematic relationship." *Criminology,* 35:659–675.

Reiss, Albert J. Jr. (1986). "Co-offender influences on criminal careers." In *Criminal Careers and "Career Criminals."* Vol. II. Alfred Blumstein, Jeffrey A. Roth, and Christy A. Visher (eds.). Washington, DC: National Academy Press.

Schuessler, Karl. (1973). *Edwin H. Sutherland: On Analyzing Crime.* Chicago: University of Chicago Press.

Sutherland, Edwin H. (1924). *Criminology.* Chicago: Lippincott.

——. (1937). *The Professional Thief.* Chicago: University of Chicago Press.

——. (1939). *Principles of Criminology,* Third Edition. Chicago: Lippincott.

——. (1947). *Principles of Criminology,* Fourth Edition. Chicago: Lippincott.

——. (1956). "Development of the theory." Pp. 13–29 in *The Sutherland Papers.* Cohen, Albert, Lindensmith, Alfred, and Schuessler, Karl (eds.). Bloomington: Indiana University Press.

Vold, George B. and Thomas J. Bernard. (1986). *Theoretical Criminology,* Third Edition. Oxford: Oxford University Press.

Warr, Mark. (1993a). "Age, peers, and delinquency." *Criminology,* 31:17–40.

——. (1993b). "Parents, peers, and delinquency." *Social Forces,* 72:247–264.

——. (1996). "Organization and instigation in delinquent groups." *Criminology,* 34:11–37.

——. (1998). "Life-course transitions and desistance from crime." *Criminology,* 36:183–216.

Warr, Mark and Mark C. Stafford. (1991). "The influence of delinquent peers: What they think or what they do?" *Criminology,* 29:851–866.

Social Learning Theory

Ronald L. Akers
University of Florida

The Social Learning Theory discussed in this essay is one that I originally proposed with Robert L. Burgess as a reformulation of Edwin H. Sutherland's differential association theory of crime to integrate it with behavioral principles of learning (Burgess and Akers 1966b). It is a general theory that has been applied to a wide range of deviant and criminal behavior. It has much in common with, incorporates basic insights from, and has implications for policy and programs similar to general social/cognitive and behavioral learning theories as developed by Albert Bandura and other psychologists (1977; Bandura and Walters 1963; Rotter 1954; Skinner 1953). Gerald Patterson and others have also applied psychologically based social learning principles to delinquent and deviant behavior (Jessor and Jessor 1977; Patterson et al. 1975; 1992; Patterson and Chamberlain 1994; Patterson 1995). A common feature of all such approaches is a primary focus on overt, observable behavior, but with a readiness to incorporate cognitive variables and processes as part of the basic learning mechanisms. Unlike the other social learning approaches, my theory is linked directly to the criminological theory of Sutherland. First, a brief statement of his theory.

Sutherland's Differential Association Theory

Edwin H. Sutherland's "differential association" theory in its final version was proposed in the form of nine statements (1947, 6–7):

1. Criminal behavior is learned.

2. Criminal behavior is learned in interaction with other persons in a process of communication.

3. The principal part of the learning of criminal behavior occurs within intimate personal groups.

4. When criminal behavior is learned, the learning includes (a) techniques of committing the crime, which are sometimes very complicated, sometimes very simple, and (b) the specific direction of motives, drives, rationalizations, and attitudes.

5. The specific direction of motives and drives is learned from definitions of the legal codes as favorable or unfavorable.

6. A person becomes delinquent because of an excess of definitions favorable to violation of law over definitions unfavorable to violation of law.

7. Differential associations may vary in frequency, duration, priority, and intensity.

8. The process of learning criminal behavior by association with criminal and anticriminal patterns involves all of the mechanisms that are involved in any other learning.

9. Although criminal behavior is an expression of general needs and values, it is not explained by those general needs and values, because noncriminal behavior is an expression of the same needs and values.

The first proposition of the theory is that criminal behavior is learned, and the terms *learned* and *learning* are included in other statements as well. Criminal behavior is learned in a process of symbolic interaction with others, mainly in primary or intimate groups. Although all nine statements constitute the theory, it is the sixth statement that Sutherland identified as the "principle of differential association." This is the principle that a person commits criminal acts because he or she has learned "definitions" (rationalizations and attitudes) favorable to violation of law in "excess" of the definitions unfavorable to violation of law.

It is not a simple theory of running around with "bad companions." Rather, the theory explains delinquent and criminal behavior by referring to the person's exposure to and learning of criminal and noncriminal "patterns" and "definitions." The seventh principle in the theory makes it clear that this is not a simple process of only criminal or only noncriminal association, but a process that varies according to what Sutherland called the *modalities* of association. That is, if persons are exposed first (priority), more frequently, for a longer time (duration), and with greater intensity (importance) to law-violating than to law-abiding associations, then they are more likely to deviate from the law.

Akers' Social Learning Theory

The Burgess-Akers Behavioral Reformulation of Differential Association Theory

Sutherland asserted in the eighth statement of his theory that all the mechanisms of learning are involved in criminal behavior. However, beyond a brief comment that more is involved than direct imitation, he did not explain what the mechanisms of learning are. These learning mechanisms were specified by Burgess and Akers (1966b) in the "differential association-reinforcement" theory of criminal behavior. Burgess and Akers proposed a full reformulation of Sutherland's theory that retained the principles of differential association, combining them with, and restating them in terms of, the learning principles that had been developed up to that time by behavioral psychologists. They retained the concepts of differential association and definitions from Sutherland's theory, but conceptualized them in more behavioral terms, and added concepts and propositions from behavioral learning theory. The main principle added was differential reinforcement, whereby operant behavior (the voluntary actions of the individual) is conditioned or shaped by rewards and punishments. But the learning principles on which Burgess and Akers drew also included the conditioning of involuntary reflex behavior, discriminative stimuli (the environmental and internal stimuli that provide cues or signals for behavior), schedules of reinforcement (the rate and ratio in which rewards and punishments follow behavioral responses), and other principles of behavior acquisition and modification.

Thus, Burgess and Akers revised Sutherland's nine-statement theory into seven statements by combining the first and eighth, dropping the ninth statement, and revising each of the statements in his theory using behavioral concepts and propositions (Burgess and Akers 1966b).

1. Criminal behavior is learned according to the principles of operant conditioning.

2. Criminal behavior is learned both in nonsocial situations that are reinforcing or discriminative and through that social interaction in which the behavior of other persons is reinforcing or discriminative for criminal behavior.

3. The principal part of the learning of criminal behavior occurs in those groups which comprise the individual's major source of reinforcement.

4. The learning of criminal behavior, including specific techniques, attitudes, and avoidance procedures, is a function of the effective and available reinforcers, and the existing reinforcement contingencies.

5. The specific class of behaviors that are learned and their frequency of occurrence are a function of the reinforcers which are effective and available, and the rules or norms by which these reinforcers are applied.

6. Criminal behavior is a function of norms that are discriminative for criminal behavior, the learning of which takes place when such behavior is more highly reinforced than noncriminal behavior.

7. The strength of criminal behavior is a direct function of the amount, frequency, and probability of its reinforcement.

The Central Concepts and Propositions of Social Learning Theory

Akers subsequently developed the reformulated theory referring to it as *social learning* and applying it to criminal, delinquent, and deviant behavior in general (Akers 1973; 1977; 1985; 1998). Rather than concentrate on Burgess and Akers' original seven statements, he explicated the theory primarily by identifying and explaining four central concepts: (1) differential association, (2) differential reinforcement, (3) definitions, and (4) imitation. He devised specific measures of these and other concepts, and tested central propositions about the effects of the social learning variables on crime and deviance (Akers et al. 1979; Akers 1985; Akers and Cochran 1985; Akers 1992; 1998). Akers' development of the theory—which includes such concepts as imitation, anticipated reinforcement, and self-reinforcement—makes social learning theory "soft behaviorism" (Akers 1985, 65) that is closer to the social and cognitive learning theories mentioned above, such as Albert Bandura's (1973; 1977; 1986; Bandura and Walters 1963), than to the orthodox operant behaviorism of B.F. Skinner (1953; 1959) with which Burgess and Akers began. Social learning theory retains all the differential association processes in Sutherland's theory (albeit clarified and somewhat modified) while adding the explanatory power of differential reinforcement and other principles of behavioral acquisition, continuation, and cessation (Akers 1985, 41). It offers an explanation of crime and deviance, which embraces variables that operate both to motivate and control criminal behavior, and both to promote and undermine conformity.

> [T]he principal behavioral effects come from interaction in or under the influence of those groups with which one is in differential association and which control sources and patterns of reinforcement, provide normative definitions, and expose one to behavioral models. . . .
>
> Deviant behavior can be expected to the extent that it has been differentially reinforced over alternative behavior (conforming or other deviant behavior) and is defined as desirable or justified when the individual is in a situation discriminative for the behavior. (Akers 1985, 57–58)

> The probability that persons will engage in criminal and deviant behavior is increased and the probability of their conforming to the norm is decreased when they differentially associate with others who commit criminal behavior and espouse definitions favorable to it, in-person or symbolically are relatively more exposed to salient criminal/deviant models, define it as desirable or justified in a situation discriminative for the behavior, and have received in the past and anticipate in the current or future situation relatively greater reward than punishment for the behavior. The probability of conforming behavior is increased and the probability of deviant behavior is decreased when the direction of these variables, on balance, is reversed. (Akers 1998, 50)

Differential Association. Differential association refers to the process whereby one is exposed to normative definitions that are relatively more favorable or unfavorable to illegal or to law-abiding behavior. Differential association has both behavioral *interactional* and *normative* dimensions. The interactional dimension is the direct association and interaction with others who engage in certain kinds of behavior, as well as the indirect association and identification with more distant reference groups. The normative dimension is the different patterns of norms, values, and attitudes to which an individual is exposed through this association.

The groups with which one is in differential association provide the major social contexts in which all the mechanisms of social learning operate. They not only expose one to definitions, they also present one with models to imitate and with differential reinforcement (source, schedule, value, and amount) for criminal or conforming behavior. The most important of these groups are the primary ones of family and friends, though they may also be secondary and reference groups. Neighbors, churches, school teachers, physicians, the law and authority figures, and other individuals and groups in the community (as well as mass media and other more remote sources of attitudes and models) have varying degrees of effect on the individual's propensity to commit criminal and delinquent behavior. Those associations which occur first (priority), last longer (duration), occur more frequently (frequency), and involve others with whom one has the more important or closer relationships (intensity) will have the greater effect.

Definitions. Definitions are one's own attitudes or meanings that one attaches to given behavior. That is, they are orientations, rationalizations, definitions of the situation, and other evaluative and moral attitudes that define the commission of an act as right or wrong, good or bad, desirable or undesirable, justified or unjustified.

In social learning theory, these definitions are both *general* and *specific*. General beliefs include religious, moral, and other conventional values and norms that are favorable to conforming behavior and unfavorable to committing any deviant or criminal acts. Specific definitions orient the person to particular acts or series of acts. Thus, one may believe that it is morally wrong to steal and that laws against theft should be obeyed, but at the same time one may see little wrong with smoking marijuana and rationalize that it is all right to violate laws against drug possession.

The greater the extent to which one holds attitudes that disapprove of certain acts, the less one is likely to engage in them. Conventional beliefs are *negative* toward criminal behavior. Conversely, the more one's own attitudes approve of a behavior, the greater the chances are that one will do it. Approving definitions favorable to the commission of criminal or deviant behavior are basically *positive* or *neutralizing*. Positive definitions are beliefs or attitudes that make the behavior morally desirable or wholly permissible. Neutralizing definitions favor the commission of crime by justifying or excusing it. They view the act as something that is probably undesirable but, given the situation, is nonetheless all right, justified, excusable, necessary, or not really bad to do. The concept of neutralizing definitions in social learning theory incorporates the notions of verbalizations, rationalizations, techniques

of neutralizations, accounts, disclaimers, and moral disengagement (Cressey 1953; Sykes and Matza 1957; Lyman and Scott 1970; Hewitt and Stokes 1975; Bandura 1990). Neutralizing attitudes include such beliefs as, "Everybody has a racket," "I can't help myself, I was born this way," "I am not at fault," "I am not responsible," "I was drunk and didn't know what I was doing," "I just blew my top," "They can afford it," "He deserved it," and other excuses and justification for committing deviant acts and victimizing others. These definitions favorable and unfavorable to criminal and delinquent behavior are developed through imitation and differential reinforcement. Cognitively, they provide a mind-set that makes one more willing to commit the act when the opportunity occurs. Behaviorally, they affect the commission of deviant or criminal behavior by acting as internal discriminative stimuli. Discriminative stimuli operate as cues or signals to the individual as to what responses are appropriate or expected in a given situation.

Some of the definitions favorable to deviance are intensely held radical ideologies and fervent moral stances that provide strong motivation for criminal acts of terrorism and law-violating acts of civil disobedience. For the most part, however, definitions favorable to crime and delinquency do not "require" or by themselves provide strong positive motivation for crime. Rather, they are conventional beliefs so weakly held that they provide no moral restraint or are positive or neutralizing attitudes that facilitate law violation in the right set of circumstances.

Differential Reinforcement. Differential reinforcement refers to the balance of anticipated or actual rewards and punishments that follow or are consequences of behavior. Whether individuals will refrain from or commit a crime at any given time (and whether they will continue or desist from doing so in the future) depends on the past, present, and anticipated future rewards and punishments for their actions.

The probability that an act will be committed or repeated is increased by rewarding outcomes or reactions to it (e.g., obtaining

approval, money, food, or pleasant feelings—positive reinforcement). The likelihood that an action will be taken is also enhanced when it allows the person to avoid or
escape aversive or unpleasant events—negative reinforcement. Punishment may also be
direct (positive), in which painful or unpleasant consequences are attached to a behavior; or indirect (negative), in which a reward or pleasant consequence is removed.
Just as there are modalities of association,
there are modalities of reinforcement—
amount, frequency, and probability. The
greater the value or amount of reinforcement for the person's behavior, the more frequently it is reinforced, and the higher the
probability that it will be reinforced (as balanced against alternative behavior), the
greater the likelihood that it will occur and
be repeated. The reinforcement process does
not operate in the social environment in a
simple either/or fashion. Rather, it operates
according to a "matching function" in which
the occurrence of, and changes in, each of
several different behaviors correlate with the
probability and amount of, and changes in,
the balance of reward and punishment attached to each behavior (Hamblin 1979;
Conger and Simons 1995).

Reinforcers and punishers can be
nonsocial, for example, the direct physical
effects of drugs and alcohol. However,
whether or not these effects are experienced
positively or negatively is contingent upon
previously learned expectations. Through
social reinforcement, one learns to interpret
the effects as pleasurable and enjoyable or as
frightening and unpleasant. Individuals can
learn without contact, directly or indirectly,
with social reinforcers and punishers. There
may be a physiological basis for the tendency of some individuals (such as those
prone to sensation-seeking) more than others to find certain forms of deviant behavior
intrinsically rewarding (Wood et al. 1995).
However, the theory proposes that most of
the learning in criminal and deviant behavior is the result of social exchange in which
the words, responses, presence, and behavior of other persons directly reinforce behavior, provide the setting for reinforcement
(discriminative stimuli), or serve as the con-

duit through which other social rewards and
punishers are delivered or made available.

The concept of social reinforcement (and
punishment) goes beyond the direct reactions of others present while an act is committed. It also includes the whole range of
actual and anticipated, tangible, and intan-
gible rewards valued in society or subgroups. Social rewards can be highly symbolic. Their reinforcing effects can come
from their fulfilling ideological, religious,
political, or other goals. Even those rewards
which we consider to be very tangible, such
as money and material possessions, gain
their reinforcing value from the prestige and
approval value they have in society.
Nonsocial reinforcement, therefore, is more
narrowly confined to unconditioned physiological and physical stimuli. In *self-reinforcement*, the individual exercises self-control,
reinforcing or punishing personal behavior
by taking the role of others, even when alone.

Imitation. Imitation refers to the engagement in behavior after the observation of
similar behavior in others. Whether or not
the behavior modeled by others will be imi-
tated is affected by the characteristics of the
models, the behavior observed, and the observed consequences of the behavior
(Bandura 1977). The observation of salient
models in primary groups and in the media
affects both prosocial and deviant behavior
(Donnerstein and Linz 1995). It is more important in the initial acquisition and performance of novel behavior than in the maintenance or cessation of behavioral patterns
once established, but it continues to have
some effect in maintaining behavior.

The Social Learning Process

These social learning variables are all part
of an underlying process that is operative in
each individual's learning history and in the
immediate situation in which an opportunity for a crime occurs. Akers stresses that
the social learning process includes reciprocal and feedback effects between the conforming or deviant behavior and the social
learning variables that produce and sustain
that behavior. This process is one in which
the balance of learned definitions, imitation

of criminal or deviant models, and the anticipated balance of reinforcement produces the initial delinquent or deviant act. The facilitative effects of these variables continue in the repetition of acts, although imitation becomes less important than it was in the first commission of the act. After initiation, the actual social and nonsocial reinforcers and punishers affect whether or not the acts will be repeated and at what level of frequency. Not only the behavior itself, but also the definitions are affected by the consequences of the initial act. Whether a deviant act will be committed in a situation that presents the opportunity depends on the learning history of the individual and the set of reinforcement contingencies in that situation.

> The actual social sanctions and other effects of engaging in the behavior may be perceived differently, but to the extent that they are more rewarding than alternative behavior, then the deviant behavior will be repeated under similar circumstances. Progression into more frequent or sustained patterns of deviant behavior is promoted [to the extent] that reinforcement, exposure to deviant models, and definitions are not offset by negative formal and informal sanctions and definitions. (Akers 1985, 60)

Thus, the real and perceived rewarding and punishing consequences of the behavior feedback onto the behavior to affect its occurrence. Also, the theory does not hypothesize that definitions favorable to law violation only precede and are unaffected by the initiation of criminal acts. Definitions may be applied by the individual retroactively to excuse or justify an act already committed. To the extent that such excuses successfully mitigate others' negative sanctions or one's self-punishment, however, they become cues for the repetition of deviant acts. At that point they precede the future commission of the acts.

Similarly, differential association with conforming and nonconforming others influences the individual's own attitudes and behavior, but these in turn can affect association and interaction with others. It is obvious that association, reinforcement of conforming or deviant behavior, deviant or conforming modeling, and exposure to definitions favorable or unfavorable to deviance occur within the family prior to the onset of delinquency. Although the behavior of children affects the socializing and disciplinary behavior of parents, the onset of delinquency by the children cannot precede and produce the presence of the child in the family (except in the unlikely case of the late-stage adoption of a child who is already delinquent and who is drawn to and chosen by deviant parents). One's own delinquency or conformity, however, can have an effect on choice of friends. Even though one may be attracted to deviant peer groups prior to becoming involved in delinquency, associations with peers and others are most often formed initially around attractions, friendships, and circumstances, such as neighborhood proximity, that have little to do directly with coinvolvement in some deviant behavior. However, after the associations have been established and the reinforcing or punishing consequences of the deviant behavior are experienced, both the continuation of old and the seeking of new associations (over which one has any choice) will themselves be affected. Whatever patterns of conforming and delinquent behavior that have an effect on peer associations are themselves learned from previous associations, models, and reinforcement. Also, the theory would predict that the frequency and seriousness of delinquency will increase after the deviant associations have begun and will decrease as the associations are reduced. Whatever the temporal ordering, differential association with deviant peers will have a causal effect on one's own delinquent behavior (just as one's actions will have an effect on one's peers).

> Therefore, both "selection" or "flocking" (tendency for persons to choose interaction with others with behavioral similarities) and "socialization" or "feathering" (tendency for persons who interact with one another to have mutual influence on one another's behavior) are part of the same overall social learning process and are explained by the same variables. A peer "socialization" process and a peer "selection" process in deviant behavior

are not mutually exclusive, but are simply the social learning process operating at different times. Arguments that social learning posits only the latter, that any evidence of selective mechanisms in deviant interaction runs counter to social learning theory or that social learning theory recognizes *only* a recursive, one-way causal effect of peers on delinquent behavior are wrong. (Akers 1998, 56)

Social Structure and Social Learning

Akers (1973; 1985; 1989; 1997) has often proposed that social learning is the process by which social structure affects the criminal or conforming behavior of individuals. Recently, he proposed the Social Structure and Social Learning (SSSL) model illustrated below (Akers 1998).

Its [the SSSL model] basic assumption is that social learning is the primary process linking social structure to individual behavior. Its main proposition is that variations in the social structure, culture, and locations of individuals and groups in the social system explain variations in

crime rates principally through their influence on differences among individuals on the social learning variables—mainly differential associations, differential reinforcement, imitation, and definitions favorable and unfavorable and other discriminative stimuli for crime. The social structural variables are indicators of the primary distal macro-level and meso-level causes of crime, while the social learning variables reflect the primary proximate causes of criminal behavior that mediate the relationship between social structure and crime rates. Some structural variables are not related to crime and do not explain the crime rate because they do not have a crime-relevant effect on the social learning variables. (Akers 1998, 322)

The society and community provide the general learning contexts for individuals. The family, peer groups, schools, churches, and other groups provide the more immediate contexts that promote or discourage the criminal or conforming behavior of the individual. Differences in the societal or group

Figure 1
Akers' SSSL Model: Social Structure and Social Learning in Crime

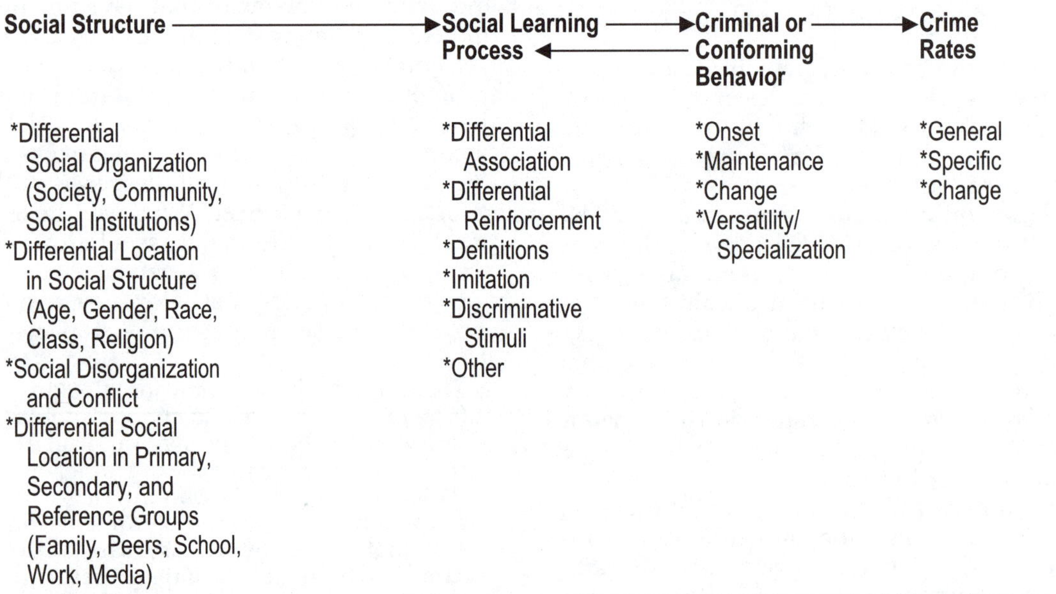

Social Structure ⟶	Social Learning Process ⟶ ⟵	Criminal or ⟶ Conforming Behavior	Crime Rates
*Differential Social Organization (Society, Community, Social Institutions) *Differential Location in Social Structure (Age, Gender, Race, Class, Religion) *Social Disorganization and Conflict *Differential Social Location in Primary, Secondary, and Reference Groups (Family, Peers, School, Work, Media)	*Differential Association *Differential Reinforcement *Definitions *Imitation *Discriminative Stimuli *Other	*Onset *Maintenance *Change *Versatility/ Specialization	*General *Specific *Change

Adapted from Akers (1998, 331).

rates of criminal behavior are a function of the extent to which cultural traditions, norms, social organization, and social control systems provide socialization, learning environments, reinforcement schedules, opportunities, and immediate situations conducive to conformity or deviance. Where individuals are located in the social structure is indicated by age, sex, race, class, and other sociodemographic and socioeconomic characteristics. These characteristics relate to the groups of which persons are likely to be members, with whom they interact, and how others around them are apt to respond to their behavior. These variables affect which behavioral models and normative patterns to which persons are exposed and the arrangements of reinforcement contingencies for conforming or law-violating behavior. Social learning is hypothesized as the behavioral process by which social disorganization, group/culture conflict or other social structural variables specified in macro-level theories induce or retard criminal actions in individuals.

Empirical Validity of Social Learning Theory

Research on Social Learning Variables

The testability of the basic behavioral learning principles incorporated in social learning theory has been challenged because they may be tautological. That is, the way in which the principle of reinforcement is often stated by behavioral psychologists makes the proposition true by definition. They define reinforcement by stating that it occurs whenever behavior has been strengthened and then state that, "If behavior is reinforced, it will be strengthened." If reinforcement means that behavior has been strengthened, then the hypothesis really means that, "If behavior is reinforced, it is reinforced." Hence, this is an obviously true statement that cannot be tested and explains nothing.

Another criticism charges that the theory hypothesizes a one-way temporal sequence in which differential peer association always precedes delinquency although, in truth, de-

linquency often precedes association with delinquent friends (Thornberry et al. 1994). Some have argued that the relationship between delinquency and peer associations is entirely spurious because both the delinquency and associations are caused by some third factor. Further, youth become delinquent first, and then seek out other delinquent youths as friends. Rather than delinquent associations causing delinquency, delinquency causes delinquent associations. Delinquents have an excess of delinquent friends simply because "birds of a feather flock together." Differential peer associations with delinquent friends is almost always a consequence rather than a cause of one's own behavior. Association with delinquent peers takes place only or mainly after peers have already independently established patterns of delinquent involvement. Choice of delinquent friends is based on similarity of delinquent behavior, and no deviance-relevant learning takes place in peer groups. From this point of view, therefore, association with delinquent friends has an effect on neither the onset nor acceleration, the continuation nor cessation, of delinquent behavior (Hirschi 1969; Gottfredson and Hirschi 1990; Sampson and Laub 1993). This would mean that it never happens that "if you lie down with dogs you get up with fleas."

These criticisms, however, may be off the mark. Burgess and Akers (1966a) identified the tautology problem and offered one solution to it. They separated the definitions of reinforcement and other behavioral concepts from nontautological, testable propositions in social learning theory and proposed criteria for falsifying those propositions. Others as well have proposed somewhat different solutions (Liska 1969; Chadwick-Jones 1976). Moreover, the variables in the process of reinforcement are always measured separately (and hence, nontautologically) from measures of crime and deviance in research on social learning theory.

Also, the theory does not propose a simple one-way causal process. As shown above, feedback effects are built into the social learning concepts (e.g., the reinforcement concept that behavior has rewarding or punishing consequences which feed back upon the behavior). Furthermore, the reciprocal relationship between one's own conduct and one's definitions and association with friends is clearly recognized in social learning theory. Therefore, the fact that delinquent behavior may develop independently of peer associations and have an effect on those associations does not contradict this theory. It would contradict the theory if the individual's level of delinquent involvement stayed the same or decreased, rather than increased, after greater association with delinquent peers. Research has not yet found this to be the case. Instead, the findings from several studies favor the process proposed by social learning theory, which recognizes both direct and reciprocal effects. (Andrews and Kandel 1979; Krohn et al. 1985; Sellers and Winfree 1990; Elliott and Menard 1991; Empey and Stafford 1991; Kandel and Davies 1991; Esbensen and Huizinga 1993; Warr 1993; Menard and Elliott 1994; Thornberry et al. 1994; Akers and Lee 1996).

Research testing the effects of social learning variables on criminal, delinquent, and deviant behavior has consistently found strong relationships in the theoretically expected direction between social learning variables and criminal, delinquent, and deviant behavior. When social learning theory is tested against other theories using the same data collected from the same samples, it is usually found to have greater support than the theories with which it is being compared (for instance, see Akers and Cochran 1985; White et al. 1986; Matsueda and Heimer 1987; Kandel and Davies 1991; McGee 1992; Benda 1994; Burton et al. 1994).

There is abundant evidence to show the significant impact on criminal and deviant behavior of differential association in primary groups such as family and peers. The role of the family is usually as a conventional socializer against delinquency and crime. It provides anticriminal definitions, conforming models, and the reinforcement of conformity through parental discipline; it promotes the development of self-control. But deviant behavior may be the outcome of internal family interaction (McCord 1991). It is directly affected by deviant parental models, ineffective and erratic parental supervision and discipline in the use of positive and negative sanctions, and the endorsement of values and attitudes favorable to deviance. Patterson has shown that the operation of social learning mechanisms in parent-child interaction is a strong predictor of conforming/deviant behavior (Patterson 1975; 1992; 1995; Snyder and Patterson 1995). In some cases, parents directly train their children to commit deviant behavior (Adler and Adler 1978). And in general, parental deviance and criminality is predictive of the children's future delinquency and crime (McCord 1991). Moreover, youngsters with delinquent siblings in the family are more likely to be delinquent, even when parental and other family characteristics are taken into account (Rowe and Gulley 1992; Lauritsen 1993).

Delinquent tendencies learned in the family may be exacerbated by differential peer association (Lauritsen 1993; Simons et al. 1994). Research has shown that the best single predictor of the onset, continuance, or desistance of crime and delinquency is differential association with conforming or law-violating peers. More frequent, longer-term, and closer association with peers who do not support deviant behavior is strongly correlated with conformity, while greater association with peers who commit and approve of delinquency is predictive of one's own delinquent behavior. It is in peer groups that the first availability and opportunity for delinquent acts are typically provided. Virtually every study that includes a peer association variable finds it to be significantly and usually most strongly related to delinquency, alcohol and drug use and abuse, adult crime, and other forms of deviant behavior. This and the other major predictors of delinquency (prior problem behavior, parental and family factors, deviant attitudes and beliefs, and low school achievement) reflect social learning processes of association, definitions, imitation, and reinforcement (Akers 1998). There is a sizable body of research literature that shows the importance of differential associations and definitions in explaining crime and delinquency. Many studies using direct measures of one or more of these social learning variables find that the theory's hypotheses are upheld. (Among these are Matsueda 1982; Winfree and Griffiths 1983; Elliott et al. 1985; Dembo et al. 1986; White et al. 1986; Sellers and Winfree 1990; Warr and Stafford 1991; McGee 1992; Stafford and Warr 1993; Winfree et al. 1993, 1994; Warr 1996). The theory is also supported by cross-cultural research (Kandel and Adler 1982: Junger-Tas 1992; Bruinsma 1992; Zhang and Messner 1995).

In addition to the positive findings by other researchers, support for the theory comes from research conducted by Akers and his associates in which all of the key social learning variables are measured. These include tests of social learning theory by itself and tests that directly compare its empirical validity with other theories. The first of these was a self-report questionnaire survey of adolescent substance abuse involving 3000 students in grades 7 through 12 in eight communities in three midwestern states (Akers et al. 1979). The second was a five-year longitudinal study of smoking among 2000 students in junior and senior high school in one midwest community (Akers and Lee 1996). The third project was a four-year longitudinal study of conforming and deviant drinking among elderly populations (1400 respondents) in four communities in Florida and New Jersey (Akers and La Greca 1991). The fourth and fifth studies were conducted on rape and sexual coercion among samples of 200 and 500 college males (Boeringer et al. 1991).

The findings in each of these studies demonstrated that the social learning variables of differential association, differential reinforcement, imitation, and definitions, singly and in combination, are strongly related to the various forms of deviant, delinquent, and criminal behavior studied. The social learning model produced high levels of explained variance, much more than other theoretical models with which it was compared. The combined effects of the social learning variables on adolescent alcohol and drug use and abuse are very strong. High amounts (from 31 percent to 68 percent) of the variance in these variables are accounted for by

the social learning variables. Social bonding models account for about 15 percent and anomie models account for less than 5 percent of the variance. Similarly, adolescent cigarette smoking is highly correlated with the social learning variables. These variables also predict quite well the maintenance of smoking over a three-year period. They fare less well, however, when predicting which of the initially abstinent youngsters will begin smoking in that same period. The social learning variables do a slightly better job of predicting the onset of smoking over a five-year period. The sequencing and reciprocal effects of social learning variables and smoking behavior over the five-year period are as predicted by the theory. The onset, frequency, and quantity of elderly drinking are highly correlated with social learning, and the theory also successfully accounts for problem drinking among the elderly. The social learning variables of association, reinforcement, definitions, and imitation explain the self-perceived likelihood of using force to gain sexual contact or committing rape by college men (55 percent explained variance). They also account for the actual use of drugs or alcohol, nonphysical coercion, and physical force by males to obtain sex (20 percent explained variance).

The research by Akers and others has also included some evidence on the hypothesized relationship between social structure and social learning. Differences in levels of marijuana and alcohol use among adolescents in four types of communities (farm, rural-nonfarm, suburban, and urban), and the differences in overall levels of drinking behavior among the elderly in four types of communities, are mediated by the social learning process. The relationship of age to adolescent substance use is almost completely explained by the operation of the social learning variables at different ages. Correlations of adolescent drug use and smoking, elderly alcohol abuse, and rape to sociodemographic variables of age, sex, race, and class are substantially reduced when the social learning variables are taken into account. These findings show results that are predicted by social learning theory. However, at this time, there has not been enough research to confirm the relationship between social learning and the social structure expected by the theory. (For more information on these and other studies on social learning theory, see Akers 1998.)

Applications of Social Learning Theory to Treatment and Prevention of Criminal and Delinquent Behavior

If criminal and delinquent behavior are acquired and sustained through the social learning process of association, imitation, definitions, and reinforcement in naturally occurring environments, then it should be possible to modify that behavior in a more law-abiding direction, at least to some extent, by deliberately manipulating that same process or the environmental contingencies that impinge on the process. This is the underlying assumption for the application of the social learning principles to prevent or change deviant behavior. Reliance on one or more of the explanatory variables in social learning theory forms the implicit or explicit theoretical basis (often in combination with guidelines from other theories) for many types of group therapies and self-help programs; positive peer counseling programs; gang interventions; family and school programs; teenage drug, alcohol, and delinquency prevention/education programs; and other private and public programs. A broad range of behavior modification programs based on learning principles, including both group and individually focused techniques, are operating in correctional, treatment, and community facilities for juveniles and adults. (See Bandura 1969; Stumphauzer 1986; Morris and Braukmann 1987; Akers 1992; Lundman 1993). It is not possible to review all these programs here, but some examples will serve to show how social learning principles have been put into practice in the treatment, control, and prevention of delinquency and crime.

One of the first programs to make use of created prosocial peer groups as an instrument to change delinquent behavior was the Highfields project (Weeks 1958). Highfields was a residential alternative treatment program for delinquent boys, who were allowed to go to school, jobs, and other activities during the day and return to the facility at night. There were no educational, vocational, or individual counseling activities. The principal treatment activity was regular participation in Guided Group Interaction (GGI) sessions. These were peer groups (guided by an adult staff) in which common problems could be discussed and a group atmosphere created that encouraged nondelinquent attitudes and behavior. At the end of the program, the boys had developed attitudes more favorable to obeying the law, and those who changed their attitudes the most were more likely to succeed and stay out of trouble later. However, the changes were not great and were more noticeable among the black than the white youth. The Highfields boys did slightly better than a comparison group of boys who had been committed to the state reformatory school (about 6 percent better when adjustments for in-program failures were made) in avoiding reinstitutionalization, but again this primarily was due to the differences observed among the black youth. The Essexfield program in the 1960s built upon the Highfields experience in using similar peer group sessions to affect changes in delinquent behavior and attitudes, but in a nonresidential setting. The Essexfield boys were not more successful in staying out of future trouble than those who were given either regular probation supervision or assigned to Highfields, but they did do somewhat better than those who had been sent to the state reform school, at least in the short run.

Donald R. Cressey (1955) proposed that both juvenile and adult treatment/reformation groups, whether naturally occurring or deliberately organized as an intervention technique, are based on the principle of differential association because such groups attempt to influence their members to acquire an excess of law-abiding over criminal definitions. The reformation process consists of some offenders joining with some noncriminals to change the criminal behavior of other offenders in the group by reducing their exposure to definitions favorable to crime and enhancing exposure to prosocial definitions. Cressey proposed that the effects of such a process comes from what he

termed *retroflexive reformation,* in which the offender really affects his own balance of definitions favorable and unfavorable to criminal behavior more than he affects other's. That is, in agreeing to participate in the group to help reform others, the criminal comes to accept the prosocial purpose and values of the group while alienating himself more from procriminal groups.

This retroflexive reformation may have been operating along with other processes in a prison and probation program designed and evaluated by Andrews (1980) who applied three major social learning principles of contingency (differential association and reinforcement), quality of interpersonal relationships, and self-management (self-monitoring and self-reinforcement) to change attitudes and behavior of convicted offenders. Manipulation of the associations and reinforcers produced significant changes toward less adherence to criminal definitions. Similarly, the more skilled the outside volunteers who worked with the groups were in creating cohesive groups (based on the principle of intensity of primary group relationships), the more likely they were to influence inmates to develop anticriminal attitudes. Adult probationers in the program developed greater respect for the law and were less likely to repeat criminal offenses. Prisoners assigned to self-management and prosocial-attitude groups changed their own attitudes in a law-abiding direction and had lower recidivism rates.

The Provo (Pinehills) Experiment (Empey and Erickson 1972) was also a program designed as a semiresidential alternative to regular juvenile probation or incarceration in a state training school for delinquent boys. It drew from the principle of differential association and the GGI techniques of Highfields with peer groups of adjudicated delinquents assigned to the Pinehills group home. With clear but nonintrusive guidance from adult counselors, a prosocial, antidelinquent peer culture was cultivated by giving the boys in the Pinehills program the authority to form groups, orient new boys coming in, set standards and rules for behavior, determine punishment for rule violation, and decide when a boy was ready to be released from Pinehills. The boys gained recognition and status in the group for conforming rather than antisocial behavior. The intent was to use this peer-group interaction to motivate adolescents toward conformity rather than deviance.

The Provo project was designed as an experimental evaluation study in which the juvenile court randomly assigned boys either to the Pinehills facility, to the secure-custody state training school, or to a regular juvenile probation caseload in the community. However, the experimental design did not last, as the judges began purposely rather than randomly assigned boys to Pinehills because they became convinced it was having a strong positive effect on the boys. This was based on early findings that the boys who participated in the peer groups at Pinehills were much less likely to be repeat offenders than those committed to the state institution. However, their recidivism was about the same as for the boys who had been placed on regular probation. The Provo project ended before planned because it ran into some opposition from county officials and received no additional public funding when its private funds ran out (Lundman 1993).

Later community based residential programs moved beyond the exclusive peer-group focus of the Highfields and Provo projects to create more of a family environment and to apply specifically the behavioral principle of differential reinforcement in order to modify behavior. The best example is Achievement Place (in the 1960s) and its successor Teaching Family (since the 1970s). The Teaching Family group homes became "perhaps the most systematic, and certainly the most long-lived and widely disseminated, application of the behavioral approach with juvenile offenders. . . ." (Braukmann and Wolf 1987, 135). The Teaching Family model involves a married couple ("teaching parents") and six to eight delinquent or "at-risk" youths living together as a family. A "token economy" is in effect in which the youth can earn reward-earning points by proper behavior or can have points taken away for improper behavior in the home and at school. The "parents" are responsible for teaching social, academic, and pre-vocational skills and maintaining mutually reinforcing relationships with the adolescents. But the youth in the home also operate a peer-oriented self-government system. Thus, in addition to the shaping of behavior by the teaching parents, the Teaching Family model promotes conforming behavior through exposure to a prosocial peer group.

Studies show that this model works quite well to maintain good behavior and retard delinquent behavior while in the Teaching Family. However, outcome evaluations in many states showed little difference in subsequent delinquent behavior between those who had been in the Teaching Family group homes and youth in control groups who had participated in other types of programs. The delinquency-inhibiting effects on the adolescents' behavior did not survive their release back to their families and environments, which did not have the systematic behavior modification used in the Family Teaching group homes (Braukmann and Wolf 1987).

Over the years, a great many other delinquency prevention and treatment programs based on peer-led and adult-led groups have been developed in school and community settings, often referred to as "positive peer culture" or "peer culture development" groups (Gorman and White 1995). The theoretical assumptions of these programs are that "if affiliating with negative role models encourages the development of deviant behaviors, then sufficient exposure to positive role models might diminish the appeal of deviant friends and hence foster more conventional social ties and behaviors" by gaining more social rewards for conformity than deviance (Gorman and White 1995, 138). Unfortunately, too many of these positive peer groups have been too artificial, made up of youth from diverse backgrounds who are not friends and have no real influence over one another. Therefore, the positive peer culture technique has not yet been shown to be effective in delinquency reduction or prevention (Gorman and White, 1995).

Alcohol and drug education/prevention programs have also employed various "social influence and skills" strategies and techniques that reflect social learning assumptions. They are designed to teach about the various influences that can affect drug-using and abstaining decisions (especially peers, media, family) and how to deal with and resist these influences. The effort is made to help develop and improve the social skills needed to interact with and get along with others without using substances. Sometimes, they are peer-oriented and involve student peers in role-playing, sociodrama, and modeling drug-free behavior (Akers 1992; Botvin et al. 1995; Gorman and White 1995).

They have increased knowledge about drugs and alcohol and changed attitudes toward drugs to some extent. Some also appear to have at least some modest, short-term effects on reducing or preventing drug behavior. The most effective programs in influencing both attitudes and behavior in the longer term are "peer programs" that include learning refusal, social, and life skills (Tobler 1986; Akers 1992; Botvin et al. 1995). It should be noted, however, that even the best programs have not had large effects and it has not been firmly established that social learning programs will produce the desired short-term and long-term effects of reductions in the prevalence of substance use not only among white, middle-class youth but also lower-class black and Hispanic youth.

Many of the programs reflective of social learning theory are also compatible with and reflect assumptions in social bonding theory, which emphasizes family supervision and discipline, the adolescent's attachment and relationships in the family and peer groups, commitment to conventionality, conventional beliefs, and involvement in conventional activities (Hirschi 1969), and with self-control theory (Gottfredson and Hirschi 1990), which also emphasizes family socialization and disciplinary practices.

For over two decades, Gerald R. Patterson and his colleagues at the Oregon Social Learning Center (Patterson 1975; Dishion et al. 1992; Patterson and Chamberlain 1994; Snyder and Patterson 1995) have been conducting research and testing social learning programs with families as well as peer groups to control or change delinquency and adolescent deviance. Their "coercive family" model proposes that the child's behavior and ways of relating to others are "learned in the family, and under more extreme conditions carry over to a child's interactions with others outside the family, including peers and teachers" (Dishion et al. 1992, 254–255).

> [P]oor parent discipline practices increase the likelihood of child coercive responses, and high rates of child coercion impede parents' attempts to provide evenhanded, consistent, and effective discipline. It is in this sense that parental limit-setting for behaviors such as lying, stealing, or fighting often fail in the quagmire of the child's arguments, excuses, and counteraccusations. (Dishion et al. 1992, 258)

Patterson's Adolescent Transition Program (ATP) involves targeting family management skills in parent-focus and parent- and teen-focus groups as compared to teen-focus and self-directed change. In the parent groups, several sessions are held with a therapist to help parents develop monitoring, discipline, problem-solving, and other effective parenting and family skills through instructions, discussion, and role-playing. The teen-focus group and individual sessions involve at-risk youth in the preteen and early adolescent years (ages 10 to 14) to develop and improve self-control, prosocial goals, prosocial peer associations, and communication skills. There were some reductions in antisocial behavior among the youth by the end of the program related to improvements in parental disciplinary and socialization practices (Dishion et al. 1992).

Most other family- and school-based programs directed toward children and youth also draw upon social learning theory, as well as from bonding theory and developmental psychology. These range from Head Start and other generalized children-oriented programs to early-intervention programs specifically geared to prevent misconduct and delinquency (OJJDP 1995). They attempt to reduce the "risk factors" and promote "protective factors" in the family, school, and community by providing social, economic, and learning resources to school children and families, often in minority, dis-

advantaged, and high-risk neighborhoods (Jessor 1996).

The best-known and most carefully done of these is the long-running Social Development Model (SDM) project of J. David Hawkins and his associates in Seattle (Weis and Hawkins 1981; Hawkins et al. 1991; 1992; Gorman and White 1995). The SDM combines strengthening attachment and commitment to the family and school (social bonding theory) with positive reinforcement, modeling, and learning prosocial attitudes and skills (social learning theory). The project aimed to develop strong bonds to family and school in childhood as protective factors against current misconduct and against future delinquency. These serve as preparation for learning prosocial skills, antidrug attitudes, and refusal behavior in later childhood and early adolescence.

In the SDM project, students entering the first grade were randomly assigned to "intervention" or to "control" classrooms in eight Seattle schools. Thereafter, students were added to both groups as they entered grades one to four. By the time the initial cohort of students entered the fifth grade, the program was expanded to include all fifth-grade students in 18 elementary schools. The program was meant to enhance opportunities, develop social skills, and provide rewards for good behavior in the classroom and families.

For the students in the intervention groups at school, the teachers utilized "proactive classroom management," interactive teaching, cooperative learning, and other innovative techniques to strengthen bonds to school and teach social skills for interacting properly with others. At the same time, parenting-skills training was offered on a voluntary basis to parents of students in grades one to three. This training involved parents' learning better to monitor their children's behavior, to teach normative expectations for the children, and to provide consistent discipline in applying positive reinforcement for desired behavior and negative consequences for undesirable behavior. Parents were also encouraged to increase shared family activities, involve their kids in family activities and times together, provide a positive home environment, and cooperate with teachers to develop the children's reading and math skills. The idea was not only to teach parents who may not be skillful in doing these things, but also to offer support for parents who are already doing them.

The program is ongoing and longer-term effectiveness will be tested later, but its progress thus far has been evaluated by comparing 199 students in the intervention group with 709 in the control group at the time they were in the fifth grade. Questionnaires were administered to the students asking them about perceived opportunities, social skills, prosocial and antisocial attitudes, attachment and rewarding experiences in the family and school, academic performance, peer interaction, as well the extent to which they had become involved in misbehavior at school or home, delinquent activity, and alcohol and drug use. Instructional practices of the teachers, family disciplinary practices, and family involvement were also measured.

The findings from the evaluation showed that the intervention group (20 percent) was somewhat less likely than the control group (27 percent) to have initiated alcohol use. Relatively fewer (45 percent) in the intervention group than in the control group (52 percent) had engaged in some other forms of misconduct or problem behavior. The intervention made the most difference for white boys, somewhat less difference for white and black girls, and no difference for black boys. The intervention group scored higher on commitment and attachment to school, but the control group actually did better on standardized academic achievement tests. The family intervention had small but statistically significant effects on the attitudes and behavior of the children (Hawkins et al. 1991; 1992).

Conclusion

Akers' social learning theory combines Sutherland's original differential association theory of criminal behavior with general behavioral learning principles. The theory proposes that criminal and delinquent behavior is acquired, repeated, and changed by the same process as conforming behavior.

While referring to all parts of the learning process, Akers' social learning theory in criminology has focused on the four major concepts of differential association, definitions, differential reinforcement, and imitation. The process based on these concepts will more likely produce behavior that violates social and legal norms than conforming behavior—when persons differentially associate with those who expose them to deviant patterns, when the deviant behavior is differentially reinforced over conforming behavior, when individuals are more exposed to deviant than conforming models, and when their own definitions favorably dispose them to commit deviant acts.

Social learning principles have been applied to treatment and prevention programs (mainly directed toward adolescents but also to adults) in peer, family, school, and institutional programs. There is evidence that some of these programs have been or can be effective, but at this time the empirical findings for many of the programs show modest and mixed success. However, the research evidence on how well the social learning theory explains crime and delinquency strongly supports the empirical validity of the theory. Research conducted over many years has consistently found that social learning is supported as an explanation of individual differences in delinquent and criminal behavior. The hypothesis that social learning processes mediate the effects of socio-demographic and community variables on deviant and conforming behavior has been infrequently studied, but the evidence so far suggests that it will also be upheld.

References

Adler, Patricia and Peter Adler. (1978). "Tinydopers: A case study of deviant socialization." *Symbolic Interaction*, 1:90–105.

Akers, Ronald L. (1973). *Deviant Behavior: A Social Learning Approach*. Belmont, CA: Wadsworth.

——. (1977). *Deviant Behavior: A Social Learning Approach*, Second Edition. Belmont, CA: Wadsworth.

——. (1985). *Deviant Behavior: A Social Learning Approach*, Third Edition. Belmont, CA: Wadsworth. Reprinted 1992. Fairfax, VA: Techbooks.

——. (1989). "A social behaviorist's perspective on integration of theories of crime and deviance." Pp. 23–36 in *Theoretical Integration in the Study of Deviance and Crime: Problems and Prospects*. S. Messner, M.D. Krohn, and A. Liska (eds.). Albany: State University of New York Press.

——. (1992). *Drugs, Alcohol, and Society: Social Structure, Process, and Policy*. Belmont, CA: Wadsworth.

——. (1997). *Criminological Theories: Introduction and Evaluation*, Second Edition. Los Angeles: Roxbury

——. (1998). *Social Learning and Social Structure: A General Theory of Crime and Deviance*. Boston: Northeastern University Press.

Akers, Ronald L. and John K. Cochran. (1985). "Adolescent marijuana use: A test of three theories of deviant behavior." *Deviant Behavior*, 6:323–346.

Akers, Ronald L., Marvin D. Krohn, Lonn Lanza-Kaduce, and Marcia Radosevich. (1979). "Social learning and deviant behavior: A specific test of a general theory." *American Sociological Review*, 44:635–655.

Akers, Ronald L. and Anthony J. La Greca. (1991). "Alcohol use among the elderly: Social learning, community context, and life events." Pp. 242–262 in *Society, Culture, and Drinking Patterns Re-examined*. D.J. Pittman and H.R. White (eds.). New Brunswick, NJ: Rutgers Center of Alcohol Studies.

Akers, Ronald L. and Gang Lee. (1996). "A longitudinal test of social learning theory: Adolescent smoking." *Journal of Drug Issues*, 26:317–343.

Andrews, D.A. (1980). "Some experimental investigations of the principles of differential association through deliberate manipulation of the structure of service systems." *American Sociological Review*, 45:448–462.

Andrews, Kenneth H. and Denise B. Kandel. (1979). "Attitude and behavior: A specification of the contingent consistency hypothesis." *American Sociological Review*, 44:298–310.

Bandura, Albert. (1969). *Principles of Behavior Modification*. New York: Holt, Rinehart, and Winston.

——. (1973). *Aggression: A Social Learning Analysis*. Englewood Cliffs, NJ: Prentice Hall.

——. (1977). *Social Learning Theory*. Englewood Cliffs, NJ: Prentice Hall.

——. (1986). *Social Foundations of Thought and Action: A Social Cognitive Theory*. Englewood Cliffs, NJ: Prentice Hall.

——. (1990). "Selective activation and disengagement of moral control." *Journal of Social Issues*, 46:27–46.

Bandura, Albert and Richard H. Walters. (1963). *Social Learning and Personality Development*. New York: Holt, Rinehart, and Winston.

Benda, Brent B. (1994). "Testing competing theoretical concepts: Adolescent alcohol consumption." *Deviant Behavior*, 15:375–396.

Boeringer, Scot, Constance L. Shehan, and Ronald L. Akers. (1991). "Social contexts and social learning in sexual coercion and aggression: Assessing the contribution of fraternity membership." *Family Relations*, 40:558–564.

Botvin, Gilbert J., Eli Baker, Linda Dusenbury, Elizabeth M. Botvin, and Tracy Diaz. (1995). "Long-term follow-up results of a randomized drug abuse prevention trial in a white middle-class population." *Journal of the American Medical Association*, 273:1106–1118.

Braukmann, Curtis J. and Montrose M. Wolf. (1987). "Behaviorally based group homes for juveniles offenders." Pp. 135–159 in *Behavioral Approaches to Crime and Delinquency: A Handbook of Application, Research, and Concepts*. E.K. Morris, and C.J. Braukmann (eds.). New York: Plenum.

Bruinsma, Gerben J.N. (1992). "Differential association theory reconsidered: An extension and its empirical test." *Journal of Quantitative Criminology*, 8:29–49.

Burgess, Robert L. and Ronald L. Akers. (1966a). "Are operant principles tautological?" *Psychological Record*, 16:305–312.

——. (1966b). "A differential association-reinforcement theory of criminal behavior." *Social Problems*, 14:128–147.

Burton, Velmer, Frances Cullen, and David Evans. (1994). "Reconsidering strain theory: Operationalization, rival theories, and adult criminality." *Journal of Quantitative Criminology*, 7:155–199.

Chadwick-Jones, J.K. (1976). *Social Exchange Theory: Its Structure and Influence in Social Psychology*. London: Academic.

Conger, Rand D. and Ronald L. Simons. (1995). "Life-course contingencies in the development of adolescent antisocial behavior: a matching law approach." Pp. 55–99 in *Developmental Theories of Crime and Delinquency*. T.P. Thornberry (ed.). New Brunswick, NJ: Transaction.

Cressey, Donald R. (1953). *Other People's Money*. Glencoe, IL: Free.

——. (1955). "Changing criminals: The application of the theory of differential association." *American Journal of Sociology*, 61:116–120.

Dembo, Richard, Gary Grandon, Lawrence La Voie, James Schmeidler,and William Burgos. (1986). "Parents and drugs revisited: Some further evidence in support of social learning theory." *Criminology*, 24:85–104.

Dishion, Thomas J., Gerald R. Patterson, and Kathryn A. Kavanagh. (1992). "An experimental test of the coercion model: Linking theory, measurement, and intervention." Pp. 253–282 in *Preventing Antisocial Behavior: Interventions from Birth Through Adolescence*. J. McCord and R.E. Tremblay (eds.). New York: Guilford.

Donnerstein, Edward and Daniel Linz. (1995). "The media." Pp. 237–266 in *Crime*. J.Q. Wilson and J. Petersilia (eds.). San Francisco: ICS.

Elliott, Delbert S., David Huizinga, and Suzanne S. Ageton. (1985). *Explaining Delinquency and Drug Use*. Beverly Hills, CA: Sage.

Elliott, Delbert S. and Scott Menard. (1991). "Delinquent friends and delinquent behavior: temporal and developmental patterns." Institute of Behavioral Science, University of Colorado.

Empey, LaMar T. and Maynard L. Erickson. (1972). *The Provo Experiment: Evaluating Community Control of Delinquency*. Lexington, MA: Lexington.

Empey, LaMar T. and Mark Stafford. (1991). *American Delinquency: Its Meaning and Construction*. Belmont, CA: Wadsworth.

Esbensen, Finn-Aage and David Huizinga. (1993). "Gangs, drugs, and delinquency in a survey of urban youth." *Criminology*, 31:565–590.

Gorman, D.M. and Helene Raskin White. (1995). "You can choose your friends, but do they choose your crime? Implications of differential association theories for crime prevention policy." Pp. 131–155 in *Crime and Public Policy: Putting Theory to Work*. H. Barlow (ed.). Boulder, CO: Westview.

Gottfredson, Michael and Travis Hirschi. (1990). *A General Theory of Crime*. Palo Alto, CA: Stanford University Press.

Hamblin, Robert L. (1979). "Behavioral choice and social reinforcement: Step function versus matching." *Social Forces*, 57:1141–1156.

Hawkins, J. David, Richard F. Catalano, Diane M. Morrison, Julie O'Donnell, Robert D. Abbott, and L. Edward Day. (1992). "The Seattle social development project: Effects of the first four years on protective factors and problem behaviors." Pp. 139–161 in *Preventing Antisocial Behavior: Interventions from Birth Through Adolescence*. J. McCord and R.E. Tremblay (eds.). New York: Guilford.

Hawkins, J. David, Elizabeth Von Cleve, and Richard F. Catalano, Jr. (1991). "Reducing early childhood aggression: Results of a primary prevention program." *Journal of the Academy of Child and Adolescent Psychiatry*, 30:208–217.

Hewitt, John P. and Randall Stokes. (1975). "Disclaimers." *American Sociological Review*, 40:1–11.

Hirschi, Travis. (1969). *Causes of Delinquency*. Berkeley: University of California Press.

Jessor, Richard. (1996). "Risk behavior in adolescence: A psychosocial framework for understanding and action." Pp. 138–143 in *Juvenile Delinquency*. J.G. Weis, R.D. Crutchfield, and G.S. Bridges (eds.). Thousand Oaks, CA: Pine Forge.

Jessor, Richard and Shirley L. Jessor. (1977). *Problem Behavior and Psychosocial Development*. New York: Academic.

Junger-Tas, Josine. (1992). "An empirical test of social control theory." *Journal of Quantitative Criminology*, 8:9–28.

Kandel, Denise and Israel Adler. (1982). "Socialization into marijuana use among French adolescents: A cross-cultural comparison with the United States." *Journal of Health and Social Behavior*, 23:295–309.

Kandel, Denise and Mark Davies. (1991). "Friendship networks, intimacy, and illicit drug use in young adulthood: A comparison of two competing theories." *Criminology*, 29:441–469.

Krohn, Marvin D., William F. Skinner, James L. Massey, and Ronald L. Akers. (1985). "Social learning theory and adolescent cigarette smoking: A longitudinal study." *Social Problem*, 32:455–473.

Lauritsen, Janet L. (1993). "Sibling resemblance in juvenile delinquency: Findings from the national youth survey." *Criminology*, 31:387–410.

Liska, Allen E. (1969). "Uses and misuses of tautologies in social psychology." *Sociometry*, 33:444–457.

Lundman, Richard J. (1993). *Prevention and Control of Juvenile Delinquency*, Second Edition. New York: Oxford University Press.

Lyman, Stanford M. and Marvin B. Scott. (1970). *A Sociology of the Absurd*. New York: Appleton-Century-Crofts.

Matsueda, Ross L. (1982). "Testing control theory and differential association." *American Sociological Review,* 47:489–504.

Matsueda, Ross L. and Karen Heimer. (1987). "Race, family structure, and delinquency: A test of differential association and social control theories." *American Sociological Review,* 52:826–840.

McCord, Joan. (1991). "Family relationships, juvenile delinquency, and adult criminality." *Criminology,* 29:397–418.

McGee, Zina T. (1992). "Social class differences in parental and peer influence on adolescent drug use." *Deviant Behavior,* 13:349–372.

Menard, Scott and Delbert S. Elliott. (1994). "Delinquent bonding, moral beliefs, and illegal behavior: A three-wave panel model." *Justice Quarterly,* 11:173–188.

Morris, Edward K. and Curtis J. Braukmann (eds.). (1987). *Behavioral Approaches to Crime and Delinquency: A Handbook of Application, Research, and Concepts.* New York: Plenum.

OJJDP, Office of Juvenile Justice and Delinquency Prevention. (1995). *Delinquency Prevention Works.* Washington, DC: U.S. Department of Justice.

——. (1975). *Families: Applications of Social Learning to Family Life.* Champaign, IL: Research.

Patterson, Gerald R. (1995). "Coercion as a basis for early age of onset for arrest." Pp. 81–105 in *Coercion and Punishment in Long-Term Perspectives.* Joan McCord (ed.). Cambridge: Cambridge University Press.

Patterson, G.R., D. Capaldi, and L. Bank. (1991). "The development and treatment of of childhood aggression." Pp. 139–168 in *The Development and Treatment of Childhood Aggression.* D. Pepler and R.K. Rubin (eds.). Hillsdale, NJ: Erlbaum.

Patterson, G.R. and Patricia Chamberlain. (1994). "A functional analysis of resistance during parent training therapy." *Clinical Psychology: Science and Practice,* 1:53–70.

Patterson, G.R., John B. Reid, and Thomas J. Dishion. (1992). *Antisocial Boys.* Eugene, OR: Castalia.

Patterson, G.R., J.B. Reid, R.Q. Jones, and R.E. Conger. (1975). *A Social Learning Approach to Family Intervention.* Vol. 1. Eugene, OR: Castalia.

Rotter, Julian. (1954). *Social Learning and Clinical Psychology.* Englewood Cliffs, NJ: Prentice Hall.

Rowe, David C. and Bill L. Gulley. (1992). "Sibling effects on substance use and delinquency." *Criminology,* 30:217–234.

Sampson, Robert J. and John H. Laub. (1993). *Crime in the Making: Pathways and Turning Points Through Life.* Cambridge: Harvard University Press.

Sellers, Christine S. and Thomas L. Winfree. (1990). "Differential associations and definitions: A panel study of youthful drinking behavior." *International Journal of the Addictions,* 25:755–771.

Simons, Ronald L., C. Wu, Rand D. Conger, and F.O. Lorenz. (1994). "Two routes to delinquency: Differences between early and late starters in the impact of parenting and deviant peers." *Criminology,* 32:247–276.

Skinner, B.F. (1953). *Science and Human Behavior.* New York: Macmillan.

Snyder, James J. and Gerald R. Patterson. (1995). "Individual differences in social aggression: A test of a reinforcement model of socialization in the natural environment." *Behavior Therapy,* 26:371–391.

——. (1959). *Cumulative Record.* New York: Appleton-Century-Crofts.

Stafford, Mark and Mark Warr. (1993). "A reconceptualization of general and specific deterrence." *Journal of Research in Crime and Delinquency,* 30:123–135.

Stumphauzer, Jerome S. (1986). *Helping Delinquents Change: A Treatment Manual of Social Learning Approaches.* New York: Hayworth.

Sutherland, Edwin H. (1947). *Principles of Criminology,* Fourth Edition. Philadelphia: Lippincott.

Sykes, Gresham and David Matza. (1957). "Techniques of neutralization: A theory of delinquency." *American Journal of Sociology,* 22:664–670.

Thornberry, Terence P., Alan J. Lizotte, Marvin D. Krohn, Margaret Farnworth, and Sung Joon Jang. (1994). "Delinquent peers, beliefs, and delinquent behavior: A longitudinal test of interactional theory." *Criminology,* 32:47–84.

Tobler, Nancy. (1986). "Meta-analysis of 143 adolescent drug prevention programs: Quantitative outcome results of program participants compared to a control or comparison group." *Journal of Drug Issues,* 16:537–567.

Warr, Mark. (1993). "Age, peers, and delinquency." *Criminology,* 31:17–40.

——. (1996). "Organization and instigation in delinquent groups." *Criminology,* 34:11–38.

Warr, Mark and Mark Stafford. (1991). "The influence of delinquent peers: What they think or what they do?" *Criminology,* 4:851–866.

Weis, Joseph G. and J. David Hawkins. (1981). "Preventing delinquency: The social development model," in *Preventing Delinquency*. Washington, DC: Government Printing Office.

Weeks, H. Ashley. (1958). *Youthful Offenders at Highfields*. Ann Arbor: University of Michigan Press.

White, Helene R., Valerie Johnson, and A. Horowitz. (1986). "An application of three deviance theories for adolescent substance use." *International Journal of the Addictions*, 21:347–366.

Winfree, L. Thomas, and Curt T. Griffiths. (1983). "Social learning and marijuana use: A trend study of deviant behavior in a rural middle school." *Rural Sociology*, 48:219–239.

Winfree, L. Thomas, G. Larry Mays, and Teresa Vigil-Backstrom. (1994). "Youth gangs and incarcerated delinquents: Exploring the ties between gang membership, delinquency, and social learning theory." *Justice Quarterly*, 11:229–256.

Winfree, L. Thomas, Christine Sellers, and Dennis L. Clason. (1993). "Social learning and adolescent deviance abstention: Toward understanding reasons for intiating, quitting, and avoiding drugs." *Journal of Quantitative Criminology*, 9:101–125.

Wood, Peter B., John K. Cochran, Betty Pfefferbaum, and Bruce J. Arneklev. (1995). "Sensation-seeking and delinquent substance use: An extension of learning theory." *Journal of Drug Issues*, 25:173–193.

Zhang, Lening and Steven F. Messner. (1995). "Family deviance and delinquency in China." *Criminology*, 33:359–388.

8

Labeling or Social Reaction Theories of Crime

Introduction

The positive school of criminology had a major impact on how scholars viewed crime. Although biological, psychological, and sociological versions of positivism exhibit profound differences, they also share important common conceptual ground. For example, each of these versions presumes a certain "correctness" about the legal order. That is, they all assume something is inherently bad about behaviors that are defined as crime by the substantive criminal law, and that there is agreement or consensus in society about the inappropriateness of those behaviors. Thus, positivism assumes that the rules or norms of a society are given and taken for granted, that substantial consensus exists about which behaviors are wrong and forbidden, and that the law accurately identifies only those behaviors that everyone agrees should merit social blame and punishment.

In the criminology literature, this view is referred to as the "normative view" of law. Its central premise is that the law reflects social agreement as to acts that should be declared wrong and harmful. Taking the content of the law for granted, the question that positivist criminologists of all stripes directed their attention to, then, is why do some people fail to conform their conduct to behavior that everyone agrees is bad and wrong? What causes people to act that way and break agreed-upon norms of behavior? The answer to that question could be found in persons' biological make-up, in their personalities, their family structures, types of neighbor-

hoods, or the kinds of friends they hang around with. What was seldom if ever questioned was the very foundation of the normative position on law: the belief that there was agreement or consensus in society about the definition of what constituted harmful, wrong, or criminal behavior. Law was accepted as given, as was the position that the state and its legal system operated to enforce the law when it was violated. What was unexamined, therefore, was any role that the state or agencies of the state may have in producing crime. David Matza (1969) eloquently described the positive criminologists' scientific posture of ignoring the role that the state (Leviathan, in his words after Hobbes [1651] and the Classical Theorists) may play in the generation of crime:

> The scholar's or scientist's way of becoming partially blind is, inadvertently perhaps, to structure fields of inquiry in such a way as to obscure obvious connections or to take the connections for granted and leave the matter at that. The great task of disconnection—it was arduous and time-consuming—fell to the positive school of criminology. Among their most notable accomplishments, the criminological positivists succeeded in what would seem the impossible. They separated the study of crime from the workings and theory of the state. That done, and the lesson extended to deviation generally, the agenda for research and scholarship for the next half-century was relatively clear, especially with regard to what would not be studied. Scientists of various persuasions thereafter wandered aimlessly, leaving just a few possibilities uncovered, considering how deviation was produced. Throughout, a main producer remained obscure, off-stage due to the fortunate manner in which fields of inquiry were divided. The role of the sovereign, and by extension, instituted authority was hardly considered in the study of deviant behavior. That lofty subject, unrelated to so seamy a matter as deviation, was to be studied in political science. There, as in the curriculum in government or political sociology, Leviathan had little bearing on ordinary criminals. And in criminology, the process of becoming an ordinary criminal was unre-

lated to the workings of the state. It was, it must be granted, a pretty neat division. . . .Until the relation between organized authority and crime became a topic of conjecture and research, a crucial part of the process of becoming deviant was omitted. (143–144)

In sum, Matza observed that positive criminologists became "blind" by restricting their study of crime to the criminal offender and her immediate surroundings, thereby deliberately ignoring the complicity of the state and state apparatuses in the production of crime and deviance.

Beginning in the mid-1960s, however, an emerging group of scholars gave much more serious attention to the following questions: (1) "What makes some kinds of acts and not others criminal or deviant?" and (2) "What makes some kinds of persons and not others criminal or deviant?" This group of scholars has been given various titles, but we think what describes them best are the names *labeling theory* or *social reaction theory*. The latter is particularly well suited to this group which tried to reorient the field of criminology away from a concern with what causes some people to do crime toward a greater concern with what happens when persons, especially those with power and authority, respond or react to some behavior in a negative manner. Instead of assuming that some acts are inherently or naturally bad and criminal, and then seeking to understand what causes some people to commit these acts, those in the social reaction tradition tried to understand why some behaviors are treated as if they were crimes and what happens when people with such are treated as if they were criminal. Rather than focusing on causation, then, these scholars were interested in social reactions to behavior. As we will see in this chapter, social reaction/labeling theory represents a major break with positivism on some important issues, not the least of which is the source of law.

The social reaction school of deviance became especially popular in the 1960s, but we can trace its history a little further back in time than that. Although he devoted relatively little space in his large criminology volume to the subject, Frank Tannenbaum

(1938) wrote that reactions by authorities to the annoying behavior and minor deviance of youths may turn "spunky" kids into "bad" kids, pushing them into serious and frequent criminal acts. However, the foundation for social reaction/labeling theory was probably laid down a little later by Edwin Lemert (1951) in his groundbreaking book, *Social Pathology*. But it was not until the 1960s that the theory really "caught on" and became a prominent theoretical perspective in the study of crime and deviance.

The fact that this social reaction theory or school of deviance became popular in the early and mid-1960s should not be too surprising. As you will see in this section, social reaction/labeling theory can be thought of as an "anti-authority" theory. It argues that the creation and enforcement of rules and laws is based, at least in part, on social and political power wherein those with power make and enforce rules against those who are poor, a minority, or socially and culturally outcast. And it argues that in trying to "do something about" crime and other kinds of deviance, the actions of organized authorities often make things worse. In other words, the state or government can make the lives of the deviants it processes even worse than they were before. This profound skepticism that government can do good, and more often than not does great harm, reflected the sentiments of a large number of people (crime and deviance scholars included) who were actively involved in antigovernment work of their own in the civil rights, antidraft, and antiVietnam War movements. The 1960s were a tumultuous period, but more importantly, a period when a large segment of the public had great doubts about the benevolence of their government. A theory whose foundation is built on that doubt was sure to become popular both in and out of the halls of academia.

As implied by the comments of Matza quoted above, one of the truly important contributions social reaction scholars made to the study of crime was putting directly under the microscope a "main producer" of crime that up to this point had received very little attention—Leviathan or the state. Before the work of the labeling or social reaction theorists, criminologists were not interested in the study of the state. This was the field of inquiry conceded to political scientists or political sociologists. But social reaction theorists made the simple observation that, after all, the state actually makes crime by deciding that some behaviors are so harmful or injurious that they deserve to be called criminal (rather than simply inappropriate behaviors or behaviors not to be tolerated), and it makes criminals by applying definitions of crime to people.

In bringing into full view the role of the state in the creation of laws that define deviance, social reaction theorists called attention to the role of power and conflict in deviance. They also raised the idea that although state agencies may intend to do good in their dealings with deviants (i.e., they may try to reform or rehabilitate them), what they may actually do is to move them closer to a life of crime. That is, these well-intentioned efforts to cure or reform may "tag" or label people as deviant or "not normal," with the consequence that others then begin to treat them as not normal. In turn, because others treat them as different, criminals and other deviants begin to think of themselves as not normal, and then act in accordance with this self-perception. What the labeling and social reaction scholars did, then, was to put on the table the following issue: "What happens when a society responds to deviance in a particular (usually negative) manner?" If nothing else, they raised some issues—such as the importance of social reactions to deviance and the role of conflict in deviance creation—that most criminologists previously had ignored or dramatically downplayed.

Levels of Social Reaction

Collective Rule-Making

As alluded to above, the theme that is absolutely central to social reaction/labeling theory is the process of social reaction that others have to our behavior. There are several different levels at which reactions to deviance may occur or play out. The first level refers to collective action or rule-making (Schur 1971). Some persons can be so offended by a particular kind of behavior that

they take it upon themselves to have this behavior given the official designation of "criminal" or "deviant." Notice again that in this relativistic view the "deviantness" or "criminality" of behavior is not a feature or inherent characteristic of the act, but is a label bestowed or given to the act by others. One of the first and most prominent labeling theorists, Howard S. Becker (1963), stated this principle as follows:

> *social groups create deviance by making the rules whose infraction constitutes deviance,* and by applying those rules to particular people. . . . From this point of view, deviance is not a quality of the act the person commits, but rather a consequence of the application by others and sanctions to an "offender.". . . Deviant behavior is behavior that people so label. . . . Whether an act is deviant, then, depends on how other people react to it. (9, 11)

One theme of the social reaction perspective, therefore, is that some behaviors get the label of "deviant" or "criminal" given to them because of the concerted efforts of some group. One, perhaps strong, way to state this is to say, "Look, virtually anything can be defined as deviant." It could be "A," "B," or even "C," and there is nothing distinctive about the act itself that can tell us it is deviant. It only becomes so when someone decides to treat it that way, and wants to convince us that he or she are correct in this characterization.

One example would be the efforts of groups like the Women's Christian Temperance Union (WCTU) and the Anti-Saloon League in the early 1900s to have the making and sale of alcohol characterized as a criminal act (Gusfield 1955; 1963). They believed that alcohol consumption was "evil," that it destroyed lives and families, that it threatened the very moral fabric of society. They also tried to convince others of this point of view, seeking to enlist people in their cause to "do something about" the problem of drinking. The work of prohibitionists was successful when in 1919 the United States Congress, over a Presidential veto, passed the National Prohibition Act (also called the Volstead Act). As the Eighteenth Amendment to the Constitution, this act prohibited both the importation and manufacturing of alcoholic beverages in the United States. In other words, the manufacturing and selling of alcoholic beverages, which had once been legal, suddenly became a criminal act. In support of the view that deviance is not an inherent quality of an act, social reaction scholars would note that the behavior of making liquor stayed the same after Prohibition. What changed was the reaction to the behavior.

Social reaction at the level of collective rule-making frequently occurs because of the special efforts of a very committed and dedicated person or core group of people who are active in the crusade to have a particular behavior declared deviant or criminal. This person or persons are instrumental in drawing attention to how bad the act it, how much harm it is producing, how its practitioners are morally degenerate, and that if nothing is done, how this behavior will do irreparable damage to society. In the social reaction literature, these very active and vocal opponents of a given behavior have been called *moral crusaders* or *moral entrepreneurs* (Becker 1963).

These terms are very descriptive. Both indicate that the field of battle is high moral ground. The struggle is whether or not a particular behavior is an immoral and reprehensible act, which requires that we "do something about it," or if it fits within the definition of tolerated, even if not approved, conduct. Social reaction at the level of collective rule-making is, therefore, a pitched battle over morality. The fact that it involves a crusade implies that there are two morally unequal and opposing forces—the forces of good and evil. In Western European history, the Crusades are portrayed as an attempt of godly Christian forces (the good) to recapture the holy lands from the pagan Ottoman Empire (the evil). A crusade, therefore, clearly implies a contest between holiness and profanity, and a moral crusade implies a struggle between the morally upright and the morally degenerate. The term *entrepreneur* suggests that someone organizes, directs, or creates interest in the movement to get a given behavior declared deviant or criminal. Just as a business entrepreneur

has to "drum up interest or business" for her product among potential customers who may initially lack such interest, the moral entrepreneur has to create concern over the alleged deviant behavior, thus generating public support to "do something about it."

In American history, there are numerous examples of moral crusades and moral entrepreneurs. We just mentioned the role of the WCTU in the early 1900s. One of the most vocal women in the WCTU, driving not only the Prohibition movement but also woman's suffrage and other progressive causes, was Carrie Nation. It was in no small measure due to her work in visibly demonstrating the evils of alcohol use (e.g., lost jobs, broken families, spirals into crime and prostitution) to the rest of the United States that the Prohibition movement was successful in criminalizing the manufacture of alcoholic beverages. In his book, *Outsiders*, Howard Becker (1963) detailed how the Federal Bureau of Narcotics and its commissioner, Harry Anslinger, were successful in portraying the marijuana user as a morally weak dissolute who was at the complete mercy of his habit, and marijuana itself as a "gateway" drug that led to other, more dangerous kinds of addictions and perversions. Through a vivid (supposedly actual) story of what happens to the marijuana user, Anslinger implied that it is nothing less than the destroyer of youth (Anslinger and Cooper 1937):

> An entire family was murdered by a youthful addict in Florida. When officers arrived at the home they found the youth staggering about in a human slaughterhouse. With an ax he had killed his father, mother, two brothers, and a sister. He seemed to be in a daze. . . . He had no recollection of having committed the multiple crime. The officers knew him ordinarily as a sane, rather quiet young man; now he was pitifully crazed. They sought the reason. The boy said he was in the habit of smoking something which youthful friends called "muggles," a childish name for marijuana. (150)

In part because of the successful demonization of marijuana use by the Federal Bureau of Narcotics, marijuana became a feared drug and marijuana users a threatening group. In response to this moral threat, the nonmedical use of marijuana and other opiate drugs was effectively criminalized with the passage in 1937 of the Marijuana Tax Act. Although legal in a majority of states as late as 1930, the use of marijuana now had become criminal behavior (Becker 1963, 135).

A final example of a moral crusade refers to the efforts undertaken by Anita Bryant against gays and lesbians. In 1977, the Miami-Dade County (Florida) Commission passed an ordinance that made it illegal to discriminate (e.g., in public-sector jobs or housing) on the basis of sexual orientation. Anita Bryant, a former Miss America and entertainer who also happened to be a devout Baptist, was appalled by the action of the county commission. She reasoned that, among other things, the ordinance sent the wrong message—that the county approved of homosexual conduct. She feared that because homosexuals could not reproduce, they would need to recruit new members into their ranks, most likely among innocent youths. She formed a group called "Save Our Children," who took it upon themselves to "educate" the Miami metropolitan area public about the dangers and threat posed by homosexuals, with the ultimate goal of having the ordinance repealed. Ms. Bryant's group was extremely well financed, connected, and organized (it was backed by both the Baptist and Roman Catholic churches in Miami-Dade County). Initially, her opponents were virtually unorganized. Only minor gay rights groups spoke on behalf of the ordinance and general tolerance for one's sexual orientation. With a well-organized campaign of speeches, demonstrations, and television opportunities, Bryant and Save Our Children succeeded in casting homosexuals as threatening to the moral fabric of society. In a referendum, the ordinance was overturned by a 2–1 vote. Ironically, the defeat of the referendum galvanized the gay and lesbian community. They became much more organized, developing their own message and campaign for civil rights. In December of 1998, the Miami-Dade County Commision passed a new antidiscrimination ordinance (by a 7–6 vote), which immediately was resisted by religious conservatives who promised to have the new ordinance repealed.

There is one important point not to get confused about. According to social reaction theory, deviance is frequently "created" when moral crusades led by moral entrepreneurs have certain behaviors, that were once at least tolerated, made into criminal or deviant acts. This does not mean, however, that just anyone can create a movement to criminalize acts that they find inappropriate, disgusting, or immoral. Not every moral crusade catches on and not everyone can be a successful moral entrepreneur. Not only did the social reaction theorists argue that deviance is often socially created by collective action, they also brought into focus the issue that this rule-making capacity is easier for some people than others.

Social reaction theorists were among the first scholars to highlight the importance of power differentials in the rule-creation process. By this they meant that the creation of rules (the criminalizing of once-tolerated acts) is generally in the hands of the politically, socially, culturally, and economically powerful and is directed against the powerless. The importance of political power in the making of rules was early on argued by Becker (1963): "[D]istinctions of age, sex, ethnicity, and class are all related to differences in power, which accounts for differences in the degree to which groups so distinguished can make rules for others" (18). What social reaction theorists argue, therefore, is that at the level of collective rule-making, efforts to create rules are more a matter of conflict than moral agreement or consensus. Rules are created when a *powerful* group feels threatened or offended by the actions of a powerless group and attempts to have their actions given the designation "criminal." Hence, the critical role played by power and conflict in deviance and crime is the second important theme of the social reaction perspective.

The foregoing perspective of the social reaction theorists was contrary to the positive criminologists' belief that law reflected consensus in society. John Lofland (1969) perhaps stated the social reaction point of view best when he observed that "deviance is the name of the conflict game in which individuals or loosely organized, small groups with little power are strongly feared by a well-organized, sizable minority or majority who have a large amount of power" (14). Lofland considers deviance to be the result of a "game" involving conflict between powerful and well-organized groups who fear or feel threatened by the actions of a smaller, less organized group with substantially less power.

Keep in mind that, at the time the Volstead Act was enacted, prohibition groups like the Anti-Saloon League and the WCTU were more powerful and far better organized than either the manufacturers or users of alcoholic beverages (prohibition groups had the support of the majority of the business community because their platform promised stable, i.e., nonalcoholic, workers). In addition, prohibition groups won the public relations campaign and succeeded in convincing others that alcohol use was a threat to the very existence of stable and orderly society. Because this well-organized, powerful, well-connected, and threatened group was able to characterize the behavior of those it was trying to "reform" as sinful, wasteful, and destructive, and the threatening group lacked the political muscle to fight back, the former was able to criminalize the making of alcohol. Similarly, the Federal Bureau of Narcotics was well-organized, politically powerful, and successful in promoting marijuana as a dangerous drug leading to untold human misery (prostitution, unemployment, addiction, even murder). Marijuana users had neither organization nor political power and could not stop the criminalizaton of the drug. Likewise, Anita Bryant and her religious supporters were for many years both more organized and more politically powerful than their opponents— individual homosexuals or loosely-knit groups of homosexuals. Bryant, like other moral entrepreneurs before her, was initially successful in portraying the behavior of her foes as morally degenerate and dangerous. As a result, she was successful in getting the public to think that homosexuals were threatening to recruit new members by infiltrating public schools and the Boy Scouts.

Organizational Processing

We have just argued that social reactions to behavior occur at the level of collective rule-making. There is a second level of possible social reaction. This occurs when agencies or institutions of society attempt to enforce or apply these rules to those who have committed the suspect behavior (Schur 1971). Once some behaviors are given the label of "deviant" or "criminal," a set of social institutions usually follow to make sure the rules are enforced. After all, the rules supposedly were created to "do something about" behavior that is viewed by some as threatening. Now, something must be done to or done about the threat.

Thus, enforcement agencies (e.g., the police, courts, regulatory agencies, correctional or mental health institutions) react to occurrences of the now deviant behavior by arresting, prosecuting, counseling, and institutionalizing. At this level, reactions are made by formal agents of social control in their official capacity against persons who allegedly have broken the rule. At the level of collective rule-making, then, social reactions are made to behaviors as deviant and rules are created. However, at the level of organizational processing, social reactions are made to individuals. That is, attempts are made to enforce the rule and apply a definition or label *to the person* as deviant. In the first instance, behaviors are given labels; and in the second, persons are given labels.

For example, in response to the Volstead Act, the Federal Bureau of Investigation (FBI) and agents of the Federal Bureau of Narcotics mounted enforcement campaigns against illegal "bootleggers" of alcohol. To show that they took this new enforcement task seriously, the FBI hired approximately 1,500 new agents for prohibition duty. Federal (and state) judicial and correctional systems had to respond in kind. Violation of the Volstead Act meant a federal criminal offense, trial in federal court, and possible confinement in a federal correctional facility. Other kinds of organizational processing of deviants occur everywhere in society. Civil courts have commitment hearings to determine if a person's behavior is so bizarre that he warrants treatment or confinement in a mental institution. Diagnostic committees in mental health facilities have case reviews, in which persons are examined and labeled as "manic depressive," "paranoid schizophrenic," or some other type. Juvenile courts have hearings to determine if a youth's conduct has placed him beyond the control of his parents, necessitating the label of "child in need of supervision" (CHIN), or even a delinquent.

Just as in the case of collective rule-making, the processing of would-be deviants at the organizational level is embedded in a context of power and conflict. In other words, the attempt at the organizational level to enforce rules and apply labels to persons is not generally a consensual process in which the ones being labeled agree with and support the claim being made by others that they are "deviant." The application of labels, no less than the creation of rules, occurs in the throes of conflict and within a context of power differentials. Recall Howard Becker's (1963) contention that social groups create deviance by reacting to the behavior of particular kinds of people. Elsewhere in his book, he states that rules are much more likely to be enforced against those who lack the resources and power to effectively resist such enforcement efforts:

> The degree to which an act will be treated as deviant depends also on who commits the act and who feels he has been harmed by it. Rules tend to be applied more to some persons than others. Studies of juvenile delinquency make the point clearly. Boys from middle-class areas do not get as far in the legal process when they are apprehended as do boys from slum areas. . . . Similarly, the law is differentially applied to Negroes and whites. (12–13)

Becker (1963) also makes the more general point that "[t]hose groups whose social position gives them weapons and power are best able to enforce their rules" (18). In addition to demographic characteristics of persons, John Lofland (1969, 61–103) has systematically discussed other personal attributes that make some people more or less vulnerable to attributions of being deviant, such as the strength of their self-esteem or personal identity and their social integration

in a conventional life with conventional others.

What Becker, Lofland, and other social reaction theorists are suggesting is that committing an act alleged to be wrong might be necessary, but it is not sufficient to account for enforcement or labeling. In addition to the commission of an act, labels are more likely to be applied and are more likely to be successfully applied against the powerless. This means that whether or not one is labeled a deviant or criminal depends in part upon what one has done, but also on who one is—one's social class, ethnicity, education, or family background. The position of social reactions theorists that rule enforcement is in part determined by one's personal attributes has been referred to in the literature as the "status characteristics hypothesis" (Paternoster and Iovanni 1989).

Thus, whether or not one will be successfully labeled by others is partially determined by one's status or status attributes (e.g., social class, gender, race). Because social reaction theorists themselves have at times been unclear about this hypothesis, let us unambiguously restate it. The hypothesis predicts that whether a label is successfully applied depends *in part* on what one has done and *in part* on who one is. The implication of this is that one can expect a more potent social reaction (a more serious label) from authorities when the alleged infraction is of a more serious rule, and when one either lacks the resources to resist the reaction or, because of one's personal attributes one more closely resembles commonly held stereotypes about the "kind of person" likely to break such a rule. Although there may be some disagreement over exactly how large of an influence social characteristics can be expected to have on labeling outcomes (Tittle 1980; Akers 1997), a reasonable point of departure would be to predict that such characteristics should have a substantial effect.

In their attention to the enforcement of rules and the imposition of labels, social reaction theorists have traditionally been concerned with the official enforcement of rules. That is, they have focused their attention on the attempt by formal institutions of social control to "do something about" deviance (e.g., the police, criminal and juvenile courts, correctional institutions, schools, mental health institutions, and social agencies for the disabled). Social control theorists have, therefore, been less concerned with informal attempts at labeling. By *informal* we mean labels that are applied by individual persons or agencies who do not have a formal social control function (e.g., parents, friends, employers, neighbors).

In part, this emphasis on formal labeling simply reflects the history of social reaction theory. One of the anchors of the theory was a paper by Harold Garfinkel (1956), who discussed the conditions that contributed to successful labeling. Labeling events were called "status degradation ceremonies," after which one's status shifts (shifted downward or degraded) from that of nondeviant to deviant. Garfinkel argued that these ceremonies are most effective in changing someone's status when they are formal, that is, when they involve an institutionalized ceremony, such as a public trial. This emphasis on formal deviance processing was later amplified in Matza's (1969) argument that the effective labeling of a person as deviant (a process he refers to as "signification") is enhanced when it is "organized authority" (the state or Leviathan) that is pitted against the individual:

> Persons unrelated to organized authority may signify too, but not so potently, or meaningfully. Besides, non-authoritative members of society who choose to collaborate in the control of deviant behavior can be discounted or otherwise put in place—at least in principle. . . . Confronted with a more mighty authority, however—Leviathan and not that of mere peers—the subject's authority over the process may be dwarfed. (144–145)

Because of this theoretical history, then, the kinds of social reactions that were traditionally studied were predominantly the formal social control reactions of organized authorities against subjects.

The tradition of examining the effect of formal reactions to deviance and crime, however, does not preclude the fact that informal social reactions are also important components of the theory. Professor Ross Matsueda (who provides an excellent overview of labeling theory in the next essay) has developed a labeling theory of informal social reactions that is anchored in symbolic interactionism—one of the theoretical roots of social reaction/labeling theory (see also Wellford and Triplett 1993). He demonstrates that a concern with the informal social reactions of parents, teachers, and friends is entirely compatible with social reaction theory. Moreover, he convincingly argues that informal sanctions are probably more important than formal sanctions because they are more often experienced than formal reactions, are given by social others who are more important in the lives of those being labeled than formal authorities, and generally occur earlier in life when they can have their greatest impression. We will return to Matsueda's theory of informal social reactions momentarily. For now, it is important simply to remember that social reactions to deviant and criminal behavior can consist of either the responses of formal institutions of control or the informal reactions of those closest to us in our daily lives.

The Reaction to the Reaction

There is a third level of reaction that is of concern to labeling and social reaction scholars. This occurs when those being labeled respond to the treatment of those who are enforcing the rule. In other words, the person to whom the label is applied has his or her own response to the reaction—a reaction to a reaction. According to the labeling/social reaction view, the process of being labeled as "deviant" or "criminal" is a harmful, malignant, or stigmatizing experience. Although those enforcing the rule may have intentions to reform, rehabilitate, or even cure the one at whom their efforts are directed, a likely consequence of these efforts is instead that things get worse—even more deviant acts are generated. This process was vividly described by Tannenbaum (1938) as the "dramatization of evil":

> The process of making the criminal, therefore, is a process of tagging, defining, identifying, making conscious and self-conscious; it becomes a way of stimulating, suggesting, and evoking the very traits that are complained of. If the the-

ory of relation of response to stimulus has any meaning, the entire process of dealing with the young delinquent is mischievous insofar as it identifies him to himself or to the environment as a delinquent person. The person becomes the thing he is described as being. (19–20)

What Tannenbaum is alluding to here is the fact that attempts to "do something about" the rule-breaking may backfire because people internalize the negative labels that others are imposing—labels like "troublemaker," "misfit," "delinquent," or "bully."

The most systematic attempt to explain and understand the reaction of the individual to the fact of her labeling was by Edwin Lemert (1951; 1967). Lemert drew an important distinction between what he called "primary" and "secondary deviance." Primary deviance occurs for a wide variety of reasons—cultural, psychological, social—and is responded to, if at all, by attempts to normalize the behavior (e.g., "boys will be boys"). Consequently, acts of primary deviance are not a part of one's self-identity, which instead continues to revolve around nondeviant roles and activities. When primary deviance is reacted to in a stigmatizing, negative manner, however, "problems of adjustment" are created.

The one being labeled a deviant, for example, is told that he is a special kind of person—the kind who would commit such a deviant act. That is, rather than being a conventional person who also happens to have broken a rule, the social reaction implies that he is a *rule-breaker*. Matza (1969) refers to this attempt to stick the one being labeled with a new identify as the "process of signification"—the person comes to signify or represent what she has done:

> To signify is to *stand for* in the sense of representing or exemplifying. . . . To be signified a thief does not assure the continuation of such pursuits; but it *does* add to the meaning of a theft in the life of the perpetrator, and it *does* add to the meaning of that person in the eyes of others. . . . To be signified a thief is to lose the blissful identity of one who among other things happens to have committed a theft. It is a

movement, however gradual, toward being a thief and representing theft. (156)

Perhaps you are wondering how one's identity in the eyes of others can change so dramatically as a result of being labeled. Becker (1963, 32–34) argued that this is because a deviant identity is a "master status." This is the most important status we have; all other roles or positions we occupy are secondary. The deviant identity is the one that others come to know us by. To follow up on Matza's example, we may be a husband, a father, a son, a carpenter, a Roman Catholic, a union member, a Democrat, a basketball fan, and someone convicted of selling drugs. But the experience of public trial and conviction for drug selling will turn us, in the eyes of those around us, first and foremost into a drug pusher. All other traits or statuses will recede into the background.

The problem for the one being labeled or signified, of course, is that she reacts to the new identity which has been attributed to her by others. The one being labeled, therefore, must come to terms with her new label or definition of herself. Although we may ignore or resist attempts to signify us as a thief, a prostitute, or a junkie (a process known as "deviance disavowal"), consistent and pervasive imputations that we are deviant make resistance difficult. Social reaction theory's anchor in symbolic interactionism implies a belief in the *social* self—that our identities about ourselves are strongly influenced by what others think about us.

This idea was developed by Charles H. Cooley (1902). He argued that our self-identity can best be understood as a "looking-glass self." We first create an identity about ourselves and take it out into the world, others react to what we have presented ourselves as being, and we then respond to the reactions of others. What we think about ourselves, then, is heavily influenced by what others think about us and what kind of person we are. When others refer to and treat us like deviants, it is difficult for us to resist these claims for long, and as a result we begin to think of ourselves as deviant. In the words of Tannenbaum quoted above, we become the thing that we are described as being. Alteration of one's own personal identity, then, is a consequence or problem of adjustment that those being labeled must deal with.

Another problem of being thought of as a deviant is that others may respond to one's new "spoiled" status by rejection and avoidance. This is described by labeling theorists in various ways. Becker (1963) notes that as a result of being labeled, one tends to be excluded from previous conventional groups, and more generally from the "ordinary means of carrying on the routines of everyday life open to most people" (34–35). This exclusion would include such things as jobs, families, neighborhood groups, and voluntary organizations. Becker also implies that an exclusion from the conventional routines of life is followed by a closer relationship with deviant routines and persons. Schur (1971, 69–81) captures much the same process with the term "role engulfment." He argues that when deviant labels are applied, persons being labeled tend to get "caught up in" the deviant role, organizing their identities and activities around that identity. That is, one who is role-engulfed both thinks of oneself and is thought of by others in terms of the deviant identity. Not surprisingly, one's behavior becomes similarly organized around the deviant role and increasingly distant from normal or conventional ones.

As one's personal identity moves toward a closer fit with a deviant one, and one finds oneself excluded from the conventional routines of life, there is a third consequence of deviant labeling—one is at greater risk of committing additional deviant or criminal acts. Rule-breaking that is done in response to deviant labeling is referred to as "secondary deviance." Although primary deviance is peripheral to one's identity, secondary deviance is a an expression of that identity. Lemert (1967, 63) noted that secondary deviance occurs in response to the problems that are created by social reactions to primary deviance. According to social reaction/labeling theory, then, reactions to deviant and criminal behavior create problems that those being labeled must react or respond to. One possible response is greater involvement with rule-breaking. The simple prediction is that social reactions to deviance create more deviance.

Recent Social Reaction/Labeling Theories

The immediate professional response to the arguments of social reaction/labeling theory was generally positive. We noted earlier how it resonated with many of the sentiments of the time, and it led to a great deal of theorizing and empirical work. The research testing various predictions of the theory is voluminous, yet there is really no solid consensus in the field as to the validity of the theory. There is even no real consensus as to the burden of proof the theory must meet (Tittle 1980; Paternoster and Iovanni 1989; Akers 1997). We refer the interested reader to treatments of this abundant literature (Gove 1980; Shoemaker 1996; Akers 1997).

Although labeling theory was at one time very popular among those who studied crime and deviance, its appeal began to wane by the early 1980s. In part, this reflected the hostility (at worst) or ambiguity (at best) of empirical research that did not soundly endorse the theory. Moreover, the antiestablishment sentiments of the theory did not resonate well among a new generation of scholars who had not experienced, and could not relate to, the political tumult of the 1960s. By the mid-1980s, then, social reaction/labeling theory had fallen into disfavor. Like many other criminological theories that have taken a beating, however, labeling theory was "down but not out." Recently, there has been a revival of interest and work in the social reaction tradition, which has involved significant modifications or extensions of the original theory.

One modification of the theory has been undertaken by Professor Ross Matsueda and his colleagues (Bartusch and Matsueda 1996; Heimer and Matsueda 1994; Matsueda 1992). Matsueda moved away from the traditional concern in social reaction theory with the reactions of organized authorities and developed an informal labeling theory. His informal social reaction theory posits that youths who commit initial acts of misbehavior frequently get reacted to or labeled by parents, neighbors, teachers, and other kids. These labels are not official designations of deviant character, but are informal "appraisals," such as "you are a bad kid" or "you are the type of kid who will wind up in jail one day." Those on the receiving end of these appraisals then begin to think of themselves in those very same terms. Ultimately, they act in ways (committing crimes) that are consistent with the appraisals of others and their own self-assessment. In this way, informal labels lead to additional misbehavior or secondary deviance. Matsueda and his colleagues have found empirical support for their informal social reaction theory (Bartusch and Matsueda 1996; Heimer and Matsueda, 1994; Matsueda 1992), and this work promises some very intriguing avenues for additional research. Professor Matsueda describes his theory in the next essay of this chapter.

A second revitalization of social reaction/labeling has involved a more fundamental reworking of the theory. According to deterrence theory, you will remember, social reactions to crime in the form of punishment should result in less crime. Both specific and general deterrence are premised on the idea that reactions by authorities will inhibit or lower crime. Labeling theory proffers the opposite prediction—that social reactions by organized authorities will most likely result in additional crime (secondary deviance). The empirical literature with respect to both theories has been equivocal—sometimes reactions to crime seems to reduce crime, sometimes they make things worse.

Theories independently developed by John Braithwaite (1989) and Lawrence W. Sherman (1993) have attempted to reconcile these inconsistent findings. Sherman has developed what he calls a "theory of criminal defiance." His theory attempts to explain why official criminal sanctions have a labeling effect and increase crime under some conditions, have a deterrent effect and decrease crime under other conditions, and at still other times seem to have no effect on crime. He argues that critical variables in the sanctioning process are the manner in which sanctions are imposed and the extent to which the one being sanctioned or labeled is integrated in (bonded to) a conventional life. Sanctions can be imposed either in a manner that shows deference to and respect for the rights and dignity of subjects, or they can be imposed in a way that shows authorities' contempt. When sanctions are imposed on subjects in a manner that shows respect for them as persons and treats them fairly, and when the authorities' condemnation is directed at the act rather than the person, the reaction is likely to be one of felt shame and remorse. Shame and remorse in turn are thought to be primary emotional states that drive the inhibition of crime. When sanctions are imposed disrespectfully, with little regard to their fairness, and when the label imposed by authorities is directed against the person, however, Sherman argues that subjects are more likely to react with their own anger and defiance. When angry and defiant subjects are also poorly bonded, in that they have few or weak connections to a conventional lifestyle (i.e., they are not married or unemployed), sanctions are likely to "boomerang" and lead to increased deviance. When angry and defiant subjects are well bonded or when well-bonded subjects are treated disrespectfully by authorities, however, sanctions are likely to have no effect on behavior because the defiant and deterrent effects are counterbalancing. When well-bonded subjects are treated with respect by authorities, sanctions are likely to reduce involvement in crime.

John Braithwaite (1989) has further developed the idea that the manner in which sanctions are imposed is a critical variable in social reaction kinds of theories. Braithwaite, too, argues that sanctions will have different effects depending on the manner in which they are imposed by authorities, whether the reaction by authorities targets the offending person or the offensive act, and the extent to which the subject is integrated in the social order. Professor Braithwaite will develop the full implications of his theory of reintegrative shaming in the last essay of this chapter.

References

Akers, Ronald L. (1997). *Criminological Theories*. Los Angeles: Roxbury.

Anslinger, Henry J. and Courtney Ryley Cooper. (1937). "Marijuana: Assassin of youth." *American Magazine*, 124:19–20, 150–153.

Bartusch, Dawn Jeglum and Ross L. Matsueda. (1996). "Gender, reflected appraisals and labeling: A cross-group test of an interactionist theory of delinquency." *Social Forces*, 75:145–177.

Becker, Howard S. (1963). *Outsiders*. New York: Free.

Braithwaite, John. (1989). *Crime, Shame, and Reintegration*. Cambridge: Cambridge University Press.

Cooley, Charles H. (1902). *Human Nature and the Social Order*. New York: Charles Scribner's Sons.

Garfinkel, Harold. (1956). "Conditions of successful degradation ceremonies." *American Journal of Sociology*, 61:420–424.

Gove, Walter R. (1980). *The Labeling of Deviance*, Second Edition. Beverly Hills, CA: Sage.

Gusfield, Joseph R. (1955). "Social structure and moral reform: A study of the women's Christian Temperance Union." *American Journal of Sociology*, 61:223.

——. (1963). *Symbolic Crusade: Politics and the American Temperance Movement*. Urbana: University of Illinois Press.

Heimer, Karen and Ross L. Matsueda. (1994). "Role-taking, role commitment, and delinquency: A theory of differential social control." *American Sociological Review*, 59:365–390.

Hobbes, Thomas. [1651] (1968). *Leviathan*. Baltimore, MD: Penguin.

Lemert, Edwin M. (1951). *Social Pathology*. New York: McGraw-Hill.

——. (1967). *Human Deviance, Social Problems, and Social Control*. Englewood Cliffs, NJ: Prentice Hall.

Lofland, John. (1969). *Deviance and Identity*. Englewood Cliff, NJ: Prentice Hall.

Matsueda, Ross L. (1992). "Reflected appraisals, parental labeling, and delinquency: Specifying a symbolic interactionist theory." *American Journal of Sociology*, 97:1577–1611.

Matza, David. (1969). *Becoming Deviant*. Englewood Cliffs, NJ: Prentice Hall.

Paternoster, Raymond and LeeAnn Iovanni. (1989). "The labeling perspective and delinquency: An elaboration of the theory and an assessment of the evidence." *Justice Quarterly*, 6:359–394.

Schur, Edwin. (1971). *Labeling Deviant Behavior*. New York: Harper and Row.

Sherman, Lawrence W. (1993). "Defiance, deterrence, and irrelevance: A theory of the criminal sanction." *Journal of Research in Crime and Delinquency*, 30:445–473.

Shoemaker, Donald J. (1996). *Theories of Delinquency*, Third Edition. New York: Oxford University Press.

Tannenbaum, Frank. (1938). *Crime and the Community*. Boston: Ginn.

Tittle, Charles R. (1980). "Labeling and crime: An empirical evaluation." Pp. 241–263 in *The Labeling of Deviance*, Second Edition. Walter R. Gove (ed.). Beverly Hills, CA: Sage.

Wellford, Charles F. and Ruth A. Triplett. (1993). "The future of labeling theory: Foundations and promises." Pp. 1–22 in *New Directions in Criminological Theory*. F. Adler and W.S. Laufer (eds.). New Brunswick, NJ: Transaction.

Labeling Theory

Historical Roots, Implications, and Recent Developments

Ross L. Matsueda
University of Washington

Unlike most criminological theories, which emphasize the causes of crime, labeling theory focuses mainly on societal reactions to deviance. Although there is much disagreement among labeling theorists—and many do not even consider labeling theory a formal theory—most would agree that this theory is interested in two major questions. First, how does society label some people and their behavior as deviant? Second, what effects do those labels have on the future lives and behavior of the people labeled? For example, they hypothesize that deviant labels are not randomly distributed to members of society, but are more likely to be applied to members of disadvantaged classes, ethnic minorities, and other groups that society has stereotyped as deviant or criminal. Labeling theory also hypothesizes that labeling can have negative consequences. Negative labeling—such as calling a child a "bad kid," placing unruly students in a special class for troublemakers, or publicizing an ex-convict's record—often stigmatizes individuals, lowers their self-esteem, and isolates them from conventional society. The result may be more deviant behavior than would have occurred without the labeling. That is, society's reaction may end up amplifying the very behavior it was trying to reduce. These ideas have led some labeling theorists to call for reducing negative labeling by diverting young offenders away from the juvenile justice system and deinstitutionalizing minor offenders and the nonchronically mentally ill.

This essay provides an overview of theoretical developments, empirical research, and policy implications of labeling theory. It begins by reviewing symbolic interactionism, the broader theoretical perspective underlying most labeling theories. It then discusses the early development of labeling theory, emphasizing the classic works of Tannenbaum, Lemert, Becker, and Erikson. This is followed by a discussion of the controversy over the treatment of actual deviance, criticisms from Neo-Marxist and positivist criminologists, and a summary of recent theoretical developments. Finally, the policy implications of judicious nonintervention are discussed in historical context.

Underlying Perspective: Symbolic Interactionism

Symbolic interactionism is a school of thought based on the ideas of George Herbert Mead, John Dewey, W.I. Thomas, Charles Horton Cooley, and others. Herbert Blumer (1969) coined the term "symbolic interactionism" to refer to the writings of these scholars, which emphasize the way that meaning arises in social interaction—through communication using language or symbols. Symbolic interaction follows the philosophical school of American pragmatism in assuming that social reality consists of an ongoing social process. We should think of society not as a static structure containing functional positions, but rather as an ever changing process. We should think of social order not as an unchanging property of society, but rather as an outcome of interaction and negotiation between members of society. Similarly, we should view members of society as not only adapting to a changing society and social groups, but also helping to constitute that society and those social groups. Symbolic interaction focuses on this process: How does society constrain the behavior and interactions of its members? How do members of society constitute larger social groups, institutions, and societies through social interaction?

Mead (1934), the most important figure among symbolic interactionists, argued that a fruitful approach to studying society begins with the analysis of face-to-face interaction. In a process of communication using language—or to use Mead's term, "significant symbols"—individuals construct shared meanings and understandings. Perhaps the most important shared meaning concerns one's self. The self arises through role-taking, the process of taking the role of the other, viewing one's self from the perspective of the other, and controlling one's behavior accordingly. For example, when adults call a youth a "bad kid" or a "troublemaker," the youth may come to see himself as a bad kid and a troublemaker. That is, he may eventually adopt an identity as a bad kid or troublemaker. In this way, the self is a reflection of appraisals made by significant others (Matsueda 1992). Cooley (1922) used the term "looking glass self" to emphasize that one's self is a reflection of how others see one.

Identity formation is influenced by important or significant others, who tend to be members of one's primary groups, such as families and peer groups. These are sometimes called "reference groups" because they provide an individual with a perspective, a point of reference, and a comparison group. By taking the roles of "reference" groups one comes to see oneself from the perspective of the group. In this way, symbolic interactionists link organized social groups to an individual's self or identity.

Symbolic interactionists hypothesize that the identity thus developed influences an individual's behavior. Mead argued that reflective behavior, which entails self-conscious thinking, is a form of role-taking that occurs in the mind and helps people consider the consequences of their behavior before acting overtly. Self-conscious consideration of alternative lines of action is like engaging in an imaginative rehearsal of the behavior in advance (Dewey 1922). Thus, people are able to rehearse various lines of action in their imagination before carrrying out the action in the same way that actors rehearse scenes before going onstage. Moreover, because role-taking involves considering lines of action from the standpoint of reference groups, it follows that behavior is controlled by social groups. Self-control is actually *social* control.

For example, a youth who has been insulted by a friend may consider responding by attacking the friend but then reconsider after taking the role of the other. The youth realizes that if he attacks, the friend will have a very negative view of him. Similarly, he realizes that if he does nothing—turns the other cheek—he will be viewed by his friend as a weak coward. Therefore, he responds by returning the insult rather than attacking. The act of thinking and contemplating is a form of role-taking in which an individual engages in an imaginative rehearsal of possible lines of action (attacking, insulting, or turning the other cheek).

In sum, symbolic interactionism implies that the labeling or appraising of indviduals by social groups affects the individuals' identities or social selves. Those identities, in turn, influence subsequent behavior through taking the role of the other. Therefore, symbolic interactionism provides a general behavioral theory from which the specific propositions of labeling theory can be derived. When viewed historically, it is clear that labeling theory is loosely based on interactionist principles.

The Early Development of Labeling Theory

Tannenbaum's Dramatization of Evil.

Perhaps the earliest formal statement of a labeling perspective was made by Frank Tannenbaum (1938) in his book, *Crime and the Community*. Tannenbaum described the labeling process, which he called a "dramatization of evil." He argued that conflict arises between the youth and community over the definition of the situation. From the standpoint of the youth, the acts of breaking windows, climbing over roofs, and stealing from street vendors are forms of play, adventure, excitement, mischief, and fun. But from the standpoint of the community, these acts are forms of evil, nuisance, and delinquency, which require control, chastisement, and punishment (Tannenbaum 1938, 17). Repeated conflict between the youth and community causes a polarization and hardening of attitudes. The community gradually shifts from defining specific acts as evil to defining *the individual* as an evil person. Soon the youth's companions, hang-outs, speech, and personality come to be regarded with suspicion. Conversely, the youth gradually shifts from feeling a sense of injustice at being wrongly accused and punished to recognizing that the community defines him (and his group) as different, bad, and evil. Ultimately, this causes a change in self-identity of the youth, who comes to view himself as delinquent, and further integrates him in gangs, which provide escape, security, and special rules. The youth responds to negative labeling in different ways, sometimes actively resisting with aggression, sometimes fleeing. At this point, the group is susceptible to the influence of older, more experienced youth, who may lead others into overt delinquent acts. The experiences of arrest and incarceration intensify the hardening process, opening up the world of the delinquent to formal institutions of control and other incarcerated youth.

Thus, for Tannenbaum, random acts of misbehavior in play groups come into conflict with the adult community, not because the children are inherently bad, but because their behaviors are disapproved by adults. This sets in motion a process of escalating conflict, in which adults label youths as "bad" or "evil," the youths respond with resistance within their groups, which in turn elicits increased negative labeling as adults combat the escalating deviance. Often, then, the "person becomes the thing he is described as being" (Tannenbaum 1938, 20). An important implication is that society's response to youth misbehavior, including deterrence and rehabilitation, often makes matters worse. At least in some cases, had the child's early acts of misbehavior been essentially ignored—attributed to normal child immaturity—the child would have aged out of the misbehavior, rather than continued on a path of crime.

Lemert's Primary and Secondary Deviance

These ideas lay dormant for over a decade until Edwin Lemert (1951) published *Social Pathology*, in which he distinguished his concepts, *primary* and *secondary deviance* (he clarified and developed these concepts later—see Lemert 1972). *Primary deviance* refers to initial acts of deviance that arise from original causes (some combination of social, cultural, psychological, and physiological factors) and have only minor consequences for a person's status, social relationships, or subsequent behavior. Primary deviance tends to be situational, transient, and idiosyncratic. Indeed, Lemert (1972, 42) noted that most people "violate many laws during their lifetimes" and that the average law-abiding citizen commits many acts that technically are crimes, but are not serious enough to be viewed as crimes either by the perpetrator or the rest of society. Secondary deviance, in contrast, is explicitly a response to societal reactions to deviance and has major consequences for a person's status, relationships, and future behavior. *Secondary deviance* occurs when society's response to initial deviance (e.g., stigmatization, punishment, and segregation) causes fundamental changes in the person's social roles, self-identity, and personality, resulting in additional deviant acts. Whereas the primary deviant's life and identity are organized around conventional activities, the "secondary deviant's life and identity are organized around the facts of deviance" (Lemert 1972, 41).

For Lemert, societal reactions are reactions to deviance—at least deviance in the eyes of the social audience. His work suggests that societal reactions can be warranted—society is responding to behaviors that are objectively deviant—or unwarranted—society is falsely responding to behaviors that are not objectively deviant. If society labels as a murderer one who has actually murdered another person, the label is warranted; if society labels as mentally ill a person who was merely eccentric, the label is unwarranted. Lemert (1951, 56) uses the term "putative deviation" to refer to "that portion of the societal reaction which has no foundation in objective behavior" (see Rains 1975). Presumably, the social scientist determines whether a societal reaction is putative or not.

But what does the "societal reaction" consist of? Society's responses to crime and deviance are highly variable, ranging from expression of moral indignation to formal prosecution, stigmatization, and punishment. The most important societal reaction is the response of social institutions of control, such as the criminal justice system and mental health institutions. Processing in the criminal justice system stigmatizes the individual at every stage—from arrest, detention and court appearance to sentencing and punishment. Lemert noted that often the labeled criminal faces more scrutiny and is subjected to more rules (e.g., terms of probation and parole; rules in jails and prisons) than other members of society. The process leading to secondary deviance is not immediate but unfolds over time, as primary deviants are reacted to by agents of social control with stigmatization and degradation ceremonies. The result may be that deviance becomes a "master status," organizing the deviant's life (Lofland 1969). Garfinkle (1956) argued that degradation ceremonies are likely to be successful when denouncers establish legitimacy with their audiences and demonstrate that the values shared by the audience are violated by the deviant. Goffman (1963) observed that "normals" often structure situations to avoid encounters with deviants because they fear "guilt by association." Thus, labeling can segregate individuals from conventional realms even in the absence of physical obstacles, such as incarceration. Goffman also discussed ways in which individuals seek to minimize their stigma by managing the information that others have about their identities. He made the important point that stigmatization is a process of interaction between society and the individual, in which the individual can play an important role in negotiating and combating stigma.

Becker's Moral Entrepreneurs, Moral Crusaders, and Outsiders

Labeling theory became a dominant view of deviance and crime with the simultaneous publication of Howard Becker's (1963) wide-ranging and highly-influential book, *Outsiders,* and related papers by Kitsuse (1962) and Erikson (1962). Working within the framework laid down by Tannenbaum and Lemert, Becker made three important con-

tributions to labeling theory. First, he offered an explicit labeling definition of deviance, arguing that "deviance is *not* a quality of the act the person commits, but rather a consequence of the application by others of rules and sanctions to an 'offender'" (Becker 1963, 9). Second, he expanded the definition of societal reactions to include the creation and enforcement of social rules. Third, he applied the ideas of symbolic interactionism to describe the process of becoming a marijuana user, developing a deviant culture, and initiating a deviant career.

Becker (1963) provided the first formal labeling definition of deviance. He rejected the conventional sociological view of deviance and crime as violations of agreed-upon rules or laws on two grounds. First, such a definition falsely assumed that rule-violators constitute a homogeneous category. Second, the definition failed to recognize that deviance is created by society. Becker (1963, 9) defined deviance explicitly as a social creation in which "social groups create deviance by making the rules whose infraction constitutes deviance, and by applying those rules to particular people and labeling them as outsiders." Society creates deviance not by creating the social institutions and structures that cause deviant behaviors—as etiological theories of crime argue. Instead, society creates deviance by making rules and then labeling people for violating those rules. This implies that deviance is a label and not a behavior: "The deviant is one to whom that label has successfully been applied; deviant behavior is behavior that people so label" (Becker 1963, 9). At the same time, Kitsuse (1962) defined deviance similarly as a process by which societal members "interpret behavior as deviant, define persons who so behave as a certain kind of deviant, and accord them the treatment considered appropriate to such deviants" (248). Similarly, Erikson (1962, 11) argued, "Deviance is not a property *inherent in* certain forms of behavior; it is a property *conferred upon* these forms by the audiences which directly or indirectly witness them."

Becker's second major contribution to labeling theory was his conceptualization of societal reactions to include rule-creation and enforcement. He argued that the process of creating deviance begins not at the point when a person is labeled deviant—for allegedly violating some rule—but rather earlier, when social groups and moral crusaders first create those rules. According to Becker (1963, 9), "Social groups create deviance by making the rules whose infraction constitutes deviance, and by applying those rules to particular people and labeling them as outsiders." Rule creation is often instigated by moral crusaders, who are typically from upper classes, motivated by humanitarian concerns, and preoccupied with the substantive ends (rather than the logistical means) of their crusades. Moral crusaders are able to bring attention to the problem using the mass media, and they can marshal support from various interest groups that may have disparate interests in seeing the rule passed. Moral crusades tend to have a natural history, beginning with a broad set of values (e.g., self-determination or the protestant work ethic), deriving specific rules based on those values, and then creating a bureaucratic system to enforce those rules.

Unlike moral crusadors, rule enforcers—police, prison guards, security—tend to be more concerned with the bureaucratic imperatives of enforcement than with the actual substantive content of the rules. Becker observed that rules are almost never enforced uniformly to all that fall under its purview, but rather are selectively enforced. Law is more likely to be enforced against members of the lower class or racial minorities, and the reasons for selective enforcement are highly variable, often having to do with organizational and political imperatives. Police may perceive that delinquency is largely a problem of lower-class minorities and view upper-class white rule-violators as good kids having adolescent fun. Or they may respond to public outcry against drunk driving or prostitution and step up their enforcement. In general, the powerless may be more susceptible to labeling than others, even when committing the same infractions. These observations led to a major distinguishing proposition of labeling theory: Social control institutions disproportionately label the disadvantaged and powerless as deviant, regardless of their actual behavior (e.g., Paternoster and Iovanni 1989). In this way, labeling theory became linked to group conflict theories, which depicted society as segmented into groups disagreeing over values and interests (see Quinney 1970). Laws were viewed as an expression of one group's political power over others, as powerful groups could mobilize the law to sanction behaviors that violate their interests or values. Law enforcement was also viewed as an expression of social control of politically weak groups.

The Functions of Deviance for Society

Kai T. Erikson's (1962) essay on the sociology of deviance adopted a structural functionalist view and asked the question, "What positive functions does deviance serve for a society?" In fact, this question had been raised long ago by two classic theorists, Emile Durkheim and George Herbert Mead.

For Durkheim (1964), punishment of criminals, which requires criminal acts that violate laws, serves two important functions in society. First, punishment reaffirms the moral order of society. Criminal acts violate values, beliefs, and morals that we hold dear, and thereby threaten the bonds that hold society together. Were criminals to go unpunished, the strength of our moral beliefs would be undermined. Therefore, society reacts with outrage and passion in punishing criminals, often doing so in a very public way to restore the moral order. Second, punishment also serves to define moral boundaries in a society. Durkheim (1964) notes that what constitutes crime and deviance is not universal, but instead is relative to a given society, and therefore, members of society face the problem of distinguishing deviant from normal behavior. This is done by punishing criminals: Each time an act is punished, the line between moral and immoral behavior is explicitly drawn for members of society. In a "society of saints," in which there is no violence, theft, or robbery, crime would still exist, but would consist of trivial acts of deviance that we would consider merely "bad taste." Those trivial acts would be punished, which reinforces the moral order and defines moral boundaries. This implies that a certain amount of deviant behavior is "normal"—that is, functional—for society.

Mead (1918) argued similarly that punishment allows members of society to express impulses of outrage and hostility at the criminal, impulses that are normally restrained. This expression creates a strong emotional identification with conventional society and a feeling of anger at the criminal.

Erikson (1962, 1966) drew on Durkheim's ideas, expanding labeling theory to include the functions of deviance for society. Erickson (1962) noted that labeling entails a very explicit process of selection. Even hardened criminals engage in conventional routine behavior most of their days, but society singles out a "moment of deviation"—a small island of deviance in a sea of conformity—as a measure of the kind of person he or she "really is." The result may be jail or hospitalization. Erikson (1966) argued that this very selective labeling occurs in a community to define moral boundaries and to develop a sense of group identity. Labeling is not a quiet act of censure, but rather, as in the case of a criminal trial, a public ceremony used to announce the moral boundary, degrade the deviant, and thereby reaffirm the community's identity. Moreover, Erikson (1966) observed that the societal reaction to deviance (e.g., imprisonment, rehabilitation, and hospitalization) does not appear to reform the criminal, which is their manifest or announced function. Instead it appears to stigmatize the offender, segregate the offender with other deviants, and set up a feeling of distrust by the community. The result is a self-fulfilling prophecy in which deviants return to their deviant ways. Erickson concludes that societal reactions must serve a latent function of providing society with a pool of offenders for defining moral boundaries and reaffirming social solidarity.

In his classic book, *Wayward Puritans*, Erikson (1966) examined the Salem witchcraft trials in early Puritan settlements, showing that criminal laws and punishments were invoked against alleged witches in ways that defined moral boundaries and reaffirmed the moral order. The Puritans expressed their emotional hysteria by condemning the witches and labeling them sinners, criminals, and agents of the devil, which in turn helped reduce the factions and tensions between Puritans, Quakers, and other religious sects within the society.

The Controversy Over Actual Deviance

Societal Reactions to What?

A significant controversy emerged over the role of actual deviance. If deviance is defined as a label or societal reaction, then is the initial behavior (i.e., "primary deviance" to use Lemert's term) that gave rise to the label *not* deviance? Becker (1963, 20) created confusion and controversy with his famous four-fold table of "types of deviant behavior," which cross-classifies "rule-breaking" behaviors by behaviors "perceived as deviant":

TYPES OF DEVIANT BEHAVIOR

	Obedient Behavior	Rule-Breaking Behavior
Perceived as Deviant	Falsely Accused	Pure Deviant
Not Perceived as Deviant	Conforming	Secret Deviant

Here, conforming and pure deviant behaviors are straightforward, the former referring to obedient behavior that is perceived as obedient, the latter referring to rule-violating behavior that is perceived as deviant. If deviance consisted only of these two categories—that is, if the other cells were zero—labeling would not be problematic, statistics on criminals would be accurate, and etiological and labeling theories would study the identical phenomenon. Of more interest are the diagonal cells. The falsely accused is the conforming person who is labeled a deviant anyway. This is the criminal who receives a "bum rap," the normal person whose eccentricity is viewed as mental illness, the effeminate heterosexual male who is labeled gay. The secret deviant is one who violates societal rules but is not labeled a deviant. Labeling theorists focused on this category, particularly with the finding of self-report delinquency surveys suggesting that virtually everyone admits to committing at least one act of delinquency. They concluded that deviance is largely a societal reaction rather than an objective act.

But this table contains an internal contradiction first pointed out by Gibbs (1966) and then Pollner (1974). If deviance is defined not as a "quality of the act," but rather as a reaction or label by a social group, then how can there be "obedient" or "rule-breaking" behavior independent of the societal reaction? Those are presumably "qualities of the act." Becker (1973) stated this concisely: "If we begin by saying that an act is deviant when it is so defined, what can it mean to call an act an instance of secret deviance? Since no one has defined it as deviance, it cannot, by definition, be deviant; but secret indicates that *we* know it is deviant, even if no one else does" (186–187).

This contradiction led to much confusion, out of which three distinct resolutions emerged. First, most labeling theorists followed Lemert's (1951, 1967) writings, which emphasized the societal reaction component of deviance but allowed for variation in whether the reaction is warranted or not. Indeed, he defined putative deviance as "that portion of societal reaction" that is unwarranted. Thus, blind persons are often treated as if they were hard of hearing even though their hearing is fine, and runaway girls are often treated as sexually delinquent when they are not. Becker (1963) himself adopted such a position, suggesting the term "potentially deviant" to apply to behaviors that have yet to be labeled deviant.

Second, others, including Kitsuse (1962), maintained a labeling definition of deviance as a label and not objective behavior, and simply refused to take a stance on "actual" deviance (Rains 1975). This led to studies of how the social reality of deviance is constructed in social interaction, including ethnomethodological studies (Garfinkle 1967), studies of the medicalization of deviance (Conrad and Schneider 1980), and studies of the social construction of social problems (Spector and Kitsuse 1977).

Third, still others have recently taken some of the ideas of labeling theory and incorporated them into new causal theories of not only secondary deviance, but also primary deviance and crime. These theories include Link's modified labeling theory of mental illness (Link et al. 1989), Braithwaite's (1989) theory of reintegrative shaming, and Matsueda and Heimer's symbolic interactionist theory of differential social control (Matsueda 1992; Heimer and Matsueda 1994).

Social Construction and Ethnomethodology

A version of labeling theory emerged in the 1970s associated with social constructionists and ethnomethodologists, who ignored the question of whether or not actual deviance existed prior to labeling, and instead studied the ways in which deviance is constructed or accomplished in interaction. Their views are sometimes called the "interpretive paradigm," in contrast to those of positivist criminologists who adhere to the "normative paradigm" (Wilson 1970; Hawkins and Tiedeman 1975). The normative paradigm assumes that actual deviance exists and can be identified by observing who violates norms. Norms or rules, in turn, have an objective existence independent of the occasions of their use, and can be identified by social scientists. For example, crimes of burglary exist and can be identified by violations of laws (which are norms) proscribing breaking and entering with intent to steal. These laws exist in objective reality and can be used to identify burglars, who are people who violate these laws.

The interpretive paradigm, in contrast, does not assume that actual deviance (or norms) exists, and instead studies the ways in which society creates deviance (and norms) in everyday interaction. Proponents of the interpretive paradigm argue that norms and laws—indeed all rules—are *inherently* vague and have to be interpreted to fit a given situation. We cannot specify a rule so precisely that it fits all possible cases. For example, burglary is defined by "breaking and entering a dwelling house with intent to steal," but whether a given case fits this definition is not always clear. Is an outhouse a dwelling house? Does stumbling drunk into a house constitute breaking and entering? Social constructionists argue that we use stereotypes and typifications to fit the legal category to a particular case. Often, practical considerations enter into the social construction. For example, based on stereotypes of burglars, prosecutors may view the stumbling drunk as "not really" a burglar, and not press charges in part because they do not want to waste valuable court time on the case, or they feel society would not benefit from a conviction. Thus, constructionists are not seeking to "discover" whether the behavior "really" is a burglary or not—as if the truth is out there waiting to be discovered. Instead, they want to study how it is that members of society interpret the law to fit the case and, in this way, construct the law in each situation.

Ethnomethodologists adopt the interpretive paradigm and examine structures of interaction, such as the organization of turn-taking in conversations, the three-part narrative structure in storytelling, and the structure of openings and closings in interactions. Within interactions, these structures are devices used by people to accomplish or display things we take for granted (e.g., gender, power, or deviance). From this standpoint deviance is not something external to the interaction, but rather is accomplished in the interaction through the use of conversation and language devices. For example, in labeling a child "mentally retarded," clinicians and parents often engage in a sequence of making, accepting, or disputing proposals concerning the child's problem. They succeed in achieving intersubjective agreement that there is some problem and then negotiate specific diagnoses or labels (Maynard 1991).

In an early classic study, Kitsuse and Cicourel (1963) argued that official statistics of deviant behavior reflect the process of labeling in society rather than the process producing actual deviant behavior in society. Official crime statistics, for example, are produced by a labeling process, which includes underreporting of crimes to police, recording and charging decisions made based on organizational reasons, and plea-bargaining decisions on the basis of extra-legal factors. Thus, official statistics are produced by "the actions taken by persons in the social system which define, classify and record certain behaviors as deviant" (Kitsuse and Cicourel 1963, 135). Therefore, these researchers advocated studies of the production of crime statistics by social organizations.

Sudnow (1965) followed this suggestion in a classic study of plea bargaining. He showed how prosecutors exercise their discretion in dealing with criminal cases, which are each unique and complex. That is, prosecutors construct typifications, called "normal crimes," then fit cases into these categories, as a way to deal with large groups of cases routinely and quickly. The typifications are based on the lawyer's common-sense knowledge, including statutory requirements of law, but also extralegal factors, such as characteristics of the offender, and the timing and location of the alleged offense. See Maynard (1988) for a review of other constructionist and ethnomethodological studies.

Medicalization of Deviance

An offshoot of labeling theory developed in the late 1970s is a view referred to as the "medicalization of deviance." Here the politics of labeling focuses on the power of the medical profession to succeed in defining a range of deviant acts as medical problems, which instantly transforms them into maladies treatable by the medical model. According to Conrad (1975), medicalization refers to the process of "defining behavior as a medical problem or illness and mandating or licensing the medical profession to provide some form of treatment for it"(12). Once the deviant act is medicalized, other approaches to explaining, treating, and policy making are ignored. Examples of medicalization include mental illness, alcoholism, drug addiction, violence, and hyperactivity. Each of these forms of deviance, according to Conrad (1975), has become increasingly defined as a medical problem. As genetic and pharmacological research has advanced, the scientific basis for defining the etiology (biochemical) and treatment (pharmacological) of deviance has gained strength.

In some instances, defining deviant behavior as an illness can reduce stigma by transforming deviance from a bad or evil act in need of punishment to a medical problem in need of treatment. For example, alcoholism is viewed as disease rather than a character defect; hyperactivity is viewed as an illness rather than a disruptive, disobedient child. But proponents of the medicalization perspective emphasize the negative consequences of medicalizing deviance (Conrad 1975; Conrad and Schneider 1980). Once defined as a medical problem, the deviant behavior is removed from public discourse and placed in the domain of the medical profession, which exerts a monopoly over illness by virtue of its power and prestige. The deviant behavior is individualized—divorced from its social context, separated from its political implications, and encapsulated in hospitals and clinics. Moreover, deviance is defined as an individual malady, never a social system problem. Hyperactivity is a neurological problem, not a problem of the organization of school classrooms; violence is a brain disorder or genetic defect, not a problem of social inequality; depression is a chemical disorder, not a problem of social relations. As a medical problem, the deviant behavior is subject to social controls that are legitimate in the world of medicine (e.g., using psychoactive drugs or psychosurgery). Some recent research has combined medicalization with ethnomethodology and examined the ways doctors and patients accomplish diagnoses of illnesses in conversation (e.g., Maynard 1991).

Critique of Labeling: Conflict, Marxist, and Positivist

During the late 1960s and early 1970s, labeling theory blossomed. Studies of labeling various forms of deviance proliferated. The journal *Social Problems* became a scholarly forum for developing the labeling perspective. The concept of labeling became widespread, entering into popular discourse, including policy debates about deviance. Public policies that drew upon labeling ideas were implemented (e.g., deinstitutionalization of the mentally ill and diversion of juvenile delinquents from the justice system). By the mid-1970s, however, labeling theory had come under attack. Criticism came from two disparate sources: conflict theorists and Neo-Marxists, who argued that labeling theory's analysis of rule-creation and enforcement was rudimentary, and positivist criminologists, who argued that actual deviance *did* exist and the concept of secondary deviance was empirically *bankrupt*.

Conflict Theory's Criticisms

Conflict theorists, such as Austin Turk (1969) and Richard Quinney (1970), extended labeling theory's views on the creation and selective enforcement of rules by developing a political theory of law. The conflict framework assumes that society is held together not by consensus over basic values and beliefs, but rather by coercion or force, as politically powerful groups impose their values on other groups. Thus, the dominant political groups, such as upper classes, use the law as a weapon against behaviors that violate their values and threaten their privileged positions. Criminals and deviants are simply people whose behaviors threaten the interests of the powerful classes. By passing laws against such threatening behaviors, the powerful are able to mobilize law enforcement and punishment against other classes, using their political power to protect their interests. The behaviors of the subordinate classes are not inherently deviant or criminal, but are simply labeled as deviant. Therefore, to understand crime we should look not at the criminal, but rather at the distribution of power in society that leads to the labeling of powerless individuals and their behaviors as criminal. Thus, rather than destroying labeling theory with a devastating critique, early conflict theorists merely chastised labeling theorists for not developing a political theory of society to augment the theory of labeling individuals.

Neo-Marxist Critique

Neo-Marxist and radical criminologists offered a more fundamental critique of labeling theory, as well as all other theories of crime. Marxian criminologists (e.g., Taylor, Walton, and Young 1973; Quinney 1977), argued that it was not enough to show that criminal laws reflected conflict and power differentials in society, as shown by labeling and conflict theories. Following the writings of Karl Marx, they argued that capitalism is at root an economic system of two opposing classes, capitalists and workers. Capitalists exploit labor by degrading their work, paying them less than they are worth, and reaping profits at their expense. They use the law to control the masses, punishing those who threaten the stability of the inequitable system. Thus, rather than serving society as a whole, criminal law is an instrument of the ruling capitalist class to secure the legitimacy of capitalism. The legal precepts of equality in the eyes of the law are false capitalist ideologies that serve to mystify the essence of capitalist laws as instruments of the ruling class (Quinney 1977).

According to Marxists, criminologists should be demystifying the law, showing how it favors not simply *some* powerful segments of the population, but rather a *specific* historical group, the capitalist class. Eventually, such critiques will help workers overcome false consciousness (based on capitalist ideologies), realize *class* consciousness (based on the interests of all workers), and recognize that they can rise up, overthrow capitalism, and effect a more equitable system. For Marxists, anything short of this actually works in capitalism's favor. That is, any discussion of crime and law that fails to critique capitalism will contribute to capitalist ideology by further mystifying the essence of law in capitalist society. Thus, Marxists maintain that labeling theorists have contributed to the mystification of law and deviance. This criticism of labeling theory assumes that Marxist theories reveal the true essence of society, law, and deviance under capitalism. Such an assumption received some support during the 1970s, but that support has waned today, making the Marxian critique of labeling less resonant.

Positivist Criminologists' Critique

A significant criticism of labeling, which survives today in many circles, was made during the 1970s by positivist criminologists—those who believe that the proper study of crime uses methods of the natural sciences, (e.g., formulating scientific laws, using the concept of causality, and using experimental or statistical methods). This criticism has two prongs: a criticism of the labeling definition of deviance for ignoring actual deviance, and a criticism of the propositions of labeling theory, including the hypotheses of deviance amplification and secondary deviance.

Gibbs (1966) first raised the problem of actual deviance, noting that if deviance is defined as a societal reaction, one cannot speak of actual deviance existing independent of societal reaction. He also noted that labeling theorists sometimes sound like they are proposing more than a mere definition of deviance, suggesting a theory of deviant behavior as well. If so, he maintained, labeling theory needs to explain why actual deviant *acts* (not *reactions*) are greater in some populations and not others, are committed by some individuals and not others, and are labeled in some societies but not others.

This led other positivist researchers to treat the processes of deviance amplification and secondary deviance as if they were causal explanations of deviant behavior. In many cases, critics of labeling theory claimed to have invalidated labeling theory but, in fact, tested hypotheses that did not follow from labeling theory (Paternoster and Iovanni 1989). For example, some argued that labeling theory implies that extralegal characteristics of offenders (e.g., race or social class) should be the most important factors explaining labeling outcomes, more important than actual rule-breaking. But labeling theories never argued that extralegal factors should have greater effects on labeling than actual rule-breaking. Instead, they simply pointed to the importance of power differentials in the labeling process (e.g., Becker 1963). Indeed, most labeling theorists responded that the labeling perspective is not a causal theory—that is, an organized set of propositions explaining some phenomena—but rather it is a perspective pointing to the importance of the labeling process (Becker 1973). Lemert (1976, 244) dryly noted that "labeling theory seems to be largely an invention of its critics."

Empirical Evidence on the Positivist Critique

Paternoster and Iovanni (1989) critically reviewed the empirical evidence on labeling theory, identifying two hypotheses from the theory: (1) the status characteristics hypothesis, in which attributes of individuals (e.g., age, gender, race, and class) affect who is labeled; and (2) the secondary deviance hypothesis, in which negative labels cause problems of adjustment and future deviance. In reviewing evidence on the former, Paternoster and Iovanni (1989) argued that labeling theory predicts that labeling will vary by status characteristics even when holding constant prior deviant behavior. However, labeling theory does not require that status characteristics are the most important determinant of labeling, as some researchers assume. Stated this way, the empirical research is equivocal. Studies examining the effect of status characteristics on police decisions to arrest, juvenile court intake decisions, and juvenile court sentencing dispositions sometimes find effects of age, social class, gender, and race, but at other times do not. Paternoster and Iovanni (1989) suggest that research needs to consider differential labeling throughout the juvenile justice system to examine effects that cumulate throughout the system; it should also examine the social conditions under which differential labeling may occur.

In reviewing research on secondary deviance, Paternoster and Iovanni (1989) argued that labeling theory implies more than the simple hypothesis that negative labeling increases future deviance. Rather, secondary deviance implies a long causal chain of events including negative labels, objective and perceived opportunities, and deviant self-images. Moreover, some groups (defined by gender, race, or class) may be more vulnerable to these events, implying that the chain of events may interact with social groups. Empirical research, however, has focused merely on the effects of labeling on future deviance or simply examined personal identity or objective opportunities separately. Such research has not contradicted labeling theory, but neither has it yielded strong support. A couple of recent exceptions are worth noting. Hagan and Palloni (1990) find that official labeling of parents and sons interacts to produce greater delinquency by sons. They conclude that labeling leads to the intergenerational reproduction of a criminal class, supporting the ideas of Mead, Tannenbaum, and Lemert. Triplett and Jarjoura (1994) estimate a multivariate causal model and find that informal labeling exerts significant effects on decisions to continue delinquency already initiated. Findings such as these support Paternoster and Iovanni's (1989, 387) call for a "revitalization of a labeling theory of delinquency" that specifies a causal model of delinquency and subjects that model to empirical test.

New Theoretical Directions

Three recent theoretical developments have moved beyond labeling theory's preoccupation with societal reactions to take up Paternoster and Iovanni's (1989) challenge to develop a theory of the causes of deviant behavior. In a sense, they have responded to Becker's (1973) call for an interactionist theory of all aspects of deviance, including primary deviance, reactions to deviance, and secondary deviance. Unlike previous theorizing in labeling theory, each of these three new approaches has taken a positivist, quantitative approach, seeking to explain behavior and test that explanation using experimental and statistical methods.

Link's Modified Labeling Theory

Bruce G. Link and his colleagues (1987; 1989) have focused on mental illness, beginning with Scheff's labeling theory of mental illness. Scheff (1966) outlined a classic labeling approach, in which a person's residual rule violation is labeled mentally ill by others based on societal conceptions of mental illness. That label, in turn, constrains the person to adopt the role of a mentally ill person, organize an identity around that role, and ultimately "become" mentally ill.

Link et al. (1989) expanded this theory to a five-stage process of labeling. The first stage concerns the extent to which people believe that mental patients will be devalued and discriminated against by the community. Both patients and other community members will learn these beliefs through socialization. The greater the belief, the more likely mental patients will expect to be rejected by the larger community, and the more likely other community members will in fact reject mental patients. In the second stage, the person is officially labeled by treatment agencies, which makes societal conceptions of mental illness relevant to the self. In the third stage, the patient responds to the labeling with three possible responses: (1) *secrecy*, whereby the treatment history is concealed from employers, relatives, or potential lovers; (2) *withdrawal*, in which the patient limits interactions to those who accept his illness and stigma; and (3) *education*, in which the patient seeks to minimize stigma by enlightening others. Each of these responses suggests that patients view stigmatization as a threat to self. The fourth stage entails negative consequences of labeling for a patient's life. This can arise directly from the patient's beliefs about the community's devaluation and discrimination against mental illness (stage 1) or from the patient's responses to labeling, secrecy, withdrawal, and education (stage 3). The result is that the patient may have lower self-esteem, fewer social network ties, and poorer job prospects. In the fifth stage, the patient is more vulnerable to repeat episodes of mental illness because of the labeling and stigma outlined in stages 1 to 4.

Link and his colleagues found empirical support for this perspective, particularly for steps 1 to 4 (Link et al. 1987; Link et al. 1989). Patients and nonpatients alike believe that mental patients will be rejected by most people. Patients believe that coping mechanisms, like secrecy and withdrawal, are advisable for mental patients. Finally, the stigma of labeling undermines social support derived from relations within households and the community.

Braithwaite's Reintegrative Shaming

A second new extension of a labeling perspective is John Braithwaite's (1989) work on shame and reintegration. Braithwaite (1989) began with the observation that labeling and stigmatization sometimes increase crime but sometimes do not. His theory of reintegrative shaming seeks to identify the conditions under which secondary deviance occurs. For Braithwaite, secondary deviance occurs when society's response to crime stigmatizes the offender as an outcast. Cut off from conventional society, the offender is likely to affiliate with subcultural groups—assuming the individual has a taste for subcultures and has the structural opportunity to affiliate—which further ensnares him or her in a web of criminality. In contrast, when community disapproval—particularly public shaming—is followed by reacceptance into the community of law-abiding citizens, the offender is likely to refrain from crime. Such reintegrative shaming effectively reduces crime because (1) social disapproval is embedded in the wider context of social acceptance, (2) the effect of stigmatization and being pushed into subcultures is minimized, and (3) shaming and repentance builds a person's conscience, which will reduce future crimes in the absence of external controls.

Braithwaite (1989) argued that reintegrative shaming is more effective in communitarian societies characterized by interdependencies based on mutual obligations, trust, and group loyalties. In these societies (e.g., Japan), members are intertwined in each other's lives and, thus, more likely to be affected by shaming and more likely to engage in shaming behavior. In contrast, within individualistic societies (e.g., the United States), members are less collectively-oriented and more individualistic; therefore, disintegrative shaming is more likely to occur, stigmatizing offenders and pushing them toward subcultures. Within a society, those individuals who are most committed to a community (e.g., women, employed, older persons) are more likely to engage in shaming behavior, more likely to respond to shaming themselves, and less likely to deviate. Finally, shaming begins in early child socialization within the family, as parents punish children while expressing love for the child rather than expressing rejection. As the child develops, socialization relies less on shaming and more on internal controls, appealing to the child's own standards of right and wrong and respect for others. Shaming is needed primarily as a refresher. Braithwaite's theory of reintegrative shaming seeks to integrate and synthesize traditional causal theories of crime. The concept of stigmatization is derived from labeling theory; the concept of subcultural affiliation is derived from differential association and differential opportunity theories; and the notion of commitment to society is derived from control theories. This general strategy of integration, which remains sensitive to contradictory underlying assumptions, is also pursued by Matsueda and his colleagues.

Matsueda and Heimer's Differential Social Control

Matsueda (1992) and his colleagues (Heimer and Matsueda 1994; Heimer 1996; Bartusch and Matsueda 1996) have returned to the symbolic interaction principles of George Herbert Mead in developing a theory of differential social control. Matsueda (1992) and Heimer and Matsueda (1994) argue that a symbolic interactionist theory of delinquency provides a theory of self-control and social control. As such, this theory explains not only labeling and secondary deviance, but primary deviance as well. They begin with the concept of role-taking. Most of our everyday activities are routine and do not require extensive thought. Behaviors are a stream of habitual responses to routine situations. When, however, a situation becomes problematic—that is, the habitual responses somehow do not work properly—the person stops and engages in reflection, thinking, or cognition. Cognition consists of role-taking: the person takes the role of the other, views the problematic situation from the standpoint of significant others, and evaluates alternative lines of action from the perspective of others. If the response to the line of action is negative, the person repeats the role-taking, considering another alternative from the standpoint of others. This serial process of cognition—which is an imaginative rehearsal of alternatives—continues until the problem is resolved.

This implies that the self is a reflection of appraisals made by significant others, including organized groups, such as generalized others and reference groups. Therefore, self-control is social control, because the self is derived from social groups. Matsueda (1992) incorporated labeling hypotheses into this perspective, arguing that negative labeling by parents, teachers, and peers would influence future delinquency through the role-taking process. Furthermore, the differential labeling process predicts that socially disadvantaged youth are more likely to be labeled in part because of their greater delinquency and in part because of discrimination. He found support for a causal chain in which parental appraisals affected reflected appraisals, which in turn affected delinquency, but failed to find strong support for the status characteristics hypothesis.

Heimer and Matsueda (1994) expanded the role-taking process to include learned definitions of delinquency, anticipated reactions to delinquency, and delinquent peers. They used the term "differential social control" to emphasize that social control through role-taking can take a conventional direction (e.g., when taking the role of conventional groups) or a criminal direction (e.g., when taking the role of criminal groups). They also showed how classical theories of crime could be viewed as special cases of differential social control. Their analyses supported the hypothesis that reflected appraisals, delinquent peers, and delinquent attitudes affect delinquent behavior. Heimer (1996) and Bartusch and Matsueda (1996) used differential social control to explain gender differences in delinquent behavior, finding that the role-taking process varied somewhat by gender, but explained substantial variance in the gender gap. Finally, Matsueda and Heimer (1997) applied it to explain delinquency through the life course, arguing that symbolic interaction provides a biosocial theory of development and selection into life-course roles, a theory of the meaning of those roles, and a theory of how those roles affect crime.

Policy Implications: Judicious Nonintervention

Theoretical Rationale of Nonintervention

The policy implications of labeling theory can be summarized by a general principle: "leave kids alone whenever possible" (Schur 1973, 155). Lemert (1967, 96) termed this *judicious nonintervention*, in which the juvenile court would be used as a last resort, after all other remedies had failed. Schur (1973) used the term *radical nonintervention* to emphasize not only a "hands off" policy, but also an emphasis on changing society (including some laws) over changing individual youth. More specific policies can be derived from the core propositions of labeling theory.

The proposition of secondary deviance stipulates that primary deviance often results in a dramatization of evil, which in turn leads to barriers to conventional groups, affiliation with delinquents, and a delinquent identity, all of which leads to secondary deviance. It follows that policies that minimize stigmatization of youth will minimize secondary deviance. Diversion programs, in which youth are diverted away from the juvenile justice system, reduce the stigmatizing effect of juvenile detention and the juvenile court. For those juveniles who are sent to court, replacing the label "juvenile delinquent" with something less maligning, such as "Persons in Need of Supervision," can reduce stigma; and expunging the court records of juveniles can reduce the consequences of stigma.

Deinstitutionalization of nonserious offenders—particularly status offenders—also reduces stigmatization, association with other inmates, and delinquent self-images. Similarly, "mainstreaming" nonchronic mental patients reduces the stigma of mental hospitalization, allowing patients to function in the community. An extreme version of these policies, consistent with the writings of Tannenbaum and Lemert, eliminates stigmatization by simply ignoring the alleged nonserious deviance. A less radical and more politically palatable version diverts the youth or mental patients into the community where they can be observed or treated outside of an institutional context.

The labeling proposition of rule creation postulates that moral entrepreneurs create rules favoring some groups (e.g., powerful groups) over others (e.g., powerless youth). Examples of the overreach of the juvenile justice system are status offenses—juvenile offenses (e.g., running away, smoking cigarettes, and violating curfews) that would not be criminal if committed by an adult. It follows that a policy of decriminalizing all but the most serious juvenile offenses would minimize the spiraling process of deviance amplification.

Finally, the proposition of selective enforcement specifies that moral enforcers selectively label and stigmatize individuals based on stereotypical conceptions of criminals. Those preconceptions typically depict criminals as members of disadvantaged classes, who lack political power to combat the label. The result is a self-fulfilling prophecy, in which the disadvantaged are disproportionately stigmatized and vulnerable to secondary deviance, which reaffirms the initial stereotype. It follows that policies that protect the rights of the accused, provide justice, and enforce due process will help reduce the disproportionate labeling and secondary deviance of disadvantaged groups. For example, the ideology of the juvenile court emphasized diagnosis and treatment of juvenile delinquents, in contrast to the due process and punishment of adult criminals. But the result was that many juveniles were denied their right to due process in the name of treatment. Reform of this system emphasized giving juveniles the same legal rights as adults.

Diversion and Deinstitutionalization Programs

Many of these policies were implemented to reform the juvenile justice system during the late 1960s. Indeed, labeling theory served as the theoretical justification for much of the reform movement. At this time, Lemert was a consultant to the President's Commission on Law Enforcement and Administration of Justice, Task Force on Juvenile Delinquency. His report drew explicitly on his writings on labeling theory, noting the potentially stigmatizing effects of the juvenile court and outlining his proposal of "judicious nonintervention" (Lemert 1967, 96–97). Here, Lemert suggested using the juvenile court as a last resort for extraordinary cases. Moreover, the juvenile court, he maintained, should be a court of law, administering justice and punishment, and not a treatment agency, attempting to remedy parent and child problems. The latter, according to Lemert (1967, 97), would result in a "conflict and confusion of values and objectives." Other chapters of the Task Force Report echoed the need for reforming the juvenile court to protect the rights of juveniles, reduce stigmatization, and eliminate the conflict of punitive and treatment responses.

The Task Force Report reflected increasing dissatisfaction with the traditional juvenile court, increasing calls for reform and increasing acceptance of labeling theory. It also helped promote these trends. While the report was being written, the Gault decision ruled that juveniles should enjoy many of the same rights to due process as adults, including the right to counsel, notice of charges, and trial by jury. Other decisions followed. The result was that after two decades, the juvenile court incorporated substantial formal legal procedures to protect the rights of juveniles.

Other policies, however, had equivocal effects. Juvenile diversion programs exploded during the 1970s, fostered in part by legislative mandates and federal and state funding. A diversion program takes an offender who otherwise would have entered (or penetrated deeper into) the justice system, and turns him or her away, either to no program, a community treatment program, or a treatment program run by the justice system (Klein 1979, 153). The judicious and radical nonintervention polices promoted by Lemert (1967) and Schur (1973) imply diverting first-time and nonserious offenders directly into the community. Diversion programs, however, rarely follow this policy of "true diversion" (Cressey and McDermott 1973). Instead, diversion typically entails some form of treatment, such as counseling, skill enhancement, and vocational training,

and often under the purview of juvenile justice personnel. More troubling is the finding that diversion programs often target juveniles who would otherwise merely be counseled by police, rather than referred to the justice system. Moreover, many referrals to diversion programs come not from the justice system, but rather from families, schools, and welfare agencies. Thus, rather than reducing the net of official labeling, the programs may have had the unintended consequence of increasing the net of official control (Klein 1979).

A similar story emerges with deinstitutionalization (Empey and Stafford 1991). The Juvenile Justice and Delinquency Prevention Act of 1974 provided federal funds to deinstitutionalize status offenders. In 1976, the national Deinstitutionalization of Status Offenders (DSO) program funded state and county programs to eliminate status offenders from detention and confinement. Such programs suffered from two weaknesses (Klein 1979). First, the definition of status offenders was not clear, particularly given that status offenders often commit delinquent acts. Second, juvenile justice personnel typically followed the conventional wisdom of using early identification and treatment. The result, according to Klein (1979, 162) was that deinstitutionalization programs were often applied to youth who were "not likely to have been institutionalized in any case." Maxson and Klein (1997) argued that more recent DSO programs fail to articulate state legislative mandates, and that agencies merely "do what they want to do." A similar conclusion may be drawn from programs to deinstitutionalize serious offenders, such as the Massachusetts Experiment, in which the Commissioner of Youth Services abruptly closed secure juvenile facilities throughout the state. Offenders were provided treatment in the community, but the result may be that "instead of having 'institution kids,' we now have a new group of 'agency kids'" (Coates, Miller, and Ohlin 1978).

In his assessment of diversion and deinstitutionalization programs, Klein (1979) noted a litany of obstacles to implementation, including ambiguous theory, vague definitions of appropriate clients and overall objectives, and resistance by entrenched juvenile justice professionals. He also identified three unintended consequences of such programs: alternative encapsulation, relabeling, and net-widening. Ironically, each of these consequences actually increased stigmatization and labeling, the very things the programs were intended to reduce. *Alternative encapsulation* refers to removing juveniles from the juvenile justice system only to insert them into another system—social service, mental health, or welfare. *Relabeling* refers to deliberately altering the juvenile's status to retain control. Status offenders may be reclassified downward as dependent and neglected or upward as delinquent. *Net-widening* refers to increasing rather than decreasing the reach of the juvenile justice system.

These processes make it difficult to evaluate diversion and deinstitutionalization programs, but it is probably safe to conclude that there exists no strong evidence of reduced re-offending for juveniles who have been diverted or deinstitutionalized over alternatives. Yet, research has not used strong research designs, such as randomized experiments, in which treatment groups (diverted or deinstitutionalized youth) are comparable to control groups (nondiverted and institutionalized youth). Moreover, the programs have not implemented the judicious nonintervention implied by labeling theory. It is probably safe to say that the policy implications of labeling theory have not been tested rigorously. Recent trends toward policies of getting tough on crime suggest movements away from nonintervention toward increased labeling. Singer (1996) uses the term *recriminalization* to refer to the recent phenomenon of treating violent juvenile offenders as adult criminals.

At best, a strategy of nonintervention will reduce labeling effects only. It will not change other social conditions—identified by recent causal theories reviewed above—that generate primary deviance, such as disorganized communities, weak social controls of families and schools, role-taking in delinquent peer groups, and learning of delinquency.

Conclusion

Labeling theory has been one of the most significant perspectives in the study of crime and deviance. The seminal ideas of Tannenbaum, Lemert, Becker, and Erikson led to an exciting set of studies and controversies in the 1970s. Research on the social construction of labeling, the medicalization of deviance, and the effects of labeling and stigmatization exploded during the 1970s. Policies of diversion and deinstitutionalization of juveniles were implemented in part to reduce the negative effects of labeling. The concept of labeling diffused from academic circles to policy circles, and eventually to everyday public discourse.

At the same time that labeling theory was enjoying attention from researchers and policy makers, it came under attack from critics. Many of the criticisms were based on misrepresentations and misunderstandings—treating labeling theory as if it were a formal scientific theory containing interrelated propositions, presuming that all labeling theories claimed to be an etiological theory of criminal behavior, and assuming that all labeling theories claimed that actual deviant behavior did not exist. Nevertheless, other criticisms were on firm ground, noting the inconsistent and contradictory treatment of actual deviance, identifying the limitations of labeling theory as a complete theory of deviance, and noting the limits of policies of nonintervention in dealing with crime.

A recent resurgence of interest in labeling theory has led to promising theoretical directions. Perhaps the most promising developments are those that draw out the insights of labeling theory, combine them with broader sociological theories of crime and deviance, and construct a causal theory of primary deviance, labeling, and secondary deviance. These integrated theories imply other policies beyond nonintervention, including primary prevention in communities, families, and schools as well as general deterrence. For example, Braithwaite's theory of reintegrative shaming suggests that social institutions should avoid the stigmatizing effects of harsh impersonal punishment characteristic of the criminal justice system. Such formal punishment should be used only as a last resort. In its place, other social institutions (families, schools, and communities) should express disapproval and shame the offender, while at the same time reaffirming affection and membership by reintegrating the offender back into society. This line of theorizing, research, and policy can be augmented by a second promising line of research that uses advances in sociolinguistics, conversation analysis, and language studies to identify the micro-structures of talk used to accomplish labeling in everyday interaction. These studies open up the black box of labeling dynamics by examining the moment-by-moment construction of labeling. Finally, a third line of research on the social and political processes leading to legislation can provide the context for studies of criminal behavior and the construction of labeling. For example, Singer (1996) traces the passage of New York's juvenile offender law, which sends 13 to 15-year-old violent offenders directly to criminal court, to mass media constructions of the problem of juvenile violence, and political considerations in a reelection year. Once passed, the law has a strong effect on labeling of juveniles, secondary deviance, and the symbolic meaning of juvenile violence in the community. More generally, theory and research along these three lines promise to breathe new life into the labeling perspective, integrate it into broader social science theory, and maintain the resurgence of interest in labeling theory.

References

Bartusch, Dawn Jeglum and Ross L. Matsueda. (1996). "Gender, reflected appraisals, and labeling: A cross-group test of an interactionist theory of delinquency." *Social Forces*, 75:145–177.

Becker, Howard S. (1963). *Outsiders: Studies in the Sociology of Deviance*. New York: Macmillan.

——. (1973). "Labeling theory reconsidered." Pp. 177–212 in *Outsiders: Studies in the Sociology of Deviance*. New York: Free.

Blumer, Herbert. (1969). *Symbolic Interaction: Perspective and Method*. Englewood Cliffs, NJ: Prentice Hall.

Braithwaite, John. (1989). *Crime, Shame, and Reintegration*. Cambridge: Cambridge University Press.

Coates, Robert B., Alden D. Miller, and Lloyd E. Ohlin. (1978). *Diversity in a Youth Correctional System: Handling Delinquents in Massachusetts*. Cambridge, MA: Ballinger.

Conrad, Peter. (1975). "The discovery of hyperkinesis: Notes on the medicalization of deviant behavior." *Social Problems*, 23:12–21.

Conrad, Peter and Joseph W. Schneider. (1980). *Deviance and Medicalization: From Badness to Sickness*. St. Louis, MO: Mosby.

Cooley, Charles H. (1922). *Human Nature and the Social Order*, Revised Edition. New York: Scribners.

Cressey, Donald R. and Robert A. McDermott. (1973). *Diversion from the Juvenile Justice System*. Ann Arbor: National Assessment of Juvenile Corrections, University of Michigan.

Dewey, John. (1922). *Human Nature and Conduct*. New York: Modern Library.

Durkheim, Emile. (1964). *The Division of Labor in Society*. New York: Free.

Empey, LaMar T. and Mark C. Stafford. (1991). *American Delinquency: Its Meaning and Construction*, Third Edition. Belmont, CA: Wadsworth.

Erikson, Kai T. (1962). "Notes on the sociology of deviance." *Social Problems*, 9:307–314.

——. (1966). *Wayward Puritans*. New York: Wiley.

Garfinkle, Harold. (1956). "Conditions of successful degradation ceremonies." *American Journal of Sociology*, 61:420–424.

——. (1967). *Studies in Ethnomethodology*. Englewood Cliffs, NJ: Prentice Hall.

Gibbs, Jack P. (1966). "Conceptions of deviant behavior: The new and the old." *Pacific Sociological Review*, 9:9–14.

Goffman, Erving. (1963). *Stigma: Notes on the Management of Spoiled Identity*. New York: Simon and Schuster.

Hagan, John and Alberto Palloni. (1990). "The social reproduction of a criminal class in working-class London, circa 1950–1980." *American Journal of Sociology*, 96:265–300.

Hawkins, Richard and Gary Tiedeman. (1975). *The Creation of Deviance: Interpersonal and Organizational Determinants*. Columbus, OH: Merrill.

Heimer, Karen. (1996). "Gender, interaction, and delinquency: Testing a theory of differential social control." *Social Psychology Quarterly*, 59:39–61.

Heimer, Karen and Ross L. Matsueda. (1994). "Role-taking, role-commitment, and delinquency: A theory of differential social control." *American Sociological Review*, 59:365–390.

Kitsuse, John I. (1962). "Societal reaction to deviant behavior: Problems of theory and method." *Social Problems*, 9:247–256.

Kitsuse, John I. and Aaron V. Cicourel. (1963). "A note on the use of official statistics." *Social Problems*, 11:131–139.

Klein, Malcolm W. (1979). "Deinstitutionalization and diversion of juvenile offenders: A litany of impediments." Pp. 145–201 in *Crime and Justice: An Annual Review of Research*, Vol. 1. N. Morris and M. Tonry (eds.). Chicago: University of Chicago Press.

Lemert, Edwin M. (1951). *Social Pathology: A Systematic Approach to the Theory of Sociopathic Behavior*. New York: McGraw-Hill.

——. (1967). "The juvenile court—quest and realities." Pp. 91–106 in President's Commission on Law Enforcement and Administration of Justice, *Task Force Report: Juvenile Delinquency and Youth Crime*. Washington, DC: Government Printing Office.

——. (1972). *Human Deviance, Social Problems, and Social Control*, Second Edition. Englewood Cliffs, NJ: Prentice Hall.

——. (1976). "Response to Critics, Feedback and Choice." Pp. 244–249 in *The Uses of Controversy in Sociology*. L. Coser and O. Larsen (eds.). New York: Macmillan.

Link, Bruce G., Francis T. Cullen, James Frank, and John Wozniak. (1987). "The social rejection of ex-mental patients: Understanding why labels matter." *American Journal of Sociology*, 92:1461–1500.

Link, Bruce G., Francis T. Cullen, Elmer Struening, Patrick E. Shrout, and Bruce P. Dohrenwend. (1989). "A modified labeling theory approach to mental disorders: An empirical assessment." *American Sociological Review*, 54:400–423.

Lofland, John. (1969). *Deviance and Identity*. Englewood Cliffs, NJ: Prentice Hall.

Matsueda, Ross L. (1992). "Reflected appraisals, parental labeling, and delinquency: Specifying a symbolic interactionist theory." *American Journal of Sociology*, 97:1577–1611.

Matsueda, Ross L. and Karen Heimer. (1997). "A symbolic interactionist theory of role transitions, role commitments, and delinquency." Pp. 163–214 in *Advances in Criminological Theory, Vol. 7, Developmental Theories of Crime and Delinquency*. New Brunswick, NJ: Transaction.

Maxson, Cheryl L. and Malcolm W. Klein. (1997). *Responding to Troubled Youth*. New York: Oxford University Press.

Maynard, Douglas W. (1988). "Language, interaction, and social problems." *Social Problems*, 35:311–334.

——. (1991). "Interaction and asymmetry in clinical discourse." *American Journal of Sociology*, 97:448–495.

Mead, George Herbert. (1918). "The psychology of punitive justice." *American Journal of Sociology*, 23:577–602.

——.(1934). *Mind, Self, and Society*. Chicago: University of Chicago Press.

Paternoster, Raymond, and LeeAnn Iovanni. (1989). "The labeling perspective and delinquency: An elaboration of the theory and assessment of the evidence." *Justice Quarterly*, 6:359–394.

Pollner, Melvin. (1974). "Sociological and common-sense models of the labelling process." Pp. 27–40 in *Ethnomethodology*. R. Turner (ed.). Harmondsworth, UK: Penguin.

Quinney, Richard. (1970). *The Social Reality of Crime*. Boston: Little, Brown.

——. (1977). *Class, State, and Crime*. New York: McKay.

Rains, Prudence. (1975). "Imputations of deviance: A retrospective essay on the labeling perspective." *Social Problems*, 23:1–11.

Scheff, Thomas J. (1966). *Being Mentally Ill: A Sociological Theory*. Chicago: Aldine.

Schur, Edwin M. (1973). *Radical Nonintervention: Rethinking the Delinquency Problem*. Englewood Cliffs, NJ: Prentice Hall.

Singer, Simon I. (1996). *Recriminalizing Delinquency: Violent Juvenile Crime and Juvenile Justice Reform*. Cambridge: Cambridge University Press.

Spector, Malcolm and John I. Kitsuse. (1977). *Constructing Social Problems*. Menlo Park, CA: Cummings.

Sudnow, David. (1965). "Normal crimes: Sociological features of the penal code in a public defender office." *Social Problems*, 12:255–276.

Tannenbaum, Frank. (1938). *Crime and the Community*. Boston: Ginn.

Taylor, Ian, Paul Walton, and Jock Young. (1973). *The New Criminology*. London: Routledge and Kegan Paul.

Triplett, Ruth A. and G. Roger Jarjoura. (1994). "Theoretical and empirical specification of informal labeling." *Journal of Quantitative Criminology,* 10:241–276.

Turk, Austin. (1969). *Criminality and Legal Order.* Chicago: Rand McNally.

Wilson, Thomas P. (1970). "Conceptions of interaction and forms of sociological explanation." *American Sociological Review,* 35:697–710.

Reintegrative Shaming

John Braithwaite
Australian National University

Shame and Crime

The pivotal concept of the theory in *Crime, Shame, and Reintegration* (Braithwaite 1989) is reintegrative shaming. According to the theory, societies have lower crime rates if they effectively communicate shame about crime. They will have a lot of violence if violent behavior is not shameful, high rates of rape if rape is something men can brag about, and endemic white-collar crime if business people think law-breaking is clever rather than shameful.

That said, there are ways of communicating the shamefulness of crime that increase crime. This process is called *stigmatization*. Reintegrative shaming communicates shame to a wrongdoer in a way that encourages him or her to desist; however, stigmatization shames in a way that makes things worse. So what is the difference?

Reintegrative shaming communicates disapproval within a continuum of respect for the offender; the offender is treated as a good person who has done a bad deed. Stigmatization is disrespectful shaming; the offender is treated as a bad person. Stigmatization is unforgiving (i.e., the offender is left with the stigma permanently), whereas reintegrative shaming is forgiving (i.e., ceremonies to certify deviance are terminated by ceremonies to decertify deviance). Put another way, societies that are forgiving and respectful while taking crime seriously have low crime rates; societies that degrade and humiliate criminals have higher crime rates.

Low Crime Societies

African societies are among those which use reintegrative shaming quite extensively. The Nanante, for example, exemplifies an institution of reintegrative shaming that deals with crime in a ritually serious but reintegrative way.

The Nanante

An Afghan criminologist at the University of Edinburgh, A. Ali Serisht, pointed out (after the publication of *Crime, Shame, and Reintegration* in 1989) that the Pushtoon, the largest ethnic group in Afghanistan, have an institution called Nanante similar to the conferencing notion I discussed in that book. The Nanante is a ceremony in which the criminal offender brings flour and other food and kills a sheep for a community feast. Often this will be held at the victim's house, where the victim will participate in cooking the food the offender brings. At the ceremonial part of the event, the offender is not told that he is bad and in need of reform, but rather that "You have done an injustice to this person." At the same time, the offender is assured that "You are one of us and we accept you back among us." The police and courts have virtually no presence in communities that rely on the Nananate.

Japan is the developed society that has perhaps the heaviest reliance on reintegrative shaming as an alternative to humiliating or outcasting criminals. It has a very low crime rate and is the only nation in which the evidence indicates a sustained decline in the crime rate over the past half century. This has been accomplished with a low imprisonment rate—37 per 100,000 population, compared to over 600 in the United States. Guy Masters' (1995, 1997) research shows that Japanese schools use reintegrative methods for controlling delinquency very similar to the restorative justice conferences we describe later.

Delinquency in the Japanese Classroom

The students would then be asked by their home room teacher to explain their actions. This would often be done at the child's home in front of the parents. Finally, a meeting with all the students and parents would be arranged, and with any other people that might be involved.

For instance, if a fight had occurred with students from another school, or an item had been stolen, then these individuals would also be present. The police might also attend and make comments. In these meetings, the teachers would start by talking about the student and then the incident. Those involved would be expected to talk about the effect that it had had. The students would be expected to explain why they did it, and to apologise to everybody there. The parents would often then apologise to the injured party, as would the teachers. The students would then have a separate meeting with their home room teacher again, to discuss that meeting, and, as teachers said to me, to stress what the individual student had learnt from the situation. The more serious the incident the more meetings would be arranged. . . . For these incidents there was never any specific punishment per se, just the process of the meetings. . . . There was a strong feeling that students should not be given up on. . . . Even with the persistent trouble makers, a common comment was always that, 'This time—I think that they might learn'. . . . When talking about persistent trouble makers, one teacher commented that: 'Young children make mistakes. They do bad things, but that doesn't make them bad people. Our job is to look after them when they make these mistakes, until they learn to look after themselves.' It would appear that they [teachers] look after them by showing them how serious what they have done is, and how it has hurt others." (Masters 1995, 27–29)

Lewis (1989) identified the following four principles from her observations of discipline in Japanese classrooms: "(1) minimizing the impression of teacher control; (2) delegating control to the children; (3) providing plentiful opportunities for children to acquire a 'good girl' or 'good boy' identity; and (4) avoiding the attribution that children intentionally misbehave" (35).

Stigmatizing other human beings is a common human frailty because stigmatizing the debased identity of others is a way of shoring up one's own identity. Stigmatization is an ineradicable fact of existence in all societies, including Japanese society. Reintegrative societies, however, have well-developed cultural scripts and rituals for ending stigmatization with ceremonies of apology and forgiveness. "Pig, Pig, Pig" is another example from the work of Masters (1997) of how stigmatization can be responded to by reintegrating the offender back into a community of care.

Pig, Pig, Pig

"The incident began during the morning roll call when the boy in charge called a girl by her (unappreciated) nickname of 'pig.' The girl was offended and refused to answer, so the boy raised his voice and yelled the word several times. . . . Later that morning during the break, several children gathered around the girl and chanted 'pig, pig, pig.' Deeply hurt . . . she ran away from the group. For the remainder of the school day she did not speak a word; that afternoon she went home and would refuse to return for a week. The teacher in charge of the class had not been present during the periods when the girl was insulted, so she did not appreciate what had happened."

"Later that day, the girl's mother called to ask what had gone on. Immediately, the principal began a quiet investigation in cooperation with the teacher. By that evening, parts of the story were known, and the principal visited the child's home to apologise to her parents. The next day, and on each successive day until the problem was solved, special teachers' meetings were held with all present to seek a solution. On three occasions the principal or the girl's homeroom teacher went to the girl's home and talked with her. The final resolution involved a visit by the entire class to the girl's home, where apologies were offered along with a request that the insulted girl forgive her friends. Two days later she returned to school, and two weeks later the teacher read a final report to the regular teachers' meeting and then apologised for having caused the school so much trouble." (Cummings 1980, 118–119, cited in Masters 1997)

Reintegrative Shaming in Western Societies

Contemporary Western societies are rather stigmatic compared to much of Africa and Asia. However, they are not as stigmatic as they used to be. We no longer put criminal offenders in the stocks, where they can suffer all manner of degradation up to and including rape. We no longer require poor students to wear a dunce's cap. Indeed, our schools and our childrearing practices in families have become much more reintegrative over the past two centuries.

Moreover, the evidence is strong that American families that confront wrongdoing while sustaining relationships of love and respect for their children are the families most likely to raise law-abiding citizens (see Braithwaite 1989, 71–83). Laissez-faire families that fail to confront or that just "natter" at misbehavior (Patterson 1982) and stigmatizing families that reject and degrade both experience a lot of misbehavior (Baumrind 1971, 1978).

Robert Sampson and John Laub's (1995) celebrated analysis of the Gluecks' data on the life course of American offenders and nonoffenders supports this conclusion: "What seems particularly criminogenic is harsh, unreasoning, and punitive discipline combined with rejection of the child. Stigmatizing punishment, by the family as well as the State . . . appears to backfire" (122).

Research that Toni Makkai and I have conducted on the enforcement philosophy of nursing home inspectors in Australia, the United States, and the United Kingdom suggests that inspectors are ineffective when they are tolerant and nonjudgmental in the face of failures by nursing home management to meet standards of care for old people required by the law (Makkai and Braithwaite 1994). Nursing home compliance with the law actually declines following inspections by tolerant and understanding inspectors. It declines even more sharply after visits from inspectors with a stigmatizing approach to wrongdoing. The inspection teams that did best at improving compliance were those who believed in clearly communicating that failure to meet legal standards would not be tolerated, yet who believed in doing so in a way that showed respect, avoided humiliation, used praise when things improved, and believed in being both tough and forgiving.

Lawrence Sherman (1993) has interpreted his research on U.S. policing as suggesting that when police stigmatize offenders, this engenders defiance. Respectful policing, which involves procedural fairness, politeness, and giving the offender the benefit of a presumption that he is a good person who may have done a bad act, builds commitment to the law. Sherman has embarked on an ambitious program of experimental criminology to test these hypotheses more directly.

Why Should Shaming Reduce Crime?

Most Westerners believe we learn to refrain from crime by fear of punishment. Does this fit your own behavior very well? Some of the time it probably does. But think about the person who has done most to make your life difficult in the past year. Did you consider murdering him or her to deal with this? For most readers of this book, the answer will be no. You chose another course not because you considered murder as an option and then concluded that the risks outweighed the benefits from getting the difficult person out of the way. More likely, you refrained from murder because it was simply unthinkable to you; it was right off your deliberative agenda. My theory is that it is exposure early in our lives to the idea of the shamefulness of murder that puts it off the deliberative agenda of responsible citizens. This is why it makes no difference to most people whether the punishment for murder is the electric chair or prison.

What matters in a culture, according to the theory, is moral clarity about the evil of killing other people. This is why homicides go up after wars (Archer and Gartner 1976). It is why television that communicates the message that the best way to deal with violence is through violence, that those who wrong us can sometimes deserve to die for it, is a problem. Sadly, the ethnographic evidence is that murderers in America often believe they are agents of justice, purifying the world of the evil person they are wasting (Katz 1988).

When we do something wrong, the people who are in the best position to communicate the shamefulness of what we have done are those we love. A judge waving his finger at us from on high is in a rather poor position to be able to do this. We do not care so much about his opinion of us because we have been given no reason to respect him as a human being, and we will probably never meet him again. It is family we love and friends we respect who have most influence over us. Precisely because their relationships with us are based on love and respect, when they shame us they will do so reintegratively (respectfully).

Why Should Stigmatization Make Things Worse?

In contrast, when people shame us in a degrading way, this poses a threat to our identity. One way we can deal with the threat is to reject our rejectors. Once I have labelled them as dirt, does it matter that they regard me as dirt? There is a profound connection here between the theory of reintegrative shaming and subcultural theory in criminology. When respectable society rejects me, I have a status problem; I am in the market for a solution to this status problem. Criminal subcultures can supply that solution.

Albert Cohen (1955), for example, speaks of a child who does poorly at school as rejected in the status system of a school that values respect for property and control of aggression. A delinquent subculture of children, who have been similarly rejected by the status system of the school, can proffer a collective solution to that status problem. The subculture of school failures may value contempt for property and toughness rather than control of aggression. That is, the very values against which disrespected children fail can be the basis for respect in a delinquent subculture.

Stigmatization, therefore, increases the attractiveness of criminal subcultures. Disrespect begets disrespect. Because you don't respect me, I won't respect you or the rules you value. I have no hope of seeking out a respected identity under your values; thus, delinquent subcultures look more promising to me as a basis for respect.

Criminal subcultures neutralize the shame that would otherwise be experienced as a result of lawbreaking. Often subcultures invert shame, so that it is mobilized against those who are too "weak" to stand up to the law and the authorities. In the Mafia, for example, it is a matter of great shame to cooperate with law enforcement.

Mainstream law and order cultures that are highly stigmatizing therefore nurture criminal subculture formation; they create a market for an oppositional identity. Once those who are rejected by the stigmatizing culture are in the clutches of the criminal subculture, it does more for them than allow them to take pride in what the stigmatizers take to be a matter of shame. The criminal subculture also provides practical resources—communicating knowledge, for example, about how to disarm an alarm system, how to sell drugs, or how to evade tax.

Integrating Criminological Theories

The reintegrative-disintegrative (stigmatizing) distinction is a shunt that switches the criminologist onto different modes of explanation. When there is stigmatization, we have just seen that the propositions of subcultural theory are more likely to come true. When shaming is reintegrative, the propositions of control theory are more likely to be true. By this I mean that attachment to parents and other agents of conventional morality is more likely to reduce crime. Young people are more likely to continue to believe in the rules those agents of conventional morality uphold and to be influenced by them.

Labeling theory is obviously the other mainstream theory that has the conditions of its validity specified by the theory of reintegrative shaming. Labeling, according to the theory, will actually reduce crime when it is respectful, focused on the act rather than the person, and terminated by ceremonies of forgiveness and apology following disapproval. When it is stigmatizing, however, labeling will only make things worse.

The entire framework of the theory of reintegrative shaming can be accommodated within a differential association framework (Sutherland and Cressey 1978). Although it is a useful theoretical framework (see Chapter 7), differential association lacks specificity in what it implies and rejects. The theory of reintegrative shaming, however, can give it some specificity of meaning. Reintegrative shaming is the key process for communicating definitions unfavorable to crime. Stigmatization pushes the stigmatized away from those definitions and into the clutches of criminal subcultures that communicate definitions favorable to crime—e.g., "Rich people can afford to be robbed and they themselves rob people like me all the time by their rip-offs."

The connection of opportunity theory to the theory of reintegrative shaming is more indirect, but nevertheless powerfully important. Unemployment and school failure close off legitimate opportunities. At the same time, they also cut off interdependency with other citizens. School failure tends to sever ties of interdependency with the school as the school failures reject their rejectors from the school community. Further, unemployment takes the employed out of interdependency with other citizens in the world of work. Because the unemployed often deal with the shame of losing their job by rejecting the world of workmates and employers, they become less vulnerable to the reintegrative possibility of social control.

But there is a much more profound way that unemployment breaks up communities of care. Families racked by unemployment are more likely to disintegrate. When children lose the caring love of a mother, father, or other extended family members whose attachment is primarily to the alienated partner, the web of reintegrative influence become less powerful. Those whose presence or love is lost to us are no longer in a position to shame us reintegratively when we err or to praise our fortitude when we resist opportunities for wrongdoing. If dad is a hated male identity in a family culture dominated by a bitter mom, then a boy is more at risk from the supportive male identity a criminal subculture may supply. A boy will always be in the market for some sort of male identity. If it is the case that unemployment (and poverty and failure more generally) opens up conflicts in struggling families, and splits them physically or emotionally by disrespect, then the love and respect needed to render socialization effective will be lacking.

Blocked opportunities, therefore, undermine interdependence and community, and this weakens reintegrative capability (and promotes stigmatization). Stigma further reduces legitimate opportunities. Once we are labeled a criminal, it is hard to get a job (Hagan 1993).

Conditions of widespread stigmatization and unemployment are breeding grounds for criminal subcultures that offer solutions to those who have status problems as a result of these afflictions. They also offer practical illegitimate opportunities—ways of making a living by selling drugs, for example.

Stigmatizing processes apply equally, I argue, to crimes of the powerful. The nursing home owner is stigmatized by the state as a crook, a rapacious person who preys on vulnerable old people. A nursing home industry subculture of resistance to the regulatory requirements of the state can supply a solution to his status problem. They project that it is nit-picking bureaucrats with their red tape and whinning old people who have never had it so good (together with their antibusiness advocacy groups) who are bringing the country down. Instead, it is aggressive business people who make the country strong. The business subculture of resistance also helps share knowledge about legal tactics to resist the demands of the regulators and the resident advocates.

So the theory works at the top of the class structure as well as at the bottom. Regulatory stigmatization closes off a legitimate opportunity to accumulate wealth (say through enjoying a positive reputation as an ethical provider). This fosters criminal subculture formation. The criminal subculture of the business community then constitutes illegitimate opportunities of a much more damaging sort than can be created in the slum. If you have the capital of Nelson Bunker Hunt and W. Herbert Hunt, you can even try to manipulate an entire global market for a commodity like silver (Abolafia 1985). Great wealth means enormously superior capability to constitute both legitimate and illegitimate opportunities (Braithwaite 1991). The blocked legitimate opportunity of unemployment or school fail-ure is not relevant to them; but when their opportunities are blocked by, say, a new tax law, they have inexorable capabilities to con-stitute new illegitimate opportunities through offshore tax havens and other schemes.

Societies that structure their opportuni-ties very unequally will have more of both crimes of the powerless and crimes of the powerful. There will be more systematic blockage of legitimate opportunities to the poor. And there will be more capacity for ruthless exploitation of illegitimate opportu-nities by the rich when more unsystematic causes block their legitimate opportunities. For both the crimes of the powerful and the crimes of the powerless, stigmatization is relevant to formation of and attraction to criminal subcultures. And reintegrative shaming is vital to the control of both types of crime.

Communities

Reintegrative shaming, according to the theory, will be more widespread in societies where communities are strong, where citi-zens are densely enmeshed in loving, trust-ing, or respectful relationships with others. Obviously, it follows from the theory that shaming is more likely to be powerful and reintegrative where communities are strong and caring. Strong communities are also the key resources for the prevention of criminal subculture formation. Frank T. Cullen (1994) has reviewed the considerable evi-dence that "social support" is of central im-portance to crime prevention. Sampson, Raudenbush, and Earls (1997) have shown that "collective efficacy, defined as social co-hesion among neighbors combined with their willingness to intervene on behalf of the common good, is linked to reduced vio-lence" (918). Chicago neighborhoods with more collective efficacy, more social trust, had less crime. Consistent with the theory I have outlined above, the negative effect of poverty on crime was mediated through col-lective efficacy. Across U.S. cities, Chamlin and Cochran (1997) have shown that more "altruistic" cities, as measured by charitable contributions, have lower crime rates, an

outcome which they interpret, in part, in terms of the communitarian aspects of the explanation of crime in *Crime, Shame and Reintegration*.

The Structure of Shame and the Pattern of Crime

Relations of power explain why some kinds of crime are defined as more shameful than others. In societies where women are particularly powerless, violence against women by those who own them will not be defined as very shameful. As a result, the the-ory predicts that violence against women will be among the deepest crime problems in such societies. Where business power reigns supreme and workers have little clout, occu-pational health and safety crimes will not be defined as very shameful. So there will be a lot of that kind of crime. Where bankers de-fine what is shameful, bank robbery will be shameful and insider trading by bankers will not. This class structure of shame will cause people to believe that bank robbery is a major problem when it is not. It will cause them to be blind to the corporate crimes of bankers as a central crime problem, when the reality is that the best way to rob a bank is to own it.

An interesting implication of this analysis is that our deepest crime problems are the very problems we are in the best position to do something about. Social movement poli-tics is the crime prevention strategy I have in mind. If structural inequalities of power are the reason family violence and corporate crime against workers and bank customers are not shameful (and, therefore, are wide-spread), then a women's movement that communicates the shamefulness of violence against women, a trade union movement that denounces health and safety crimes, and a consumer movement that exposes the rip-offs of banks can have major effects.

Restorative Justice

This kind of social movement politics seems to me the most important crime pre-vention implication of the theory. A second important implication is that restorative jus-tice will be more effective than retributive justice. The Nanante and the disciplinary practices in Japanese schools are examples of restorative justice at work in civil society. That is, civil society rather than the state is the most important site for restorative justice. Families, schools, and indigenous communities are the preeminently important sites for restorative justice in civil society for preventing crimes of the powerless. And workplaces are the most important sites for restorative justice to prevent crimes of the powerful.

In recent years, state-run restorative justice programs as an alternative to court have become increasingly important in the criminal justice systems of all Western societies. Restorative justice means restoring victims, restoring offenders, and restoring communities. These objectives take priority over punishment. Key *values* of restorative justice are healing rather than hurting, respectful dialogue, making amends, caring and participatory community, taking responsibility, remorse, apology, and forgiveness. Restorative justice is also a *process* that involves bringing together all the stakeholders—victims, offenders and their friends and loved ones, representatives of the state and the community—to decide what should be done about a criminal offense.

The native peoples of North America have strong traditions of restorative justice that are being revitalized through healing circles or sentencing circles. These circles traditionally put the problem, not the person, in the center of a community discussion about a crime (Melton 1995). In many if not all U.S. states now and in all Canadian provinces, European-Americans are learning from the restorative justice wisdom of the first American nations. Circle processes are being discovered as richly applicable to people brought up in a European civilization. There is appeal in the sheer simplicity of victims and their loved ones, offenders and their loved ones, and caring members of the community sitting in a circle to discuss the consequences of a crime and what can be done to put it right. At the end of a circle or a restorative justice conference, an agreement is reached, which will often by signed by the offender, the victim, and a police officer. The idea is that if this agreement is implemented, there is no need for the matter to go to court. Agreements can include compensation payments to victims, apology, community work, undertakings to enter drug rehabilitation programs, surrender of weapons or of a motor vehicle, moving from living on the street to living with a member of one's family, and so on.

Most programs seek to reduce the imprisonment rate by pretrial diversion. Yet others cut in at more advanced stages of the criminal justice process. For example, the John Howard Society of Manitoba has a program mostly limited to running restorative justice conferences in cases where a prosecutor has already recommended prison time of more than six months (Bonta, Rooney, and Wallace-Capretta 1998). The idea is to see if the meeting can come up with an agreement that will persuade a judge to keep the offender out of prison. The program seems to be having some success in accomplishing this.

A great deal of research is underway in many nations about the effectiveness of restorative justice processes. So far, the results are most encouraging (Braithwaite 1999), but it is far too early for criminologists to be able to form an opinion as to whether they really work as a better way of doing justice. The theory of reintegrative shaming predicts that restorative justice processes will be more effective than criminal trials in reducing crime because by putting the problem rather than the person in the center, direct denunciation by someone whom you do not respect (e.g., a judge, the police) is avoided. At the same time, shame is difficult to avoid when a victim and her supporters, as well as the family of the offender, all talk through the consequences that have been suffered, emotionally as well as materially, as a result of the crime. This discussion of consequences structures shame into a restorative justice process; the presence and support of those who care most for us structure reintegration into the ritual. The objective is to get the offender to acknowledge shame through apology and making amends; this, according to Retzinger and Scheff (1996), is better than bypassing shame, leaving shame to fester below the surface in a variety of unhealthy ways. Equally, it is an objective to help victims to heal the shame they so commonly feel.

Integrating Normative and Explanatory Theory

Let us now think about the difference between explanatory and normative theory. So far we have been discussing an explanatory theory of crime—an ordered set of propositions about the way the world is. A normative theory is an ordered set of propositions about the way the world ought to be. My research agenda has been to integrate explanatory and normative theories, something that is not common in contemporary criminology. Jeremy Bentham's theory of crime is the most influential example of an attempt to unify an explanatory theory (deterrence) and a normative theory (utilitarianism).

It seems to me that the theory of reintegrative shaming could be a dangerous theory (albeit less dangerous than deterrence) unless it is integrated with a normative theory of what should be shamed. My argument is that conduct should be subject to shame when doing so will increase freedom as nondomination. Freedom as nondomination or "dominion" has been conceived by Philip Pettit and me (Braithwaite and Pettit 1990; Pettit 1997) as a republican conception of freedom. This normative theory implies that a more decent way to run a criminal justice system is with the minimum level of punishment that is possible while enabling the state to maintain its promises to the security of citizens. It means that punishing people only because they deserve it makes no moral sense. Equally, shaming people for no better reason than that they deserve it, in a way that increases the amount of oppression in the world, is morally wrong.

Republican political theory also means active citizenship and community building. This commends the social movement politics and restorative justice that we argued was also an implication of the explanatory theory in *Crime, Shame, and Reintegration*.

Conclusion

There has not been space in this essay to recount why I think the theory of reintegrative shaming explains the most powerful relationships that have been demonstrated by criminological research—why women commit less crime than men, why young people commit more crime than older folk, why big cities have more crime, why residential mobility (moving one's household) is associated with crime, why school failure is a cause of crime, why entering a happy, secure relationship with a partner and getting a satisfying job turns people away from crime, why crime in the suites does more damage than crime in the streets (see Braithwaite 1989).

This is the first ambition of the theory: to give a better fit to the established facts than is provided by other theories. I found the best way to accomplish that was to integrate the explanatory power that does reside in other criminological theories. The theory of reintegrative shaming is an explicit attempt to integrate the insights of control, subcultural, opportunity, learning (e.g., differential association) and labeling theories of crime. Integration with opportunity theory has been especially important because a key ambition was a theory that accounted for both crimes of the powerless and crimes of the powerful. My first contribution to criminological theory in the book *Inequality, Crime, and Public Policy* (Braithwaite 1979) was a work in the opportunity theory tradition (for the paper where I do most to work through this integration, see Braithwaite 1991). Finally, I seek to integrate normative and explanatory theories because of the belief that integration with explanatory theory is the path to more powerful and morally convincing normative theory, and integration with normative theory is the path to more powerful explanatory theory.

In the process of mutual adjustment of the categories of explanatory and normative theories, my conclusion is that the republican prescription of liberty, equality, and community (fraternity/sorority) is the path both to a more decent society and to a safer one (Braithwaite and Parker 1999). The agendas of liberal-egalitarian social movements, such as the women's movement, the environment movement, the human rights movement, and the social movement for restorative justice, seem to me practical vehicles for such transformation. It is, therefore, the influence of their work that is particularly commended to the critical scrutiny of criminological researchers. This means a less state-oriented criminology than we have now.

References

Abolafia, Mitchel Y. (1985). "Self-regulation as market maintenance: An organization perspective." Pp. 312–347 in *Regulatory Policy and the Social Sciences*. R.G. Noll (ed.). Berkeley: University of California Press.

Archer, Dane and Rosemary Gartner. (1976). "Violent acts and violent times: A comparative approach to post-war homicide rates." *American Sociological Review*, 41:937–963.

Baumrind, D. (1971). "Current patterns of parental authority." *Developmental Psychology Monograph*, 4:1–2.

Baumrind, D. (1978). "Parental disciplinary patterns and social competence in children." *Youth and Society*, 9:239–276.

Bonta, James, Jennifer Rooney, and Suzanne Wallace-Capretta. (1998). *Restorative Justice: An Evaluation of the Restorative Resolutions Project*. Ottawa: Solicitor General Canada.

Braithwaite, John. (1979). *Inequality, Crime, and Public Policy*. London: Routledge and Kegan Paul.

Braithwaite, John. (1989). *Crime, Shame, and Reintegration*. Melbourne, Australia: Cambridge University Press.

Braithwaite, John. (1991). "Poverty, power, white-collar crime, and the paradoxes of criminological theory." *Australian and New Zealand Journal of Criminology*, 24:40–58.

Braithwaite, John. (1999). "Restorative justice: Assessing optimistic and pessimistic accounts." Pp. 1–27 in *Crime and Justice: A Review of Research*. Vol. 25. M. Tonry (ed.). Chicago, IL: University of Chicago Press.

Braithwaite, John and Christine Parker. (1999). "Restorative justice is republican justice." Pp. 103–126 in *Restoring Juvenile Justice: An Exploration of the Restorative Justice Paradigm for Reforming Juvenile Justice*. Lode Walgrave and Gordon Bazemore (eds.). Monsey, NY: Criminal Justice Press.

Braithwaite, John and Philip Pettit. (1990). *Not Just Deserts: A Republican Theory of Criminal Justice*. Oxford: Oxford University Press.

Chamlin, Mitchell B. and John K. Cochran. (1997). "Social altruism and crime." *Criminology*, 35:203–227.

Cohen, A.K. (1955). *Delinquent Boys: The Culture of the Gang*. Glencoe, IL: Free.

Cullen, F.T. (1994). "Social support as an organizing concept for criminology: Presidential address to the Academy of Criminal Justice Sciences." *Justice Quarterly*, 11:478–527.

Cummings, W. (1980). *Education for Equality in Japan*. Princeton, NJ: Princeton University Press.

Hagan, J. (1993). "The social embeddedness of crime and unemployment." *Criminology*, 31:465–491.

Katz, J. (1988). *Seductions of Crime: Moral and Sensual Attractions of Doing Evil*. New York: Basic.

Lewis, C. (1989). "Cooperation and control in Japanese nursery schools." Pp. 28–44 in *Japanese Schooling: Patterns of Socialisation, Equality, and Political Control*. James Shields (ed.). University Park: Pennsylvania State University.

Makkai, T. and J. Braithwaite. (1994). "Reintegrative shaming and compliance with regulatory standards." *Criminology*, 32:361–385.

Masters, G. (1995). "The family model of social control in Japanese secondary schools." Unpublished manuscript, Lancaster University.

Masters, G. (1997). *Reintegrative Shaming in Theory and Practice*. Ph.D. dissertation, Lancaster University.

Melton, Ada Pecos (1995). "Indigenous justice systems and tribal society." *Judicature*, 126:126.

Patterson, G.R. (1982). *Coercive Family Process*. Eugene, OR: Castalia.

Pettit, P. (1997). *Republicanism*. Oxford: Clarendon.

Retzinger, S. and T.J. Scheff. (1996). "Strategy for community conferences: Emotions and social bonds." Pp. 315–336 in *Restorative Justice: International Perspectives*. B. Galaway and J. Hudson (eds.). New York: Criminal Justice Press.

Sampson, R. and J.H. Laub. (1995). *Crime in the Making: Pathways and Turning Points Through Life*. Cambridge, MA: Harvard University Press.

Sampson, R.J., S. Raudenbush, and F. Earls. (1997). "Neighborhoods and violent crime: A multilevel study of collective efficacy." *Science,* 277(5328):918–924.

Sherman, L.W. (1993). "Defiance, deterrence and irrelevance: A theory of the criminal sanction." *Journal of Research in Crime and Delinquency,* 30:445—473.

Sutherland, E. and D. Cressey. (1978). *Criminology,* Tenth Edition. New York: Lippincott.

9

Radical and Feminist Theories of Crime

Introduction

In this chapter, you will learn about two different but related theories of crime which, because of a lack of better terminology, we refer to as "radical" and "feminist" theories. In one sense, these two types of theories are very different and warrant the separate treatment that they are getting in this chapter. However, a common thread exists between them because they both can be considered "countercultural" or critical theories of crime. By countercultural, we mean that both radical and feminist theories pursue lines of inquiry that other more "traditional" theories—e.g., strain, social learning, and social control—do not. Radical and feminist theories of crime are "critical" theories, unlike these more traditional theories. They are critical in the sense that they question some very basic assumptions about the nature of social order and law that other theories more readily accept. For example, radical and feminist criminologists question the belief held by more traditional theorists that the criminal law reflects a social consensus about what is appropriate and inappropriate conduct. The radical and feminist view is that rather than consensus and agreement, social order is produced out of political conflict and coercion. For both types of theory, therefore, the issue of inequality in society is a key theoretical variable. Furthermore, because the notion of conflict is central to both radical and feminist theories, and because both draw upon themes from conflict theory, we also briefly discuss some conflict theories in criminology.

The two essays that follow provide more background information about radical and feminist perspectives. In the first essay, Professors Michael J. Lynch and Paul B. Stretesky discuss where radical theory in crime came from and where it is likely to be going in the next few years. In the second essay, Professors Meda Chesney-Lind and Karlene Faith give a comparably detailed discussion of feminist theories of crime. First, however, a brief review of radical and feminist criminology.

Radical Theories of Crime

What Makes a Theory a "Radical" Theory?

Although this is a good question, we probably will not have an equally good answer. This is because radical theory in criminology is not homogeneous. There is no one radical theory of crime; rather, there are many (Marxism, postmodernism, peacemaking, anarchism, cultural criminology, left realism, left idealism, constitutive criminology, and abolitionism). Unfortunately, for any clear presentation of the theory, each of these different "schools" or brands of radical criminology emphasizes somewhat differently what it believes are distinctive features of the "crime problem." As a result, there is no real agreement, either within the field of criminology generally or among radical criminologists themselves. Nevertheless, as you will discover from reading the essay by Lynch and Stretesky, different versions of radical criminology do share some important common ground.

Essentially, we agree with Shoemaker's (1996), Cullen and Agnew's (1999), and Beirne and Messerschmidt's (2000) assessment that the essence of any radical theory of crime is a concern with the issues of inequality and power differentials. It is probably no exaggeration to say that radical criminologists more than any other group of crime scholars have consistently contended that formal efforts at social control, such as the operations of the criminal justice system, benefit the affluent and powerful at the expense of the less affluent and powerless. Though there are subtle differences among them, all versions of radical theory adopt a "conflict" perspective on the law and the legal and criminal justice systems. This conflict view argues that both in its enactment and enforcement, criminal laws primarily serve the interests of the politically and economically powerful rather than some general or public interest. This means that the content and enforcement of law protects the privileged position of those in power and is used as a device to control and discipline those in the lower classes of society.

There are several implications that follow from this position. One is that among radical criminologists there is little interest in discovering the "motivation" for crime. Radical criminologists spend little or no time trying to understand the reasons why some people commit crimes while others do not. In the traditional sense, then, they are not interested in the "causes" of crime, and would not even claim that persons commit crime because of peer pressure, disorganized communities, inadequate socialization, weak social bonds, or faulty biologies. To most radical criminologists (and we must remember to be careful here because the subfield of radical criminology is so diverse), the "cause" of crime resides in the fact that American society is characterized by economic and political conflict. Those with economic and political power use it to their advantage by criminalizing the behaviors of the powerless. As a result, "crime in the street" is met with the power of the criminal law, the police, courts, and penal system, while "crimes in the suite" (organizational, white-collar, corporate, and political crimes) are defined either as shrewd business practices or as mere civil violations.

A second implication of the radical point of view is that given the fact that the "root cause" of crime lies in economic and political inequality, current strategies for dealing with the crime problem will not work at best and are injurious and destructive to the powerless at worst. Consistently, radical criminologists are critical of the use of the criminal justice system as a remedy to crime. Their view is that traditional crime control strategies are frequently too punitive—they involve more police, longer terms of imprisonment, and capital punishment, for exam-

ple. If one of the most powerful causes of crime is an inequality of economic and political power and the consequences of such powerlessness (e.g., unemployment, poverty, feelings of helplessness and anger), then arresting and imprisoning more offenders for longer periods of time is not going to do much to solve the problem. In fact, it most likely will make matters worse, not only because the real causes go unresolved, but also because social control efforts fall heavily on the backs of the poor and powerless. More punitive crime control strategies fail to get at the root causes of crime, therefore, and disproportionately affect the poor and powerless.

A third implication of the radical perspective follows from the one above. Radical criminologists are fairly uniform in their call for a dramatic restructuring of American society. If crime is due to power inequalities, then if we are truly serious about reducing crime, we must be willing to do something about the effects of this inequality, such as unemployment, poverty, inadequate housing and educational facilities for the poor, racism, and sexism. Even though some radical criminologists (left realists and peacemakers) would adopt minor efforts at reforming the criminal justice system, most have little faith that a system that essentially serves the interests of the powerful will ever be able to reform itself.

In sum, although they are a very diverse group of scholars, radical criminologists would share a common agenda. This common agenda includes the beliefs that:

- Modern Western societies are characterized by a class system wherein a select few have abundant wealth and political power while the majority are powerless.

- The wealthy use their political power to protect their privileged position in society. This means that both the content and enforcement of criminal laws benefit the wealthy and disadvantage the less affluent.

- The criminal law does not, therefore, reflect the interests of all members of society, but more strongly reflects the interests and concerns of the wealthy.

- Criminals are not qualitatively different from noncriminals. They do not commit crimes because there is something wrong with them or because something compels them to do it. Rather, criminals are generally those poor and powerless members of society who are substantially affected by class conflict in the form of unemployment, poverty, and feelings of discrimination.

- Punitive criminal justice practices will not remedy the root causes of crime and will not reduce the amount of crime in society. Harsh sanctions will only further impoverish and make helpless the lives of the poor, who are disproportionately the targets of criminal justice sanctions.

- The criminal justice system must be made more equitable and fair, and criminal justice policy should be devoted to more broadscale social reform that reduces political and economic inequality.

Early Radical Criminology

It is somewhat difficult to trace the beginning of radical theory in criminology. However, a very early theory considered to be radical was developed by a Dutch criminologist and socialist, Willem Bonger (1916), who in his theory sought to directly apply the philosophy of Karl Marx to the study of crime. According to Bonger, all capitalist societies have one major effect—they all generate and foster feelings of egoism rather than altruism among their members. That is, because capitalism is driven by the profit motive, it encourages people to think of their own needs first, promotes greed and selfishness, and discourages social sentiments. This egoistic seed that resides in each person in a capitalist society gives way to "criminal thoughts," which include acting in ways that benefit oneself, even if it is contrary to the interests of others. All persons in capitalist society develop egotistical feelings and act in ways that advance their own interests. Thus, capitalists do things like fix prices, manufac-

ture adulterated products, or maintain unsafe working conditions in order to keep costs down, and workers do things like steal and act violently. Unfortunately, due to the powerlessness of the working class, it is only their behaviors and not the behaviors of those in power that get the label criminal. Moreover, since crime is endemic to capitalist society, the only way to reduce crime would be to replace capitalism with an economic system that fosters social rather than individual sentiments—like socialism.

The Roots of Radical Criminology in Conflict Theory

Bonger's theory of capitalism and crime did not capture the interest of criminologists, however, and it really had no substantial impact on the field of criminology. In fact, throughout the early and middle 1900s, the field of criminology was dominated by the positive school and its interest in the biological, psychological, and sociological causes of crime. Nevertheless, there were occasional efforts at a radical explanation of criminological issues. For example, Georg Rusche and Otto Kirchheimer (1939) proposed that during any historical period the dominant form of punishment was heavily influenced, if not determined, by the prevailing form of economic production. They argued that the rapid growth of the industrial penitentiary beginning in the eighteenth century had come about from a desire to exploit the virtually free and limitless labor of the poor and criminal. Another influence for radical criminology issued from scholars housed at the University of California, Berkeley, School of Criminology, during the late 1960s and early 1970s. Out of this active group came such work as Tony Platt's (1969) attempt to link the juvenile court reform movement in Chicago during the early 1900s to the desire of economic elites to create social order out of what they feared was urban chaos. With these two exceptions, from the early 1900s until the early 1970s, there was really no organized and systematic radical criminology point of view.

There were, however, occasional attempts to apply a nonradical conflict model to the study of crime. Even though a "conflict" view is not the same as a "radical" view, one common theme is shared by the two approaches. In conflict theory, as in radical theory, the law is thought to reflect the interests of a politically dominant group or groups, rather than reflect some degree of general social agreement or consensus. Conflict theorists see society as comprised of diverse groups, each trying to pursue its own interests. Groups that have greater political power are able to influence the creation and enforcement of laws so that they are benefited by them. In other words, powerful groups make sure that their values are contained in the law, while powerless groups are made subject to them.

Thorsten Sellin (1938) was one of the first criminologists to spell out a conflict view of crime. Sellin argued that modern society is a pluralist society, that is, it consists of diverse groups, each with its own "conduct norms" or preferred and approved ways of behaving. Sellin was specifically referring to conduct norms within different immigrant groups in the United States in the early 1900s. Italians had different ways of behaving from Germans, and the Irish, and those from Eastern Europe, who all had different ways of behaving from those already assimilated into U.S. culture. Crime occurs when, because of a lack of political power, the conduct norms of one group are not reflected in the law, as the conduct norms of immigrant groups were not adopted into U.S. law. Simply behaving in a way that is conforming to one's own culture (Italian, German, or Irish), then, could cause conflict with the law and put one at high risk of being deemed a criminal. In this view, the ultimate "cause" of crime is a conflict of cultures and the brute political fact that the law reflects the conduct norms of only some and not all groups.

In the 1950s, the criminologist George B. Vold (1958) elaborated Sellin's culture conflict explanation of crime. Rather than a conflict of immigrant versus established cultures, Vold argued that American society is comprised of diverse interest groups (business vs. labor; teachers vs. administrators; casino owners vs. religious groups), and that each interest group has its own unique agenda it wishes to advance via collective action. Because the interests of each group tend to be competitive, the satisfaction of one group's interest is usually at the expense of that of another. Hence, there is conflict among interest groups. Reflecting his conflict view of society, Vold argued that some groups have the political power to ensure that the law captures their interests at the expense of others. Crime occurs, therefore, because politically powerless groups have not been able to secure their interests through the legislative process (i.e., they lose the political game and their behaviors are made criminal). In addition, some acts that were once legal later become criminal because of the efforts of other interest groups to have them criminalized.

After being dormant for decades, a conflict perspective on crime emerged again in the late 1960s and early 1970s. This conflict perspective was actually an elaboration of labeling/social reaction theory. Recall that one of the theoretical positions of labeling theory is that what specific behaviors get labeled as crime is based largely on political power (e.g., in the creation of the Prohibition Act, the political power of the Women's Christian Temperance Union was greater than that of the supporters of alcohol consumption). Recall also that it was theorists in the labeling/social reaction tradition who first put the role of the state in the creation of crime on the criminological table. Conflict theorists felt, however, that labeling/social reaction theory was not capable of a full exploration of the role of political and economic power in the creation of crime.

One particular type of theory that emerged during this period of conflict theory revival was developed by Austin T. Turk (1969) and outlined in his book, *Criminality and the Legal Order*. Like other conflict theorists, Turk is more interested in explaining why some acts and some actors get treated as criminal, rather than in individuals' motivations for crime. Turk argues that modern society is characterized by power conflicts between authorities and subjects. Authorities make and enforce the rules that are applied to subjects and include formal agents of social control, such as judges, prosecutors, and the police. A key concept in Turk's theory is the notion of criminalization. Criminalization occurs when authorities confer the status of "criminal" on the behavior of subjects. Criminalization is most likely to occur whenever the subjects' behavior is so threatening that a fundamental law is being resisted, when authorities have substantially more power than subjects, and when subjects make clumsy, unrealistic, or unsophisticated moves that threaten authorities.

At about the same time that Turk was writing about the conflict between authorities and subjects, Richard Quinney (1970) was developing his own conflict theory of crime. Quinney's thesis was that modern pluralistic society was held together not by consensus (agreement) but by coercion (the exercise of power). Power is defined as the ability to influence the behavior of others. Some groups in society have and exercise power, while others do not and are subject to it. Reminiscent of the labeling tradition, Quinney further argues that crime is not a quality that is inherent in an act, but is a quality that is bestowed on it through the process of political conflict. In other words, groups with power are successful in having the behaviors of their opponents characterized as harmful, dangerous, and criminal. Thus, crime is created, and created through a social and political process. Persons without political power, therefore, are at greater risk of having their behaviors legislated as criminal than those in more powerful positions.

The conflict view of crime, then, relates criminal behavior to the actions of political minorities who lack the power to translate their values or norms into law. Power in modern society is unequally distributed, and those with political power make and enforce rules against those without power. With this view, conflict theorists defined criminalization as essentially the product of a political process. It was up to radical criminologists to move to the position that criminalization is largely the result of *economic* rather than political forces.

Early and More Recent Radical Perspectives on Crime

Perhaps the best and earliest attempt to state a radical view of crime was found in the work of three British criminologists—Ian Taylor, Paul Walton, and Jock Young (1973). In their book, *The New Criminology*, Taylor and his colleagues delivered a sharply critical review of all previous criminological theorizing. They also proposed an outline of what a truly social (radical) theory of crime should contain. Although skeptical of a purely Marxist theory, these theorists noted that any theory of crime must nonetheless accommodate the fact that criminal behavior is an inevitable consequence of the exploitation of the working class by a capitalist means of production. To them, most criminals are not, however, prerevolutionary figures fighting for the overthrow of an unjust regime. Rather, they are committing crimes that simply enable them to exist as well as they can in a society that has continuously brutalized them. The contribution of Taylor, Walton, and Young to radical criminology was more energizing than substantive. They may not have developed an explicitly radical theory of crime, but they laid the foundation for others who did.

One of these new radical criminologists was Richard Quinney, who moved from his conflict position in 1970 to an explicitly Marxist theory of crime in subsequent years (1974; 1980). In two books, *Critique of Legal Order* (1974) and *Class, State, and Crime* (1980), Quinney's concern was not what motivates persons to commit crimes, but why some acts and some persons get criminalized. His answer was that modern American society is a class society characterized by a struggle between the capitalist class and the working class. The capitalist class owns the means of economic production and constitutes the dominant class. Members of the capitalist class use their economic and political power to their advantage. Essentially, the ruling economic class employs the state as its personal agency of social control. It uses the state and state institutions, such as the armed forces internationally and police forces domestically, to secure its long-term economic interest and continue its economic and political dominance. In making this argument, Quinney adopts what is known as an *instrumentalist* view of the state. Thus, the ruling economic class employs the state as its instrument to further its own ends at the expense of other classes, particularly the working class.

In Quinney's (1980, 59–66) theory, lower- and working-class persons commit crimes of accommodation and resistance, acts committed in order to survive the brutal conditions imposed by the capitalistic class. These would include most of what we know as "street crime," such as armed robbery, burglary, drug dealing, and other predatory and economic crimes, as well as what he would call *politically conscious acts of rebellion.* Members of the capitalist class also commit acts that cause physical injury and economic loss. Such acts include bribery of government officials, white-collar and corporate crimes, and environmental pollution. Although they are alleged by radical criminologists to cause much greater damage and social injury than street crimes, these behaviors of the capitalist class, what Quinney (1980, 51–59) calls *acts of domination and repression,* are not likely to be met with the full force of the criminal law and the criminal justice system. The capitalist class uses such behaviors to secure its position of economic and political dominance, and so they are not likely to be criminalized.

The form that radical criminological theory took in the 1970s was primarily Marxist, along the lines outlined in Richard Quinney's theory in the preceding paragraphs. Throughout the decade of the 1970s, then, radical criminology was synonymous with Marxist criminology. Beginning in the mid-1980s, however, radical criminology underwent a period of intense theoretical development and diversification. Although in the past there had been some conceptual homogeneity within the ranks of radical criminologists, there was now great theoretical diversity. For example, in response to the Marxist position adopted by what were termed *left idealists,* a group of radical criminologists developed a position known as *left realism* (Lowman and MacLean 1992; Matthews and Young 1992). Both groups are politically radical or on the left of the political spectrum but differ with respect to one fundamental issue.

Left idealists are said to be idealists because they hold out the hope that capitalism will be overthrown in the short run and replaced with a more humane mode of production—socialism. Left idealists maintain a more hardline stance towards criminal justice reform, thinking any attempt to reform a corrupt system will only prolong its existence. Left idealists also concentrate their intellectual work on understanding the state and the connection between the capitalist state and a capitalist economy. That is, they are less concerned with what might be considered more mundane criminological issues.

Left realists, on the other hand, argue that crime is a very real problem for the working and lower classes because most crime victimizes them, and because the criminal justice system disproportionately incarcerates their members and miserably fails to improve their lives. Left realists are critical of what they might term the "lofty" policy implications of left idealism, which are to replace the capitalist mode of production with a more equitable one (Matthews and Young 1992). Left realists have put forth a more pragmatic set of policy goals, while not abandoning their belief that capitalism bears the brunt of the responsibility for working- and lower-class crime. They have called for crime victimization surveys in working-class communities to document and characterize the intraclass nature of most crime. They also have argued for various reforms of the criminal justice system, such as a reduction in imprisonment as a solution of first resort to the crime problem, crime victim compensation and restitution programs, and informal community based social control working in tandem with police.

While radical criminologists were splitting into left realists and left idealists in Europe (particularly Britain), in the United States a group of radical criminologists had joined forces to construct what they called *peacemaking criminology* (Pepinsky and Quinney 1991). Peacemaking criminology can perhaps be thought of as a combination of left-wing radical politics and spiritual humanism. Peacemaking criminology asserts that there is a great deal of misery and suffering in the world, and that the function of criminology is the creation of social justice and peace and an end to human suffering. It is an almost utopian perspective that fosters the reconciliation of all conflict and discord and the creation of a world without unemployment, poverty, racism, sexism, ageism, or want. Like left realists, peacemaking criminologists seek reforms of the criminal justice system, whose current punitiveness they decry as creating "negative peace." Such reforms include victim compensation and restitution programs, alternatives to incarceration, and more widespread use of mediation and arbitration in criminal law matters.

A recent radical perspective in criminology is *postmodernism*. As described by two of its spokespersons, postmodern criminology rejects the scientific method of positive criminology (Henry and Einstadter 1998; Beirne and Messerschmidt 2000). It takes the view that there are no external "truths" or "facts" to be discovered by the scientific method and systematic data collection. Rather, they assert that criminologists need to move away from objective research methods as their typical strategy for understanding crime and employ what they call "alternative discourse and meaning" (Henry and Einstadter 1998, 417). This seems to entail a much more subjective understanding of criminological issues and the belief that all accounts or understandings of crime are equally valid and important.

The most recent offshoot of the radical school is *constitutive criminology*, which is viewed by its proponents as a more developed postmodern view (Henry and Milovanovic 1991; 1996). Constitutive criminology can be viewed as criminology's version of literary criticism and "deconstruction." Constitutive criminologists argue that much of our understanding of crime is wrapped in myths and "code words" that convey political and ideological messages (i.e., crime is black male misbehavior, crime needs to treated with harsh measures, criminals choose to do crime, etc.). The consequence of these myths is that they degrade criminals and delude the public about crime.

They would argue for the complete restructuring of the way crime is thought of and spoken about so that human dignity is honored.

Feminist Theory

As you have seen in this book, the theoretical assumptions we make are inextricably linked to the way in which we interpret empirical observations of social research. Depending on the theoretical position used to understand data, the data can take on different meanings. Although a few early criminological researchers examined women's delinquency, crimes committed against women and committed by women have only recently become a topic of interest for criminologists. Moreover, most early works explained the etiology of female deviance as either biological or psychological and were always filled with sexist stereotypes (Lombroso 1920; Thomas 1923). Advocates from the women's movement and other victims rights groups in the 1960s and 1970s helped illuminate violence against women as a serious social problem. Simultaneously, the magnifying glass was also cast on the unique status of female offenders.

Unfortunately, the majority of criminological theories in use at that time had been developed primarily by men using data almost exclusively from samples of men and boys. As such, feminist scholars asserted, the extant knowledge about women, including victimization of women and offending by women, was distorted by the exclusion of women from scholarly discourse. Because of the perceived inadequacies of existing theories to explain violence committed by and against women, feminist theories emerged to "situate the everyday events of women's and men's lives in an analysis that links our personal and collective experience to an understanding of the structure of gender relationships in society and culture" (Andersen 1999, 324).

As you will see, feminist scholarship has added more than theory to the discipline of criminology. For example, Simpson (1989) stated that ". . . [feminist theory] is best understood as both a world view and a social movement that encompasses assumptions and beliefs about the origins and consequences of gendered social organization as well as strategic directions and actions of social change" (606). This chapter highlights three versions of feminist theory: liberal feminist theory, socialist feminist theory, and radical feminist theory. To fully understand contemporary feminist theories, however, they must first be situated within their rich historical background.

A Brief History

As was the case with radical criminology, even though there is no single feminist theory in criminology, all feminist theories have certain assumptions in common. The primary assumption shared by the majority of feminist theories is that women's and men's positions in society are the result of social, not natural or biological, factors. The historical roots of feminist theory date back to 1792 when Mary Wollstonecraft completed the first major work of feminist theory, *A Vindication of the Rights of Woman* (Donovan 1992). Wollstonecraft's concern with "subservience to authority" was a central theme in her work. She believed the perceived weakness of women was the result of their lack of liberty and their dependence on men. The philosophy of liberalism emerging on many fronts during this time is related to the concept of *individual liberty* and the emphasis on human reason as the basis for humanitarian change. For example, the "natural rights of the individual" spoken of by Enlightenment thinkers, such as John Locke, were concurrently coming to the forefront of government philosophical treatises, such as the American Declaration of Independence (1776) and the French Declaration of the Rights of Man (1798). Feminists like Wollstonecraft were simply trying to ensure that women would be entitled to the same "natural rights" that were being sought by men. Unfortunately, the male theorists who enforced the natural rights doctrines emerging in the Western world at that time did not accept this feminist position; the only persons who had natural rights, they believed, were white male property-owning heads of families.

The next major attempt to ensure equal rights for women was the "Declaration of Sentiments" drafted by Elizabeth Cady Stanton and issued in Seneca Falls, New York, in 1848 (Rossi 1974). Whereas the Declaration of Independence sought to overthrow the "absolute despotism" of the King of Great Britain, the Declaration of Sentiments' despot was man himself. It stated, "The history of mankind is a history of repeated injuries and usurpations on the part of man toward women, having in direct object the establishment of an absolute tyranny over her." This clearly sets down the roots of women's oppression by a system of domination established by men. In essence, the Seneca Falls document declares that the oppression of women as a class or group has been a historically pervasive and systematic subjugation by men.

During the same time, across the Atlantic, a book by John Stuart Mill (although the ideas therein he attributed to his wife, Harriet Taylor Mill), called *The Subjection of Women*, first published in 1851, inspired the British suffrage movement. In this work, Mill defined human liberty as a natural right and one that should not be denied on the basis of any individual or group characteristic. In this work, Mill also described the social conditions that were used to create gender-specific arrangements as well as attitudes that were used to discredit the claim of women's equality. Foretelling the thoughts of contemporary behaviorist theorists in psychology, Mill postulated that the perception of women being naturally subjected to men as universal was simply the result of social learning. Because women had historically been subservient to men, Mill believed, it was impossible to make claims about natural gender differences.

These ideas are central to contemporary *liberal feminist* theory, which is centered on the premise of equality and the capacity for existing democratic social institutions to create equal rights and equal opportunity for women. Similar to Mill's early work, liberal feminists emphasize gender socialization as the origin of gender differences, "thereby assuming that changes in socialization practices will result in more liberated and egalitarian gender relations" (Andersen 1999, 325). In general, the basic tenets of liberal feminist theory are that the inequality of women has arisen because as a group, they have been denied their rights and have been socialized to accept their subservient position relative to men. Discrimination is thus a central concept for liberal feminists. In this view, all will be fine once women have truly achieved equality with men in political, economic, and social institutions.

Critics of this philosophy assert that this is optimistic at best and completely wrong at worst. "What about the inherent structural inequalities of our social systems that have propagated sexist societies in the first place?" critics ask. In addition, critics contend that liberal feminist theory does not explain the effects of race and class stratification in women's lives. For example, asserting that women should be equal to men is only the beginning. Which men should women be equal to (Eisenstein 1981)? Gender equality, critics assert, would only allow some women equality with some men. The conditions of oppression that produced gender as well as race and class inequality in the first place would remain unchanged. To speak to these issues, so-called radical alternatives to the liberal perspective emerged. These perspectives place more emphasis on the development of gender as a social, economic, and political category.

The historical roots of these more radical feminist perspectives are also situated in the nineteenth century. Perhaps the most notable influence was Karl Marx and Friedrich Engels' essay, *The Communist Manifesto*, originally published in 1848. The resulting theoretical perspective has often been called *dialectical materialism*, the central thesis of which states that the material conditions of people's lives shape their behavior and their beliefs. As Catherine A. MacKinnon (1982) succinctly stated, "Marxist theory argues that society is fundamentally constructed of the relations people form as they do and make things needed to survive humanly. Work is the social process of shaping and transforming the material and social worlds, creating people as social beings as they create value. It is that activity by which people

become who they are. Class is its structure, production its consequence, capital its congealed form, and control its issue" (1).

Marx and Engels defined production as the labor humans perform to satisfy their immediate needs. Systems of production that distort human potential must be transformed by changing social relations, more specifically, through revolution. According to Marx, capitalism was one of those systems of production. In capitalist societies, Marx observed, the economic infrastructure was divided into two classes: capitalists, who owned the means of production, and the proletariat, who sold their labor to capitalist owners in exchange for wages. The only way to end the tyranny of private ownership of the means of production and the accumulation of profit by the few was by reorganizing the means of production through revolution. Where did women fit into this picture? According to Marxists, women's oppression was a reflection of the more fundamental form of oppression by class. Once oppression by class was obliterated through revolution, sexism would also disappear. Thus, women will be liberated once class oppression has ended. Radical feminists, on the other hand, do not believe that gender oppression will end with the elimination of class oppression. Although radical feminism shares a lot of common theoretical ground with Marxist criminology, this point is essentially where the two part company.

Socialist feminist theory, which emerged in the 1970s, asserted that although capitalism was a significant source of women's oppression, the sexual division of labor was the primary source of oppression. Consequently, eradicating class oppression by itself, these scholars believed, would not necessarily eliminate sexual inequality as well. Evidence of this, of course, lies in observations of women in socialist countries, such as China and Cuba. In these cases, the only real effort by the revolutionary leadership for ending traditional sex roles has been limited to making women's labor available to the political regime. However, feminists argue that freeing women to work outside the home is just one aspect of equality, particularly because socialist societies still allow men freedom from work within the home. As MacKinnon (1982) stated, "Feminists do not argue that it means the same to women to be on the bottom in a feudal regime, a capitalist regime, and a socialist regime; the commonality argued is that, despite real changes, bottom is bottom. . . . Neither technology nor socialism, both of which purport to alter women's role at the point of production, have ever yet equalized women's status relative to men" (9). Despite assertions such as these, a basic premise of socialist feminist theory is that women should have full access to public industry "and the right to earn a living wage" (Mitchell 1971, 148). The exclusion of women from public industry and their restriction to the private world of the family, socialist feminists believe, form the basis for their subordination.

Socialist feminists believe that while capitalism remains a significant source of women's oppression, gender relations are equally important. With this view, other important questions arise, such as "What is the relationship between the mode of production and biological and social reproduction?" This and similar questions have illuminated the relationship between the family and the economy. For example, as a result of industrialization during the nineteenth century, the family changed from a unit of production to a unit of consumption. It was during this time that the private labor of women in the domestic and private realm became separated from publicly productive labor (Zaretsky 1976). This former sphere was, of course, reserved for those who could afford to stay home. Even though most working-class, poor, and minority women worked outside of their homes, women's work still became ideologically defined as caring for the emotional needs and maintenance of the family. Thus, socialist feminist theory argues that it is the interaction of women's role in reproduction, sexuality, and the socialization of children with the economic mode of production that subordinates women to men (Mitchell 1971). A change in women's status, social feminists believe, will occur only when women are allowed full entry into the system of production and, at the same time have equal status in family relations.

Critics of socialist feminist theory, however, maintain that this theory still does not explain the emergence of men's dominance over women to begin with.

While *radical feminist* theory has taken many directions, many of these theorists situate the source of women's oppression squarely on the shoulders of patriarchy and patriarchy alone (Daly 1978). *Patriarchy*, as defined by radical feminists, is a "sexual system of power in which the male possesses superior power and economic privilege" (Eisenstein 1981, 17). In essence, radical feminism views all systems of domination, including those based on class, as extensions of the underlying politics of male supremacy.

Some strains of radical feminism assert that sexuality is the key variable in women's oppression. For example, MacKinnon (1982) stated, "Sexuality is to feminism what work is to Marxism: that which is most one's own, yet most taken away . . . the molding, direction, and expression of sexuality organizes society into two sexes—women and men—which division underlies the totality of social relations" (1–2). MacKinnon proposed that through rape, sexual harassment, incest, and other violence, men exercise their sexual power over women.

The implications of radical feminist theory for social change are more dramatic and as such are very different from those of socialist feminists. Radical feminists contend that as long as the "state" has modes of operation and underlying assumptions based on men's power, women will never be able to overcome their subordination through actions of the state. Because the cause of women's oppression lies in the fundamental nature of political and economic institutions, radical feminist theory asserts that revolutionary changes are needed in both the systems of capitalism and patriarchy.

In sum, there is no single feminist theory, and the contributions of feminist scholars to the field of criminology have been informed by three primary perspectives (i.e., liberal, socialist, and radical feminism). Moreover, important new feminist scholarship, particularly by women of color, has compelled us to examine the more intricate relationships existing between race, class, and gender (Andersen and Collins 1998) to remedy the "add [gender] and stir" mentality that pervades criminological theorizing in general (Simpson 1989).

Feminist Theory and Criminology

Liberal, socialist, and radical feminist theory each have made unique contributions to the field of criminology. Feminist thought has illuminated the fact that female crime and victimization must be seen within the larger societal context of gender, race, and class relations. From a feminist perspective, what is considered crime is established by the powerful in society who define some acts as criminal in order to protect their own interests (Messerschmidt 1986).

Some feminist scholars have focused their attention on women as criminals. This research has concentrated on several research questions, including "How are women's crimes linked to gender relations?" and "Has the evolution of gender relations created more opportunities for women to commit crimes and if so, what types of crime?" Historically, if research on women's criminality and deviance was done at all, it was limited to behaviors that were linked with women's sexuality, such as prostitution and promiscuity. Nothing typifies this pattern more than the double standard placed on promiscuity for males and females; only among young girls is promiscuity seen as a social problem.

Feminist scholars have importantly noted that women's deviance cannot be separated from the social context in which they live. For example, research on girls' gangs has shown that young women find solidarity in gang membership that they may not experience in their home environments. In addition, the gang provides a haven for young girls to cope with the many problems they have associated with sexism, racism, and class inequality (Campbell 1989; Joe and Chesney-Lind 1995). Unlike earlier research, then, these types of feminist analyses place women's deviance within the social context of gender, race, and class relations that exist in society.

Relatedly, feminist scholars studying women's crime have also pointed to the strong connections between women's involvement in crime and their victimization. Daly (1994), for example, has called this the "reproduction of harm," meaning that women who have been emotionally and sexually abused, raised in families that are marginalized by poverty, and subjected to violence in relationships with men are more likely to become deviant or engage in criminal behavior. In addition, other research has shown that women's crime often directly or indirectly benefits men (Miller 1986) and that many women are coerced into crime by their male partners (Richie 1996).

The differential treatment of male and female offenders in the criminal justice system, from adjudication to incarceration, has also been a topic of concern for feminist scholars. Regarding adjudication, early research argued that judges gave female offenders more lenient sentences than men convicted of the same crime because of chivalrous and paternalistic attitudes toward women. More recent research, however, has suggested that once the influence of a defendant's prior record is controlled, the other factors related to a judge's sentence are not so much chivalry, but the status of both male and female defendants' work and family obligations (Daly 1989). That is, females are given more lenient treatment than men because of the belief that women are more indispensable to the stability of the family. This research suggests that judges are not so much protecting women as they are seeking to protect children and families.

For those females who find themselves sentenced to prison, institutions "primarily designed, built, and run by men for men" (Church 1990, 20) are usually what await them. Few prisons today provide the special services required for the needs of female inmates, particularly their reproductive needs, or their needs to sustain maternal ties to their children or both (Ingram-Fogel 1993). Gender stereotypes also shape the vocational training women receive in prison. For example, although vocational training for men allows them the potential to obtain a well-paying job in such trades as mechanics and carpentry, vocational training for women, to the extent that it exists at all, is usually restricted to stereotypical female jobs that offer little hope of advancement, such as laundresses or beauticians (Morash, Harr, Robin, and Rucker 1994).

Feminist analyses have also made other important contributions to the study of women's victimization. The results of the first national survey of family violence was not published until 1980 (Straus, Gelles, and Steinmetz 1980). This survey brought to light the problem of violence within the family from spouses, partners, and other intimates that women must confront. Only after such national attention did the U.S. Department of Justice begin to redesign its National Crime Victimization Survey to more accurately measure incidents of intimate partner violence and other violence against women, such as rape (Bachman and Taylor 1994). It was no surprise to feminists to see that once women were finally asked about their experiences with intimate perpetrated violence, a very different picture of women's vulnerability was revealed compared to the stereotypical notions held by society. For example, data from the redesigned National Crime Victimization Survey showed that it was not the stranger lurking in the bushes that posed the greatest threat to women. Women were more likely to be both assaulted and raped by people they knew and often loved compared to strangers (Bachman and Saltzman 1995; Tjaden and Thoeness 1998).

The acknowledgment of violence against women as a serious social problem was just the beginning. Feminist scholars and other victim's rights groups next worked diligently to make sure the criminal justice system responded to violence against women in the same way it responded to other forms of violence. For example, although statutes vary by state, most state legislatures and the federal government enacted rape reform statutes aimed at increasing the probability of alleged rape offenders being treated in court like all other individuals being tried for a violent crime (Bachman and Paternoster 1993; Horney and Spohn 1991). Other efforts were mobilized to ensure that offenders who as-

saulted their intimate partners would be treated similarly to other violent offenders by police. For example, mandatory arrest policies for these assaults have been implemented in most jurisdictions across the country. In addition, the historical 1994 Violence Against Women Act implemented by the United States Congress instituted a number of other penalties aimed at deterring intimate partner assaults. For example, the Lautenburg Bill attached to the Act made it illegal for someone convicted of assault, including misdemeanor assault against intimate partners, to own a firearm.

In sum, feminist scholars have advanced criminological theory by illuminating both society's emphasis on masculinity as a socially learned pattern of aggression and domination along with the larger political and economic status of women in patriarchal and capitalist systems in which this socialization occurs. This theorizing has, in turn, helped transform society's antiquated notions and sexist stereotypes concerning violence committed by and against women.

References

Andersen, Margaret L. (1999). *Thinking About Women: Sociological Perspectives on Sex and Gender*, Fifth Edition. Boston: Allyn and Bacon.

Andersen, Margaret L. and Patricia Hill Collins. (1998). *Race, Class, and Gender: An Anthology*, Third Edition. Belmont, CA: Wadsworth.

Bachman, R. and R. Paternoster, (1993). "A contemporary look at the effects of rape law reform: How far have we really come?" *The Journal of Criminal Law & Criminology*, 84(3):554–574.

Bachman, R. and L.E. Saltzman. (1995). *Violence Against Women: A National Crime Victimization Survey Report*. NCJ-145325. Washington, DC: Bureau of Justice Statistics, U.S. Department of Justice.

Bachman, R. and B. Taylor. (1994). "The measurement of rape and family violence by the redesigned National Crime Victimization Survey. *Justice Quarterly*, 11:702–714.

Beirne, Piers and James Messerschmidt. (2000). *Criminology*, Third Edition. Boulder, CO: Westview.

Bonger, Willem. [1916] (1969). *Criminality and Economic Conditions*. Reprint edited by Austin T. Turk. Bloomington: Indiana University Press.

Campbell, Anne. (1989). *Girls in the Gang.* Cambridge, UK: Basil Blackwell.

Church, George J. (1990). "The view from behind bars." *Time,* 136, 20–22.

Cullen, Francis T. and Robert Agnew. (1999). *Criminological Theory: Past to Present.* Los Angeles: Roxbury.

Daly, Kathleen. (1989). "Rethinking judicial paternalism: Gender, work-family relations, and sentencing." *Gender & Society,* 3:9–36.

Daly, Kathleen. (1994). *Gender, Crime and Punishment.* New Haven, CT: Yale University Press.

Daly, Mary. (1978). *Gyn/Ecology: The Meta-Ethics of Radical Feminism.* Boston: Beacon.

Donovan, Josephine. (1992). *Feminist Theory: The Intellectual Traditions of American Feminism.* New York: Continuum.

Eisenstein, Zilla. (1981). *The Radical Future of Liberal Feminism.* New York: Longmans.

Henry, Stuart and Werner Einstadter. (1998). *The Criminology Theory Reader.* New York: New York University Press.

Henry, Stuart and Dragan Milovanovic. (1991). "Constitutive criminology: The maturation of critical criminology." *Criminology,* 29:245–263.

——1996. *Constitutive Criminology: Beyond Postmodernism.* London: Sage.

Horney, J. and C. Spohn. (1991). "Rape law reform and instrumental change in six urban jurisdictions." *Law and Society Review,* 25, 117–153.

Ingram-Fogel, Catherine. (1993). "Hard time: The stressful nature of incarceration for women." *Issues in Mental Health Nursing,* 14, 367–377.

Joe, Karen A. and Meda Chesney-Lind. (1995). "Just every mother's angel: An analysis of gender and ethnic variations in youth gang membership." *Gender & Society,* 9, 408–431.

Lombroso, N. (1920). *The Female Offender.* New York: Appleton.

Lowman, John and Brian D. MacLean. (1992). *Realist Criminology: Crime Control and Policing in the 1990s.* Toronto: University of Toronto Press.

MacKinnon, Catherine A. (1982). "Feminism, Marxism, method, and the state: An agenda for theory." Pp. 1–30 in *Feminist Theory: A Critique of Ideology.* Keohane, N.O., Rosalda, M.A. and Gelpi, B.C. (eds.). Chicago: University of Chicago Press.

Marx, Karl and Friederick Engels. (1970). *The Communist Manifesto.* New York: Pathfinder.

Matthews, Roger and Jock Young. (1992). *Issues in Realist Criminology.* London: Sage.

Messerschmidt, James. (1986). *Capitalism, Patriarchy, and Criminology: Toward a Feminist Criminology.* Totowa, NJ: Rowman and Littlefield.

Mill, John S. [1851] (1970). *The Subjection of Women.* New York: Source.

Miller, Eleanor M. (1986). *Street Women.* Philadelphia, PA: Temple University Press.

Mitchell, Juliet. (1971). *Woman's Estate.* New York: Pantheon.

Morash, Merry, Haarr, N. Robin and Lila Rucker. (1994). "Comparison of programming for women and men in U.S. prisons in the 1980s." *Crime and Delinquency,* 40, 197–221.

Platt, Anthony M. (1969). *The Child Savers.* Chicago: University of Chicago Press.

Pepinsky, Harold E. and Richard Quinney. (1991). *Criminology as Peacemaking.* Bloomington: Indiana University Press.

Quinney, Richard. (1970). *The Social Reality of Crime.* Boston: Little, Brown.

——(1974). *Critique of Legal Order: Crime Control in Capitalist Society.* Boston: Little, Brown.

——(1980). *Class, State, and Crime,* Second Edition. New York: Longman.

Richie, Beth. E. (1996). *Compelled to Crime: The Gender Entrapment of Battered Black Women.* New York: Routledge.

Rossi, Alice A. (1974). *The Feminist Papers: From Adams to de Beauvoir* (1973). New York: Bantam.

Rusche, Georg and Otto Kirchheimer. (1939). *Punishment and Social Structure.* New York: Columbia University Press.

Sellin, Thorsten. (1938). *Culture, Conflict, and Crime.* New York: Social Science Research Council.

Shoemaker, Donald J. (1996). *Theories of Delinquency,* Third Edition. New York: Oxford University Press.

Simpson, Sally S. (1989). "Feminist theory, crime, and justice." *Criminology,* 27, 605–632.

Straus, M.A., R. Gelles, and S.K. Steinmetz. (1980). *Behind Closed Doors: Violence in the American Family.* New York: Anchor.

Taylor, Ian, Paul Walton, and Jock Young. (1973). *The New Criminology.* New York: Harper and Row.

Tjaden, P. N. and Nancy Thoennes. (1998). *Prevalence, Incidence, and Consequences of Violence Against Women: Findings from the*

National Violence Against Women Survey. National Institute of Justice and Centers for Disease Control and Prevention, U.S. Department of Justice.

Thomas, W.I. (1923). *The Unadjusted Girl.* Boston: Little, Brown.

Turk, Austin T. (1969). *Criminality and the Legal Order.* Chicago: Rand-McNally.

Vold, George B. (1958). *Theoretical Criminology.* New York: Oxford University Press.

Zaretsky, E. (1976). *Capitalism, the Family, and Personal Life.* New York: Harper and Row.

Radical Criminology

Michael J. Lynch
University of South Florida

Paul B. Stretesky
Colorado State University

Criminology textbooks tend to lump critical theories of crime together, as if all critical theories were the same. This results in a superficial examination of critical explanations of crime. To avoid this problem, this essay examines one form of critical perspective, radical criminology (on other forms see Arrigo 1995; Ferrell and Sanders 1995; Henry and Milovanovic 1996; Milovanovic 1994, 1995; DeKeseredy and Schwartz 1996; Schwartz and Friedrichs 1994).

Radical criminology examines how forms of inequality, oppression, and conflict affect crime and law. Consequently, radicals are interested in how structural inequalities evident in a society's class, race, and gender structures affect (1) participation in crime, (2) how crime is defined, and (3) the making and enforcement of laws. To answer these issues, radicals examine crime relative to the social, economic, and political structures and forms of inequality found in a given society at a particular moment in history (Lynch and Groves 1995). As a result, radical explanations pay close attention to history and culture. Thus, even though general "rules" are useful for describing the content of radical criminology, in practice, radical explanations of crime vary depending upon the historical era and cultural system to which they are applied. Taking this historical and cultural preference into account, this essay focuses primarily on modern U.S. society.

In contemporary American society, three forms of inequality—race, class, and gender—stand out. Each form of inequality has an impact on an individual's life course, the nature of power, and who holds power within society. These forms of inequality and their impact on crime are examined below.

When radicals speak about race, class, and gender, they use these terms differently than traditional criminologists. For traditional criminologists, race, class, and gender tend to be interpreted as characteristics of individuals, and are used to identify subjects of study as "middle-class," "African American," or "female." For radicals, race, class, and gender are both identities and structures. As structures, race, class, and gender contain culturally and historically specific "rules" that define (1) the types of power groups possess, (2) a group's social and economic positions within society, and (3) the opportunities for success people from these groups typically possess. As identities, race, class, and gender tell us about social expectations concerning the behavior of people from different groups and the ways in which people act to construct themselves (their identities). For example, "middle-class" defines a location in U.S. social structure, which in turn defines the types of power persons can access and wield, their opportunities or pathways to success, and the forms of oppressive conditions which they control or which control them. But, being "middle-class" also defines behavioral expectations, and we expect middle-class people to behave in particular ways. We identify middle-class people by what they wear, where they live, and the schools they attend. Similarly, being African American (or white or Hispanic) or female (or male) affects a person's access to power and success and our behavioral expectations and responses. In short, a person's structural location carries with it different forms of access and different behavioral expectations. For radicals, these differences are evidence of inequality, and these inequalities help explain the probability that people located in different structural locations will engage in crime or will be labeled as criminals.

To explain this view, we first examine the nature of inequality in U.S. society. Next, we examine some background issues necessary to understand the radical view of crime. This discussion is followed by an examination of the relationship between class, race, gender, economic power, and inequality. We then examine the radical view on street crime, corporate crime, and environmental justice. The final section of this essay examines some policy implications related to this view.

Class, Race, and Gender: Social Stratification and Economic Inequality

Radical analysis stems from the observation that societies are based on unequal social relationships characterized by a conflict between the "haves" and "have-nots" (Marx and Engels 1995, 1970). The nature and form of these conflicts vary historically and culturally. Despite the relative nature of this claim, radicals view conflict and inequality as the basis of most crime. As a result, it follows that the best way to reduce crime is to eliminate social, economic, and political inequality.

For radicals, unequal societies are characterized by a lopsided distribution of power. The more unequal a society, the greater a problem crime becomes. Inequality also has important implications for individuals living within a society. Inequality means that some people will have less (or more) access to life chances for success, and that success is a function of a person's structural position within society. Because many people occupy similar structural locations, their opportunities for success (or failure) are also similar. Radicals focus on race, class, and gender inequality to explain patterns of crime because people who occupy these structurally defined positions have similar sets of opportunities and behave or are treated in similar ways or both. Evidence of how race, class, and gender structure success and crime is examined later in this essay.

Crime and Inequality: An Overview

There are two ways to examine the influence of inequality on crime. With respect to street crime, radicals argue that those denied equal access to life chances for success will be more likely to (1) engage in crime or (2) have their behaviors defined and labeled as criminal (or both). A few brief examples il-

lustrate this point. Studies indicate that criminal law, the most coercive form of social control society can render, tends to focus on the lower classes and minorities. Policing, for instance, is concentrated in lower-class and minority communities, and prisons primarily house people who are lower-class and minorities. Historically, crimes such as vagrancy and loitering were enacted to control the working and lower classes (Chambliss 1964; Harring 1983). Throughout history, drug laws have served similar functions, typically focusing on controlling drugs commonly used by minorities and the lower class (Brownstein 1991, 1996, 2000).

Inequality and the emphasis on acquiring power also helps explain the crimes of the powerful. Two issues are important here. First, inequality and power help explain why law focuses on the lower classes while neglecting the equally harmful behavior of the powerful (Reiman 1998). Second, our culture's emphasis on power and wealth helps explain why people with power use illegal means to obtain even more power (Friedrichs 1996; Simon 1999). In short, for radicals, the forms of inequality, power, and conflict that are part of the organization of American society can be used to explain the crime of the lower classes (and minorities and women) as well as the crimes of the upper classes.

Class Inequality and Crime: Background

In examining the relationship between inequality and crime, early radicals focused on social class, basing their views on Marx's analysis of capitalism. The emphasis on class was a defining characteristic of radical criminology, which distinguished it from all other forms of criminology. A brief overview of this position is presented below.

For Marx, the history of all societies was the history of class conflict, or the opposition of the "haves" and "have-nots." But Marx was particularly interested in examining how these conflicts played out in capitalist societies. There, conflicts revolve around the opposition of capitalists and workers. Capitalists, who own and control the machinery of production and capital, need workers to carry out their objectives of accumulating capital, and capitalists' economic power results from their ability to control and exploit the labor of workers. Capitalists also possess the ability to translate their economic power into political power. In modern societies this occurs through activities such as campaign contributions and lobbying.

Marx argued that capitalists have a particular set of interests to protect, and that their primary interest is establishing circumstances conducive to profit-making. Marx demonstrated that capitalists' profits are directly related to workers' wages, and that it was in the capitalists' best interests to keep wages to a minimum.

In contrast, workers' interests revolve around increasing wages, and in general, activities that advantage capitalists disadvantage workers. Further, whereas capitalists are relatively powerful, workers are relatively powerless, having little influence over law-making and economic processes. Nevertheless, throughout history, workers have struggled to obtain their share of society's power and wealth, demanding expanded employment opportunities, higher wages, better working conditions, and health care and retirement benefits. Workers have relied on strikes, work slowdowns, and work stoppages to achieve these goals. Sometimes, when these avenues fail or are closed off, they turn to crime as an alternative to legitimate means to success (Quinney 1980).

Law is an important method of "mediating" the conflicts between these classes. Numerous laws defining property rights, wage levels, and working conditions have been passed throughout history. Traditional criminologists argue that these laws reflect widely shared values that represent the interests of all people in society—a view commonly called consensus theory. In contrast, radicals suggest that laws generally (though not always) favor the best interests of capitalists and that most laws, even criminal laws, have a distinct advantage for the powerful, protecting the social, economic, and political organization of society that serves as the basis of the powerful's privileged position.

As noted, this class view of crime and law is unique to radical criminology. Employing

this view, early radicals were acknowledged for highlighting the effects of class and inequality on crime, and for focusing attention on crimes of the powerful. But radicals were also criticized for their "singular focus" on class and crime (see Inciardi 1980). This unidimensional focus on class has, however, been addressed by radicals (e.g., Messerschmidt 1986), and they have since incorporated other important dimensions of inequality in their explanations of crime, especially racial and gender inequality (e.g., Messerschmidt 1993, 1997; Schwartz and Milovanovic 1996). Today, a radical view that fails to acknowledge the important effect each of these structures has on crime is considered inadequate (see Schwartz and Milovanovic 1996; Lynch, Michalowski, and Groves 2000).

Despite these additions, class remains an important element of radical theories of crime. Further discussion of the radical view of class is presented in the next section.

The Radical Economic Model

For radicals, classes are defined by how people relate to a society's economic system or mode of production. The contemporary American economy is based on capitalism and is a blend of manufacturing and service sector production. In the mid-1970s, the U.S. economy shifted from a highly concentrated form of manufacturing capitalism to service capitalism. Capitalism is one example of a mode of production. Other examples include socialism, communism, and feudalism, to name a few.

Each mode of production entails specific relations to production, or more simply, a class system. People located in different classes possess different degrees of economic, political, and social power (theoretically, this distinction does not apply to communism, though in practice, self-proclaimed communist nations have been class societies). Class divisions also determine the kinds of conflicts that will emerge in society. Under capitalism, the most important conflicts are between the owners (capitalists) of the productive forces (also called the means of production) and workers.

Radicals employ a two-class model as a heuristic device. Contemporary U.S. society, however, has more than two classes (Wright, 1978), which can be defined as follows: (1) capitalists or owners of large companies, (2) managers of large businesses, (3) self-employed owners of small businesses (categories two and three comprise the petty-bourgeois or small capitalists), (4) professionals, such as doctors, lawyers, or teachers, (5) workers, from those who work on mass-production lines (manufacturing workers), to clerical and fast-food employees (service workers), to construction or unskilled workers (laborers) and (6) groups that have no relationship to production, or the surplus or marginalized populations. Surplus populations consist of the unemployed, partially employed, and underemployed as well as migrant workers, the homeless, and career criminals (whom Marx called the lumpenproletariat). In U.S. society, these populations are distributed as follows: capitalists, 2 percent; the "middle class" (two, three, and four), 15 percent; workers, 65 percent; surplus population, 18 percent (Perlow 1988).

For radicals, class membership is important because it affects people's access to power. Research has shown that being born into a particular class significantly impacts a person's life chances for success and, more often than not, people remain part of the class into which they are born (Frank and Cook 1995). Most Americans don't define class in terms of a person's relationship to production, but rather with respect to income or wealth. To make our discussion relevant to the way most Americans think about class, we next review information on wealth and income.

Class, Wealth, and Income: Inequality in U.S. Society

Decisive evidence of social stratification and inequality in the United States emerges when examining the distribution of our nation's wealth (stored-up capital represented by savings and property holdings and other assets) and income.

One way to assess inequality is to examine the concentration of wealth—the ratio of

wealth owned by the richest 20 percent of the population compared to the poorest 20 percent of the population. These data indicate that the United States has the most lopsided class system of any advanced nation in the world. It also has one of the highest rates of crime. In Japan, this ratio of inequality is four; in Germany, five; in the United States, this ratio is nine (U.N. Development Program 1993). In other words, the richest 20 percent are twice as far removed from the poor as the rich in other nations. Other measures paint a similar picture of inequality. In Britain, the richest 1 percent of the population owns 18 percent of the wealth; in France and Canada, this figure is about 25 percent; in Sweden 16 percent. In the United States, the richest 1 percent owns 39 percent of the wealth (Wolff 1995).

Faced with these facts, people argue that in America, the land of opportunity, things have improved for those at the bottom of the social structure over time, and that competition and hard work—the invisible hand of market systems—have reduced inequality. Evidence indicates otherwise: today, the wealthy have more and the poor less than they once did. Economist Edward Wolff (1995) noted that federal data "show that between 1983 and 1989 the top 20 percent of wealth holders received 99 percent of the total gain in marketable wealth, while the bottom 80 percent of the population got only 1 percent" (58). This trend was more exaggerated between 1989 to 1992 (Wolff 1995). Increasing inequality is revealed in the following as well: in the United States, the number of millionaires and billionaires increased at the same time that home-ownership and retirement savings declined for middle-income families (Wolff 1995, 1995b). Other data show a hardening of class lines and a polarization of wealth and classes in the United States over the past fifty years (Perlow 1988).

Income Inequality

Inequality is also evident in the unequal distribution of income. In 1994, the top 20 percent of income earners took home about half of all income, while the bottom 20 percent received only 3.6 percent (U.S. Census

Bureau 1999). The "super rich"—the top 5 percent—took home nearly 22 percent of all income. This picture of income inequality becomes more exaggerated if we consult a broader period of time, and available evidence suggests that income inequality has widened over the past 50 years (Currie and Skolnick 1984, 100–107). In recent years, the lowest 20 percent of income earners saw their share of income decline from 4.0 percent to 3.6 percent (1967–1999). In contrast, income for the top 1 percent more than doubled during a time when median income was relatively stable and the cost of living doubled (1979–1989) (Frank and Cook 1995, 5). Contrary to capitalist ideology, these facts indicate little hope for the vast majority of people within the lower class—and increasingly, the middle class—to improve their economic conditions. Wealth and income, in other words, trickle up, not down, and many of the wealthy are so well off that they are referred to as the "super rich" (Perlow 1988) or the "top-out-of-sight" (Fussell 1997).

Increasing inequality calls into question the idea that hard work gets you ahead. Frank and Cook (1995) argue that despite working harder and longer, U.S. workers are worse off today than 30 years ago, working longer hours for reduced wages, accumulating more personal debt, and having less in savings and retirement benefits (Frank and Cook 1995; Schor 1995). In short, the rich are getting much richer, while most of the rest of us are working harder and losing ground.

Many object to this depiction of American society, citing evidence of "people they know" who "made it." The big picture, however, suggests that these kinds of success stories are rare. National statistics indicate that many more people failed to achieve economic success, are in the same place they were decades earlier, or have seen their economic circumstances decline (Barlett and Steele 1992; Frank and Cook 1995). In sum, the 1980s and 1990s accelerated a growing pattern of inequality that has characterized the American class system over the past 50 years.

Inequality and the Shift from a Manufacturing to a Service Economy

The accelerated path of inequality in the United States can be explained by economic transformations that occurred over the past 25 years. In the mid-1970s, the United States began to shift from a manufacturing to a service economy. In a nutshell, this shift caused a decline in high-wage manufacturing or blue-collar employment as these jobs were shifted to nations with lower wage rates; a rise in low-wage, service sector and menial employment; declines in the quality and quantity of rewards associated with white-collar work; high levels of unemployment among minorities residing in urban areas; and decreases in leisure time (Schor 1995; Frank and Cook 1995; Wilson 1997).

To this point, we have reviewed inequality as it relates to income, wealth, and social class. In the United States, inequality is also a function of gender, race, and ethnicity.

Gender and Economic Inequality

Economic inequality has an important gender dimension. Historically, women have less access to economic and political power than men, and this remains true today despite claims that affirmative action has eliminated discrimination against women (see Carnoy 1994; Lynch 1996; Lynch and Patterson 1996). Recent reviews of income data have generated misleading conclusions concerning gender income disparity, noting, for example, that over the past fifteen years women's incomes have increased relative to men's incomes. On its face, this statement is true. But it is true not because women are being paid more, but rather because men's wages have declined (Amott 1995, 207). The decline in men's wages can be explained relative to the shift to a service economy, which displaced men from manufacturing jobs and high-paying white-collar employment. This transformation has had little effect on women, who have traditionally been employed in low-wage service sector jobs (Figart and Lapidus 1996, 1998). On average, women earn only 73 percent as much as men (U.S. Census Bureau 1999). This gender wage disparity is evident across all forms of

employment, and even women in high-status positions (physicians, lawyers, and ac-
countants) earn significantly less than men
in those fields (Ruth 1995; Figart and
Lapidus 1998). Occupational and income
gender inequality has numerous adverse impacts on women, which may help explain the
increase in female crime over the past two
decades. Contributing to gender inequality
is the increasing number of women who live
in female-headed households that are at or
below the poverty level, a process called the
feminization of poverty (Messerschmidt
1986; Kozol 1995; Rotella 1995; Sklar 1995).

Race, Ethnicity, and Economic Inequality: Racism and Inequality

In the United States, economic inequality
has important racial and ethnic dimensions.
For example, although women are disadvantaged relative to men, not all women are
equally disadvantaged; minority women suffer greater economic disadvantages than
white women. The effect of race and ethnicity helps explain why minorities are more
likely than whites to have lower incomes, or
be part of the lower classes, and are more
likely to turn to crime or to be labeled as
criminals.

To be sure, relative to whites, African-
Americans and Hispanics are economically
disadvantaged. In 1998, for instance, median family income for whites was nearly
$42,000, while black ($25,400) and Hispanic
($28,330) median family incomes were
about one-third lower (U.S. Census Bureau
1999). Further, the unemployment rate for
black males is more than twice that for white
males (U.S. Department of Labor 1996). Employed African-American men are usually
paid less for the same work, or are more
likely to be restricted to minimum wage,
poorly paid service sector jobs (Carnoy
1994). Even though the middle and working
classes lost ground over the past 20 years,
these losses had a greater impact on blacks
than whites (Carnoy 1994, 15–29).

Racism is a powerful structural force that
negatively impacts African-Americans. In
the United States, racism has meant that African-Americans not only hold lower-paying

jobs but are also spatially segregated
(Massey and Denton 1993). Segregation en-
sures that African Americans remain detached from economic structures that would
promote their financial independence and
revitalize their communities (Massey and
Denton 1993).

It is commonly assumed that racism and
segregation have diminished since the Civil
Rights Movement. However, Massey and
Denton's (1993) analysis of racial segregation in the United States shows that African-
American communities have become more
segregated over the past 30 years as the result of institutionalized racism, which has
contributed to poor economic circumstances in African-American communities.
Given these poor economic conditions, it is
no surprise that crime is higher in minority
communities than in white communities.
Any sensible crime policy must include
means of dismantling institutional discrimination and methods for revitalizing the economic base in minority communities.

The Disadvantages of Being at the Bottom

Many indicators show that the quality of
life—evident in levels of illness, mental
health difficulties, inadequate housing, limited access to health care, problems of self-
esteem, or living in proximity to pollution
and hazardous waste—declines as we de-
scend the economic ladder. It is important to
remember that these indicators are not qualities of poor people but rather result from living within a particular class and racial context that carries with it certain liabilities.

Compared to the middle and upper
classes, the poor have less access to quality
education, making it difficult for them to escape poverty (DiMaggio 1982; DiMaggio and
Mohr 1985). Lower-income people also have
less access to things the affluent take for
granted, such as telephones, computers, and
the Internet (e.g., Associated Press 1998) and
are more likely to have hazardous waste sites
in their neighborhoods, to live near polluting
industries, and to suffer from environmentally induced health problems (Gilman 1995;
Knox 1996, 1994, 1992a, 1992b; Knox and
Gilman 1997; Stretesky and Lynch 1999).
And last but not least, poor persons are more

likely to be victims of violent crime. It is important to remember that these general class-linked life-chance factors are negatively enhanced for minorities.

How are the inequalities reviewed above related to crime? We will discuss these explanations in the next section.

The Causes of Crime: A Radical View

Crime and Social Structure

Radical criminologists locate the causes of crime within society's structure. Societies contain a variety of structural inequalities, which vary from one society to the next. The idea that crime varies with the social and economic features of a society gives rise to the claim that "a society gets the type and amount of crime it deserves" (Lynch, Michalowski and Groves 2000). In other words, the way a society is organized, the kinds of economic, racial, and gender stratification systems it contains, shapes the kinds and amounts of crime found within that society. Thus, explaining crime requires knowing about the kinds of economic, class, racial, and gender systems that operate in that society, as well as the kinds of laws and mechanisms for enforcing the law that are in operation in that society. In this view, crime is not simply the result of factors that cause crime, but is also shaped by the forms of law and the ways in which the law is enforced.

Macro versus Micro Explanations

Typically, traditional theories of crime employ a micro-level perspective to examine why individuals commit crime. In contrast, radicals employ macro-level models to examine rates of criminal offending and how the level of crime found in a society relates to its social, cultural, and economic structures. Consistent with their preference for macro-level explanations, radicals argue that it is possible to predict the level of crime in society without examining individuals' behaviors, and radical analyses of crime rates in the United States have produced very accurate predictions (Lynch, Groves, and Lizotte 1994; for review, see Lynch, Michalowski, and Groves 2000).

Connecting Structure, Inequality, and Crime

Radicals hypothesize that societies characterized by extensive networks of economic (class) and social (race and gender) inequality will have higher levels of crime than more equal societies. For radicals, crime is not the simple result of aberrant individual behavior; rather, it is caused by structural circumstances, indicating that the behavior of individuals is greatly influenced by the kinds of societies in which they live (Mills 1959).

Rather than address the broader hypothesis set out above, radicals have concentrated their efforts on explaining crime in capitalist societies (United States, England, Canada, and Australia), and most radical criminologists work in or come from these countries. As a result, radical analyses of crime explore how the inequalities and processes that characterized capitalism produce crime. This focus was inherited from the studies of crime by Friedrich Engels (Marx's friend and coauthor, who was himself a capitalist) and the Dutch criminologist Willem Bonger. We briefly review their work below, updating their view where necessary. This review is cursory and omits many subsequent studies by radical criminologists.

Friedrich Engels

In 1845, Engels published a study of the English working class, which included his observations on crime. What follows is a description of Engels' observations and some background information needed to make sense of those observations.

As noted, capitalist society contains two primary classes: one that owns and one that labors. The working class survives by selling its labor to the capitalist class. Capitalists need to purchase labor because applied labor produces the products the capitalist class sells. The capitalist class wants to purchase labor at the lowest possible price, and it suppresses labor costs to maximize profits. Historically, and when Engels was writing, the most important means of suppressing labor costs was labor-saving technology—machinery. Machinery intensifies labor, making it more efficient, reducing the number of workers required in the manufacturing process. Technological advances benefit capitalists by lowering the cost of doing business. In contrast, technological advances negatively impact the working class. First, these advances decrease the number of jobs as machine labor replaces human laborers, generating an unemployed population that we referred to earlier as the surplus or marginal population. Second, the generation of a surplus population increases competition for available jobs, which also contributes to a decline in wages. Engels (1973, 173) argued that job loss and declining wages can explain (in rationally understandable terms) why marginalized and even employed workers increasingly turn to crime to supplement their incomes.

This theme appears in contemporary writings of radical criminologists. Richard Quinney (1979, 1980) and David Gordon (1971), for example, argued that crime is a rational response to systems of inequitable distribution that characterize capitalism. Left with no legitimate alternatives for survival, marginalized people may turn to crime. Spitzer (1975) suggested that marginalized populations suffer a reduction in social attachments and a reduced stake in conformity that enhances the probability of criminal behavior. Because capitalism's tendency to marginalize whole groups of people is unique in the history of economic systems, capitalism is seen as responsible for the resulting levels of criminal behavior.

Under capitalist systems, competition is generally viewed as a positive force that improves products, generates innovations, and decreases prices. This view, Engels argued, neglected competition's negative consequences, which include: an increase in the surplus population, a reduction in wages, and the erosion of working-class solidarity that result from competing for a limited number of jobs. Competition also caused capitalists to violate the law to produce commodities more cheaply. Consequently, Engels viewed competition over resources as a cause of crime by the masses (1964, 224; 1973, 168–173), the businessman (1964, 201–202, 209) and the middle classes (1981, 49). In short, Engels demonstrated how cap-

italism generates crime. In capitalist systems, crimes are typically committed to survive and enhance profit and are the by-product of intense competition and individualism.

Willem Bonger

Bonger (1916), like Engels, argued that capitalism's intense competitive spirit produces crime. Bonger argued that capitalist systems socialize people to view themselves as individuals and to look out for themselves (for a modern example, see O'Connor 1985). The result is a population that does not consider how their actions might harm others. Capitalism societies, in other words, produce egoistic people, and Bonger argued that egoism generates crime among all classes. Although Bonger believed egoism was evenly distributed among all classes, he noted that the powerful's political strength enabled them to perform exploitive acts without having those acts treated/labeled as criminal. This explains why more lower-class individuals are processed by the criminal justice system than upper-class individuals.

Both Bonger and Engels emphasized an idea that came to characterize radical criminology, namely, that crime is not confined to the lower or working classes, and that many harmful acts are not treated as crimes because the people who committed them are powerful. Even though traditional criminologists focus on street crimes committed by the lower classes, radicals have concentrated on equally serious acts committed by businesses and corporations that escape legal controls, or which are defined as harms by administrative and regulatory laws. These laws are enforced by agencies, such as the Securities and Exchange Commission (SEC) which oversees stock transactions; the Occupational Safety and Health Administration (OSHA), which polices workplace safety; the Food and Drug Administration (FDA), which regulates the quality and safety of foods and drugs; and the Environmental Protection Agency (EPA), which regulates pollution and environmental laws, among others (see Frank and Lynch 1992;

Friedrichs 1996; Simon 1999; Lynch, Michalowski, and Groves 2000). We examine these crimes below.

Corporate Crime

In 1992, the Justice Department estimated that street crime costs approximately $18 billion. This substantial sum pales in comparison to the costs of the following in dividual corporate crimes: business frauds—$400 billion; governmental frauds—$164 billion; and EPA estimates of lost work time due to illness, diseases, and damage to buildings associated with pollution—$23 billion. Recently, Reiman (1998) estimated the total costs of corporate crime at $1 trillion, nearly 60 times the cost of all street crimes committed in the United States!

Monetarily, it is clear that corporate crime costs society much more than street crime. But corporate crimes are also more violent, causing extensive deaths and injuries (Frank and Lynch 1992). For example, the odds of workplace injures are 11 times greater than the odds of being the victim of a violent crime (Lynch, Michalowski, and Groves 2000). Unnecessary surgeries and inadequate medical care cause twice as many deaths as homicides (Reiman 1998, 78–80). Approximately 10,000 people die each year from preventable workplace accidents (injuries that could have been prevented if corporations had followed the law), while another 100,000 people die due to preventable diseases contracted in the workplace (deaths that could have been prevented if corporations had protected workers from toxic substances; see Kramer 1984). Together, these deaths, which corporations allow by their inactions, are four times higher than the number of homicides in the United States. In addition to these known deaths and injuries, countless others are caused by the marketing of unsafe foods, drugs, cosmetics, households chemicals, life-threatening herbicides and pesticides, and the aggressive advertising of tobacco and alcohol (Karliner 1997; Feagin and Lavelle 1996; Glantz et al. 1996; Gibbs 1996; Friedrichs 1996; Simon 1999; Frank and Lynch 1992).

Typically, we have assumed that the deaths and injuries corporations cause are "accidents." This excuse for corporate violence has been employed to legitimize criminological neglect of this form of violence. It is now well established, however, that corporate executives knowingly allow faulty products and dangerous chemicals to reach the marketplace. A few examples should suffice to make this point.

In the 1970s, executives at Ford Motor Company allowed Pintos to be produced even though they possessed evidence that rear-end collisions could cause gas tank leaks and explosions (Cullen, Maakestad, and Cavander 1987). The staff at CBS's *60 Minutes* recently unearthed evidence that a similar problem plagued Ford Mustangs produced during the 1960s, and that Ford had evidence of this design flaw. Similar allegations have surfaced concerning cars GM produced in the 1970s. In 1984 in Bhopal, India, Union Carbide dismantled safety equipment designed to prevent the leak of deadly gases at its production facility. A gas leak occurred at that plant, killing 2,500 and injuring as many as 200,000 people (Lynch, Nalla, and Miller 1988). Tobacco company executives have keep secret evidence of tobacco's toxicity since 1955, and in the early 1990s during testimony before Congress, they argued that to their knowledge tobacco was safe (Glantz et al. 1996). The pharmaceutical firm Wyeth-Ayerst was one of two companies to produce and sell FEN/PHEN, a diet drug, even though evidence from 30 years of research indicated severe health consequences associated with the use of the drug and its compounds (Lynch, Michalowski, and Groves 2000). Many pharmaceutical and chemical companies knowingly sell products banned in the United States (to protect public health and safety) to other countries that lack strict drug and chemical regulations (Silverman, Lee, and Lydecker 1982; Weir and Shapiro 1982). Thousands of other documented cases exist that show that corporations knowingly endanger public health in various ways (see Frank and Lynch 1992; Friedrichs 1996; Gibbs 1995; Feagin and Lavelle 1996; Karliner 1997; Simon 1999). These cases establish that corporate executives purposefully place people at risk of injury and death for the sake of economic gain. For radicals, such acts are more reprehensible than street crimes because the scope of harm is so much greater.

In the early 1970s, radical criminologists including Herman and Julia Schwendinger, Richard Quinney, William Chambliss, Paul Takagi, Tony Platt, Jock Young, Ian Taylor, and Paul Walton, among others, advanced a theoretical perspective that questioned the definition of crime, which they saw as narrowly focused on the behavior of the lower classes. These radicals sought to broaden our understanding of crime and were responsible for redirecting attention toward the kinds of corporate crimes discussed above. Traditional criminologists criticized this approach, arguing that it excluded an explanation of the crimes of the lower classes (e.g., see Inciardi 1980). This criticism was based upon a narrow reading of radical criminologists' work, which reveals that this criticism has no merit. For example, Taylor, Walton, and Young's (1973) classical book, *The New Criminology*, was devoted almost wholly to explaining street crimes; Chambliss' (1964) work on delinquency and vagrancy included clear examples of explanations of lower-class crime; and Herman and Julia Schwendinger (1970, 1985), Tony Platt (1978), and Richard Quinney (1980) also devoted significant attention to explaining lower-class crimes (see also Colvin and Pauly 1983; Greenberg 1985, 1993; Hagan 1994). It is not possible to review each of these views here. Instead, we present a unified radical explanation of crime that draws on ideas (rather than specific theories) contained in the work of radical criminologists.

The Causes of Crime: A Unified Radical Approach

Crime is not caused by one factor, but rather by many forces coming together. Thus, to explain crime, theories of crime must incorporate a wide variety of explanatory styles capable of shifting across different "levels of analysis" (Groves and Lynch

1990). Radical criminology is primarily associated with macro-level theorizing; that is, theories about how social, economic, class, racial, and gender structures affect crime rates in a given society. Macro-level theory is an example of one kind of level of analysis. Radicals, however, have also examined how other levels of analysis affect crime, including intermediary (institutional) social structures (Colvin and Pauly 1983), group structures (Schwendinger and Schwendinger 1985), cultural conditions (Ferrell and Sanders 1995), and individual level conditions (Barak 1998). Contemporary radicals rely on mixed levels of analysis to explain crime, relating each level to one another. Radicals call this kind of multilevel, relational model "contextual analysis" (Mills 1959; Groves and Lynch 1990). The term "contextual analysis" means to place crime in its context, which radicals see as a mix of macro-intermediary, and micro-level structures and conditions.

Our contextualized model of crime draws upon the insights of a number of radical criminologists. We begin with several broad observations related to America's cultural and economic system. These conditions provide the context against which we explain crime. Before beginning, we offer the following qualifying statements. First, due to space limitations, our discussion omits an important aspect of radical theories of crime, namely, how law-making and enforcement, which are also products of contextual factors, shape crime. In addition, our discussion is limited to street crime (for corporate crime, see Friedrichs 1996; Simon 1999; Lynch, Michalowski, and Groves 2000).

Background Factors for a Contextualized Radical Explanation of Crime

The United States is a capitalist society based on inherently unequal class divisions that translate into varying abilities to access political power and to purchase culturally valued goods. Following Merton's theory of anomie, radicals argue that cultural values are widely shared within a society, while the ability to achieve culturally valued goals is not. To paraphrase Merton, U.S. society socializes citizens to expect certain rewards and the attainment of socially desirable positions. Consequently, most Americans have similar life goals. Not all U.S. citizens, however, possess the ability to attain culturally prescribed goals. The higher the class into which an individual is born, the greater likelihood that a person will have access to wealth, power, and institutions acting as pathways to success. In the terms of another popular theory of crime, we can say that those from higher social classes have preferable life courses that maximize success and minimize the probability of engaging in crime and being labeled criminal (Sampson and Laub 1993).

Class is not the sole determinant of success. A good education is also a means to success. Here, too, the lower class is at a disadvantage, beginning with its initial entry into the public educational system. Lower-class public schools have fewer resources, such as computers, textbooks (that are likely outdated), and libraries, and physically they are in worse states of repair. In addition, where teachers can select assignments, experienced teachers are more likely to choose better schools with more facilities and are less likely to choose assignments in lower-class public schools. Not only are these schools deprived of resources and better teachers, they suffer from environments inconducive to learning. For example, evidence indicates that students attending lower-class schools are less likely to succeed in school (Rusk 1995). Empirical evidence also notes that schools in poor neighborhoods are more likely to be situated near hazardous waste sites that contain chemicals known to negatively impact cognitive processes (Lynch and Stretesky 1999).

Parental wealth has clear effects on the schools children attend, and the more wealth parents have, the greater the choice in schooling options. For example, affluent parents dissatisfied with the schools their children attend can opt to send them to private schools. Across the United States, numerous private schools cater to the children of the elite. Entry into these schools estab-

lishes a life course or pathway to success that enhances access to better educational institutions and better jobs later in life. This same kind of hierarchy characterizes U.S. universities and colleges, and only those with adequate economic resources can afford the more than $20,000 annual tuition costs at the most prestigious schools in our nation, compared to the $3,000 to $4,000 it costs to attend many state universities.

The kinds of schools children attend are a consequence of the structural location of children in society. Young children cannot choose the school they attend—that is determined by where their parent(s) can afford to live or by other factors such as redlining, a form of housing discrimination. Thus, children's life chances are intergenerational and depend upon the circumstances of their parents.

Race and ethnicity also have important impacts on life chances for success. Earlier, we noted that the United States is characterized by a system of institutionalized racism that segregates whites, blacks, and Hispanics. Institutionalized racism limits minorities' life chances for success. Proportionate to their representation in the population, more blacks and Hispanics are poor than whites, and fewer attend college or earn high school degrees. In addition, blacks and Hispanics face forms of institutionalized racism that do not impact whites. Further, although the lower classes have more limited chances for success than people from classes above them, lower-class (and within other classes as well) minorities have fewer chances for success than whites. Thus, it is not surprising that minorities are more likely to engage in street crimes compared to whites. In sum, being a member of a particular class structures (affects) the life chances a person has for success. At the same time, American culture promotes the belief that anyone can be successful. The structure of life in American society and its ideological beliefs are clearly at odds on this point. People who fail to achieve the goals promoted by our society sometimes resort to crime as an alternative means of obtaining goods society tells us are measures of success. And sometimes they resort to crime as an alternative to market mechanisms that have excluded them from participation.

Economic conditions also impact racial differences in criminal participation. As noted, minorities' chances for success have decreased over the past two decades. The decline in minorities' life chances can be traced to the mid-1970s economic restructuring in the United States. This economic transformation had its greatest impact on urban minorities who, because of past employment discrimination, were closely tied to entry-level manufacturing jobs in inner cities (Frank and Cook 1995; Wilson 1996). As the economy shifted from manufacturing to service provision and manufacturing jobs were eliminated, minorities were most hard hit. Further, the late 1970s and early 1980s were also marked by an economic recession and increased unemployment (Box 1987). That period was also accompanied by a general tendency toward inflation and a decline in relative wages (a decline in purchasing power and wages; Frank and Cook 1995). In recent years, employment has increased, but largely in low-wage sectors, and has had its greatest impact on whites. Ironically, throughout this period, black educational attainment rose, while white educational attainment remained constant (Carnoy 1994). Despite this rise in educational attainment, black employment did not expand as rapidly as white employment, while black income fell relative to white income (Carnoy 1994).

To increase profit, owners of productive forces engaged in corporate downsizing, shifting manufacturing to foreign nations and increasing the use of technology in the manufacturing sector. Each of these economic changes reduced the number of well-paying jobs and elevated unemployment. These conditions have been especially detrimental to African-Americans, and in cities like Detroit, where machine labor replaced human labor on automobile assembly lines, rates of unemployment for young black males are nearly 30 percent. Crime among this population is also high.

In the modern era, the contraction of manufacturing extended unemployment until increased employment was generated by expanding service industries. The creation of newly marginalized populations who could not find meaningful employment corresponds with the rise in crime that occurred in the 1970s and 1980s. In the broadest sense, marginalized workers find themselves in social conditions where they are detached from making a contribution to society. As Spitzer (1975) noted, these populations lack a stake in conformity, which makes crime an attractive alternative means of survival. It should also be noted that this process impacts employed workers as well, especially those whose economic status has declined due to economic transformation and increased use of technology, contributing to conditions that could propel them to commit crime (Lynch, Groves and Lizotte 1994).

It bears mention that the recent decline in crime corresponds with increased employment opportunities in the manufacturing and service industries. In contrast, traditional criminologists have suggested that these declines are due to rising rates of imprisonment. This analysis misses the mark because imprisonment rates have increased in the United States since 1972. Recent analysis suggests that there is little correlation between rising rates of incarceration and crime (Irwin and Austin 1994; Lynch 1999).

In sum, by examining patterns and trends in crime in the United States, we see that they correspond to changes in the social and economic structure of the country. Crime, whether measured by official statistics or self-reports, is higher among the lower rather than the middle or upper classes, and is higher among minorities relative to whites. Crime is also higher in urban areas, especially in regions marked by the greatest declines in capital investment and social capital, such as school resources (Hagan 1994). Empirical evidence demonstrates that crime rates are related to processes that generate high rates of profit (Lynch, Groves, and Lizotte 1994) and that unemployment, economic inequality, and poverty are also related to crime trends. Other studies indicate that the shift from a manufacturing to a service economy also had an impact on crime. Importantly, these economic conditions had their greatest negative impact on minorities, which helps explain why these groups are overrepresented in the criminal justice system (though this cannot be done without analyzing patterns of discrimination).

Towards a New Direction: The Study of Environmental Justice

As noted, radical theories of crime are in a constant state of change, adapting to transformations that occur in society. The changing nature of radical criminology can be illustrated by examining green theorizing and environmental justice research.

The concept "green" is widely associated with environmentally friendly products and is often employed as an advertising gimmick. Framed more broadly, thinking green means showing concern for the connection between natural resource conservation and human welfare. At its most extreme level, being green is a political commitment to clean production practices that minimize human and environmental harms. This movement began to take shape in the early 1960s following publication of Rachel Carson's (1962) book, *Silent Spring*, and green movements grew out of more general environmental concerns that characterized the 1960s and 1970s. By the 1980s, the green movement had been formed, encompassing theoretical explanations connecting environmental pollution, race, ethnicity, class, and gender inequality—areas that also hold concerns for radical criminologists. For example, in *Dumping in Dixie*, Robert Bullard (1990) examined how racism affected the location of environmental hazards (toxic dumps). Vandana Shiva (1988) exposed the role of women as activists in green movements. More recently, economist James O'Connor (1998) called for an integration of environmental (green), class- and race-based (red) analysis. These works signaled the emergence of a perspective that exposed how the negative impacts of environmental pollution stem from oppressive and unequal race, class, ethnic and gender structures that characterize U.S. society.

In recent years, criminologists have begun to take green issues seriously (Frank and Lynch 1992; Clifford 1997; South 1998;

South and Beirne 1998). One example of this concern involves the study of environmental justice (see Lynch and Stretesky 1998, 1999; Stretesky and Hogan 1998; Stretesky and Lynch 1999). Environmental justice examines whether environmental harms (e.g., pollution, toxic waste dumping) are distributed evenly among social groups, or whether specific groups are overexposed to these harms.

Radicals are interested in four primary issues that relate to environmental justice: (1) ways in which corporate polluters maintain their power through dangerous, environmentally harmful production, distribution, and waste disposal practices; (2) the types of environmental crimes corporations engage in, and the social control responses (if any) these activities elicit; (3) patterns of environmental victimization related to race, class, and gender; and (4) solutions to the problem of environmental injustice. We explore these points below.

Corporations employ many tactics to maintain their power and protect their economic positions. Of prime importance are legislative lobbying (e.g., attempts to derail legal protections that limit harmful corporate behaviors that affect the environment and humans) and the production of scientific evidence that depicts chemical and pollution harms as minimal or nonexistent (Karliner 1997; Feagin and Lavelle 1996; Stauber and Rampton 1995). For example, between 1979 and 1995, twelve chemical companies and their employees donated nearly nine million dollars to congressional candidates (Feagin and Lavelle 1996, 124). One recipient, Representative Charles Hatcher, introduced legislation to forbid local governments from regulating pesticides. If implemented, this legislation would eliminate the additional protection local governments have traditionally applied to pesticide manufacturing above and beyond federal regulations. Representative Charles Stenholm, also a recipient of chemical industry contributions, pushed legislation to allow manufacturers to sue the U.S. Environmental Protection Agency for undue economic hardship caused by the agency. This close connection between corporations and government raises an interesting question posed by radical criminologist David Simon (1999, 122): "Who speaks for the interests of school children, minority groups, the poor, the mentally retarded, renters, migrant-workers—in short, for the relatively powerless" where environmental regulations are at issue?

Another successful industry tactic is hiring former governmental employees, especially former heads of regulatory agencies, to gain insight into regulatory processes and to act as lobbyists and consultants on avoiding compliance with existing regulations. Between 1990 and 1995, chemical industries hired 136 former government officials (Feagin and Lavelle 1996) including John Byington, former head of the Consumer Product Safety Commission (CPSC). In his new role, Byington recommended that the chemical industry refute all studies by CPSC with its own research; use CPSC rules to sue the government for arbitrary and capricious actions; win over government personnel who are already sympathetic to claims made by industry; use legislation and lobbying to stall CPSC's progress; and hire attorneys to attend CPSC hearings.

The chemical industry also uses lawsuits (SLAPPs: strategic lawsuits against public participants) to harass public interest groups that push for industry regulation (Rebovich 1998). In addition, many environmentally destructive industries have employed criminal tactics to influence legislation and other environmental regulatory processes. For example, in the 1970s and 1980s, several chemical and oil companies admitted making millions in illegal payments from secret funds to foreign government officials to gain a market advantage over competitors (Simon 1999). Many also engaged in various forms of illegal dumping (e.g., midnight dumping) to dispose of hazardous waste. Combined, legal and illegal chemical dump sites place an estimated 25 million people at risk of disease and death in the United States. The estimated cost for cleaning up the worst of these sites (EPA Superfund sites) is $100 million. This is an important criminological issue since the EPA estimates that 90 percent of all Superfund sites contain illegally dumped hazardous waste.

Our society has become so reliant on dangerous chemicals that nearly everyone is exposed to some type of environmental hazard in his daily life. However, minorities and the poor are disproportionately exposed to a wider variety, and higher concentrations, of toxic hazards because toxic chemical production facilities and dump sites are closer to the communities in which they live (Bullard 1990; Mohai and Bryant 1992; Moses 1993; Krieg 1995; Pollack and Vittas 1994; Ringquist 1996; Stretesky and Hogan 1998; Institute of Medicine 1998; Stretesky and Lynch 1999). Two arguments are often offered to explain this pattern of race and class bias.

One argument suggested that the poor and minorities live near hazardous waste sites by choice because properties in affected areas are inexpensive and attract the economically impoverished. A second argument holds that the placement of these facilities is unplanned. Existing evidence suggests that both explanations are wanting. Radicals (Stretesky 1996; Stretesky and Hogan 1998) have countered the choice argument, offering data demonstrating that the placement of hazardous waste sites does not alter the racial or economic characteristics of an area. Also, consider the following policy for placing waste-to-energy facilities offered by Cerrell Associates (1996) to the State of California:

> All socioeconomic group[s] . . .resent the nearby siting of . . .[disposal] facilities, but the middle and upper socioeconomic strata possesses better resource to effectuate their opposition [A] . . .great deal of time, resources and planning could be saved and political problems avoided if officials and companies look for lower socioeconomic neighborhoods that are . . .heavily industrialized . . .with little, if any, commercial activity [to place disposal facilities] . . . .Middle and higher . . .[class] neighborhoods should not fall within the one-mile and five-mile radius of the proposed site. (43, 117)

Cerrell's siting advice illustrates how race and class affect the placement of hazardous waste facilities. Given this advice, it should come as no surprise that these facilities are disproportionately found in lower-class and minority communities. Because hazardous waste siting decisions disproportionately affect the poor, they are also likely to disproportionately affect minorities. Interestingly, studies funded by the toxic waste industry find no relationship between race and hazardous waste siting (e.g., Anderton et al. 1994). Our own independent assessments of this relationship, utilizing several different data sets (hazardous waste production; waste disposal; chemical accidents) and locales (Tampa, Florida; the State of Florida; the United States), however, demonstrated a consistent race effect.

Studies of environmental justice are important for a number of reasons. First, proximity to hazardous waste production and disposal sites increases the likelihood of contracting certain diseases and illnesses. Because facility proximity is linked to the geography of race and class, the health consequences associated with hazardous chemicals in the United States are not evenly distributed among the population. In short, because adverse health consequences can be predicted by knowing the race and class of an area, an institutionalized system of injustice exists. Second, some of the chemicals found in hazardous waste sites also have adverse impacts on behavior. Many hazardous waste disposal facilities contain high levels of heavy metals, such as lead, which have detrimental impacts on children's learning abilities and behavior. In brief, this means that some portion of minority and lower-class children's poor school performance may be a result of the unequal distribution of hazardous substances and may, in turn, affect their progress through life, enhancing the probability that these children will turn to crime as they grow up. In addition, hazardous waste facilities also have high levels of pesticide contaminants. It is well known that overexposure to pesticides (and lead) produces aggression, which may explain why rates of violent crime (assaults and homicides) are higher in lower-class and minority communities.

Finally, the study of environmental justice underscores the need for social transformation as an appropriate mechanism for dealing with crime and injustice. To a large degree, the production and disposal of hazardous waste is the result of the way things are currently produced. In many manufacturing areas, alternative production methods that generate less (or even none) of the toxins that result from current production practices already exist. But, corporations avoid these alternatives because they are more costly, and show little concern for the general public's health. In short, the problem is that corporations make hazardous waste production and disposal decisions based on profit margins. These profit margins exclude calculations of the human and environmental harms these practices generate. There is a clear need to de-emphasize profit as the basis for decision making, a difficult task within the current profit-oriented social and economic structure that characterizes the United States.

Policy Implications

Radicals are often accused of failing to offer policies that would reduce crime. Such criticisms neglect the work radicals have undertaken on policy initiatives to reduce crime for a variety of reasons. First, radical criminological policies often deal with broad-scale social and economic changes that involve institutions outside of the criminal justice system—the institution most traditional criminologists would alter to affect crime. As a result, traditional criminologists fail to grasp the central idea of radical criminology; namely, that the causes of crime are located in social and economic institutions, and that criminal justice policy changes will thus have little impact on reducing crime. Indeed, the history of the effectiveness of criminal justice policy changes demonstrates the general inability of these policies to significantly reduce crime.

Examples of radical crime policies follow. Economic inequality is a source of crime that can be shown to differentially impact lower-class and minority communities, and women. During the economic restructuring that occurred in the United States over the past 25 years, crime has tended to increase in lower-class and minority communities and also among women. Solutions to crime must, therefore, remedy these inequalities. These policies should also be connected to programs for change developed by environmentalists that reduce the production and disposal of toxic waste in lower-class and minority communities (Roseland 1997). This strategy requires reorganizing production and forcing global corporations to reinvest in communities they have withdrawn resources from in the past. Rather than view minority communities as locations for toxic waste, corporate executives must be educated (and, if education fails, coerced) to see these communities as viable sites for local production practices that are sensitive to minimizing environmental damages. Many such alternatives exist, some of which are just as profitable as traditional, polluting producing techniques (Roseland 1997). One example is the "eco-city," which enhances local economic activity, provides stability to communities now deprived of an economic base, helps attach people to their local communities and the U.S. economy, decreases unemployment, and produces fewer pollutants. These outcomes are consistent with policies offered by both radical and traditional criminologists for reducing crime.

Second, radicals have offered numerous policy initiatives related to altering the criminal justice process to reduce crime (see Reiman 1998; Lynch, Michalowski, and Groves 2000 for review). Many, such as gun-control, are consistent with policies offered by traditional criminologists as well as policy makers.

Third, radicals suggest equalizing punishment for corporate offenders. This suggestion has been criticized because it argues for more punishment. There is no denying the accuracy of this criticism. In response, radicals argue that without broad social and economic changes, the only way to protect the public from corporate crime is to increase the penalties for these offenses. In the case of corporate crime, this strategy makes sense because the motivation for corporate offenses is clearly economic and, as studies have shown, is part of the calculations corporate executives make when deciding whether or not to engage in unlawful activities.

Conclusion

This chapter has reviewed the central ideas behind one form of critical theorizing, radical criminology. Much more could be written on this topic, and whole books have been written on materials omitted from our discussion. Thus, for those of you who are intrigued by any of the ideas we have presented, we suggest that you investigate radical and critical criminology further, digest these ideas, and compare them to those offered by traditional criminology and reach your own conclusions concerning the appropriateness of each of these views.

References

Amott, Theresa. (1995). "Shortchanged: Restructuring women's work." In *Race, Class and Gender.* M. L. Anderson and P.H. Collins (eds.). Belmont, CA: Wadsworth.

Anderton, Andy, P. Rossi, J. Oakes, M. Fraser, E. Weber, and E. Calabrese. (1994). "Hazardous waste facilities: Environmental equity issues in metropolitan areas." *Evaluation Review,* 118:23–140.

Arrigo, Bruce. (1995). "The peripheral core of law and criminology: On postmodern social theory and conceptual integration." *Justice Quarterly,* 12, 3:447–472.

Barak, Gregg. (1998). *Integrating Criminologies.* Boston: Allyn and Bacon.

Bartlett, D.L. and J.B. Steele. (1992). *America: What Went Wrong?* Kansas City, MO: Andrews and McMeel.

Bonger, Willem. (1916). *Criminality and Economic Conditions.* Boston: Little, Brown.

Box, Stephen. (1987). *Recession, Crime and Punishment.* London: Tavistock.

Brownstein, Henry. (1991). "The media and the construction of random drug violence." *Social Justice,* 18:85–103.

——. (1996). *The Rise and Fall of a Violent Crime Wave: Crack Cocaine and the Social Construction of a Crime Problem.* Albany, NY: Harrow and Heston.

——. (2000). *The Social Reality of Violence and Violent Crime.* Boston: Little, Brown.

Bullard, Robert. (1990). *Dumping in Dixie: Race, Class and Environmental Justice*. Boulder, CO: Westview.

Carnoy, Martin. (1994). *Faded Dreams*. Cambridge, MA: Harvard University Press.

Carson, Rachel. (1962). *Silent Spring*. New York: Houghton Mifflin.

Cerrell Associates. (1996). *Political Difficulties Facing Waste-to-Energy Conversion Plant Siting*. Los Angeles: Waste Management Board.

Chambliss, William. (1964). "A sociological analysis of the law of vagrancy." *Social Problems*, 12:67–77.

Chambliss, William and Robert Seidman. (1982). *Law, Order and Power*. Reading, MA: Addison-Wesley.

Clifford, Mary. (1997). *Environmental Crime: Enforcement, Policy and Social Responsibility*. Gaithersburg, MD: Aspen.

Colvin, Mark and J. Pauly. (1983). "A critique of criminology: Toward an integrated structural-Marxist theory of delinquency production." *American Journal of Sociology*, 90, 3:513–551.

Cullen, Frank, W. Maakestad, and G. Cavander. (1987). *Corporate Crime Under Attack*. Cincinatti, OH: Anderson.

Currie, Elliott and Jerome Skolnick. (1984). *America's Problems*. Boston: Little, Brown.

DeKeseredy, Walter and Martin Schwartz. (1996). *Contemporary Criminology*. Belmont, CA: Wadsworth.

DiMaggio, P. (1982). "Cultural capital and school success." *American Sociological Review*. 47:189–201.

DiMaggio, P. and J. Mohr. (1985). "Cultural capital, educational attainment and marital selection." *American Journal of Sociology*. 90:1231–1261.

Engels, Fredrick. (1981). "Demoralisation of the English working class." In *Crime and Capitalism*. D. Greenberg (ed.). Palo Alto, CA: Mayfield.

——. (1973). *The Conditions of the Working Class in England*. Moscow: Progress.

——. [1844] (1964). "Outlines of a critique of political economy." In *The Economic and Philosophic Manuscripts of 1844*. D. Struik (ed.). New York: International.

Feagin, Dan and Marianne Lavelle. (1996). *Toxic Deception: How the Chemical Industry Manipulates Science, Bends the Law, and Endangers Your Health*. Secaucus, NJ: Carol.

Ferrell, Jeff and C.R. Sanders (eds.). (1995). *Cultural Criminology*. Boston: Northeastern University Press.

Figart, D.M. and J. Lapidus. (1998). "Will comparative worth reduce race-based wage discriminiation?" *The Review of Radical Political Economics*. 30(3):14–24.

Frank, Nancy and Michael J. Lynch. (1992). *Corporate Crime, Corporate Violence*. Albany, NY: Harrow and Heston.

Frank, Robert and Phillip Cook. (1995). *The Winner Take All Society: Why the Few at the Top Get So Much More than the Rest of Us*. New York: Penguin.

Friedrichs, David O. (1996). *Trusted Criminals*. Belmont, CA: Wadsworth.

Fussell, Paul. (1997). *Class*. New York: Ballentine.

Gibbs, Lois. (1995). *Dying From Dioxin*. Boston, MA: South End.

Gibbs, Lois. (1996). "Toxic struggles: The theory and practice of environmental justice." In *Forward*, R. Hofrichter (ed.). Philadelphia, PA: New Society.

Gilman, E.A. (1995). "Childhood cancers: Space-time distribution in Britain." *Journal of Epidemology and Community Health*. 49(2):158–163.

Glantz, Stanton, J. Slade, L.A. Bero, P. Hanauer, and D.E. Barnes. (1996). *The Cigarette Papers*. Berkeley: University of California Press.

Gordon, David. (1971). "Class and the economics of crime." *The Review of Radical Political Economy*, 3(3):51–72.

Greenberg, David F. (1985). "Age, crime and social explanation." *American Journal of Sociology*, 91:1–21.

——. (1993). *Crime and Capitalism*. Philadelphia, PA: Temple University Press.

Greer, Jed and Kenny Bruno. (1996). *Greenwash: The Reality Behind Corporate Environmentalism*. New York: Apex.

Groves, W., Byron Lynch, and Michael J. Lynch. (1990). "Reconciling structural and subjective appoaches to the study of crime." *Journal of Research in Crime and Delinquency*. 27(4):348–375.

Hagan, John. (1994). *Crime and Disrepute*. Thousand Oaks, CA: Pine Forge.

Harring, Sidney. (1983). *Policing in a Class Society*. New Brunswick, NJ: Rutgers University Press.

Henry, Stuart and Dragan Milovanovic. (1996). *Constitutive Criminology: Beyond Postmodernism*. London: Sage.

Inciardi, James (ed.). (1980). *Radical Criminology: The Coming Crisis*. Beverly Hills, CA: Sage.

Institute of Medicine. (1998). *Toward Environmental Justice: Research, Education and Health Policy Needs.* Washington, DC: National Academy Press.

Irwin, John and James Austin. (1994). *It's About Time: America's Imprisonment Binge.* Belmont, CA: Wadsworth.

Karliner, Joshua. (1997). *Corporate Planet.* San Francisco: Sierrra.

Kozol, J. (1995). "Homeless in America." In *Issues in Feminism.* S. Ruth (ed.). Palo Alto, CA: Mayfield.

Knox, E.G. (1996). "Spatial clustering of childhood cancers in Great Britain." *Journal of Epidemology and Community Health.* 48(4):369–376.

——. (1992). "Leukaemia clusters in Great Britain, 1: Space-time interaction." *Journal of Epidemiology and Community Health.* 46(6):566–572.

——. (1994). "Leukaemia clusters in childhood: Geographical analysis in Britain." *Journal of Epidemiology and Community Health.* 48(4):369–376.

Knox, E.G. and E.A. Gilman. (1997). "Hazard promitities of childhood cancer in Great Britain from 1953–1980." *Journal of Epidemiology and Community Health,* 51:151–159.

Kramer, Ron. (1984). "Corporate criminality." In *Corporations as Criminals.* E. Hochstedler (ed.). Beverly Hills, CA: Sage.

Krieg, Eric. (1995). "A socio-historical interpretation of toxic waste sites." *The American Journal of Economics and Sociology,* 54:1–14.

Lynch, Michael J. (1996). "Class, race, gender and crime." In *Race, Class, Gender and Criminology.* M. Schwartz and D. Milovanovic (eds.). New York: Garland.

——. (1999). "Beating a dead horse: Is there any empirical evidence for a deterrent effect of imprisonment?" *Crime, Law and Social Change,* 38:1–17.

Lynch, Michael J. and W. Byron Groves. (1989). *Primer in Radical Criminology.* Albany, NY: Harrow and Heston.

——. (1995). "In defense of comparative criminology." In *Advances in Criminological Theory* Vol. 5. F. Adler and W. Lafuer (eds.). New York: Transaction.

Lynch, Michael J., W. Byron Groves, and Alan Lizotte. (1994). "The rate of surplus value and crime: A theoretical and empircal examination of Marxian economic theory and criminology." *Crime, Law and Social Change,* 21:15–48.

Lynch, Michael J., Raymond J. Michalowski and W. Byron Groves. (2000). *Primer in Radical Criminology,* Third Edition. Monsey, NY: Willow Tree.

Lynch, Michael J., Mahesh K. Nalla, and Keith Miller. (1988). "Cross-cultural perceptions of deviance: The case of Bhopal." *Journal of Research in Crime and Delinquency,* 26(1):7–35.

Lynch, Michael J. and E. Britt Patterson. (1996). "Thinking about race and criminal justice: Racism, stereotypes, politics and academia." In *Justice with Prejudice.* M.J. Lynch and E. Britt Patterson (eds.). Albany, NY: Harrow and Heston.

Lynch, Michael J. and Paul Stretesky. (1998). "Uniting class, race and criticism through the study of environmental justice." *The Critical Criminologist,* 9(1):1, 4–6.

——. (1999). "Class, race, gender, and critical criminology: A comment on Milovanovic's dislocations and reconstructions." *The Critical Criminologist,* 9(3):4–8.

Marx, Karl. [1867] (1976). *Capital,* Vol. I. New York: International.

——. [1848] (1981). "Crime and capital accumulation." In *Crime and Capitalism.* D. Greenberg (ed.). Palo Alto, CA: Mayfield.

Marx, Karl and Fredrick Engels. [1848] (1955). *The Communist Manifesto.* Arlington Heights, IL: Crofts.

——. [1846] (1970). *The German Ideology.* New York: International.

Massey, Douglas and Nancy Denton. (1993). *American Apartheid.* Cambridge, MA: Harvard University Press.

Messerschmidt, James. (1986). *Capitalism, Patriarchy and Crime.* Totowa, NJ: Rowman and Littlefield.

——. (1993). *Masculinities and Crime.* Lanham, MD: Rowman and Littlefield.

——. (1997). *Crime as Structured Action: Gender, Race and Class in the Making.* Thousand Oaks, CA: Sage.

Michalowski, Ray. (1998). "International environmental problems." In *Environmental Crime.* M. Clifford (ed.). Gaithersburg, MD: Aspen.

Mills, C. Wright. (1959). *The Sociological Imagination.* New York: Oxford.

Milovanovic, Dragan. (1994). *A Primer in the Sociology of Law.* Albany, NY: Harrow and Heston.

——. (1995). "Dueling paradigms: Modernist vs. postmodernist thought." *Humanity and Society,* 19(1):1–22.

Mohai, Paul and Bunyan Bryant. (1992). "Environmental racism: Reviewing the evidence." Pp. 161–78 in *Confronting Environmental Racism,* R. Bullard (ed.). Boston: South End.

Moses, Marion. (1993). "Farmworkers and pesticides." In *Confronting Environmental Racism*. R. Bullard (ed.). Boston: South End.

O'Connor, James. (1985). *Accumulation Crisis*. New York: Basil Blackwell.

——. (1998). *Natural Causes: Essays in Ecological Marxism*. New York: Guilford.

Perlow, Victor. (1988). *Super Profits and Crises*. New York: International.

Platt, Tony. (1978). "Street crime: A view from the left." *Crime and Social Justice*, 9:26–34.

Pollock, Philip and Elliot Vittas. (1979). *Criminology*. Boston: Little, Brown.

——. (1994). "Who bears the burdens of environmental pollution? Race, ethnicity, and environmental equity in Florida." *Social Science Quarterly*, 76:294–310.

Quinney, Richard. (1979). *Criminology*. Boston, MA: Little, Brown.

Quinney, Richard. (1980). *Class, State, and Crime*. New York: Longman.

Rebovich, Donald. (1998). "Environmental crime research: Where we have been, where we should go." In *Environmental Crime*. M. Clifford (ed.). Gaithersburg, MD: Aspen.

Reiman, Jeffrey. (1998). *The Rich Get Richer and the Poor Get Prison*. Boston: Allyn and Bacon.

Ringquist, Evan. (1996). "Equity and the distribution of environmental risk: The case of TRI facilities." *Social Science Quarterly*, 78:811–829.

Roseland, Mark. (1997). *Eco-City Dimensions*. Gabriola Island, BC: New Society.

Rotella, Elyce. (1995). "Women and the American economy." In *Issues in Feminism*. S. Ruth (ed.). Palo Alto, CA: Mayfield.

Rusk, David. (1995). *Cities Without Suburbs*. Washington, DC: Woodrow Wilson Center Press.

Ruth, Shelia. (ed). (1995). *Issues in Feminism*. Palo Alto, CA: Mayfield.

Sampson, Robert J. and John Laub. (1993). *Crime in the Making: Pathways and Turning Points Through Life*. Cambridge, MA: Harvard University Press.

Schor, Juliet. (1995). *The Overworked American*. New York: Basic.

Schwartz, Martin and David O. Friedrichs. (1994). "Postmodern thought and criminological discontent: A new metaphor for understanding violence." *Criminology*, 32:221–246.

Schwartz, Martin B. and Dragan Milovanovic (eds.). (1996). *Race, Gender and Class in Criminology*. New York: Garland.

——. (1985). *Subcultures of Delinquency*. Beverly Hills, CA: Sage.

Schwendinger, Herman and Julia Schwendinger. (1970). "Defenders of order or guardians of human rights?" *Issues in Criminology*, 5:113–126.

Shiva, Vandana. (1988). *Staying Alive: Women, Ecology, and Development*. Atlantic Highlands, NJ: Zed.

Silverman, Milton, P. Lee, and S. Lydecker. (1982). *Prescription for Profit: The Drugging of the Third World*. Berkeley: University of California Press.

Simon, David. (1999). *Elite Deviance*. Boston: Allyn and Bacon.

Sklar, Holly. (1995). "The upper class and mothers in the hood." In *Race, Class and Gender*. M. Anderson and P. Collins (eds.). Belmont, CA: Wadsworth.

South, Nigel. (1998). "A green field for criminology: A proposal for a perspective." *Theoretical Criminology*, 2:211–234.

South, Nigel and Piers Beirne. (1998). "Editor's introduction to special issue: For a green criminology." *Theoretical Criminology*, 2:147–148.

Spitzer, Steven. (1975). "Toward a Marxian theory of deviance." *Social Problems*, 22:638–651.

Stauber, John and Sheldon Rampton. (1995). *Toxic Sludge is Good For You!* Monroe, ME: Common Courage.

Stretesky, Paul B. (1996). "Environmental Equity?" *Social Pathology*, 2(3): 293–298.

Stretesky, Paul and Michael Hogan. (1998). "Environmental justice: An analysis of superfund sites in Florida." *Social Problems*, 45:268–287.

Stretesky, Paul and Michael J. Lynch. (1999). "Environmental justice and the predictions of distance to accidental chemical releases in Hillsborough County, Florida." *Social Science Quarterly*, 80:830–843.

Taylor, Ian, I.P. Walton and J. Young. (1973). *The New Criminology*. London: Routledge and Keegan Paul.

United Nations Development Program. (1993). *Human Development Reprot*. New York: United Nations

U.S. Bureau of the Census. (1999). *Wealth and Income in the United States*, 1998. http://www.census.gov.

U.S. Department of Labor. (1996). *Employment and Unemployment in the U.S.* http://www.dol.gov.

Weir, and Shapiro. (1982). *Circle of Poison*. San Francisco: The Food Institute.

Wright, Erik Olin. (1978). *Class, Crisis and the State*. London: New Left.

Wolff, Edward N. (1995). *Top Heavy: A Study of the Increasing Inequality of Wealth in America*. New York: Twentieth Century Fund Press.

What About Feminism?

Engendering Theory-Making in Criminology

Meda Chesney-Lind
University of Hawaii at Manoa

Karlene Faith
Simon Fraser University

Criminology has long suffered from what Jessie Bernard called the "stag effect" (Bernard 1964). It has attracted male scholars who wanted to study and understand outlaw men, hoping perhaps that some of the romance and fascination of this role would rub off. As a result, what came to be known as the field of criminology was actually the study of male crime and, largely, male victimization. Predictably, theorizing about crime and justice followed much the same intellectual trajectory, and theories that were generated to discuss "crime," "victimization," and "crime policy" were actually theorizing male deviance and criminality, in the main.

Feminism challenged the overall masculinist nature of criminology by pointing to the repeated omission and misrepresentation of women in criminological theory. As Maureen Cain (1990) explained, "women and girls exist as Other: that is to say, they exist only in their difference from the male, the normal" (2). Women's crime was overlooked almost completely and female victimization was ignored, minimized, and trivialized. So severe has been this distortion that some feminist scholars have wondered, aloud, as to whether feminist criminology is not, in fact, an oxymoron (Stanko 1993, cited in Heidensohn 1995, 66).

Leaving this question open for the moment, it is crystal clear that feminism has dramatically challenged criminology. Because of the enormity of girls' and women's victimization, the silence on the role of violence in women's lives was the first to attract the attention of feminist activists and feminist scholars. Take, for example, the issue of wife battery. Once dubbed a private, personal matter and routinely ignored by the criminal justice system, its dimensions and consequences are now becoming known. In the United States, the former surgeon general, C. Everett Koop[1] estimated that three to four million women are battered each year; roughly half of them are single, separated, or divorced. In addition, population-based surveys indicate that 21 to 30 percent of U.S. women will be beaten by a partner at least once in their lives.[2] Battering also tends to escalate and become more severe over time. Almost half of all batterers beat their partners at least three times a year.[3]

The health consequences of such violence are immense. Battery is the greatest single cause of injury to women, accounting for more injuries than auto accidents, muggings and rape combined. It also provides the primary context for many other health problems. Battered women are four to five times more likely to require psychiatric treatment and five times more likely to attempt suicide than nonbattered women.[4]

Because of years of feminist activism, though, excellent work exists on the problem of women's victimization—especially in the areas of sexual assault, sexual harassment, sexual abuse, and wife battery (see, for example, Martin 1977; Estrich 1987; Dziech and Weiner 1984; Schechter 1982; Buzawa and Buzawa 1990; Scully 1990; Russell 1986; Rush 1980). Compared to the wealth of literature on women's victimization, girls and women who are labeled as "delinquent" or "criminal" have received far less scholarly attention.[5]

What would criminology look like if women's experience of crime and victimization was at the center rather than the periphery of scholarly inquiry? Suddenly, men have a gender, not just women; and male behavior is no longer normalized. Male violence against women, in particular, takes on a very different meaning if women's relative nonviolence is the normal response to life and men's aggression the aberration. The violence, fear, and victimization that are so much a part of many women's lives (that is, the other side of male violence) are suddenly important areas of study and research. One can immediately see why feminist perspectives have so invigorated criminology and criminological theory. The progress, though, has been uneven.

In the United States, for example, the construction of woman as victim has made the greatest headway. The recognition of women's victimization, while long overdue, had some effects unanticipated by feminist activists and scholars. Specifically, the discovery of "domestic violence" supplied mainstream criminologists with "new" crimes to study, and new men to jail (particularly men of color). Most importantly, this approach to wife battery did not fundamentally challenge androcentric criminology. Its appeal is, in part, a product of the fact that the victimized woman does not challenge core notions of patriarchal ideology; she— the plundered waif—after all, needs male protection and assistance. None of these comments should be taken to mean that women's victimization is not horrific, but rather that the study of women's victimization (long considered, in some circles, to be coextensive with feminist criminology) caused the least resistance in the field itself.

The study of women in conflict with the law and out of control, as noted above, has not developed as fully.[6] Perhaps the existence of these women suggests that male domination is not as complete as it might be. These women were certainly trouble for theories of male criminality, which were long described as theories of crime. So the "offending" women were ignored, and those who studied them did so from the very edges of the field.

This has meant, of course, that the lives of women on the economic margins, who were the overwhelming victims of this control, were left largely undocumented and unexplained. Their race and their class simply placed them outside a slightly modified criminology where men (assumed to be poor and nonwhite) are criminals and women (as-

sumed to be docile, good, and white) are victims.

The relative paucity of scholarship on the topic of "unruly" women (Faith 1993) has permitted two troubling trends to develop, particularly in the United States and Canada. First, the lack of solid scholarship has permitted the occasional discovery of "bad" women during periods when this would serve patriarchal interests. In the 1970s, the female offender was touted in the media as a by-product of the then-emerging social movement which was seeking legal and social equality for women (Chesney-Lind 1989). In more recent years, the discovery of girls, and women's violence, in the form of girls in gangs, has again been blamed on the women's movement (see Chesney-Lind 1993; and DeKeseredy 1999). More importantly, the lack of a robust body of scholarship about women and crime has meant that when the women's prison population in the United States tripled in the 1980s and continued soaring in the 1990s, there was virtually no information about the women being jailed with the exception of media hype about violent, drug-dependent women of color in conflict with the law.

Should we undertake the project of what might be called engendering criminology given its androcentric (or male-oriented) history? We contend that given the primacy of crime as a social problem, and the profound impact that current crime policies have on women and men at the economic and racial margins, we have no choice. We as feminist scholars shoulder many burdens, but perhaps the most daunting is the one articulated by Liz Kelly (quoted in Heidensohn 1995, 71): "Feminist research investigates aspects of women's oppression while seeking at the same time to be a part of the struggle against it."

Some contend that it is important that feminists should begin a conscious process of contributing to the development of criminological theory. Clifford Shearing (1998) defines theory as "the set of claims about the world that we use to go on from one space-time moment to the next. Theory makes living possible" (16). Paul Rock and Simon Holdaway (1998) analyze the dearth of criminological theorists in contemporary times, and the reasons so many criminologists do theory under the table, but are reluctant to name theory-making as one of their professional activities: "Criminology has a tacit division of labor. There are a number of scholars, a small minority perhaps, who self-consciously call themselves theorists. . . . The fact that criminology is an ineluctably empirical discipline serves as a constant check and brake on its propensity to theorize" (2, 5).

Feminist researchers have certainly avoided naming themselves as theorists, and not simply because criminology is largely empirical (or fairly tied to numerical data on the dimensions of crime and victimization). Instead, many women scholars approach the process of theory-making with a considerable degree of ambivalence—despite its obvious importance. Theory-making is often seen as elite, intellectual activity, and women scholars have long been either reluctant to or discouraged from engaging in such high-status and, some might contend, self-enhancing activities. Indeed, a look at the earliest years of feminist criminology displays the reticence of even pioneering women scholars to name their actions as theory-making. They preferred, instead, to document the specific ways in which the field of criminology had forgotten about women, and gender, without daring to call their work "theoretical."

It is clear, though, that feminist theories as well as a variety of traditional criminological theories affected the early work of feminist criminologists. Perhaps it is time, three decades after the birth of feminist criminology, to sketch out a few of the major trends within feminist theorizing, and document the impact of these theoretical perspectives on the important field of feminist criminology (and particularly the scholarship on the experience of girls and women in the areas of crime and criminal justice).

An equally important task is to critically examine and rethink all the traditional schools of criminological theory, with an eye towards gender and feminist theory (see, for example, Gelsthorpe and Morris 1990). In this work, though, we will focus on the ways in which contemporary feminist theories have helped create feminist criminology and might ultimately invigorate criminology and criminological theorizing as well.

What Criminology Could Gain from Feminist Theory

It is not necessarily obvious that the field of criminology and criminological theory-making in particular has anything to gain from a consideration of the many strands of contemporary feminist theory. For this reason, a brief discussion of *why* we think engendering criminology is important might be a good start to this essay.

First, there is no denying that a longstanding focus on social class (and particularly the crime-prevention link) can be found in most if not all traditional theories of crime and delinquency. It is also clear that the field has not had nearly the same intense interest in gender. This situation is ironic because a strong relationship between social-class position and delinquency and crime has been shown to be problematic, while it is clear that gender has a dramatic and consistent effect on delinquency and crime causation (Hagan, Gillis, and Simpson 1985; Hagan 1989). Indeed, the gender gap in serious crimes, particularly violent crime, is robust, significant, and longstanding. As an example, in 1997, 84 percent of those arrested for murder, forcible rape, robbery, and aggravated assault were male.

The second irony, and one that consistently eludes even contemporary criminological theorists, is that although academicians have had little interest in female offenders, the same can not be said about other elements of the criminal justice system. Indeed, even though adult women in prison have sometimes been called the "forgotten offenders," our work on the early history of the separate justice system for youths reveals that concerns about girls' immoral conduct was really at the center of what some have called the "child-saving movement" that set up the juvenile justice system (Platt 1969; Messerschmidt 1987; Schlossman and Wallach 1978).

In this essay, we argue that criminology must begin to do more than consider gender as a *variable*. Instead, in order to begin to fully explain both the gender gap in crime— particularly violent crime—as well as the sometimes perplexing responses of the criminal justice system to girls and women, as both victims and offenders, we must *theorize* gender. This means thinking about the way in which the sex/gender system affects and shapes crime, victimization, and criminal justice.

The sex/gender system, while it varies across cultures, functions as a system of social stratification, in which both men and women and the tasks performed by them are valued differently—with men and the work they do valued more highly. Exploring the interaction between crime and the sex/gender system (or patriarchy) means recognizing the importance of the following interrelated components in contemporary society:

- The social construction of gender categories on the basis of biological sex.

- A sexual division of labor in which specific tasks are allocated on the basis of sex, and;

- The social regulation of sexuality, in which particular forms of sexual expression are positively and negatively sanctioned. (Renzetti and Curran 1999, 3)

To *theorize gender* means to begin to systematically think about the links between the observed patterns of women's victimization, women's offending, and women's experience with the criminal justice system within the context of patriarchy. It is also possible to rethink male crime, victimization and experiences with the criminal justice system with this same lens, that is, to place male behavior in its patriarchal context as well. To best undertake that sort of thinking, though criminologists must become familiar with the best theoretical work on the sex/gender system in contemporary society—which is to say the major schools of modern and postmodern feminist theory.

Schools of Feminist Thought

The inclusion of women in criminological research was catalyzed by the second wave of the feminist movement in the late 1960s and early 1970s.[7] As might be expected, feminist scholars of this period brought the insights of feminist theories into their groundbreaking work. The best known of the early theoretical influences were the notions of *liberal feminist theory, socialist feminist theory,* and *radical feminist theory.*

New schools of thought, though, have continued to appear on the feminist theoretical landscape and they, too, are of clear relevance to criminology. *Postmodern feminist theory* analyses focus important attention on the role of professional and bureaucratic language (or "discourse") in the domination of one group over another. These theorists also direct attention to the "construction" of truth in such cultural outlets as the media, which, as we shall see, can play a very critical role in the public's perception of the crime "problem."

Although feminism, by definition, is grounded in women's experience, critical male scholars have increasingly adopted feminist perspectives in their own research on men and male behavior as well as women (Messerschmidt 1993). A focus on different *masculinities* encourages research on the links between the pressure to conform to particular aspects of manhood and male involvements in crime.

Most recently, *multicultural feminist theory* has called attention to important differences among women, particularly the experiences of women of color and women of Anglo-European heritage. Recognition of diversity is clearly vital to the study of women and crime or criminal justice (because girls and women of color are over-represented among those in U.S. prisons), and for this reason, this literature is particularly relevant to feminist criminologists.[8]

In sum, the separation of feminist theories into clear, distinct "ideal types" (or labels) is fraught with difficulties,[9] given cross-fertilizations and the resultant hybrid theories.[10] In addition, very few feminist criminologists label themselves as to which kind of feminism they represent. However, exploring the major types of feminist theory, and illustrating their impact on the field of feminist criminology, will clearly show how vital these perspectives are to a criminology that includes girls and women.

Liberal Feminist Theory

Liberal feminist theory was and is deeply influenced by notions of individual rights, equality, and freedom (Mill [1869] 1971). This perspective emphasizes notions of "women's rights," was deeply influenced by the French and American revolutions, and was extremely influential in the first wave of feminism. As an example, a key document from that era, the Seneca Falls Declaration of Sentiments of 1848, contains the following statement: "We hold these truths to be self-evident: that all men and women are created equal" (quoted in Rossi 1973, 416).

Liberal feminism focuses on the effects of the differential socialization of males and females, sex stereotyping of the workplace, and the legal and political disenfranchisement of women. Liberal feminism has traditionally sought to remedy these problems through education, integration, and litigation (Lorber 1998, 19).

Within the field of criminology, liberal feminist theory has highlighted the many discrimination and equity issues that exist in the criminal justice system. Here, we find stark examples. Take the fact that when Sandra Day O'Conner, the first woman on the U.S. Supreme Court, graduated in the top 10 percent of her Stanford Law School class in 1952, the only job she was offered was as a legal secretary (Doyle and Faludi 1995, 263). Influential early work in this area focused on issues of inequality, such as barriers to women's employment in policing, the law, and the judiciary (see Price and Sokoloff 1982/1995, Part 3).

Research on the differential treatment and sentencing of girl and women offenders also relies heavily on the liberal feminist intellectual tradition. Until 1968, for example, Pennsylvania women routinely received indeterminate sentences to reformatories for offenses for which men received short jail terms (Pollock-Byrne 1990, 167). Similarly, research on the sentences given by the juvenile justice system, in its early years, documented discrimination against girls. For example, in Chicago (where the first family court was founded), one-half of the girl delinquents, but only one-fifth of the boy delinquents, were sent to institutions between 1899 and 1909. Other jurisdictions showed much the same pattern: in Milwaukee between 1901 and 1920, twice as many girls as boys were committed to training schools (Schlossman and Wallach 1978, 72); and in Memphis females were twice as likely as males to be committed to training schools between 1900 and 1907 (Shelden 1981, 70).

The pattern of inequitable sentencing continued until very recently, particularly for girls charged with noncriminal, status offenses like running away from home. In a study of a juvenile court in Delaware in the 1970s, researchers found that first-time female status offenders were more harshly sanctioned (as measured by institutionalization) than males charged with felonies. For repeat status offenders, the pattern became even starker, with females six times more likely than male status offenders to be institutionalized (Datesman and Scarpitti 1977, 70).

Finally, liberal perspectives also focused attention on the dramatic differences in the programs available to male and female prisoners. A classic Michigan case, *Glover v. Johnson*, 478 F. Supp. 1075 ([E.D. Mich.] 1979), illustrates the point quite clearly: at the time the suit was brought, males in Michigan prisons had access to twenty-two vocational programs while women had access to only three (Pollock-Byrne 1990, 169).

The limits of the liberal perspective revolve around the fact that equality has often translated into treating girls and women *as if they were boys or men*. Recent efforts to "equalize" conditions in the justice system, for example, have resulted in women being incarcerated in prisons designed to hold dangerous male prisoners, women being placed on chain gangs, and women being sentenced to prison for longer sentences—all in the name of equality (see Chesney-Lind 1997).

Marxist and Socialist Feminism

Karl Marx had little to say about crime and punishment; he exalted the working class and generally dismissed all "criminals" as the "dangerous classes." However, an activist and academic revival of Marxism in the 1960s and 1970s led to a revival of perspectives that dealt with the importance of economic inequities and conflict and extended these notions to the study of crime (see Quinney 1970; 1980).

Marx also had little to say about women or gender, because his paradigm tended to stress the notion that all problems would be solved by a class-based revolution. Prior to the second wave of feminism, even modern Marxists ignored women's work in the home, in the outside work force, and in the criminal justice system (Rusche and Kircheimer 1939). As a consequence, Marxist feminists grappled with the contradictions of a Marxism that hierarchized revolutionary priorities, with women and children still coming in last (Eisenstein 1979; Barrett 1980; Sargent 1981).

It was socialist feminists who recognized that familial reproduction and the nuclear family are as important to the needs of capitalism as production in the workplace, starting with a stable work force (see Zaretsky 1978). Moreover, they recognized that patriarchy affected the ways by which men controlled women's productivity (Rowbotham, 1973). Critical socialist-feminist scholars have been prominent among researchers of women, crime and punishment, and criminology itself. They give weight to the interactive effects of patriarchy and capitalism in explaining the social and material conditions of women's lives. They differ from their Marxist-feminist ancestors in that they view women's interests as inherent in, rather than subordinate to, the interests of working-class struggles. They recognize the gender factor as well as the economic factor in the division of labor and the distribution of criminalization (Snider 1994).

Socialist and Marxist theory clearly influence studies of the corporate victimization of women, with focus on the ways in which corporations have systematically neglected the health of women workers, or worse, profited from women's anxieties about their appearance (as in the case of silicone breast implants) (Chapple 1998). Few Marxist feminists, though, with notable exceptions such as Angela Davis (1981), have specifically focused in their work on the criminal justice system.

A criminology influenced by Marxist and socialist feminist theory would stress the notion that crime for both women and men occurs in an economic context. Even heavily sexualized women's crimes, such as prostitution, are far more about "work" and "money" than about sex—hence, the appearance of unions to represent prostitutes (see Jaget 1980). This theoretical perspective might also focus on the growth of what some have called the "prison industrial complex" and the specific meaning of these corporate interests for women. Take, for example, the growth of women's prisons in the United States. In the mid-1970s, only about half the states and territories had separate prisons for women, and many jurisdictions confined women inmates in men's prisons or in women's prisons in other states (Singer 1973). Between 1980 and 1990, however, the number of women in prison had increased threefold, and suddenly, the nation had 71 female-only facilities. A short five years later, in 1995, the number of prisons for women had jumped to 104—an increase of 46.5 percent in half a decade (Chesney-Lind 1998).

Marxist or socialist feminist theory would take note of the fact that the spiraling increase in the imprisonment of adult women is part of a larger, arguably international increase in reliance on imprisonment as a response to social problems—particularly the drug problem. As a direct result of the building boom in corrections, corrections budgets are by far the fastest-growing segment of state budgets—increasing by 95 percent between 1976 and 1989. During this same period, state expenditures for lower education dropped slightly (2 percent), higher education dropped by 6 percent, and state expenditures for welfare (excluding Medicare) dropped by 41 percent (Donziger 1996, 48). This means that monies that once supported low-income women and their children in the community, as well as the dollars to provide women with educational opportunities, are being cut back dramatically at the same time that monies to arrest, detain, and incarcerate women on the economic margins are being increased.

Socialist and Marxist feminism, predictably, has been affected by the wholesale collapse of communist nations which embraced Marxist principles, but failed to address gender inequality or the sexual and physical victimization of women. The latter shortcoming, in particular, was to set the stage for a more contemporary form of feminist theorizing that is inclusive of, but is not primarily concerned with, the political economy.

Radical Feminist Theory

The search for a paradigm that would adequately address the "micro-inequalities" (Lorber 1998, 66) in women's daily lives, as well as provide a language for the pervasive physical and sexual violence against girls and women, propelled some toward a new type of feminist theory. Radical feminist analysis posited the power imbalance between men and women—patriarchy—as the central and, some would contend, first oppression. Pioneer radical feminists, such as Kate Millet (1970), Phyllis Chesler (1972), Mary Daly (1978), and Susan Griffin (1981), saw the sex/gender system as the foundational power imbalance within human societies.

Radical feminists focused national attention, arguably for the first time, on the pervasive nature of women's experience of men's physical and sexual violence. For this reason, radical feminism propelled the feminist agenda into a whole new area of public life—publicizing and theorizing about the issues of wife battery (Martin 1977; Pizzey 1974), rape (Brownmiller 1975), child sexual abuse (Butler 1978), and sexual harassment (MacKinnon 1989).

Radical activists lobbied for shelters and more effective legislation, and actively confronted cultural norms that accepted a man's right to discipline, control, and punish his family in any way he chose (Faith and Currie

1993; Stanko 1985). Despite a predictable backlash against some of the notions advanced by radical feminism, today there is a virtual consensus among feminists of all stripes that violence against women and children is a priority issue.

What may be less well understood is that violence against girls and women is also inextricably connected to female delinquent and criminal behavior. As an example, research on the characteristics of girls in the U.S. juvenile justice system clearly shows the role played by physical and sexual abuse in girls' delinquency. According to a study of girls in juvenile correctional settings conducted by the American Correctional Association (1990), a very large proportion of these girls—about half of whom were of minority backgrounds—had experienced physical abuse (61.2 percent). More than half of these girls (54.3 percent) had experienced sexual abuse, and for most this was not an isolated incident; a third reported that it happened 3 to 10 times and 27.4 percent reported that it happened 11 times or more. Most were 9 years of age or younger when the abuse began. Again, while most reported the abuse (68.1 percent), reporting the abuse tended to result in no change (29.9 percent) or in making things worse (25.3 percent) (American Correctional Association 1990, 56–58).

Given this history, it should be no surprise that the vast majority had run away from home (80.7 percent), and of those who had run, 39 percent had left home 10 or more times. Over half (53.8 percent) said they had attempted suicide, and, when asked the reason, they said it was because they "felt no one cared" (American Correctional Association 1990, 55). Finally, what might be called a survival or coping strategy is criminalized; girls in correctional establishments reported that their first arrests were typically for running away from home (20.5 percent) or for larceny theft (25.0 percent) (American Correctional Association 1990, 46–71).

Detailed studies of youth entering the juvenile justice system in Florida have compared the "constellations of problems" presented by girls and boys entering detention (Dembo, Williams, and Schmeidler 1993; Dembo et al. 1995). These researchers have found that female youth were more likely than male youth to have abuse histories and contact with the juvenile justice system for status offenses, while male youth had higher rates of involvement with various delinquent offenses. Further research on a larger cohort of youth (N=2104) admitted to an assessment center in Tampa concluded that "girls' problem behavior commonly relates to an abusive and traumatizing home life, whereas boys' law violating behavior reflects their involvement in a delinquent life style" (Dembo et al. 1995, 211). Clearly, the experience of violence and victimization plays a central rather than peripheral role in the understanding of girls' delinquency (and, as we shall see, women's crime as well), and these insights are largely due to radical feminist theorizing.[11]

Radical feminism is not without shortcomings. Specifically, the focus on women as victims has been criticized for rendering girls and women as incapable of action or agency. In many early radical feminist paradigms, nearly all women were *de facto* victims. Radical feminist theory has also been criticized on the grounds of promoting "biological essentialism." That is, some of the theories suggest that women have certain innate qualities and attributes as women, and men likewise as men, based on male and female sexuality. In contrast, most academic feminist strands of theory presumed the social construction of gender and sex roles and pointed to diversities among women.

Masculinities

The focus on male violence against women ultimately refocused the gender lens, particularly in criminology, on men and male behavior, and especially on male violence. Until the 1980s, few criminologists had taken gender or masculinity into account. This is true despite the fact that, for many decades, men have accounted for about 90 percent of those arrested for violent crime. In the main, critical criminology (like sociology) has been focused instead on the power of social class in predicting delinquency and crime. Hence, the fact that women in those economically marginalized environments did not engage in the same activities provoked little attention.

An early exception might be Albert Cohen (1955) in his study of delinquent boys. He explicitly recognized the function of masculinity in facilitating antisocial behavior among male youth. Cohen notes that the delinquent's response "however it may be condemned by others on moral grounds, has at least one virtue: it incontestably confirms, in the eyes of all concerned, his essential masculinity. The delinquent is the rogue male" (Cohen 1955, 139–140).

It remained for other theorists, therefore, to flesh out this insight by taking the feminist insights about gender and applying them to male behavior, and particularly male violence. The work of Connell (1987), in particular, focuses on the notion that there exists a "hegemonic masculinity"—the masculinity of economic success, racial privilege, and visible heterosexuality that marks some men as powerful and other men and all women as powerless.

Messerschmidt's work (1986; 1993) extended the focus on masculinity specifically into the study of male crimes by exploring not only the crimes of privileged men (white-collar crime), but also the role played by social and political powerlessness in generating violent street crime. In this sense, Messerschmidt explores the ways in which certain forms of doing masculinity actually facilitate violence. He also explores the same powerlessness of women whose relatively few crimes are predominantly nonviolent, and finally he examines how other forms of doing masculinity, among privileged men, can produce corporate crime.

Those who employ masculinity theories often document how particular crimes by men are in accordance with the particular masculinity valued within their specific social location. In the process of committing the crime, they are constructing their own gender. Gay-bashing is a crime that explicitly defends masculinist heterosexuality; crimes of sexual assault against women and children similarly stem from power imbalances built from gendered presumptions of authority and rights.

A good example of how masculinity studies can influence criminology comes from work by Schwartz and DeKeseredy (1997) on campus sexual assault. The authors review research which suggests that each year between 15 and 30 percent of women on college campuses in North America report experiences that meet the legal definition of sexual assault. They attempt to make sense of what some might call an epidemic of violence by privileged men, noting that "men do not grow up in a culture that promises and urges complete equality between men and women" (Schwartz and DeKeseredy 1997, 47). They forge an important link between sexual assault and hegemonic masculinity.

Schwartz and DeKeseredy explain how men are surrounded with messages that failure is feminine, depersonalized sex is macho, boys must at all costs avoid being too friendly with girls, and men's worldview is built around a sense of heterosexual entitlement. They note that "a male [who is] motivated to prove masculinity by scoring by any means necessary, who has no empathy for his sexual partner/victim, and who is sure he has a right to do so," can, and will, be completely indignant when his behavior is labeled as rape. Such men are convinced they are victims of a "feminazi conspiracy" because, in their view, "they did nothing wrong." These "violent, irresponsible, misogynist, privileged men" (Schwartz and DeKeseredy 1997, 72) are, in fact, unsure of their own ability to measure up to the impossible standards of hegemonic masculinity. So, they actively seek out opportunities to prove their masculinity—normalizing their objectification and violence against women with the active support of their peer groups.

The groups that Schwartz and DeKeseredy zero in on as problematic on campus are fraternities and sports teams. A horrific, and apparently real, example of a fraternity newsletter documents precisely how groups of young privileged men objectify women and normalize sexual violence (Schwartz and DeKeseredy, 1997, 111). The newsletter includes an account of a gang rape in which two inebriated males "decide to give this girl what she needs and just throw her in the middle of the party room and everyone got laid." Schwartz and DeKeseredy remind us here that studies repeatedly show that alcohol is a factor in 66 percent of acquaintance rapes occurring on college campuses.

Masculinity studies, like the work just described, focus attention on "social values that encourage men's violence and sexual exploitation of women" (Lorber 1998, 149). These theories also explore distinctions and power differences between different types of masculinities. The pimp, the gang banger, the factory worker who steals tires, and the corporate executive who embezzles have different resources and therefore commit different crimes. Young men of color who commit street crime, such as robbery and other theft, assault, and drug possession or trafficking, are most apt to be punished; white-collar and corporate men who commit "suite" crime are much less likely to be prosecuted for their offenses.

The system that should respond to crime is itself heavily masculine and male dominated. Men, across age lines, are the dominant presence in law enforcement and criminal justice occupations, from the police to the judges. Masculinity theorists show ways by which the state, as a network of patriarchal agencies and institutions, generates masculinist violence and crime, just as it is in charge of controlling and punishing it. It is not surprising, then, that traditional crime policies have stressed what might be called masculine values of control and punishment instead of what might be characterized as feminine impulses, such as reintegration and restorative justice.

The shortcoming of masculinity theories might be the fact that, despite borrowing from the rich feminist theoretical terrain, they do not really offer a new theoretical perspective (Lorber 1998, 156). Beyond this, some might even say that refocusing on men in the area of crime research, although useful, also runs the risk of revisiting some of the androcentric excesses of the field's early years. Other, newer perspectives within feminist theory, however, do offer considerably different and exciting possibilities for future feminist research on women and men. We will briefly consider two of these:

postmodern feminism and multiracial feminism.

Postmodern Feminism and Criminology

What has come to be known as postmodernism is actually the collection of myriad strands of postmodernist thought that critique and deconstruct "modernity"— the period in Western history that began with the Enlightenment. This is an intellectual tradition that, while stressing democracy, equality, and rationality, also accommodated both the development of capitalism (out of feudalism) and the resistance of working people to exploitation by the owners of production. Ultimately, it gave birth to the first wave of feminism during the late nineteenth century at the height of the Industrial Age.

Contrary to Enlightenment rhetoric, the modern period has come to represent structured inequality and stratified, industrialized societies founded on hierarchies of power, ownership, and privilege. Postmodernists note that, in the modern period, in addition to status accrued through economic wealth and structural class position, power is increasingly gained by new professionals who have acquired and constructed special knowledges (Foucault 1980). It is this emphasis on culture and the production of knowledge, rather than on structure, that is an earmark of postmodernism.

Foucault notes that expert knowledges are inextricably linked with the discourses of power—law, psychiatry, medicine, and so on—which determine "truths." As expressed by deconstructionist Anne Worrall, "[I]t is those who have power who are authorized 'to know' and whose 'knowledge' is afforded privilege." She points out that to examine a statement, one must consider the identity of the author, the grounds on which the discourse is based, the audience to whom it is directed, the object of discussion, and the objective or purpose of the assertion (Worrall 1990, 7–8). In other words, "knowledge" is not necessarily an expression of "truth," and it is never neutral.

The postmodern emphasis on the production of knowledge is certainly relevant to the study of criminology, and particularly feminist criminology. The field has recently been struggling with the role of the media in the creation of both public attitudes and policies regarding criminals, crime, and punishment; and postmodernism can certainly help here. For example, a recent study by the American Bar Association found that, with reference to rates of violent crime, "in no instance is the rate higher than 20 years ago and in most categories it is now substantially lower." Murder rates, as an example, were higher in 1933 than in 1992 (American Bar Foundation 1995, 4). Similarly, recent data released by the U.S. Department of Justice show that murder, rape, robbery, and aggravated assaults are at a 23-year low (Bureau of Justice Statistics 1997, 1).

Even though crime levels have remained relatively stable or decreased, the public perception is clearly that crime is out of control. Between 1989 and 1994 the proportion of citizens who reported that they were "truly desperate" about crime increased from 34 percent to 62 percent (Madriz 1997). Another study found that the number of Americans naming crime as the nation's "most important problem" increased sixfold between June of 1993 and January of 1994 (*Media Monitor* 1994, 1).

Why the disconnect? Simply put, while the United States may not be suffering from a crime wave, it does appear to have experienced a media crime wave during the last decade or so. Many sources indicate that the coverage of crime has increased dramatically in recent years; *Media Monitor,* for example, noted a tripling of crime news stories on primetime television news between 1989 and 1993. In fact, stories about crime and drugs were the leading news stories in the decade with economic news placing a distant second; the early 1990s saw the networks air nearly 10,000 crime stories compared to 6,673 stories on the economy, and about the same number of stories on the former Soviet Union (6,047) (*Media Monitor* 1997, 1).

Current media treatments of crime and violence, in particular, have facilitated a "war on crime" that seems increasingly to have replaced the cold war on the U.S. political and economic landscape. Savvy politicians have clearly capitalized on people's fear of criminal victimization and embraced the crime issue to win elections. Meanwhile, more principled political figures find themselves effectively silenced by the unrelenting media crime wave and the resultant public clamor for punishment. Like earlier political grandstanding on the communist threat, which was virtually risk free, today there appears to be no safer spot in the political arena than to advocate getting tough on crime. But the effects, particularly with regard to imprisonment, of the political focus on crime have also been undeniable and horrific. U.S. prison populations climbed from 200,000 in 1973 to 1.2 million in 1997 (Bureau of Justice Statistics 1998), and they are still climbing. Clearly, the control of information and the power to disseminate certain "truths" has had huge consequences for crime policy, largely irrespective of the actual level of crime.

Postmodernism has clearly encouraged the "deconstruction" of media knowledge, linking these ideas to those of the privileged and powerful, whose interests they represent. At the same time, postmodernism's emphasis on deconstruction, and knowledge as relatively arbitrary, has caused some to criticize the field. It does seem telling that ideas disputing the notion of truth emerged precisely at the moment that white men lost the ability to control knowledge production exclusively, and women and people of color began to express themselves in writing. A disciplinary reliance on relatively obscure, theoretical jargon, and the absence of a clear way for deconstruction to deal with pressing social problems, such as the nation's increasing imprisonment rate, has led some scholars to seek new ways to talk about gender, race, and class.

Multiracial Feminism and Criminology

Multiracial feminism stresses the notion of a "matrix of domination" (Collins 1990)—focusing attention on a system of interlocking inequalities of gender, race, and class. The perspective continually stresses that each of these systems interacts with the others and cannot be successfully understood separately. The field has particularly focused attention on the fact that the predominantly white and middle-class women's movement had, in its focus on gender alone, essentially ignored the diversity of women's experiences, lives, and communities.

Multicultural feminist theory emphasizes both structure and culture in the understanding of crime among African-American women. Ritchie's (1996) work on the involvement of "battered black women" in crime is a good example of the insights that can be gleaned from a multicultural feminist perspective. She documents how the personal experience of sexual and physical violence and battering combines with the impacts of institutional racism and discrimination to produce a unique and criminogenic pattern of "gender entrapment" for African-American women. Living in economically marginalized communities, these battered women are trapped both because of their larger cultural loyalties to African-American men and because they feel they cannot go to the police for protection. One woman Ritchie interviewed put it bluntly: "The station-house is full of drug-using, prostitute-using, women-hating men. . . . I learned early in my life that the cops were dangerous to my people" (Ritchie, 1996, 95). As a result, abused African-American women often feel they have no choice but to stay in abusive relationships. Staying, nevertheless, often means that they are virtually forced to engage in petty crimes like drug dealing, forgery, and prostitution, either because their batterer demands it or because it is their only choice to survive economically.

Multiracial feminism has correctly identified the criminal justice system as a major site of "group-based experience" (Collins 1997, 278). There is no clearer example of Collins' point than the special meaning of the imprisonment frenzy discussed earlier for people of color. Crime is increasingly understood as a code word for race in contemporary U.S. politics, and it is widely understood that when politicians talk about being "tough on crime" they are really talking about increasing the numbers of African Americans in the nation's prisons and jails.

The data on this trend are also irrefutable. Mauer and Huling (1995, 3) now estimate that roughly one out of three African-American men between the ages of 20 and 29 are under some form of correctional supervision. One scholar commenting on this trend observed "'prison' is being re-lexified to become a code word for a terrible place where blacks reside" (Wideman, cited in Schiraldi, Kuyper, and Hewitt 1996, 5).

In a related trend, some of us (see Bloom, Chesney-Lind, and Owen 1994) have noted that the war on drugs has also become an undeclared war on women. The overall number of women in prison in the United States has quintupled since 1980—a trend explained largely by the implementation of gender-blind, get-tough policies on drug and other offenders. This new national zeal for imprisoning women has taken a special toll on women of color. Between 1986 and 1991, for example, the number of African-American women incarcerated for drug offenses rose by 828 percent. The number of Hispanic women in prison for these offenses increased by 328 percent, and the number of white women imprisoned for drug offenses increased by 241 percent (Mauer and Huling 1995).

Multicultural feminism offers both to criminology and to feminist theory a way of understanding how the major systems of inequality—race, gender, and class—intersect. This is not to say that multicultural feminism is without problems. Different minority groups (Asians, African-Americans, Native Americans, and Latinos) have considerably different experiences with the systems of repression (see Joe 1996). Moreover, like Marxist feminism, the perspective always struggles with balancing the importance of gender against other social identities—in this instance race. For criminology, however, the emphasis on race is vital, because theorizing race, gender, and class are essential to the growth of a powerful feminist criminology.

Wrapping It Up: The Future of Feminist Criminology

Most feminists approach theory-making with a great deal of trepidation. Among other things, we are well aware that the early history of research on women and crime, in particular, is littered with grandly terrible theorizing—particularly about women's offending. We also tend to be hesitant to make global statements about the situation of all girls and women, because we, as criminologists, are keenly aware of the complex ways that race, gender, and class intersect to affect the female experience.

We hope this essay has shown that feminist theories offer much to criminological theorizing. Clearly, the understanding of women's experience of crime, victimization, and justice requires thinking about and theorizing gender and crime. We have also argued that feminist theories reminded criminology that men also have a gender, and that thinking about gender and male criminality could offer new insights.

Much work lies ahead. The crucial question that haunts all research and theorizing on gender will eventually also haunt criminology and criminological theory. How do we explain the vast differences in the involvement of women and men in criminal behavior—particularly violent behavior? How do we explain discriminatory criminal justice policies? When should we focus on theories that explore *similarities* between women and men, and when should we probe *differences?* Finally, can we theorize in ways that also capture the valuable differences *among* women?

There is an urgent need for criminologists to engage in solid research- and theory-building so as to challenge the crime myths that are played out in the media regarding women's crime and crime generally. Racism is clearly at the heart of much that passes as "truth" about crime, and the consequences of this misinformation for communities of color in the United States are devastating. Beyond this, the backlash against abundant solid research on the dimensions of girls' and women's victimization continues unabated (see Roiphe 1993; Wolf 1993). It is essential that feminist criminologists not be intimidated by such attacks and that we continue to do work on this vital issue, both empirically and theoretically.

Finally, there is the responsibility of feminist criminology to research and theorize girls' and women's crime as well as official responses to that behavior. Howe discusses the value of Pat Carlen's work (1983; 1985; 1988; 1990), which stresses the importance of applying research findings to policy-making. "Academics must not let 'theoretical rectitude' deter them from 'committing themselves as *academics* and as *feminists*' to campaigns on behalf of women lawbreakers" (Carlen 1990, 111–12; Howe 1994, 214).

Research consistently documents that victimization is at the heart of much of girls' and women's lawbreaking, and that this pattern of gender entrapment, rather than gender liberation, best explains women's involvement in crime. That is, although most women who are victimized do not become criminals, the vast majority of imprisoned girls and women have been the victims of severe and chronic abuse. We have also seen, particularly in the United States, an increased willingness to incarcerate women and girls, often deploying the rhetoric of "equality" to justify this response. Good, clear thinking on both the theoretical and policy level will be necessary for us to respond to the unique questions that an understanding of gender poses for the field of criminology. So, for feminist criminologists, the "to do" list is quite long. Even though activism to improve the situation of girls and women is clearly necessary, it is also necessary that we continue to build feminist theories and use these insights to improve the situation for all—girls and women as well as boys and men.

Notes

1. C. Everett Koop. (May 22, 1989). "Violence Against Women: A Global Problem." Address by the Surgeon General of the U.S. Public Health Service at a conference of the Pan American Health Organization, Washington, D.C.

2. National Committee for Injury Prevention and Control. (1989). *Injury Prevention; Meet-*

ing the Challenge. New York: Oxford University Press.

3. M. A. Straus, R. J. Gelles, and S. Steinmetz. (1980). *Behind Closed Doors: Violence in the American Family.* New York: Doubleday.

4. E. Stark, A. Flitcraft. (1991). Cited in L. Heise. (1991). "Violence Against Women; The Missing Agenda." In Koblinsky et al., (eds). *Women's Health: A Global Perspective.* Westview.

5. Early but important exceptions to this generalization are Issues in Criminology 1973; Smart 1976; Crites 1976; Bowker, Chesney-Lind, and Pollock 1978; Chapman 1980; Jones 1980.

6. There has, though, been an encouraging outpouring of work on women offenders in the last decade. See Belknap 1996, Chesney-Lind 1997, and DeKeseredy 1999 for reviews of this recent work.

7. The women's movement has traditionally been divided into two historic "waves," despite the fact that work on the status of women can be dated well before the first of these events, and continued in a rather clear form after the first "wave" had passed. Generally, however, the first "wave" is recognized as starting with the Seneca Falls Convention in 1848, and the second "wave" is dated to the publication of Betty Friedan's influential book, *The Feminine Mystique,* in 1963.

8. This same issue relates to differences between and among lesbians and heterosexual women.

9. Feminist typologies of feminism began with the work of Alison Jaggar and colleagues in 1978 (Jaggar and Struhl 1978), and typologies appeared in the appendices of articles on feminist criminological theory (see Daly and Chesney-Lind 1988).

10. In 1991, two Canadian scholars stated: "For the past twenty years, theoretical and militant debates and positions have co-existed, mutually influencing, interpenetrating, clashing, even contradicting each other in the discursive space occupied by women" (Descarries-Bélanger and Roy 1991, 1).

11. Radical feminist theory has created a rich intellectual tradition that has, in turn, further splintered into three types: radical materialist, woman-centered, and radical lesbian (Descarries-Bëlanger and Roy 1991, 14–17). Space, unfortunately, does not permit a full exploration of each of these important strands of contemporary radical feminist theorizing.

References

American Bar Foundation. (1995). "Reducing crime by increasing incarceration." *Researching Law*, Winter, 6(1):1–6.

American Correctional Association. (1990). *The Female Offender: What Does the Future Hold?* Washington, DC: St. Mary's.

Barrett, Michíle. (1980). *Women's Oppression Today: Problems in Marxist Feminist Analysis.* London: Verso Editions.

Belknap, Joanne. (1996). *The Invisible Woman: Gender, Crime and Justice.* Belmont, CA: Wadsworth.

Bernard, Jessie. (1964). *Academic Women.* University Park: Pennsylvania State University.

Bloom, Barbara, Meda Chesney-Lind, and Barbara Owen. (1994). *Women in Prison in California: Hidden Victims of the War on Drugs.* San Francisco: Center on Juvenile and Criminal Justice.

Bowker, Lee, Meda Chesney-Lind, and Joycelyn Pollock. (1978). *Women, Crime and the Criminal Justice System.* Lexington, MA: DC Heath.

Brownmiller, Susan. (1975). *Against Our Will: Men, Women, and Rape.* New York: Bantam.

Bureau of Justice Statistics. (1997). "Criminal victimization, 1973–1995." Washington, DC: U.S. Department of Justice.

Bureau of Justice Statistics. (1998). *Prisoners in 1997.* Washington, DC: U.S. Department of Justice.

Butler, Sandra. (1978). *Conspiracy of Silence: The Trauma of Incest.* San Francisco: New Glide.

Buzawa, Eve and Carl Buzawa. (1990). *Domestic Violence: The Criminal Justice Response.* Newbury Park, CA: Sage.

Cain, Maureen (1990). "Realist philosophy and standpoint epistemologies for feminist criminology as a successor science." Pp. 124–140 in *Feminist Perspectives in Criminology*, Loraine Gelsthorpe and Allison Morris (eds.). Buckingham, UK: Open University Press.

Carlen, Pat. (1983). *Women's Imprisonment: A Study in Social Control.* London: Routledge.

Carlen, Pat. (ed.). (1985). *Criminal Women.* Cambridge, MA: Polity.

Carlen, Pat. (1988). *Women, Crime, and Poverty.* Milton Keynes: Open University.

Carlen, Pat. (1990). *Alternatives to Women's Imprisonment.* Milton Keynes: Open University.

Chapman, Jane Roberts. (1980). *Economic Realities and the Female Offender.* Lexington, MA: Lexington.

Chapple, C.L. (1998). "Dow Corning and the silicone breast implant debacle: A case of corpo-

rate victimization of women." In *Masculinities and Violence.* Lee Bowker (ed.). Thousand Oaks, CA: Sage.

Chesler, Phyllis. (1972). *Women and Madness.* New York: Doubleday.

Chesney-Lind, Meda. (1989). "Girls' crime and woman's place: Toward a feminist model of female delinquency." *Crime and Delinquency*, 35(1):5–29.

Chesney-Lind, Meda. (1993). "Girls, gangs and violence: Reinventing the liberated female crook." *Humanity and Society*, 17:321–344.

Chesney-Lind, Meda. (1997). *The Female Offender: Girls, Women, and Crime.* Thousand Oaks, CA: Sage.

Chesney-Lind, Meda. (1998). "The forgotten offender: Women in prison." *Corrections Today*, 12:66–73.

Chesney-Lind, Meda and Randall G. Shelden. (1998). *Girls, Delinquency, and Juvenile Justice.* Belmont, CA: Wadsworth.

Cohen, Albert L. (1955). *Delinquent Boys: The Culture of the Gang.* New York: Free.

Collins, Patricia Hill. (1990). *Black Feminist Thought: Knowledge, Consciousness, and the Politics of Empowerment.* Boston: Unwin Hyman.

Collins, Patricia Hill. (1997). "Comment on Hekman's 'truth and method: Feminist standpoint theory revisited': Where's the power?" *Signs*, 22:375–79.

Connell, R.W. (1987). *Gender and Power.* Stanford, CA: Stanford University Press.

Crites, Laura (ed.). (1976). *The Female Offender.* Lexington, MA: Lexington.

Daly, Kathleen and Meda Chesney-Lind. (1988). "Feminism and criminology." *Justice Quarterly*, 5(4):497–538.

Daly, Mary. (1978). *Lyn/Ecology: The Meta-Ethics of Radical Feminism.* Boston: Beacon.

Datesman, S. and F. Scarpitti. (1977). "Unequal protection for males and females in the juvenile court." In *Juvenile Delinquency: Little Brother Grows Up.* T.N. Ferdinand (ed.). Newbury Park, CA: Sage.

Davis, Angela. (1981). *Women, Race, and Class.* New York: Random House.

DeKeseredy, Walter. (1999). *Women, Crime, and the Canadian Criminal Justice System.* Cincinatti, OH: Anderson.

Dembo, R., James Schneidler, Camille Chin Sue, Polly Borden, and Darrell Manning. (1995). "Gender differences in service needs among youths entering a juvenile assessment center: A replication study." *Journal of Correctional Health Care*, August, 2(2):291–216.

Dembo, R., L. Williams, and J. Schmeidler. (1993). "Gender differences in mental health service needs among youths entering a juvenile detention center." *Journal of Prison and Jail Health,* 12:73–101.

Descarries-Bélanger, Francine Roy and Shirley Roy (1991). *The Women's Movement and Its Currents of Thought: A Typological Essay.* Ottawa: Canadian Research Institute for the Advancement of Women/Institut Canadien de recherches sur les femmes.

Donziger, Steven (ed.). (1996). *The Real War on Crime.* New York: Harper Perennial.

Doyle, James A. and Michele A. Faludi. (1995). *Sex and Gender: The Human Experience.* Madison, WI: Brown and Benchmark.

Dziech, B.W. and Weiner, L. (1984). *The Lecherous Professor.* Boston: Beacon.

Eisenstein, Zillah (ed.). (1979). *Capitalist Patriarchy and the Case for Socialist Feminism.* New York: Monthly Review.

Estrich, Susan. (1987). *Real Raper.* Cambridge: Harvard University Press.

Faith, Karlene. (1993). *Unruly Women: The Politics of Confinement and Resistance.* Vancouver: Press Gang.

Faith, Karlene. (1994). "Resistance: Lessons from Foucault and feminism." Pp. 36–66 in *Power/Gender: Social Relations in Theory and Practice.* H. Lorraine Radtke and S.J. Henderikus (eds.). London: Sage.

Faith, Karlene and Dawn Currie. (1993). *Seeking Shelter: A State of Battered Women.* Vancouver: Collective.

Feinman, Clarice. (1980). *Women in the Criminal Justice System.* New York: Praeger.

Foucault, Michel. (1980). *Power-Knowledge: Selected Interviews and Writings 1972–1977.* Colin Gordon (ed.). New York: Pantheon.

Friedan, Betty. (1963). *The Feminine Mystique.* New York: Dell.

Gelsthorpe, Loraine and Allison Morris (eds.). (1990). *Feminist Perspectives in Criminology.* Buckingham, UK: Open University.

Griffin, Susan. (1981). *Pornography and Silence: Culture's Revenge Against Women.* New York: Harper.

Hagan, John. (1988). *Structural Criminology.* New Brunswick, NJ: Rugers University Press.

Hagan, John, A.R. Gillis, and John Simpson. (1985). "The class structure of gender and delinquency: Toward a power-control theory of common delinquent behavior." *American Journal of Sociology,* 90:1151–1178.

Heidensohn, Frances, (1995). "Feminist perspectives and their impact on criminology and criminal justice in Britain." Pp. 63–85 in *International Feminist Perspectives in Criminology.* Nicole Hahn Rafter and Frances Heidensohn (eds.). Buckinham: Open University Press.

Howe, Adrian. (1994). *Punish and Critique: Towards a Feminist Analysis of Penality.* London: Routledge.

Issues in Criminology. (1973). *Women, Crime, and Criminology,* Fall, 8:3.

Jaget, Claude (ed.). (1980). *Prostitutes: Our Life.* Bristol, UK: Falling Wall.

Jaggar, Alison and Paula R. Struhl (eds.). (1978). *Feminist Frameworks: Alternative Accounts of the Relations Between Men and Women.* New York: McGraw-Hill.

Joe, Karen. (1996). "The life and times of Asian-American women drug users: An ethnographic study." *Journal of Drug Issues,* 26(1):125–142.

Jones, Ann. (1980). *Women Who Kill.* New York: Fawcett Columbine.

Lorber, Judith. (1998). *Gender Inequality: Feminist Theories and Politics.* Los Angeles: Roxbury.

MacKinnon, Catharine. (1989). *Toward a Feminist Theory of the State.* Cambridge, MA: Harvard University Press.

Madriz, Esther. (1997). *Nothing Bad Happens to Good Girls: Fear of Crime in Women's Lives.* Berkeley: University of California Press.

Martin, Del. (1977). *Battered Wives.* New York: Pocket.

Mauer, Marc and Tracy Huling. (1995). *Young Black Americans and the Criminal Justice System: Five Years Later.* Washington, DC: The Sentencing Project.

Media Monitor. (1994). "Crime down, media crime coverage up." January/February:3(1).

Media Monitor. (1997). "Network news in the nineties: The top topics and trends in the decade." July/August:11(3).

Messerschmidt, James W. (1986). *Capitalism, Patriarchy, and Crime: Toward a Socialist Feminist Criminology.* Totowa, NJ: Rowman and Littlefield.

Messerschmidt, James W. (1993). *Masculinities and Crime: Critique and Reconceptualization of Theory.* Totowa, NJ: Rowman and Littlefield.

Mill, John Stuart. [1869] (1971). *On the Subjection of Women.* Greenwich, CT: Fawcett.

Millett, Kate. (1970). *Sexual Politics.* New York: Doubleday.

Pizzey, Erin. (1974). *Scream Quietly or the Neighbors Will Hear.* London: If Books.

Platt, Antony M. (1969). *The Childsavers*. Chicago: University of Chicago Press.

Pollock-Byrne, Joycelyn. (1990). *Women, Prison, and Crime*. Pacific Grove, CA: Brooks/Cole.

Price, Barbara and Natalie Sokoloff (eds.). (1982). *The Criminal Justice System and Women*. New York: Clark Boardman.

Price, Barbara and Natalie Sokoloff (eds.). (1995). *The Criminal Justice System and Women: Offenders, Victims, and Workers*, Second Edition. New York: McGraw-Hill.

Quinney, Richard. (1970). *The Social Reality of Crime*. Boston: Little, Brown.

Quinney, Richard. (1980). *Class, State and Crime*. New York: Longman.

Renzetti, Claire and Dan Curran. (1993). *Women, Men and Society*. Boston: Allyn and Bacon.

Ritchie, Beth. (1996). *Compelled to Crime: The Gender Entrapment of Battered Black Women*. New York: Routledge.

Rock, Paul and Simon Holdaway. (1998). "Thinking about criminology: 'Facts are bits of biography.'" Pp. 1–13 in *Thinking About Criminology*. Simon Holdaway and Paul Rock (eds.). Toronto: University of Toronto Press.

Roiphe, K. (1993). *The Morning After: Sex, Fear and Feminism on Campus*. Boston: Little, Brown.

Rossi, Alice (ed.). (1973). *The Feminist Papers*, pp. 413–421. New York: Columbia University Press.

Rowbotham, Sheila. (1973). *Woman's Consciousness, Man's World*. New York: Penguin.

Rusche, Georg and Otto Kirchheimer. (1939). *Punishment and Social Structure*. New York: Russell and Russell.

Rush, Florence. (1980). *The Best Kept Secret: Sexual Abuse of Children*. New York: McGraw-Hill.

Russell, Diana. (1986). *The Secret Trauma*. New York: Basic.

Sargent, Lydia (ed.). (1981). *Women and Revolution: A Discussion of the Unhappy Marriage of Marxism and Feminism*. Boston: South End.

Schechter, Susan. (1982). *Women and Male Violence*. Boston: South End.

Schiraldi, Vincent, Sue Kuyper, and Sharon Hewitt. (1996). *Young African Americans and the Criminal Justice System in California: Five Years Later*. San Francisco: Center on Juvenile and Criminal Justice.

Schlossman, Steven and Stephanie Wallach. (1978). "The crime of precocious sexuality: Ffmale juvenile delinquency in the progressive era." *Harvard Educational Review*, 48:65–94.

Schwartz, Martin D. and Walter S. DeKeseredy. (1997). *Sexual Assault on Campus*. Thousand Oaks, CA: Sage.

Scully, Diana. (1990). *Understanding Sexual Violence*. Boston: Unwin Hyman.

Shearing, Clifford. (1998). "Theorizing—Sotto Voce." Pp. 15–33 in *Thinking About Criminology*. Simon Holdaway and Paul Rock (eds.). Toronto: University of Toronto Press.

Shelden, Randall. (1981). "Sex discrimination in the juvenile justice system: Memphis, Tennessee, 1900–1971." In *Comparing Male and Female Offenders*. M.Q. Warren (ed.). Beverly Hills, CA: Sage.

Singer, Linda R. (1973). "Women and the correctional process." *American Criminal Law Review*, 11:295–308.

Smart, Carol. (1976). *Women, Crime and Criminology: A Feminist Critique*. London: Routledge and Kegan Paul.

Snider, Laureen. (1994). "Criminalization: Panacea for men who assault women, but Anathema for corporate criminals." Pp. 101–124 in *Social Inequality/Social Justice*. Dawn H. Currie and Brian D. MacLean (eds.). Vancoucer: Collective Press.

Stanko, Elizabeth A. (1985). *Intimate Intrusions: Women's Experience of Male Violence*. Boston: Routledge and Kegan Paul.

Stanko, Elisabeth A. (1989). "Missing the mark: Police battering." Pp. 46–59 in *Women, Policing and Male Violence*, Jill Hanmer, Jill Radford and Elizabeth Stanko (eds.). London: Routledge.

Stanko, Elizabeth. (1990). *Everyday Violence: How Women and Men Experience Physical and Sexual Danger*. London: Pandora.

Stanko, Elizabeth. (1993). "Feminist criminology: An oxymoron?" Paper presented to the British Criminology Conference, Cardiff, England.

Wolf, Naomi. (1993). *Fire with Fire*. New York: Random House.

Worrall, Anne. (1990). *Offending Women: Female Lawbreakers and the Criminal Justice System*. London: Routledge.

Zaretsky, Eli. (1978). "The effect of the economic crisis on the family." In *U.S. Capitalism in Crisis*. Radical Political Economic Collective (eds.). New York: Union of Radical Political Economics.

10

Theoretical Development in Criminology

Falsification, Integration, and Competition

Introduction

Now that you are at the last chapter of the book, you must have a sense of being completely overwhelmed by the sheer number of theories that criminologists have put forward to explain crime and criminals. You have read about biological theories, rational choice and routine activities, strain, control, social learning, social reaction/labeling, feminist, Marxist, and social disorganization theories in the course of this book, and it is a little frightening to think that there are some criminological theories (a nontrivial number, in fact) that have been left out because there simply is not enough space to cover them. You may also be thinking that even though some of these theories may certainly be necessary in that they provide what you think is an accurate, correct explanation of the causes of crime, other theories fail this test.

You might be wondering, as a result, whether we really need all of these theories. Perhaps we could whittle the existing number down to a few strong, convincing, and useful ones. Sounds like a good idea, but how will criminology "clean its house" and keep the number of theories in its professional community within some reasonable limit? In this respect, criminology is not different from any of the other social or even the natural sciences. Other disciplines, especially newer ones, generally face an equal abundance of theoretical explanations for what they study. In response, science has generated a few procedures to evaluate theory: (1) theoretical falsification, (2) theoretical integration, and (3) theoretical competition (Hempel 1966; Popper, 1959; Stinchcombe, 1968).

Theoretical Falsification

In the very first chapter, we suggested that one of the bases upon which theory is and should be evaluated is its cognitive or empirical validity. This simply refers to the extent to which a theory "fits the known facts." Probably the most important function of theory is to organize and explain a set of known facts so it seems reasonable that one clear standard to expect of a theory is how well it actually explains those facts. For example, an astronomical theory that is able to accurately account for the motions of the planets in our solar system (e.g., Kepler's laws of planetary motion) can be said to have passed this hurdle of the empirical validity test. However, a second theory, whose predictions are found to be at odds or inconsistent with the known motions of planets, is likely to be suspect or outright rejected on the basis that it is false. That is, it cannot account for the known facts. Thus, good theories can be reconciled with known facts and bad theories cannot.

Related to the capacity to account for known facts is the standard that a good theory is one whose predictions are held up. Let us say that the combination of two chemicals, x and y, result in an entirely new chemical z, which is not simply the sum of the two. A chemical theory that predicts the unknown chemical combination is attractive as a good theory. A theory which failed to predict the new chemical would be far less attractive. Theories can be evaluated, then, to the extent that they can be shown to harmoniously exist with or be hostile to a set of known facts or with a set of predictions that the theory makes. Such theories can be said to possess empirical or cognitive validity. In other words, the theory can be empirically verified. On the other hand, theories that cannot account for known facts or whose predictions are not borne out lack empirical validity and thus are falsified. The process of falsification, then, is a good way to determine which theories are good and should be kept versus which are bad and might be discarded by the field.

As with theories in other fields, there is a set (probably limited) of "known facts" with which any criminological theory must be compatible. For example, we have noted that males are more criminal than females, younger people more than older, urban more than rural, poor more often than rich. Theories of crime that harmonize with these known facts are empirically valid, while those that cannot account for such facts are falsified. Similarly, each criminological theory makes predictions about the distribution of criminal activity across persons or places. Crime should be higher among those feeling strain and anger and in communities that are socially disorganized, for example. When the predictions of a criminological theory are shown to be true, the theory is supported and, on that basis, seems a theory worth keeping. A theory that makes untrue predictions, however, is falsified and becomes a candidate to be discarded, letting the empirically "strong" theories stand. Because science places a high value on empirical accuracy, then, the process of empirical verification and falsification seems a reasonable basis on which to evaluate a theory, and the basis on which a discipline can determine precisely those theories it will retain.

Although the foregoing seems a reasonable strategy for evaluating theory and winnowing down the number of theories in a field, it is a strategy that often breaks down in practice. You may have noticed two things about each of the theories discussed in this book: (1) each enjoys some degree of empirical support, and (2) each is able to provide a convincing explanation as to why it may not enjoy a great deal of empirical support. That is, proponents of a theory also give what seems to be a credible account as to why the theory might not fit some known facts very well or why some of the theory's predictions have proven in some research studies to be empirically false. When empirical studies fail to support a theory, proponents of that theory can argue that the research was flawed in some manner (the wrong sample

of subjects, the wrong measures of key theoretical variables, the wrong statistical strategy, the wrong. . .) In other words, it is notoriously difficult to sift through these many criminological theories, retaining some and eliminating others, because all have some empirical validity and can celebrate the "good news," and all have ways to minimize or discount the "bad news" (the poor fit with facts or false predictions). Because it is difficult (though not impossible) to "knock down" a theory with the empirical evidence, we have the present situation of numerous theories, each with a legitimate claim to some authority and credibility.

It is not likely, then, that a criminological theory will find itself completely lacking in empirical validity. As we have seen, what is more probable is that the theory is able to explain some but not all of the known facts of crime, and that some but not all of its predictions will be found to be true, and that proponents of the theory can offer very convincing accounts for its failure. As a result, historically, it has been rare that a criminological theory has been completely dismissed by those in the discipline because it lacks empirical validity. Possessing some truth, even empirically weak theories linger and limp along, winning some converts along the way and ensuring their virtual immortality. Evaluating the cognitive validity of a set of criminological theories, therefore, is not likely to be a productive exercise in theoretical development. But perhaps there is an alternative strategy to simply outright accepting or rejecting a theory. If all theories have some but not total or even strong empirical validity, maybe some theories can be combined into a new theory in such a manner that the new theory is better than its component parts. This is the notion of "theoretical integration."

Theoretical Integration

Perhaps reflecting a sentiment in the discipline that there are too many explanations of crime that clutter the theoretical landscape, the idea of theoretical integration has recently received a lot of attention in criminology (Messner, Krohn, and Liska 1989).

When scholars talk about the process of theoretical integration, however, each usually has a slightly different idea about what that process would entail. In spite of this lack of an agreed definition, there is some common ground among the different approaches to theoretical integration that we can exploit to our benefit. For our purposes, we will take theoretical integration to entail the combining of parts of two or more pre-existing theories into a separate new theory that promises to provide greater explanatory power, prediction, or understanding of crime causation than its component theories alone. Theoretical integration implies that the theories being integrated are able to form a meaningful explanatory link. They must, therefore, share important common theoretical ground. Simply taking the explanatory variables from one theory and combining them with those of another is not sufficient to constitute theoretical integration. The explanatory variables must be meaningfully (i.e., theoretically) linked.

Do not think for one moment, however, that the business of theoretical integration is either going to be easy to do or easy to understand. It is a lot like buying a car. In the abstract, it sounds like a great idea; but when you leave the house to go do it, things get complicated really fast (e.g., new vs. "previously owned?" buy vs. lease vs. lease with option to buy? whether to get that "undercarriage protection?" how to finance . . .). The complexity in this case arises because those who have written about theoretical integration have suggested several different types of integration as well as several more strategies for actually implementing theoretical integration.

Intradisciplinary Versus Multidisciplinary Integration

At perhaps the most general level, theoretical integration can take place either from among a set of theories within the same discipline (*intradisciplinary*), or the theories can exist in different disciplines and the integrated theory becomes *multidisciplinary*. For example, the integrated theory that Elliott, Huizinga, and Ageton (1985) built to explain juvenile delinquency combines three theories—strain, social control, and social learning theories—all of which are considered sociological theories of crime. More recently, Matsueda and his colleagues (see Chapter 8) have combined several sociological theories into an integrated labeling theory.

Most attempts at theoretical integration have been intradisciplinary. Wellford (1989) thinks that this is not a productive approach to integration and has vocally argued for the development of multidisciplinary criminological theory. He has suggested that before criminologists can even begin to understand the complexities of crime, they must draw upon the knowledge of several disciplines—biology, economics, sociology, and psychology. For example, Terrie Moffitt's (1993) account of offending over the life course combines explanatory variables from biology and psychology (because of birth trauma some children experience brain and neural damage, which leads to a diminished capacity to process information and communicate) with those from sociology (poor parenting, being in the lower class, delinquent peers, and social learning) to account for two distinct kinds of offender. One kind consists of those who become involved in offending in childhood and continue throughout life (the life-course-persistent offender) and the other includes those who initiate offending during adolescence and desist when they enter early adulthood (the adolescent-limited offender). Unlike other approaches to theoretical integration, Moffitt's is multidisciplinary.

Single-Level Versus Multi-Level Integration

There is also a difference between theories that are integrated within a single level of analysis and those that cut across levels of analysis or are multilevel. Recall that the level of analysis of a criminological theory depends upon whether the theory is an attempt to explain variations in the level of offending across persons (the micro- or individual level of analysis) or variations in the rates of offending across groups or geographical units, such as neighborhoods or nations (the macro- or structural level of analysis). Some efforts at theoretical integration are single-level in that they combine parts of different theories at the same level of analysis. For example, the integrated theories of Elliott, Huizinga, and Ageton (1985) and Moffitt (1993) mentioned in the previous paragraph both deal with the individual level of analysis. Micro-level integration, then, integrates different theories, each of which explains the involvement of individuals in crime. The institutional anomie theory of Messner and Rosenfeld (1994) that you read about in Chapter 6 however, integrates two different macro-level theories of crime. This theory combines an emphasis on culture (the theme in the U.S. cultural system of the unrestrained pursuit of financial success) with the social disorganization of communities (the dominance of the economic sector and corresponding weakness of institutions of social control, such as the family).

More rare are attempts to integrate theories at the micro-level with those at the macro-level into what is frequently referred to as a multilevel integrated theory of crime. Such integrated theories explain crime by emphasizing the influence that larger structural forces have on individuals and their actions. One example is John R. Hagan's (1989; Hagan, Simpson, and Gillis 1987) power-control theory of gender and delinquency. Power-control theory attempts to explain male-female differences in delinquency with reference to two levels of explanation: (1) one's class position in a capitalist economic system and the relation between class position and family structure (the macro part of the theory), and (2) differences in the manner in which male and female children are socialized and supervised (the micro part of the theory).

More specifically, Hagan argues that there are two types of family structures, "patriarchal" and "egalitarian." In patriarchal families, the father is employed in a job that places him in control over others, while the mother is either not employed or employed in a job that places her under the control of others. In egalitarian families, both parents are employed in jobs that give them control

and power over others. In patriarchal families, female children are socialized very differently than male children. Females are taught to be risk averse and are provided greater supervision; males, however, are more likely to be left alone and are encouraged to be risk takers. Thus, in patriarchal families, female children are under tighter social control. Differences in the socialization of male and female children also exist in egalitarian families, but to a much lesser degree. The effect of these different experiences with power and control is what explains the consistently observed gender differences in delinquency. That is, males, are predicted to commit more frequent acts of common delinquency. In locating the causes of delinquent offending in both social structural power relations and differences in control exercised over individuals within families, Hagan's power-control theory is an example of a multilevel integrated theory of crime. The inclusion of power relations characteristic of one's class position is the macro-component of the theory, while its inclusion of different childrearing practices for male and female children is the micro-component.

Conceptual Versus Propositional Integration

Once the disciplinary nature of the integration is decided upon, as well as the level of analysis at which the integration will occur, one still must decide on the type of theoretical integration to conduct. Liska, Krohn, and Messner (1989) have suggested two broad types of theoretical integration—conceptual and propositional (see also Akers 1997). In *conceptual integration*, which Liska and his colleagues claim is generally the easier of the two to pull off, the concepts and explanatory variables of at least one less general theory are simply absorbed into those of a more general theory. In other words, the concepts of the less general theory are simply taken to be more specific manifestations of those from the more general theory. Since the concepts of the more general theory include those from the less general theory (and a lot more), the less general theory is absorbed or integrated into the more general one.

For example, Akers (1989; 1997, 208–210) has argued that many micro-level theories of crime can be integrated into social learning theory because their concepts can be simply subsumed under comparable and more general social learning concepts. He refers to this type of integration as "conceptual absorption." As one instance of this absorption, he notes a concept in Hirschi's (1969) social control theory called "moral beliefs." In social control theory, moral beliefs refer to something like conscience (i.e., moral positions that control rule-breaking). If I refrain from committing assault because I think it is wrong or improper to use violence against another person, I am being restrained by my moral beliefs. Akers claims that the social control concept of moral beliefs is simply a specific instance of the more general social learning notion of "definitions favorable and unfavorable to the violation of the law." The "definitions" concept from social learning theory is more general in that it contains both restraints and inducements to crime, as well as restraints and inducements to noncrime. Social learning theory, therefore, can conceptually absorb the concept of moral beliefs, Akers argues, because "definitions" includes all the conceptual ground covered by moral beliefs, but the idea of moral beliefs is more conceptually narrow and does not include things covered by the concept of definitions.

As another example of conceptual absorption, Akers (1990) has argued that deterrence and rational choice theories could be subsumed as special cases under social learning theory. He states that the key explanatory concepts of deterrence/rational choice theory—the formal and informal costs of crime, the expected benefits of crime and noncrime, and any attendant moral costs due to shame and embarrassment—are simply more specific instances of a general social learning theory concept (i.e., differential reinforcements and punishments). Akers' position (1990, 655–657, 669–670) is that differential reinforcements and punishments include the full range of consequences that both increase the likelihood of criminal behavior and inhibit it. Moreover, as a more general theoretical concept, this notion includes rational learning mechanisms not directly implicated by deterrence and rational choice theories, such as learning by imitation. Because they contains more general theoretical concepts, Akers (1990) concludes that deterrence and rational choice theories do not say anything different than social learning theory. In fact, they say a lot less. Thus, the entire content of these two theories could simply be incorporated into or absorbed by the new theory:

> Thus, social learning incorporates reward and punishment in the explanation of crime, and the concept of differential reinforcement applies to the balance of the full range of formal and informal rewards and punishments, from the most "rational" calculation of this balance to the most irrational responses to it. Rational choice does not add more; indeed, it is more limited. (671)

Propositional integration is a more formal effort because it entails linking the propositions, and not just the concepts, of two or more theories into a new combined theory. The key word is "linking"—to be considered theoretical integration, rather than simply usurpation, a propositionally integrated theory must actually meaningfully connect or relate the propositions of different theories into the new theory. Based in part on work previously done by Hirschi (1979), Liska, Krohn, and Messner (1989, 5–15) have suggested three different strategies for integrating theoretical propositions: (1) side-by-side or horizontal integration, (2) end-to-end or sequential integration, and (3) up-and-down or deductive integration.

In *side-by-side* or *horizontal integration*, the field of inquiry is partitioned into different components. One theory is assumed to explain one component, and one or more other theories explain other components. The integrated theory is simply the sum of the different components. As Liska and colleagues (1989) point out, one way to divide the field of criminological inquiry is to have one theory explain some types of crimes (say, instrumental ones) and other theories explain other types (say, highly emotional ones). This is the logic behind what are known as "typological" theories in criminology. For example, Gibbons (1994, 61–62) constructed a typological theory of crime that included twenty distinct types of offenders, each involving a somewhat unique causal pathway to crime. These offender types include professional thieves, naive check forgers, white-collar criminals, psychopathically violent offenders, incest offenders, and amateur shoplifters. Gibbons divided the field of inquiry into several different kinds of crime, each with its own explanation. The integrated typological theory is simply all the separate explanations of crime combined.

More recently, the developmental psychologist Terrie Moffitt (1993) has constructed a more simple two-pathway model to crime. In her taxonomy, there are only two distinct groups of offenders, the life-course-persistent offender and the adolescent-limited offender, which are created by two different causal processes. The life-course-persistent offender is the product of biological and psychological abnormalities and has early behavior so erratic and undisciplined that it easily overwhelms parents (particularly poor parents with limited resources to provide assistance). These behaviorally difficult children are not easily socialized (disciplined) and, as a result, they commit antisocial acts early in life and continue throughout life. The antisocial behavior of the adolescent-limited offender, however, is not the product of faulty socialization. These youths are generally well adjusted, until they hit adolescence, where their desire to flex their adult muscles conflicts with the fact that they are still dependent on their parents. This independence is expressed in acts of rebellion and resistance (e.g., petty delinquency, drinking, sexual promiscuity), which they learn from more antisocial youths. Essentially, normally well-socialized but rebellious adolescents learn from and mimic the behavior of the life-course-persistent offender. And, as you can perhaps now see, the process that drives the adolescent offender is closely tied to social learning theory.

Unlike their life-course-persistent counterparts, adolescent-limited offenders generally cease offending when they begin to enter into adult roles. Moreover, the short-lived antisocial period of the adolescent-limited offender is not caused by biological or psychological dysfunction, but by peer association and the strains of adolescence. Moffitt's taxonomic theory, therefore, is a side-by-side integration of biopsychological and sociological theories of crime. Biological and psychological factors are presumed to account for the offending of one class of offender (the life-course-persistent offender), while more sociological factors account for another (the adolescent-limited offender).

In *end-to-end* or *sequential* integration, theories are combined in such a way that the independent variables (the "cause") in one theory are linked to another theory in such a way that they become the dependent variables (the "effects") in the integrated theory. In this way, the concepts of two or more theories provide a causal chain or sequence that identifies (1) the immediate or most proximate causes of crime, (2) the intermediate or middle causes, and (3) the most remote causes. Perhaps the most well-known example of this type of integration is Delbert Elliott and colleagues' (1985) proposed integration of strain, social control, and social learning theories. In their integrated theory, the most distant cause of crime is strain within the family and school. Family and school strain have a direct effect on the formation of social bonds. When there is stress and conflict within families and when youths are alienated from school personnel, socialization breaks down and a strong social bond to conventional life is not established. Weak social bonds, the intermediate cause of delinquency, leads youths to seek out the companionship and support of delinquent others. It is from these delinquent peers that youths learn delinquent definitions, receive social reinforcement for antisocial behavior, and imitate the acts of their delinquent friends. Delinquent peers are, therefore, the most immediate cause of delinquency.

Notice how the end-to-end sequencing works in this integrated theory. Social bonds and delinquent peers are independent variables in social control and differential association/social learning theory, respectively. In the integrated theory of Elliott and colleagues, these two are both dependent variables and independent variables. They are dependent variables in that they are influenced by family and school strain; they are independent variables in that they are either indirectly or directly related to delinquent offending. This example of end-to-end integration is illustrated for you in Figure 1.

Up-and-down or *deductive* integration is probably the most rare strategy in the social sciences for theoretical integration. Such a theory consists of more abstract theoretical constructs than those of the theories that comprise it. Quite possibly, the only deductively integrated theory was Burgess and Akers' (1966) attempt to integrate differential association theory within social learning theory (Liska, Krohn, and Messner 1989). They took Sutherland's notion of the "learning of definitions favorable and unfavorable to the violation of law within intimate primary groups" and translated it into the more abstract and general principles of behavioral learning theory. Sutherland's theory, then, consisted of more specific deductions from the more general reinforcement theory of Burgess and Akers.

For example, they took Sutherland's proposition that "the principal part of the learning of criminal behavior occurs within intimate personal groups" and translated it into "the principal part of the learning of criminal behavior occurs in those groups which comprise the individual's major source of reinforcements" (Burgess and Akers 1966, 146). Burgess and Akers' reformulation is more general than Sutherland's original proposition because they propose that the learning of criminal and noncriminal definitions can occur in contexts other than the individual's primary group. Granted, the lion's share of the learning of definitions may take place with those in our primary groups, but it can also include learning from the mass media (e.g., television, movies, video games) and from groups that we identify with but might not be highly involved with or committed to (what Burgess and Akers [1966] refer to as "reference" rather than "primary groups"). Because Sutherland's original proposition is a special case of Burgess and Akers' reformulation, it is subsumed under that. The integration, therefore, is "up and down."

Theoretical Competition

There is a third, alternate approach to theoretical development—*theoretical competition.* Rather than accommodating itself with

Figure 1
Example of End-to-End Theoretical Integration

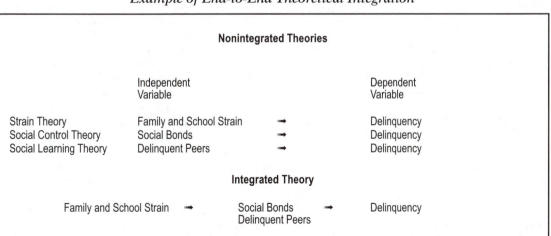

other theories (e.g., theoretical integration), however, theoretical competition is based upon a strategy of opposition and conflict. This is a strategy similar to falsification, but one concerned only about the empirical validity of one theory compared with others. In the process of theoretical competition, each theory pits itself against other theories so the question becomes, "How does one theory stack up against another?" Thus the goal of each theory is to make itself as strong a competitor as possible—that is, as attractive a suitor to prospective supporters as it can be, and as unattractive as possible for those who wish to stage a "hostile takeover." Instead of being inviting and friendly to other theories, then, in theoretical competition, a theory is confrontational and quarrelsome. Instead of gaining strength (clarity, coherence, organization, explanatory power, internal consistency) by trying to blend or integrate itself into another theory, in theoretical competition each theory is left alone to develop its strengths and strengthen its weaknesses. Finally, in theoretical competition each theory tries to make a distinctive name for itself by emphasizing its differences from other theories.

As you can well imagine, when in opposition to competitors, theorists are called upon to emphasize the strengths of their theory and minimize its weaknesses. Hirschi (1989) has stated more eloquently than anyone else the posture that a theory must adopt when in this type of competition:

> [T]he first purpose of oppositional theory construction is to make the world safe for a theory contrary to currently accepted views. Unless this task is accomplished, there will be little hope for the survival of the theory and less hope for its development. Therefore, oppositional theorists should not make life easy for those interested in preserving the status quo. They should instead remain at all times blind to the weakness of their own position and stubborn in its defense. Finally, they should never smile. (45)

What should not be lost in Hirschi's eloquence is his point that theoretical competition forces a theory to become better by developing itself—for example, by sharpening its concepts, clearly noting its scope conditions, and providing clear and testable propositions. In fact, he argues that being forced to compete with others is the only hope for the development of a theory. Without undergoing very careful work by its proponents, there is "little hope for the survival of the theory." As an alternative to theoretical integration, then, theoretical competition is based on the strategy of keeping theories separate, and developing them as far as possible. Constantly at war with other theories, the choices are either to improve or surrender. It is the Darwinian notion of the "survival of the fittest" in the theoretical world. Those in favor of this approach argue that this forces theories to become clear and better able to do what they are supposed to do—explain crime and criminals (Hirschi 1989, 44).

Proponents of theoretical competition have a second argument against those who wish to integrate theories. They claim that in the rush to combine theories, integrationists have ignored crucial differences and distinctions among them so that the combined integrated theory is unfaithful to its parts (what Hirschi 1989, 44, has derided as "some integrated stew"). Hirschi (1979, 1989), for example, would argue that Elliott and colleagues' (1985) attempt to integrate social learning, strain, and social control theories ignored the fundamental tension that exists between strain and control explanations of crime. Strain theories take conformity to norms as given so that they must explain what motivates people to break rules—their answer, people are under strain. Control theories like Hirschi's, however, take self-interest as given and presume that people will do whatever they need to do to secure the things they want, even if it involves crime. Given the tendency for self-interest, what they must explain is why people do *not* commit crimes. Hirschi's (1989) point is that these are two fundamentally different approaches to the study of crime—so different that they cannot be accommodated or reconciled.

Any attempt to integrate two such diametrically opposed theoretical positions can only come at the expense of one of the theories, which must take a back seat to the other.

In their integration, Elliott et al. (1985) do essentially that; they put the constant motivation-for-crime assumption of control theory in the back seat. In Hirschi's (1979, 34) own terms, these scholars "use the terms and ignore the claims of control theory." They essentially argue that the process of social bonding can produce either conventional or antisocial outcomes. In a similar way, the controversy about accommodating different theoretical positions continues to haunt others who argue for integrated theory.

Forced to compete against one another, inadequate theories will be proven to be such and eventually abandoned, it is argued, while those that survive will go on to become more accepted by the field with each successful test. As Liska and Messner (1999, 214) note, a particularly useful strategy might be the development of "crucial" or "critical" tests. That is, hypotheses would be used to verify a key part of one theory while falsifying an equally key element of another theory (see Hempel 1966, 25–28). For example, labeling and deterrence theories make entirely different predictions about the effects of formal sanctions. Labeling theory predicts that the imposition of formal sanctions would have cascading effects; it would result in the imposition of a deviant label, the internalization of a deviant self-identity, exclusion from conventional routines, closer association with deviant others, and additional (secondary) deviance. Deterrence theory, however, would predict that crime would diminish in this case because formal sanctions would increase the cost and reduce the profit of committing crimes. It would appear simple to devise a set of "critical tests" that would pit labeling theory against the deterrence prediction regarding the effect of formal sanctions. However, we know that rarely do these tests prove to be "critical" in any sense. Theories whose predictions are not confirmed can claim any number of extenuating excuses as to why the outcome turned out as it did. In fact, numerous such "critical tests" of theory in the criminological literature have not resulted in closure, so it is difficult to be very hopeful about the prospects for theoretical competition.

A final point about theoretical competition: There are other bases on which to compare theories in addition to their explanatory power, and some theories may be preferred on these other grounds. For example, a community of scholars can compare theories in terms of the work agenda or "puzzles" that they pose (Kuhn 1970). A given theory may be very weak in its current explanatory power, but may contain a set of intriguing research questions. One theory may be preferred over another, therefore, because of its potential rather than its current standing.

Two recent examples come immediately to mind. When Gottfredson and Hirschi (1990) published their general theory of crime, they could argue that their notion of time-stable differences in self-control was compatible with the known facts of crime, but they could not claim on the basis of existing empirical evidence that the theory was capable of explaining crime better than other theories. What their theory did do, however, was raise some intriguing questions about doubtful issues, such as an initial propensity to commit crime, the importance of family socialization, the stability of crime over the life course, and the many manifestations of low self-control. It was a captivating theory because it posed all sorts of research and theoretical questions—it was a rich treasure box of "puzzles."

The same could be said of what is now thought of as their competitor, Sampson and Laub's (1993) theory of age-graded informal controls. Although Sampson and Laub's analyses with the Gluecks' data certainly showed that their theory possessed explanatory power, the field provided no consensus that it was more capable in that regard than, say, social learning theory. What was appealing about their theory, however, was the puzzles that it posed—"given stability, is there still the possibility of significant changes in offending over the life course?" "Can events and experiences later in life affect someone's offending pattern that has already been well established?" "What are the implications of not adequately considering one's initial propensity to offending when examining these later life events and experiences?" Like Gottfredson and Hirschi's, the theory put forth by Sampson and Laub was rich in research, theoretical puzzles, and potential—no small part in understanding why both theories have captured the attention of large numbers of criminologists.

Theoretical Elaboration

As a compromise between theoretical integration and competition, Thornberry (1989) has suggested the strategy of theoretical elaboration. He warns us of going to either extreme in following the integration or competition strategies of theoretical development. For example, when pushed too far, theoretical integration leads to "theoretical mush" (51), and extreme theoretical competition ignores important commonalities among theories. The strategy of theoretical elaboration is instead based on the following ideas. Unlike theoretical integration, which starts with two or more theories and attempts to create a new theory by combining different elements from each, it starts with one base theory. This one theory is then made more comprehensive or "elaborated" by what Thornberry (1989, 56) calls *logical extension*. The example Thornberry (1989, 57) provides is Hirschi's (1969) social control theory. Social control theory presumes that there is variation in the social bond that connects persons to conventional society, thus providing a restraint on purely self-interested behavior, such as crime. Hirschi was not really interested in explaining what produced these variations in the social bond, just that they occurred and were related to delinquency and crime. Thornberry would elaborate Hirschi's theory by explicitly including a set of explanatory factors to account for variations in the social bond. Some candidate factors might be whether or not the family was "broken" by divorce or separation, the criminality of the parents, or even the community within which the family lived, and their social class or ethnicity. The new, elaborated theory would then be more comprehensive because it would provide an explanation of both variations in the social bond and variations in criminality. Notice that this specific example of theoretical elaboration is remarkably similar to an end-to-end or sequential integration.

Thornberry (1987) has provided his own elaborated theory of delinquency and adult offending in what he calls an *interactional theory of delinquency*." In this theory, Thornberry elaborates the basic theoretical structure of social bonding and social learning theories by adding two-way causal direction. He argues that there are structural determinants of social bonding (e.g., attachment to the family) and social learning (e.g., delinquent peers) variables, such as the social organization of the community, social class, and race. These background structural factors influence the formation of a bond to conventional society; a weak bond is not sufficient to cause delinquency, however, unless there are delinquent peers to learn from. Involvement with delinquent peers and delinquent acts in turn further weaken the social bond, leading to greater involvement with delinquent peers and more delinquency. Because elaboration theory is in its early stages, criminological scholars are not certain if it presents any substantial differences vis-a-vis theoretical integration.

A Recent Example and Movement Beyond Strategies of Elaboration and Competition

There are two essays in this final chapter of the book. The first, by Professor Charles R. Tittle, presents an example of one type of integrated theory of crime, called "control-balance" theory. Control balance is a general theory of crime and deviance in that it offers one comprehensive explanation not only of diverse forms of criminality (violent, property, drug, and other crimes) but also of non-criminal forms of deviance (sexual perversions, cult membership). It is an integration of deterrence/rational choice, strain, social learning, and social control theories. As Professor Tittle explains, control balance describes a ratio. It refers to the amount of control that one experiences or is subject to relative to the amount of control that one can exercise over others. The ratio of control experienced to control exercised determines the probability that someone will commit deviance; that is, the greater the imbalance in either direction, the higher the risk of deviance.

Moreover, the theory also predicts the specific form the deviance will take depending upon the magnitude of the imbalance. Those who exercise more control over others than have control extended over them are said to have control "surpluses." The type of deviance committed will depend upon the magnitude of the surplus. Those with small control surpluses will tend to commit acts of exploitation (e.g., price fixing, contract killings), while those with the greatest surplus will tend to commit decadent acts of deviance (e.g., sexual cruelty, sadistic torture). Those who are more controlled than controlling are said to have control "deficits." The type of deviance committed here too will depend upon the magnitude of the deficit. Those with a small control deficit will tend to commit acts of predation (e.g., criminal acts of physical violence), while those with the greatest deficits will tend to commit acts of submissive deviance (e.g., allowing oneself to be sexually degraded or abused). Professor Tittle's (1995) theory is relative new, and a stream of empirical research to test the theory has yet to be completed.

In his essay, Professor Thomas J. Bernard tackles the problem of theoretical abundance in criminology from an entirely different direction. He argues that both the theoretical integration and competition strategies have proven to be unproductive for the field. He claims that the essence of all criminological theories is the identification of risk factors for crime, factors that make criminal activity more or less likely to occur. For example, a poor relationship with one's parents is a risk factor for social control theory, as is weak parental supervision. Because all criminological theories identify risk factors, all have something to say about crime. Bernard's position is that the question we should be asking of our theories is, "Do the risk factors that this theory identifies explain criminal conduct?" The question is entirely an empirical one for Bernard. Those risk factors that appear to be strongly associated with crime should be retained, while those only

weakly related should be discarded. As he readily acknowledges in his essay, this approach is very empirical and the issue that Bernard will ultimately have to address is whether any enumeration of risk factors constitutes a "theory" of crime.

References

Akers, R.L. (1989). "A social behaviorist's perspective on integration of theories of crime and deviance." Pp. 23–36 in *Theoretical Integration in the Study of Deviance and Crime.* S.F. Messner, M.D. Krohn, and A.E. Liska (eds.). Albany: State University of New York Press.

——. (1990). "Rational choice, deterrence, and social learning theory in criminology." *Journal of Criminal Law and Criminology,* 81:653–676.

——. (1997). *Criminological Theories: Introduction and Evaluation.* Los Angeles: Roxbury.

Burgess, R.L. and R.L. Akers. (1966). "A differential association-reinforcement rheory of criminal behavior." *Social Problems,* 14:128–147.

Elliott, D.S., D. Huizinga, and S.S. Ageton. (1985). *Explaining Delinquency and Drug Use.* Beverly Hills, CA: Sage.

Gibbons, D.C. (1994). *Talking About Crime and Criminals.* Englewood Cliffs, NJ: Prentice Hall.

Gottfredson, M. and T. Hirschi. (1990). *A General Theory of Crime.* Palo Alto, CA: Stanford University Press.

Hagan, J.R. (1989). "Micro- and macrostructures of delinquency causation and a power-control theory of gender and delinquency." Pp. 213–228 in *Theoretical Integration in the Study of Deviance and Crime.* S.F. Messner, M.D. Krohn, and A.E. Liska (eds.). Albany: State University of New York Press.

Hagan, J.R., J.H. Simpson, and A.R. Gillis. (1987). "Class in the household: A power-sontrol theory of gender and delinquency." *American Journal of Sociology,* 92:788–816.

Hempel, C. (1966). *Philosophy of Natural Science.* Englewood Cliffs, NJ: Prentice Hall.

Hirschi, T. (1969). *Causes of Delinquency.* Berkeley: University of California Press.

——. (1979). "Separate and unequal is better." *Journal of Research in Crime and Delinquency,* 16:34–37.

——. (1989). "Exploring alternatives of integrated theory." Pp. 37–50 in *Theoretical Integration in the Study of Deviance and Crime.* S.F. Messner, M.D. Krohn, and A.E. Liska (eds.). Albany: State University of New York Press.

Kuhn, T.S. (1970). *The Structure of Scientific Revolutions* Second Edition. Chicago: University of Chicago Press.

Liska, A.E., M.D. Krohn, and S.F. Messner. (1989). "Strategies and requisites for theoretical integration in the study of crime and deviance." Pp. 1–19 in *Theoretical Integration in the Study of Deviance and Crime*. S.F. Messner, M.D. Krohn, and A.E. Liska (eds.). Albany: State University of New York Press.

Liska, A.E. and S.F. Messner. (1999). *Perspectives on Crime and Deviance* Third Edition. Upper Saddle River, NJ: Prentice Hall.

Messner, S.F., M.D. Krohn, and A.E. Liska. (1989). *Theoretical Integration in the Study of Deviance and Crime: Problems and Prospects*. Albany: State University of New York Press.

Messner, Steven F. and Richard Rosenfeld. (1994). *Crime and the American Dream*. Belmont, CA: Wadsworth.

Moffitt, T.E. (1993). "Adolescence-limited and life-course-persistent antisocial behavior: A developmental taxonomy." *Psychological Review*, 100:674–701.

Popper, K. (1959). *The Logic of Scientific Discovery*. New York: Basic.

Sampson, R.J. and J.H. Laub. (1993). *Crime in the Making: Pathways and Turning Points Through Life*. Cambridge: Harvard University Press.

Stinchcombe, A. (1968). *Constructing Social Theories*. New York: Harcourt, Brace, and World.

Thornberry, T.P. (1987). "Towards an interactional theory of delinquency." *Criminology*, 25:863–891.

——. (1989). "Reflections on the advantages and disadvantages of theoretical elaboration." Pp 51–60 in *Theoretical Integration in the Study of Deviance and Crime*. S.F. Messner, M.D. Krohn, and A.E. Liska (eds.). Albany: State University of New York Press.

Tittle, C.R. (1995). *Control Balance: Toward a General Theory of Deviance*. Boulder, CO: Westview.

Wellford, C.F. (1989). "Towards an integrated theory of criminal behavior." Pp. 119–128 in *Theoretical Integration in the Study of Deviance and Crime*. S.F. Messner, M.D. Krohn, and A.E. Liska (eds.). Albany: State University of New York Press.

Wilson, J.Q. and R.J. Herrnstein. (1985). *Crime and Human Nature*. New York: Simon and Schuster.

Control Balance

Charles R. Tittle
Washington State University

Suppose you ask a question in this class and your teacher says, "That is the stupidest question any student has ever asked; how did you get into college anyway?" How do you imagine it would make you feel, and what do you think you would do about it? If you are like most people, you would probably feel humiliated, become conscious of your inability to control what happens, and you would want to show the teacher and the other students that you are not the lowly nincompoop implied by the teacher's remark. But what could you do?

An Illustrative Overview

There are several things you might do if you were humiliated by a professor. For one thing, you might make up your mind to study really hard, to "ace" the next test, to succeed in life, and later, after having succeeded, contact that teacher and recall the putdown. Such a response could be called "conformity." However, you might not be able to do those things, and if you did, it would take years; the other students who witnessed the debasement probably would not learn about your triumph; and before too long the pain of the moment would fade, causing you to lose that motivation to succeed in life.

A quicker, more satisfying reaction would be to slug the professor. We'll call this reaction "predation." An assault is not hard to do, and it would overcome your humiliation while giving you a feeling of control. The problem, of course, is that slugging the professor would probably cause you a lot more trouble than it is worth. The teacher may slug you back, the police may arrest you, the university may expel you, and your future plans to go to law school may be jeopardized; in any case you probably wouldn't get credit for the course. So, you probably won't take that kind of drastic action.

You might also start to denigrate the teacher to your friends, give her a poor mark on the student evaluations at the end of the term (even though in other respects this is an excellent teacher), be sullen and uncooperative during the rest of the semester, show contempt when she tries to make a joke in class, or possibly even make loud, disruptive noises. Such actions constitute a form of deviance (usually noncriminal) called "defiance." This, too, is easy to accomplish, and though it will be less gratifying than having slugged the teacher, it will at least help restore your sense of dignity and give you a measure of control over your own destiny. But there is also a potential cost associated with this conduct—you are not likely to do well in the class and the poor grade may affect your future. This cost, however, is much less than that associated with punching the teacher.

Still another possibility is simply to capitulate. In this maneuver, you decide that nothing you can do will help overcome your sense of degradation. You imagine that anything you might do will be met with a response by the teacher that produces even more humiliation and accentuates your lack of control. So you sit quietly, do everything the teacher asks or implies, stop imagining any other possibilities, and accept a permanent state of subordination in that class. If you do this, it is "submission," which may or may not be deviant, depending on how surrender of the human spirit is viewed in your social context. Submission, of course, is not satisfying but it may reflect your feelings of helplessness, and it at least allows you to get through the semester, perhaps even with a good grade.

If you are from a wealthy, influential family you might have other options. One is to get somebody else to commit predation on your behalf ("exploitation"). For instance, you could ask your father to threaten to stop donating money to the university, or you could ask him to make trouble with the Board of Regents unless that teacher is disciplined or fired. Perhaps you could hire a private detective to gather dirt for jeopardizing the teacher's marriage. You might even employ some thugs to assault the teacher. All of these acts would restore your sense of control, and if you are highly positioned socially, it would be easy to do with little possibility that it would be costly to you. The teacher may not even learn you are responsible for those bad consequences, and the chances that the police will find out who assaulted the teacher or hired the thugs is slight. In other words, on balance, some of these things might be an advantageous response. The trouble is, you probably are not socially situated so as to make it possible.

An additional rare possibility, which would be conceivable only if you are exceptionally wealthy or powerful and are attending a private university owned by your family, or one that you could buy, would be to shut down the school. That way all the teachers could be dismissed, and you could establish a different school staffed with hand-picked professors whom you liked or who would do your bidding. Such deviant reactions (they are deviant because they violate normative expectations in such a way as to be socially unacceptable) that involve pursuing personal goals through broad scale actions with almost no regard for the consequences they have for others is called "plunder."

A final, almost unheard of reaction to your humiliation at the hands of the teacher might be to adopt a completely decadent lifestyle. In doing so, you would ignore all social rules and live a life of complete selfishness that shows utter disregard for the social system that produced your debasement. If you did this, you would lose all sense of direction in your life; you would pursue any and all impulses, including any whimsical pleasures, desires, and cruelties; and your actions would be completely without awareness or concern for others. Of course, you could resort to such decadence only if you were unbelievably wealthy or powerful so that you did not have to worry about sustenance or about what others might think or do about your behavior.

The Causal Process

Although there are many ways to deal with a teacher's humiliating response to a question, not all of the possibilities are equally likely. What influences what you are actually likely to do? According to control balance theory, the most important thing is the extent to which a possible response promises to overcome your sense of humiliation, weighed against the potential costly consequences of committing that act or acts. The greater the value of the act for extending your sense of control (thereby countering feelings of degradation) relative to the potential consequences of your actions (magnitude and potentiality of counter-controlling responses), the greater the chances that you will do it. This balancing of the control you might gain from deviant behavior against the control that will likely be directed back at you is called "control balancing." According to the theory, how the calculation turns out largely determines what you will do when you are provoked.

The control balancing process is similar for all people in all provocative situations, but it does not always unfold in the same way. For one thing, some people start with a lot more relative control than do other people. Those people with a lot of control can contemplate doing more serious things without worrying so much about what will happen in return. For example, if you are from a wealthy and influential family, your response to the hypothetical insulting teacher is probably going to be different from that of a student from a low-income family. That is because the potential counter controls that a wealthy student's deviant actions might elicit are less potent than those for a student with less initial control. In addition, no matter what a person's chances of stimulating counter control, that person may do no deviance because he is inhibited by moral considerations. Perhaps such a student has been taught from an early age to respect teachers and, as a result, has internalized the belief that it would be wrong to misbehave in a classroom. Conditions, such as morally based respect for teachers, that intervene into the control balancing process, are called "contingencies."

Control balance theory, therefore, postulates that there is a fundamental underlying process that leads to deviant behavior and that people's concerns about control are central to it. The process begins with some situational provocation, usually one that stimulates feelings of humiliation, that calls up an individual's awareness of his or her relative control potentiality. The theory contends that the likely outcome depends on how the provoked individual's ability to exercise control compares to the control that is likely to be exercised back if he or she commits various acts of deviance. However, because this underlying process of balancing is affected by a number of other things, criminal or deviant behavior results when a peculiar set of conditions converge.

Key Conditions

The most important condition is the person's *control ratio*, or "the extent to which an individual can potentially exercise control over circumstances impinging on him, relative to the potential control that can be exercised by external entities and conditions against the individual." Other conditions must also come together for deviance to occur: (1) a predisposition toward being motivated for deviance, (2) situational provocation that reminds a person of a control imbalance, (3) the transformation of predisposition into actual motivation for deviance, (4) opportunity for deviant response, and (5) the absence or relative weakness of constraint, so that the mental process of "control balancing" will result in a perceived gain in control. Altogether, then, there are six important conditions involved in deviant behavior. Each is considered separately, and then we will see how they fit together.

Control Ratio

Everybody has a global, *general control ratio* that roughly reflects their *typical* ability to exercise control relative to being the object of control. This global control ratio reflects all of one's statuses, roles, personal and physical characteristics, organizational contacts, and interpersonal relationships. All people also have numerous *situational control ratios* that represent their ability in specific circumstances to exercise control relative to being controlled.

A person's general control ratio suggests his or her average probability of being able to control rather than being controlled. Situational control ratios, however, focus on concrete contexts, such as at home, in a work situation, on a date, at school, or on the athletic field. An individual's control ratio, then, is not fixed; it varies from place to place, from time to time, and from situation to situation. Yet in general, and in any given context, one's control ratio conceivably can be estimated empirically.

Control ratios depend on individual characteristics as well as social or organizational variables. For example, almost all students exercise less control than that to which they are subject; they have a general control deficit—a ratio less than one. Because most students are relatively young, they have little control over adults, even though adults can exercise much control over them; because students are subordinates in classes and other university contexts, they have little control over professors and administrators, although professors and administrators have a lot of control over them; because most students do not have occupations or careers, they have relatively few economic resources that might enable them to control commodities and services, even though economic circumstances exercise a great deal of control over them; and in interpersonal relationships, students may or may not have a favorable balance of control, depending on many things.

Despite the fact that most students have general control deficits, some specific students may have control surpluses in their group of residential friends (because of being highly respected), and they might have large surpluses of control in dating relationships (because somebody is in love with them or because they are exceptionally attractive and pleasant). Moreover, students who generally have control deficits may on occasion see those ratios boosted or lowered. Thus, a solitary student confronting a large number of professors may have a large control deficit, but if numerous students confront one professor, because of the shared collective control inherent in large numbers, each student's control ratio may be enhanced. Similarly, although students may generally have control deficits, the magnitude of those deficits may vary from course to course. In one class, a student may impress the professor with her intelligence or diligence, thereby gaining control from the professor's willingness to assume that student has some degree of mastery of the material. In another class, the student may have less control because the professor has low tolerance for any student mistakes.

Deviance grows from a process involving several sequential steps. Control ratios are important for all of those steps. You'll see later why that is true, and I will outline how the control ratio's influence is played out, but for now you should remember five things about control ratios: (1) control ratio is the key concept and variable in control balance theory, (2) some control ratios may consist of equal parts of control to be exercised and to be suffered; that is, they may be about equal to one, (3) control ratios may be unbalanced, reflecting either a deficit (a ratio less than one) or a surplus (a ratio greater than one), (4) control ratios are not entirely fixed because they may change as individuals change locales and social statuses or assume new roles; nevertheless, they can be characterized as more or less stable, and (5) individuals differ with respect to their control ratios.

Predisposition to Be Motivated

Although one's control ratio is the most important variable in explaining the probability and form of deviance a person is likely to commit, it does not work alone. In fact, it is only when a series of variables, including the control ratio, converge in particular ways that deviant behavior occurs. First, one has to be predisposed toward deviant motivation. Almost anyone may have such predisposition, but it does not become obvious without some blockage of a person's basic goals. Predisposition stems from the convergence of three inputs: (1) desire for auton-

omy, (2) an unbalanced control ratio, and (3) blockage of goals.

Autonomy Seeking

A necessary element in all deviant behavior, because it fuels the balancing process, is an underlying urge for autonomy. Such a desire is probably instilled in us as infants. It is expressed as an urge to escape control exercised against us and to extend our control over other people and circumstances. Because infants must depend for all their needs on others and on circumstances over which they have no control, they come to resent it. That resentment causes them to want to escape dependency. In addition, because caregivers are the first important people in everybody's lives, infants identify with caregivers; that is, they want to be like them. Because caregivers are controllers, identification with them produces a desire to extend control over others. Hence, everybody has a latent desire to escape the control that is arrayed against them and to extend their own control.

The theory, therefore, assumes a desire for autonomy in all people in more or less equal amounts. This assumption may be wrong, but like all assumptions, its correctness cannot be directly determined. Theories always begin with some conditions that are taken for granted (Savelsberg 1999). Eventually, the theoretical implications that flow from the assumptions may find little empirical support, thereby indirectly challenging the initial assumptions and the theory based on them. But at least temporary acceptance of beginning assumptions is necessary before one can begin to appreciate the implications of a theory. Such acceptance, however, is not the same as believing the assumptions or being committed by faith to their truth. Instead, it is like buying a ticket to the circus. A ticket allows you to get into the big top to see what is going on. You may not like what you see, and you may want your money back (that is, you may want to reject the assumption), but the ticket is the price for finding out if you like the show.

It is also important to note that some assumptions in any theory are "fundamental," while others are "convenient." Fundamental assumptions are so crucial that the entire theory depends on their accuracy. Assumptions of convenience, however, are made in order to develop theoretical implications more precisely and fully. It is like saying, "Let's pretend such and such is true in order to see where this leads us." In the case of control balance theory, the assumption that all people desire autonomy is fundamental, while the assumption that the degree to which people desire autonomy is more or less constant is one of convenience. The assumption that the degree of autonomy seeking varies little from person to person was made to enable the development of detailed implications of the interrelationships in the theory. It is possible that at a future date the theory can be reformulated with the degree of autonomy desired by individuals being treated as a variable. A reformulation in which people differ in their desires for autonomy would yield far more complex predictions than now. Even though it is convenient to assume that the degree of autonomy desired is more or less constant from person to person, the assumption that all people have some desire for autonomy is so basic that it cannot be changed without destroying the theory.

Control Ratios and Predisposition

Desire for autonomy is one thing that affects predisposition for deviant motivation, but predisposition also depends on unbalanced control ratios. The greater the imbalance in the control that one can exercise relative to that to which he is subject, the greater will be the likelihood of that person's predisposition toward becoming motivated for deviance. Because everybody desires autonomy, unbalanced control ratios are latent sore spots that can, under certain conditions, flare into motivation for deviance. This is not to say that those with balanced control ratios are never motivated for deviance. Those with unbalanced control are simply more likely to become motivated, and so their degree of predisposition is greater.

Think back to the student humiliated by the teacher. That student, as all people presumably do, generally desires autonomy. She wants to escape control from others and from environmental constraints; in other words, the student wants to be a master of her own fate. In addition, she probably has a control imbalance—most likely a deficit, although some students, because of family or personal circumstances, may have a surplus. The professor's remarks would not matter to the student if that student did not desire autonomy, and it probably would not matter as much if the professor were dealing with somebody of equal control, say another professor of similar rank and stature. A putdown between equals has less force because it implies almost certain tit for tat, and it does not humiliate like an insult from a person of either lesser or greater control potential.

Goal Blockage

As noted in the paragraphs above, predisposition to become motivated for deviance depends on a desire for autonomy and on a control imbalance. In addition, predispositions are linked to blockages of human goals. If a person were, without restraint or barrier, accomplishing all of his or her goals, including the goal of exercising control, then the issue of deviance would almost never arise. If all of the goals of the student in our example were being accomplished, she would probably not be a classroom student in the first place, would not be asking questions of the professor, and would not be in a position to become humiliated and then contemplate a response.

Convergence to Produce Predisposition

Thus, the degree of predisposition for deviant motivation depends on how three things come together; the three things consist of a constant and two variables. The constant is the desire for autonomy that everybody has. The variables are (1) the extent to which the person's impulses (or goals) are blocked and (2) an imbalance of control. When these three things converge for an individual, that person is then in a state of readiness to experience motivation for deviant behavior.

Motivation

Provocation

Although many people are predisposed, they only occasionally actually become motivated for deviant behavior. Motivation occurs when a person becomes acutely aware of his control imbalance and realizes that deviant behavior can change that imbalance, either by overcoming a deficit or by extending a surplus. The conditions that transform predisposition into actual motivation exist in situations that a person may encounter. Those conditions consist of provocations and things that cause people who experience them to feel debased or humiliated. Sometimes predisposed people encounter situations that vividly remind them of their control imbalance. Such situational provocations may include, but are not limited to, the following: (1) somebody tells an individual what to do, especially in a commanding, harsh tone, (2) a person is jilted by a boyfriend or girlfriend, (3) bills arrive on top of other bills that have piled up, (4) an individual's authority is questioned, or some rights a person thought she had are questioned, (5) an individual is pushed while waiting in line, (6) a person is stopped by the police, (7) someone is denied admission to a club, (8) an individual is hungry but is denied food because he has no money, or (9) a student gets a sharp or hostile reaction from a professor (as happened to our hypothetical student at the beginning of this essay).

All such situations, and many more, remind people of what their control imbalances are. For most students, these kinds of events would remind them that they have deficits of control. A few students, however, would be reminded that they have control surpluses; being reminded of a control surplus usually occurs when a person realizes that superior control is not at that moment producing the advantages that the person would normally expect. Situational provocations, then, alert the predisposed person to a control imbalance that otherwise she would have been only vaguely aware of, and situational provocations stimulate the alerted individual to search for some mechanism that might help change the imbalance. When a person wants to try to change a control imbalance quickly, deviant behavior often comes to mind.

Debasement

Acute awareness of a control imbalance, however, is usually not enough to motivate deviance. There must also be some negative emotion generated by the situation—a feeling of being debased, humiliated, or denigrated that intensifies the thought that deviance is a possible response to the provocations. Negative emotions produced by situational provocations are inside the person, but they grow out of external circumstances. How potential provocations are interpreted depends partly on individual characteristics. Sometimes provocation is unusual and directly humiliating in a way that would debase just about anybody; such was the case with our example of the professor denigrating the student's intellect. At other times, however, provocation of some specific individuals stems from ordinary, routine events that ordinarily would not provoke most people or generate emotions of debasement. For instance, students routinely take examinations in college classes. Because it is an expected, everyday occurrence, taking an exam usually does not provoke acute awareness of a control imbalance. Occasionally, however, an individual student, say an older person who has returned to school or a teacher who has decided to obtain an advanced degree, will find examinations humiliating. Such people often think that being tested is beneath their dignity. To them, mere announcement of an exam may activate awareness of a control imbalance and evoke a feeling of debasement.

Convergence to Generate Motivation

Predisposed people—those for whom a desire for autonomy has converged with a control imbalance and some goal blockage—can sometimes become motivated to commit deviant acts. They do so when situations remind them of a control imbalance in a humiliating way. Motivation can be said to exist when deviant behavior comes to be perceived as a means to alter a control imbalance, thereby permitting the person to overcome debasement or humiliation. Motivation to commit deviance, therefore, is a variable. It may not occur at all, it may develop moderately, or it may be intense.

Opportunity

Although motivation depends somewhat on predisposition and is an essential element of deviant conduct, motivation does not always lead to deviant behavior; whether it does or not depends on other variables.

One of them is simple opportunity. Opportunity means that circumstances are such that a potential deviant act is possible. No matter how strongly motivated people are to steal automobiles, they cannot do it unless there are automobiles to be stolen, and they cannot do it if the automobiles within their purview are impossible to steal. All deviant behavior requires opportunity; and according to control balance theory, when motivation is strong and there is opportunity, some form of deviance is highly likely. When an individual becomes acutely aware of his or her control imbalance, grasps the idea that deviance will help, and in addition is situated so that opportunity to commit one or another of those potentially helpful deviances exists, then we can expect that individual to commit some form of deviance.

Seriousness and Control Balancing

Because opportunity for a variety of deviant acts is usually omnipresent, motivated people have a high probability of doing some deviance. However, they will not commit just any specific kind of deviance that one might imagine; instead, they will commit one of a set that is reasonable for them, given their control ratio, degree of motivation, and quality of opportunity. If we could measure all, or most, forms of deviance that a motivated person might potentially commit (that is, for which there are opportunities) we would expect them to commit some of those acts but not others (how they choose among the possibilities will be discussed shortly).

Even though the specific acts likely to be committed are contingent on several simultaneously operating variables, the theory predicts that some form of deviance will be committed (as opposed to conforming behavior) when a person has become motivated. For any particular specific deviant act, say vandalism, the theory does not predict that a motivated person will commit it, even with good opportunity to do so. The reason has to do with the control balancing process, which hinges on possible counter controlling responses.

A potential deviant—a person with motivation and opportunity—contemplates committing forms of deviance that hold the promise of producing the greatest effect—that is, those kinds that most quickly and effectively lead to short-term change in control. However, those deviances with the greatest potential payoff are also the ones that will most likely bring forth counter controlling responses. The degree to which a given deviant act is likely to provoke counter control reflects the "seriousness" of the act. Any person with an urge to do something about his or her control ratio will, therefore, contemplate the most serious form of deviance for which there is an opportunity. However, because the most serious forms of deviance activate the strongest counter control, resorting to that serious act may not be a realistic means of altering a particular person's control imbalance. In fact, for some people, the potential counter control that would be activated by serious acts of deviance would actually cause them to end up with less relative control than that with which they started.

Because of this, a motivated individual will tend to avoid those acts of deviance that appear too costly, given his or her control ratio (and various risk factors). For example, those with high control surpluses can contemplate, and are likely to commit, serious deviant acts that have great value for extending their control surpluses. But those with high control deficits are likely to avoid serious deviant acts, even though such acts would be especially useful for altering their control ratios. So, although motivated persons will do some kind of deviance, the exact kind they are likely to do depends on the seriousness of the potential acts possible in the specific context as well as on their specific control ratios.

The motivated person with a substantial control deficit will abandon the idea of very serious deviant acts as a way of altering the control imbalance. Instead of a very serious deviant response, such as slugging somebody, the individual with a moderate control deficit will slide down the scale of seriousness in search of a less serious deviant act, such as vandalizing an automobile. By contrast, a person with a large surplus of control can realistically contemplate very serious deviant acts (but of a different order called "autonomous deviance") to extend her control after having become motivated. These more serious acts might include buying and shutting down the school in our example of the humiliated student. However, a person with a small surplus of control can only contemplate a less serious autonomous act, such as hiring someone to find dirt on the professor.

Constraint

The control balancing process by which individuals decide what forms of deviance to use in altering a control imbalance involves an additional, very important variable called "constraint." Constraint is present to a greater or lesser extent in situations where deviance might be possible. It refers to the likelihood or perceived likelihood that potential control will actually be exercised. Constraint is made up of three components: (1) the familiar control imbalance, which influences practically all of the variables in the causal process specified by control balance theory; (2) situational risk, or the specific chances of discovery and activation of potential counter-controlling responses (which are affected by things like lighting, presence of observers, physical evidence, and chance); and (3) seriousness, which rests on the emotional feelings of victims and others as well as on the perceived harm implied by particular acts of deviance (remember that seriousness is the amount of potential counter control for a given deviance in a particular situation). Together these variables represent the costs associated with specific acts of deviance; it is those costs that motivated individuals must take into account in seeking a solution to their "control problem."

Control Balancing

The import of constraint will become clearer if you think about the hypothetical student with whom we began our discussion. That student is predisposed toward deviant motivation by virtue of an unbalanced control ratio, a blockage of her goals (to get the question answered, to make an impression on the professor or other students, or whatever), and her basic desire for autonomy that everybody shares. The student becomes motivated toward deviance by the provocative situation in the classroom where, in asking a question and receiving an insulting response, she realizes that the professor, and probably a lot of other people and circumstances as well, exercise more control over her than she can exercise in return. Moreover, that realization is accompanied by an emotion of having been denigrated, which inspires the thought that various types of deviance, such as slugging the professor, becoming sullen, hiring a private detective, and so on, will help change her control ratio and restore her lost dignity. There is, of course, opportunity for several of these options, no matter who the student is, and there is opportunity for a few of the options only for some select subset of students who might be in this situation. Thus, according to the theory, such a student is likely to do something deviant.

Exactly what she will do depends partly on constraint. The student will want to do serious forms of deviance because serious deviance will most dramatically alter her control imbalance and overcome the denigration. But the more serious the acts, the greater the potential counter control that might be activated; hence, some students can contemplate doing more serious things in response to their humiliation than can other students. In addition, risk factors, which are greater for some students than for others and for some deviant acts than for other deviant acts, have to be taken into account. Therefore, the acts that a given person can realistically contemplate depend on the individual's control ratio, the seriousness of the act, and situational variables like risk (chances of actually being found out). Moreover, the likelihood of a person committing the most serious forms of deviance depends partly on the strength of motivation, which in turn is linked to the nature of the provocation and the degree of debasement experienced by the person. Finally, how a person actually acts—even when motivation is strong, opportunity is present, and constraint is small—is influenced by various contingencies, such as moral feelings, personal self-control, and social affiliations with members of the audience that might witness the acts.

In short, the deviance-generating process is complicated and highly conditional; that is, it depends on a number of variables. Those variables are identified in the theory, and how they come into play is spelled out. Therefore, despite the complexity, one can use the theory to explain what occurs and to predict what probably will occur, provided there are good indicators of the relevant variables.

So far you have been told what the main variables in the theory are, but the role of "contingencies" has not yet been explicated. Before considering contingent variables, you need to contemplate a diagram of the causal process. Figure 1 uses arrows to illustrate the interconnection of various influences in the unfolding of deviance. To trace

Figure 1
Causal Linkages of Control Balance Theory

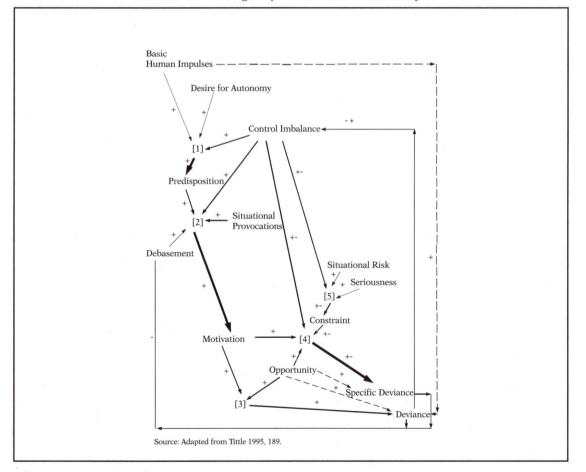

Source: Adapted from Tittle 1995, 189.

the process as it has been described above, start in the upper left-hand corner. Note that the first juncture in the process is indicated by a bracketed 1. That nexus, where a blockage of basic human impulses, a desire for autonomy, and a control imbalance come together is the "predisposition" we discussed before.

In examining the diagram, note that some of the arrows are darker and wider than others; this signifies importance or strength of influence. Consider the first nexus where the arrow for a control imbalance is slightly larger and darker than the other arrows. A control imbalance is highlighted because it is the most important of the three influences on predisposition. Observe also that the diagram includes some dotted arrows. They are used to acknowledge that some connections among the variables are possible, even though they are not specifically accounted for within the explanatory scheme of the theory. For instance, blockage of basic human impulses sometimes leads directly to deviance. This might occur when a very hungry person impulsively steals food—not because of the need to alter a control imbalance but simply to avoid starvation. Similarly, opportunity is sometimes so great that deviance results even in the absence of motivation. Finally, be cognizant of the arrows that go backward to some of the variables. This signifies that deviance has a reverse effect on some of the variables. According to the theory, deviance reduces the feelings of debasement that gave rise to deviant motivation in the first place, and it may increase or reduce the control imbalance at the heart of the sequence of influences leading to deviant behavior. These effects are shown by the reverse arrows.

While Figure 1 depicts the flow of influences ultimately leading to deviant outcomes, it does not convey the cognitive and emotional processes underlying the interconnection of the variables. For instance, the emotional feeling that an individual experiences when he is humiliated or debased must be imagined; it cannot be pictured. Similarly, the underlying control balancing process—weighing gain from deviance against cost from constraint—that goes on

in nexus [4] must be understood from the earlier qualitative account because it cannot be diagrammed.

You can grasp the import of the theory more fully by considering Figures 2 and 3. Figure 2 depicts the idea that, taking into account the various causal linkages of the theory, as well as the contingencies that we will discuss later, the average overall probability of some form of deviance depends on the magnitude of a control imbalance, conceived as either a deficit or a surplus. Notice that in the middle of the first row of the figure is the word *Balanced*, while to the left is a *minus* and to the right is a *plus*. Below that is the Probability of Deviance. In the middle, where control ratios are more or less balanced (the person exercises as much control as that to which he is subject), we expect low levels of deviance, indicated by the center point of the arrowed V. As a control imbalance increases in the surplus direction (*plus*, indicating more control exercised than is experienced) or in the deficit direction (*minus*, indicating less control exercised than is experienced), the probability of some unspecified kind of deviance increases (note that this probability refers to some among all possible types of deviance, not a given, particular form of deviance).

Figure 2
Control Imbalance and Probabilities of Deviance

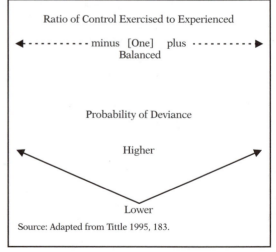

Source: Adapted from Tittle 1995, 183.

Figure 3 shows how the seriousness of potential deviant behaviors interacts with control imbalances to generate various probabilities of actual behavior. In the figure, the arrows extending outward from the middle Balanced, zone signify continua of increasing control imbalance—a deficit to the left and a surplus to the right. There are also two slanted arrows representing increasing degrees of seriousness, but note that seriousness is not a single continuum from one side of the figure to the other. Instead, there are two different continua, one for seriousness of "repressive" deviance—that associated with control deficits—and another for seriousness of "autonomous" deviance—that associated with control surpluses. The two general categories of deviance, repressive and autonomous, are regarded as qualitatively different (Tittle 1997).

Figure 3 shows that on the deficit side, the seriousness of likely deviance decreases as the extent of a control deficit increases. Thus, the most serious forms of repressive deviance are most likely to be committed by those with the smallest control deficits. Those with the greatest deficits are likely to do the least serious deviance because that is the only kind of deviance they can realistically contemplate doing. Individuals with small control deficits, on the other hand, can imagine getting away with more serious deviant acts; they probably will not face overwhelming possibilities of counter control. On the opposite, autonomous, side of the diagram, the most serious deviance is likely to be committed by those with the greatest control surplus—again because they can anticipate extending their control with the least chance of counter control. And those with relatively small control surpluses can imagine getting away with only the least serious forms of autonomous deviance.

Explaining Specific Types of Deviance

The argument that increasingly serious forms of deviance, either of the repressive or the autonomous types, are most likely for

Figure 3
Continua Representing Variations in Control Ratio and Predicted Forms of Deviance Associated with Positions on Those Continua

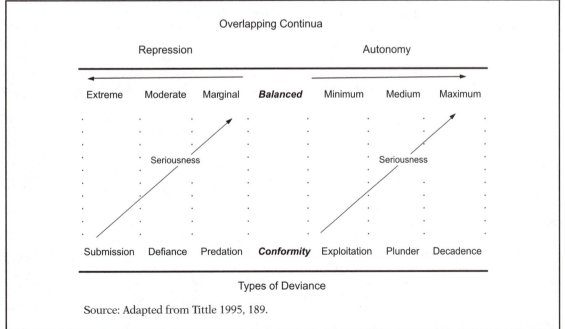

Source: Adapted from Tittle 1995, 189.

those with smaller deficits or larger surpluses of control will be more salient if you imagine that the continua of seriousness are subdivided into categories, each encompassing approximately one-third of each continuum. These subdivided categories can then be identified with types of deviance that are likely to be committed by individuals with the specified degree of control imbalance.

To meaningfully subdivide the continua, however, one must assume that the various kinds of deviance supposedly falling in the zones of the continua are, in fact, characterized by the degrees of seriousness implied by the zone wherein they lie. Presently there are no data concerning the seriousness (as defined in the theory) of all potential acts of deviance relative to each other. Identification of specific types of deviance likely to occur in the various zones of seriousness is, therefore, somewhat problematic. Earlier, when I suggested that students experiencing humiliation at the hand of a teacher might resort to one or another form of deviance, I was speculating that predation is more serious than defiance and that exploitation is less serious than plunder. I really do not know that, so it is actually more accurate to say that those students would most likely resort to the most serious forms of deviance possible, given their control ratios and other conditions. Nevertheless, because it is interesting to speculate, those types of deviance that I assume are most likely to be committed by individuals with the associated control ratios are shown at the bottom of the diagram.

Things Explained

Conformity

In the middle of Figure 3, corresponding to the balanced zone of control ratios, is conformity, which in the theory is taken to mean *behavior consistent with social norms that is undertaken with full awareness of possible alternative, nonacceptable behavior.* When people can exercise about as much control as that to which they are subject (when their control ratios are about one), they are less likely to experience the conditions leading up to deviant motivation, and even when they do become motivated for deviance, they

are less likely to do it because of the more or less equal possibility of counter controlling responses. Counterposed to conformity are the various forms of deviance. They will be described in seesaw fashion, moving out from the center of the diagram from one side to the other.

The Least Serious Autonomous Deviance

On the surplus side of the balanced zone, in the first third of the autonomous continuum, are assumed to be acts of exploitation in which *individuals or groups use third parties as intermediaries or use structural or organizational arrangements to coerce, manipulate, or extract property from individuals or groups to benefit the exploiter without regard for the desires or welfare of the exploited.* Exploitation includes activities like corporate price fixing, profiteering from manufacturing processes that endanger workers, influence peddling by political figures, contract killings, employment of religious injunctions to solicit financial contributions for the personal use of evangelists, and, of course, the various exploitative acts committed against the professor by one of our hypothetical insulted students—which, you will recall, includes (1) having a parent threaten to cease donating money to the university unless the professor is fired, and (2) hiring a private detective to gather dirt for revenge.

Though such acts are probably generally regarded as quite serious, they are probably among the least serious forms of autonomous deviance. According to the theory, such acts will be most characteristic of those with the lowest control surpluses. Remember that those with minimum control surpluses are most liable for these acts because, even though such individuals might desire to do more serious things in order to extend their control when provoked, they must take into account the potential counter control that their actions would stimulate. These exploitative acts, of course, are not generally possible at all for people with control deficits.

The Most Serious Repressive Deviance

On the opposite side of the balanced zone, in the first third of the repressive continuum out from the center, we are likely to see acts of predation. They involve *direct physical violence, manipulation, or property extraction by an individual or group for the benefit of the predator, who acts without regard for the desires or the welfare of the individual or group that is the object of predation.* Predation includes theft, rape, homicide, robbery, assault, fraud, price gouging by entrepreneurs, coercive pimping, sexual harassment, and even acts like parental use of guilt to elicit child attention. Recall that in the case of the humiliated student, slugging the professor would qualify as predation. Predatory acts are assumed to be the most serious forms of repressive deviance, and they are most likely to be undertaken by people with relatively small deficits of control—because, given that their control deficits are not great, they can anticipate being able to manage the counter control that is likely to result.

Moderately Serious Autonomous Deviance

The second approximate third of the autonomous continuum encompasses acts that are assumed to be more serious than exploitation; they are characterized as "plunder." Plunderous behavior is that in which *individuals or organizations selfishly pursue their own ends with little awareness or regard for much else, particularly how their behaviors might affect others.* The acts included in this category are things like autocratic behaviors of medieval kings and nobles who destroyed peasant fields while hunting foxes, oppressive taxation of poverty-stricken peoples to provide wealth to corrupt rulers, massive pollution by giant oil companies with accompanying price increases to recover costs of cleanup, attempted genocide directed against racial or ethnic groups by powerful segments of the population, unrealistic taxes or work requirements imposed by occupying armies or slave holders, or the arrogant destruction of forests and animals by early explorers. In the hypothetical case of a provoked student, described at the beginning of this essay, recall that plunder implies things like buying and shutting down the university. Clearly only those with a considerable control surplus can afford to do such things.

Moderately Serious Repressive Deviance

In contrast, the second third of the repressive continuum is assumed to include acts in which the *individual perpetrator expresses contempt for, or hostility toward, a norm, a set of norms, or toward the individual, group, or organization with which that norm is associated.* Such acts are called "defiance," and they include youthful violation of curfews, vandalism, mocking denigrations of company officials by striking workers, sullenness by a marital partner, exaggerated obedience by employees, political protests, and in the case of the angered student, denigration of the teacher to other students and being loud and disruptive or sullen in class. Those with substantial, but not overwhelming, control deficits are likely to commit defiance, although they would prefer to do more serious things. The reason they do not actually commit the more serious acts is because they cannot realistically expect to handle the consequences that more serious deviance would imply for them.

The Most Serious Autonomous Deviance

Extremely serious autonomous deviance, that in the last third of the continuum out from the middle, is assumed to consist of *random, impulsive acts guided by no consistent or rational life organization, reflecting the perpetrators' momentary whims.* This zone might include excessive or unusual forms of sexual expression, such as group sex with children, cruel debauchery, humiliation of people for entertainment, and nonsensical pleasure-seeking or destruction, as in sadistic torture. Only those with very large control surpluses can be decadent and imagine getting away with it.

The Least Serious Repressive Deviance

Those with the greatest control deficits are likely to *lose all sense of personal autonomy, as well as the ability to visualize alternatives to obedience.* Consequently, they basically give up and become submissive. They adopt passive, unthinking, slavish patterns of obedience to the expectations, commands, or anticipated desires of others. Such behaviors might include eating slop on command, helping repress others to please power holders, allowing oneself to be physically abused, humiliated, or sexually degraded, or as in the case of our student exemplar, conforming to routinized patterns of the class without contemplating or questioning whether there is an alternative. Because the surrender of all efforts toward personal autonomy is probably regarded as unacceptable in many modern societies, including the United States, it is a form of deviance within those societies, albeit perhaps the least serious form. Remember, however, that this cannot be known for sure until survey data are collected to ascertain whether, and to what degree, submissive behavior is regarded as unacceptable.

Submission is especially interesting, partly because it has a different rationale than do the other forms of deviance described previously (Braithwaite 1997). In all of the other types of deviance, an individual or a group uses deviance in an active way. In those cases, deviance serves a purpose and, in that sense, can be said to be instrumental or functional. Submission, however, is passive; it represents almost complete capitulation to superior control and cession of imaginative contemplation. Submission, therefore, is qualitatively different from other forms of deviance. It is not adopted in order to overcome a control imbalance, but instead represents surrender to superior control.

In addition, submission is not the same as conformity. External manifestations might appear similar—those conforming and those submitting are not causing any trouble and they are ostensibly following social rules. Adhering to social expectations with full volition and with ability to visualize the possibility of doing something different (conformity) is a far cry from obedience born of demoralizing defeat. In using control balance theory to account for documented patterns of behavior, such as variations by gender, race, or social class, one

must be careful to recognize the distinction between conformity and submission.

Finally, although the theory is designed to explain deviance, and in that effort also explains submission (as well as conformity, which is the residual category), it is important to note that submission is not necessarily deviant in all societies. In some societies, submission is normative (nondeviant), at least for some categories of people, such as women in Muslim contexts. But here one should be reminded that the theory predicts submissive type behavior when an individual or group is confronted with overwhelming control, without regard for the deviant or nondeviant status of submission.

Contingencies

So far, the underlying causal process of control balancing, along with the sequence and convergence of events involved in deviance, have been presented. The theory contends that these basic processes are always at work in such a way that they produce typical outcomes. However, the theory is not deterministic; it does not assert that under various circumstances such and such form of deviance will inevitably occur. For instance, although people with substantial, but not overwhelming, control deficits will probably commit some forms of defiance from time to time, all people with a modest control deficit are not invariably slated for defiance. As you learned earlier, a given person must be provoked and debased, have opportunity for various kinds of defiance, and not face too much constraint, which is at least partly determined by characteristics of the situation. But even then, neither defiance nor any other kind of deviance may occur. That is because a number of other variables impinge on the control balancing process to affect how fully it unfolds.

Conditions that may intervene into the control balancing process are called "contingencies." There are a lot of them, which, for convenience, can be classified as either personal, organizational, or situational in character. Among the personal contingencies are perceptual accuracy, moral feelings, habits, personality, ability to commit the deviance at issue, desire to do things that compete with deviance as alternatives, and previous deviance. Depending on these variables, a particular individual in a given set of circumstances will manage the events, feelings, and thoughts identified in control balance theory somewhat differently. For instance, whether a situation is provocative—that is, whether it brings to mind in an acute way a person's control imbalance—and whether it implies debasement depends partly on perceptual characteristics of the individual. What one person finds routine, such as being asked to wait in a line, another finds provoking. And what some experience as debasing simply rolls off the backs of others. Using our student example, some individuals to whom a professor responds caustically will not take umbrage. They might perceive it as a learning moment, and rather than being demeaned or humiliated, they may perceive that they have done themselves proud by being bold enough to ask a question in the first place. Furthermore, such perceptual differences enter into interpretation of opportunity and assessment of constraint.

In similar ways, the other personal contingencies noted above, such as moral commitments, affect how the control balancing process unfolds and the extent to which it produces the outcomes specified earlier. But there are other contingencies besides characteristics of individuals. Various kinds of organizational arrangements that exist in specific situations in which deviance might be a possibility, as well as those in which the individual is generally enmeshed, are relevant. Subcultural affiliations represent one of the most important organizational contingencies, at least for young people.

Imagine that the hypothetical student we have been using as an example is well integrated into a student subculture that shares and promotes the idea that respect for students on the campus must be enhanced, and that a number of her subcultural peers are also in the class. Such a person will be more easily provoked and more thoroughly humiliated than someone with a similar control ratio who is not part of such a subculture. Moreover, in contemplating potential counter control that might be stimulated by a de-

viant act, a subculturally-involved student will feel more capable of resisting than would a student with a similar general control ratio who is not enmeshed within a supportive peer network. Finally, the student's response to the professor's putdown may be emboldened by a desire to enhance her stature among the other members of the subculture. In that case, potential counter control from authorities is less relevant than potential control from peers. As result of all of this, the control balancing process will manifest itself somewhat differently, and with less force, for a subcultural participant than for a student who is not in such a subculture.

Finally, there are some situational contingencies that come into play. Although opportunity, risk, and provocation are part of the fundamental control balancing process, they also vary situationally in ways that may affect the "normal" control balancing process. Some opportunities are better than others, the chances of misbehaviors being discovered vary enormously from one context to the other, and the degree of provocation implicit in given situations is not equal. Where opportunity is maximum, risk is highest, and provocation is most intense, the control balancing process will transpire with greatest efficiency. But when either opportunity or risk or provocation is less than maximum, one can expect outcomes to be affected. How they are affected can be spelled out, and from such theorizing, one can derive more precise hypotheses than would be possible by focusing exclusively on the central causal process of the theory.

One strength of control balance theory is its explicit recognition of contingencies of various kinds. The theory attempts to specify the direction and, in some cases, the likely magnitude of their effects on the causal processes at work (see Tittle 1995, Chapter 8). The theory, then, provides explanation and prediction of deviance and of submission, even when submission is not deviant, by reference to a central causal process. In that balancing process, individuals weigh the possible gain in control that would be obtained from deviant behavior against potential counter control that the deviance is likely to stimulate. Control balancing is embedded within networks of converging conditions, and the fullness with which the theoretical process unfolds is affected by particular specified contingencies that may influence any or all of the variables and conditions in the theoretical chain of causes.

Background of the Theory

Control balance is a relatively new theory (Tittle 1995). It was developed as an exemplar to illustrate a particular method of theory building—called "theoretical integration"—involving the merging of parts of pre-existing theories. It grew out of a conviction that all extant theories are in one way or another too narrow, too exclusively focused on one or another causal element, too imprecise, or that they lack the ability to spell out a full causal process. The method that led to its development specifies that theories should do the following: (1) focus on abstract rather than concrete commonalities of different behaviors (in this case, seeing disparate acts as having an underlying purpose of advancing one's relative control); (2) be focused around a central causal process (in this instance, control balancing) into which various inputs (largely incorporated in other theories already in the arena) can flow; and (3) articulate how various components of the theory interlink in causal sequences to produce specific outcomes. In addition, the particular mode of theoretical integration that led to control balance implies that a theory must contain statements about how contingencies that are not part of the theory itself affect the operation of the causal processes in the theory.

Hypotheses and Evidence

As you have seen, control balance attempts to do all of the things that a theory should ideally do. Its internal structure, therefore, appears to be an advancement, yet theories must do more than exhibit good technical structure. Above all, they must explain the phenomena within their domains, which in the case of control balance mainly includes *behaviors that the majority of a given group regards as unacceptable or that typi-*

cally evokes a collective response of a negative type (called deviance). "Explaining" means that a theory must answer questions of "why" and "how" for a critical audience of scientists. Scientists insist that theories produce intellectual satisfaction—satisfy their curiosities about why and how—and they want them to be consistent with empirical reality. Finding out if a theory works empirically involves two things: (1) logically assessing the adequacy with which the theory handles known facts, and (2) ascertaining how well it holds up in empirical tests of specific hypotheses derived from the theory.

This theory seems to account for variations between sexes, ages, races, places of residence, those more or less bonded socially, and socioeconomic categories in certain criminal, delinquent, and deviant activities that have been measured (see Tittle 1995, Chapter 9). Space limitations preclude a discussion here showing how that is so, but it is important to note the difficulty of assessing whether the theory "fits the facts," given that the "facts" themselves are often problematic and the existing data do not correspond with the concepts set forth in the theory. Applying the theory to explain familiar variations in demographic distributions of deviance requires assumptions about the average overall control ratios of those occupying specific single statuses. Because there are currently no data suitably reflecting control ratios among those in single statuses, much less the general control ratios for people who occupy multiple statuses, such assumptions may be inaccurate. In addition, assumptions about control ratios based on single statuses, even if they were correct and were good estimators of general control ratios, ignore the individual distinctions in control ratios that characterize different people with similar demographic statuses. That is why it is a mistake, for example, to use femaleness as a proxy measure of a control deficit (see Jensen 1999; Jensen and Westphal 1998).

Furthermore, the theory's domain is far wider than the range of deviances covered in extant data sources; as a result, focusing only on specific, currently measured offenses is likely to underestimate the theory's power. For example, the theory suggests that, in general, people with modest control deficits are likely to engage in some form of defiance. Because more females than males are probably a little more likely to have modest control deficits (this is an assumption, since actual measures of control ratios by sex have not been undertaken), one would expect them to engage a bit more frequently in defiance. To check this out, one would need to have measures of most forms of defiance that females and males respectively might have an opportunity to commit—in order to see if, overall, females commit more kinds of defiance more frequently than males. But current measures of defiance are extremely limited. They most often concern things like vandalism, drug use, and mental illness, and they rarely include those kinds of defiance that are most likely available to females (such as sullenness, crying, withholding sexual favors, or refusal to perform certain household or school duties). So, if one looks only at available data about defiance and confines comparisons to those few offenses that have been studied, one is likely to draw erroneous conclusions about the theory (Tittle 1999).

Not only is the compatibility of the theory with known variations in deviance somewhat uncertain, but at this point there are too few direct tests to judge the empirical adequacy of the theory (at this writing only Piquero and Hickman 1999). If one takes account of the various stages in the theoretical process leading to control balancing and ultimately to deviance, and also makes allowance for the various contingencies that may intrude, the theory yields hundreds of hypotheses that can be tested. Some of those hypotheses are especially provocative because they predict outcomes that are not obvious from conventional thinking. For instance, conventional thinking suggests that the most oppressed people will be the ones most likely to turn to acts like theft, assault, and homicide. But control balance theory suggests that predation will be more likely among those with relatively small control deficits than among those with great control deficits. The theory also suggests that the relationship between its causal variables and different outcomes is not linear—a prediction that is unusual in conventional thinking, which assumes linearity in most causal effects.

The most important, and the most general, hypotheses to be derived from the theory are as follows: (1) the greater a control imbalance, in either direction from a central point of balance, the greater the total probability of deviance, and (2) the type of deviance most likely to occur depends on the control ratio of the person and the seriousness of the acts—with control deficits being associated negatively with seriousness of the likely act and control surpluses being associated positively with seriousness of the potential act. Given these rich empirical possibilities, there may soon be a body of direct evidence bearing on the theory.

Policy Relevance

Control balance theory was not developed with potential policy applications in mind. It was intended as an exemplar of a particular form of theory building and as an explanatory mechanism for understanding (explaining) and predicting deviance. Nevertheless, the theory contains potential directives for those who wish to draw on it for formulating policy to deal with crime and deviance (Braithwaite 1997). One obvious, general thing it tells those who wish to reduce deviance is to move more people to a state of balance in their control ratios. For instance, rates of crime and deviance, particularly defiance and to some extent predation, are especially high among young people. Control balance theory suggests that is because most youth have control deficits. Although implying massive social transformations, it might be possible to increase the control that youth can typically exercise to a point where it is about equal to that which they experience.

Contemplating such policies, however, calls attention to the difficulty of making effective social changes requiring large, structural modifications, especially within a politically charged environment. Few adults would appreciate efforts to usurp their power in order to enhance the control ratios of youth and, in any case, large shifts in control would be impractical because the subordination of youth hinges on economic dependency that is linked with modern postindustrial systems of production. Those systems of production are intricately woven into modern societies and lifestyles, making their modification both difficult and undesirable to most people.

Furthermore, enhancing the control that youth can exercise would have to be carefully aimed toward balance—because increasing the control that young people have could move some who currently have modest control deficits up to the point where they have slight deficits, thereby decreasing their probabilities of committing defiance but at the same time increasing their probabilities of predation. In addition, if increased control by youth were bought at the price of reduced control among adults, there might be some shifting of conforming adults into unbalanced control zones where they become liable for more deviance. Because public policy in a democracy with large numbers of competing interests seldom reflects finely calibrated solutions, tinkering with control ratios among youth could have adverse consequences.

A more realistic approach might be to focus on the variables that accompany the causal sequences set forth in the theory. In that vein, policy makers could attempt to reduce the motivation and opportunity for deviance, or increase the constraint. Because motivation results from predisposition as it converges with situational provocation and debasement, one type of social policy might focus on educational programs to alert more people to the potential negative consequences of reminding individuals or groups of their control imbalances, especially when such provocation implies degradation or humiliation. In other words, an improved climate of mutual respect and dignity among people should reduce the potential for deviance because it would generally lessen the frequency and intensity of deviant motivation. This might be an especially important lesson for law enforcement personnel who confront minorities and other subordinates. Alternatively, possibly through educational programs in the schools or communities,

more individuals could be taught how to manage their own emotions so that provocative situations would less often be interpreted as demeaning.

In addition to policies aimed at reducing deviant motivation, a wise society might attempt to reduce the opportunities for deviance—or at least the opportunities for the kinds of deviance that are of most concern to the population as a whole. Citizens could be encouraged and trained to guard their property more effectively or make it physically more secure; educated to understand and avoid exploitation and plunder; alerted to the value of prudent movements; and inspired to make suicide and other forms of defiance more difficult. In addition, the availability of dangerous drugs could be further restricted. Some of these things are already being promoted, but some are not. In particular there is a dearth of information and guidance about how citizens can avoid being victims of powerful individuals or corporations.

Furthermore, the principles of control balance suggest that increased constraint could reduce deviance that is of most concern to society. Consistent with social policies already in existence, increased surveillance in places of likely predation as well as enhanced general readiness to counter deviant actions should help reduce the most serious forms of deviance. Perhaps the places currently with the weakest constraint should be targeted for modification and tagged for attention in an overall effort to stimulate the willingness of citizens and victims to counter potential deviance with restraining control. Such places would include the offices and conferences of those with surplus control where exploitation and plunder are hatched.

However, if increased constraint were too obvious, or if people were too ready to activate counter control, enhanced efforts at constraint could produce more, rather than less, deviance. More constraint might lead to more deviance by helping to provoke people with control imbalances toward deviant motivation. Remember that provocation consists of being reminded of one's control imbalance. When the police, or other authorities, are too ubiquitous or intervene too readily in ordinary affairs, their effect is likely to generate greater provocation of people's awareness of their control imbalances, resulting in increased motivation for deviance.

In contemplating the principles of control balance, one should keep in mind that many policies that the theory might seem to suggest, while potentially reducing some forms of deviance, probably would increase other forms. For instance, restricting opportunities for rape by encouraging women to learn self-defense, not to go places alone, and to avoid unguarded encounters with males might reduce the rate of rape, but it would not dissipate the motivation to use some other form of predation by males who become motivated to use deviance to alter their control imbalances. Hence, a decline in rape might be accompanied by a rise in purse snatching or an increase in male homicide. Similarly, increasing the constraint associated with burglary might diminish the rate of burglary but simultaneously elevate the rate of fraud or vandalism. Still, a carefully thought out social policy might deliberately trade a reduction in rape for an increase in purse snatching or diminution of burglary for an elevation of fraud and vandalism, and some might even advocate trading declines in rape for increases in male homicide.

Finally, social policies could be focused on changing contingencies that intrude into the control balancing process at various places in the chain of events leading to deviance. A number of policies might help larger proportions of the population become inclined toward, and better equipped for, nondestructive responses to control imbalances. For instance, ways might be explored to improve the general level of morality so that more people find various forms of deviance personally distasteful. In addition, programs might encourage people to use nondeviant alternatives to enhance their control. And helping social institutions—such as families, schools, and community organizations—to mold the personalities of youngsters to be less impulsive and more empathetic could affect how control balancing plays out.

It is clear, then, that one can draw on control balance theory in formulating social policies for combatting deviance. However, most of the policies so derived are too broad-based to have much practical import, and the ones that are the most focused and, therefore, most pragmatic are not unique to this theory. For example, reducing opportunities and enhancing constraints for the most destructive types of deviance are commonly suggested maneuvers. What is not commonly recognized, but what is explicit in control balance reasoning, however, is that many of the most "practical measures" will not reduce the overall level of deviance but instead will likely change the form of deviance that is committed. Reduction in overall rates of deviance would most likely come from the broadest policy implications of control balance. One of those overarching, but probably impractical, policies would be to alter the relative distributions of control among citizens so that there is more balance. Another is to intervene in the conditions of everyday life so that individuals with control imbalances less often face provocative circumstances that remind them of their control situations or generate negative emotions of degradation. Given the difficulty of accomplishing such objectives, deviance is likely to remain as an ever present feature of modern societies.

Conclusion

Control balance theory portrays deviant behavior as emerging from situations where an individual becomes aware of, and is made to feel humiliated by, a control imbalance. To overcome the imbalance and the feelings it generates, the individual resorts to deviant behavior. However, the type of deviance that results represents a compromise between the potential gain in control implied by the deviant behavior and the potential counter-controlling consequences of the contemplated act. Exactly how this process plays out is influenced by numerous contingencies.

References

Braithwaite, John. (1997). "Charles Tittle's control balance and criminological theory." *Theoretical Criminology*, 1:77–97.

Jensen, Gary F. (1999). "A critique of control balance theory: Digging into details." *Theoretical Criminology*, 3:339–343.

Jensen, Gary F. and Lori Westphal. (1998). "Gender and conformity: Submission vs. reasonable choices." Paper presented in March at the annual meeting of the Academy of Criminal Justice Sciences, Albuquerque.

Piquero, Alex and Matthew Hickman. (1999). "An empirical test of Tittle's control balance theory." *Criminology*, 37:319–340.

Savelsberg, Joachim. (1999). "Human nature and social control in complex society: A critique of Charles Tittle's control balance." *Theoretical Criminology*, 3:331–338.

Tittle, Charles R. (1995). *Control Balance: Toward a General Theory of Deviance.* Boulder, CO: Westview.

——. (1997). "Thoughts stimulated by Braithwaite's analysis of control balance theory." *Theoretical Criminology*, 1:99–109.

——. (1999). "Continuing the discussion of *control balance." Theoretical Criminology*, 3:344–352.

Integrating Theories in Criminology[1]

Thomas J. Bernard
Pennsylvania State University

As is obvious from reading the various chapters in this book, there are many different theories in criminology, most of which seem to contradict each other. This is a problem for the field of criminology. Because a whole bunch of famous criminologists seem to disagree with each other about almost everything, students may be tempted to conclude that we really don't know much about crime.

Most criminologists think it would be desirable to reduce the number of criminology theories. The problem is that criminologists vigorously disagree about how that should be done. The most common view is that the different theories make contradictory predictions. These contradictory predictions can be subjected to competitive testing in which research determines which predictions are supported by the data and which are not. Theories that are falsified by this process can then be discarded, thus reducing the total number of theories. This is the traditional scientific method: reducing the number of theories through theoretical competition and falsification.

More recently, however, some criminologists have argued that the process of theoretical competition and falsification has failed as a method of reducing the number of criminology theories. These criminologists generally argue that the different theories make different, but not contradictory, predictions. Therefore, the different theories can be combined with each other through various forms of integration. Integration, then, is an alternative to falsification as a way to reduce the number of theories in criminology, and has arisen as a result of the perceived inability of theoretical competition and falsification to accomplish this goal.

Elliott's Integrated Theory

In 1979, Elliott, Ageton, and Cantor offered an early version of an integrated theory, arguing that integration is the key to a more powerful explanation of delinquency. In this paper, they explicitly attempted to combine strain, control, and social learning perspectives in order to explain delinquency and drug use with greater power. Several years later, Elliott, Huizinga, and Ageton (1985) provided a more complete version of their integrated theory and included a more in-depth defense of theoretical integration. These attempts at integration, and the responses to them by those who opposed integration, raised most of the issues that still form the current debate.

Elliott and his colleagues attempted their integration of criminology theories in two steps, first by integrating strain with social control theories, and then by integrating the combination of strain and control with social learning theory. Strain theory was described as arguing "that delinquency is a response to actual or anticipated failure to achieve socially induced needs or goals (status, wealth, power, social acceptance, etc.)" (Elliott, Huizinga, and Ageton 1985, 14). Control theory was then described as arguing that the strength of an individual's bonds to conventional society is inversely related to the probability that the individual will engage in delinquent behavior. Sources of weak social controls include inadequate socialization in the family and social disorganization in the community or society. These two theories were integrated by arguing that the probability of delinquency should be highest when an individual experiences both more strain *and* less control. They also argued that, in addition to decreasing social controls, social disorganization could increase the likelihood of strain. Finally, they argued that strain itself should reduce social controls. Thus, Elliott and his colleagues proposed a number of connections between strain and control theories.

After integrating strain and control theories, Elliott's groups added social learning theories. These theories were described as arguing that delinquency is affected by the balance between the rewards and punishments associated with both conforming and deviant patterns of socialization. With respect to adolescents, families and schools generally reinforce conventional or law-abiding behaviors, and this does not vary much from one child to the next. In contrast, peer groups are more likely to reinforce deviant behavior, but this varies quite a bit among different adolescents. Elliott therefore argued that the amount of exposure to delinquent attitudes and behavior within the peer group is the primary factor that affects the probability of delinquent behavior.

Where control theory is interested in the strength of (conventional) socialization, learning theory is interested in its content (deviant versus conforming socialization). Elliott therefore found it necessary to modify control theory, taking into account the type of group to which the individual bonds. According to control theory, there are no strong bonds to deviant groups, because deviance itself consists in purely self-interested behavior. Thus, deviant groups consist of sets of people who are purely self-interested. These people have no actual bonds to other members of the group, and the group itself stays together only to the extent that this furthers the self-interests of each group member.

In contrast, Elliott argued that individuals could form strong bonds to deviant social groups. Deviant behavior is most likely when there are strong bonds to deviant groups and weak bonds to conventional groups, while it is least likely when there are strong bonds to conventional groups and weak bonds to deviant groups.

The final step was to integrate all three theories: strain, social control, and social learning (Elliott, Huizinga, and Ageton 1985, 66). In their view, everything starts with strain, inadequate socialization, and social disorganization. These three factors all lead to weak conventional bonding, such as to families and schools. Then, youths with such weak conventional bonds can develop strong delinquent bonds. The result is increased likelihood of delinquency.

The Falsification Versus Integration Debate

In a response to Elliott, Ageton, and Cantor's 1979 paper, Travis Hirschi (1979) argued forcefully against integration as a strategy in criminology. He stated that most criminology theories are contradictory in that their assumptions are incompatible. Theories must be tested on their own, for internal consistency and explanatory power, or against other theories. Theories can only be integrated if they essentially argue the same thing, and criminology theories do not. Hirschi concluded that, for criminology theories, "separate and unequal is better."

In the more complete version of the integrated theory published in 1985, Elliott, and colleagues responded to Hirschi's arguments against integration. They began by arguing that the "oppositional tradition" in criminology (i.e., theoretical competition) had failed. The oppositional tradition refers to the falsification process, in which the different theories are competitively tested against each other. They also argued that any individual theory could only explain 10 to 20 percent of the variance in illegal behavior. As Elliott, Huizinga, and Ageton say, "stated simply, the level of explained variance attributable to separate theories is embarrassingly low, and, if sociological explanations for crime and delinquency are to have any significant impact upon future planning and policy, they must be able to demonstrate greater predictive power" (125).

In a separate article, Elliott (1985) went on to argue that theoretical competition is generally pointless because most of the time different theories explain independent portions of the variance in crime. Because there are multiple causes of crime, different theories that incorporate different causal factors aren't necessarily incompatible. Elliott concluded that criminologists should synthesize such theories, achieving a greater explanation of deviant behavior, rather than allowing them to remain in competitive isolation.

Hirschi (1989) then expanded on his own argument against integration, sardonically discussing the fall of the "oppositional tradition" and the recent movement toward theoretical integration. He acknowledged that criminology theory has failed to advance despite the prevalence of theory competition. However, he did not see integration as a solution to this problem. In particular, he objected to the compromises made to control theory that have been required by integrationists in order to make its assumptions compatible with those of other theories. Hirschi argued that integrationists ignore the fact that the different criminology theories are incompatible, and they plod ahead anyway. But, the integrative attempt has been dirtied, tainted by the decision to ignore contradictory assumptions.

The Strain/Control/Cultural Deviance Interpretation

A number of other criminologists besides Elliott have attempted integration of criminology theories (summarized in Bernard and Snipes 1996), while a number of criminologists besides Hirschi have objected to integration as a strategy (summarized in Tittle 1985). But the issues in the debate have remained largely the same since the Elliott-Hirschi exchange. Among those who favor integration, I probably have the most radical view, proposing the most wide-ranging integration of theories based on the most fundamental re-interpretation of criminology theories.

My position on integration can be summarized in four points. First, I argue that, up to this point, *the integration debate in criminology has assumed the validity of the strain/control/cultural deviance interpretation of criminology theories.* Those who favor integration, such as Elliott, largely start from this interpretation and then propose some changes in the theories in order to integrate them. For example, Elliott proposes some changes in control theories in order to integrate them with strain and cultural deviance theories. Those who oppose integration also assume the validity of the strain/control/cultural deviance interpretation. For example,

Hirschi objects to the changes proposed by Elliott, arguing that if you must change control theory in order to integrate it with other theories, then you have not integrated it at all. Rather, you are proposing an entirely new theory that does not include control theory and therefore should be tested against it.

Second, I argue that *the strain/control/cultural deviance interpretation virtually requires Hirschi's position on integration, because within that interpretation the various criminology theories are contradictory and therefore cannot be integrated with each other.* That is, if one of these theories is true the others must be false (Liska 1971; Agnew 1992).

But third, I argue that the *strain/control/cultural deviance interpretation of criminology theories itself is wrong.* In particular, I have argued that the strain/control/cultural deviance interpretation seriously distorts "strain" and "cultural deviance" theories. That distortion, rather than the theories themselves, makes the integration of criminology theories impossible. In order to describe my position on integration, I therefore need to describe my interpretation of strain and cultural deviance theories.

Fourth, *I present a new interpretation that more accurately represents the content of criminology theories.* This interpretation views theories as identifying the risk factors associated with an increased or decreased likelihood of crime. There can be many such risk factors, so the competition among theories does not result in the falsification of some theories and the verification of others. Instead, the competition among theories is empirical: it is about whether particular risk factors associated with particular theories explain a lot or a little of the variation in crime. Consequently, the risk factor approach is highly integrative, in which virtually all criminology theories can be integrated with each other.

I begin the discussion of my position by describing the problems I see in the "strain" and "cultural deviance" interpretations of criminology theories.

What Do Strain Theories Argue?

Hirschi (1969) describes strain theories as proposing variable drives to crime, especially frustrations arising from limited legitimate opportunities for economic success or social status. Merton (1938), Cohen (1955), and Cloward and Ohlin (1960) are said to be examples.

But I have argued that this interpretation severely distorts so-called "strain" theories. In Bernard (1984, 1987a, 1987b), I argue that Merton (1938), Cohen (1955), and Cloward and Ohlin (1960) do not propose a "variable drive" to crime in the social psychological sense of proposing that "more frustration" is associated with "more crime." Criminals might indeed be frustrated by their structural conditions, but none of these theories asserts a causal connection between frustration and criminal behavior. Rather, each theory makes a macro-level structural argument linking rates and distributions of crime to socially structured contexts. For example, in Bernard (1987a), I summarized Merton's argument in four propositions:

1. The value attached to the goal of monetary success varies in different cultures. . . .

2. At the cross-cultural level, variations in the value attached to monetary success are positively related to rates of utilitarian, profit-oriented criminal activity.

3. Rates of utilitarian criminal behaviors in different groups are inversely related to the access those groups have to legal means of acquiring wealth.

4. Access to the legal means of acquiring wealth varies according to social structural location. Specifically, in U.S. society, there is a positive relation between access to legal means of acquiring wealth and social class position, with the lowest social class having the least access and the highest social class having the most access.

Nothing in these propositions argues that people who are more frustrated tend to commit more crime. In addition, nothing in these propositions contradicts Hirschi's argument that people who are more controlled tend to commit less crime.

Far from being contradictory, I argue that Hirschi's theory and Merton's theory make a very similar argument at one particular point (Bernard 1987c). In Hirschi's theory, commitment measures the extent to which an individual's self-interests are legal. People who are "committed" (in Hirschi's sense) will engage in few illegal actions because few of their self-interests are illegal. But Merton's theory actually makes a very similar argument about criminals. He argues that people who are "strained" (in Merton's sense) will engage in many illegal actions because many of their self-interests are illegal (see Stinchcombe 1975, 12; Cullen 1983, 36–37).

These two assertions do not contradict each other in any way. Rather, they actually are the same assertion phrased differently. In particular, "strained" people are not necessarily "frustrated" in a social psychological sense because they simply are pursuing their own self-interests (see Cullen 1983, 82). Essentially, Hirschi describes the "structuring" of legal actions while Merton describes the "structuring" of criminal actions.[2]

Criminologists should not assume the strain/control/cultural deviance interpretation of these theories when discussing whether they can be integrated with other criminology theories. At minimum, the above interpretation of these theories should be considered. This interpretation not only makes integration impossible, but it forms the basis for a wide-ranging integration, as described below.

What Do "Cultural Deviance" Theories Argue?

In general, cultural deviance theories are said to argue that people are socialized into cultures, that some cultures contain deviant norms, and that when people conform to these cultures they engage in deviant behavior. Culture itself consists in ultimate human values and is said to be independent of structure. The term *cultural deviance* reflects the assertion that the person conforms to the culture but the culture itself is deviant (Kornhauser 1978, 34). Four theories frequently are described as cultural deviance theories: those of Sutherland and Cressey (1978), Miller (1958), Wolfgang and Ferracuti (1967), and Akers (1985).

But these four theories actually argue that shared ideas are the crucial intervening variable between social structural conditions and criminal behavior. This assertion bears almost no resemblance to the cultural deviance argument presented above. Shared ideas are described as an immediate cause of criminal behavior, but in each theory the source of those ideas is said to lie in social structural conditions.

The relation between "culture" and "structure" in cultural deviance theories is most clear in Akers' (1985) social learning theory, which focuses on "definitions favorable to deviant behavior." Akers (1985) argues that these definitions arise in a structural context, which is then experienced in terms of differential reinforcement. Thus, Akers' theory "specifies the process by which social structure shapes individual behavior" (66).

Since 1986, I have been arguing that no criminology theory has ever advanced the "cultural deviance" argument described by Hirschi and Kornhauser (Vold and Bernard 1986, 227–229). More recently, several other criminologists have also objected to the cultural deviance interpretation (e.g., Akers 1996; Matsueda 1997; but see Costello 1998). For example, Sullivan (1989) presented a cultural explanation of youth crime but explicitly rejected the cultural deviance characterization. Based on modern anthropology theory, Sullivan argued:

> The notion that culture is a package of beliefs and customs handed down unthinkingly from one generation to the next with no modification of content or function is largely discredited. In that form, culture appears as a mysterious, exogenous force that drives human behavior inexorably and unalterably, and its contents as a mere list of traits that have accumulated accidentally. . . . The black box conception of culture . . . was at the heart of the mistaken theories of the "culture of poverty". . . .[These theories] maintained that poor people are poor because they share and transmit to their children a set

of defective values, including unwillingness to defer gratification, a sense of fatalism about their conditions, and an inability to submit to authority. (242–243)

Sullivan then defined culture as "the shared understandings of those in like circumstances" (244) and proposed a cultural explanation of youth crime that is rooted in the structure of the situation (246–249). In this explanation, shared or "cultural" ideas are the crucial intervening variable between social structure and individual action.

Criminologists should not simply assume the cultural deviance interpretation of these theories when considering whether they can be integrated with other criminology theories. At minimum, the structural interpretation of these theories, as described above, should also be considered. That structural interpretation makes integration with other criminology theories both possible and desirable.

From Falsification to Risk Factors

In my view, the strain/control/cultural deviance interpretation is fatally flawed, and all arguments about integration based on it are simply wrong. But integrating criminology theories requires some overall interpretation of those theories, some understanding of how the theories relate to each other. My view is based on three conclusions that I have reached after considering the current state of criminology theories and what we must do in order to achieve scientific progress in the field.

First, in my view, the most important characteristics of theories are *the location of independent variation and the direction of causation*. These are fancy (and precise) terms for describing "what causes what" in the theory.

A well-known example can illustrate the meaning of these terms. Criminologists agree that delinquent kids tend to have delinquent friends, but they disagree strongly about "what causes what." Some criminologists argue that the direction of causation is from the delinquent friends to the delinquent behavior. That is, they argue that having delinquent friends increases the likelihood that a kid will engage in delinquent behavior. In these theories, the delinquent friends are the location of independent variation—that is, the delinquent friends are the cause and the delinquent behavior is the effect.

Other criminologists, however, argue that delinquent kids tend to select other delinquent kids as friends. That is, the direction of causation is from the delinquent behavior to the delinquent friends. Having delinquent friends, in their view, does not *cause* delinquency. Instead, engaging in delinquent behavior *causes* the kid to select other delinquents as friends. In this case, the delinquent behavior is the cause and the delinquent friends are the effect. Thus, independent variation is found in the delinquent behavior itself, and the direction of causation is from the delinquent behavior to the delinquent friends.

I argue that we should focus on the location of independent variation and the direction of causation when we interpret theories. This focus clarifies how the theories relate to each other and, therefore, clarifies whether they can be integrated with each other. This focus also leads to a very different analysis of criminology theories than the strain/control/cultural deviance interpretation.

For example, Gottfredson and Hirschi's (1990) theory of low self-control and Kornhauser's (1978) theory of community control both describe themselves as "control" theories. But they are very different theories if you look at them from the point of view of location of independent variation and the direction of causation. Kornhauser argues that mobility, heterogeneity, and poverty in urban neighborhoods "cause" the individual-level characteristics of the people in those neighborhoods. In contrast, Gottfredson and Hirschi argue that people with low "self-control" tend to end up in particular social structural locations, such as those with high mobility, ethnic heterogeneity, and poverty. Thus, these two theories describe different sources of independent variation and different directions of causation. These are fundamentally different theories, despite the fact that they both are "control" theories.

Second, I have come to the conclusion that falsification should be abandoned as a criterion for evaluating criminology theories. I have long been concerned with criminology's failure to falsify theories. I originally raised this issue in a 1990 article titled "Twenty Years of Testing Theories: What Have We Learned and Why?" (Bernard 1990). After arguing that no criminology theories had ever been falsified, I went on to make a variety of suggestions about how criminology theories ought to be constructed so that they would be more falsifiable.

The "Twenty Years" article emphasized how to falsify theories, but now I have concluded that this approach cannot succeed. The problem is that crime is such a complex phenomenon that virtually anything can influence it at least some of the time. Thus, no reasonable criminology theory can ever be falsified, no matter what it asserts, because that assertion will turn out to be true at least some of the time.

Third, I do not believe that abandoning falsification is essentially a pessimistic or fatalistic conclusion because falsification is not the only scientific way to deal with criminology theories. Rather, *I think we need to shift from falsification to a "risk factor" approach that deals in structured probabilities.* This shift will make criminology much more capable of scientific progress.

Falsification requires an "all or nothing" conclusion (the theory is either verified or falsified) based on competitive testing and statistical significance. In contrast, the "risk factor" approach allows a graduated conclusion (a theory may explain a little or a lot of the variance) based on location of independent variation and direction of causation. Where the falsification approach is competitive (if one theory is true, then others must be false), the risk factor approach is integrative (many factors may influence crime, some having larger and some smaller effects).[3]

With falsification, the entire causal chain proposed by the theory is supposed to be evaluated. This makes research quite complex. The "risk factor" approach, in contrast, focuses directly on variables rather than theories, and the issue is which variables are sources of independent variation with respect to the dependent variable. Variables that are not actual sources of independent variation are excluded from consideration, even if they otherwise are quite interesting from a theoretical standpoint. Once variables associated with independent variation have been identified, then the question is not one of falsification or verification, but rather the strength of the relationship—i.e., whether a little or a lot of the variation can be explained by the variable.

By interpreting theories in terms of their sources of independent variation and directions of causation, the policy options that might reduce crime become apparent. This has not always been the case in the past. Criminology theories often describe crime in terms that are intuitively appealing but not particularly clear in terms of what they are actually saying from a policy point of view (Gibbs 1985). The policy implications of the theory draws one's attention directly to the sources of independent variation within the theory. This focus on policy implications also is consistent with good theorizing because, as Lewin pointed out in his famous aphorism, there is nothing as practical as a good theory.

Jeff Snipes and I presented an extensive theoretical defense of this approach (Bernard and Snipes 1996) in an article that analyzed the content of criminology theories and argued that it is theoretically justified to take a "risk factor" approach to them. To further demonstrate this point, we used this approach as the basis for organizing and interpreting the material in the Fourth Edition of *Theoretical Criminology* (Vold, Bernard, and Snipes 1998). What I want to do here is provide a practical analysis of how to interpret the field in these terms, based on the conclusion to that edition.

Interpreting Criminology Theories from a Risk Factor Approach

In my view, most criminology theories are based on two commonsense observations. The first observation is that *some people are more likely than others to engage in crime, re-gardless of the situation they are in.* The theories that are based on this observation attempt to identify the individual characteristics that cause these differences in behavior. The other observation is that some situations are more likely to have higher crime rates regardless of the characteristics of the people who are in them. The theories that are based on this observation attempt to identify the characteristics of those situations that cause these differences in crime rates. There is no contradiction between these two types of theories—they simply are separate scientific problems.[4]

In the Fourth Edition of *Theoretical Criminology*, we reviewed a wide range of criminology theory and research and concluded that *the following characteristics of individuals seem to increase the probability that a person will engage in criminal behavior, regardless of the situation that person is in* (see Vold, Bernard, and Snipes 1998, 323–324):

1. A history of early childhood problem behaviors and of being subjected to poor parental childrearing techniques, such as harsh and inconsistent discipline; school failure and the failure to learn higher cognitive skills such as moral reasoning, empathy, and problem solving.

2. Certain neurotransmitter imbalances such as low seratonin, certain hormone imbalances such as high testosterone, central nervous system deficiencies such as frontal or temporal lobe dysfunction, and autonomic nervous system variations such as unusual reactions to anxiety.

3. Ingesting alcohol, many illegal drugs, and some toxins such as lead; head injuries; pregnancy or birth complications.

5. Thinking patterns that focus on trouble, toughness, smartness, excitement, fate, and autonomy; an exaggerated sense of "manliness"; a tendency to think in terms of short-term rather than long-term consequences; a tendency to see threats everywhere and to believe that it is appropriate to respond to threats with extreme violence.

6. Chronic physiological arousal and frequent experience of negative emotions, either because of an inability to escape from negative situations or because of a tendency to experience negative emotions in a wider range of situations than other people.

7. Association with others who are engaged in and approve of criminal behavior.

8. Weaker attachments to other people, less involvement in conventional activities, less to lose from committing crime, and weaker beliefs in the moral validity of the law.

In addition, the following individual differences seem to increase the probability that a person will be a victim of crime:

9. Frequently being away from home, especially at night; engaging in public activities while away from home; associating with people who are likely to commit crime.

This summary represents a wide range of different theories in criminology. Often these theories are stated in such a way as to make it appear that they contradict each other. In my view, that simply is not the case. Rather, I would argue that the competition among all the different theories is largely empirical, over which factors explain more and which explain less of the variation in crime.

It is important to recognize that there are multiple causes of crime and that these multiple causes can interact with each other to produce a greater effect than one would expect from simply adding the two separate effects together. For example, one particularly important area of interaction may be in the area of biosocial theory. Biological and social variables may independently increase the likelihood that an individual may engage in crime. In addition, biological and social factors may interact, so that certain biological characteristics may have a large impact on crime under some social circumstances but little or no impact under others.

A second type of criminology theory assumes that there are some situations that are associated with higher crime rates, regardless of the characteristics of the individuals who are within them. The theories, therefore, attempt to identify variables in the situation. These theories tend to be more complex and descriptive, and it is sometimes hard to determine the location of independent variation. To the extent that is true, the policy recommendations of the theory will be vague. In addition, situations with high crime rates often have a large number of variables, all of which are correlated with each other and all of which are correlated with crime—e.g., poverty, inequality, high residential mobility, single-parent families, unemployment, poor and dense housing, the presence of gangs and illegal criminal opportunities, inadequate schools, and a lack of social services. It can be extremely difficult to determine which (if any) of these variables is causally related to high crime rates, and which have no causal impact on crime at all. Finally, the number and complexity of these theories means that many are left out or shortchanged in the following discussion.

In spite of these daunting problems, we reviewed a wide range of criminology theory and research and concluded that *the following situations seem likely to have higher crime rates, regardless of the people who are in these situations* (Vold et al. 1998, 329–330):

1. Economic modernization and development is associated with higher property crime rates. Property crime tends to increase until the society is quite highly developed and then to hold steady at a high level. The processes that result in this pattern of crime involve changes in routine activities and in criminal opportunities, which eventually are balanced by the increasing effectiveness of countermeasures.

2. Economic inequality is associated with higher rates of violence. The process may involve feelings of frustration and relative deprivation.

3. Cultures which emphasize the goal of material success at the expense of adhering to legitimate means are associated with high rates of utilitarian crime; an unequal distribution of legitimate

means is associated with an inverse distribution of utilitarian crime; in situations without legitimate means to economic success, the development of illegitimate means is associated with increased utilitarian crime while the lack of such development is associated with increased violent crime; in these structural situations, the inability to achieve status by conventional criteria is associated with status inversion and higher rates of nonutilitarian criminal behavior. The processes involved in these structural patterns either involve frustration or the simple tendency to engage in self-interested behavior.

4. Neighborhoods with poverty, frequent residential mobility, and family disruption have high crime rates. The processes involve neighborhood anonymity resulting in social disorganization.

5. Poverty, urban environments, racial discrimination, and social isolation are associated with high rates of extreme violence associated with trivial conflicts and insults. The process involves chronic physiological arousal, which generates cognitions about when it is appropriate to become angry and the extent of violence that is appropriately used when one is angry.

6. Media dissemination of techniques and rationalizations that are favorable to law violation are associated with increased rates of law violation. The process involves direct learning of techniques and rationalizations, and indirect learning by observing the consequences criminal behaviors have for others.

7. Societies that stigmatize deviants have higher crime rates than those that reintegrate them. The process involves blocked legitimate opportunities and the formation of subcultures.

8. Societies in which some people control others have higher crime rates than societies in which people control and are controlled by others in approximately equal amounts. The process involves people's natural tendency to expand their control.

As with the individual difference theories described above, this summary represents a wide range of different theories that often are stated in such a way as to make it appear that they contradict each other. In contrast, I would argue that the competition among these theories is empirical, over which factors explain more and which explain less of the variation in crime rates. Similarly, it is important to recognize multiple causes of crime rates and that these multiple causes can interact with each other to produce a greater effect than one would expect from simply adding the two separate effects together. For example, it may be that neighborhood disorganization may interact with economic inequality at the societal level, to produce much higher neighborhood crime rates than would otherwise be expected.

It certainly may be true, and it is even quite likely, that some of the above arguments are false. But that is an empirical question about each particular assertion. Empirical support for one of these arguments would not imply a lack of support for any other argument. To that extent, depending on their empirical support, all these theories can be integrated into a single theory that describes the characteristics of societies with higher or lower crime rates.

Conclusion

Criminology actually has made a great deal of progress in the last 40 years, but our conception of science hides that progress because it focuses on falsification as a standard of science progress. Despite an enormous burst of research activity, no criminology theories have been falsified in at least 40 years. We need to abandon falsification as the standard for scientific progress and turn to integration based on a risk factor approach. We need to stop the competitive testing of criminology theories, and to focus instead on integration by looking at theories in terms of their variables and the relations among them. The essential question should be: which variables are related to crime, and in which ways?

A second major advantage of my approach is that it makes theory directly relevant to policy implications. Looking at theories in terms of the location of independent variation and the direction of causation draws attention directly to what causes crime and what can be done about it.

For example, consider those two long lists that I just reviewed in the preceding section of this essay. The first list describes *characteristics of individuals that seem to increase the probability that a person will engage in criminal behavior, regardless of the situation that person is in.* The second list describes *the situations that seem likely to have higher crime rates, regardless of the people who are in these situations.*

Ask yourself: Which of the factors from those two lists can and should be manipulated by government intervention to reduce crime? Some factors probably cannot be manipulated by government intervention, and some that can be manipulated probably should not be for ethical or practical reasons. But the remaining factors would be the focus of the policy implications of criminology theory and research.

Probably the major objection to my approach is the sense that it treats theory with a certain disrespect. When I first presented these ideas at an annual meeting of the American Society of Criminology, one of the audience members asked me if I was going to rename the Vold book *Theoretical Criminology.* I thought that suggestion was quite amusing, as did the audience, but it raises a real issue. Does the risk factor approach largely eliminate theory from criminology and convert it into an atheoretical empirical enterprise?[5]

I do think the risk factor approach reduces the role of theory in criminology, but I do not see that as a problem. In contrast, I believe that the problem lies in the way we have treated theory in the past. In my view, criminologists have tended to reify (make things out of) theories and deify (made gods out of) theorists. I would argue that the risk factor approach puts theories in their proper place in the scientific process.

In my view, the role of theory in the scientific process is to identify variables and the order or organization among them. Once it has done this, then the role of research is to see if those variables act in the real world the way theory says they will act. New theory is then called for because the results of research never completely conform to the predictions of the old theory. Theory, like research, should be a fleeting phenomenon, one that appears at a particular point in the scientific process, serves its useful function, and then disappears in later theoretical revisions and reformulations. Theory should never be reified. What remain are the variables, the order or organization among them, and the effects those have on crime.

Notes

1. I want to thank Jeff Snipes because this essay relies heavily on work I did with him, especially Bernard and Snipes (1996) and Vold, Bernard, and Snipes (1998).

2. An additional difference is that Hirschi's argument is at the individual level (i.e., individuals with less control tend to commit more crime), while Merton's argument is at the aggregate level (i.e., the distribution of legitimate opportunities is inversely related to the distribution of utilitarian criminal behavior).

3. This raises what is usually described in terms of "levels of explanation." See Bernard and Snipes (1996). In general, I believe that talking about "levels of explanation" confuses the situation, and that it is much more useful to talk instead about the dependent variable. Most criminology theories either explain the behavior of individuals or explain the rates and distributions of criminal behavior in societies. A few additional theories explain the behavior of groups. Simply stating what the theory explains is much more direct and clear than talking about the "level of explanation."

4. This is comparable to the approach taken in Albert J. Reiss and Jeffrey A. Roth, eds., *Understanding and Preventing Violence*, vol. 1, Washington DC: National Academy Press, 1993, ch. 3. See also Robert J. Sampson and Janet L. Lauritsen, "Violent Victimization and Offending: Individual-, Situational-, and Community-Level Risk Factors," pp. 1–114 in Reiss and Roth, eds. *Understanding and Preventing Violence*, vol. 3, National Academy Press, Washington DC, 1994. It is also quite comparable to what Cressey (1960) described in terms of epidemiology and individual be-

havior. There are also other theories in criminology that describe how criminal law enactment and enforcement bureaucracies behave. These theories are not discussed here or in the Bernard and Snipes (1996) article due to space considerations (p. 343). However, they are discussed in Vold, Bernard, and Snipes (1998). In addition, integrating these theories with the other two types was discussed in Thomas J. Bernard (1989), "A Theoretical Approach to Integration," pp. 137–59 in S.F. Messner, M.D. Krohn, and A.E. Liska, eds., *Theoretical Integration in the Study of Deviance and Crime*. Albany: State University of New York Press.

5. Jeff Snipes and I addressed this issue at some length, attempting to justify this approach in theoretical terms (Bernard and Snipes 1996).

References

Agnew, R.S. (1992). "Foundation for a general strain theory of crime and delinquency." *Criminology,* 30:47–87.

Akers, R.L. (1985). *Deviant Behavior: A Social Learning Approach*. Belmont, CA: Wadsworth.

——. 1996. "Is differential association/social learning cultural deviance theory?" *Criminology,* 34(2):229–247.

Bernard, T.J. (1984). "Control criticisms of strain theories." *Journal of Research in Crime and Delinquency,* 21:353–372.

——. (1987a). "Testing structural strain theories." *Journal of Research in Crime and Delinquency,* 24:262–280

——. (1987b). "Reply to Agnew." *Journal of Research in Crime and Delinquency,* 24:287–290.

——. (1987c). "Structure and control." *Justice Quarterly,* 4(3):224–409.

——. (1990). "Twenty years of testing theories: What have we learned and why?" *Journal of Research in Crime and Delinquency,* 27:325–347.

Bernard, T.J. and J.B. Snipes. (1996). "Theoretical integration in criminology." *Crime and Justice: A Review of Research,* 20:301–48.

Cloward, R. and L.E. Ohlin. (1960). *Delinquency and Opportunity*. New York: Free.

Cohen, A. (1955). *Delinquent Boys*. New York: Free.

Costello, B.J. (1998). "The remarkable persistence of a flawed theory: A reply to Matsueda." *Theoretical Criminology,* 2(1):85–92.

Cressey, D.R. (1960). "Epidemiology and individual conduct." *Pacific Sociological Review,* 3:47–58

Cullen, F.T. (1983). *Rethinking Crime and Deviance Theory*. Totowa, NJ: Rowman and Allenheld.

Elliott, D. (1985). "The assumption that theories can be combined with increased explanatory power." Pp. 123–149 in *Theoretical Methods in Criminology*. R.F. Meier (ed.). Beverly Hills, CA: Sage.

Elliott, D., S. Ageton, and R. Cantor. (1979). "An integrated theoretical perspetive on delinquent behavior." *Journal of Research in Crime and Delinquency,* 16:3–27.

Elliott, D., D. Huizinga, and S.S. Ageton. (1985). *Explaining Delinquency and Drug Use*. Beverly Hills, CA: Sage.

Gibbs, J. (1985). "The methodology of theory construction in criminology." Pp. 23–50 in *Theoretical Methods in Criminology*. R.F. Meier (ed.). Beverly Hills, CA: Sage.

Gottfredson, M.R. and T. Hirschi. (1990). *A General Theory of Crime*. Stanford, CA: Stanford University Press.

Hirschi, T. (1969). *Causes of Delinquency*. Berkeley: University of California Press.

——. (1979). "Separate but unequal is better." *Journal of Research in Crime and Delinquency,* 16:34–38.

——. (1989). "Exploring alternatives to integrated theory." Pp. 37–49 in *Theoretical Integration in the Study of Deviance and Crime*. S.F. Messner, M.D. Krohn, and A.E. Liska (eds.). Albany: State University of New York Press.

Kornhauser, R.R. (1978). *Social Sources of Delinquency*. Chicago: University of Chicago Press.

Liska, A. (1971). "Aspirations, expectations, and delinquency." *Sociological Quarterly,* 12:99–107.

Matsueda, R.L. (1997). "Cultural deviance theory: The remarkable persistence of a flawed term." *Theoretical Criminology,* 1(4):429–52.

Merton, R.K. (1938). "Social structure and anomie." *American Sociological Review,* 3:672–82.

Miller, W.B. (1958). "Lower-class culture as a generating milieu of gang delinquency." *Journal of Social Issues,* 14(3):5–19.

Reiss, A.J. and J.A. Roth (eds.). (1993). *Understanding and Preventing Violence*, Vol. 1. Washington, DC: National Academy Press.

Sampson, R.J. and J.L. Lauritsen. (1994). "Violent victimization and offending." Pp. 1–114 in *Understanding and Preventing Violence*. A.J. Reiss and J.A. Roth (eds.). Vol. 3. Washington: National Academy Press.

Stinchcombe, A.L. (1975). "Merton's theory of social structure." In *The Idea of Social Struc-*

ture. L. Coser (ed.). New York: Harcourt Brace Jovanovich.

Sullivan, M.L. (1989). *Getting Paid*. Ithaca, NY: Cornell University Press.

Sutherland, E.H. (1949). *White Collar Crime*. New York: Dryden.

Sutherland, E.H. and D.R. Cressey. (1978). *Criminology*. Philadelphia: Lippincott.

Tittle, C.R. (1985). "Prospects for synthetic theory." Pp. 161–78 in *Theoretical integration in the Study of Deviance and Crime*. S.F. Messner, M.D. Krohn, and A.E. Liska (eds.). Albany: State University of New York Press.

Vold, G.B. and T.J. Bernard. (1986). *Theoretical Criminology*, Third Edition. New York: Oxford University Press.

Vold, G.B., T.J. Bernard, and J.B. Snipes. (1998). *Theoretical Criminology*, Fourth Edition. New York: Oxford University Press.

Wolfgang, M.E. and F. Ferracuti. (1967). *The Subculture of Violence*. London: Tavistock.